People and Computers
Partners in Problem Solving

People and Computers
Partners in Problem Solving

John F. Vinsonhaler
Michigan State University

Christian C. Wagner
Oakland University

Castelle G. Gentry
Michigan State University

West Publishing Company
St. Paul   New York   Los Angeles   San Francisco

This book is dedicated to our wives, Jeane, Debbie, and Nancy, and to our families

Chapter Opening 1 Courtesy of National Aeronautics and Space Administration; *Figure 1–1*, p. 3 (a) Fran Heyl Associates. Photo by Philip Harrington; (b) Sun Microsystems, Inc; (c) Courtesy of International Business Machines Corporation; (d) Courtesy of Radio Shack, a division of Tandy Corporation; *Figure 1–2*, p. 6 (a) Courtesy of Apple Computer, Inc.; (b) Courtesy Cray Research, Inc.; (c) Courtesy of International Business Machines Corporation; *Figure 1–3*, p. 6 Courtesy of Insignia Solutions; *Chapter Opening 2* Courtesy of International Business Machines Corporation; *Figure 2.1*, p. 22 Photo by Kurt Stepnitz; *Figure 2–2*, p. 24 (a, b), *Figure 2–3*, p. 27 (a-b) Courtesy of International Business Machines Corporation; *Figure 2–4*, p. 30 (a) Courtesy of Sperry Univac Corporation; (b) Courtesy of International Business Machines Corporation; *Figure 2–5*, p. 34 (a) Courtesy of Sperry Univac Corporation; (b), *Figure 2–6, p. 37 (a-b), Figure 2–7*, p. 41 Courtesy of International Business Machines Corporation; *Figure 2–10*, p. 45 Dan McCoy/Rainbow; *Figure 2–11*, p. 46 Name of product is: NEXPERT OBJECT—A rule based on w/object representation hybrid expert system shell; *Chapter Opening 3* Photo by Kurt Stepnitz; *Chapter Opening 4* Courtesy of International Business Machines Corporation; *Figure 4–1*, p. 107 Photo by Kurt Stepnitz; *Figure 4–2*, p. 111, *Figure 4–3*, p. 118 Courtesy of International Business Machines Corporation; *Figure 4–4* p. 124 Photo by Kurt Stepnitz; *Figure 4–6*, p. 132 Courtesy of CompuServe, Incorporated; *Figure 4–7*, p. 136, *Chapter Opening 5* Photo by Kurt Srepnitz; *Chapter Opening 6* Courtesy of WordPerfect Corporation; *Chapter Opening 7* Photo by Kurt Stepnitz; *Chapter Opening 8* dBase III Plus is a registered trademark of Ashton-Tate Corporation. All rights reserved. *Chapter Opening 9, Figure 9–1*, p. 369 Courtesy of International Business Machines Corporation; *Chapter Opening 10* Reproduced by permission of Hayes Micrcomputer Products, Inc., (copyright symbol followed by year date in Hayes copyright notice), Hayes Microcomputer Products, Inc.; *Chapter Opening 11, Chapter Opening 12* Photo by Kurt Stepnitz.

Copyediting: Pam McMurray
Text Design: John Edeen
Text Illustrations: Rolin Graphics
Composition: Clarinda Company
Cover Design: Diane Beasley
Cover Image: Audrey LaCross

Library of Congress Cataloging-in-Publications Data

Vinsonhaler, John F.
    People and computers : partners in problem solving / John F.
Vinsonhaler, Christian C. Wagner, Castelle G. Gentry.
        p.   cm.
    Includes index.
    ISBN 0-314-93903-2
    1. Electronic data processing.   I. Wagner, Christian C.   II. Gentry,
Castelle G.   III. Title
QA76.V52 1989
004--dc19   88-29333
                                                          CIP

Contents

Computer Hardware   53

4 Common Computer Software Systems and Their Use   105

5 Computer Software: Operating Systems   147

Word Processing Software   193

Spreadsheet Software 251

Data Base Management Software 307

Graphics Software   361

Communications Software   411

Programs, Programming Languages, and Programming Software   445

Computer Programming and Systems Design   479

Preface

For many years computer literacy has been the focus of the first undergraduate computer course. Computer literacy is commonly defined as the computer knowledge essential to a literate, functioning member of society. In practice this concept has usually been translated into a course that provides a general survey of the abstract ideas associated with the computer, reviews the uses of computers by organizations rather than by individual people in science and industry, discusses the social impact, and gives a brief experience with a programming language or a simple applications program.

Many current trends are causing a gradual change in this approach: the growing number of college students who have already been introduced to computers, either in high school or through work experience; the growing demand in the professions (e.g., business, law, medicine, teaching, and engineering) for a sophisticated understanding of computers; and the growing tendency for nearly every college graduate to become a direct hands-on user of personal computers and applications software (e.g., word processing, spreadsheet, data base management, graphics, and communications software) as a means for increasing personal productivity.

Computer Competency

The central thesis of this book is that traditional computer literacy no longer meets the needs of the modern college student and that it must be replaced by a new concept that we term *computer competency*. Computer competency emphasizes making people comfortable, effective users of computers in their chosen professions and in workplaces increasingly dominated by personal computers and applications software. In our view, a first course in computer competency should emphasize the three essential features uniquely embodied in this textbook: personal productivity applications, learning how to learn about software, and depth of contents.

■ Productivity Applications

This book focuses on the reader as a person who uses a variety of applications or productivity software to solve problems or perform other tasks on a personal computer. It also assumes that the power, complexity, and variety of both hardware and software will grow rapidly, as will linkages to mainframe computer services and data bases. This should be a realistic scenario for the typical college graduate of the 1990s. Thus, the text emphasizes personalizing the computer for the student and includes many demonstrations of using software applications for typical personal and professional tasks, such as communicating, planning, and analyzing.

The Case Studies   An anecdote at the beginning of each chapter presents the computer hardware or software discussed in the chapter in a situation that the reader can relate to; where appropriate, the anecdote illustrates the typical use of software to solve a simple problem from beginning to end. The case study for the chapter on hardware, for example, describes a student's experience in buying a personal computer. The case study in the chapter on operating systems describes a student trying to get a new piece of software to work with his version of DOS. In addition, each chapter on applications software includes a second case study that describes a more complex application. The chapter on communications software, for example, describes the gleefulness of a first-time user of a CompuServe-like service. In the case studies and throughout the chapters, screens showing what the software user actually sees are integrated directly into the text instead of in the separate figures used in most books.

The ISPCO Generic Approach   Exclusive training for a specific software or hardware system is of questionable value for a college student, since any particular hardware or software system is likely to be obsolete by the time the student graduates. This is not to say that experience with specific hardware and software is unnecessary, only that the student's chances of transferring this knowledge to the next generation of computers is greatly enhanced if he or she also learns the generic model that underlies the particular system. The ISPCO generic model used in this text is a common one used by many instructors. According to this model, the major functions of any computer hardware or software component can be organized in terms of *input, storage, processing, control,* and *output.*

Like most good ideas, the ISPCO approach is simple: when teaching students about computing, organize the instruction around these five functions, with the ISPCO model providing a general framework into which the student can fit his or her knowledge of how computers work. Thus information on hardware, for example, is presented in the context of the model, i.e., in terms of input devices, storage devices, processing and control devices, and output devices. Software is examined from the same perspective: each function and command is associated with input, storage, processing, control, or output. This generic approach was first suggested to us by the research literature on cognitive schema, which contains many studies that show that organizing learning in this manner provides a powerful aid to understanding, retention, and generalization. After years of teaching experience with the ISPCO model, we can say with confidence that this simple model is a powerful key to student understanding.

■ Learning to Learn

This text has evolved around the principle that students are best served by knowledge that is *transferrable* to new situations and is *richly structured* to give a deeper, more mature understanding. Rather than guessing at the manner by which students could acquire such knowledge and abilities, we began the development of this text with a careful analysis of research in reading comprehension, cognitive psychology, and artificial intelligence concerning the organization of human memory and the means by which is is developed. From this study, we developed the unique combination of instructional features used in this text. These features have been classroom-tested on more than a thousand students at two different universities. Some of these features have already been mentioned—including case studies to take advantage of the greater retention of anecdotes, compared to simple statements of information, embedding screen examples in the text, and using the ISPCO model as an advanced organizer. Two more features are important in helping students to learn: ISPCO frames and ISPCO scripts provide a means of transferring learning to new hardware and software.

ISPCO Frames A frame is a method used in artificial intelligence (AI) research to represent declarative knowledge (i.e., factual information about things). Frames use slots for the attributes that define an object, e.g., a simple frame for cars would have a slot for the color (red, blue, silver, . . .), style (two-door, four-door), manufacturer (GM, Ford, Toyota, . . .), and so on. Individual objects are represented by inserting specific values into the slots (e.g., this car is a red, two-door Ford). More complex ideas can be represented by hierarchically grouping frames that share (inherit) attributes. In this textbook, we have applied this idea to knowledge about software and hardware. Thus the frames in this text are figures that give short definitions for each of the ISPCO functions and commands discussed in the chapter and provide blank spaces in which the student can insert information on specific systems. The slots are grouped by ISPCO function. When students use these frames to operate or describe software, they learn not only the commands for the particular system but also the underlying ISPCO structure. Exercises in the text require students to fill in the blank slots with the commands for the specific software available to them; the completed frames can then be used in laboratory assignments. Blank frames and frames with filled-in values for major software systems (e.g., Word, WordPerfect, Lotus 1-2-3, dBASE III, AppleWorks, and Microsoft Works) are provided in the ancillary materials that accompany the text. These frames can be copied and handed out to students or used in lectures.

ISPCO Scripts Scripts are devices used in AI research to represent procedural knowledge (i.e., knowledge about actions). A script contains a sequence of actions common to many repeated activities of the same type (e.g., the script for eating in a restaurant consists of sitting at a table, ordering food, eating the food, paying, and so on). In this text, scripts summarize what one does whenever one uses a particular type of software, e.g., a word processor to write a paper or a spreadsheet to prepare a budget. When students use scripts to operate specific software, they learn not only the steps for that particular software system but also the general procedure for the software type.

Several points about scripts and frames should be kept in mind. These concepts come directly from the cognitive sciences. It has been demonstrated in psychological and AI research that they are the devices by which effective learners remember complex information. Research has also shown that teaching with these devices improves learning and retention. In addition, the scripts and frames provide a complete summary of virtually all of the major concepts in each chapter.

■ Depth of Coverage

Most beginning computer textbooks lack the depth necessary to meet the average student's needs, let alone the growing public demand for excellence in undergraduate education and for material that challenges the good student. Although software has become easier to use, it has at the same time become more complex and more demanding in terms of computer sophistication. For example, contrast Visicalc and Excel. Excel is clearly easier to use, since it has graphic menus that use a mouse and it has on-line help, but it also has many more commands and is capable of much more sophisticated operations (such as graphics, spreadsheet merging, and cut-and-paste between applications). Similarly, hardware has become generations more powerful and complex. The early personal computers had only one simple microprocessor, floppy disks, and impact printers. Today, personal computer hardware commonly includes multi-processing and coprocessing chips, hard disks, 3.5- and 5.25-inch floppies, CD-ROM, laser printers, and modems. All of this sophistication means that students must know more rather than less about computers.

Increased depth is provided in many areas in this text. The chapter on hardware discusses the real computer—the main circuit board, the microprocessor chips, and expansion slots—and the central role of these components in determining hardware and software compatibility. The chapter on operating systems discusses what really happens when an operating system is booted, what is involved in installing an applications software package, and how device drivers support hardware compatibility.

There are separate chapters on all five types of applications software (word processing, spreadsheets, data base management, graphics, and communication). The chapter on data base management provides a technically accurate discussion of all four basic operations (data record definition, data record entry, report definition, and report generation) with realistically complex examples. Hierarchical, network, and relational models are defined with easy-to-understand examples. The chapter on graphics gives an unparalleled coverage of chart graphics construction and the use of the major paint graphics tools such as the encircler, the mover, and the pencil. The chapters on programming and system development examine such fundamental software engineering topics as the system development life cycle, structured design, and very high level programming languages. A cursory glance at any of the chapters will reveal these and many more interesting features.

Typical Chapter Contents

Perhaps the best way to show how all these ideas are combined is to summarize the contents of the typical chapter such as chapter 6, Word Processing Software.

First case study

This is an anecdote about a student writing, saving, and re-editing a term paper to illustrate the sequence of actions and the functions used in a simple word processing application.

ISPCO organization figure

This figure summarizes the input, storage, processing, control, and output functions used with word processors. It is followed by sections on each of the five functions.

Input functions and commands

Descriptions of how to input text and commands from the keyboard are provided. Examples are given from representative word processing software such as WordPerfect and MacWrite.

Storage functions

Descriptions of the storage functions and commands for file directory and file creation, saving, loading, and deleting are given in this section. Typical examples are provided.

Processing functions

This section includes descriptions of the processing functions and typical commands for editing text (insert, delete, copy, cut and paste, find, replace), formatting text, preparing indexes, using spelling checkers and thesauruses, and so on. The examples use representative text and typical word processing software.

Control functions

Descriptions and typical commands are summarized for macro and similar functions.

Output functions

Descriptions and typical commands are given for formatting, selecting fonts, and generating printed and disk file output with word processors.

Second case study

This anecdote is about a more complex word processing problem involving a mailmerge task. Steps and typical commands are illustrated.

Scripts and frames for word processing

This section gives the ISPCO Frame for the functions and commands discussed in the chapter, with spaces where the students can record commands for the specific software used by their class. It also presents ISPCO Scripts for common applications of word processors.

Computer insights

Computer Insights are short, high-interest essays on topics that relate to the chapter. They often discuss specific hardware systems (e.g., the PS/2, the Macintosh II, and the NeXT computer) or specific software systems (e.g., in chapter 6, WordPerfect, Microsoft WORD, and other word processors are summarized).

Chapter review

Objective questions and exercises keyed to the major objectives of the chapter are included at the end of each chapter. Correct answers are given in the text book appendix.

Ancillary Materials

Instructor's guide The text and the instructor's guide are designed to permit the instructor to teach several types of courses with the text. The materials in the Guide and in the text are organized so that the instructor can select what chapters to exclude or emphasize. Chapters 1 through 5 provide a basic introduction to computing, including historical perspectives, computer hardware, a brief introduction to the different types of software, and a complete discussion of operating systems. Most courses should cover these chapters. Chapters 6 through10 provide a thorough treatment of word processing, spreadsheet, data base, graphics, and communications software. These chapters are designed for a course that emphasizes the use of personal computers and productivity software. Chapters 11 and 12 introduce the student to programming, programming software, and system design. These chapters are designed for a course that emphasizes programming (a later edition of this book will include a BASIC programming appendix). For each chapter, the instructor's guide includes a summary, a list of objectives, suggested activities, and test items, all organized so that some chapters may be skipped and others emphasized. (It is our hope, however, that instructors will encourage their best students to read all of the chapters).

Blank and filled-in frames   As noted previously, blank versions of the chapter frames are included in the ancillary materials. These frames are identical to those in the text, except that they provide more space in which to write command summaries and are suitable for duplication. Also included in the ancillary materials are similar frames in which the blanks have been filled in for widely used hardware (e.g., the IBM PC, the IBM PS/2, the Apple II, and the Macintosh) and software (e.g., WordPerfect, Microsoft WORD, Lotus 1-2-3, VP-Planner, dBASE III Plus, MacPaint, Kermit, AppleWorks, and Microsoft WORKS). These frames can be duplicated for lectures or handed out as feedback for student exercises.

Transparency masters for main figures   Transparency masters for the instructor are provided for all of the most important figures in the text.

Computerized test bank   The test bank includes questions that were not included in the text chapters and that are suitable for testing purposes. Software to support test preparation is also provided.

Software systems and student manuals   Software diskettes and student manuals suitable for use with the text are available from the publisher. Student versions of WordPerfect, Lotus 1-2-3, VP-Planner, and dBASE III PLUS are currently available.

Acknowledgments

John Vinsonhaler and Chris Wagner conceptualized and wrote the text and figures for all chapters except chapter 12, which was written with the assistance of Jeane Vinsonhaler. Computer Insights, the glossary, and the end-of-chapter materials were written by Cas Gentry, Chris Wagner, and John Vinsonhaler. The instructor's guide was organized and written by Cas Gentry, who also prepared the photographic illustrations. Many significant ideas for the book were provided by Jerry Westby, by our colleagues in computer and cognitive sciences, and by our students in the classes that were taught using the many drafts of this textbook and ancillary materials.

Truly, this book could not have been written without the strong support provided by our editor, Jerry Westby, and West Publishing. Jerry and his panel of reviewers made major contributions that improved the organization and contents of the text. Our production editor, Deanna Quinn (and in the final stages, Sharon Walrath), translated our ideas and manuscripts into a delightful, beautifully illustrated book. Deanna also served as our patient guide through the jungle of textbook production.

As any author knows, authors both love and hate their reviewers. After viewing the final product that our panel helped us create, our feelings have turned to fond appreciation. Our sincerest thanks go out to the following reviewers for the many hours spent helping us improve this book:

Gerald W. Adkins
Georgia College

Gary Armstrong
Shippensburg State College

John Avitable
Rutgers University—The State University of New Jersey

James J. Ball
Indiana State University

Curtis Bring
Moorhead State University

Donald Cartlidge
New Mexico State University

William R. Cornette
Southwest Missouri State University

Richard Daughenbaugh
University of South Alabama

George Farrimond
Southern Oregon State College

Robert Fritz
American River College

Homer Gerber
University of Central Florida

Barbara Ann Greim
University of North Carolina—Wilmington

Lorinda Hite
Owens Technical College

Randall Hock
Saginaw Valley State College

Robert Horton
University of Wisconsin—Whitewater

Earl Jackson
North Texas State University

Betty L. Jehn
University of Dayton

Dana L. Johnson
North Dakota State University

Edward Keefe
Des Moines Area Community College

Richard L. Kimball
University of Maine at Presque Isle

Le Roy Kratzer
Foothill College

Ronald Lancaster
Bowling Green State University

John Lane
Edinboro State College

John Lawson
Towson State University

David R. Lee
San Jose State University

Patricia M. Milligan
Baylor University

Paul Paulson
Central Michigan University

William E. Pracht
Texas Tech University

Leonard Presby
William Paterson State College

Tom Richard
Bemidji State University

Charles Riden
Arizona State University

Robert Riser
East Tennessee State University

Harold Sackman
California State University at Los Angeles

Laura Saret
Oakton Community College

Jerry F. Sitek
Southern Illinois University at Edwardsville

Timothy Sylvester
College of DuPage

Charles M. Williams
Georgia State University

Margaret Zinky
Phoenix College

Functions of Human and Computer Problem Solving

Essential Chapter Concepts

When you are finished with this chapter, you should know:

- Why you need to learn about computers.

- What range of computer knowledge you need.

- How this text will facilitate your learning about computers.

Functions of Human and Computer Problem Solving

INPUT   STORAGE   PROCESS   CONTROL   OUTPUT

This book explores the relationship between people and **computers.** People can solve many types of problems more effectively if they use computers to help them. People and computers can work together, each doing the tasks to which they are best suited. With this partnership, many existing tasks can be performed more efficiently and new tasks that would otherwise be impossible can also be done.

The operation of a space vehicle, the most complex type of machine ever created, provides an example of a good working relationship between people and computers. These vehicles are not controlled and operated by people alone, but by a partnership between people and computers. People provide the high-level control of the space vehicle and express this control through commands to computers. The computers then monitor and control many lower-level motors, sensors, and other devices. There is a natural shifting of tasks between people and computers. In this book, we hope to foster such a partnership between people and computers by emphasizing the increased range of tasks that can be performed by people using microcomputers, minicomputers, mainframe computers, and computer networks. *The time for standing in awe of the computer is long past. It is time for the average person to accept and use computers as everyday tools.* Thus, the purpose of this book is to help you become *computer competent,* i.e., to help you become a confident, effective user of computers both in your chosen profession and in your personal life. Computer competence is one sure path to greater personal productivity in a society increasingly dependent on computers and on computer knowledgeable people.

computer
A tool that can input, store, process, and output information and control the sequence of these actions. A modern electronic computer is adaptable to a wide variety of uses because the instructions that control the computer's actions are stored in memory and can be altered to meet changing needs.

information society
A society characterized by (1) a shift from jobs in production to jobs in information processing, (2) a growing need for a better educated work force with computer skills, and (3) greater productivity (more goods for less cost) due to better use of information in the production process.

America is rapidly becoming an **information society** based on computers and information networks. What is an information society? It is a new social structure that has arisen from relatively recent technological advancements in computing. Throughout history, major technological innovations have altered the way people are employed and hence the structure of society. The information society is just the most recent accommodation to technological change.

To better anticipate the magnitude and importance of the information so-

1.1

Why Learn About Computers?

ciety, one need only consider the social changes that have followed other periods of technological advancement. In the United States, three major technological societies preceded the current information society. Each society can be categorized by the occupation of the majority of its people: farmer, laborer, and clerk.

From the establishment of our country until the late nineteenth century, farming was the major source of employment in the U.S. During the eighteenth and much of the nineteenth century, agriculture accounted for 90% of this country's employment (today less than 3% of the U.S. population work in farming). The technological advances of the industrial revolution brought about the next societal change: the ascendance of the American laboring class and their powerful trade unions. As was true for agriculture in the farming society, the number of people involved in industry crested and then waned. The next major employment shift occurred in the mid- to late 1960s, when the increasing size and complexity of government, business, and the military created a society in which clerical jobs were the major occupation.

Today, computer and communication technology is rapidly altering the social structure of this country again, this time giving us an information society in which a large number of jobs will be filled by technicians, many of whom must be skilled in developing and using information processing systems. A major indicator of this move to a technician-centered job force is the growing demand on higher education: there are currently more people employed in universities than in agriculture. Our country has a growing need for people with better education, technical skills, and computer sophistication for jobs ranging from using the simple scanners in a grocery check-out line to conducting advanced medical tests and procedures, operating complex transportation systems, and developing modern robots and automation.

Why has the U.S. society so rapidly shifted from past occupations to new ones, from farmer, to laborer, to clerk, to technician? Productivity is certainly the most significant driving force. The quantity and quality of goods and services that can be produced from a given amount of resources has increased with each occupational shift. Technology has changed agricultural productivity by a factor greater than 75. In the eighteenth century, a farmer could feed himself and 1 other person. In this century a farmer can feed himself and 150 other people. The productivity gains resulting from computerized factories with industrial robots could be even more dramatic. For example, with advances in automation it may become possible to profitably sell a sports car that costs $35,000 today for a price of $3,500.

As the information society matures, a minimum knowledge of computers and their use will become an assumed skill for all employed people, much like the ability to read or drive a car is now assumed. Even now, most companies prefer job candidates with some level of computer knowledge. This preference is merely a hint of what will come in the future. Knowledge about computers will profoundly affect people's employment opportunities throughout their lives. Professional careers will require much more sophisticated knowledge about computers and skill in using computers than those demanded of the average person. In short, the skilled use of computers in your area of specialization (e.g., in sales, personnel, investment, science, business, engineering, medicine, education, or law) will become a prerequisite for the more interesting and rewarding jobs. Just some of the many professional uses of computers today are shown in Figure 1–1.

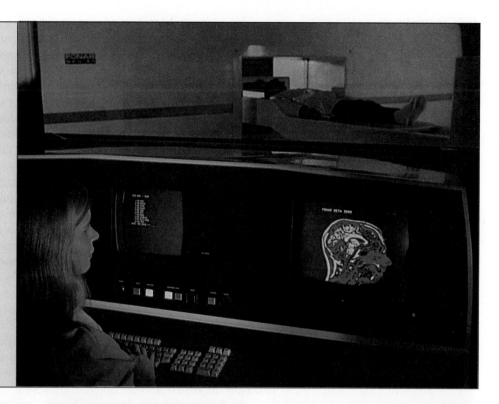

Figure 1–1 Computers in the Professions. Professions from every walk of life, whether physicians, engineers, musicians, or business professionals are using computers more and more to help solve their problems.

Many students don't know what they should learn about computers. This is no surprise considering the various opinions among professional educators on the appropriate content for an introductory computing course. At one time, introductory courses taught students how to program in BASIC (Beginners All-Purpose Symbolic Instruction Code is an easy-to-use language for giving instructions to a computer). Other courses have focused on how computers are used by different groups of professionals, such as business executives or physicians. This text takes a different approach. It shows how a person like you can use computers to solve real-world problems as a student or professional. The text emphasizes a working knowledge of computing and familiarity with both single-**user** personal computers and large mainframe computers shared by many users.

1.2

What Should I Learn About Computers?

user
A person responsible for applying a computer program to the processing of data and determining the usefulness of the program in solving his or her problems.

ISPCO model
The organizing framework for this text; it shows the most significant aspects of any computer hardware or software in terms of five functions: input, storage, processing, control, and output.

input
Accepting information from the environment, e.g., when a human sees or when a computer detects the keys pressed at its keyboard.

storage
Retaining information.

processing
The manipulation of information inside a computer or person.

control
The *order* in which the input, storage, processing, and output tasks are performed.

output
Sending information into the environment, e.g., when a human speaks or when a computer prints.

In learning how to use computers, the reader will be confronted with many learning tasks. The first will be to learn some new vocabulary. *Byte, modem, microprocessor, software, spreadsheet,* and many other new words must be committed to memory. In addition, many words that the reader has used since childhood now take on new meanings: *bit, instruction, input, storage, processing, control,* and *output* are just a few examples. To help with this new vocabulary, definitions of major terms are given in the margins of this text and collected together in the glossary at the end of the text (don't worry about the terms just listed—their definitions will come later).

Along with the vocabulary of computers, the reader must learn the structure of computers, that is, how computer hardware and software systems are organized. The vocabulary terms must be tied together so that, for example, the relationship between a bit and a byte is well understood. This need for students to learn the structure of computing is one of the driving forces behind the development of this text. Later in this chapter, a coherent organizational scheme based on a model called the **ISPCO model** will be presented; it will be used throughout the text to aid the reader's understanding of the structure behind computing (ISPCO is an abbreviation for the major computer functions of **input, storage, processing, control,** and **output**).

With the vocabulary and structures well in hand, the last step in becoming a computer user is the experience of actually using a computer. This step often presents problems for new users, because using a computer is not something that can be learned by reading alone. Just as a book cannot teach someone how to throw a baseball, (demonstration, practice, and feedback are required), it cannot teach someone how to use a computer. Computers must be experienced.

The only way to become a computer user is to sit down and use one. Much of computer use deals with a series of physical interactions that cannot be easily described in words. For example, a simple instruction like "type your

Computer Insights
Computer Hardware: The Basic Components of Large and Small Computers

A computer is composed of a collection of separate parts in the same way that a component stereo system has a separate turntable, tape deck, amplifier, tuner, and speakers.

Basically, a computer needs the parts that perform the five functions of input, storage, processing, control, and output. The most common way of inputting data into a computer is with a typewriterlike keyboard. The most common output devices are television monitors and paper printers. Storage of a computer comes in two parts: (1) very fast but limited internal memory that is built out of electronic circuits and called RAM (random access memory) or ROM (read only memory) and (2) slower but indefinitely large memory on magnetic disks. Finally, the processing and control hardware of a computer is combined in one component called a *microprocessor* or *central processing unit* (the brain of the computer). All of these pieces are tied together with a variety of wires and connectors.

At present, the major difference between a giant, million-dollar supercomputer and the most inexpensive, small personal computer is a matter of degree, not concept. The small computer will generally use slower electronic circuits and have only one of each type of component. The supercomputer can have more than one processing unit, many keyboard-television monitor combinations, dozens of disk drives, and many times the RAM and ROM, all using the fastest circuits available.

Large and small computers are manufactured by many different computer companies that change the design of their hardware frequently. Thus, there is a great variety of computers in use, increasing the complexity and confusion that face a new computer user. (For more about hardware see Chapter 3.)

name" seems to require little more than the ability to type the correct letters on a computer keyboard, but there are underlying details that must be known. For example, if the user makes a mistake while typing, he or she must know how to correct the error. The user must also know how to tell the computer when the name has been completely typed. To respond to the simple phrase "type your name," then, the user needs to know a number of details of computer use, but it is just not reasonable to attempt to describe all these details in a textbook.

Hence, a new user must practice using computers; it is easier to *show* proper computer use than to *tell* about it. This book assumes, therefore, that the reader has access to computer hardware and software; the text is designed to support the reader who can spend time in hands-on practice with the computer. It contains many convenient summaries that are to be used while sitting at the computer. Practice is indispensable.

■ The Beginning of Structure: Generic versus Specific Knowledge

When learning about any technological product, there is a distinction between generic and specific knowledge. Generic knowledge can be applied to virtually all examples of a particular product. For example, in all of the different makes and models of cars, there is a switch that controls the headlights and another the windshield wipers. No matter how these switches are set up in any particular car, the concepts are the same. Specific knowledge, on the other hand, is more detailed and immediately useful, but it cannot be transferred from one product to another. For example, the headlights on a particular car may be turned on by pulling the knob on the left of the steering wheel while the wipers are controlled by twisting the stem on the steering column; this knowledge is specific knowledge that would be useless to the user of another make of car that has controls in different locations.

Knowledge of computers can also be generic or specific. Computer technology generally comes in two parts, **hardware** and **software.** Generic knowledge of hardware can be applied to any manufacturer's product. Specific knowledge of hardware can be applied to just one machine (e.g., to an IBM Personal Computer). Similarly, generic knowledge of software can describe how an entire class of software products works (e.g., all word processing systems), while specific knowledge details how one particular product functions (e.g., the specific word processing system named Word Perfect). To give just a small indication of the number of hardware and software systems that exist today, Figure 1–2 shows a variety of hardware systems, while Figure 1–3 illustrates the diversity of software available.

As the figures indicate, an extensive variety of hardware and software is available today. Because of this variety, this text will emphasize generic knowledge over specific knowledge. First of all, the number of different computing systems makes the memorization of specific knowledge an impossible task. Second, computer hardware and software change rapidly due to technological advancement. Thus, knowledge specific to particular computer hardware or software is not nearly as useful as generic knowledge that can adapt to changing computer systems. Finally, generic knowledge is easier to transfer from place to place. When leaving one school or job for another, the chances are good that the new situation will use different computer hardware and software than the old. Generic knowledge can be easily applied to a new situation,

hardware
The physical devices making up a computer system.

software
Computer programs that contain sets of instructions for the computer to follow. When the computer follows the instructions, some desired task is performed. Software is often used to refer both to computer programs and to documentation for their use.

Figure 1–2 A Variety of Computer Hardware. This figure showing some computer hardware exhibits the Cray 2 supercomputer (middle), and two of the most powerful microcomputers, the Macintosh II (left) and the IBM Personal System/2 (right).

whereas specific knowledge of the old system may be of little use with the new one.

In this text, then, we will be less concerned with the specifics of any particular computer system than with the underlying concepts that enable the user to understand all computing systems. Thus, knowledge gained from this text will *not* soon be made obsolete by rapidly changing hardware and software technology. As computer technology changes, new and different computing systems can still be organized by the conceptual frames of reference presented here.

■ The Overall Structure: The ISPCO Model of Computer Functions

model
A representation of a process, concept, or device that is less complex than the real thing, e.g., a scale model of an airplane represents only the physical dimensions of the plane. See also ISPCO model.

Underlying the entire contents of this text is a **model** of computer functioning called the ISPCO model. This model describes all actions that a computer can perform in terms of only five basic functions. When information about computers is organized in terms of these five functions, the reader can understand and recall it more easily and can see the similarities that exist in all of computing. Specifically, the ISPCO model states that a computer is capable of the following functions:

1. inputting information (I)
2. storing information (S)

Figure 1–3 A Variety of Software. The computer software systems shown here represent only a small sample from a growing mountain of such packages.

Table 1.1 The ISPCO Model of Human and Computer Functions

ISPCO Function	Human Ability	Computer Analogue
Input: Means of receiving data from environment	sight, touch, hearing, taste, smell	keyboards and many other kinds of input devices
Storage: Means of retaining data	memory, remembering	electronic circuits, magnetic disks, and other computers
Processing: Means of manipulating data	adding, subtracting, etc.	adding, subtracting, etc.
Control: Means of sequencing all the tasks	choosing and scheduling tasks to be performed	executing instructions in computer programs
Output: Means of sending data out to the environment	writing, speaking, movement, other nonverbal means	printer, video screen, and many other output devices

3. processing information (P)
4. controlling the sequence of functions being performed (C)
5. outputting information (O)

Although this concept may sound imposing, it should not be. When functions of a computer are compared to human thought processes, the five parts of the model can be easily understood. Both people and computers can (1) perceive information about their environment (input), (2) remember those perceptions (storage), (3) operate on these perceptions (processing), (4) make decisions on what to do next (control), and (5) act on their environment (output). Computers are machines that extend human thinking. To the extent that these five functions represent human thought processes, they also represent the functions of a computer. Table 1.1 relates these human and computer functions by giving meaning and examples of each.

These five functions of a computer are central to the understanding of the concepts presented in this text, and they should be committed to memory. (The abbreviation ISPCO is derived from the first letter of each of the five functions.)

The ISPCO model of computer functioning is well accepted as a model in the computer field, and it will be used to organize and present material throughout this textbook. The functioning of all computer hardware and software will be broken down and described in terms of input, storage, processing, control, and output. Frequent figures will be provided to help orient the reader to the specific ISPCO functions being discussed.

Let us consider an example in which we will use the ISPCO model to organize our knowledge about a particular computer operation. The following ISPCO case study is illustrated in Figure 1–4.

Case Study

Larry Miles was broke. It was Saturday night and he had a date, but he'd forgotten to get money from his bank. So he decided to go to his bank's 24-hour automated teller, "Compu-teller," and withdraw $100. He was glad he had asked the bank to connect his checking account to the automated machine!

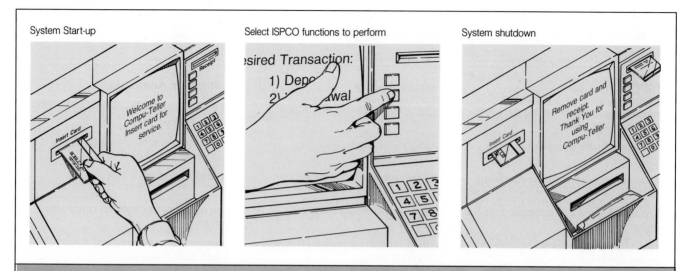

System Start-up   Select ISPCO functions to perform   System shutdown

Figure 1–4   The Larry Miles Case Study: Using an Automatic Teller Computer

He raced his car over to the bank, pulled up next to the automated teller machine, and rolled down his window. Then the interaction between Larry and the machine went like this:

1. Larry pushed his automated teller card into a special slot on the front of the Compu-teller. He could hear some kind of machinery whirring and clunking in the background before the plastic screen that covered the rest of the Compu-teller began to rise.
2. The small screen at the top of the Compu-teller flashed a message to Larry: "Enter your PIN number:". Larry knew that PIN stood for "personal identification number," a secret code number that protected his account. Larry had to enter it using a small numeric keyboard on the machine. If the proper PIN were not entered, the machine would not give access to his account. In that way, no one else could use Larry's teller card. Responding to the message, Larry typed in the four digits of his secret number.
3. Larry typed his PIN correctly, and the machine responded with a new message on the screen. It looked like this:

```
Hello, Larry Miles
What would you like to do?

1 = Deposit money to account
2 = Withdraw money from account
3 = Check status of account
4 = Quit using compu-teller

Push the button corresponding to your choice.
```

4. Larry pressed the number 2 on the keyboard. The screen on the machine immediately changed to request the amount of money he wished to withdraw:

```
Enter amount to withdraw:

Press the CANCEL key if you make an error.
Press the ENTER key if the value is correct.
```

In response to the request, Larry pressed the keys 1 0 0 . 0 0 ENTER to get $100.

5. The machinery whirred again and a small door on the side of the machine opened. Sitting inside the door were five $20 bills. Larry took the money.

6. Larry triggered an electric eye when he took the money. The machine knew that he had taken it, so the money door slowly closed.

7. The teller machine then displayed its original screen asking Larry what to do. He pressed a 4 to terminate the interaction. A printed receipt of the transaction was ejected through a slot near the top of the machine. Larry took the receipt and noted that he now had $574.12 in his account. Finally, the Compu-teller pushed Larry's card out through the slot and lowered the plastic shield back over itself. Larry took the card and left for his date.

To better understand what happened in this interaction and to be able to generalize from it, let's organize Larry's trip to the bank using our ISPCO model (remember, ISPCO stands for *input, storage, processing, control,* and *output*). In fact, we can examine Larry's trip in two different ways within the ISPCO model. First, let's consider the specific *sequence of events* that Larry went through at the bank. Some of the steps that he used when he withdrew the money are identical every time he uses the machine. For example, the interaction is always started up by inserting the teller card and terminated when the plastic shield is lowered back over the controls. Other steps may vary depending on the type of interaction. For example, if Larry uses the teller machine to deposit money or check on the status of his account, a different set of steps than those for withdrawal must be used. But for any specific task, the steps are always the same.

The second way of looking at the trip to the teller machine is to consider the *alternative capabilities* that are available every time Larry uses the machine. No matter when he uses it, the machine always has the same set of input, storage, processing, control, and output capabilities. Once started, the machine can always accept inputs from the small keyboard and generate outputs to the screen and money drawer, and it can remember Larry's account balance and update it as needed. Like the automated teller, every computer has a number of ISPCO capabilities that are common to all of its uses and which define the range of tasks it can perform.

■ Scripts

The sequence of events that occurred between Larry and the teller machine is an example of a **script**. In the theater, an actor's script describes the characters in a play, the scenery, the required props, and most importantly, the sequence of interactions that occur between the characters. Psychologists and computer scientists have borrowed the word *script* to describe how people and intelligent computer systems remember sequences of events. For example, whenever someone talks about "eating at a restaurant," a number of thoughts come to mind including things like: the characters (a hungry person, a waiter, a cook, and a cashier), the props (tables, menus, food, and drink), and a sequence of events (be seated, order the food, wait for the food, eat the food, pay for the food). Such scripts are the basic mechanisms by which people remember sequences of actions.

In this text, an ISPCO script is the sequence of input, storage, processing, control, and output commands that a person must issue in order to get a computer system to complete a particular task. Much of learning to use computers, then, is learning the appropriate ISPCO scripts. To aid with that learning, this text will present many case studies so that the reader can understand, develop, modify and remember scripts for working with computers. Consider the ISPCO script that summarizes the interaction that Larry just had with the teller machine. There were three essential parts to the interaction:

script (ISPCO script)
A summary listing of the sequential steps required to complete a specific task using a computer.

1. *Start-up* The first element in the script is Larry starting up the system. He inserted his card and keyed in his personal code to begin the interaction.
2. *Select ISPCO Functions* Once the system was started up, Larry selected the various ISPCO functions that he wished the machine to perform. He *input* to the machine that he wanted to withdraw money (he pressed button 2), then he read the machine's *output* (on the screen) asking how much he wanted. He *input* the amount of money he wanted (by pressing the keys to make the number 100.00) and he received an *output* of money (from the cash door). The machine retrieved his previous balance from *storage* (although Larry couldn't see it happening), performed a *process* of subtracting the withdrawal from his account, and then remembered the remaining balance in its *storage*. The machine then gave a printed *output* (receipt) showing Larry's remaining balance. Throughout this interaction, the *control* of the activities (the ordering of the tasks involved) is shared between Larry and the machine. Sometimes Larry specified the order of tasks to be performed (as he chose to make a withdrawal instead of a deposit) and sometimes the computer defined the order (as it subtracted the withdrawn amount from Larry's total balance).
3. *Shutdown* The last element of the script is the shutdown when Larry collected his receipt and teller card and left the machine.

This simple interaction between a person and an automated teller machine provides a basic description of every interaction between a *person* and *a computer*. Every interaction with a computer follows a similar script or sequence of actions: there is a start-up procedure, a series of ISPCO functions, and a method for shutdown. As we proceed through this text, more specific scripts for using many varieties of computer hardware and software will be given. These scripts will provide ready answers to such questions as "How do I type a letter on a word processor?" by showing the steps required to perform the task.

THE SIMPLEST ISPCO SCRIPT

1. *START UP THE COMPUTER SYSTEM.* This step includes turning on electrical power, finding appropriate disks, and so forth.

2. *CHOOSE VARIOUS ISPCO ACTIONS.* Some mechanism is provided for the user to enter ISPCO commands and data.

3. *SHUT DOWN THE COMPUTER SYSTEM.* This step includes possibly saving data onto disk or other permanent storage and turning off electrical power.

■ Frames

frame (ISPCO frame)
An illustration that summarizes the generic or general input, storage, processing, control, and output capabilities of hardware or software systems; frames provide places for the reader to enter information on his or her specific system.

Although Larry and the teller machine interacted in a particular manner on this occasion, there are a number of characteristics that are true of the teller machine *independent* of the actions that are being performed. For example, the teller machine can generate three varieties of output, namely, it can print information on its screen, it can print a receipt, and it can dispense money. These underlying capabilities of the machine are always present regardless of whether they are used during a particular interaction. An illustration of a computer system's functional abilities is called a **frame**.

Like a script, a frame is a simple memory concept. It represents information about objects that does not change over time. For example, when you find out that a friend bought a new car, you immediately ask what model? what color? what size engine? or manual or automatic? You never ask, how many wheels does it have? because you already know the answer—this information never changes. Both the varying information (e.g., color) and the constant information (e.g., number of wheels) are part of a person's understanding of a car, even though they are not explicitly stated in every case.

In this text, an ISPCO frame will describe software or hardware in terms of the structures and functions that do not change over time. It summarizes all of the possible ISPCO functions that a computer system can perform. This text will provide explicit and detailed ISPCO frames for all common varieties of computer software systems so that the reader of the text can easily organize any particular computer system in terms of the general descriptions in the ISPCO frames. An ISPCO frame helps a computer user organize the many aspects of computer use. Major concepts throughout the text will be summarized in such frames. The boxes on the left side of the frame will always be filled in to describe the precise concepts being referenced. The boxes on the right will be empty except for prompts; in these boxes the users can fill in specific details for their own systems right next to the generic concepts they have learned from the text.

Let's consider the ISPCO functions that Larry's teller machine might perform over the course of many visits.

1. *Input.* The Compu-teller machine can accept a certain variety of inputs. Larry can insert his automatic teller card, he can input arbitrary choices when the computer gives him a set of options, and he can input an amount to be deposited or withdrawn. In addition, when depositing money, he physically inputs a check or cash to the machine.

2. *Storage.* The Compu-teller must store and recall many things. Larry's real PIN must be remembered so that it can be compared to the one entered by the card user. The machine must also remember Larry's previous balance and any change that is made to it. If a withdrawal is made, it must remember the date, time, and amount of withdrawal. If a deposit is made, it must remember the date, time, and amount of deposit, and it must remember to have the deposit double-checked by a person.

3. *Processing.* The Compu-teller must compare the PIN that was entered by Larry with the true one in its memory. It must subtract any withdrawal from the account and add (when verified) any deposit to the account.

4. *Control.* The computer program that drives the Compu-teller controls the order in which the I, S, P, and O functions occur. For example, the program requires the entry and verification of a PIN before access to an account is allowed.

5. *Output.* The Compu-teller can output a wide variety of messages to its screen or on its printed receipt. When a withdrawal is made, it can output cash if the PIN is correct and the account balance is adequate.

These functions are summarized in the ISPCO frame. Note that a frame is essentially a list of all of the ISPCO functions that a particular computer system can perform.

A Simple ISPCO Frame

	Underlying Concept	Specifics for Larry Miles' System
ON/OFF	START-UP: Method for starting up an automated bank-teller system. Usually includes a plastic card and a secret identification code.	Needed to start up: bank card received from bank Secret code: 55342 Procedure: Insert card into slot. When screen asks for PIN, type in secret code number and press ENTER.
ON/OFF	SHUTDOWN: Method for terminating the interaction with an automated bank-teller system. Usually by choosing QUIT on a menu.	Procedure: Press CANCEL at any time to get to the main list of options on the screen. When on this screen, type the number 4 to terminate the interaction. Remember to retrieve money, card, and receipt.
INPUT	INPUT: Possible inputs include identification codes, commands, cash and check deposits, and dollar amounts for processing.	Input devices: Numeric keypad for entering PIN, dollar amounts, and some command selections; other keys for canceling, confirming commands, et cetera. Slot for accepting envelopes with cash or checks (no coins); and another slot for accepting card.
STORAGE	STORAGE: Automated tellers must have access to all information about accounts—deposits, withdrawals, balance, identification codes, and so on.	Storage devices: Unknown. Clearly it knows Larry's secret PIN, account balance, what he types in, et cetera, but this information is hidden in the bank somewhere. Irrelevant to Larry's use, except that it won't let him withdraw money he doesn't have!
PROCESS B = 2 + C	PROCESS: an automated teller can generally allow deposits, balance inquiries, withdrawals, fund transfers, and the like.	Processing: It allows deposit or withdrawal of funds from checking and transfer to or from checking or savings. It will not give any access to other accounts at the bank (like an IRA). It allows loan payments but Larry doesn't have any loans.
CONTROL	CONTROL: Shared between the user (when options are selected) and the computer (when its program runs).	Control: Compu-teller controls initially by demanding correct PIN. Then user controls by choosing option. Then computer controls processing for that option. The computer and user continue to switch control back and forth in this way throughout the interaction.
OUTPUT	OUTPUT: Possible outputs include money, messages to screen, and printed receipt. Messages inform user about the interaction's status.	Outputs: Balances are printed on receipts. Command options are displayed on screen. Each action performed is documented on the printed receipt. Money (in bills) comes out of drawer on the bottom.

It is of critical importance that the reader understand these three concepts: the ISPCO model, ISPCO scripts, and ISPCO frames. To review, the *ISPCO model* states that most of the important characteristics of any hardware or software system can be described in terms of five computing functions: input, storage, processing, control, and output. This may sound like a simple idea, but the ISPCO abbreviation provides a very effective organizer for computing instruction.

The *ISPCO script* is a *summary of the steps* for performing certain computing tasks. The most general script says that all interactions with a computer begin with some type of start-up procedure, continue with an arbitrary sequence of ISPCO functions controlled by a person and computer, and terminate with a shutdown process. Most chapters in this text will include more specific scripts that tell the reader how to perform particular types of actions with software or hardware.

Finally, the *ISPCO frame* is a *summary of a computer system's capabilities*. It lays out all possible input, storage, processing, control, and output functions available in the system. The ISPCO model, ISPCO scripts, and ISPCO frames organize the material in the text, and they demonstrate the underlying similarities that exist across computer systems. They cannot, however, include all aspects of computer operations. For example, the ISPCO scripts and frames in this chapter's case study do not include any information about the creation of the **computer program** that runs the Compu-teller. (This was done by employ-

computer program
A procedure for solving a problem with a computer; a list of instructions that directs the computer to perform certain tasks to produce the desired results.

Computer Insights
Computer Software: The Varieties of Common Software

Seven varieties of computer software are in very common use: word processors, spreadsheets, data base management systems, graphic systems, communication systems, programming systems, and operating systems. Although these software systems will be described in detail later in the text, a brief description of each type of system follows.

Word processors are used to create documents. They work with two types of data: text and formatting commands. The words that the user wants to write are the text; formatting commands tell how the text should be placed on the page (e.g., what parts should be centered or underlined, and how big the top, bottom, left, and right margins should be). Since documents frequently need changes, word processors are capable of deleting, inserting, or altering the text and the formatting commands, all under user control. The final output of a word processor is a printed document.

Spreadsheets are used to create tables of data arranged in rows and columns. Each location in the table can have one of three things in it: a number (like 8.44), a name (like "payrate"), or an equation that gives an answer based on numbers in other locations of the table (like "grosspay is payrate times hours"). Because the data in the table may change, spreadsheet software provides processes that can delete, insert, or alter what is placed at any table location. The final output of a spreadsheet is a table of data consisting of formulas, words and numbers.

Data base management systems are used to maintain a set of data and generate reports from the data. They work with a set of related data collected into a group called a *record*. A record can contain both words (like "City: Chicago") and numeric data (like "payrate: $5.44"). The major processes available can delete, insert, or alter records, select a subset of records based on some criteria (like "payrate > $5.00"), and generate reports based on the data. The final output of a data base management system is a printed report based on all or a subset of the records.

Graphic systems are of two general types: those that generate business charts (like pie charts) from a set of data, and those that allow the drawing of an arbitrary picture. The chart generating systems are straightforward: the user enters the data to be graphed, the labels for the graph, the type of graph, and other relevant parameters, and then the graph is printed in its final form. The picture drawing systems are very different in that the user actually composes a picture from scratch. The user draws pieces of a picture using some type of drawing or pointing device, edits the picture by inserting, deleting, or changing portions of the picture, and finally prints out the completed image.

Communication systems have the simple purpose of sending data back and forth from one computer to another. The user must first issue a set of commands to inform the system of various communication parameters (the telephone number of the other computer, how fast to send and receive data, etc.). The connection between the local computer and the remote one must then be initiated. Once the connection is completed, the user can operate as though the local computer were the remote computer by entering commands at the local keyboard, having the remote computer process the command, and printing the results on the local screen. Alternatively, the user can request that files of data on one computer be sent to the other.

Programming systems help people write computer programs by accepting a set of instructions from the user in some formal language and then translating these instructions into a form the computer can understand and process.

Operating systems exist on all computers and underlie all other varieties of computer software. The operating system is the computer program that knows how to use the computer hardware. Other software (e.g., a word processor) then uses the programs of the operating system to access the hardware of the system to read the keyboard, print to the screen, use a printer or disk drive, and so forth.

operating system
A set of programs that manages the hardware and software resources of a computer system and enables the user to interface with application programs and peripheral devices. It controls the execution of computer programs and may provide scheduling, debugging, input/output control, accounting, compilation, storage assignment, data management, and related services.

ees of the bank, who had to analyze the tasks to be performed by the teller, synthesize a solution to these tasks, and finally translate the solution into a computer language understandable by the system.) However, the ISPCO devices will prove effective in organizing and directing your thinking about computer hardware and a wide variety of software including **operating systems**, **programming languages**, and the **applications software** packages for **word processing**, **spreadsheets**, **data base management**, **graphics**, and **communication**.

1.3

What Can I Learn From This Text?

programming language
A language suitable for expressing commands that can be executed by a computer (e.g., BASIC).

applications software
Computer programs written to help with particular tasks for a particular set of users. In contrast, *systems software* includes computer programs such as operating systems used to manage and program the computer.

word processing software
An applications program that enables a user to generate and edit arbitrary documents.

spreadsheet software
An applications program that aids the user with the manipulation of tabular data like that found on an accountant's ledger sheet.

data base management system (DBMS)
A set of programs designed to store an interrelated collection of data and allow it to be accessed for a variety of purposes and by a variety of users within an organization.

graphics software
Programs that enable users to create visual displays on screen, paper, film, or other media. The visual displays are generally of two types: business graphs like bar charts or pie charts and arbitrary graphic images like pictures of space shuttles or tennis shoes.

communications software
Applications programs that enable two or more computers to interact with one another.

This text focuses on the use of applications and **programming software** to solve problems. To sharpen this focus and place the discussion of software in its proper perspective, the text includes a history of how computers have evolved, an extensive review of current computer hardware and operating systems, and a thorough coverage of a wide variety of applications software. All of this information is organized and summarized by ISPCO scripts and frames. The ISPCO model is the key to understanding and learning about computers from this text.

Chapter 2 uses the ISPCO functions as a basis for a conceptual history of computing; it will ignore details and focus on historical trends. The oldest "computers" were nothing more than counting frames, like the abacus, that performed the storage function only. Many, many years later came the next evolutionary step, a computer that was capable of storing and processing numbers, such as a mechanical calculator. Computing devices have gradually taken on more and more of the ISPCO functions; today all five functions are commonly performed by computing systems.

Chapter 3 introduces the reader to the hardware of computing in terms of the ISPCO functions. Thus, hardware will be described as input devices (e.g., keyboards, mice, and voice recognition), as storage devices (e.g., floppy disks, RAM, and ROM), as processing and control devices (e.g., microprocessors), and as output devices (e.g., printers and screens).

Beginning with chapter 4 and continuing to the end of the text, a wide variety of applications and programming software will be explored. Operating systems, word processors, spreadsheets, data base management systems, graphics systems, communications systems, and programming languages are all described in detail using ISPCO frames and scripts to help the reader gain on overall perspective of each type of software.

All the chapters of the text are organized as follows:

1. *The Organizing Frame of Reference.* Each chapter begins with an elaboration of the ISPCO model to serve as an organizing base for the chapter. Be sure to study this figure before reading the chapter.
2. *Essential Chapter Concepts.* Each chapter states general goals of the chapter so that the reader knows the general concepts he or she is expected to learn.
3. *The Initial Case Study.* Chapters begin with an anecdote or case study. These case studies give the reader vicarious experience in using computers by presenting people who are trying to solve real-life problems. The case studies provide a first approximation of the ISPCO script that characterizes the use of a particular software or hardware system. The reader should focus on the case study's

general problems and how they are solved rather than on a precise understanding of every detail.

4. *The Main Contents of the Chapter.* Most chapters are organized into sections that discuss the ISPCO functions of the hardware or software covered by the chapter, e.g., the ISPCO functions involved in the use of a word processor.

5. *Other Case Studies.* Some chapters also include a second case study to help the reader put the use of the hardware or software into a more complete perspective.

6. *ISPCO Frames and ISPCO Scripts.* Each chapter ends with a concise description of the chapter contents arranged into an ISPCO frame similar to that shown for the Compu-teller. The ISPCO frame summarizes the major contents of the chapter.

   In addition, there may be one or more ISPCO scripts that explicitly list the steps required to perform common activities described in the chapter. In the same way that Larry Miles' use of the bank teller was summarized by an ISPCO script, so will common uses of hardware or software be described.

7. *The Chapter Review.* Each chapter ends with a detailed list of specific objectives that the reader should attain and a set of questions designed to test achievement of each objective. Other activities may also be suggested.

To find out how well you have understood this introductory chapter, complete the review in the following section.

programming software
A set of software designed to help people prepare computer programs. Programming software is usually associated with a particular programming language, such as BASIC or Pascal.

Chapter 1 Review

Expanded Objectives

The objectives listed below are an expansion of the essential chapter concepts listed at the beginning of the chapter. The review items that follow are based on these expanded objectives. If you master the objectives, you will do better on the review items and on your instructor's examination on this chapter.

After reading the chapter, you should be able to:

1. give valid reasons for learning about computers.
2. recognize the value of generic over specific knowledge of computers.

3. compare people and computers in terms of the ISPCO functions.
4. recognize the necessary interaction between people and computers.
5. match ISPCO functions with their definitions.
6. match a list of computer tasks with their ISPCO functions.
7. give valid reasons for using scripts and frames.
8. recognize the defining characteristics of frames and scripts.
9. match randomly ordered tasks with specific script events.

Review Items

Completing this review will give you a good indication of how well you have mastered the contents of this chapter and prepare you for your instructor's test on this material. To maximize what you learn from this exercise, you should answer each question *before* looking up the answers in the appendix. The number of the corresponding expanded objective is given in parentheses following each question.

Complete the following clusters of items according to the directions heading each set.

A. *True or false.*

____ 1. To successfully compete in the world market, both business and industry will continue to transfer tasks from people to computers. (4)

___ 2. A tax program written for an Apple personal computer will generally work just as well on any IBM computer, since all the machines are so similar. (2)

___ 3. Unfortunately, because of differences in computer systems, we cannot usefully generalize from one computer to another. (2)

___ 4. In the near future, computerized data bases (e.g., banking records) will have little impact on the average person. (1,4)

___ 5. People who have access to electronic information systems will have a decided advantage over those who do not. (1)

___ 6. New jobs will increasingly require skill in using computer systems. (1,4)

___ 7. The computer is a useful tool, but it cannot perform any functions analogous to the intellectual functions performed by people. (3)

___ 8. The interaction between people and computers is increasing. (4)

___ 9. The complexity of the computer field will make it virtually impossible for the average person to understand and use computers at an effective level. (2)

___ 10. A frame summarizes the sequence of steps for accomplishing a computer task. (8)

___ 11. A script summarizes concepts that can be generalized across many uses of software and hardware. (8)

B. *For this cluster of items, match the function on the left with the appropriate description on the right. (To confound guessing, two inappropriate descriptions have been included in the list on the right.) (5)*

___ 12. input
___ 13. control
___ 14. output

a. the manipulation of data
b. the presentation of data to the computer user

___ 15. processing
___ 16. storage

c. the checking of errors in output
d. the retention of data
e. the repair of computer hardware
f. the computer's reception of data
g. the sequencing of tasks performed by the computer

C. *Match the function on the right with the appropriate activity on the left. These questions concern a computer that balances a checkbook. (6)*

___ 17. the computer subtracts a withdrawal to get the new balance

___ 18. the computer displays the correct balance on the computer screen

___ 19. the computer saves the balance on disk until needed next time

___ 20. the computer chooses to add the amount of a deposit to the current balance

___ 21. the computer accepts the amount of a deposit from the user at the keyboard

a. input
b. output
c. control
d. processing
e. storage

D. *Match the task on the right with the script event on the left. These questions concern typing a letter on a computer. (9)*

SCRIPT EVENT	TASK
___ 22. start-up	a. saving a letter to memory
___ 23. select input	b. printing a letter
___ 24. select storage	c. changing parts of a letter
___ 25. select processing	d. turning the computer on
___ 26. select output	e. turning the computer off
___ 27. shutdown	f. type in a letter

2

The Evolution of Computer Hardware and Software

Essential Chapter Concepts

When you are finished with this chapter, you should know:

- How the modern computer fits into the age-old human search for tools to help people think and solve problems.

- How the evolution of computers, from prehistory to the present day, can be viewed as a transfer of the five information processing functions from people to computers.

- What the major historical trends in computing evolution have been: the increase in person/computer contact, the increase in capacity of input, storage, processing, control, and output, and the increase in the variety of problems that can be aided by computer.

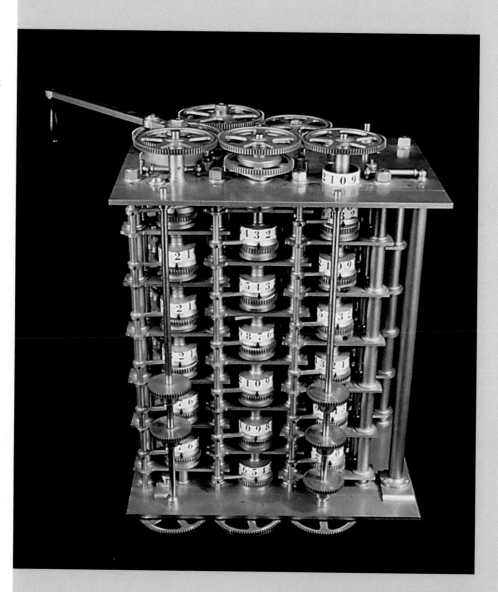

Computer Hardware and Software

INPUT	STORAGE	PROCESS	CONTROL	OUTPUT

Hardware: As computer hardware evolves, it performs more and more of the ISPCO functions.

Software: Instructions move from memorized or written steps to elaborate programs stored in computer memory.

People: People with technical skills use whatever hardware and software is available to solve their problems.

Even the casual observer cannot help noticing the immense effect that the electronic computer has had on the modern world. The major reason that computers have had such an imposing effect is that the computer is the first human invention capable of performing all five of the intellectual functions (input, storage, processing, control, and output) without direct human supervision. The importance of computers has been further magnified by improvements in computer hardware and software that permit almost any individual or group to have access to increasingly powerful computing machines.

To provide a basis for organizing and understanding the constantly changing field of computing, we will begin with a review of the evolution of computing. This review is not intended to convey innumerable facts and details but instead to demonstrate the human needs and trends that have propelled the historical evolution of computing. As the review proceeds, the reader will find that the ISPCO model can serve as a base around which computer knowledge can be organized. This review will set the stage for discussions of hardware and software in later chapters.

As we will do throughout this text, we will begin this chapter with a case study that highlights the purpose and many of the concepts of the chapter. In this case study, we are concerned with the lack of enthusiasm with which most students approach the history of computing. They have the same opinion that Sarah did as she talked with her teacher, Professor Jones:

"Okay, Sarah," said Ms. Jones, "you said you had some questions about the course so far. Sit down and tell me what they are."

2.1

Why Study History?

Case Study

Sarah sat down and plunged right in. "Well, I want to know why we have to study computer history. I really hate memorizing dates and places and things like that. I figure instructors like history and find it interesting, but it's not really what I want. I want to know how to use computers to do all of the things I see other people doing with them."

Professor Jones sighed. She'd answered this question so many times outside of class, she ought to put it in her lecture! "Sarah, there are lots of good reasons to study computer history. To begin with, surveys show that one in five people are so afraid of computers that they avoid using them. History shows that computers are just modern versions of friendly old tools people have used for centuries. Knowing this makes many people less apprehensive and more realistic about computers and learning to use them."

"An early chapter on history also helps apprehensive students get started in computers in a less technical setting. It gives them time to prepare themselves for actually using the computer by learning, for example, the location of the computer lab or how to use a computer keyboard, screen, and disk."

"Okay," said Sarah, "that's reasonable. But I'm not afraid of computers. What good is it for me?"

Professor Jones continued her lecture. "The basic problem is that you have the wrong view of history. Although some instructors emphasize trivial items such as dates and places, the really important part of any history is the perspective it gives. What events actually happened and why? What were the important trends and their causes? These historical insights help you make your personal decisions about computing. Sooner or later, we all have to make decisions about computers."

Sarah wasn't convinced. "But how does knowing history help me make decisions?"

Professor Jones answered, "We have to be able to evaluate current trends and separate important developments from fads and advertising hype. We have to decide what computers to purchase or use, what knowledge we need about computing, and how computers can improve our own lives. Knowing what happened in the past can greatly assist us in having the proper perspective and not being caught up in every fashion advocated by some popular computing magazine. For example, as a student, if you had the money, would you go out and buy a computer? If so, how would you select it?"

"Well," said Sarah, "I guess I would buy the most powerful computer I could afford. I read an article that said most people should own a computer, even students in high school."

"You know, Sarah, that's exactly what lots of people thought who ran out and bought 'home computers' a few years ago," Professor Jones replied. "It turned out that the home computer fad caused otherwise intelligent people to ignore one very important thing: computers are only used if they are useful, that is, if they can help solve problems people need to solve. Most home computers weren't designed properly and completely enough to be useful. They lacked the software and the storage and output devices necessary for them to be used by the home owner or student. Computers were primarily useful for elementary programming and game playing. They couldn't do most things that average people needed done or cared about. The home computer market failed and companies lost millions of dollars. Some even dropped out of the computing industry. The moral to this story is that when you buy computer hardware without deciding what you want to do with it, you are probably wasting your money. After a good history of computing, you would know this and you would be less likely to repeat the mistakes of earlier days."

"As another example," continued Professor Jones, "Yesterday a computer science student asked me if he should learn the new computer language named Ada. The answer was clear from the historical perspective. The computer language COBOL has been used for more computer programs than almost any other language because the U.S. Department of Defense decreed that all programs written for it would have to be done in COBOL. The Department of Defense has just changed its standard language from COBOL to Ada. It's likely that the importance of Ada will come to equal that of COBOL, so, of course, the student would be wise to learn the language Ada!"

"When you look at the trends in computing," Professor Jones finished, "you gain a much deeper understanding of the field. You will see that computers are not magical devices that solve all problems. You will see that the driving force in computer development is ordinary people who are trying to solve problems that are important to them. They need good intellectual tools to help them, and modern day computers are the best intellectual tools we have been able to invent. That old saw about necessity being the mother of invention is really true in computing."

"Okay, okay! I'm convinced," Sarah said. "So, if we look at how people solved problems with computers in the past, we might be able to make more intelligent decisions about our own use of computing today." Sarah leaped up and hurried out of the office exclaiming, "Where's that history chapter? Let me at it!"

"These days," mused Jones to herself. "everybody's a comedian. But at least, maybe she'll read the chapter now!"

Although Sarah will probably find the history of computing far less exciting than the actual use of computers, she should be willing to take the time to understand this history. The diverse perspectives of computer history provide a simple and solid foundation on which to relate the concepts of modern computing systems.

<table>
<tr><td colspan="5">**Computer Hardware and Software**</td></tr>
<tr><td>INPUT NOT AVAILABLE</td><td>STORAGE</td><td>PROCESS NOT AVAILABLE</td><td>CONTROL NOT AVAILABLE</td><td>OUTPUT NOT AVAILABLE</td></tr>
</table>

Hardware:	Performs only the storage function for aiding with manual computation.
Software:	Procedures memorized by people.
People:	Perform the other functions of IPCO mentally.

2.2

Aids to Manual Calculation from Prehistory to 1650

Five thousand years ago (around 3000 B.C.), numerical systems and counting were largely unknown. As these concepts began to evolve, people searched for ways to simplify the problem of counting and remembering. Indeed, the earliest "computers" were devices that aided with manual calculation by helping with the human problem of remembering numbers. Consider the problem of a hypothetical sheepowner named Isaac.

Each spring after lambing, Isaac had his herder, Jacob, move his flock of sheep to the highlands where they could graze on the rich grasses over the summer. However, this spring Isaac was hesitating, for he had come to suspect that Jacob was selling off some of the sheep for his own profit.

Case Study Isaac, the Sheepowner

Isaac pondered the question, How can I make sure that Jacob does not steal my sheep? One night, he had an inspiration. "Before sending my flock to the highlands," he said to himself, "I'll have my sheep pass, one at a time, through a narrow gate. As each sheep passes the gate, I'll drop a stone into a leather bag. When autumn comes and Jacob returns the sheep, I'll pass them through the same gate, but this time removing a stone for each sheep that passes through. If the bag is empty after the last sheep passes, then I'll know that all my sheep have been returned. If I end up with more stones than sheep, Jacob is in deep trouble!"

abacus
A primitive computer used for storing numbers according to the location of counters that slide back and forth in groves or on rods.

Like Isaac's bag of stones, the first primitive computers were quite limited. Of the five computing functions of input, storage, processing, control, and output, they could perform only the storage function for numeric values. All other computing functions were performed by the human mind. Figure 2–1 summarizes some of the ancient tools used for manual calculation. Of all these tools, the **abacus** was probably the most important.

The abacus first appeared around 1000 B.C., with many variations existing across the cultures of Egypt, Greece, Rome, and pre-Columbian Mexico and Peru. The abacus began as a counting frame, that is, a wooden board with grooves. Numbers were represented by pebbles placed in the grooves. Eventually, each groove represented a place value in the decimal system (units, tens, hundreds, and so on).

The software for primitive computers like the abacus consisted of the memorized sequences of steps that people performed. When these steps were followed, they caused changes in what was stored in the computer and thus yielded the desired calculations. Abaci (abaci is the plural of abacus) were used by clerks for business records, as well as by engineers and pre-scientists. Astronomical calculators are thought to have been used in religious rites and in the making of agricultural decisions. Although the devices of this era seem

Figure 2–1 Manual Calculation in Ancient Times. Each of these, the abacus, the caliper, and the hour glass, represented important innovations in manual calculation, in its time.

primitive, with these few aids and incredible ingenuity, the ancients created structures like the Roman aqueducts and the arched bridges of central Spain, which, amazingly, are still in use today.

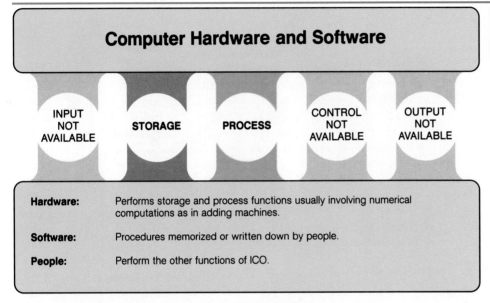

Computer Hardware and Software

| INPUT NOT AVAILABLE | STORAGE | PROCESS | CONTROL NOT AVAILABLE | OUTPUT NOT AVAILABLE |

Hardware: Performs storage and process functions usually involving numerical computations as in adding machines.

Software: Procedures memorized or written down by people.

People: Perform the other functions of ICO.

The next step in computer evolution was the creation of **mechanical computers** capable of storage and processing. One of the people credited with the invention of early mechanical computers was the French scientist, mathematician, and philosopher Blaise Pascal.

mechanical computer
A computer that operates through levers and cogged wheel gears rather than through electrical means. Also referred to as mechanical calculators.

**Case Study
Pascal, the
Accountant**

Blaise Pascal was a talented teenager in Paris about 1640 A.D. His father was a tax auditor who had the tedious task of summing long columns of decimal numbers to balance the accounts of clients. Blaise set for himself the task of helping his father.

As a solution to his father's problem, Pascal invented one of the first adding machines. It used cogged wheels for storage and processing of information. Unlike the abacus, this machine could automatically carry across place values from units to tens, tens to hundreds, and so on. Pascal's invention greatly aided with the laborious summing of numbers in an accounting ledger.

The major evolutionary change in computers of this period was the creation of hardware able to both store and process information. Humans continued to perform the other computing functions—input, control, and output.

The mechanical computer was introduced in the mid-seventeenth century when the adding machine with automatic carrying was developed. In subsequent years, more and more complex numerical computers capable of automatically adding, subtracting, multiplying and dividing were created. The processing of non-numeric information (ie., information other than numbers) was made possible by the use of **punched paper tape** and **punched paper cards.** For example, simple music boxes led to non-numeric mechanical computers controlling entire mechanized orchestras programmed, in part, by punched pa-

punched paper tape
A continuous paper strip used as an input and storage medium; machine-readable programs and/or data is coded by a pattern of punched holes.

punched cards
Small rectangular cards used as an input and storage medium; machine-readable programs and/or data is coded by a pattern of punched holes.

per tape or cards. At the close of this period, a Frenchman named Joseph-Marie Jacquard developed a punched card system that was able to control the weaving of cloth in a textile mill. Two of the mechanical computers from this era are shown in Figure 2–2.

The major hardware breakthrough during this period was the invention

Figure 2–2 Early Mechanical Computers. Pascal's manual calculator (bottom) went from design to application rapidly, but it took over one hundred years for technology to catch up with the design requirements of Babbage's Analytical Engine (top).

of the **cogged wheel.** The cogged wheel represented numbers via positions on the wheel and processed numbers for addition, subtraction, and so on, by movement of the wheel. For example, addition would begin by storing one number in the calculator by setting the wheels to particular positions. A second number was then added to the original by repositioning the wheels. Mechanical interconnection of the wheels permitted carrying across place values during addition. When the calculation was finished, the results were read directly by noting the final positions of the wheels.

With this mechanical computer technology as a base, in 1812 Charles Babbage proposed a computer capable of all the ISPCO functions except control. He called it the **difference engine** because it was designed to produce numeric tables by the mathematical technique called the method of differences. Babbage never actually completed the development of his difference engine because of technical difficulties, lack of patience on the part of governmental sponsors, and an interest in the design of a newer and better computer. Some years later, however, a Swedish engineer, George Scheutz, succeeded in building a working model.

The new idea that turned Babbage away from the difference engine was the design of his **analytic engine.** This was the first proposal for a general purpose computer capable of all five ISPCO functions. The principal improvement was the provision for a programmable control unit. This control unit could perform different sequences of machine operations based on the patterns of holes punched in pasteboard cards. Unlike the difference engine, which could perform only a small set of tasks, the analytic engine could be programmed with these cards to perform widely differing computations. Although Babbage described all the basic ideas necessary for modern computers, the lack of an adequate technological base delayed the development of such machines for over one hundred years.

The software for mechanical computers was more formal than that for simple aids to manual calculation. The procedures that clerks used to operate the mechanical calculators were written down and were essentially the first computer programs.

With the hardware of mechanical calculators and the software of written

cogged wheel
A gear used in early calculators to automatically carry place value from units to tens, from tens to hundreds, and so on.

difference engine
A mechanical computer envisioned by Charles Babbage; it would perform mathematical computations using the method of differences.

analytic engine
A mechanical computer proposed by Charles Babbage but never completed by him. It was to be the first true computer capable of all five ISPCO functions.

Computer Insights
Profiles in Computing: Augusta Ada Byron

The history of computing described so far has included few female contributors. In no way is this due to anything other than the historical reality of a less enlightened time. Of special note, therefore, is one of the first women to contribute to the underlying conception of the computing field, Augusta Ada Byron.

Augusta Ada Byron was the daughter of Lord Byron, the poet, and was an excellent mathematician. She encountered the work of Charles Babbage in a French paper on his difference and analytic engines. After contacting Babbage, she translated this paper into English and added her own notes on the subject. Included in these notes was the first com-

puter program, which was intended to compute a mathematical series of numbers. In addition, Byron realized that when a sequence of instructions had to be repeated during a calculation, it was unnecessary to make a second copy of the instructions. The same set of commands could be reused by going back and repeating the instructions until some condition was met; in programming this repetition of commands is called a *loop*.

In honor of her role as the first computer programmer, the U.S. Department of Defense named its newly designed computer language *Ada*.

procedures, the variety of computer applications and the number of people using them vastly increased. Many businesses regularly used computers to perform jobs formerly done by people. Perhaps as a result, the first signs of fear or hatred of computers began to emerge in the nineteenth century. During this period, for example, over eleven thousand Jacquard looms (automated textile looms) were put into use in France, resulting in substantial job losses for textile workers. Disgruntled workers, in attempts to wreck the machines, threw wooden shoes or *sabots* into the works of the loom. The French word *sabotage* is said to be derived from this practice.

2.4

Electromechanical Computers: 1900–1945

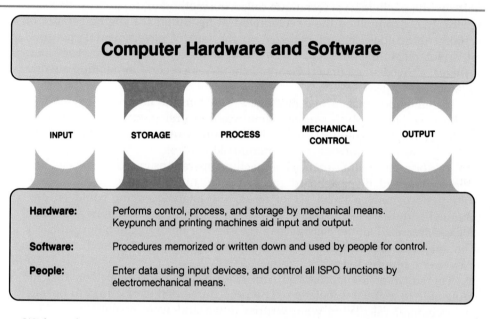

Computer Hardware and Software

INPUT   STORAGE   PROCESS   MECHANICAL CONTROL   OUTPUT

Hardware:	Performs control, process, and storage by mechanical means. Keypunch and printing machines aid input and output.
Software:	Procedures memorized or written down and used by people for control.
People:	Enter data using input devices, and control all ISPO functions by electromechanical means.

With each new improvement in computer hardware, computer applications spread. The greater the improvement, the greater the demand for the device, and the demand, in turn, stimulated other hardware improvements. The next step in the evolution of the hardware for computing was the development of **electromechanical computers.** The need for such machines arose from problems in handling massive amounts of data, problems like those faced by Herman Hollerith.

electromechanical computer
A type of early computer in which data was represented by cogged wheels and processing was performed by altering the positions of the wheels using small, electrically driven motors.

**Case Study
Hollerith, the
Census Taker**

In 1885, Herman Hollerith was faced with a serious problem. Hand tabulation of the 1880 United States census was proceeding with glacial slowness, even with the use of mechanical calculators. In fact, the tabulation of the last census would not be finished until long after 1890, when the next census data was to be collected. Hollerith envisioned himself lagging further and further behind.

Hollerith solved his problem by adding electricity to the punched card concepts of Jacquard's loom and Babbage's difference engine. He created an electromechanical computer that could automatically input data via punched cards, accumulate the data, and output the results. The punched cards, about the size of a dollar bill of that era, eventually became standardized with 12 rows and 80 columns. Each column could be used to hold some numeric value like the number of children in a family; the specific value was determined by which hole in the column was punched out. The added speed and processing power of this new type of computer allowed Hollerith to complete the census data by 1888 and the 1890 census in less than three years.

The electromechanical phase in the evolution of computing technology had its beginnings in the 1880s and continued through 1945, culminating in the realization of Babbage's dream of a general-purpose computer. Basic developments in this period included the steady refinement of mechanical computing through the use of small electric motors to automatically move the gears that represented data. Fundamental to all of these developments was the idea of representing information as holes punched into paper cards and as changes in the state of electrical circuits.

In this period, most of the hardware functions previously performed by humans were gradually taken over by computers. Input was no longer directly performed by humans. Instead, information was punched into paper cards or tape and input under machine control. Similarly, output was provided by electromechanical printers attached to the computers. The computer continued to increase its capacity for storing and processing information. The main hardware task left to people was control. Even this function could be performed by computer hardware by the close of World War II. Two electromechanical computers are shown in Figure 2–3.

Hollerith's invention began this era of computing, and another computing milestone occurred in 1937, when Howard H. Aiken of Harvard University proposed to the Computing-Tabulating-Recording Company that the first fully automatic calculating machine be built. This collaboration resulted in the Harvard Mark I, which was completed in 1944. The MARK I weighed 5 tons, could store 72 numbers and could perform 3 additions every second or a multiplication every 3 seconds. It included facilities for storage and processing and for control by means of instructions on punched tape. In addition, the Mark I set many precedents for succeeding computers. For example, it provided a special set of circuits (an **instruction register**) that would break each instruction on the paper tape into two parts: an **operation code** that told which process to perform, and an **address** that designed a particular storage location containing the data to use during the process.

The software introduced with mechanical computers continued to be important in electromechanical computers. However, one new element was introduced—a primitive program that was stored on a **plug board.** A plug board was a large board containing many electrical connections that could be easily altered by unplugging and replugging wires. The operation of the machine would depend, in part, on the pattern of wires plugged into the board. For example, setting the plugs one way might cause the machine to sum the numbers in columns 1 through 10 of all cards processed, while another plug setup might sum numbers in columns 11 through 20 instead. Plug boards were the first means through which the computer could control its own functions by means of internally stored sets of instructions.

instruction register
A set of circuits inside a computer where instructions to the computer are placed for decoding and execution. Instructions include operation codes and addresses for data to be processed.

operation code
The part of a computer instruction that indicates what operation (e.g., addition or subtraction) is to be performed on the data.

address
The part of a computer instruction code that specifies a particular storage location for data in memory; in other instances, the location of a particular input, storage, processing, control, or output device of a computer.

plug board
A simple device for programming early computers. The pattern of electrical connections in the computer could be altered by a board with many plugs connected by wires. Changing the connections between the plugs changed the program.

Figure 2–3 Electromechanical Computers. Two of the more famous of the electromechanical computers were the Harvard Mark I (left), the first successful general purpose computer, and Hollerith's Tabulating Machine (right), used to compute the census.

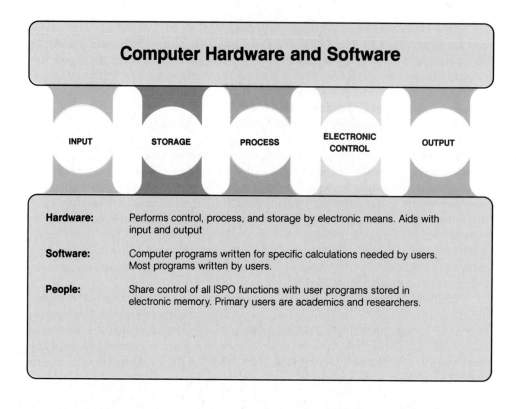

Computer Hardware and Software

INPUT   STORAGE   PROCESS   ELECTRONIC CONTROL   OUTPUT

Hardware:	Performs control, process, and storage by electronic means. Aids with input and output
Software:	Computer programs written for specific calculations needed by users. Most programs written by users.
People:	Share control of all ISPO functions with user programs stored in electronic memory. Primary users are academics and researchers.

With hardware and software now capable of performing tasks useful to a large number of people, the foundations of the computer industry were laid. Large business computing firms were established to serve the increasing need of business, industry, and science for faster and more automatic calculating devices. Hollerith's punched card machines grew into accounting machines capable of performing most business accounting functions. Hollerith's company, the Tabulating Machine Company, was part of the Computing-Tabulating-Recording Company, the firm that became IBM. Eventually, IBM developed a vast marketing prominence in the field of business machines; this situation later permitted IBM to seize the dominant position in the computer industry.

2.5

Noncommercial Electronic Computers: 1945–1950

The next major step in the evolution of computers was the creation of **noncommercial electronic computers.** These machines placed the input, storage, processing, and output functions under the control of a program stored in the computer itself and operated at speeds much greater than those of electromechanical computers.

Case Study The Ultra Story

If necessity is the mother of invention, then wars, as major sources of "necessity," must inspire their share of inventions. World War II, in which over 55 million people were killed, certainly provided awesome necessities. Largely unprepared at the beginning, the Allies turned to a variety of technological inventions in their search for survival.

By 1940, Germany had developed a secret coding machine called the Enigma. The Enigma was a coding machine that used a frequently changed secret "key" to scramble letters in messages in such a way that they could only be deciphered by another Enigma set to the same key. If this key could be discovered quickly enough, the code could be broken. Germany's finest mathematicians and code specialists estimated that no human or computer could discover their secret coding key rapidly enough to be useful. The Allies desperately needed to determine a way to break the codes!

The British solved the problem by building a better and faster computer with solely electronic mechanisms; its code name was the Ultra System. With significantly faster capabilities for control, storage, and processing, and using a captured Enigma machine as a model, the Ultra System could break German codes. According to some military historians, the resulting intelligence was a key factor in determining the outcome of World War II.

During the noncommercial phase of electronic computing, the primary way to acquire an **electronic computer** was to build one! As a result, this period of computer development was dominated by the people able to build computers, specifically, academic researchers, engineers, and scientists. Two of the first noncommercial electronic computers are shown in Figure 2–4.

In this period, the technological base of computers switched from electromechanical devices to electronic circuits using **vacuum tubes.** The computers based on this technology have historically been referred to as **first generation computers.** The most significant improvement brought about by these first generation machines was that they were able to perform all of the hardware functions of previous computers, namely, input, storage, processing, control, and output, but *at electronic speeds:* in 1945 computers were capable of performing roughly one calculation per second, but by 1950, they were performing thousands of calculations per second.

Based on these expanding technologies, J. P. Eckert, Jr., and J. W. Mauchly of the Moore School of Electrical Engineering at the University of Pennsylvania built the Electronic Numerical Integrator and Calculator (ENIAC) in 1946 as a true, general purpose, electronic computer. It could be pro-

noncommercial electronic computers
Computers developed between 1945 and 1951, when computers were not sold commercially. To acquire a computer during this period, an organization had to build one.

electronic computer
A computer in which data is handled electronically, that is, by electrical currents, thus permitting rapid performance of input, storage, processing, control, and output, especially compared to earlier mechanical computers.

vacuum tube
A basic electronic switching device used in first generation computers.

first generation computers
The first computers to handle data electronically through the use of vacuum tubes. If a vacuum tube was conducting electricity, it represented a 1 and if it was not conducting, a 0.

Computer Insights
Profiles in Computing: John von Neumann

Many of the theoretical foundations of present-day computing have been attributed to the mathematical genius John von Neumann (pronounced "von Noýman"). One example is the idea of the stored program. A stored program computer keeps the instructions that define its processing in storage much in the same way it keeps data. With this system, one computer can perform widely different functions by changing the stored instructions. This stored program concept was first implemented by Arthur Burks, Herman Goldstein, and von Neumann during the development of the EDVAC computer.

Most computers today are called von Neumann machines because they are designed using the concepts first proposed by von Neumann. By using stored programs, a computer like a little home computer can be a video game one minute, a letter-writing system the next minute, a checkbook-balancing system the next, and an income tax aid the next. When the computer is started up, it does a very simple thing: it copies a program from a computer disk into storage. Then this stored program is executed. Different disks load different programs that perform different tasks.

Von Neumann contributed greatly to our modern technological society. An often quoted story was that on days when he was in the mood, he would spend the morning visiting his colleagues gathering up their most troublesome theoretical problems and think about them over lunch. Then in the afternoon, he would retrace his steps and give each of the scientists the solutions for most of their problems.

Figure 2–4 Noncommercial Electronic Computers. The computer instructions for ENIAC (top), the first electronic computer, were accomplished through switching wires by hand. The ENIAC was soon followed by the EDVAC which could be programmed through internally stored instructions, an idea conceived by John von Neumann, pictured here.

grammed to perform a wide variety of information processing tasks by having a technician reprogram the computer by rewiring its program panels using as many as 6000 switches. ENIAC was the first machine to use electronic circuits exclusively for the function of information storage, processing, and control (although patent lawyers have argued successfully in court that an earlier machine by John Atanasoff contained all of the essential design principles).

Computer Insights
Profiles in Computing: Commodore Grace Murray Hopper

Anyone who programs a computer owes a debt to Grace Hopper, who was instrumental in the development of "people-oriented" computer programming languages. Grace Hopper was born in New York City in 1906. After receiving a B.A. in mathematics and physics from Vassar, she joined the U.S. Naval Reserve and remained in the military until retirement. Hopper found her way into computing at Harvard while working as a programmer on the MARK I. Later, she joined the Eckert-Mauchly Corporation to work on the UNIVAC I.

Hopper had a unique view of programming for that time: programming ought to be made easier for people to do. She worked to make programming easier by helping to develop programming languages that were simpler for people to read and write. Specifically, Hopper developed the first compiler and the first compiler for symbolic languages. Just as a knowledgeable human can translate a book written in French into English, a compiler translates a set of instructions in a quasi-human language into another language that the computer can understand. Grace Hopper's inspired view of what programming languages should be like led her to develop COBOL (COmmon Business Oriented Language), the first English-like language for computer programming.

In this and in other work, Hopper was always a staunch foe of the establishment. In her office, she kept a ship's clock that was probably the only one in the U.S. Navy that ran backwards!

In 1945, before the ENIAC was actually completed, John von Neumann proposed a means for overcoming the tedious and time-consuming programming task required by the ENIAC design. His idea was to store the program in the computer's memory, where, like any other data, it could be modified. Changing a program thus became relatively easy when contrasted with shifting thousands of wires. In 1951, von Neumann implemented this idea with his new machine, the Electronic Discrete Variable Automatic Computer (EDVAC). The important feature of EDVAC was its large storage, which allowed the retention of programs in memory.

The major improvement in programming during this era was the development of **machine language programming.** To get a computer to perform a particular set of processes, a programmer was no longer required to rewire boards but could use a symbolic equivalent. The codes for a set of instructions were represented as a string of 0's and 1's (the equivalent of whether a plug was in or out of a particular hole in a plug board). These codes were then placed into computer storage by flipping switches on the computer's control panel. Once the code was stored in memory, the computer could be instructed to perform the sequence of commands that the codes represented.

During this time period, three-fourths of the new machines were one of a kind, with financial support for their development coming from universities and government. Applications of electronic computers were primarily focused on research problems, and the users were physicists, engineers, and scientists, but the necessary technical developments for commercial computers were completed in this era.

In 1951, just after the close of this period, Remington Rand sold the first UNIVAC I to the Bureau of the Census and began the commercial sale of first generation hardware. With the UNIVAC I, Remington Rand had an early lead over IBM in commercial computing. As the computing industry began to grow, professional organizations such as the Association for Computing Machinery (ACM) were established to further the new field of computing.

machine language programming
The most primitive computer programming language, in which all instructions are made from strings of 0's and 1's. Machine language is the only language the computer processes directly. Any other programming language must be translated into machine language before it can be used.

2.6

Batch Processing Computer Systems: 1950–1965

Computer Hardware and Software

INPUT   STORAGE   PROCESS   BATCH CONTROL   OUTPUT

Hardware:	Performs all ISPCO functions. Overall control by operating system that performs tasks in batches. Each task controlled by user program.
Software:	Batch operating systems, programming language software, user applications software.
People:	Use computers widely in business and government. Users provide most input data by keypunching. Users create programs in FORTRAN and COBOL to solve specific problems.

batch operating system
An operating system able to manage the processing of a sequence of computer users' jobs, *one at a time,* without human intervention.

As the computing field moved into the era of widely available commercial electronic computers, there was a gradual improvement in the control functions available to users. The first new control mechanism was the **batch operating system,** which developed in response to problems faced by people like a hypothetical computer pioneer, Phil.

Case Study
Phil, the Physicist

Phil had long been fascinated by the computer and had actually assisted in the design of one of these electronic monsters. Because of his recognized expertise, Phil's bosses had made him responsible for the care and feeding of one such machine that had been installed across the hall from his office. There was only one problem: everyone in the company wanted to begin using this new wonder, and Phil discovered, much to his dismay, that increasing amounts of his time were being used to start up the computer and assist company personnel in using the computer. He didn't mind their use of the machine, but the use of his valuable research time for this relatively trivial task was another matter! How did Phil escape his dilemma?

Having kept close tabs on the development of computers across the country, Phil decided to follow the lead of others and create a special type of computer program called a batch operating system. He set aside a few months and busily began creating a computer program that would read in other people's programs and perform the tasks they requested! After working long and hard on it, he named it POS (for Phil's Operating System). POS would read a user's cards into the computer and treat each card as a command from the user that would control what processing was performed next.

Once he had the program operating, Phil locked his door tightly and refused to answer the phone. Users wanting to use the computer were greeted by a big sign that said, "Place your punched cards here. Your job will be run during the night and you can pick up the results in the morning." After setting up the system, Phil had to worry about users' needs only twice a day. He would go over to the computer at 5 P.M., load all of the punched cards into a punched card reader, and start up his POS program. POS would then read in the cards for the first job and perform the computing tasks described thereon. After the completion of job 1, POS would continue with job 2, job 3, and so on. Phil would then leave POS to work on its own: reading cards, computing, and printing output! The next morning he would sort and package the cards and any printed output that had been generated and place them in a basket with a sign that informed the users, "This basket contains the finished jobs brought in yesterday."

In the beginning, commercial computers were operated by the user. The marketing of the first commercial electronic computer, the UNIVAC I, made available the power of computers to business, industry, and government. Computers like the IBM 650 arose as rent-by-the-hour machines used to process a single user job at a time. User tasks were described on punched cards or magnetic tape and then input to the computer for execution.

As the anecdote about Phil relates, this single-user-at-a-time philosophy was eventually replaced by a batch operating system in which the tasks for different users could be combined together into stacks or batches and executed as a sequence of jobs at a later time. Users of batch processing systems were frequently idle while waiting for their turn in the processing queue. The turn-around time (the time a user waited for output after inputting a job) could range from hours to days. The user felt distant from the computer and from those who ministered to it. If anything went wrong with a computer job, it was generally assumed to be the user's fault. Examples of the computing systems in this time period are given in Figure 2–5.

The technological base for single-user and batch computers began with first generation components based on the vacuum tube and evolved into what is called second generation technology. **Second generation computers** were based on a crystallized or solid-state version of the vacuum tube called the **transistor.** Because of this astounding improvement in hardware fabrication (the inventors of the transistor were later awarded a Nobel prize), the cost of computer circuitry plummeted while reliability and processing capacity increased dramatically.

A second advancement in hardware during this era was made in 1952 by Jay W. Forrester of the Massachusetts Institute of Technology. He completed the development of magnetic core storage and installed this new storage system in a computer that had been in operation at MIT for several years, the Whirlwind I. The design of the **magnetic core memory** was based on magnetizing small iron washers. Each of these washers was capable of two magnetic states, magnetized in a clockwise direction or magnetized in a counterclockwise direction. These magnetized states could be interpreted as representing a 1 and a 0, so the **binary number system** could be used to store data in the magnetic core memory. The use of magnetic core technology greatly increased machine reliability and computing speed.

Software advances followed quickly on the heels of the hardware improvements. Although programs could be entered as strings of 0's and 1's on any computer, special programs were written to read in more English-like computer commands and translate them into the 0's and 1's the computer needed. An **assembler** was a program that would accept abbreviations for machine language commands (e.g., LOAD REGISTER1,LOCATION4) and store the corresponding 0's and 1's (e.g., 01001101 0100100100001110) in the computer's memory. Clearly, it was a lot easier for a person to remember and type in the former command rather than the latter. A **compiler** was an even more complicated

second generation computers
Electronic computers that used the transistor as the technological base for electrical circuits.

transistor
An electronic switch that determines whether the current is flowing or not, and can thus represent the required one (on) or zero (off) state in a computer; used in second generation computers.

magnetic core memory
Internal computer memory using tiny rings of metal, each able to store a single bit of data; used for many years until replaced by semiconductor devices.

binary number system
The representation of numbers using only zeros and ones. The binary number system is discussed in chapter 3.

assembler
A computer program that reads an assembly language program and creates a corresponding machine language program that can be processed by the computer hardware.

compiler
A computer program that translates a program written in a high-level language into a program written in (approximately) machine language that the computer can actually execute.

Figure 2-5 Batch Processing. The UNIVAC I (top) was the first of the commercially marketed electronic computers (note a young Walter Cronkite on the right). The IBM 704 was IBM's first truely successful electronic computer (bottom).

computer program that would accept much more abstract commands (e.g., COMPUTE PAY AS THE PRODUCT OF HOURS AND RATE) and translate them into a set of many 0 and 1 commands. Compiled languages were even easier for people to comprehend and use than the languages of assemblers. (Assemblers and compilers will be covered in chapter 11. The reader does not yet need to be concerned about understanding them in detail.)

In the years 1950 through 1955, the commercial computer industry came of age, with a shift away from one-of-a-kind machines to many-of-a-kind commercial models. Vigorous competition for the lead in computer sales arose between Remington Rand and IBM. The first IBM entry into computing (the IBM 650) was not completed until 1953, two years after the release of UNIVAC I. Even though IBM had helped Aiken build the Mark I, its executives failed to realize the potential market for large computers and it continued to concentrate its efforts during the next few years on the production of accounting equipment. Changes in the IBM executive suite and the obvious success of UNIVAC finally jolted IBM into the production of commercial computers. The IBM 704, which made use of the new magnetic core storage, was a booming success.

As the computing industry continued to develop after 1955, two major patterns emerged: rapid growth and continued dominance by IBM. In the ten-year period from 1955 to 1965, the number of computers in the United States increased from an estimated 1000 to 30,000, most made by IBM. By 1965 IBM had built an estimated 70–80% of the 10 billion dollars worth of computers in use in the United States, more than ten times as many computers as were produced by its nearest competitor, Remington Rand.

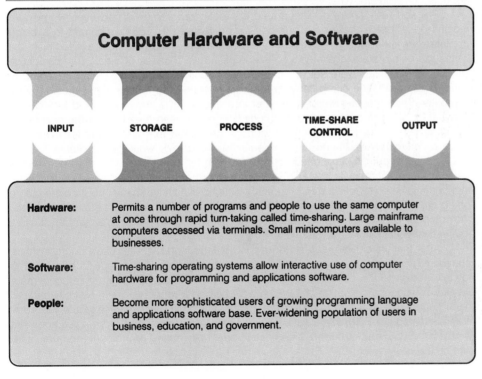

Computer Hardware and Software

INPUT   STORAGE   PROCESS   TIME-SHARE CONTROL   OUTPUT

Hardware: Permits a number of programs and people to use the same computer at once through rapid turn-taking called time-sharing. Large mainframe computers accessed via terminals. Small minicomputers available to businesses.

Software: Time-sharing operating systems allow interactive use of computer hardware for programming and applications software.

People: Become more sophisticated users of growing programming language and applications software base. Ever-widening population of users in business, education, and government.

2.7

Time-sharing Computer Systems: 1965–1975

The need for ever more control over the hardware and software of computing systems led to the next stage in computer evolution, namely, the **time-sharing computer system.** The needs that motivated this change in computing software and the characteristics of the resulting systems are highlighted by the experiences of Polly, a hypothetical computer programmer at a local bank.

timesharing
The simultaneous use of one computer by more than one user, often accomplished by time-slicing, i.e., a very rapid turn-taking enforced by the operating system of the computer. In this turn-taking, each user gets a "slice" of time to run his or her program.

Case Study
Polly, the
Programmer

Polly had worked as a computer programmer at a large bank for over a year and was becoming very good at her job. Although a brilliant programmer, Polly had one real problem: she was a very poor typist. Typically, after working out a very carefully designed computer program, she would go to the keypunch machine, sit down, and begin an agonizing series of keystrokes. When her program was finally keypunched, Polly would try to look through her stack of four hundred cards to see if any typing errors remained. Hoping that there were none, she would make the trip to the computer room and deposit the cards in a stack to be run later in the day on the now famous POS system.

With the computer run set, Polly would return to her work space and try to forget her nagging doubts about the accuracy of the job she had just submitted. Even when involved in the difficult task of creating written documentation for her program, her mind would keep returning to the possibility that some silly error might keep her program from running. Four hours later, she would rush back to the computer room only to discover that she had mistyped her name! The computer, in its narrow way, was not programmed to give access to the mistyped name and had not run her program at all! Polly would quickly retype the card and resubmit the job. After another four-hour wait, she might discover that a second simple typing mistake in one of the computer commands had invalidated all of her results.

Eventually, Polly's threshold for frustration was reached, and she called up the POS company and demanded to talk to the company president, Phil. Phil calmed her concerns by telling her that at that very moment a new system was being set up that would alleviate her problem. What was that solution?

Phil and his team of engineers and computer programmers had been working for months on a system called Phil's Time-Sharing System (PTSS). In contrast to a batch processing system, which worked on one job at a time, PTSS did not have to finish one whole job before starting another. To accomplish this, a series of direct communication links called terminals were set up. Each terminal consisted of a typewriter keyboard to send messages to the computer and a typewriter printer to receive messages from the computer. The computer was so fast that in a fraction of a second it could look at one terminal for a user's command and, if none had been given, then look at the next terminal, then the next, and so on until it found a command that was ready for execution. Once a command was found, the computer would start to work on the problem, but it would stop periodically and check other terminals for commands. As more commands came from more terminals, the PTSS program would correctly schedule all of the seemingly simultaneous requests by giving only a little bit of its time to any one problem before going on to the next one. This process was called time-slicing or time-sharing, because the computer's immense speed permitted it to allocate its time across a number of users in a seemingly simultaneous manner.

After that, when Polly sat down to work, she no longer sat at a keypunch. Instead, she would type (still agonizingly slowly) at a terminal. She would type in her name to identify herself to the computer and would immediately, as far as she was concerned, receive a response indicating whether she had typed it properly. Then, as Polly entered each successive command into the computer, the computer would execute the command immediately. Polly was always aware of how far her work had progressed and what problems, if any, had occurred. Needless to say, Polly called up Phil and congratulated him on the new system.

mainframe computer
A large computer with powerful peripheral devices able to store huge amounts of data and serve many users at the same time.

terminal
A single device that embodies both the input and output functions. It often includes a computer keyboard for input of data to the computer and a television screen or printer for output of data from the computer.

We have already noted that computer technology (like most engineering and scientific endeavors) is cumulative. Old or even ancient methods continue to be used if they are cost-effective. Written procedures such as checklists, which were first used in the nineteenth century, are still used in operating complex machinery today.

Thus, even as new technologies and procedures were made available, many computer installations continued to use the older batch methods while beginning the use of time-sharing. But gradually this era saw the replacement of most batch processing services by more effective time-sharing services, which allowed many users to simultaneously share a large computer and use a variety of hardware and software resources. Time-shared computers were both large and small. Some were capable of simultaneously servicing hundreds of users, while others were limited to just a few. Most often, however, the computer was a centralized **mainframe** designed to serve users through a network of **terminals.** Figure 2–6 provides a view of time-sharing computer systems.

The most important trends in the computer hardware of this time period were size and cost reduction, leading to the development of **third generation computers.** Third generation hardware was based on **integrated circuit technology,** through which hundreds of second generation components could be combined on a single **integrated circuit chip** made out of silicon. As an example of the improvements that were possible with integrated circuits, the IBM 360 Model 50 occupied a single small cabinet instead of a complete room, yet it had a thousand times the computing power of older machines. Integrated circuits used in the IBM 360 increased processing speed, reduced machine cost and machine maintenance, and permitted faster computation and wider distribution of computers.

The major software innovation of this time was clearly the new **operating system software** that allowed time-sharing and **teleprocessing.** An operating system (like POS or PTSS) is just a computer program, but it controls the use

third generation computers
Computers that used integrated circuits as the technological base for their electronic circuits.

integrated circuit technology
The fabrication of entire circuits with many transistors using the same material from which transistors are made. With this technology, large circuit boards can be replaced by tiny pieces of semiconductor material.

integrated circuit chip
A complete circuit containing a large number of transistors imprinted on a small piece of silicon. Used for virtually all aspects of computer hardware fabrication.

operating system software
Programs designed to operate computers with minimal human supervision; discussed in chapter 5.

teleprocessing
The use of communication networks to permit users to interact with remotely located computers.

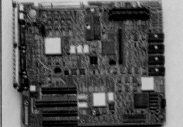

Figure 2–6 Time-Sharing Systems. Announced in 1964, the IBM System/360 time sharing computers (right) represented the first upwardly compatible family of computers, permitting the same programs to operate on all members. The integrated circuit board, in the left picture, made systems like the 360 possible by combining hundreds of electronic elements on a single chip, a major key to size and cost.

of all of a computer's hardware and software. It decides which users are allowed to use which devices and on which schedule. An operating system that permits time-sharing allows more than one person to work at the same time, and each user can behave as if he or she is in complete control of a large computer, even though several persons are using the machine simultaneously. In time-sharing, the programs of two or more users working at different terminals are stored together in the computer's memory. Control of the computer switches back and forth from one terminal to another and from one part of memory to another. Besides enabling ready access by users, time-sharing increases resource efficiency by dividing the cost of computing among its many users.

The concept of teleprocessing arose quite naturally from time-sharing. Since a user was not using the computer directly but was using a terminal to communicate with the computer, the distance between the computer and the terminal was not important. In teleprocessing, special communication lines or just ordinary telephone lines were used to connect a terminal to a computer. A user could be in a different room, building, city, or state from the computer and still have access to the system.

Just as important as the software improvements in operating systems were advances in the software used to support the use of programming languages. Many new programming languages were created for a variety of ap-

Computer Insights
Computer Hardware: Micros, Minis, and Mainframes

During the 1950s, all computers were *mainframe* computers, so named because they were constructed from racks or frames into which electronic circuit boards were inserted. In the 1960s, the miniaturization of electronic components allowed complete computers to be created on a single electronic circuit board. These computers were called *minicomputers* to distinguish them from larger mainframe systems. Finally, in the 1970s it became possible to place entire computers on a single silicon chip, and the name *microcomputer* was coined for such systems.

The differences between mainframe computers, minicomputers, and microcomputers were clear at that time. A microcomputer was a computer in which the processing unit consisted of a single chip with limited amounts of storage. It was based on older and slower technology and was used by and priced for individual users. The minicomputer, in contrast, was a larger system that required an entire circuit board for its processor, could process two to four times the amount of data at one step, and had a storage capacity several times that of a microcomputer. A minicomputer could generally support simultaneous use by a number of users. Finally, the mainframe computer was much more expensive, could process even more information at a single step, and had much larger storage capacities. It was primarily used by large business and organizations.

In recent times, most of these distinctions have broken down. It is common, for example, to find an older mainframe system costing millions of dollars in one room and in the next a newer minicomputer costing far less than the mainframe but having comparable memory and processing capacities. Similarly, there are new microcomputers with greater memory and processing capabilities than older minicomputers.

The primary distinctions that remain are the cost and purpose of the system. Microcomputers are still used primarily by individuals and cost from $1,000 to $10,000 for a basic system with peripherals. Micros are primarily personal computers; the largest manufacturers are IBM and Apple.

Minicomputers primarily serve groups of users or small organizations. Their cost ranges from $10,000 to $100,000 including most peripherals. They are actually the midrange of computers between the personal and mainframe computers. Digital Equipment Corporation and Wang are two of the leading minicomputer firms.

Mainframe computers cost from several hundred thousand to several million dollars. These machines are designed to serve large organizations or computer networks with hundreds or thousands of users. Many have specialized functions, e.g., serving as a centralized national data base for a large corporation. Other larger computers called *super computers* can cost tens of millions of dollars; they can perform calculations that are virtually impossible on other machines. IBM, Control Data, and Cray are three of the leading manufacturers of mainframe computers.

plications areas. Specialized languages were developed for nearly all existing fields of computer applications, and literally hundreds were formulated for some well-recognized areas.

The computer industry as a whole experienced tremendous growth in this time period, but it was a growth with many problems. As more and more businesses and industries began to use computers, it was soon discovered that computers were not the answer to every problem. Many a company purchased a shiny new computer only to discover that the expected benefits of computerization never arrived. Applications software that performed a desired task with accuracy and precision was difficult to find. Software seemed to always lag behind hardware. Knowledge of how the human task of computer programming should be done was nonexistent, and many untrained people tackled the creation of large software systems. As a result, many businesses became wary of the computers that could send an ordinary taxpayer a tax refund of $12 million or a water bill for $200,000.

Computer Hardware and Software

| INPUT | STORAGE | PROCESS | NETWORKING CONTROL | OUTPUT |

Hardware: Links networks of mainframes, minicomputers, and micro- or personal computers to give individual users control over substantial computing resources.

Software: Network software allows any computing systems to be linked together. Personal computer use leads to "user friendly" software for nonskilled users in operating systems, programming, and applications.

People: Almost universally accept the computer as a tool to increase productivity in any profession. The microcomputer makes computers accessible to all.

2.8

Personal Computers and Networks: 1975–?

computer network
A linking of two or more computers so that information can be shared among them.

personal computer
A computer designed primarily for use by an individual or a few individuals. The control and processing may be performed by more than one microprocessor chip. They typically cost less than $10,000.

microprocessor
A single silicon chip that performs the control and processing functions of a small personal computer.

minicomputer
A small computer that can service more than one user at a time through ten or fewer terminals. The cost of a minicomputer is typically less than $100,000.

The last stage of evolution that we can describe in this text is the one in which we are now living. It is the era in which arbitrary **computer networks** are being created by combining **personal computers,** which are designed primarily for individuals and use one or more **microprocessors** (small computers built on a single semiconductor chip), **minicomputers** (a broad range of medium power computers), and mainframe computers (the largest, most powerful class of computers, including supercomputers). At the same time, the hardware available to the average person is becoming more varied, more powerful, and cheaper! Mainframe computer hardware capability that cost literally millions of dollars two decades ago is now available in personal computers and costs only hundreds of dollars. The advancing hardware has the power to run more varied and more complex software, and the software is much easier to use. Where these ever-increasing capabilities will lead us is unclear. But let us consider the beginning of this era with one last vignette concerning our hypothetical computer professionals, Polly and Phil.

Case Study
The Computer
Explosion

Our programmer, Polly, has risen through the ranks of the banking community and is now, thankfully, in a position that does not require much typing. She is the director in charge of all computer applications for a large chain of metropolitan banks, and she is having problems.

The first problem seems to be the need for computing resources. The bank has in recent years bought the largest available PTSS (time-sharing) computer system and has continued to expand its capability whenever possible. But the number of users for her computer hardware are expanding faster than her hardware capacity. She thought she had the problem solved when the company purchased 20 more disk drives (devices that read data to and from magnetic disks) and many extra megabytes (one megabyte is one million characters) of fast memory. But these purchases didn't help, because as soon as the word got around that the computer was faster and better than ever, more users were attracted, the system slowed down again, and now more people than ever before were complaining about the very slow response time of the computer. The system was good— there were just too many users. As if these problems were not enough, Polly was having a real headache trying to coordinate the data processing needs of all of the branches of the bank at their many diverse locations.

Finally, Polly couldn't take it any more and called Phil to see if anything could be done to solve the problem. "Sure. No problem," said Phil. But what was he going to do?

Always watching for trends, Phil and his group had long realized that expanded use of personal computers would be the wave of the future. Having built many large-scale systems, they embarked on the most ambitious yet: a program that would distribute computer processing tasks across many computers made by many manufacturers and in many locations. They would need to set up complex computer networks that would interconnect personal computers with each other and with larger computers so that data could be sent back and forth among them.

Phil and his group established standards that detailed what kind of messages a computer could expect to receive from another computer in the network and what types of responses it could make to these requests. Because of the plummeting price of hardware, they decided to set up small personal computer workstations (individual personal computers linked to a computer network) for individual users. These workstations would contain their own powerful computers, which would provide many of the facilities available on larger systems. When a job exceeded the capabilities of the workstation's own computer, the workstation was designed to transfer the job across the network to a larger system that would complete the task and return the solution. The computers were gradually becoming personalized for each individual user's situation and needs. They communicated with each other and with the user but were independent of each other and could perform autonomously.

Of course, this new system satisfied Polly's need, and Phil's company prospered even more. The users of this new system (Phil's Distributed Network System—PDNS, of course) rarely had to wait for anything. Whenever a new user wanted access to the system, he or she would be given a personal computer workstation. For most of the tasks to be performed, there would be no competition at all for resources; the user's personal computer would do his or her bidding. Only occasionally, when the big machine's data base or greater computing capacity was required by a number of users, was there a possibility of conflict, but even that conflict was insignificant compared to the inconvenience previously suffered by users. Since the personal computers were doing so much, the larger machines were freer to do the complex tasks for which they alone were suited.

The typical computing resource is no longer access to one or two large computers. Today, typical computer users have their own **work stations** with small but powerful personal computers, which can access a network of computers of many sizes, offering an immense array of services and data bases. Thus, the personal computer is the center of a growing web of computer and information services.

In 1982, for the first time in the history of the computing industry, the second largest corporation in total dollar volume (Digital Equipment Corporation) was not a manufacturer of mainframes but a manufacturer of small computers. This event is likely to become a historic watershed, marking the beginning of a new revolution in computing. In the 1980s and 1990s, the personal computer (in the form of a secretarial workstation, a management terminal, and so forth) will become increasingly important, as will communications, networks that include many types and sizes of computers. A few workstations are shown in Figure 2–7.

The technological base of computing hardware in this era is called fourth generation hardware. In the same way that hundreds of second generation components were reduced to a single third generation device, so can hundreds of third generation components be combined into a single **fourth generation computer.** The basis for this fourth generation hardware is **LSI** (large scale integration) and **VLSI** (very large scale integration) integrated circuits. Fourth generation hardware is now being used in so many ways that attempting to catalog even a few of them would be beyond the scope of this chapter.

The most important concept to be learned from this phase of the evolution of computer hardware is that quantum leaps will continue to be made in terms of increasing the number of functions that can be placed in a given amount of space and the speed at which these functions can be performed. The effects of the advancing technology are seen in dramatic improvements in the size, speed, cost, and capabilities of the circuits. These improvements continue on a seemingly daily basis as new and improved integrated circuit chips get smaller, faster, cheaper, more capable, and more reliable.

As technology improves, the speed and power of all personal, mini-, and mainframe computers will continue to rise. The graph in Figure 2–8 shows the historic relationship among cost, power, and applicability of computers. We can summarize these relationships easily for hardware—everything keeps getting better! Costs keep going down; size keeps going down; capabilities, speed, and reliability keep going up. *On the average, the per-dollar capability of a computer doubles every year,* i.e., next year you should be able to purchase twice as much memory or computing power as you could this year for the same amount of money.

workstation
A computing resource for use by a professional that generally includes a personal computer linked to other computing devices in some type of network.

fourth generation computers
Modern electronic computers using large scale integrated (LSI) circuits or very large scale integrated (VLSI) circuits as the technological base for their computations.

large scale integrated (LSI) circuits
Single chips containing 100–1,000 gates (basic functional units like transistors) per chip.

very large scale integrated (VLSI) circuits
Single silicon chips containing more than 1,000 gates (basic functional units). VLSI is the basis for current microprocessors (single-chip computers).

Figure 2–7 Workstations. Workstations are individual workspaces where a worker has a dedicated personal computer. These workstations can share information and peripheral devices with other computers through cable linked local area networks (LANs).

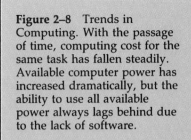

Figure 2–8 Trends in Computing. With the passage of time, computing cost for the same task has fallen steadily. Available computer power has increased dramatically, but the ability to use all available power always lags behind due to the lack of software.

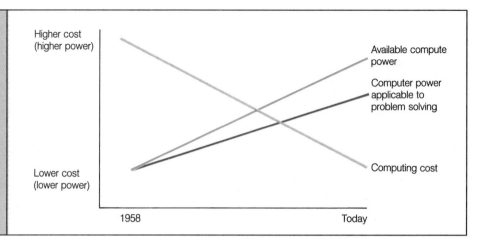

user friendly
A computer program or system that has been designed for ease of use by ordinary, nontechnical people.

Because of the ever-increasing power of hardware, trying to define the size of computers in terms of computing power is becoming pointless. What do the terms *personal* (or *microcomputer*), *minicomputer*, and *mainframe computer* mean? After all, the micros of today have developed the power of yesterday's minis; the minis have assumed the power of yesterday's mainframe computers, and the mainframes are becoming more powerful still, all at a reduced cost to the user. Today, the only enduring meaning that can be given to these terms is on the basis of their cost and the number of persons served. Personal computers usually cost less than $10,000 and serve a single individual or a small business. Mainframe computers usually cost in the millions and serve hundreds or thousands of users or large organizations. Minicomputers lie between these extremes.

Improvements in this era have not been limited to hardware. Software is becoming far more accessible, reliable, and usable. In sharp contrast to earlier periods, the watchword for software created in this era is **user friendly,** i.e., designing programs that are pleasant and easy to use. The entire notion that the user is always wrong ("Well, you obviously didn't read revision 22 in the users' manual!") has been overcome to a large degree. With the huge growth in the market for personal computers, software firms are realizing that their software and documentation must be accurate and easy to use if a software system is to become popular. Indeed, because of the burgeoning software market, the quality and variety of computer software and computer data bases are growing remarkably. However, the full power of the hardware improvements is seldom completely utilized for problem solving, because software developments for new applications usually lags well behind hardware developments.

On the industry side of computing, this era seems to be characterized by unlimited growth. Many studies indicate that the computing industry is becoming one of the major industries in the United States and in the entire world. In 1987 the gross sales for hardware alone exceeded 100 billion dollars. Today, the personal computer market exceeds 15 billion dollars annually and continues to grow. IBM alone sells more than 1 million personal computers per year.

Many new companies have tried to profit from this growth in the computing industry and have been led into a fiercely competitive market. Highly visible companies that have permanently or temporarily left the computer production industry include Osborne, Xerox, Commodore, RCA, and General

Electric. Even companies that have never left computer production have had some unsuccessful products. For example, Texas Instrument and Coleco withdrew products from the home computer market (the TI 99/4 and the ADAM, respectively), IBM had trouble marketing its PC Jr., and Apple erred with its Apple III. Companies with sufficient resources have been able to learn from their failures, while those without have dropped out of the competition.

The evolution in computing systems has not stopped or even slowed. Instead, as ever greater markets open up for computing services, research and competition continue to advance the ways in which computers can help solve human problems. Looking back over the progress of computing, we can see several important trends that can help us anticipate some of the future events in the volatile field of computing.

First, *the development of computer hardware and software is driven by people who are trying to solve real-world problems.* As the anecdotes illustrate, ancient and modern computers were created to solve human problems, beginning with Isaac and continuing to the present time.

Second, *the range and complexity of the problem-solving tasks performed by computers will forever increase.* Already the problems range from the simplest (counting) to the extremely complex (operating a multinational corporation). This trend will surely continue. In the near future, computers using **artificial intelligence** will aid us in the analysis of problems and the synthesis of solutions as well as in the preparation of computer programs.

Third, *during any given period of history, the range of practical problems that were successfully solved by computer was determined by three factors: people, hardware, and software,* as summarized in the Figure 2–9.

In the past, in today's society, and in the future, the types of problems that can be solved with computers are limited by the cost and power of the available hardware, its ease of use, the ISPCO tasks performed by the available

2.9

Computer Evolution in Retrospect

artificial intelligence
A field of study whose goal is to create computer systems that exhibit intelligent behavior (possess problem-solving skills, understand natural language, and so on). It draws eclectically upon the fields of computer science, psychology, education, linguistics, brain physiology, and other disciplines concerned with human reasoning and intelligence.

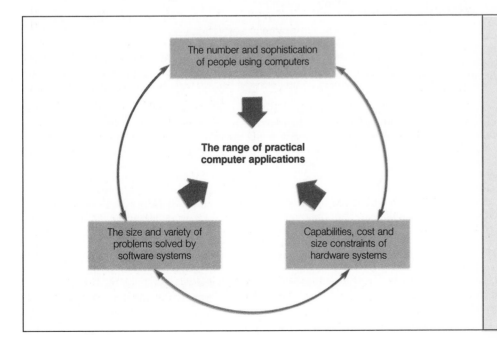

Figure 2–9 Factors Defining the Range of Computer Applications

software, and the ordinary person's knowledge of how computers can be used to solve problems. The cyclic development of practical computing applications has generally been hardware-driven, that is, a new technology allows the creation of hardware that is more powerful or smaller or cheaper than that previously available. Computer systems that were not previously economical to produce suddenly become economical, and software developers race to take advantage of the new hardware and to be the first entrepreneurs to tap a new market. The new software, in turn, changes people's attitudes toward and knowledge about computer applications. This new level of expectation stimulates more hardware development, thus repeating the cycle.

embedding of computer systems
Embedding of computer systems occurs when one computer system becomes a part of a more complex system. For example, a word processing system might be placed on a silicon chip and become part of computer hardware.

The most common technological change is frequently the **embedding of computer systems.** Computer systems are embedded by placing an entire hardware and/or software system of earlier vintage into a new system to serve as just one of its components. For example, a piece of well developed and tested software may be placed into a single integrated circuit chip and thus become a piece of hardware, making its capabilities available to any larger system. Embedding allows the ISPCO functions of one computer system to become a primitive process inside the boundaries of a larger system.

Computer Insights
Why Computer Innovations Bloom or Go Bust

Several factors determine the success of computer applications.

1. Applications that have clear objectives, solve problems that truly need solving, and meet important needs of people tend to be successful.
2. Applications that address well-understood problems for which the solution can be broken into a number of simple steps tend to be successful.
3. Applications that fit within the range of current hardware, available software, and trained people who are willing and able to use the application tend to be successful.

Some recent applications that have bloomed are credit and automated teller cards and point-of-transaction sales terminals. Credit cards and automated teller cards had all the attributes of success. There was a clear need for providing easy access to credit. Financial institutions could save money on paper work, earn money from retail stores, earn money from high interest rates, and increase retail sales. The consumer had the advantage of instant credit. The administration of computerized credit accounts was well understood, and the hardware and software were already in use.

Point-of-transaction sales (POTS) terminals have replaced the cash register in many stores. POTS are used by checkout clerks to register a purchase, usually through a laser wand or a window that reads universal product bar codes. POTS were a natural success because they had all of the required attributes: (1) people were available who could be easily trained to handle the input devices, (2) money could be saved because inventory systems could be directly linked to the sales terminal for purchasing control, and (3) inventory and purchasing management was a well-understood problem.

Some other recent computer innovations have not done well, for example, early home computers and computer-aided instruction. The first home computers lacked most of the attributes of potential success. The objective of the home computer was never clear. No demonstrable need for home computers was established. The cost of the computer itself was minimal, but to make it useful, disk drives and printers had to be purchased at substantial additional cost. Most of the tasks for which the homeowner was responsible were already being successfully accomplished without the computer, e.g., typing an occasional letter or balancing a checkbook.

The computer-aided instruction revolution predicted in the 1960s failed to materialize in the public schools because this application also lacked most of the attributes of success. No clear needs or objectives were identified for the computer in relation to the school and the teacher. Since the computer was expensive and was generally added onto the regular school costs, there was no apparent cost advantage. Few teachers were trained to use computers. These problems of hardware costs, software availability, and computer-sophisticated teachers are only now beginning to be solved.

Someday, when historians attempt to divide our current time into periods with names and time frames, the time beginning with the first noncommercial electronic computer and proceeding beyond today to some point in the future will be called the Intelligence Revolution. Historians may view this as the time when naturally occurring, biological intelligence was joined by electronic, artificial intelligence that was conceived and designed by people. From that point on in our "future history" (using the term of the science fiction author Heinlein), we will have an indispensable partner to aid in the many endeavors of our species. This exciting "future history" of the computer revolution is what the reader should relish and participate in.

Although it seems that computers can do almost anything, many things actually lie outside their current capabilities. Surprising as it may be, these limits on computer performance seem to be more a human problem than a problem intrinsic to computers. Computers can generally be programmed to perform any well-understood computational feat. Unfortunately, there are many problems that people do not understand and for which computerized solutions have thus not been devised.

These difficult computing problems are the focus of a field of research called artifical intelligence (AI). AI researchers attempt to solve difficult programming problems by successive approximations using continued interaction among the computer, the researcher, and the user. In this partnership, a partial solution is programmed, then the behavior of the computer is observed and new insights are gained. The process is then repeated with hopes that it will yield more correct solution.

■ Game Playing

One of the first problems attacked by AI researchers was the problem of teaching a computer to play a good game of chess or checkers (an example of a chess playing computer is in Figure 2–10). These researchers began by considering how people play checkers, hoping that insights based on human performance would help direct the programming effort.

A person plays checkers by selecting moves that seem likely to lead to the goal of winning. During this process, the player might try to anticipate the opponent's move. The better checker player will try to look several moves ahead ("If I move here, then the opponent will probably move there, in which case I had better move this guy . . ."). Given this rather simplistic view of the game, there seems to be no major reason why a computer couldn't be programmed to play checkers.

But before starting to write a checker-playing program, it might be wise to examine the situation a little more closely. Statisticians have estimated that there are almost 1,000,000,000,000,000,000,000 possible move sequences (i.e., games) in checkers. If the computer could check, say, 3 billion moves a second, it would only take the computer about 100 centuries to check all the possibilities! Therefore, the straightforward idea of having a computer play checkers by examining all the possibilities appears untenable, no matter how fast computers are likely to get.

Successful computer programs for playing checkers have been devised, but only after a great deal of interaction between checker-playing programs

Figure 2–10 A Computer Playing Chess. A chess-playing computer program controls a robot arm to move chess pieces against its human opponent.

and checker-playing people and after a great deal of revision and thinking about the problem of building a good checker player. These programs "think" about a game of checkers in ways similar to a human expert, that is, by being intelligent and looking for the characteristics of winning and losing board positions. There are now checker-playing computer programs that are virtually unbeatable by human opponents. These programs were developed by successive approximations with interactions between computers and humans guiding the revision process. If the task of writing a checker-playing program seems difficult, consider chess (Figure 2–10): estimates of the number of different chess games are around 1,000,000,000,000,000,000,000,000,000,000,000,000,000,000. To date, no chess-playing program exists that can beat the best human players.

■ Expert Systems

People are expert in many things. They are expert doctors, lawyers, and Indian chiefs, to name just a few. Is it possible to give computers a comparable type of expertise in various professional areas?

Consider the task of creating a computer program that could behave as a medical expert (Figure 2–11 illustrates such an "expert system"). We will first look at the circumstances that control a human doctor's behavior. A human doctor works in many different types of settings. In one instance, the patient may require a simple physical exam. In another, the patient may have some acute problem, or a chronic one, or even one that is life-threatening. The doctor must respond appropriately to all possibilities.

One portion of a physician's behavior that might be the easiest to program is the actions performed during a routine physical exam. Commonly, the doctor collects data on the patient's height, weight, age, sex, temperature, blood pressure, and respiration. Why? Probably because this data helps to determine whether the patient actually has a medical problem. The physician will

Figure 2–11 Interacting with an Expert System. Expert system development programs like this one are used to create simulation/modeling programs that can use information to make decisions, in ways similar to a human expert.

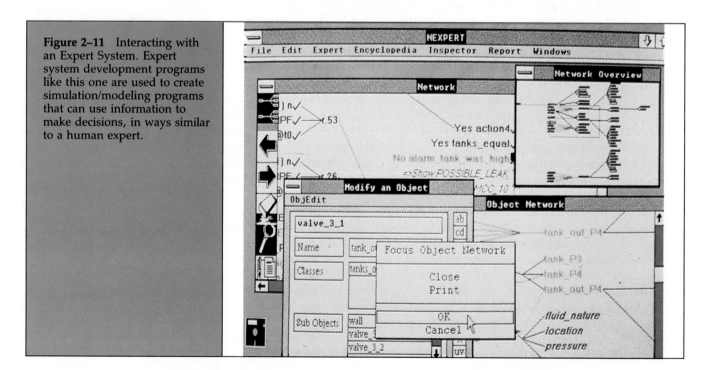

go on to check eyes, ears, nose, throat, urinary output, blood counts, and so on. The process is lengthy but straightforward. Creating a computer program to do this would be just a matter of following a series of predefined steps. But one question: what does the doctor do if the patient falls to the floor clutching his chest in the middle of the physical exam? Even in a less dramatic situation, the goals and priorities of the physical examination can drastically change in short time periods as the data on the patient unfolds.

There have been many attempts at creating expert systems. Probably the most common approach is the so-called production system. A production system is essentially a large set of rules constructed in the following form:

☐ IF (this is the situation)
☐ THEN (perform these actions)

At least a portion of a doctor's expertise could be embodied in many rules governing different types of situations, but there are still problems. There may be alternative actions for the same situation. If there are competing goals, it is possible that contradictory actions would be indicated. How are such choices and contradictions resolved? How would a computer programmer know if all those rules were consistent and correct? How could anyone be certain that the computer programmer had not mistyped a rule!

All of these various concerns have been explored. A programmer writes a program that tries to behave with expertise, sees what is wrong with it, fixes it, and tries again. Business, industry, and individuals all need expertise, and there are never enough human experts. It would seem that if computers are capable of some functions analogous to thinking (ISPCO), that designers of computer systems should be able to create computerized medical experts within the limits of those functions.

Unfortunately, the problem of creating computer experts is poorly understood. In some small problem areas, expert systems have been created and are working correctly and usefully on a daily basis. But only through the interaction between the computer expert and the people watching its performance can more accurate solutions be devised. General purpose systems that include computer programs *and* methodologies for extracting human expertise are not generally available, and the methods used by existing systems are open to debate.

■ Understanding Natural Language

Anyone new to the computer field may be appalled by the precision and formality required for communicating with computers. This specialized form of communication is now becoming less visible as software designers around the world parade their user-friendly systems. There is no question that computer systems are becoming easier to use. More and more, one can communicate in subsets of standard natural languages like English. There is some concern that this simplification may be unfortunate: the precision required in older systems often demanded that the computer users be more careful in their own thinking—always a desirable goal. But nonetheless, systems are becoming easier to use.

One might ask, however, why a communication problem exists at all? Can't we just build a computer system that understands English, tell it what we need in English, and have it ask any questions it has in English? How might this be done?

Figure 2–12 Natural Language Understanding Systems. Natural language understanding is a complex task that current computers do not do well. The first step is to accept the input sentence. The second step is to determine the underlying syntactic structure of the sentence, similar to sentence diagramming learned in grade school (a new model of language by the Residential Grammar Corporation has been used). The third step is to turn that meaning into action in the robotic world. The figure shows a robotic arm with a vision camera mounted on top carrying out the natural language command it received.

1) Input sentence: The robot put the box on the pallet.

2) Sentence diagram using Residential Grammar.

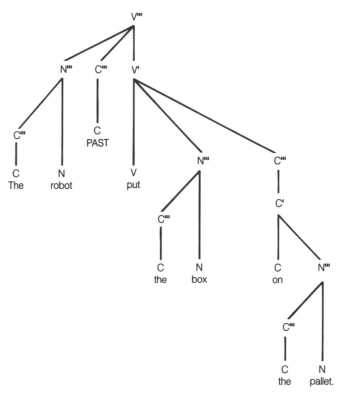

3) Knowledge representation:

   MOVE (Actor: robot, Object: box, From: unknown, To: pallet)
   INSTRUMENT (MOVE, arm)
   TIME (MOVE, 8:15 AM)

4) Perception and action

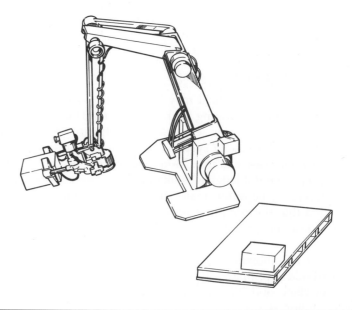

When asked *not* to think of the color of an elephant, most people find it difficult not to think of gray. This is an example of the a natural connections that exist in a person's knowledge. In some ways, this large network of interconnections may actually *be* a person's knowledge. This network works well within the human mind, but to have it work within a computer, the following problems arise: (1) defining what such a net would look like, (2) entering information into the net, (3) interpreting natural language questions asked by computer users, and (4) providing comprehensible and correct answers.

Many attempts have been made to model human thinking and language comprehension. Networks of concepts, generally called semantic nets, have been entered into computers. The systems resulting form these attempts (see Figure 2–12) have been quite good at understanding natural language within a given small area of human endeavor, e.g., a child's block set, or military aircraft.

Computer programs that effectively understand all of human language are not available. Existing attempts are made in an interactive way. A proposed method for understanding language is programmed into the computer, and its behavior is monitored. For situations in which the computer's responses are not appropriate, careful analysis is performed to discover the problems and determine how they might be repaired. Revisions are made and the cycle is repeated. In this way, the field of natural language understanding continues to fumble slowly toward the goal of creating a computer program that effectively understands a natural language. The real difficulties seem not to deal with available hardware or programming but instead with the analysis of the problem and the synthesis of potential solutions.

In all of our examples and in many other areas in the AI field, there are two constant characteristics: the problems are poorly understood and the solutions to these problems are generated by successive refinements.

Chapter 2 Review

Expanded Objectives

The objectives listed below are an expansion of the essential chapter concepts listed at the beginning of the chapter. The review items that follow are based on these expanded objectives. If you master the objectives, you will do better on the review items and on your instructor's examination on the chapter.

After reading the chapter, you should be able to:

1. identify major inventions that improved computer software and computer hardware functions.
2. match major hardware and software inventions with the individuals primarily responsible for them.
3. relate major inventions to the ISPCO functions that they performed.
4. sequence the ISPCO functions in the order in which they were transferred from people to computers.
5. discriminate among the generations of computer hardware.
6. explain some of the implications of the microcomputer for our society.
7. relate the major trends that have occurred in the development of computers (e.g., miniaturization) and their consequences.
8. explain the major software and hardware terms defined in this chapter.

Review Items

Completing this review will give you a good indication of how well you have mastered the contents of this chapter and prepare you for your instructor's test on this material. To maximize what you learn from this exercise, you should answer each question *before* looking up the answers in the appendix. The number of the corresponding expanded objective is given in parentheses following each question.

Complete the following clusters of items according to the directions heading each set.

A. *True or false.*

___ 1. The processing function was transferred to computers before the storage function. (6)

___ 2. Computer programming is an intellectual function not yet routinely transferred to computers. (6)

___ 3. The computer is the first invention capable of performing the ISPCO functions without intervention by people. (2)

___ 4. As the telephone is an extension of a person's voice, so is a computer an extension of a human mind. (2)

___ 5. Before the invention of magnetic core storage, computer programs could be stored on punched cards and paper tape. (5)

___ 6. The invention of batch operating systems enabled different users to access the same computer at the same time. (5)

___ 7. The technological base for electromechanical computers was storage and processing through cogged wheels driven by electrical motors. (3)

___ 8. The advent of general purpose computers had to wait for von Neumann's concept of storing computer programs in a computer's memory. (3,4)

___ 9. One of the most difficult tasks for a person who wishes to use a microcomputer effectively today is the need to learn machine language. (8)

___ 10. Some early computers were designed for business applications. (1)

___ 11. Assembly and compiler languages are easier to use than machine languages. (10)

___ 12. Time-sharing systems require teleprocessing. (10)

___ 13. The distinctions among micro-, mini-, and mainframe computers is becoming increasingly difficult to make on the basis of power alone. (9)

___ 14. Teleprocessing permits a person to use a computer that is some distance away. (10)

___ 15. The three major factors affecting the range of viable computer applications are: the cost and power of software, the range of available software, and the type of problem being solved. (9)

___ 16. Over time, the price and size of computer hardware are going down, while the reliability, power, and speed are increasing. (9)

___ 17. Over time, software systems will become easier to use. (9)

___ 18. Von Neumann developed the concept of storing the computer program in computer memory so that it could be easily modified. (4)

___ 19. Some operating systems enable several users to use the same computer at the same time. (5)

B. *A number of inventions which affected the evolution of the computer are listed in the left column. Match each invention with the problem that it was designed to overcome.* (5)

___ 20. counting frames, knots in rope, pebbles

___ 21. cogged wheels turned by hand

___ 22. Harvard Mark I

___ 23. EDVAC

___ 24. punched cards

a. difficult to remember numbers

b. difficult to tabulate large masses of data

c. difficult to control a computer's actions

d. difficult to add long columns of numbers

e. difficult to modify a computer's program

C. *Match the inventor on the left with his (one) invention on the right.* (4)

___ 25. Jacquard

___ 26. Hollerith

___ 27. Pascal

___ 28. Babbage

a. cogged wheel turned by hand

b. programmable textile loom

c. punched card machines

d. input of data by applying pressure on marked keys

e. difference and analytic engines

D. *Match each invention on the left with the basic function(s) it performs.* (3)

___ 29. counting board

___ 30. first mechanical calculator

___ 31. punched card machines

___ 32. electromechanical computer

___ 33. modern electronic computer

a. input

b. storage

c. processing

d. control

e. output

E. *Match each system on the left with the most appropriate description of the right.* (5)

___ 34. timesharing systems

___ 35. computer network systems

___ 36. batch systems

a. a one-user-at-a-time system

b. a multi-user and multi-computer system

c. a multi-user and single-computer system

d. a multi-computer and single-user system

F. *For each of the four generations of computers listed on the left, find the best description on the right.* (7)

___ 37. first generation

___ 38. second generation

___ 39. third generation

___ 40. fourth generation

a. transistor based

b. integrated circuit based

c. magnetic core storage based

d. very large scale integrated circuit based

e. vacuum tube based

Computer Hardware

Essential Chapter Concepts

When you have finished this chapter, you should know:

- How human information is represented in the ISPCO devices of a computer system.

- The purpose, internal functioning, and current technology of many of the ISPCO devices in a typical computer system.

- What variety of configurations can be built from simple ISPCO devices.

Computer Hardware

INPUT	STORAGE	PROCESS	CONTROL	OUTPUT
Keyboard	RAM	CPU chips	CPU chips	Printer
•	•	•		•
Mouse	ROM	Coprocessor		Screen
•	•	chips		•
Terminal	Tape			Terminal
•	•			•
Modem	Disk			Modem
	•			
	CD-ROM			

Understanding computers and using them to solve problems requires knowledge of both hardware and software. Remember that hardware refers to the physical components of the computer, while software refers to sets of instructions for the hardware (i.e., computer programs). Computers can function only when software and hardware are combined together in an appropriate manner. This chapter will focus on the hardware characteristics of computer systems.

Today, the hardware of a computer is composed of a number of separate components that are connected by a variety of wires and plugs. A small personal computer may have a single keyboard for input, a **disk drive** and **integrated circuit memory** for storage, a microprocessor for processing and control, and a screen for output. By contrast, a mainframe may consist of 60 terminals for input and output, 20 disk drives and 10 times the internal memory for storage, 3 central processors for processing and control, and 5 printers for output. (The exact meanings of all these terms will be given later in the chapter.) No matter how large or small a computer system is, the same basic principles apply to its hardware. The hardware of every computer system is a set of ISPCO devices connected by a **communication line.** A schematic example of such hardware is given in the figure on the next page.

Before we go into more detail, it is important that the reader understand exactly what we mean by computer (usually personal computer) hardware, as illustrated in the figure on page 54. In the abstract, computer hardware consists of: (1) the devices for ISPCO and (2) the communication line that links the ISPCO devices, as shown at the top of the figure. But how is this scheme translated into real pieces of equipment? In concrete form, a computer consists of (1) the **main circuit board** (or motherboard) containing the communication line hardware, (2) the microprocessor chip or chips containing the control and processing hardware, and (3) the input, storage, and output hardware. Actual hardware devices are shown at the bottom of the figure.

disk drive
A device that reads data from magnetic disks and writes data on them.

integrated circuit memory
The fastest type of storage built from integrated circuit chips.

communication line or bus
A hardware device shared by the storage, input/output and control/processing hardware. It is used to transfer information among the ISPCO hardware.

main circuit board (motherboard)
An electronic circuit board containing the power source, communication line, microprocessor and internal storage chips and expansion board slots (places in which to plug other circuit boards). The main circuit board provides the basis for the combination of other hardware to form a computer.

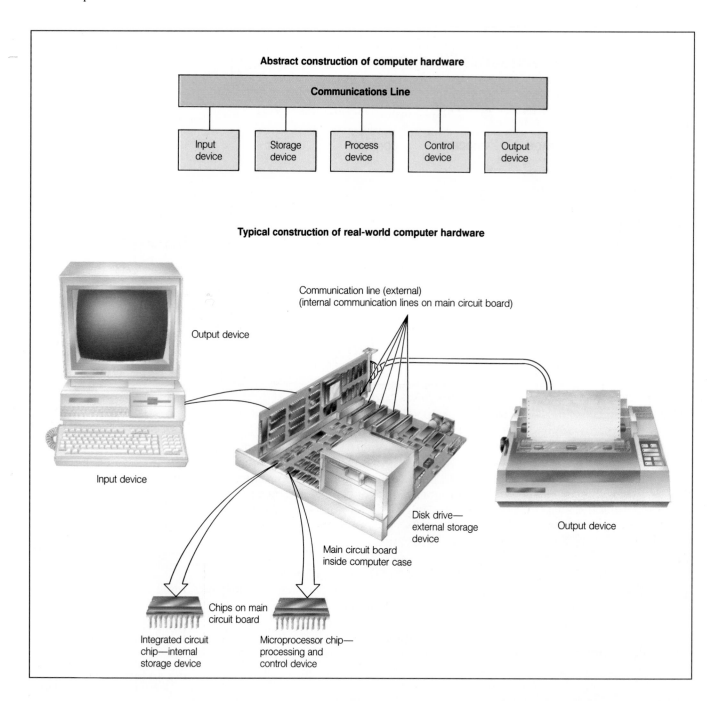

Abstract construction of computer hardware

Communications Line

| Input device | Storage device | Process device | Control device | Output device |

Typical construction of real-world computer hardware

Output device

Communication line (external)
(internal communication lines on main circuit board)

Input device

Disk drive—
external storage
device

Output device

Main circuit board
inside computer case

Chips on main
circuit board

Integrated circuit
chip—internal
storage device

Microprocessor chip—
processing and
control device

expansion slots
Places on the motherboard in which
other circuit boards may be inserted to
expand the capabilities of the
computer, e.g., to increase the size of
memory, to add a printer, and so on.

internal storage
Storage composed of integrated circuit
chips directly attached to the
motherboard.

Let's consider each of these parts in turn. The motherboard (main circuit board) links all of the hardware devices. It contains the communication line, the power source, sockets in which to plug the microprocessor and other chips, and the **expansion slots** into which other circuit boards can be plugged. The microprocessor chip is the hardware device that performs the control and processing functions. The microprocessor chip requires very fast storage, which is provided by integrated circuit memory chips that are also plugged into the motherboard. This integrated circuit memory is often called internal memory or **internal storage** since it is directly attached to the motherboard. The main circuit board (motherboard) and microprocessor combination is what really defines a computer (e.g., an IBM PS/2 Model 50 has one combination, while the Model 80 has another) and determines its ultimate power and expandability. The speed and power of the system, the amount and types of memory that can be added, and the number and types of expansion boards that can be added, are all determined by the motherboard and microprocessor combination.

The motherboard and chip combination is the major factor in determining **hardware** and **software compatibility**—that is, what hardware and software can be used with the personal computer.

The remaining devices for input, storage, and output are sometimes called **peripheral** (or **external**) **hardware** because they are added to the system and are often interchangeable across systems, e.g., the same keyboard can be used with different computers. External devices include keyboards, video screens, magnetic disk storage drives, and so on. Magnetic disk and tape storage is often called **external storage** because it is indirectly attached to the motherboard through controller hardware and is sometimes also interchangeable. Much more will be said on all this in the chapter.

hardware compatibility
The ability of hardware devices to function correctly together i.e., the ability of one device to accept and handle information processed by another device without any conversion or recoding.

software compatibility
The ability of devices to function correctly together at the software level, i.e., the ability of two devices to process data identically using the same software.

peripheral (external) hardware
Hardware devices which are not directly a part of the motherboard/ microprocessor combination. Include input and output devices and disk or tape storage. Peripherals are often interchangeable across computers.

external storage
Magnetic disk or tape storage attached through controller devices to the motherboard.

With the ever-falling prices of microcomputers, many people are first introduced to computing when they go to their nearest computer dealer to buy one. Anxious to join the computer revolution, they may arrive at the computer store in a rather naive state. As we will see in our case study about Bill, that may not be the best approach!

3.1

How Do You Buy a Computer?

Case Study

Bill was starting college in the fall and his parents had promised him a computer as a graduation present. He really would have preferred a car, new or old, but his folks thought a computer would be better. "Oh well," Bill said to himself as he pulled open the door of the computer store, "I might as well pick one out."

As soon as he entered the store, a saleswoman approached him. Her name tag said "Terry." "Good morning," she said. "Can I help you?"

"Yeah, I guess," was Bill's response. "I need to buy a computer for college next year, but I really don't know much about computers."

"Well, I'm sure we can find a machine that will make your life a lot easier," Terry said. "What college are you going to? Some schools want their students to use a particular machine."

"I'll be going to Central," Bill answered.

"The last I heard, Central didn't have a university-wide policy," said Terry. "Any machine should do, then. I guess the next thing to ask is, how much money do you want to spend?"

"My folks said I could spend up to fifteen hundred dollars," Bill replied. "Is that enough to buy anything?"

Terry said, "Oh, definitely. Computers come in all price ranges. With that amount of money, we can get you a personal computer with two disk drives, 512K of memory, a monochrome screen, and an inexpensive printer. That should be enough to get you started. Let's go over and look at a machine made by Apple that's especially made for novice users."

Bill followed Terry across the showroom floor, passing pedestal after pedestal of computer systems. Some of the screens showed beautiful, full-color images; some had little figures wandering around in some kind of arcade game. Many of the screens sat on top of boxes that housed keyboards or had slots in them. Bill thought the slots were for disks, but he wasn't sure. All of the printers sat silent as he walked by.

"You know, I'm not sure that I know what all of those words you just used really mean!" lamented Bill.

"Oh, I'm not surprised. Three months ago I didn't know any of it either," confided Terry, "but it's not hard to remember what all the pieces are if you just think of the five functions that computers have: input, storage, processing, control, and output. The keyboards are the input devices. Computers have two types of storage. One type of storage is done by electronic circuits; it is super fast and you want a lot of it. When I said '512K,' I meant that the computer would have about 512,000 chunks of internal circuit memory. The other kind of storage is on magnetic floppy disks. They're really slow compared to the circuits, but they are super cheap. That's why there are two different kinds of storage. When I mentioned a two-drive system, I meant a system that could use two floppies at once."

"As for processing and control," Terry continued, "those functions are built into the computer itself. They are part of the computer's brain. Finally, output is usually done on a TV-type screen or a printer. When I said 'monochrome,' I just meant a noncolor screen, something like a black-and-white TV, but computers usually have a black and green or black and amber screen."

Despite the supposed simplicity of the descriptions, Bill still felt dazed.

Terry turned to a microcomputer on a nearby pedestal. "Let's watch this Apple work. I'll start a demo for you." Terry turned the computer off and then on. The screen cleared, and then images started to fly across it. It seemed that this little computer could do anything! Bill watched the Apple play a video game. He watched it type out a letter to his congressman about saving the whales. He watched it draw a beautiful bar chart. He watched it simulate a car's engine, sound and all.

"Are you sure this computer only costs fifteen hundred dollars?" Bill was amazed. Maybe a computer wasn't such a bad graduation present after all! It looked like fun!

"Yep," said Terry. "It's on sale this month, and I can give you the whole setup for fourteen twenty-five plus tax. That includes a 90-day warranty on parts and labor. And Apple is a pretty reliable name in computers. People rarely need the warranty anyway."

Bill pulled out his checkbook. "Well, I think you've convinced me. Since you know all the machines and think this is a good one, I'll believe you. But what about IBM computers? I always see them advertised."

"IBM is a good machine," replied Terry, "no doubt about it. And just as important as being good, the IBM market is so big that everybody strives to make their new programs and hardware work for an IBM machine. But for your situation I think this Apple would be best. And Apple's a big company with lots of loyal hardware and software developers, too."

"Okay, sounds good to me," Bill said as he started to write out his check. He suddenly looked up, "Hey, can I write a quick note on the computer to thank my folks? It would be a real treat for them!"

"Sure. I'd be happy to help. What word processor would you like to use?" asked Terry.

"Word processor? I'm not sure what that is. I don't care."

"Well, let's use AppleTasks." Terry looked through her disks. "I can't find my copy. Let me go get one."

She came back a moment later with a small package wrapped in cellophane. "AppleTasks is a real nice system. We sell lots of copies. You know, if you buy the software right now, with your hardware, I'm sure I can cut a good deal. I can probably let you have it for only eighty dollars."

"Eighty dollars!" exclaimed Bill. "Wait a minute, I thought my machine could already write letters. Why do I have to spend another eighty dollars?"

"Oh, no, Bill. You misunderstood. That demo disk we watched only showed you the capabilities of your system. To get the computer to actually do those things, you need to buy software."

"You mean it won't play that neat video game when I get it home?" asked Bill.

Terry's reply only upset Bill further. "Well, no. That game is just like the AstroPac game, though. That only costs thirty-nine ninety-five."

"Good heavens! How much money would I have to spend to make my machine do all of those things on your demo?" Bill was almost wailing.

"Well, a chart system, a word processing system, a couple of games, and a data base system would be needed. Also, you'd probably want a surge suppressor to plug your computer into—then if there are any problems with the electricity, your computer won't get trashed. All together, I'd say you'd need to spend another eight hundred to a thousand dollars."

Bill looked rather distraught. He put his checkbook back in his pocket. "Look," he said, "I only have fifteen hundred dollars for *everything*. What can I really afford?"

Terry tried smiling to overcome Bill's negative feelings. "I'm sorry. I thought you understood about computers. Most people end up spending almost as much on software and other extra stuff as they do on the hardware. For the computers we have here, I guess we can still get you in, though. If we substitute a third-party external disk instead of the Apple drive, use this new, superlow-cost printer that just came out, and look to non-Apple software sources, we should be able to cut the cost down. Of course, there is the problem of hardware compatibility."

"Compatibility?" Bill asked. "You keep bringing up things I don't know anything about. What's compatibility?"

"Well, Bill," Terry said, "Apple makes its machines so they all work together. They sell a lot of them, so there are a lot of other manufacturers that sell parts that are supposed to work like Apple parts—they are called Apple compatibles. The problem is that they often don't work totally like Apple parts. Because of this, some software may not work properly on an Apple compatible."

Bill asked the obvious question, "Can you tell which ones won't?"

"For popular ones, we generally know," Terry responded. "Always check it out at the store, though, because when you buy software, it is generally not returnable."

Bill was numb. "Not returnable?"

"Sure. We can't let people return software. Otherwise they would take it home, make a copy on another disk and return the original. People pirate software a lot, and we just can't let that happen."

After another half hour of discussion Bill had recovered from his surprise and shock at the true cost of computing and had finally figured out how he could get a system that would provide all of the hardware and software he needed for under fifteen hundred dollars. He felt like he'd really accomplished something and learned a lot. As he took all of the boxes into his room and began to unpack them, he realized he still had a lot to learn.

The first page of the assembly instructions talked about inserting a controller card (what's that?) into a backplane slot (a what?), being sure to discharge static before touching the part (how do you do that?). As he looked at the seven different kinds of cords he had, the three different circuit boards that he somehow had to put in his computer, and the anemic instruction manual, he began to plan a second visit to the computer store for tomorrow.

Bill's experience in buying computer hardware and software is typical of that encountered by many computer novices. The prospective buyer needs to know a lot about hardware and software before stepping into the showroom. This chapter will introduce the concepts of modern computer hardware to the novice user. But, short of becoming an expert in computing, the novice buyer should check with multiple computer stores, friends, and popular consumer and computer magazines before purchasing any computer system.

3.2

The Basics of Information Representation

Computer Hardware

INPUT   STORAGE   PROCESS   CONTROL   OUTPUT

All information is represented as bits or binary numbers
composed of zeros and ones.

Arbitrary rules and codes are used to translate alphanumeric text
(e.g., a, $, etc.), whole numbers, fractional numbers, and
computer instructions into binary numbers.

Binary codes are also used to indicate where information is to be
stored or which hardware device is to receive information.

digital computer
A computer that uses only two separate values of voltage and current levels to represent information (e.g., "on" might be represented by the value 5 volts and "off" by 0 volts). On analog computers, in contrast, virtually every continuous value between on and off may be used (e.g., 5 volts, 4.264 volts, 3.5 volts, 3.43 volts). Most modern computers are digital computers because they can easily model the characteristics of analog computers.

binary digit
a single on/off switch in computer storage; the values 0 or 1.

bit
An abbreviation for *binary digit*.

The computer is an intellectual tool that can help solve human problems by automating parts of the thinking tasks of input, storage, processing, control, and output. It can help write letters, compute income taxes, or entertain with video games. It is tempting, then, to look at computer hardware in terms of the capabilities of various hardware devices, for example, this kind of computer screen is good for game playing, while that kind is better for writing letters, or one kind of processor is good for income taxes, while another is not. However, to understand how a computer really works, the reader must first understand how human concepts such as letters, income taxes, and video games can be represented inside a computer, which is built on a very different physical base than human physiology. Indeed, for a computer to do anything useful, there must always be a translation. Human instructions for the computer must be translated into a language that the hardware of the computer can process. The essential question is, *how can human information and instructions be represented inside the circuits of a computer?*

The first and almost astounding fact about modern computers is that *all information is stored through the use of on/off switches.* Letters, income taxes, or video games—all must be expressed as patterns of on/off switches. To talk about these switches more easily, we use a convention in which the on position of a switch is called a 1 and the off position a 0. Then, instead of talking about switches, we talk about numbers that contain only 0's and 1's. In fact, modern computers are more correctly called **digital computers,** because they represent all information as digits of 0 and 1.

Since only these two digits are used, they are called **binary digits,** and the term *binary digit* has been shortened to give the term **bit.** One on/off switch is thus called a bit. The bit is the smallest unit of digital information. *All information in a digital computer is stored as a sequence of bits.*

Now let's look at bits from the perspective of mathematics and base 2 arithmetic. A sequence of 0's and 1's can be viewed as a **base 2 number,** e.g., a number like 11101 means

1x16 + 1x8 + 1x4 + 0x2 + 1x1,

where each column stands for a different power of 2. Arithmetic in base 2 is similar to ordinary arithmetic in base 10, except that only 0's and 1's are allowed and the columns represent powers of 2 instead of powers of 10. When base 2 numbers become tiresome, every set of three bits can be treated as a group and converted to a base 8 or octal number; then each column represents a power of 8. Similarly, if every set of four bits is treated as a group, a base 16 or hexadecimal number results.

base 2 number
A number represented by powers of 2, e.g., in base 2, $101 = 1 \times 2^2 + 0 \times 2^1 + 1 \times 2^0 = 4 + 0 + 1 = 5$ in base 10.

Numbers in Various Arithmetic Bases

Binary	Octal	Base 10	Hexadecimal
0000	00	1	0
0001	01	1	1
0010	02	2	2
0011	03	3	3
0100	04	4	4
0101	05	5	5
0110	06	6	6
0111	07	7	7
1000	10	8	8
1001	11	9	9
1010	12	10	A
1011	13	11	B
1100	14	12	C
1101	15	13	D
1110	16	14	E
1111	17	15	F
10000	20	16	10

(Hexadecimal needs more digits than does ordinary arithmetic, so the first six letters of the alphabet are standardly used.) Despite these different ways of grouping bits, the important fact is that all information on a computer is stored as a pattern of bits.

■ The Meaning of Bits

Bits are the elemental units of computer data. All human information must therefore be represented as patterns of bits if it is to be processed by a computer. The manner by which patterns of bits stand for human concepts is not obvious—arbitrary definitions or conventions invented by people must be used. As an example, imagine that a group of people agree that the meaning of a single bit of data is:

   □ if the bit has a value of 1 then it is lunchtime
   □ if the bit has a value of 0 then it is not lunchtime

With this agreement, the message conveys specific information, namely, that it is time for lunch.

For computers to store useful information, however, they must be capable of representing more information than just whether it is lunchtime. Representing more information requires more bits. Consider a more elaborate case where four bits of information are available. With four bits, there are 16 on/off or 0/1 combinations, so 16 meanings are possible. For example, some of the four-bit combinations and their corresponding meanings under a different agreement among people might be:

- □ 0 0 0 0   means your car has a flat tire
- □ 0 0 0 1   means it is a holiday
- □ 0 0 1 0   means your neighbor's cat ate your breakfast
- □   .
- □   .
- □   .
- □ 1 1 1 1   means that your shoelace is untied

This agreement covers more information than the last one did. If the message 0 0 0 1 is sent, its meaning can be found in the list of definitions (it is a holiday). It should be clear, however, that this is a poor system. Even the simplest computers have thousands or millions of bits, so defining the meaning of all those bits would be an awesome task. What is needed instead is an understanding of the type of information represented in a computer and a set of primitive data representations out of which more complicated ones can be constructed. What is needed is some type of "alphabet" from which to build complicated "words" of meaning.

If we consider what types of information a computer might be asked to store, several kinds come to mind. First, a computer should be able to store information like people's names and addresses, or, more generally, it should be able to represent arbitrary **text**. Second, the computer needs to count, so it must be able to represent whole numbers like 1, 5, and 563 (whole numbers are also called integers). Third, to handle a simple task like balancing a checkbook, the computer must be able to represent a fraction like 453.12.

Finally, for a computer to perform tasks as directed, it must be able to represent the instructions people give it. Representation schemes for all of these types of human information are possible and common.

text
Any combination of characters such as A, B, . . . , Z, 0, 1, . . . , 9, *, ∧, and so forth.

■ Using Bits to Represent Text

A simple technique is used for representing text in a computer. A different pattern of bits is defined for each letter in the alphabet. Bit patterns for words can then be built out of these bit patterns for letters. Consider the first letter of the alphabet, *a*. How can we store that as a set of bits? Let's use four bits and start a convention that begins like:

0 0 0 0   means *a*

If 0 0 0 0 means *a*, then what would be a reasonable meaning for the pattern 0 0 0 1? The obvious answer is *b*. Continuing this reasonable pattern leads us to the following convention:

0 0 0 0 for *a*   0 1 1 0 for *g*   1 0 1 1 for *l*
0 0 0 1 for *b*   0 1 1 1 for *h*   1 1 0 0 for *m*

0 0 1 0 for *c*   1 0 0 0 for *i*   1 1 0 1 for *n*
0 0 1 1 for *d*   1 0 0 1 for *j*   1 1 1 0 for *o*
0 1 0 0 for *e*   1 0 1 0 for *k*   1 1 1 1 for *p*
0 1 0 1 for *f*

That seems like a reasonable assignment of patterns of bits to letters. The only problem is that with only four bits, there are only 16 codes, while there are 26 letters in the alphabet. Actually, with 26 lowercase letters, 26 uppercase letters, the digits from 0 to 9, and the special punctuation marks like period, comma, blank, quote, percent, and so on, many more than 26 representations are needed. As the number of different characters increases, the number of bits required to represent one character also increases.

On most computers today, a set of eight consecutive bits (a **byte**) is treated as a single unit and is used to represent a single text character. An agreement among computer vendors provides the association between a particular text character and a pattern of bits in a byte.

The most widely used agreement for assigning meaning to a byte is probably the standard code published by the American National Standards Institute. This code is called the **ASCII** (*American Standard Code for Information Interchange*) **code;** it is shown in Figure 3–1. The ASCII code defines meanings for only half of the possible byte patterns, specifically, for those bytes whose first bit is a zero. With this standard code, translating a byte value like 01000001 into a text character is just a matter of looking the character up in the **ASCII table** (01000001 represents *A*). Thus, any compli-

byte
A set of eight consecutive bits.

ASCII code
An individual element in the ASCII table; a standardized code for representing alphabetic, numeric, and other characters as bit patterns.

ASCII table
A table that lists the 128 possible patterns of seven bits (0000000, 0000001, . . . , 1111110, 1111111) and the corresponding characters of an extended alphabet that includes the full human alphabet and some additional computer characters.

Figure 3–1 The ASCII Table

Bit pattern	Symbol or name	Bit pattern	Symbol or name	Bit pattern	Symbol or name	Bit pattern	Symbol or name
0000000	NULL	0100000	SPACE	1000000	@	1100000	`
0000001	SOH	0100001	!	1000001	A	1100001	a
0000010	STX	0100010	"	1000010	B	1100010	b
0000011	ETX	0100011	#	1000011	C	1100011	c
0000100	EOT	0100100	$	1000100	D	1100100	d
0000101	ENQ	0100101	%	1000101	E	1100101	e
0000110	ACK	0100110	&	1000110	F	1100110	f
0000111	BELL	0100111	'	1000111	G	1100111	g
0001000	BS	0101000	(	1001000	H	1101000	h
0001001	HT	0101001	)	1001001	I	1101001	i
0001010	LF	0101010	*	1001010	J	1101010	j
0001011	VT	0101011	+	1001011	K	1101011	k
0001100	FF	0101100	,	1001100	L	1101100	l
0001101	CR	0101101	–	1001101	M	1101101	m
0001110	SO	0101110	.	1001110	N	1101110	n
0001111	SI	0101111	/	1001111	O	1101111	o
0010000	DLE	0110000	0	1010000	P	1110000	p
0010001	XON	0110001	1	1010001	Q	1110001	w
0010010	DC2	0110010	2	1010010	R	1110010	r
0010011	XOFF	0110011	3	1010011	S	1110011	s
0010100	DC4	0110100	4	1010100	T	1110100	t
0010101	NAK	0110101	5	1010101	U	1110101	u
0010110	SYN	0110110	6	1010110	V	1110110	v
0010111	ETB	0110111	7	1010111	W	1110111	w
0011000	CAN	0111000	8	1011000	X	1111000	x
0011001	EM	0111001	9	1011001	Y	1111001	y
0011010	SUB	0111010	:	1011010	Z	1111010	z
0011011	ESC	0111011	;	1011011	[	1111011	{
0011100	FS	0111100	<	1011100	\	1111110	|
0011101	GS	0111101	=	1011101	]	1111101	}
0011110	RS	0111110	>	1011110	—	1111110	~
0011111	US	0111111	?	1011111	—	1111111	DEL

cated textual message can be represented by the bytes of its component letters, symbols, and spaces.

Two last comments should be made about the ASCII code. First, computers use a bigger "alphabet" of symbols than do people: there are 128 ASCII codes (half of 256, since only seven bits are used), but fewer than 100 characters are generally used in natural English text. Thus, not all of the symbols in the ASCII table have a printed or written symbol, even though they all have names (e.g., the character named SOH in the chart has no single printed symbol associated with it). Second, although the ASCII table does not define the meaning of the other 128 patterns possible in a byte (those bytes that begin with a 1), a hardware manufacturer usually gives a machine-dependent meaning to these patterns, e.g., they are often used to represent special graphic symbols.

Bytes are often used to specify approximate memory size using the prefixes *kilo-* (one thousand) and *mega-* (one million). Thus, **kilobyte** (KB) means about 1000 bytes and **megabyte** (MB) means about 1 million bytes of memory.

kilobyte
Approximately one thousand bytes of information. (1024 bytes)

megabyte
Approximately one million bytes of information. (1,048,576 bytes)

■ Using Bits to Represent Integer Numbers

Textual data is only one of the types of data that needs to be represented in computer memory. Just as important is data that consists of whole numbers or integers.

The coding of integers into bit patterns seems straightforward. What whole number might the byte 00000000 represent? A good guess would be 0. What about 00000001? The obvious answer is 1. It would be reasonable to represent 2 as 00000010 and 3 as 00000011.

This scheme for assigning integer values to bit patterns treats the bit pattern as a base two number. If you need to review base arithmetic, just remember that in base 10, the number 456 can be viewed as 4 hundreds plus 5 tens plus 6 ones. Each position in the number 456 represents a different power of 10, specifically,

$$456 = (4 \times 100) + (5 \times 10) + (6 \times 1)$$

(Remember that 10 raised to the 0 power is defined to be 1.)

The same principle is used in base two, except that each position represents a different power of two. For example, the binary number 11011 represents

$$11011 = (1 \times 16) + (1 \times 8) + (0 \times 4) + (1 \times 2) + (1 \times 1)$$
$$= 16 + 8 + 2 + 1 = 27$$

(16 is 2 to the fourth power, 8 is 2 to the third, 4 is 2 to the second, 2 is 2 to the first, and 1 is 2 to the zero power.) Conceptually, this is the system used to represent whole numbers in a computer.

There are two problems, however, with this simple representation scheme. First, if only eight bits are used to represent a whole number, the range of values is limited to those from 0 (00000000) to 255 (11111111). To allow a larger range of numbers, most computers use more than one byte to represent a whole number. For example, if two bytes are used, the range of numbers would be from 0 (0000000000000000) to 65535 (1111111111111111). Many computers represent whole numbers with four or more bytes. This combination of bytes is called a **word.** Just as a byte is a set of consecutive bits, a word is a set of consecutive bytes, usually two, four, or eight.

word
A set of adjacent bytes in computer storage; the fundamental unit of information manipulated by a microprocessor or mainframe central processor.

Bit 1 sign	Bit 2 64	Bit 3 32	Bit 4 16	Bit 5 8	Bit 6 4	Bit 7 2	Bit 8 1	Value
1	0	0	0	1	0	0	1	− 9
0	0	0	0	1	0	0	1	9
1	1	1	1	1	1	1	1	− 127
0	1	1	1	1	1	1	1	127
1	0	0	0	0	0	0	0	− 0
0	0	0	0	0	0	0	0	0

Figure 3–2 Interger Numbers as Bit Patterns

The second problem with the suggested representation scheme is that there is no way to represent negative numbers. This problem is usually solved by setting aside one bit to represent the sign of a number, with 0 meaning positive and 1 meaning negative. Let's see how this works with a two-byte (16-bit) integer. With 16 bits, numbers from 0 to 65535 can be represented. By letting the first bit represent the sign of the number and the remaining 15 represent the actual number, bit patterns are split into two sets, those used for negative numbers and those for positive numbers. The numbers that can be represented are: -32767, -32767, -32766, . . . , -1, 0, $+1$, . . . , $+32766$, $+32767$. Thus, negative integers can be stored only at the expense of the range of positive integers. (Note: 1000000000000000 would seem to be a negative zero and 0000000000000000 a positive zero. Some computers allow two kinds of zeros, while others allow the negative zero to represent -32768.)

A few simple examples of eight-bit integers where the first bit represents the sign are given in Figure 3–2.

Computer Insights
Computer Hardware: Computer Families

One of the major problems in the purchase of computer hardware is the cost of computing power. One must achieve a reasonable balance between keeping the price of the hardware low and providing adequate computing power for current and future needs. Another problem arises from ever-improving hardware technology: a computing system purchased today may be made obsolete by new systems introduced tomorrow. If for any reason an existing computer system does not provide the needed power, the user must purchase new hardware and reprogram or replace existing software. To help overcome these problems, computer manufacturers have developed *computer families.*

A computer family is a set of computers with different prices and different amounts of power, but all built around the same basic design. The most important result of this common design is that the machines are supposedly *upward compatible,* that is, a machine of one level of power can be converted into any more powerful member of the family by adding new hardware devices to the existing hardware. In theory, a purchaser can thus buy the cheapest and least powerful member in the family, but the existing investment in hardware and software is not lost if his or her computing

needs increase. Instead, the user merely replaces some of the hardware or buys additional storage, processing, or other hardware to increase the power of the existing system. The problem is that hardware is not always compatible even within the same family. Most, however, are software upward-compatible, i.e., software that runs on smaller systems will also work on the larger ones. The concept of computer families and upward compatibility was first introduced in the IBM 360 line of computers in the 1960s. The problem that computer families address is of such importance that virtually all computers (everything from personal computers to large mainframes) since that time have been designed around a family of computers. Well-known families of personal computers include the IBM PC, the IBM PS/2, Apple II, and the Apple Macintosh series.

In recent years there has been interest in the concept of software families and upward compatibility on the programming side of computing. Indeed, just as a user invests in hardware, there is also an investment in software: programs, data bases, and training personnel. Hence new versions of software should be compatible (e.g., use the same data disks and commands) as older versions.

Thus there is a convention for interpreting a pattern of bits as a whole number. Positive and negative numbers can be stored in a computer, but they are limited to a certain range, which depends on how many bytes are used.

So far, we have seen two different conventions for interpreting bit patterns. If the computer were given the pattern 0000000100000001, it could be interpreted as one 16-bit integer or as two separate 8-bit text characters. The interpretation depends on how the bits are being used.

■ Using Bits to Represent Fractional Numbers

Whole numbers, however, are not adequate for many everyday problems. The ability to handle fractional numbers is also needed.

Fractional numbers are generally represented in the computer by a technique similar to **scientific notation.** Each number is represented as a fraction multiplied by a power of 10. For example, the number 456 can be represented as 0.456 times 1000 (10 raised to the power 3). The number 0.0004 can be represented as the number 0.4 times 0.001 (10 raised to the power -3). This strategy breaks a number into two parts:

1. the digits of the number (called the significant digits or the *mantissa*)
2. the position of the decimal point (the power of ten or the *exponent*).

In general, computers allow the digits of a number to range from something like -0.9999999999 to $+0.9999999999$. The decimal point may then be moved by an amount ranging from about 127 places to the left (-127) to 127 places to the right ($+127$).

Thus a fractional number is stored as a string of bits by converting it to a fraction multiplied by a power of ten and then storing the mantissa and exponent as if they were whole numbers. The exponent is always an integer and the mantissa can be treated as if it is an integer because the decimal point is always in the same place (i.e., at the beginning of the number). Such a representation often takes four bytes—one byte for the exponent and three bytes for the mantissa.

As usual, computer manufacturers have many choices of methods for representing fractions. Whatever the choice, the hardware of any system limits the maximum size and precision of numbers that can be easily represented. These limits generally restrict the use of numbers outside of a certain range. Only with special computer programs can you have numbers of arbitrary size and precision. Also, although the number representation methods described here are essentially correct, slight variations on these schemes (e.g., a number representation called two's complement) are generally used because of concerns of efficiency and hardware design. Now we can see that the 32-bit string 10001010 01001000 10100000 11110010 could be interpreted as:

1. a real number,
2. two integer numbers, or
3. four text characters.

One pattern of bits, then, can have several meanings, because there are several conventions for defining meaning.

---

scientific notation
A method used to represent fractional numbers. Numbers are represented as a number between 1 and 10, multiplied by a power of 10, e.g., 25 $= 2.5 \times 10^1$ Computers use a similar notation.

■ Using Bits to Represent Commands for the Computer

Finally, perhaps the most important representation scheme for bit patterns is the one used for representing the user's commands to the computer. Patterns of bits can also be treated as instructions telling the computer what to do next. Although we will not describe any precise method for interpreting bit patterns as computer instructions, the following example will give us some idea how instructions could be represented.

How can the 32-bit string 00 110000101010101 010101000001111 be interpreted as an instruction? Generally, the instruction convention takes the long string and breaks it into parts. Using a purely hypothetical situation, let us assume that our computer can perform only the four basic operations: addition, subtraction, multiplication, and division. The 32 bits might be broken into three parts:

1. the first 2 bits could specify which of the four operations is to be performed, e.g., 00 means add, 01 means subtract, 10 means multiply, and 11 means divide,
2. the next 15 bits represent one number,
3. the last 15 bits represent a second number.

Then the string given above would translate into:

- □   00—the code for addition
- □ 110000101010101—the code for the first number
- □ 010101000001111—the code for the second number

If the computer were asked to execute the function designated by this pattern of bits, it would add the two numbers together. This example illustrates the general technique that allows a bit pattern to be interpreted as a command for the computer.

■ Bits and Meaning

The preceding discussion highlights a simple fact of computing: if a particular type of data is needed by the computer, then a convention must be established to represent the data in computer-processable form. Generally, good choices or bad choices can be made when establishing conventions. Choices are often made to be compatible with already successful conventions. Whatever the choices are, a particular bit pattern like 0101111100010111 can be interpreted by a variety of schemes; thus, the same bit pattern can represent text, whole numbers, fractions, or computer instructions.

In our discussion of how human concepts are represented as patterns of bits, we have not considered the representation of tables of numbers or the storing of a complete student record with many types of textual and numeric data. These larger forms of data are also matters of convention, but these conventions are established during the creation of a computer program. The conventions we have discussed here are conventions of the computing machinery itself. The electronic circuits of a computer have to be put together with some primitive capabilities: the primitive forms of data described here detail the machine-level capabilities. The larger conventions will be discussed in the sections on computer programming.

3.3

Storage

Computer Hardware

| INPUT | **STORAGE** | PROCESS | CONTROL | OUTPUT |

Storage has addresses and contents.
Commands put things in and take things out.

Storage is made from circuits, magnetic, or laser media.
Storage either requires power or does not require power to hold data.
Storage is either random access or sequential access.
Storage is either read only or read/write.

RAM: circuits, requires power, random access, read/write.
ROM: circuits, no power needed, random access, read only.
Tape: magnetic, no power needed, sequential, read/write.
Disk: magnetic, no power needed, random access, read/write.
CD-ROM: laser, no power needed, random access, read/write.

As we have just seen, human concepts like names, telephone numbers, addresses, checkbook balances, and so on, are represented inside the computer as patterns of bits. These patterns of bits must be input, stored, processed, controlled, and output when the computer performs its tasks. Of the five basic processes, we will first consider storage.

Computer storage has two functions:

1. **saving** a sequence of bits that represents information, and
2. retrieving this saved information at some later time.

saving
A procedure for copying data from internal storage to an external storage device, e.g., saving data from RAM to magnetic disk.

Perhaps the simplest view of computer storage is that it consists of one long, long string of on/off switches (bits). On even the smallest computers today, the numbers of bits of storage is on the order of millions; much, much larger memories are common. Saving data into this storage requires a statement telling which of these many bits to use, whether each one used should be a 1 or a 0, and which way to interpret the stored bit patterns. This statement is essentially a message something like set the 43,621st bit to a value of 1—hardly elegant, but extremely simple. The number 43,621 is called the address within storage and the 1 is the **data** to be stored there.

data
Information provided to the computer for processing or returned to the user after processing.

Although this explanation is basically correct, few storage devices actually allow access at such a microscopic level. Most devices require the simultaneous access of at least a full byte of data, whether storing or retrieving. Thus it is not possible to set the 43,621st bit to a 1, without simultaneously setting the value of at least seven surrounding bits as well (remember, there are eight bits in a byte). Some varieties of computer storage might require a larger amount to be accessed, e.g., 1024 bytes or more.

Since the bits in storage are actually used in groups, storage is more commonly viewed as a series of consecutive, labeled slots. The label on a slot is a whole number that indicates its position within memory (e.g., the first slot, the second slot, the third slot); this label name or number is called the address. Each addressed slot is capable of holding one bit pattern of data. In Figure 3–3, we see an abstract illustration of storage: a series of slots numbered 00000, 00001, 00010, and so forth. These numbers are the addresses coded as integers. Each slot is capable of holding one bit pattern of some prescribed length. For example, the address 00000 could store the data (i.e., have the contents) 00000001.

The concept of computing storage is simple: one set of bits specifies which part of storage to use (the address) and another set of bits specifies the data (the information stored at that address). The major complexities of storage systems arise because of engineering cost-benefit concerns. The simple requirements of storage can be implemented in many different ways. Storage can be created out of very fast and very expensive electronic circuits, less fast and less expensive circuits, magnetic media like disks or tapes, or even mechanical media like punched card or paper tape. These various storage types differ in a number of important dimensions.

Address	Contents of this storage
00000	1 or more bytes
00001	1 or more bytes
00010	1 or more bytes
00011	1 or more bytes
00100	1 or more bytes
00101	1 or more bytes
•	•
•	•
•	•

Figure 3–3 Typical Computer Storage

■ Dimensions of Computer Storage

Four major dimensions of computer storage will be considered here: (1) accessibility, (2) volatility, (3) changeability, and (4) internal (fixed) or external (removable) media.

Accessibility of Storage. Computer storage may differ, first, on whether it is *random access storage* or *sequential access storage*. A storage system is random access if it takes roughly the same amount of time to access any element of storage. Random access is analogous to playing a record on a turntable—the listener can place the tone arm at any spot on the record in about the same amount of time. With sequential access storage, different parts of storage are accessed in different amounts of time. Sequential access is similar to a cassette tape—a listener can access the first song on a tape immediately, but can access the last song only after waiting for the tape to wind past intervening songs.

Volatility of Storage. The second dimension on which storage can differ is whether or not electrical power is required to maintain the data in storage. Magnetic storage devices (like tapes or disks) are nonvolatile, that is they do not require any power to keep their data; although their data can be changed, no electricity is needed to keep the change. Some other storage devices are made of electrical circuits that contain permanent and unchangeable data; these electrical circuits are also nonvolatile. They require no power since the data is "wired-in" and unalterable. There are also volatile electrical circuits with changeable data that do require power, and if the power fails, all data stored in the storage device disappears.

Changeability of Storage. The ability to change the contents of data in storage is the third dimension on which storage can vary. Read-only storage devices contain permanent data that can be read but cannot be changed. Such storage is generally used to hold programs written by the computer manufacturer. Read-write forms of storage can be altered readily; the user's programs and data are stored there.

Internal (Fixed) and External (Removable) Media. The last important storage dimension is whether or not the storage device uses a fixed internal or a removable external storage medium. Some storage devices use internal media where the bits are stored on a material that is an integral part of the computer, e.g., plugged into the motherboard. Such devices cannot be easily removed, replaced, or expanded. When they are filled, the user has little choice but to make expensive and time-consuming additions to the system. Examples of internal storage include the integrated circuit chips out of which the computer's main memory is constructed. Other devices, like floppy disk drives, use external media, where the data is stored on an easily removable material. The only part of the storage device that is built into the computer is the machinery required to read from and write to the removable medium. When the external storage medium becomes filled, the filled storage material can be removed and a new one inserted with ease. Most computer users have a large number of removable magnetic disks to use with their computer system.

Despite the differences in storage devices, they all need a storage controller. The controller is essentially a set of electronic circuits that connects the storage device to the communication line of the computer. The controller is what knows how to take an address and retrieve or store data.

■ Electronic Circuit Storage

The computer's fastest memory is the internal memory composed of integrated circuits. It is generally broken into the two parts: **RAM,** the memory in which the user's programs and data reside while in use, and **ROM,** the read only memory that contains programs and data created by the computer manufacturer. The characteristics of RAM are: *(1) it is a random access memory, (2) it uses a fixed internal medium of integrated circuits, (3) it is volatile, i.e., it requires power to hold its data, and (4) it is read-write, i.e., its contents can be changed.* The characteristics of ROM are: *(1) it is a random access memory, (2) it uses a fixed internal medium of integrated circuits, (3) it is nonvolatile, i.e., it does not require power to hold its data, and (4) it is read-only,* i.e., its contents are permanent and unchangeable. Note the large overlap in the characteristics of these two different types of memory. Of particular interest is the poor choice of names for RAM and ROM: indeed, ROM is a random access memory!

To provide a clearer understanding of the operation of integrated circuit memory, consider the analogy between computer storage and the job of an usher who seats patrons in a theater. In a theater, each seat has a label or address (e.g., row C, seat 46 is labeled C-46), and each seat can hold only one person, just as each storage location can hold only one value. The usher is equivalent to the storage controller in a computer: a particular person (content) is placed into a particular seat (storage location) designated by his or her ticket (the address). The person can be moved from one seat to another (just as a specific bit pattern can be moved from one storage location to another). The usher also needs to be able to locate a person after he or she has been seated (contents may need to be retrieved from storage).

In most theaters, the patronage of season ticket holders is extremely important; the theater reserves seats for these patrons and can count on their always being there. These patrons would be the ROM of the system: always in attendance no matter what the show. The other seats in the theater are for the various, random people who come to a particular production; they are analogous to the RAM of the system. Of course, the reserved seating for season ticket holders is the best in the house and is not mixed with the other seating.

RAM (Random Access Memory)

Electronic circuit memory built from integrated circuit chips. Its characteristics are random (equal speed) access, volatile retention (data retention requires electricity), read-write capable (contents can be changed), and fixed internal medium (can't be removed and replaced when filled).

ROM (Read Only Memory)

Electronic circuit memory with the same characteristics as RAM, except that it is read-only (contents can not be changed) and nonvolatile. Often used to provide built-in programs.

How does the usher direct the appropriate patron to seat C-46 in the theater? It would be absurd and terribly time-consuming for the usher to start at one corner of the theater and begin checking off each seat, one by one, looking for C-46! Instead, the usher can find any seat in just about the same amount of time by knowing the structure of the theater and the pattern of rows and sections. In the same way (random access), the controller for the computer memory knows the structure of the memory and can access any point in storage in approximately the same amount of time.

The external storage of data that was in RAM can also be mirrored in our theater analogy. Imagine that the stage show has to be stopped for some reason. In order to be fair, the theater manager decides to continue the show the next day at the point where it stopped. To make sure that every patron gets the proper seat for the continued performance, the manager takes a video tape picture of the audience. When everyone returns for the production the next night, the manager will turn the recording on and carefully reposition all of the patrons in the same seats as the day before. This action (as silly as it sounds here) is analogous to what the computer does when it saves the information in its internal RAM memory onto an external storage device like a disk and retrieves it at another time.

An example of current electronic circuit storage technology is included in Figure 3–4.

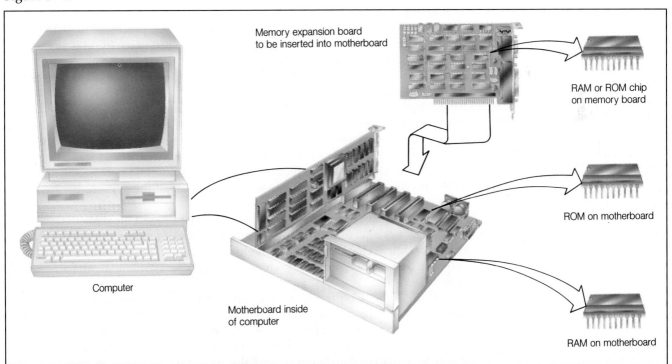

Memory expansion board
to be inserted into motherboard

RAM or ROM chip
on memory board

ROM on motherboard

Computer

Motherboard inside
of computer

RAM on motherboard

Figure 3–4 Circuit Memory (ROM and RAM). RAM and ROM are both fast, random access, integrated circuit memory chips that are positioned on the motherboard or expansion boards. They are the fastest memories in a computer. RAM requires power to retain the data it holds and can contain different data at different times. It is used, therefore, for user programs and data. ROM needs no power to hold data, but it always contains the same data, usually programs and data included by the computer manufacturer.

Computer Insights
Unlimited Computer Storage

Newer and better forms of computer hardware are always on the horizon. *Optical discs* are likely to be one of the most important storage technologies of the near future.

The same technology that created the compact disc music industry is being applied to computer storage. The compact disc stores music in digital form that is read by a laser, and the same digital form is easily adaptable to the storage of bit patterns. One compact disc can store 550 megabytes (550,000,000 bytes) of data. One compact disc can store the entire Encyclopaedia Britannica! If it existed, a six-foot square of this storage medium could hold all of the books in the Library of Congress! The only problem with compact discs at this time is that they generally are read-only—they are called CD-ROMs. But even now there are WORMs (*write once read many*) optical discs. As the density and writeability of these devices increase, they could substantially change our whole perspective on record keeping. Perhaps no computer record would ever be destroyed, since so much storage would be available. Whatever optical discs ultimately become, the ability to access such a massive data base so easily will change the way many disciplines use the computer. The problem then will become finding the relevant information needed. (For recent developments see the Computer Insight on hardware in Chapter 12.)

■ External Magnetic Storage

The general purpose of external storage is to hold data for RAM. On most computer systems, the only data that can actually be processed is data that is in RAM or ROM, the electronic circuit memories. But since ROM is unchangeable, the purpose of all the other storage on a computer is solely to hold data for later use in RAM. Thus, the major functions of external storage are saving data from RAM and loading data into RAM.

magnetic storage
Storage that is random or sequential access, nonvolatile (data retention does not require electricity), read-writable (contents can be changed), and uses either fixed or removable media (floppy disks and tape are removable while hard disks are fixed).

Another important purpose of external **magnetic storage** is to provide security for data and programs. With external storage, copies of the computer memory can be made and stored separately from the computer itself, so that any calamity to the computer hardware or environment would leave the externally stored memories unaffected. In most computer systems, the data and programs on disk are by far the most valuable part of the system, because they were created using people's time and ideas.

The two major types of external storage that use magnetic media are disks and tapes. Because disks and tape are both magnetic media, they have a number of common characteristics. To help understand these characteristics, consider a magnetic medium with which most people are familiar, the stereo cassette tape.

If an audio tape is placed into an audio cassette recorder and the user presses the record button, then whatever comes into the microphone is preserved on the tape for later listening. If what has been recorded loses favor, the tape can be reused to record another selection. When one cassette is full, it can be replaced with another and the recording process can continue. The user doesn't have to worry about losing the recording when the system is turned off, because the tape holds the music magnetically, without need of electricity. If the user has an especially nice recording that should be protected from accidental destruction, there is a write-protect tab that can be broken off the cassette top to protect the tape from further recording or erasure. Whatever the state of the recording, the user must take good care of the tape, never getting peanut butter on it or leaving it in an oven or whatever. *All of these characteristics are true of all magnetic storage media.*

Magnetic Tape Storage. Magnetic tape storage (see Figure 3–5) looks like either a reel-to-reel stereo tape deck or an audio or video cassette deck. The principles are the same regardless of appearance. *Tapes are sequential access, nonvolatile, read-write storage devices using a removable medium.*

Computer tapes are a sequential access storage media, because the part of the tape storage unit that reads the tape must pass over every inch of the tape between the current position and the desired position. Wherever the tape is positioned, it will take much less time to get to some portions of the tape (like the next spot in line) than it will to get to others (like the first or last spot on the tape).

The amount of data that can be stored on one magnetic tape is generally much larger than can be stored in the RAM at any one time. One tape can hold many types of data and programs for many purposes. Tape systems often provide a means of placing extra labels or names on the tape to separate the various sections of data and programs. For example, it might be possible to store a name like STUDENT RECORDS FOR CLASS CPS444 before the data for the specified class. If there are many such names before many sets of data and programs, a **directory** can be placed at the beginning of the tape. A directory lists the names of all data and programs on the tape as well as their locations. A directory is essentially a table of contents for a tape.

Updating a tape (changing one part of a tape's data while leaving the rest untouched) is a difficult task. Imagine that a stereo cassette is totally filled with

directory
In an operating system, a list of file names (displayed through text or graphic images) to show the data or program files stored on a disk or tape.

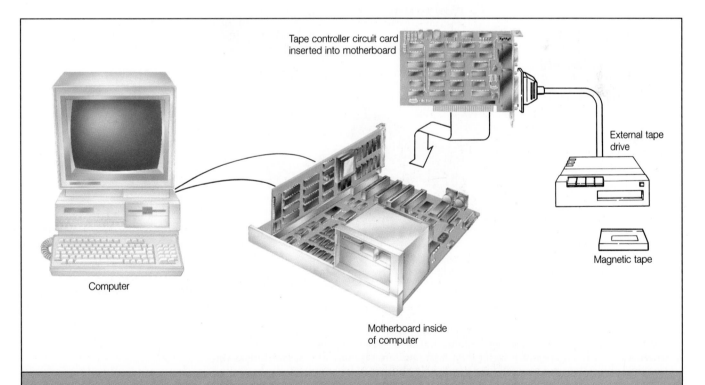

Tape controller circuit card inserted into motherboard

External tape drive

Magnetic tape

Computer

Motherboard inside of computer

Figure 3–5 Magnetic Tape Storage. Magnetic tape storage is slow in speed because it is sequentially accessed. It is, however, extremely cheap, virtually limitless, and requires no power to retain its data. Like most devices, the tape drive is controlled by a special circuit board in the backplane of the motherhood. The actual storage medium is a tape coated with a magnetic film.

songs and you want to put one new song in place of one of the old ones. What problems might arise? The task would be straightforward if the two songs happened to be exactly the same length, but how likely is that? Indeed, updating a tape often requires copying from one tape to another tape, skipping over the unwanted part, then swapping tapes to put in the new part, and when a final copy is complete, copying the whole thing back onto the original tape.

Finally, tapes are much slower than ROM and RAM, yet they are essentially unlimited in size and much cheaper as well. These cost-benefit differences make tape storage a viable alternative for computer systems.

disk
A random access circular magnetic storage medium that is divided into a series of concentric rings called tracks. The tracks are further divided into parts called sectors. Information is read from and written to the disk by rotating the disk so that various portions travel under a magnetic read/write head. The most common varieties of disks are magnetic 5.25" floppy disks, 3.5" disks, and hard disks. Recent developments include optical disks of much larger capacity.

Magnetic Disk Storage. Magnetic **disks** (Figure 3–6), another type of external magnetic storage, are *random access, non-volatile, read-write storage devices that use either a fixed or removable medium.*

Magnetic disks are basically of two types: removable and fixed. Removable disks, as the name implies, can be taken out and replaced with other disks. Like magnetic tapes, removable disks give indefinitely large storage capacity: when one gets filled, just put in another. Fixed disks, on the other hand, cannot be replaced. Instead, they act like a giant but slower addition to internal fast memory, with the improvement that the data and programs on the fixed disk do not disappear when power is turned off.

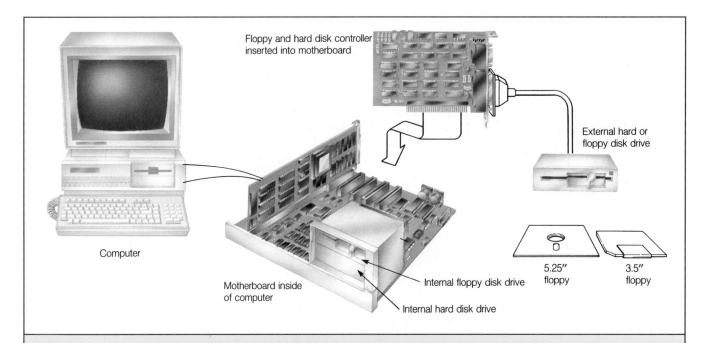

Floppy and hard disk controller inserted into motherboard

External hard or floppy disk drive

Computer

Motherboard inside of computer

Internal floppy disk drive

Internal hard disk drive

5.25" floppy

3.5" floppy

Figure 3–6 Hard Disk and Floppy Disk Storage. Disk drives are the storage mechanism of choice for a user's programs and data. Disks require no power to maintain their data, are much faster than tape, and are random access. Hard disks on personal computers are generally not removable and hence have no slot on the front for insertion. Hard disk storage is fixed, but it is generally quite large and even faster than floppy disks. Floppy disks, on the other hand, give unlimited storage because full disks can be removed from the drive and new, unused disks inserted. Floppy disks have generally been 5.25" in size, but newer floppies are 3.5" and more reliable. Either type of disk drive, hard or floppy, may be directly housed as an internal drive (in the same cabinet as the motherboard) or packaged as a separate external drive.

Disks also vary in the precise material on which the recordings are made. The most common material has been packaged as the so-called **floppy disk.** The floppy disk gets its name from the lack of rigidity of its magnetic material. Two types are in common use: the old 5.25-inch disk and the newer 3.5-inch disk. Floppy disks are generally removable. **Hard disks** are constructed of magnetic material formed into rigid platters that are sometimes connected together like a stack of phonograph records. Hard disks may be fixed or removable, but they are generally fixed, because the ever-increasing capacity of floppy disks eliminates the need for removable hard disks.

There are some important differences between disk storage and tape storage. The first important difference is speed. The disk is faster for two reasons: (1) disk drive mechanisms are inherently faster (and more expensive) and (2) unlike tape, disks are random access mechanisms (more like internal memory). The disk surface is divided into circles called tracks and the tracks are further divided into arcs called sectors. The read/write head can be positioned over

floppy disk
A low-cost, random access plastic disk that stores data magnetically. Most commonly used with personal computers.

hard disk
A rigid disk of metal coated with a magnetizable substance which is permanently mounted in a disk drive. Hard disks are faster and hold more data than floppy disks.

Computer Insights
The Apple II, the Apple Macintosh, and the Macintosh 2

The development of the Apple IIe microcomputer is now a matter of legend. In 1976, Stephen Wozniak built a small, easy-to-use microcomputer and named it the Apple I. As an employee of Hewlett-Packard, he offered his design to them, only to have it turned down. Then, at the urging of his friend Steven Jobs, Wozniak collaborated with Jobs to create the Apple Computer Corporation. They manufactured the first Apples in the garage of Job's parents.

As the company expanded, the few hundred Apple I's were succeeded by a better machine, the Apple II. By 1981, Apple was the dominant manufacturer of personal computers, with revenues of $335 million dollars. Since that time, the mainstay of Apple has been customer loyalty engendered by Apple's continued emphasis on customer support and hardware upgrades. Indeed, the Apple II has been followed by the Apple IIe, the Apple IIc, and the Apple IIgs. In each case, the company has strived to give the owners of any Apple II model the ability to upgrade their hardware to any higher-level Apple II machine. In addition, each more powerful version of the Apple II has been software compatible with the lesser versions, so that any software that runs on one machine will also run on its more powerful siblings. Finally, Apple II computers have generally provided an open structure that allows the user to insert electronic circuits and devices made by companies other than Apple. These so-called third-party vendors have brought tremendous capability and versatility to the Apple II series.

Besides the Apple II, Apple Computer Corporations has continued to develop innovative products. The initial Macintosh computer and the subsequent members of its family (the Macintosh 512K and the Macintosh Plus) gave new meaning to the phrase "user friendly." The Macintosh computer pioneered a new means of communication with the computer. Instead of having to use memorized command

words, the user selected commands using a computer screen listing the available commands, small pictures of the physical components of the system, and a pointing device. For example, to make a copy of a disk, the user could point at a picture of a disk on the screen and move it on top of a picture of a second disk—this physical action would command the computer to make the second disk be a copy of the first disk. (This graphic command technique will be described in later chapters.)

Not content to rest on its laurels, Apple has recently come out with a still newer version of the Macintosh, the Macintosh SE, as well as a substantially more powerful machine, the Macintosh II. Of these two, the Macintosh II is by far the more significant because: (1) it is an open architecture machine, so any manufacturer can design new hardware to work with it, (2) it will be able to run IBM PC software through special circuit boards that can be put into the expansion slots of its backplane, (3) it can be used with UNIX, one of the most popular operating systems today, (4) it is a powerhouse! The Macintosh II uses a fast 32-bit microprocessor (the Motorola 68020), so it can process more data at a chunk, and it provides other nice chips for math processing and memory management. Finally, it provides for extremely high-resolution full-color screens. With all of these improvements in hardware and Apple's current preeminence in user-friendly interfaces, Apple can now handle the tasks of the business world and may well take a larger share of that all-important market.

Whether Apple or any other computer manufacturer stays in the marketplace and prospers remains to be seen. But the competition provided by companies like Apple has caused major shifts in the focus of computers: a shift toward computers that are powerful yet easy for individuals to use. (See also the hardware Computer Insight Chapter 12)

any track to read any sector on the track. Which track or sector is being used does not affect the speed of access to any significant degree.

The second difference is that disk drive systems always require a table of contents or directory. The purpose of the directory is to give the names and locations of all the data and programs on the disk. On most systems, there can even be directories that point to other directories, a kind of superdirectory. In fact, these systems generally have a directory of superdirectories (should we call it a megadirectory?), and so on, to as many levels as you desire.

■ Other Storage Devices

Many different storage technologies and methods exist today and undoubtedly many others will follow. The changes that will occur will be more than just a difference in degree, more than just a little faster, a little cheaper, and a little larger. Indeed, the changes will be so great that they will require drastic changes in the ideas and practices of computer users. Consider a number of possibilities.

CD-ROM. As laser technology allows the packing of more and more storage into smaller and smaller spaces, the information available on any computer system may appear astonishing! Any computer might come with a built-in encyclopedia and dictionary. The typical computer user will need to develop effective means of using the mountains of data that will be available. We are already approaching that point with the introduction of compact-disk ROM (CD-ROM), which can store substantially more information in a given amount of space than any other external technology.

The impact of the CD-ROM goes beyond the storage of large amounts of data. What happens when we have so much memory for our own computer work that it is essentially unlimited in size? The need to ever erase anything disappears! As long as the user has an effective cataloguing system, data would never be lost (although it might be hard to find).

Associative Memories. What happens if the address for a storage location is no longer just a number but is some kind of function based on the type of data? We won't need to say "Set the 43,621st location to the name 'Smith.' " Instead, we will say "Store 'Smith' with the other surnames" and let the storage figure out what that means. Such a change could alter the very nature of computing storage as it is known today.

3.4

Input and Output

These two system functions deal with communication between the computer system and its environment. Input is a transfer of information from the environment into the computer system, while output is an action on the environment by the computer system.

Input represents the computer's ability to sense its environment. Because the computer can process only patterns of bits, all inputs to the computer must somehow be transformed into patterns of bits before they can be stored or processed.

The output of a computer system is represented by all of its abilities to take actions that affect its environment. Again, since computers process only bit patterns, the output of a computer system must be a translation of the

Computer Hardware

INPUT   STORAGE   PROCESS   CONTROL   **OUTPUT**

Keyboard:	Currently the primary means of input, differs in many dimensions across computers.
Mouse:	The primary device for pointing at images on a computer screen.
Screen:	The major interactive output device, also varies in a number of ways across computer manufacturers.
Printer:	The major permanent output device, with numerous variations.
Terminal:	A keyboard and screen combined in one unit.
Modem:	The major device for communication between two separate computer systems.

binary patterns of computer thought into the physical actions that the computer can take on the environment.

■ Input Devices

The keyboard is by far the most common input device on computers today. (see Figure 3–7). A keyboard is essentially a typewriter keyboard with electronic circuits that connect it to the computer's communication line. Whenever a key or combination of keys is pressed, a particular pattern of bits is sent down the communication line for use by other parts of the system. For example, when the letter A is pressed, the bit pattern 01000001 is placed onto the communication line; B gives a 01000010, and so on. The bit patterns given in the ASCII table are generally used. These bit patterns on the communication line enable the computer program to respond to the information that the user types at the keyboard.

A standard keyboard has anywhere from 60 to 110 or more keys. Each key can have a multitude of meanings. Just as on a typewriter, most keys have an uppercase and a lowercase meaning. One key gives a or A, depending on whether the shift key is held down. Another key gives 1 or ! depending on the shift key, and so on.

The **control key** (usually marked *control*, *ctrl*, or occasionally *alt*) works something like a shift key by allowing most keys to send out a third bit pattern called a **control character.** For example, if the control key is held down when the key marked A is pressed, the bit pattern sent is not an a or an A bit pattern but instead a control-A bit pattern. Control-A does not exist in the human alphabet, and it has no printed symbol; it exists only for the computer to use.

control key
A specially designated keyboard key that acts like a shift key in that it changes the meaning of the ordinary alphabetic keys. The A key becomes a control-A, the B key becomes a control-B, and so forth.

control character
A letter from the computer's expanded alphabet, typed by holding down the designated control key and pressing an ordinary key. The computer's alphabet includes a control-A, a control-B, and so forth.

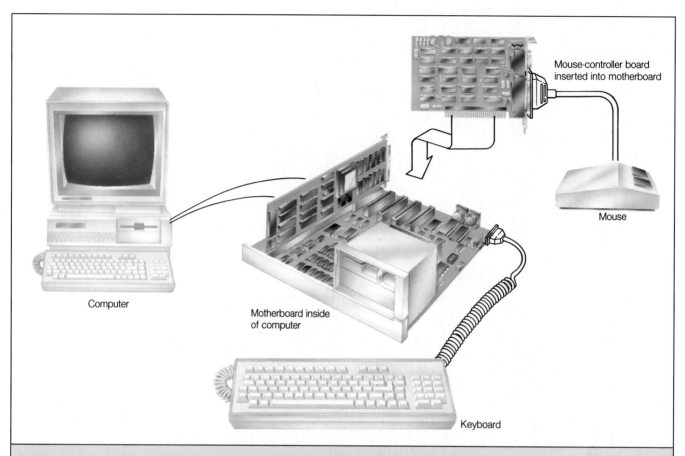

Figure 3–7 Keyboard and Mouse Input Devices. The Keyboard and the mouse are the two primary methods for input on most computer systems. Keyboards all perform essentially the same functions, but the precise placement of keys, the tactile feedback from the **keys,** and the other user-oriented factors may differ. Different mice also differ in only a few ways. The precision, durability, and price of a mouse depend on whether its technology is optical or mechanical. Mice usually come with 1, 2, or 3 buttons.

Most combinations of keys on the keyboard are used to send ASCII codes. A number of other combinations, however, perform various functions that depend on the particular computer design. For example, on the IBM-PC, holding down the three keys marked *ctrl*, *alt*, and *del* at the same time sends a signal to restart the computer from scratch; on a Tandy-1000, pressing the *hold key* causes an immediate pause in whatever the computer is doing.

Aside from the basic ability to send bit patterns onto the computer's communication line, keyboards may have a variety of other characteristics:

- *Repetition.* Most keyboards provide a simple method to repeatedly send the same bit pattern. One method is to provide a repeat key that repeats the pattern sent by any other key being pressed. Most keyboards use auto repeat keys—instead of having a separate key for repetition, every key automatically repeats if held down for more than a certain length of time.
- *Rollover.* It is easy to press a key on the keyboard before fully releasing the previous one. To prevent any loss of character data,

keyboards will generally provide what is called a two- or three-key rollover. If two or three keys are all pressed down together (they cannot be pressed simultaneously from the computer's high-speed perspective), their bit patterns will be sent along the communication line in order.

☐ *Special Function Keys.* Virtually all keyboards have some special-purpose keys. Many keyboards have a set of **function keys** labeled F1, F2, F3, . . . , F10. Other keys include *search, page up,* keys with arrows on them, and so forth. Each key will cause some special pattern of bits to be sent down the communication line.

☐ *Numeric Pads.* To allow faster entry of numeric data, many keyboards provide a small, extra keyboard to the side of the regular large one. Included on the small keypad are all of the digits 0–9 as well as other standard calculatorlike symbols.

☐ *Customized Keyboards.* Any special-purpose setting may suggest a totally nonstandard keyboard. For example, some studies of typing speeds have indicated that the traditional placement of typewriter keys is not optimal. This has led to the development of the new Dvorak keyboard that may be faster once its layout is learned. Some users prefer a keyboard with this option. Other settings, like air-traffic control, robot control, and so on, may require even more unusual types of keyboards to enter routine data.

function keys
Special keys on a computer keyboard that generate codes in the computer's extended alphabet (not in the human alphabet). There are usually 10–12 function keys labeled F1, F2, F3, . . . , F12. Any software system can then use these special keys to represent commands, e.g., F6 might mean "delete line of text" in a word processing system.

The **mouse** (also shown in Figure 3–7) is a small hand-held input device that is used as a supplement to the keyboard. It is connected to the computer by a cable. When the mouse is pressed down and moved across a flat surface, this movement is used by the microcomputer to move a corresponding pointer on the screen. The buttons on top of the mouse can also be pressed to signal the microcomputer. Thus, the mouse can be used to "point and click" at objects or places on the screen.

mouse
A hand-held pointing mechanism that controls cursor/pointer movement on a computer screen. Buttons on the mouse are used for input.

A point-of-transaction device is another common input tool. The variety of implementations are beyond the scope of this chapter. A typical example of a point-of-transaction device is a computerized cash register: as each transaction occurs, a message of coded bit patterns is sent from the register to a computer for processing. The computer can use the input for inventory control or a variety of other business functions.

Other sensory input devices are available for such things as X-ray diffractions for computer interpretation, sensors on probes sent into space, joysticks for computer games, and vision systems for robotic assembly tasks. Input systems have been devised to convert almost any natural phenomenon to patterns of bits. Through these input systems, computers can directly access a much wider range of senses than people can.

■ Output

The two most common output devices in general use are video screens and printers. Each one takes bit patterns from the communication line of the computer system and converts them into symbols or images that are comprehensible to people. The capabilities of any printer or video screen are limited only by the inventiveness of the design engineers who created it. In general, two types of data can be generated on a printer or screen: ordinary keyboard symbols or graphic images. Not all printers and screens have the power to handle graphics, but all handle text.

Video Screens.   Although the goal of any video screen is to provide sharp and clear computer images, video screens differ in a variety of ways because of cost/benefit concerns.

Possibly the most important characteristic of a screen is its resolution. All video images are made up of a series of small dots. Essentially, **resolution** is a measure of the number of dots per inch. The higher the resolution (i.e., the greater the number of dots and the closer together the dots), the clearer the picture. Many levels of resolution are now possible, as users demand ever-higher quality in visual images. A typical resolution might be about 600 dots across the screen and 400 dots down the screen. As one might expect, the more the user is willing to pay, the higher the resolution can be.

Another difference among video screens is whether the screen is a television, a monitor, or a television monitor. Monitors differ from televisions in two ways: they do not have a station selector like a television does and their resolution is much better. Video monitors are built with no intention of receiving pictures from the airwaves, so they have no station selector. Instead, they have one standard connection in back for accepting a video monitor signal. Better resolution is an important characteristic of video monitors, because precision is much more important when working at a computer screen than when watching a television show. The television monitor combines the two devices into one: you get the resolution of a monitor and the channel capability of a television. No doubt many users have enjoyed the economy of purchasing only one screen for the home rather than two.

Both one-color and full-color video screens are available. Full-color screens are more expensive than one-color screens, as might be expected, so single color monochrome screens are used in many situations where full color is not really important (e.g., typing a letter). Historically, monochrome monitors have had a green color; amber is a common alternative.

Although these are the major differences among screens, there are many other variations in their capabilities. Just a few of the possibilities are:

- □ *Size.* The physical size of screens varies greatly across systems from the small 5-inch screens of some portable computers to the large 25-inch screens of large AI workstations.
- □ *Contrast.* This is primarily a concern with screens on portable computers; screens can differ widely in the user's ability to read the screen in bright light.
- □ *Technology.* Screens can be made using different types of technology. As the technology differs, so does the amount of power required to drive the screen, the clarity of the screen, the contrast of the screen, and many other characteristics.
- □ *Intelligence.* The messages sent to computer screens can contain two types of information: (1) what data to print and (2) where and how to print it. Intelligent screens provide such things as *inverse video* (black on white instead of white on black), reduced intensity, flashing characters, or direct access to print in row X column Y of the screen. Such capabilities are quite important to some of the newer computer systems that depend on **windows.**
- □ *Variable Character Sets.* Many screens have the ability to switch between the standard English character set, and French, Spanish, or Chinese characters, or arbitrary ones defined by the user.

resolution
In computer graphic systems, resolution refers to the number of dots (pixels) in a given area on the screen. The more dots in a given area the higher the resolution or quality of the graphics.

window
A part of the video screen used by some applications programs to display information, e.g., a word processor might display information from different files by splitting the screen into different windows.

Just as computer storage devices require storage controllers, so do video screens need video controllers. A **video controller** is a set of electronic circuits that takes text or graphic specifications and figures out which dots on the screen to turn on and off. The full capabilities of a computer video system are constrained by both the screen and the controller. For example, although all video screens are, in principle, capable of drawing graphic images, not all video controllers provide the mechanisms for allowing the screen to do so. The capabilities of video controllers/screens are generally stated in terms of standards of performance, i.e., different standards specify levels of video output quality in terms of resolution and colors available.

As with most things, users get what they pay for with video controllers and screens. Higher standards of quality cost more. Anyone purchasing a video screen must seriously examine the intended use of the system to make an informed decision. The important characteristics of video output screens are summarized in Figure 3–8.

Printers. Almost everything said about video screens applies in principle to printers. For example, printers differ in their technology, their speed, their resolution, the colors they use, the sizes and qualities of paper they use, and their intelligent built-in features. They may or may not have graphic abilities and variable character sets. The prime determiner is cost.

video controller
Electronic circuits that translate text or graphic images into a pattern of lighted dots on a video screen. Often provided by a controller board inserted in an expansion slot of the motherboard.

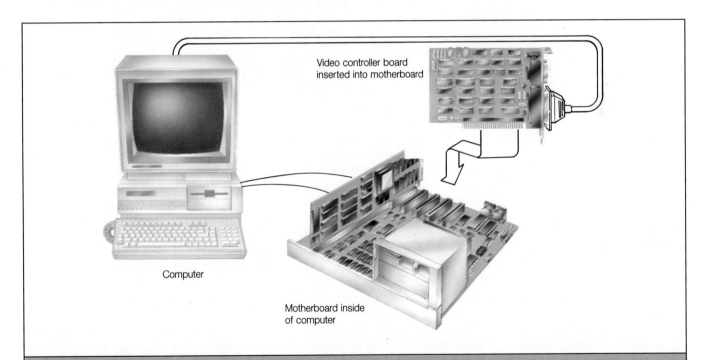

Video controller board
inserted into motherboard

Computer

Motherboard inside
of computer

Figure 3–8 Video Screens. The video display circuits of many computers are built directly into the system motherboard, but as screens with higher resolution, more colors, and larger size have been developed, it is now equally common to have an expansion board hold the video control circuits. The major characteristics of the video screen are whether it is color or monochrome, its resolution, the variety of inputs accepted, the size of the screen, and the human engineering (e.g., the brightness of the screen, the ability of the screen to swivel or tilt). As the sophistication of computer users increases, it may become common to have two or more screens attached to the same computer.

Computer Insights
The IBM PC and PS/2

As we have described, International Business Machines (IBM) is the dominant force in the mainframe computer industry. Due to an early start in the market and good customer support, IBM has always been a safe choice for computer equipment that is adequate and well serviced. As Apple and other computer manufacturers fought for supremacy in the early microcomputer market, everyone in the field wondered when IBM would join the fray and with what type of machine.

IBM finally introduced its first microcomputer, the IBM Personal Computer (IBM PC). Since that time, the IBM PC family has grown to include the IBM PC, the IBM PC XT, and the IBM PC AT. The IBM PC family and its copies have now become the dominant machine in the microcomputer market, largely because IBM was already positioned as the dominant machine in the mainframe market. Purchasing agents for companies across the country were already accustomed to dealing with IBM and were used to its good hardware, software, and service. So when these companies began to acquire microcomputers, Big Blue (the nickname for IBM) was a frequent choice.

Possibly in response to introductions by Apple computer, IBM introduced a new family of microcomputers called the IBM PS/2. The low end of the family, the PS/2 Model 30, is essentially equivalent in power to the IBM PC XT (using an Intel 8086 chip), and it comes equipped with most useful hardware connections already in place. The PS/2 Model 50 uses a more sophisticated chip, the 80286, and is the middle-level machine. Finally, the PS/2 Models, 60, 70, and 80 are much more powerful than the PC AT and have high quality graphics and very large hard disk drives. These new machines are all based on the Intel 80386 chip.

Some engineers view the design of the entire chip family on which the IBM machines are built (Intel 8088, 8086, 80286, 80386) to be a poor choice when compared to the chip family on which the Apple Macintosh is built (Motorola 68000, 68020). Many industry pundits have been disappointed by IBM's offerings. Others disagree and argue that the Intel 386 chips and the Micro Channel Architecture (MCA, the 32-bit bus in the PS/2) make the PS/2 ideally suited as a base for new software development. Historically, IBM seems to stay with safe machines of wide appeal rather than trying innovation and its inherent risks. However, it is clear that the power available on the IBM Model 70/80 microcomputer system can be augmented with third-party options to make it usable for an enormously wide range of needs. With the continuing shake-up in the microcomputer industry, however, IBM will have to continually fend off the innovations of other computer firms. (See hardware Computer Insight in Chapter 12 for more on IBM.)

dot matrix printer
A printer in which the images are created by a series of small pins impacting an inked ribbon. Different images are created by different patterns of pin strikes, that is, by having some pins impact the ribbon and others hold back as each character is printed.

laser printer
A type of printer that uses an electrostatic process to place characters on paper. Laser printers provide speed, quality, and flexibility that are currently unmatched by other printers and are the basis for the growth of desktop publishing.

impact printer
A printer that creates images by causing a letter or pin to impact an inked ribbons. Impact printers are generally of two types: dot matrix printers and daisy-wheel printers.

Printers are based on many different technologies. The most common types are **dot matrix printers**, letter quality printers, and **laser printers**. Dot matrix and letter quality printers are both **impact printers**. They form characters by causing a letter or pin to impact on an inked ribbon. Laser printers are electrostatic printers—they form letters or images using a laser to draw an electrostatically charged pattern on a drum. A toner that adheres to the pattern is used to print the pattern on paper. Dot matrix printers form all of their characters by using pins to print only a certain pattern of dots within a rectangular grid of dots. For example, a grid of 7 dots by 9 dots will print the letter A by having some of those 63 ($7 \times 9 = 63$) positions turned on to print. Because individual dots of the grid can be turned on, dot matrix printers are good for printing graphic images. Letter quality printers, on the other hand, have full-formed characters, much like a typewriter. Letter quality printers can print professional looking documents of almost any variety, but they are poor at the creation of graphic images. Finally, laser printers are based on a xerographic process like that on most copying machines. Although their images are created from a set of dots just like a dot matrix printer, the density of the dots is on the order of three hundred dots per inch. This density is so high that the human eye cannot detect irregularities. Laser printers therefore provide the best of both worlds (superior text and graphics capability) in one machine. With prices continuing to drop, laser printers are the printers of choice for most business computer users and many home users.

Printer speeds vary widely: some laser printers print many pages of the highest quality in less than a minute, while some of the cheaper dot matrix printers for home use take several minutes to print one page. On many printers the computer has control over a variety of built-in functions such as changing font sizes, forward and reverse paper scrolling, and proportional spacing, while other printers offer none of these. Most printers offer some graphics capability, but the speed and quality of the created graphics varies widely. Some printers also provide alternative character sets with a full range of mathematical or foreign language symbols.

The quality of printer output tends to be related to price: in general, the more expensive the printer, the higher the print quality. Historically, most printers have been single color (black on white) but newer technologies allows full-color graphics on any paper. The types of paper products allowed include income tax forms, standard bond paper, address labels, multipart forms, payroll checks, and so on. For most common business applications, the paper is fed into the printer by a tractor feed (wheels on each side of the paper have pins that fit into holes in the paper), but many letters are printed using friction feed (like an ordinary typewriter) or cut sheet feeders (like a typewriter, but with automatic paper feed into the printer). Printer characteristics are detailed in Figure 3–9.

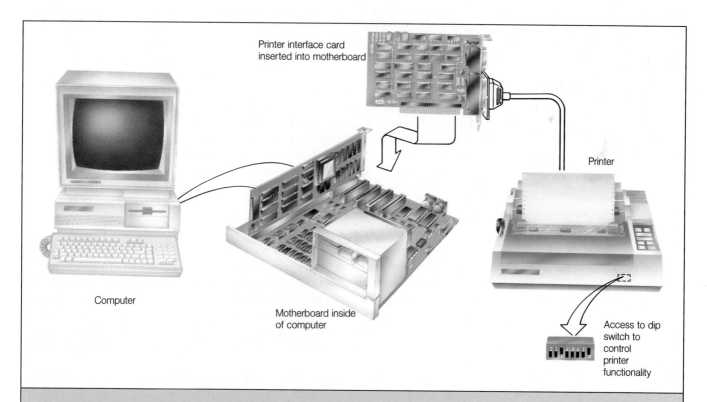

Printer interface card
inserted into motherboard

Printer

Computer

Motherboard inside
of computer

Access to dip
switch to
control
printer
functionality

Figure 3–9 Printers. Like most external devices, printers require special circuits to connect them to the computer. These circuits are usually on an expansion board but are built into the motherboard on some systems. Printers differ in the technology they use to transfer images to paper: heat, inkjet, physical impact, and xerographic processes are some of the technologies used. Whatever the technology, the characters formed are either full character or composed of varying numbers of discrete dots. The printer can be connected to the computer by either a seril or a parallel connector. The paper can be fed into the printer by friction or a tractor feed. Although dot matrix printers are widely used, xerographic or laser printers are the current standard for most computer users.

There are two real problems with existing video and printing technology. First, the characteristics of video screens and printers often do not match: one might be able to print some things on the printer that could not be previewed on the screen and vice-versa. Second, the sizes of the current devices are limited. For example, most screens cannot display the full contents of an 8.5-by-11-inch piece of paper. This limitation makes working on the screen more difficult than it need be. Neither of these criticisms is insurmountable and, in fact, some manufacturers are already addressing them.

■ Input/Output Devices

Since communication is a two-way street, it is common to combine an input device and an output device into one package—this is commonly done in a computer terminal. A terminal contains a keyboard and a video screen in one package and is connected to a computer at another location. The terminal might be augmented further by a printer that could make a copy of the screen display.

modem
A hardware device that translates bit patterns on a computer to and from audio signals that can be sent across telephone lines.

Another input-output device for computer to computer communication is called a **modem** (short for *mo*dulate-*dem*odulate). This device is shown in Figure 3–10; it is one of the standard means for connecting one computer with another. Since both computers use approximately identical alphabets based on bit patterns, their communication is not necessarily perceivable by a human, but it still must follow rules of conversation (protocols) so that they will know how to interpret any particular bit string. Modems and the general problem of computer-computer communication will be discussed in detail in Chapter 10.

The last input/output device we will mention is another computer-computer communication device that we have already covered: external magnetic storage devices. If one computer writes the data on a disk or tape, which is then read by another computer, we can view the tape or disk drive as input/output devices. Using magnetic media as a means for communication is a longstanding and efficient method for transferring data from one computer to another.

There are many other input and output devices that we have not described. An output device with great potential is the speech synthesizer, which enables the computer to actually talk. The corresponding input device is the speech recognizer, the means by which the computer can understand human speech. Speech recognition is much harder to do, but when it becomes practical, it will substantially alter computer use—one would never have to type again, and one could write the first draft of a whole book as fast as one could speak!

There are other output devices that automatically output to microfilm or to punched paper tape or cards. Other computer output can be directed to computer-controlled vehicles and robotic arms, and there is also visual input for many robotic applications.

In the future, the computer will be enhanced with many of the same senses that humans possess and some that humans do not have. The computer will have (and in some cases already has) input capabilities that are substantially superior to our own (e.g., perception of ultraviolet and infrared electromagnetic radiation). Looking into the future of computer output, today's technology already suggests that extremely high levels of precision and control that are impossible for unaided humans will be made possible through machines.

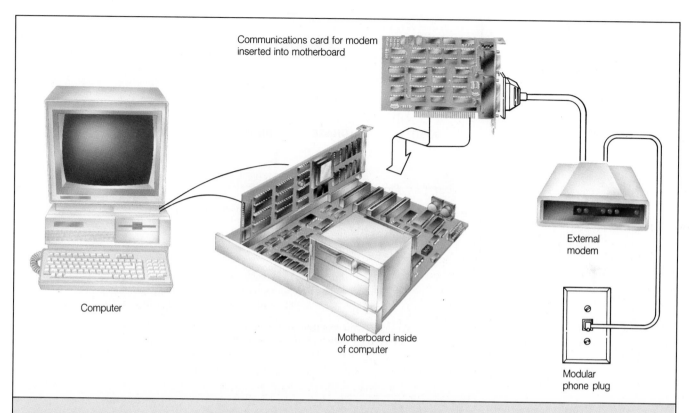

Figure 3–10 Communication by Modem. For two computers to communicate, each must have the equipment shown above. Each computer has a way to send data into a modem. The modem then converts the data into an audio signal that can be sent across a telephone line. At the other end, the second modem takes the signals from the telephone line and converts them back into computer form for the second computer to use. Since communication proceeds in both directions simultaneously, a modem both *modulates* and *demonstrates,* depending on the direction of the message. The modem shown in the figure is an external modem. Internal modems that directly connect the expansion board to the phone line are also available. As phone lines throughout the country are upgraded, there seem to be few limits on the speed of communication.

Finally, it is critical to understand the mechanisms by which the computer hardware can process patterns of bits and control all the input, storage, processing, and output functions. The processes that a computer can carry out are defined quite precisely by the underlying electronic circuits of the microprocessor or central processor. These processes represent the elemental actions available to the computer for the manipulation of bit patterns. The control function determines the order in which all the other computer functions are performed. Control is explicitly defined by the **instruction counter**, a special part of the hardware that tells the computer the location of the next instruction to perform.

In personal computers, processing and control are a function of the microprocessor chips and the motherboard combination that defines the basic computer system. Control and processing are actually performed by the micro-

3.5

Process and Control

instruction counter
A register in the microcomputer or central processing unit that gives a memory location for the next instruction to be used.

Computer Hardware

INPUT   STORAGE   **PROCESS**   **CONTROL**   OUTPUT

All computers have built-in information processing capabilities that
are a permanent part of the microprocessor
or central processing unit (CPU).

Typical built-in processes include arithmetic, relational, logical,
bit, input, output, control, and status operations.

All computers have an instruction counter that points to the
instruction in memory that should be executed next.

All computers have an instruction decoder that interprets a bit
pattern as a command to execute a process.

All computers have processing registers where processes are
applied to data.

processor chips, but these functions also involve the transfer of information
along bus or communication lines that are part of the motherboard, e. g.,
transferring data from RAM or ROM storage to the microprocessor. Similar
relationships exist in larger computers between the central processor, its fast
storage, and its communication channel hardware.

■ Processes

Computer processes manipulate patterns of bits using special-purpose electronic circuits. The method is quite simple. When a new microprocessor is
designed, the engineers decide that a particular type of manipulation (e.g.,
addition) is desired. Once this decision has been made, the designers must
then specify the electronic circuits that will perform the action. For addition,
the designers would have to specify a set of circuits that would be able to locate
the bit patterns of two numbers to be added, perform the addition, and place
the result somewhere for the rest of the system to use. The designers specify
the appropriate circuits for all the types of manipulations they wish to perform
on strings of bits, and this completed design defines the processes of the computer. These circuits, along with those for control, are part of the microprocessors of a small computer or the central processor of a large computer.

All computers can perform a minimal set of processes. Although the processes available on different microprocessors vary, a common set of bit manipulation processes is listed below:

1. *Arithmetic Processes for Whole Numbers.* Most computers can add,
   subtract, multiply, and divide two whole numbers. The whole
   numbers must be represented as bit patterns, the process must be

Computer Insights
Microcomputer Computer Chips

The heart of any computer is the processing and control unit—the place where the computer "thinks." It is not surprising that there are many different perspectives on the best design for a processing and control unit and hence many different microprocessor chips.

Each of the major computer manufacturers decides on the microprocessors that drive its computers. At the present there are three major microcomputer chip families in use. The 6502 microprocessor and its descendants (the 6502C, 65C02 and others) are used in the Apple II family. The Motorola 68000 microprocessor and its descendants (the 68010, 68020, 68030) are used in the Apple Macintosh and other machines. The Intel 8088 and its descendants (the 8086, 80286, 80386, 80486) are the chip used by IBM and its many competing clones (machines that are functionally equivalent to IBM computers but made by other manufacturers). The numbers of the various chips are generally meaningless except to identify families (e.g., the 80286 is related to 80386).

Each microprocessor chip has a number of characteristics:

1. Each chip includes within its circuits the ability to perform a variety of processes. Although the precise set of processes may differ from one chip to another, they must all be capable of simple things like arithmetic operations, references to input, storage, and output devices, and so on.
2. Each chip runs at a specific speed that determines how many processes can be performed each second, with typical values from 1MHz to 25MHz (MHz stands for megahertz). These values reflect the speed of the system clock, not necessarily the exact speed of system processes, but the higher the speed, the faster the chip.
3. Each chip has a different number and positioning of "feet" or pins that communicate between the processor chip and the underlying circuit board.

invoked, and then the answer will be available. Since only a certain number of bits are set aside to represent a whole number, the electronic circuits that do arithmetic processing must watch to see if the new number is too big to represent. If that happens, the computer circuits are smart enough to know that the answer is not correct, and they send out a message that tells the computer what happened. Some computers do not have built-in circuits to perform multiplication and division; these processes must then be built up out of repeated additions or subtractions.

2. *Arithmetic Operations on Fractional Numbers.* Many computers do not have the processes for fractional number operations built into their hardware. In these cases, fractional processes must be programmed and built up out of the integer arithmetic operations. On other computer systems, the hardware circuitry for these processes is available on an additional processing chip called a **math coprocessor**, which has the built-in circuits to perform these arithmetic operations at a much faster rate.

3. *Storage Processes.* These processes are used to initiate the storing of bit patterns in memory or their retrieval from memory. Recall from our discussion earlier that internal messages are sent down the communication line to tell the computer when to store or retrieve data. These messages come from the special electronic circuits associated with storage processes.

4. *Input/Output Processes.* These processes initiate the use of input and output devices. Just as storage access is initiated by internal messages, the various input and output devices receive instructions from input/output processes to tell them what to do. These processes access a particular part of the electronic circuits that knows how to

math coprocessor
An integrated circuit chip used to perform arithmetic processes at higher speeds than are possible with the microprocessor chip alone.

manage input and output devices and transfer data among them and the rest of the computer system.

Besides these processes, most computers include a number of other built-in operators. There can be many bit operators that change one bit pattern into another by various methods, such as converting all the 0's to 1's and all the 1's to 0's. **Relational operators** set the value of a bit to a 1 if two other bit strings are equal (or not equal, or meet some other criterion) and set it to 0 otherwise. **Logical operators** define one new bit string out of two other strings using the human concepts of "true," "false," "and," "or," and so forth. Status operators inform the system of the state of various storage, processing, input, output and other hardware. Processes like these are common to virtually all computers; they are built-in primitives that define the limits of computer performance.

■ Control

A computer can perform a set of operations, but in what order will these processes be executed? The standard method is **sequential control,** i.e., the processes are executed in the order given. Every task that the computer is to perform must be broken into steps. Sequential control says: perform the function at the top of the list first, then do the second one, then the third one, then the fourth, until the list is complete. For example, a list of steps for the computer to perform (this is actually computer program) might look like this:

1. Output the phrase "Enter X" on the screen
2. Input a number from the keyboard
3. Store the inputted value into storage location X
4. Output the phrase "Enter Y" on the screen
5. Input a number from the keyboard
6. Store the inputted value into storage location Y
7. Add values in X and Y and put result in location Z
8. Output the phrase "The value of X + Y is" to the screen
9. Output the value stored in location Z to the screen

The **default** control scheme that is built into the hardware of the computer is sequential control: *do the processes in the order given.*

Although the sequential control mechanism seems straightforward, one question remains: how does the computer know what processes to perform? That information typically comes from three sources.

First, a list of processes like the one above is always built into the computer's ROM. Read-only memory contains bit patterns that are always the same and are always there. These patterns contain representations of functions to be performed. Therefore, when you turn a computer on, it already has a list of available processes, namely, the list of processes defined in ROM; one example is a simple program called a loader, which inputs and executes other programs from disk.

A program that is in a disk drive when a computer is started up is a second source of a list of processes to perform. The loader program in ROM will have built-in capabilities to find the disk drive and ask it for a program. When the disk drive provides a program, the program is transferred into RAM and is then run. Most applications software is started up this way. For example, a video game disk is placed in the disk drive and the computer is turned on. Then the program in ROM starts, loads the video game from the disk, and then executes it.

---

relational operators
Symbols used to perform comparing operations, e.g., > (greater than) and < = (less than or equal to).

logical operators
Processes that accept true/false values as input and give back true/false answers according to particular patterns. The most commonly used logical operators are AND, OR, and NOT.

sequential control
Performing computing tasks in the order given.

default
A value or operation that is automatically used by a program if none is specified by the user.

The third source of the list of processes to perform comes from the user in the form of a computer program input from the keyboard. ROM contains the processes that enable the computer to (1) ask the user at the keyboard for a list of processes, (2) take this list and store it in memory (in RAM), and (3) perform the operations directed by this new list of processes.

Besides sequential control, there are at least three other types of control available in a computer: selection, iteration, and procedural control. The concepts behind these types of control are straightforward:

1. *Selection* (or alternation) *control* makes a choice between two sets of processes.
2. *Iteration control* repeats the same set of processes more than once.
3. *Procedural control* places one set of processes on hold, performs another set, and then comes back and finishes the first set.

These various types of control are vital to the proper programming of a computer, and a full and detailed discussion of these control mechanisms, their differences, and their uses can be found in the chapter on programming.

■ Processing and Control Hardware

Now that we have looked at the concepts behind processing and control, we can examine the hardware that actually performs these tasks. The hardware or electronic circuitry responsible for processing and control is variously called a **central processing unit** (CPU), a microprocessor unit (MPU), or sometimes just the brain of the computer. The CPU (or MPU) is primarily composed of a number of electronic devices called registers. The processing and control functions of the computer are carried out by manipulating bit patterns in these registers.

Structurally, CPU registers look just like storage devices. There are processes for putting things into registers and taking things out, but that is where the similarity ends—CPU registers can do much more than storage can. Attached to the registers are sets of special-purpose circuits that perform the many processes available in the computer; for example, the electronic circuits for addition are attached to registers. Thus, registers and the electronics attached to them are the "thinking" part of the computer. Although a wide variety of registers exists, the three principal types of registers are *instruction counters*, *instruction decoders*, and *processing registers*.

An instruction counter holds one address of storage, and the computer assumes that the next instruction to be performed is stored at that address. Whenever the instruction counter is referenced, it is automatically increased by one. In this way, whenever the instruction counter is referenced to get one instruction, it will be reset to point to the next instruction in line. This establishes the *default sequential control* scheme.

The **instruction decoder** interprets all the bit patterns that represent processing and control instructions. It knows which bit patterns represent which instructions and figures out which built-in process the computer should perform. For example, if the instruction decoder contained a bit pattern 0101000100101010, its circuitry might be designed to interpret this pattern as a command to add.

The built-in processes are actually carried out in the **processing register** or **accumulator**. For example, to add two numbers, one hardware design requires a set of two instructions: the first to load the value of one storage location into the processing register, and the second to add the value of a second

central processing unit (CPU)
The computer's "brain"; it consists of an instruction counter, an instruction decoder, and the arithmetic/logical unit for performing the various processes of arithmetic and logic. Often a single microprocessor chip.

instruction decoder
A register in the CPU that interprets bit patterns as instructions to perform built-in processes on data.

processing register or accumulator
A register in the CPU where processes are executed on data.

storage location to the current contents of the processing register. Although only three registers have been described here, computers often have multiple processing registers, variations on the registers mentioned here or other types of registers.

A simplified layout of a computer, its RAM and ROM, and its processing and control components is given in the Figure 3–11.

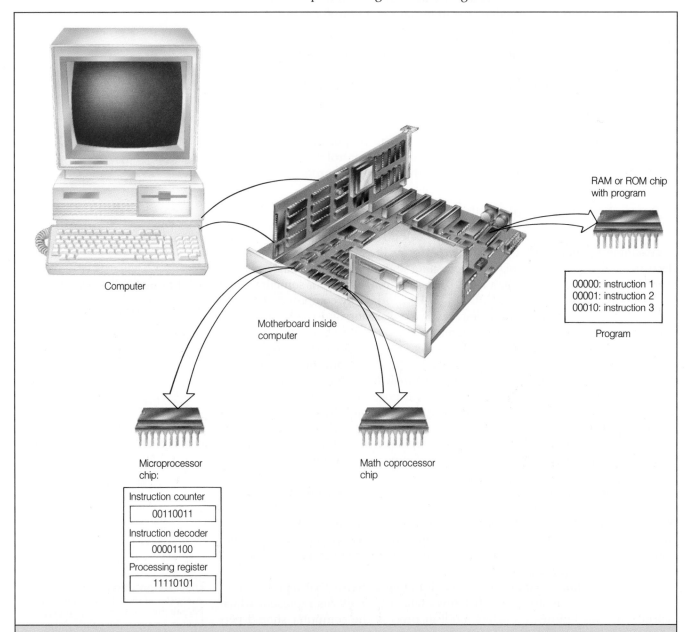

Computer

Motherboard inside computer

RAM or ROM chip with program

| 00000: instruction 1 |
| 00001: instruction 2 |
| 00010: instruction 3 |

Program

Microprocessor chip:

| Instruction counter |
| 00110011 |
| Instruction decoder |
| 00001100 |
| Processing register |
| 11110101 |

Math coprocessor chip

Figure 3–11   Processing and Control Hardware. The microprocessor provides three conceptually different kinds of registers. The instruction counter points to the next location in memory from which to extract an instruction. The instruction decoder is loaded with the binary code stored at that address, and it then proceeds to activate the appropriate circuitry to carry out the instruction. The processing register is connected to circuitry for arithmetic and other logical and bit operations. All three steps are part of executing a computer program stored in ROM or RAM.

When the computer is turned on, the instruction counter contains some initial value (like 0) that points to an instruction in ROM. The computer then proceeds in its normal operation:

1. The storage unit is sent a message telling it to get the bit pattern stored in the location pointed to by the instruction counter. This request references the instruction counter, which is automatically increased by one.
2. The storage unit reads the message, finds the addressed location, gets the value, and sends it down the communication line.
3. The processing and control unit takes this bit pattern and loads it into the instruction decoder.

Computer Insights
Robots and Advanced Automation

Robots were popularized by Karl Capek's 1920 play *R.U.R. (Rossum's Universal Robots).* The term *robot* comes from the Czeck word *robata,* meaning unpleasant or difficult work. Science fiction often depicts robots as monsters that turn against their creators. Isaac Asimov and other science fiction novelists have portrayed the robot as friend and mentor. Robots, however, are neither of these things. Robots are physical devices that affect the environment and are controlled by computer intelligence for operation without the continual assistance of a human controller.

Robots abound. Some robots weld automobile parts with speed, precision, and tirelessness unequalled by people. Others, like NASA's Mars lander and the solar system probes explore space. Still others, like cruise missiles travel thousands of miles with pinpoint accuracy while avoiding radar detection by flying so close to the ground that they actually frighten people. Robots extend our abilities to sense and affect our environment, but as with any technological advance, ethical questions sometimes arise as to their proper use.

Today's robots do not look like humans. Instead they look like spiders, torpedoes, tiny vehicles with arms (called manipulators), or one-armed TV cameras. Nonmobile robots are found on assembly lines performing fixed tasks (e.g., sorting parts or welding). Mobile robots are designed to perform more complex tasks involving the movement of the robot from place to place (e.g., performing repair tasks, maintenance, or monitoring tasks in dangerous situations). The human controller sits safely in the control area, watching TV screens and giving the robot commands to use its ISPCO functions for vision, movement, and manipulation.

Some examples of robots in use today include the PUMA manipulator from Unimate, "Moose," "Spyder," and high-tech aircraft. The PUMA is essentially a computer-controlled arm that is constructed like the human arm, with a turnable waist, a shoulder joint, an elbow joint, and three wrist joints. If shown where to place an object, it can repeat that action to within one thousandth of an inch with ease, and it can lift and work with a ten-pound object at that level of precision.

Although these actions may sound mundane, the PUMA is representative of most robots today.

Moose is a work drone. It looks like a sturdy little six-wheeled bulldozer and has a blade that can be replaced with a number of alternative tools that lift, grind, vacuum, and spray. Moose is a powerhouse that can grind its way through concrete. Moose recognizes very few commands. It is mainly operated with a joystick (like an arcade game machine) and it has a top speed of less than a half mile per hour.

Up the evolutionary ladder a bit is Spyder, the maintenance robot. It has six legs, each under the control of a microcomputer, an overall control microcomputer, manipulators, cameras, lights, and so on. It is controlled by humans using remote control consoles. Spyder is very agile and quite powerful—it can carry close to a ton. Spyder is also relatively intelligent: it can execute instructions like "walk up the stairs." In no way, however, does Spyder make much use of artificial intelligence. Robots like these are used in many hazardous industries. One was used after the Three Mile Island Nuclear Plant accident to establish the state of disrepair and radiation in the lower level of the nuclear generating plant.

Another type of robot is used for computer-controlled missiles, spaceships, and jet aircraft. These robots are specialized computer systems that use inertial guidance (super-accurate gyroscopes), satellite navigational information, and terrain pattern recognition maps to fly from one point to another, requiring human assistance only periodically. Given proper human input, a 747 jumbo jet guidance control system can, under normal conditions, fly an aircraft from any main runway at Kennedy International Airport in New York to any main runway at the San Francisco International Airport without human assistance. Similarly, the NASA space shuttle includes several guidance and control computers that aid the human crew in "flying." Indeed, manual control on re-entry is resumed only after the shuttle is well into the earth's atmosphere.

4. The instruction decoder causes the instruction to be carried out, possibly using the processing register.
5. The process is repeated.

The default control strategy (doing things in order) is enforced by the automatic incrementation of the instruction counter in step 1. If there is ever a variation in the sequential control, it is accomplished through a change in the instruction counter.

We now know how a computer really operates. But how does a bank's computer handle all of the information in its accounts? By carrying out the steps we have described at exactly this primitive a level. How does a home computer play a video game? The same way. As we will see in the programming chapter, computer programmers rarely have to work at such a detailed level, but sometimes they do, because that is how a computer runs.

3.6

Time-Sharing, Networks and Distributed Processing

Now that we have looked at a simplistic, relatively straightforward computer system, let us turn to the intricacies of more elaborate computer systems.

■ Time-Sharing Systems

A time-sharing system, as was described in a previous chapter, is a system that enables many individual computer users to simultaneously use the same physical computing devices. Recently in the personal computer field, time-sharing has come to also mean that the same user may wish to run two different jobs at the same time, e.g., using a word processor and a graphics system simultaneously. As far as this discussion is concerned, there is no logical difference between this and the situation involving time-sharing with more than one user. Either type of simultaneous use is accomplished by having the computer: (1) work on one user-task for just a few fractions of a second, (2) then work on the next user-task for a few fractions of a second, (3) and continue on with the other user-tasks until it eventually gets back to the first user-task and continues where it left off. Thus time-sharing means **turn-taking**.

turn-taking
On a time-sharing system, the determination of the sequence in which multiple users access the machine. Turn-taking is managed by the supervisory routine of an operating system.

Time-sharing is a feasible technique because computers work so much faster than people do. They work so fast that users of a time-sharing system may not even be able to detect that the computer is doing anything but their own tasks. Of course, the computer is not infinitely fast, so if there are just too many people taking turns, then the speed at which any individual user's tasks are done may become unbearably slow. The speed from the individual user's perspective is called *response time*.

In terms of hardware, a time-sharing system generally just requires more devices than a non-time sharing system, all connected to a communication line. There is often only one central processing unit connected to the line, but there are more storage devices, more varieties of output devices, more input devices, and more terminals than would be found on a single-user system. The computer terminal is frequently the major input and output device.

One of the primary advantages of a time-sharing system is that infrequently used input and output devices can be made available to many users, and the costs of these devices can be shared among those users. Another advantage is that software or stored data can be made accessible to many people.

To see the typical devices that one might encounter on a time-sharing system, look at Figure 3–12. Each of the devices shown can occur more than

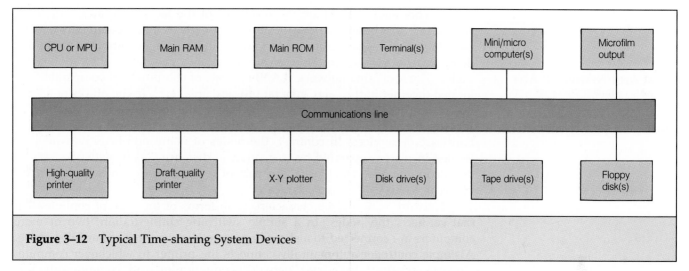

Figure 3–12 Typical Time-sharing System Devices

once and some may not appear at all in a particular time-sharing installation. There will typically be several terminals, but, beyond that, the precise hardware of time-sharing systems is of such diversity as to defy generalization. (Note that there may indeed be two CPUs to share the work or duplication of other components. These disparate devices are integrated into one system by computer programs that know what devices are there and how to make appropriate use of them.)

Such a complicated collection of devices works together through a careful signaling scheme, just as a simpler collection of devices does. Messages are constantly being sent up and down the communication line. Each message has a label that says to whom it is addressed and (perhaps) by whom it was sent. The contents of the message are examined only by the devices to which the message is sent. As more and more users access the system through terminals, the RAM of the system and the disk drives keep the data and programs of the various users separate. When a particular user gets a turn with the CPU; his or her storage is made available in RAM for fast access. When that user's turn is over, that storage may be copied onto a disk so that another user's storage may be brought into RAM for the next turn.

The previous diagram presaged one more level of complication: what if one of the devices connected to the computer communication line is actually another computer system? And what if this new computer has another computer attached to its communication line? And another and another and another? We now have **intercomputer communication** as well as the **intracomputer communication** we have already discussed. This intercomputer communication can be very complex indeed! There are two major types of concern here: networks and distributed processing.

■ Networks

Computer communications networks allow computers to communicate with each other and to share resources such as storage devices, printers, and mainframe computer power. The entities in a network are called nodes. A node can be a computer, a printer, a disk, or another network. Networks are described and classified in several ways.

One way of describing networks is terms of their nodes. Two types are very common. A centralized network connects a large computer to many

intracomputer communication
Internal communication among the ISPCO hardware devices that comprise a single computer via the internal communication bus on the motherboard.

intercomputer communication
Communication between separate computers via an external communication bus.

computer communications network
The linking of two or more computers so that files or messages can be shared among them; a computer network.

Local Area Network (LAN)
A private communications network connecting several computers by cable within a limited area such as a building or a group of buildings.

smaller computers that share the resources of the large computer, e.g., large centralized data bases. A noncentralized network connects computers of comparable size that share common resources and messages. Another method of describing networks is in terms of the physical or geographical location of the nodes. The **local area network (LAN)** consists of computers of comparable size located together in the same general physical area, e.g., in the offices of a small business or academic department. The size of the local area is determined by how far the nodes can be separated without using expensive communication hardware or services. In contrast, the nodes of many non-LAN networks are located in places separated by vast physical distances, as in networks serving large corporations. Obviously, the cost of a network depends partly on the physical distances among its nodes.

Networks can also be characterized in terms of the type of configuration that connects the nodes. In a simple switching configuration, two or more computers are connected to a shared resource like a printer or hard disk drive. A simple controller automatically connects the printer to whichever computer requests printing. In a star network configuration, all communication is through a central node computer, which is at least partially devoted to communication handling. The problem with this configuration is that if the central computer fails, the network is disconnected. The ring network configuration partly solves this problem. Each computer is essentially connected separately to a ring or circle that continuously moves messages around the circle. To send a message, a computer simply addresses it and drops it onto the ring. The failure of one computer on the ring does not disconnect the network. In a distributed network configuration, there are multiple alternative routes for linking nodes so that many computer nodes must fail before the network becomes disconnected. The major concern in distributed networking is often the cost of the hardware involved. The various forms of network connections are shown in Figure 3–13.

Once the network has been established, what happens next? In the simplest case, you might imagine that each computer in the network is a person and that the connections are telephone lines. Each person (computer) goes about his or her ordinary business but occasionally asks for some information from another person (computer). An example of a simple network might be the growing network of automatic bank teller machines: when you ask the machine for some money, it will first send a message to your bank's computer asking for your account status: if it's okay, you get the money, otherwise, forget it. Note that the automatic teller machine essentially does all of the work involved, it just needs some information from another source.

▪ Distributed Processing

distributed processing
A network mechanism in which the tasks making up a particular activity are divided among a set of separate computers.

The more complicated use of networks enters the realm of **distributed processing,** for which the analogy is less like people with telephone lines and more like a business manager with an intercom to the employees of the company. As the business manager works, information is needed from employees, to be sure, but more importantly, the manager can ask a particular employee to perform a particular set of tasks and report back when finished.

In distributed processing, one computer can ask another computer to perform a task for it. There can be many reasons for distributing various tasks across different computers. The most obvious reason is that two computers working simultaneously on a task can complete it faster than just one com-

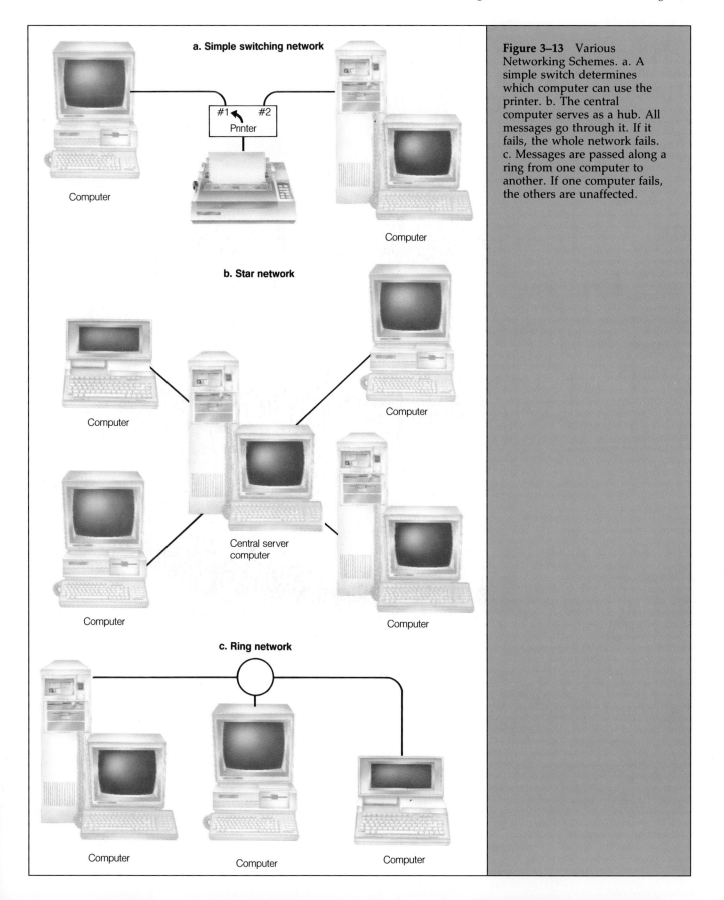

Figure 3–13 Various Networking Schemes. a. A simple switch determines which computer can use the printer. b. The central computer serves as a hub. All messages go through it. If it fails, the whole network fails. c. Messages are passed along a ring from one computer to another. If one computer fails, the others are unaffected.

Figure 3–14   Local Area Network and Distributed Processing Systems

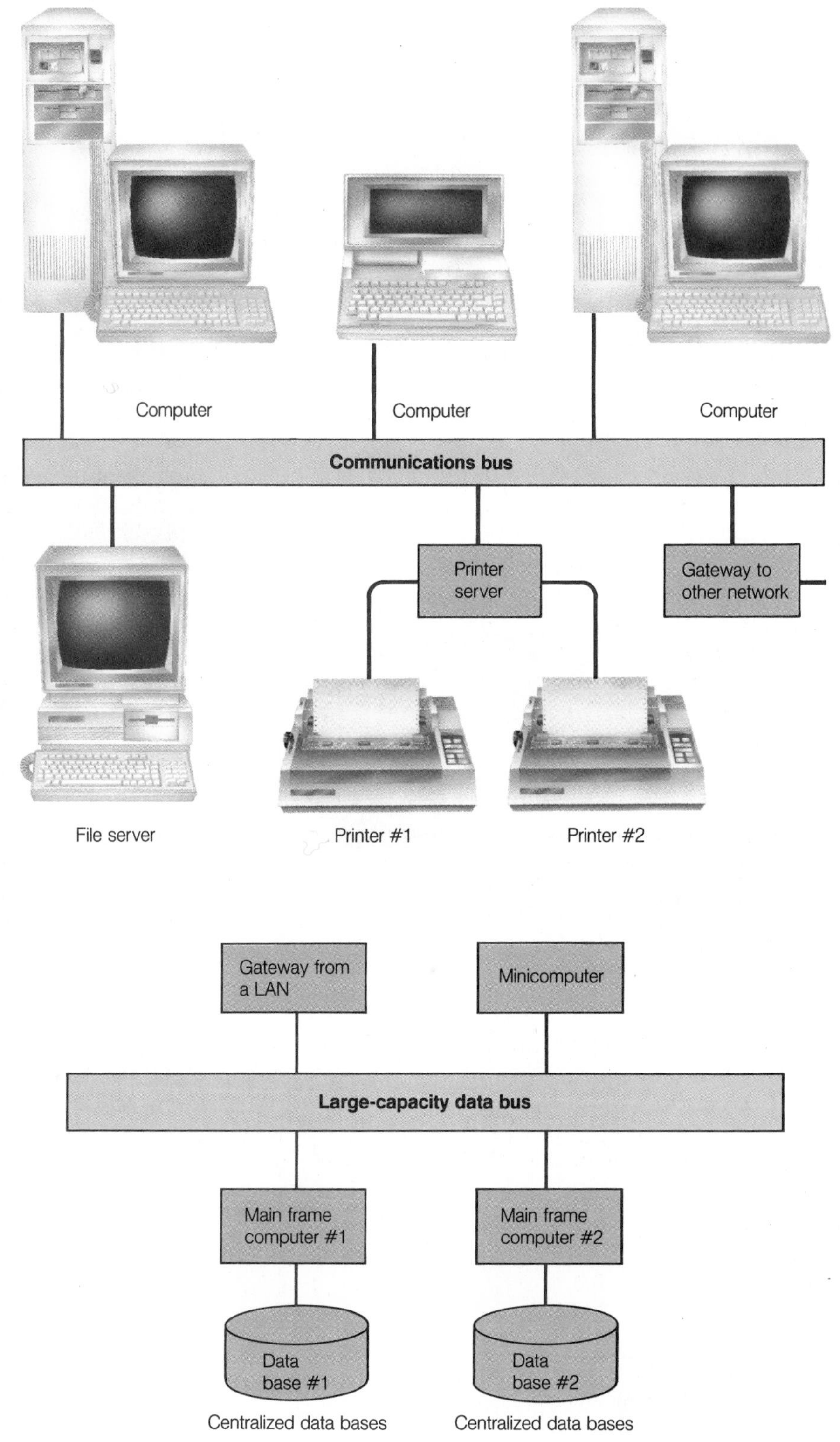

Computer

Computer

Computer

Communications bus

File server

Printer server

Printer #1

Printer #2

Gateway to other network

Gateway from a LAN

Minicomputer

Large-capacity data bus

Main frame computer #1

Main frame computer #2

Data base #1

Data base #2

Centralized data bases

Centralized data bases

puter. Secondly, some computers have been specially designed to be efficient for a particular kind of task; in the same way that an ordinary citizen might employ a lawyer for legal problems, so might an ordinary computer employ the expertise of a particular computer designed with a specific ability. Another reason for distributing the computing might be to centralize a certain type of activity in one location. For example, all confidential data could be kept on one computer; then that computer would handle all requests for that data, search the data, sort it, merge it, and so on. Figure 3–14 summarizes the major concepts behind LAN and distributed processing networks.

Other Intercomputer Connections.   In what other ways can computer hardware be connected and used? The possibilities are at least as many and as varied as the connections and relations that exist in human organizations. Think of an organization with a particular goal: a hospital, the post office, the Boy Scouts, the local bank, a school, an airline, or whatever. Across these organizations are almost uncountable variations in how tasks are allocated among people, how information flows among people, how decisions are made, and so forth. Any one of these variations could serve as a model for a computer hardware configuration. The tasks for individual computers can be terribly repetitive and menial (as are some human occupations) or extremely complex and cerebral (like other human occupations). Indeed, the computer should be viewed as a partner in the human problem-solving process. Not every task should be computerized. The computer should be viewed as another possible contributor to the eventual solution of a problem. Hence computer hardware should function as a network of assistants inside the existing human network.

Changes in computer hardware are constant and rapid. A humorous maxim in the field is that: *hardware is either experimental or obsolete, there is no middle ground!* When a computer product using a given hardware technology is ready to be sold, it has already been made obsolete by new research developments.

3.7

Hardware Summary

■ The ISPCO Frame

The hardware descriptions in this chapter are summarized in the frame for hardware use. Remember that the main purpose of an ISPCO frame is to organize the material in the chapter for easier understanding and retention.

Several things should be noted when reviewing this frame. First, the ISPCO organization provides an effective perspective on the hardware of a single computer. However, it does not consider the larger picture, that is, hardware as part of a total computer system or the connections among a number of computer systems, where the exact function of particular hardware items depends on the available software or the communication links among the computers.

Second, although the concepts of processing and control are distinct and separate, in current computing systems the processing and control hardware are generally combined into one physical device, the central processing unit or the microprocessor.

Third, the frame makes no mention of the distinctions among microcomputers, minicomputers, and mainframe computers. This is the third important idea: the much of the conceptual nature of hardware does not change significantly with the size of the system.

Finally, it can be seen that the ISPCO frame can be used to compare computer hardware systems. Since the frame summarizes the critical aspects of computer hardware, computer hardware can be evaluated by examining each of the points addressed in the frame.

Frame for Computer Hardware

	Concept	Your System
ON/OFF	AVAILABLE SOFTWARE: Hardware requires software. The names of specific software systems supported by this hardware and desired by its users are:	Software:
ON/OFF	BRAND NAME: The warranty and reputation of the computer manufacturer are major factors in hardware selection. For this hardware system, they are:	Manufacturer: Warranty: Reputation:
ON/OFF	GENERALIZED COST: The cost of hardware is measured by its dollar cost, its compatibility with other equipment, and its ability to be upgraded. For this hardware:	Dollar cost: Compatibility: Upgradability:
ON/OFF	EXPANSION SLOTS: Computer hardware adapts to the needs of a user by adding circuit cards into slots on the main circuit board. The slots in this system are:	Number of slots: Types of slots:
ON/OFF	ON/OFF: Start-up and shutdown of computer hardware require knowledge of power switches and disk handling. For this hardware, one must:	Start-up: Shutdown:
INPUT	INPUT VIA KEYBOARD: Keyboards differ on the: layout of keys, numeric input pads, cursor keys, function keys, and human engineering. This keyboard has:	Key layout: Numeric pad: Cursor and function keys: Human engineering:
INPUT	INPUT VIA MOUSE: The major characteristics of a mouse are its method of operation and the number of buttons it has. The mouse on this system has:	Method of operation: Number of buttons:

STORAGE	RAM STORAGE: Computers differ in their amount of RAM. Some systems have different types of RAM. The types and amounts of RAM on this system are:	Types of RAM: Amounts of each type of RAM:
STORAGE	RAM CARD STORAGE: RAM expansion cards plug into the slots of the main circuit board to add more memory. Amount and type are again relevant. For this system:	Types of expansion card RAM: Amounts of each type of RAM:
STORAGE	ROM STORAGE: ROM holds built-in programs. The larger the ROM, the more similar all software for the system will be. The size and contents of this ROM are:	Amount of ROM: Contents of ROM:
STORAGE	FLOPPY DISK STORAGE: Computers differ in the number, capacity (in megabytes), and types (3.5", 5.25", single- or double-sided) of disk drives. For this system:	Number of drives: Capacity of each drive: Type of each drive:
STORAGE	HARD DISK STORGE: Computers differ in the number, capacity, and speed of hard disk drives as well. For this hardware system:	Number of drives: Capacity of each drive: Speed of each drive:
PROCESSOR	PROCESSOR CHIPS: The processor determines power and speed. Upgradability improves if it belongs to a processor family. For this hardware system:	Processor: Power relative to others: Speed: Other family members:
PROCESSOR	MATH COPROCESSOR CHIPS: Special math processing chips speed math-intensive operations greatly. Other coprocessors are often available. For this hardware system:	Math coprocessor: Other available coprocessors:
OUTPUT	VIDEO SCREEN: Screens differ in color capability, resolution, graphic/text ability, and human engineering features. The screen on this system has:	Color/monochrome capability: Resolution in each mode: Graphic/text capabilities: Human engineering:
OUTPUT	VIDEO CONTROLLER: The circuit card that drives the screen also determines resolution, graphic/text ability, color ability, and so forth. This system's control has:	Color/monochrome capability: Resolution in each mode: Graphic/text capabilities:

OUTPUT	PRINTER: Printers vary in speed, quality, color and graphic ability, acceptable paper, underlying technology, and type of connections. The printer on this system has:	Speed and quality: Color and graphic abilities: Paper mechanisms: Underlying technology: Parallel/serial connections:
OUTPUT	PRINTER CONTROLLER: Printer controllers differ in speed, color and graphic ability, serial or parallel connections, buffers, and other abilities. This controller has:	Speed: Color and graphic abilities: Serial or parallel connections: Buffers and other abilities:
MODEM	MODEM: Modems are internal or external and differ in transmission speed. Most have ROM software. Status lights are useful. For this system:	Internal or external: Speeds available: ROM software capabilities: Status lights:
MODEM	MODEM CONTROLLER: External modems need serial control cards to control the characteristics and speed of the serial port. On this system:	Speeds allowed: Other port characteristics:

■ The ISPCO Scripts

The three major hardware activities faced by most users are the acquisition, installation, and maintenance of hardware. When the major concepts of computer hardware are well understood, each of these activities should be straightforward.

The steps involved in acquiring hardware center on the software that must run on the hardware, the compatibility of the hardware with other existing hardware devices (if any), and the functions available on the hardware. The major steps in hardware acquisition are summarized in the hardware acquisition script.

SCRIPT FOR HARDWARE ACQUISITION: THE NASH PRINCIPLE

1. *NEEDS ANALYSIS (N).* Study the types of applications in the textbook. Talk to computer users or join a computer club. Try out software in classes or stores. Study your personal activities and identify tasks that might be aided by the computer.

2. *APPLICATION SELECTION (A).* Select the application to be aided by computer (e.g., writing, computing budgets, drawing figures, performing statistical analyses). Then, prioritize each application and collect work samples (e.g., papers, budgets, figures). Finally, write descriptions of the software needed in terms of the work samples.

3. *SOFTWARE SELECTION (S).* Identify several software systems that meet the needs. Verify their ability with the work samples. Study reviews of software in computing magazines. Complete the frames in this text for each competing software system. Write out a list of acceptable software systems.

4 *HARDWARE SELECTION (H).*   Identify computer hardware that will run the needed software. Complete the frame for computer hardware for each competing computer system. Price the smallest and largest system you would consider. Consider computer stores versus mail order firms. Select the hardware based on what you consider to be the most important criteria: local service, brand name, hardware and software compatibility, upgradability, price, quality, ease of learning, system power, and so forth.

The installation of computer hardware can often be quite frustrating since installing hardware (i.e., connecting it to the rest of the system) is a task that is generally performed only once, so that little effort is made by manufacturers to make the installation process simple. The major steps involved in the installation of computer hardware are listed in the hardware installation script.

Finally, hardware maintenance is much the same as maintenance of any tool. Warranties cover the hardware initially. Beyond this, service contracts can be purchased to guarantee that a predetermined repair facility will repair any problem. Service contracts are essentially insurance policies. If a service contract is not purchased and something goes wrong, the user can either pay to have the device repaired or buy a new one. Because of the rapid improvement in computer technology, buying new equipment is sometimes more advisable. These concepts are described in the hardware installation and maintenance script.

SCRIPT FOR HARDWARE INSTALLATION AND MAINTENANCE

1 *FOLLOW DIRECTIONS CAREFULLY.*   Do NOT overestimate your ability. If installing new hardware is beyond you, pay for help from a local store. You can destroy computer equipment with something as simple as a static spark. If you do the work yourself, read all the directions first. Verify that all parts are present and the environment is adequate. Go through the instructions slowly.

2 *MAKE CONNECTIONS, SET DIP SWITCHES.*   Many types of connections must be made from new hardware to old hardware. Expansion cards must be pushed into slots on main circuit boards. Printers are connected to computers by parallel cables, while modems use serial cables—but they look the same. Modems are connected by attaching a phone wire to a modular telephone plug in the wall. Advanced users may actually push chips into or remove chips from sockets on boards. Once all the connections are made, check the setting of any switches on the new hardware and the old hardware—improper settings can impair function.

3 *INSTALL DEVICE DRIVERS AND TEST HARDWARE.*   Once the new hardware is set up, the software environment must often be changed to allow the new hardware to work. This is usually done via software called a device driver that knows how the new hardware works and interfaces it properly with existing software. Once installed, the hardware should be tested as widely as possible.

4 *BACK UP EVERYTHING.*   For any software you have, make backup copies on other disks. No matter how careful one is, disks can always go bad. Do not lose your ability to access hardware by carelessly losing your software.

USE DOCUMENTATION AND WARRANTY. Never misuse hardware because of lack of information. Never lose a warranty on a product by failing to follow warranty procedures.

 PROVIDE MAINTENANCE AND A GOOD ENVIRONMENT. Computer hardware requires maintenance and a quality environment. Maintenance can be prepaid through service contracts (about 10% of the purchase price, much less for nonmechanical or infrequently used hardware). The hardware's environment includes the quality of electrical power (a line conditioner is good) and the physical environment, which should be dry, cool, and dust-free.

Chapter 3 Review

Expanded Objectives

The objectives listed below are an expansion of the essential chapter concepts listed at the beginning of the chapter. The review items that follow are based on these expanded objectives. If you master the objectives, you will do better on the review items and on your instructor's examination on the chapter material.

After reading the chapter, you should be able to:

1. define and relate bits, bytes, and words.
2. explain how text, whole numbers, fractional numbers, and instructions can be represented by bit patterns.
3. explain how data flows among the ISPCO devices through the communication line.
4. describe the basic characteristics and major processes of computer storage.
5. describe the basic characteristics and major processes of computer input and output.
6. describe the four major types of processing built into computers, the main registers by which the processing is performed, and the default control strategy.
7. describe the methods by which control and processing registers, along with stored programs, are able to manage data processing.
8. recognize the variety of possible configurations of ISPCO devices within and across computers.
9. describe the characteristics and advantages of time-sharing, networking, and distributed processing.
10. recall or recognize the meanings of the major terms presented in this chapter.

Review Items

Completing this review will give you a good indication of how well you have mastered the contents of this chapter and prepare you for your instructor's test on this material. To maximize what you learn from this exercise, you should answer each question *before* looking up the answers in the appendix. The number of the corresponding expanded objective is given in parentheses following each question.

Complete the following clusters of items according to the directions heading each set.

A. *True or false.*

____ 1. One of the six major physical devices that make up a computer does not have a counterpart in the ISPCO abbreviation. (3)

____ 2. A byte is a set of consecutive bits. (1,10)

____ 3. Several words make up a byte. (1,10)

____ 4. The smallest unit of digital information is a bit. (1,10)

____ 5. Bit patterns can be used to represent whole numbers. (2,10)

____ 6. Within a word of storage, there are 256 possible bit patterns. (2)

____ 7. The computer has a larger alphabet of symbols than does the English alphabet. (2)

____ 8. On most computers, a string or pattern of eight bits is used to represent a single text character like *R*. (2)

____ 9. The string 011010 in the binary number system is equivalent to 26 in the base 10 system. (2)

____ 10. Most computers use more than one byte to represent integer numbers. (2)

____ 11. RAM contains programs that have been provided by the manufacturer and cannot be readily changed. (4,10)

____ 12. The computer's whole number representation scheme identifies a number as positive or negative depending on whether the leftmost bit is a 1 or a 0. (2)

____ 13. Data in ROM is lost when the computer is shut down. (4)

____ 14. A user's program resides in RAM when in use. (4, 10)

____ 15. Computer memory is made up of numbered slots called MPUs, which contain data. (4)

____ 16. Retrieval from magnetic tape storage is usually

faster than retrieval from magnetic disk storage. (4)

___ 17. Magnetic disks are categorized as a sequential storage medium. (4)

___ 18. Generally, RAM and ROM can hold more data than can magnetic storage tapes. (4)

___ 19. The control key on a computer keyboard is used in combination with other keys to provide access to more bit patterns than would otherwise be possible. (5)

___ 20. Although a computer keyboard typically has 60–110 keys, it is able to access more than twice as many characters. (5)

___ 21. Because of the need for interchangeable programs, keyboards, regardless of the manufacturer, are standardized. (5)

___ 22. Video monitors cannot give as fine a detail as can the screens on television sets. (5)

___ 23. A television set screen can hold more information than can a video monitor screen. (5)

___ 24. Electronic digital computers could use a base 10 number system just as easily as base 2. (2)

___ 25. Cost-benefit concerns are a major reason for the variety of ISPCO configurations among computers. (8)

___ 26. Thanks to ASCII standards, software is now largely compatible across the computers of different manufacturers. (8)

___ 27. A common means of indicating the operations to be performed is to code the first bits of a bit pattern. (2)

___ 28. The design of input and output hardware is often the result of arbitrary decisions on the part of design engineers. (5)

___ 29. All of the registers in a CPU perform the same function. (7)

___ 30. Computer processes are carried out in storage. (4,7)

___ 31. Data traveling down a communication line is routed by devices called controllers that are attached to registers. (7)

___ 32. Time-sharing on a computer is mainly a special case of turn-taking where users share computer hardware. (9)

___ 33. Distributed processing is a type of computer networking. (9)

___ 34. When a computer key is pressed, it sends a bit pattern to the communication line, which delivers it to the CPU or to one or more peripheral devices. (3)

___ 35. Protocols are the agreed-on rules by which one computer is able to converse with another. (9)

___ 36. Magnetic tape and disk drives can also be viewed as input and output devices. 94)

___ 37. Some printers are capable of printing many pages of hard copy per second. (5)

___ 38. Printers using a tractor feed depend on friction to move the·paper being printed. (5)

___ 39. Incompatibility among video screens and printers reduces their effectiveness. (5)

___ 40. A computer terminal is an external storage location for other computers. (5,10)

___ 41. A modem is used to retrieve data from a computer's disk drive or tape storage. (9,10)

___ 42. Modems permit communication among computers that are separated by distance. (9,10)

___ 43. Control in a computer is primarily concerned with the order in which system processes are performed. (7)

___ 44. The CPU (or MPU) is primarily composed of a combination of registers. (7)

___ 45. Arithmetic and logical processes are actually carried out in the processing register. (7)

___ 46. There are at least four computer processes available to all computers, regardless of make. (6)

___ 47. Sequential control permits a computer to process a list of instructions in the order given. (7,10)

___ 48. Control that permits instructions to be repeated more than once is called procedural control. (7,10)

___ 49. The type of control that permits the computer to choose one sequence of instructions over another is called alternation control. (7.,10)

___ 50. Locations that store temporary results in the CPU are called modems. (7,9,10)

___ 51. An instruction counter register holds data to be manipulated by the computer. (6,10)

___ 52. The instruction decoder register interprets bit patterns. (6,10)

___ 53. The purpose of computer time-sharing is to permit more than one user to use the same physical computing devices at approximately the same time. (9)

___ 54. One reason for using distributed processing is to take advantage of the differing capabilities of computers. (9)

___ 55. The specific configurations of devices used in time-sharing, networking, and distributed processing systems, have been standardized across the various computer systems. (9)

___ 56. One computer may have several processing registers. (8)

___ 57. Large computers often have more than one of each of the ISPCO hardware components. (8)

___ 58. CPU registers have controllers that identify messages sent to a specific register. (3,7)

B. *Match the tasks on the right with the hardware items on the left (there is only one answer per item). (7)*

___ 59. instruction decoder

___ 60. instruction counter

___ 61. processing register

a. holds addresses of instructions

b. where arithmetic tasks are executed

c. permits distributed processing

d. where bit patterns are sent for interpretation as instructions

C. *Match the appropriate alternatives on the right with the items on the left (there is only one answer per item). (4,6,7)*

___ 62. central processing unit

___ 63. directory

___ 64. RAM

___ 65. ROM

___ 66. disk

___ 67. register

a. permanent memory
b. computer brain
c. for connecting computers
d. general purpose memory
e. external memory
f. a catalog of file names
g. devices within the CPU
h. enables repetition of instructions

D. *Classify each of the following devices as an input device, an output device, an input/output device, or a storage device by placing the appropriate letter in the space provided. (5)*

___ 68. plotter

___ 69. light pen

___ 70. computer terminal

___ 71. card reader

a. input device
b. output device
c. input/output device
d. storage device

___ 72. line printer

___ 73. floppy disk

Special Exercise: The Frame for Hardware Usage

The frame contains special places for the user to write down the characteristics of real computer systems. The reader is encouraged to fill in the frame for the particular system to which he or she has access so that the concepts of this chapter can be directly applied to the reader's own hardware and software. The frame can also be used to compare different systems by filling in a frame for each one and comparing the various systems on a point-by-point basis.

The system documentation available with the software or hardware system should be the primary source of information for completing this frame.

As a person becomes familiar with different systems, each of the boxes in the frame may require expansion into even more detailed descriptions. By then, however, the user will be sophisticated enough to make such expansion.

Common Computer Software Systems and Their Use

Essential Chapter Concepts

When you have finished this chapter, you should know:

- The seven major types of software and how they perform the ISPCO functions.

- The situations in which each type of software should be used.

- The general sequence of actions involved in using the different software systems.

Computer Software

| INPUT | STORAGE | PROCESS | CONTROL | OUTPUT |

Operating system: Controls a computer's hardware and software.

Word processor: Used for entering and editing text for papers, letters and books.

Spreadsheet: Used for making tables that calculate statistics automatically.

Database manager: Used to store and retrieve data and generate reports from the data.

Graphics system: Makes charts and graphs from data.

Communication system: Sends data from one computer to another.

Programming language: Used to express human tasks in terms that the computer understands.

The remaining chapters of this book concern the successful use of computer software. This chapter will link the hardware chapter and the following chapters on software by presenting a series of short case studies that demonstrate what can be done with commonly available software. This chapter will not instruct the reader in the details of operating any particular software system. Instead, the reader should note the concepts underlying each type of software and the typical steps involved in using the software.

As the various types of software systems are examined, several common characteristics will become apparent:

1. All computer software systems use computer hardware to perform the five basic functions (input, storage, processing, control, and output).
2. Software systems differ in the types of information structures they manipulate. The type of information structure also affects which ISPCO functions are available within the system.
3. The user controls which ISPCO functions the software system performs by giving instructions in a **command language** that the computer can understand. The language may be as simple as a set of responses to a menu. This language is determined by the software type, that is, different languages are better suited to the purposes of particular types of software.

command language
A language for controlling the ISPCO tasks performed by applications software such as word processing or spreadsheet systems. These languages are usually simpler and easier to use than computer programming languages. Often they are nothing more than a simple set of responses to alternatives presented on the screen.

For example, a word processor is a type of computer program that performs ISPCO functions for letters, papers, and other documents. Word processors accept commands to input documents, save documents, process documents, and output documents, all under user and program control. Similarly, spreadsheets are programs that accept commands to perform the ISPCO functions for tables of data, while data base managers are programs that accept commands to perform ISPCO functions for **records** of data.

Seven types of software are introduced in this chapter: operating systems, word processing systems, spreadsheet systems, data base management systems, graphics systems, communications systems, and programming language systems. As the vignettes introduce these software systems and their general use, the reader should *not* try to absorb the technical details of using each system. Instead, the case studies have three purposes:

1. to give the reader vicarious experience using applications software by letting him or her "look over the shoulder" of someone applying the software to a simple, real-world problem. This experience will help the reader build up the scripts necessary to use applications software.
2. to introduce readers to the kinds of problems that each type of software is suited for and the way in which the software works. This introduction will help the reader with limited computing background understand subsequent chapters.
3. to introduce the use of the ISPCO model and scripts for applications software in a nonthreatening, high-interest context.

In this chapter, the reader should begin to see the similarities among the various applications software systems and to understand how the ISPCO model introduced in chapter 1 can be applied to software use.

record
In general, a collection of related data elements treated as a unit. In data base management systems, a collection of related fields.

4.1

Using Operating System Software

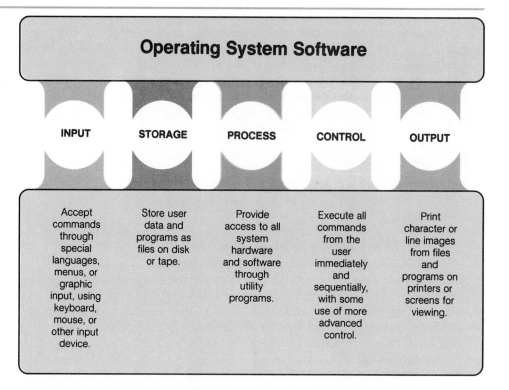

Operating System Software

INPUT	STORAGE	PROCESS	CONTROL	OUTPUT
Accept commands through special languages, menus, or graphic input, using keyboard, mouse, or other input device.	Store user data and programs as files on disk or tape.	Provide access to all system hardware and software through utility programs.	Execute all commands from the user immediately and sequentially, with some use of more advanced control.	Print character or line images from files and programs on printers or screens for viewing.

In the early years of computing, all computer systems had human operators other than the users. The computer operators took care of all the physical ministrations to the machines: they powered up the systems and later shut them down; they scheduled each user's turn with the computer hardware; and when a user needed a program or data from magnetic tape storage, computer operators would locate the appropriate reel of tape and mount it on a tape drive.

When mainframe computers began to serve multiple users and as the speed and power of mainframes increased, a new kind of program was created to perform most of the human operator's functions. These programs were called operating systems for the obvious reason that they helped operate the computer. All computers, from the largest network of mainframe computers to the smallest personal computer, now have an operating system. The operating system is a set of programs that allows the user to interact with applications programs and peripheral devices. All operating systems perform the same functions. Let us watch as Sue works with a new operating system.

Case Study

Sue was a freshman at Pleasant Community College. As part of the new curriculum set up by the computer science department, all freshman had to take an introductory computer course. Sue didn't think she would have any problem at all, since her family had a TV video game that worked like a computer. By attaching the keyboard her father had bought and inserting the BASIC language cartridge (BASIC is an easy-to-learn, high-level computer programming language) into the game slot, she had experimented a little bit, creating simple programs in BASIC.

On the first day of class, the instructor told Sue and her fellow classmates that they would be using a VAX mainframe computer for their class work. In a year or two the college would buy a larger number of microcomputers for student use, but they were not available yet. Sue listened intently to the teacher and jotted down the procedure he gave for starting up and interacting with the computer: the time-sharing system was named UNIX, computer terminals were located in room 115, the location of the power switch was

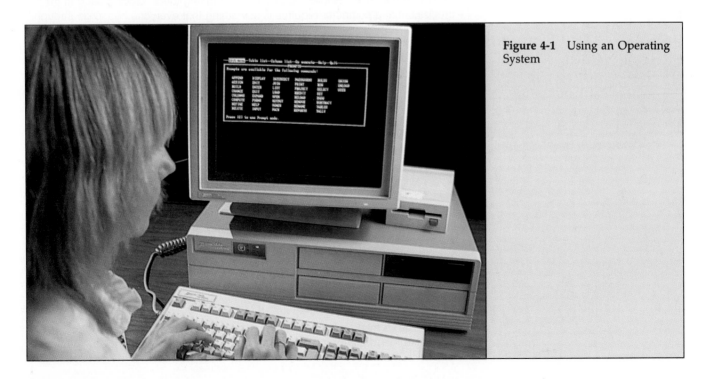

Figure 4-1 Using an Operating System

on the back. . . . . Sue's user ID (the code that would identify her to the computer) was her last name; her password (a confidential code needed to access the computer system) was her student number. The first assignment was to get onto the computer and store her name and address in the type of computer storage called a file (a named portion of disk storage). Sue knew it would be a piece of cake as she sauntered into 115.

Half an hour later, hair disheveled and with a look of despair, she trudged from the room and headed for her instructor's office. As she approached the office, she saw a line of students extending into the hallway. She was not the only one having problems! She took her place in line and leaned up against the wall to wait. As she waited, she listened in on the instructor's conversations with the students before her.

"Mr. Roberts, I hate to tell you this, but the computer is broken! It doesn't work like you said it would. I did just what you said. You said that for us to use the computer, we had to identify ourselves to the computer with those special codes you gave us. So I turned the terminal on and waited for the computer to type out 'Enter User ID:'. Then I typed in my name. It asked for my password code, and I typed in my student number. But it wouldn't let me in! I tried it a hundred different ways and it never worked!"

"Well, Bob," said Roberts, "why don't you sit down here at my office terminal and show me what you did? You see, what I told you was exactly correct. But after teaching computer classes for many years, I can guess what your problem is: you are not doing what you think you are doing! Computers are annoyingly precise and you have to be very careful."

"All right," Bob replied, "I'll show you. Turn the machine on. There . . . now the computer has printed the prompting message 'Enter User ID:'. Now I'll type in my name: M i c h a e l s carriage return. Now it asks for my password and I . . . ."

"Hold it. There is your mistake right there," said Roberts. "The computer expects you to type in your ID using lowercase letters only. You should have typed in a lowercase m.

"But that's stupid! Computers are supposed to be smart!"

"In principle, you're right. There is no excuse for a computer to be programmed like that. But unfortunately, what should be is not always what is. Don't worry about it." Roberts spoke in a comforting tone. "Getting used to the precision that a computer requires is something that everyone has to go through."

Sue sat there thinking, had she accidentally used uppercase letters when she tried to log in (identify herself to the computer)? She had tried so many combinations, she must have tried an all-lowercase ID. But had she really? It was so hard to remember! She continued to eavesdrop as the next student began.

"Mr. Roberts? I'm John Vandorn. I'm really in a hurry! I left my terminal turned on down in 115 because I got everything done and it won't let me out! I don't want to lose all of my work, so I was afraid to turn the power off. But right now anybody could sit down at my terminal and wreck something."

"Okay, let's be quick then. What part of the operating system are you running right now?" asked Roberts.

"Well, I logged onto the computer okay. It asked for my ID and password and accepted them, no problem. Then I got into the editor just like you told us so that I could store data on the computer: I typed in the command 'edit.' Then I gave it the 'append' command you described in class to add stuff. I entered my name and address and then typed in that special code that stops it, control-Z. Then I just wanted to get out of the editor, so I typed 'logout' and it just keeps coming back and saying 'undefined command'. I know that 'logout' is a good command. What's wrong?"

"You've made a very common mistake, John," replied Roberts. "You are losing track of which part of the computer software you are talking to. You see, there are many different programs that can be running while you use a computer. Each program defines its own set of legal commands. Unfortunately, there does not have to be any consistency among the different programs! On our system, 'logout' is the command that you give to the operating system to say you are done. When you are running the editor, it expects you to type in the command 'quit' when you are done. Run back to your terminal and type 'quit' to stop the editor and then 'logout' to get off the whole system."

"But, Mr. Roberts," complained John, "shouldn't the same idea have the same command? Wouldn't it make more sense to have all commands that mean 'stop the program' use the same word?"

"Well, John, that idea seems to make a lot of sense. But really, it is a harder question. It's kind of like building a car. Is there one right car that has all of the controls, all of the features, and everything else just right? If so, Detroit hasn't figured it out yet. It is often a matter of taste. Of course, a great deal of improvement is clearly needed on virtually all software systems. But computing is a new field, and it takes time to get everything right. For now, just remember that the same ideas can be handled by different commands on the computer depending on which software is running. Now hurry and log out before all of your computer time is used up or someone sits down at that empty terminal and destroys all of your work!"

Sue pulled out a piece of paper. (Ouch! That turkey John stepped on her foot as he ran back to the computer room. Oh, well.) The commands were something she needed to make note of. Working with the computer was a little more complicated than she thought. The last student before her entered the teacher's office.

"Hi, Mr. Roberts! My name is Sarah. I just had a couple of quick questions. I have all of the assignment done and I was just trying to figure out what else I could do on the system. Do you have any suggestions?"

"I'm glad to hear that at least one student could do the assignment!" exclaimed Roberts. "As for you doing anything else on the computer, Sarah, it depends on what you want to do. It is often hard to learn anything on a computer system without instruction. Computers are not like cars with just a few simple commands that everyone can almost figure out for themselves. They use many extremely complicated programs, each with its own set of commands, all interconnected or interacting in some manner. I don't want you to become exasperated trying to learn the computer by yourself."

"Well," said Sarah, "I didn't have anything special in mind. All I wanted to do was practice."

"Then, my best advice would be this," Roberts replied. "First, just practice with the commands you know. Since you know how to store data on the computer, do that a few more times with different kinds of data. You should never go too fast; learn one thing solidly before you learn another. Then, try a few of the operating system commands for making copies of your data. The data is stored in files, so try copying files, changing the names of the files or the data inside them. Try deleting a file. The first thing you always need to understand is how an operating system handles files of data. After that, our system has a good help facility (a quick guide to how a program or system should be used) built-in. Whenever you are logged in and need some help on how to use a command, you just type in the word 'help' followed by a space and the name of the command for which you need help. Then you'll get info on how to use it. Finally, try running a few of the software packages built into the system, like the ones for drawing pictures or playing chess. Those are always fun."

"Thanks, Mr. Roberts. That gives me some ideas on what to do next. See you in class."

Sue stood up. It was her turn, but instead of entering the office, she turned and headed back for the computer room. She was starting to understand the situation now.

Talking to computers did not have to make sense. It wasn't so much that computers couldn't understand anything, it was just that any particular system, like this VAX, might not be programmed in the most sensible way. Computers could *do*, but they couldn't *think*. Well, maybe if she sat down at the computer knowing that it would respond only to commands that it knew, in a very precise and limited language, she could be careful enough to get through this assignment. One thing was very clear: learning to use a computer was not something you could just learn from a textbook; you had to use one to know what they were about!

As Sue and her classmates were beginning to learn, the programs on a computer are largely arbitrary in nature. One of the most fundamental programs is the operating system. In this example, the operating system had two important functions: controlling who got access to the computer through an identification process requiring a user ID code and a password code, and storing data on the computer using an **editor**. The purpose of an operating system extends well beyond these tasks to the more general problem of controlling the use of all parts of the computer hardware and software. Operating systems on small, personal computers are often almost invisible because they start up an applications program immediately and have no login or logout function (since the microcomputer is a one-person machine). But whatever the size or type of computer, an operating system is always present to manage the use of computer resources.

editor
A program that helps users input and revise information in files (named parts of storage). Often part of another program such as an operating system or word processor.

4.2

Using Word Processing Software

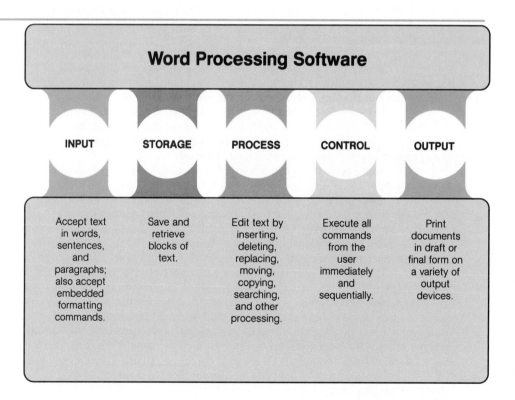

Word Processing Software

INPUT	STORAGE	PROCESS	CONTROL	OUTPUT
Accept text in words, sentences, and paragraphs; also accept embedded formatting commands.	Save and retrieve blocks of text.	Edit text by inserting, deleting, replacing, moving, copying, searching, and other processing.	Execute all commands from the user immediately and sequentially.	Print documents in draft or final form on a variety of output devices.

Word processors are computer programs that assist writers in generating, editing, storing, retrieving, and printing arbitrary text like letters, term papers, or books. They provide a wonderfully convenient way of creating documents of virtually any kind. Consider the case of Roberta, who has a term paper to write.

Roberta was a college student at Mega University. She had just returned from her history class with a new assignment, writing an essay about the new high-tech society. Since art was one of her loves, Roberta decided to write her paper on the interaction of new technology and the creative arts.

Roberta, being a very up-to-date student, had a personal computer in her room to use for her assignments (and for those all-night adventure games, of course). So she naturally planned to use a word processing system to prepare her essay assignment. Having a personal computer sure was nice. She didn't have to worry about waiting to share the terminals on the university's giant IBM mainframe or learning all of the nonsense about operating systems and commands. Oh, she knew that an operating system was somehow related to her word processor, but who cares? "Just me and my PC" was one of Roberta's favorite sayings.

Roberta took out the computer disk with the word processor on it, shoved it into the top disk drive, and turned the machine on. The disk drive whirred for a while, then the computer screen was suddenly filled with information from the word processing system.

```
The Best of All Possible Word Processors
Main Menu

Enter the letter corresponding to the command that you
wish to perform:

C(reate a new document from the keyboard)
R(etrieve an existing document from disk)
S(ave a document to disk)
P(rint a document)
Q(uit)

Choose one:_
```

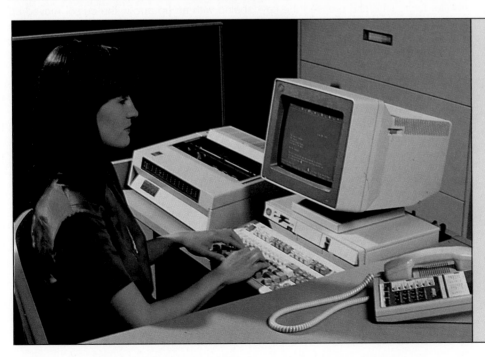

Figure 4-2 Using a Word Processor

Roberta was creating this paper from scratch, so she pushed the C key on the keyboard. The word processing system responded with an almost blank screen. One line at the very top of the screen told her that the word processor was ready to insert text (Insert) and also told her the page she was on (Pg1), the line on the page (Ln1), and the position on the line (Pos 0). Roberta knew that this line could contain other information as her word processing efforts continued.

```
Insert                              Pg 1 Ln 1  Pos 0
_
```

Roberta started typing her essay, and the characters appeared on the screen as she typed. Each new character was placed at the location of the cursor (the_line on the screen). As Roberta typed, letters appeared on the screen and the cursor moved to the right. When the cursor got to the end of a line, it jumped back to the left and down one line. Unless she wanted to leave a totally blank line on the screen, Roberta never needed to push the carriage return key, as she would on a conventional typewriter. The computer went from line to line automatically. After a few minutes, the screen looked like:

```
Insert                              Pg 1 Ln 9  Pos 43
Art and Technology: An Essay

by Roberta Dank

for History 110a

The relationship between art and technology is
characterized by a love-hate relationship.
Consider the medium of varnish-based paint:_
```

Roberta continued typing. As she typed, the cursor kept track of where she was. When she was finished with the first paragraph, she sat back and looked at it. She realized that the paragraph would sound better with a different word in the second sentence, so she used the arrow keys to move the position of the cursor to the spot she wanted to rewrite. Every time she pressed the key labeled with an up arrow, the cursor moved up a line. Similarly, the down arrow, left arrow, and right arrow keys moved the cursor in their respective directions. The movement of the cursor did not affect the text Roberta had written, it just changed the position in the paper at which any typing or deleting would be done. After the appropriate key presses, the cursor was in the second sentence before the word medium and the screen looked like:

```
Insert                              Pg 1 Ln 9  Pos 12
Art and Technology: An Essay

by Roberta Dank

for History 110a

The relationship between art and technology is
characterized by a love-hate relationship.
Consider the_medium of varnish-based paint:
          1. It provided a more permanent medium for
```

Roberta then pressed the special key marked *Del* several times. Each time she pressed the key, the character marked by the cursor was deleted from the screen and the characters to the right of the cursor were moved to the left to fill in the hole that remained. After a few more key presses, the word *medium* had been deleted and the screen looked like:

```
   Insert                    Pg 1 Ln 9  Pos 12
   Art and Technology: An Essay

   by Roberta Dank

   for History 110a

   The relationship between art and technology is
   characterized by a love-hate relationship.
   Consider the_of varnish-based paint:
        1. It provided a more permanent medium for
```

Roberta then typed in the new word she wanted and the change appeared on the screen:

```
   Insert                    Pg 1 Ln 9  Pos 23
   Art and Technology: An Essay

   by Roberta Dank

   for History 110a

   The relationship between art and technology is
   characterized by a love-hate relationship.
   Consider the acceptance_of varnish-based paint:
        1. It provided a more permanent medium for
```

Next, Roberta decided to center the title lines of her paper. To do this, Roberta hit another special key, the escape key (*esc*), to get access to the editing commands menu. Her paper disappeared from the screen and was replaced by a menu of command options:

```
   The Best of All Possible Word Processors
   Editing Commands Menu

   Enter the letter corresponding to the command that you
   wish to perform:

   D(elete block of text)        F(ind block of text)
   R(eplace block with another)  C(opy block of text)
   M(ove a block of text)        I(nsert text at cursor)
   P(rint command insertion)     S(pelling check)
   X(exit to Main Menu)

   Choose one:_
```

Centering was a print command, so Roberta pressed the letter P and another menu appeared on the screen:

```
   The Best of All Possible Word Processors
   Print Command Menu

   Enter the letter corresponding to the command that you
   wish to perform:
   C(enter text)              J(ustify both sides)
   L(eft justify text)        R(ight justify text)
   I(ndent text)              K(eep text together)
   X(exit back to Editing Commands Menu)

   Choose one:_
```

Roberta pressed the C for centering. Roberta's paper reappeared on the screen with a small window at the bottom of the screen. It asked Roberta to position the cursor at the beginning of the text to be centered and press the return key:

```
Position the cursor before the text to be centered.
Then press the return key.
```

Using the arrow keys, Roberta moved the flashing cursor to the position immediately before the title. She then pressed the return key, and another window appeared:

```
Position the cursor after the text to be centered.
Then press the return key.
```

Roberta moved the cursor to a position after her name and class number and pressed return. Immediately, all text between those two points was centered on the screen, which now looked like:

```
Insert                              Pg 1 Ln 9  Pos 23
                   Art and Technology: An Essay

                        by Roberta Dank

                        for History 110a
The relationship between art and technology is
characterized by a love-hate relationship.
Consider the acceptance_of varnish-based paint:
        1. It provided a more permanent medium for
```

Roberta continued to write new text and perform many editing options like movement, replacement, insertion, and deletion of text until she was satisfied with the final form of her paper. Then it was time to save and print the document. She called up the editing menu using the escape key and pressed X to return to the main system menu.

```
The Best of All Possible Word Processors
Main Menu

Enter the letter corresponding to the command that you
wish to perform:

C(reate a new document from the keyboard)
R(etrieve an existing document from disk)
S(ave a document to disk)
P(rint a document)
Q(uit)

Choose one:_
```

First, Roberta saved the document by pressing the S key. The word processor opened a window asking for the file name:

```
Enter the name of the file for the save:
-
```

Roberta typed in a name, and the screen looked like:

```
Enter the name of the file for the save:
History 110 paper 1_
```

The disk drive whirred as the document was saved onto the disk under the name "History 110 paper 1." When the main menu returned, Roberta then typed in the letter P to begin printing the document. A new menu appeared:

```
The Best of All Possible Word Processors
Hard copy Print Menu

Enter the letter corresponding to the command that you
wish to perform:
L(eft margin reset.     Current value =   1.0in)
R(ight margin reset.    Current value =   1.0in)
T(op margin reset.      Current value =   1.0in)
B(ottom margin reset.   Current value =   0.5in)
S(ize of page reset.    Current value =  11.0in)
N(umbering of pages.    Current value = on    )
P(rint document.)

Choose one:_
```

Since all of the current values for margins were adequate, Roberta chose P to print the paper. The paper printed out nicely and was ready to be turned in.

Our story could end here, but let's look at one last demonstration of the increased power of word processors.

Later in the term, Roberta was especially thankful for her word processing system. It was time for her to write another essay, this time for an art appreciation course she was taking. Roberta was really overloaded that week and couldn't figure out how she would get time to write the paper, when she suddenly remembered her old history paper.

Roberta started up her word processing system, but this time, instead of starting a new paper, she asked the computer to retrieve an existing document, the one entitled "History 110 paper 1."

Case Study

```
The Best of All Possible Word Processors
Main Menu

Enter the letter corresponding to the command that you
wish to perform:

C(reate a new document from the keyboard)
R(etrieve an existing document from disk)
S(ave a document to disk)
P(rint a document)
Q(uit)

Choose one:_
```

She pressed the letter R and then typed in the name of her earlier paper.

```
Enter the name of the file to retrieve:
History 110 paper 1_
```

Roberta started with this document and began revising. The title became "The History of Technology in Art." Soon Roberta was finished with the essay. It was essentially her original paper for her history class, but she had added several new insights gained from her class work since that time. She then saved this document under a new name, "Art 134 paper 1," and printed it out according to the format prescribed by her art teacher.

"You know," Roberta said to her roommate, "I'm almost starting to enjoy writing papers!"

The full complexities of a word processing system cannot be introduced in so short a story, but the basic flavor of the document creation task is represented by what Roberta did. The computer was a tool, and with the right kind of software, it provided Roberta with valuable assistance in the creation of her term papers. The use of word processing software made Roberta more productive: she was able to complete her papers in less time than usual, she made fewer errors, and the papers had better appearance.

Computer Insights
Backing Up Computer Storage

When using any type of applications software, the user will have data to store. Much user data is now stored on microcomputers, either on floppy or hard disks or in some type of battery-powered electronic circuit chips. The beginning user is all too quick to assume that once data is stored, it will be available whenever it is needed. It is important to realize that storing data in only one place on the computer is extremely hazardous to the user's mental health.

Although computer hardware and storage media improve rapidly, there is always the possibility of an error. If an error occurs, the amount of data lost can be as small as one character or as large as an entire hard disk with 40 megabytes (a megabyte is about a million characters) of data. Of course, there is a natural human tendency to feel that "it can't happen to me," but that feeling must be overcome when using the computer. Any new user should memorize the following storage procedure and apply it to all his or her data:

1. Save the data onto one floppy disk.
2. Remove that floppy disk from the drive and insert a second floppy disk.
3. Save the data onto the second floppy disk.
4. Store the two floppy disks in separate locations.

This simple procedure will guarantee that a user will always have a backup copy of his or her data in case something goes wrong with the first copy.

Another storage concern is backing up proprietary software. Proprietary software (copyrighted software written by someone else) can become unusable due to disk errors just as easily as can a user's own data. Backing up such software can be a problem, however, because proprietary software is often stored on disks that use sophisticated encoding techniques to prevent copying them. If the software is provided by a more enlightened manufacturer, the program disk will be copyable, so the user can keep a spare copy that will still be available if the original disk fails. It is then the user's moral and legal obligation not to distribute the software to other people who have not paid for it. If a disk that could not be copied goes bad, the user may have a problem. Although some copy-protected software comes with two copies in the original package, some manufacturers merely give the address for requesting replacements, and it can take a long time to request a new copy and receive it through the mail!

When considering long-term storage, beginning users should remember that floppy disks are inexpensive. Disks that can store 360K of data on a typical IBM compatible machine can be had for as little as $30 for one hundred. Most users therefore have no reason to throw away any finished data files. Of course, many intermediate versions of term papers or computer programs should not be kept, but any finished data should be placed on a floppy and archived in a closet somewhere. When that data is required someday, the cost of storing it will have been minimal and the joy at having it will be immense.

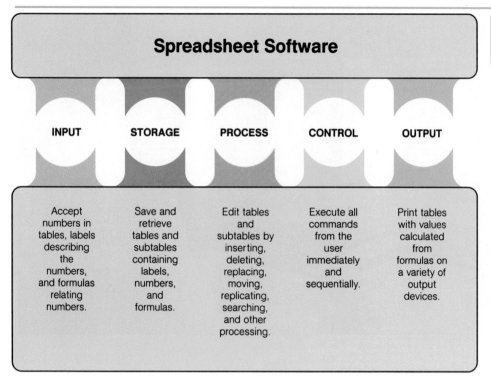

Spreadsheet Software

INPUT	STORAGE	PROCESS	CONTROL	OUTPUT
Accept numbers in tables, labels describing the numbers, and formulas relating numbers.	Save and retrieve tables and subtables containing labels, numbers, and formulas.	Edit tables and subtables by inserting, deleting, replacing, moving, replicating, searching, and other processing.	Execute all commands from the user immediately and sequentially.	Print tables with values calculated from formulas on a variety of output devices.

Using Spreadsheet Software

4.3

Electronic spreadsheet programs manipulate a different kind of data than do word processors. Instead of manipulating the words of a document, spreadsheets allow the input, storage, process, control, and output of tables of data. These tables can hold characters as a word processed document can, but the power of spreadsheets comes from their ability to store numbers and formulas based on these numbers. These formulas are especially useful for budgeting or other tasks requiring the manipulation of numeric data that may change. Spreadsheets enable the user to see the effects of making a change in one part of the data without having to go through the tedious manual readjustment of all the other data elements in the table. The readjustments occur automatically under the control of the spreadsheet software. The procedure for using such software is not necessarily complex, as we will see in the following example where Virgil has a budget problem.

Virgil was a graduate student in the psych department at Mega University. He needed to prepare a budget for a small research project. His budget was supposed to look like this:

Case Study

EXPENDITURE	1990	1991	TOTAL
Personnel	5000.	6000.	_____
Equipment	2000.	1000.	_____
TOTAL	_____	_____	_____

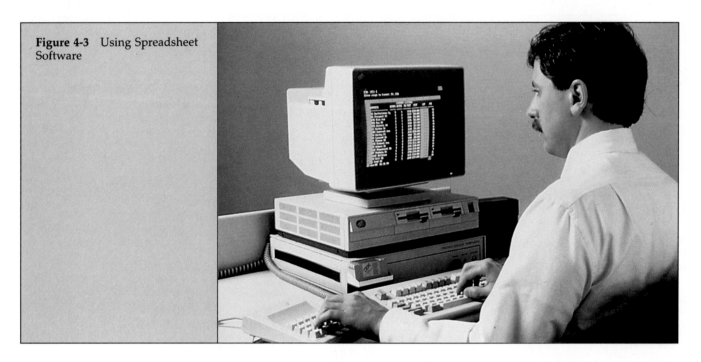

Figure 4-3 Using Spreadsheet Software

The problem was that the amounts in each category depended on the available funds at the university. Any of the amounts could change at any time.

Fortunately, Virgil had some experience using a spreadsheet program and turned there quite naturally any time tabular data was needed. Virgil arranged to use one of the departmental microcomputers, started it up, and issued the appropriate commands to the operating system to start up the spreadsheet program stored on the hard disk. The hard disk purred in the background until the spreadsheet system took over and displayed its initial screen.

```
The Best of All Possible Spreadsheets
Main Menu

Enter the letter corresponding to the command that you
wish to perform:

C(reate a new spreadsheet at the keyboard)
R(etrieve an existing spreadsheet from disk)
S(ave a spreadsheet to disk)
P(rint a spreadsheet)
X(exit to the operating system)

Choose one:_
```

Virgil had to create a brand new spreadsheet for the budget, so he pressed the C key. The system responded with a screen completely filled with little boxes, except for a couple of lines at the very top of the screen that contained information on the status of the spreadsheet. One box, A1, was in reverse video (blue on white instead of white on blue). The screen looked like this:

```
Cursor at: A1    Contents:_
              A                    B                    C
001   ┌──────────────────┐
002   └──────────────────┘
003
004
005
```

Virgil knew that using a spreadsheet was pretty simple. All he had to do was put numbers in each of the boxes of the spreadsheet to correspond to those of his written table. Then special formulas could be used to add up the contents of these boxes and give results.

The first thing that Virgil had to do was enter the titles for the table. As with most spreadsheet programs, the one Virgil used started up with box A1 as the "current box." The "current box" was shown in reverse video on the screen and was listed in the status line (the information line) at the top of the screen. New values could be entered only in the current box. Since box A1 was as good a box as any to start with the titles, Virgil just started typing the word EXPENDITURE to place that title in box A1. The results were:

```
Cursor at: A1    Contents: EXPENDITURE_
              A                    B                    C
001 ┌ EXPENDITURE_ ┐
002 └──────────────┘
003
004
```

When he hit the return key, the title was successfully entered. The current box was still box A1 as the status line indicated. To enter the next title, Virgil had to change the current box to B1 and enter a new value. As is typical for spreadsheet systems, the four arrow keys (left, right, up, and down) were used to select which box would be the current box in the table, so Virgil hit the right arrow key once. The resulting screen, with box B1 in reverse video, was:

```
Cursor at: B1    Contents:_
              A                    B                    C
001   EXPENDITURE    ┌──────────────────┐
002                  └──────────────────┘
003
004
005
```

The only differences were in the status line at the top of the screen and the reverse video portion of the screen. Virgil now typed in the year, 1990. He hit the right arrow again (making cell C1 display in reverse video) and then typed 1991.

```
Cursor at: C1    Contents: 1991_
              A                    B                    C
001   EXPENDITURE              1990    ┌──────────1991──┐
002                                    └────────────────┘
003
004
005
```

Virgil continued to enter the other data in his table by changing the current box with the four arrow keys and then typing in the data just as on a typewriter. The final result of the initial data entry was:

```
Cursor at: A5    Contents: TOTAL_

         A                 B                 C
001  EXPENDITURE          1990              1991
002
003  Personnel          $5000.00          $6000.00
004  Equipment          $2000.00          $1000.00
005 | TOTAL                                        |
```

His current cell was A5, which was displayed in reverse video. When Virgil had gotten this far, he realized that he could not fit the fourth column, which would hold the totals over the years, on the screen. To fix this, he decided to make the columns narrower. He remembered that the key marked with the symbol / had to be pressed to access spreadsheet commands, so he pressed it, and the screen changed to an editing menu.

```
The Best of All Possible Spreadsheets
Editing Command Menu

Enter the letter corresponding to the command that you
wish to perform:
C(olumn size)                      I(nsertion)
F(ormat of table entries)          D(eletion)
W(indow creation)                  K(opying)
X(exit to Main Menu)

Choose one:_
```

Virgil pressed the letter C to change the column width. A small window appeared at the bottom of the screen:

```
Enter the column to change or all:_
```

Virgil entered the word "all" and hit return. Another window then popped onto the screen:

```
Enter the width for these columns:_
```

Virgil entered the number 12 and hit the return key. The full screen reappeared as:

```
Cursor at: A5    Contents: TOTAL_

         A                 B                 C                 D
001  EXPENDITURE          1990              1991
002
003  Personnel          $5000.00          $6000.00
004  Equipment          $2000.00          $1000.00
005 | TOTAL                                        |
```

With column D on the screen, he entered the needed title into D1 by using the arrow keys to make D1 the current box and then typing in the name. Now the only thing that Virgil had to do was to compute all the totals based on the values in the table.

He changed the current box to box B5 by pressing the arrow keys appropriately. Then he typed +B3+B4 and pressed the return key. Although he typed +B3+B4, the image that appeared in box B5 was different from what was shown on the status line at the top of the page. The status line showed the formula that Virgil had typed in, while box B5 showed a value of $7000.00. Since the characters he had typed did not begin with a number or a letter, the spreadsheet software read the line as a formula. The formula said to take the value of the box B3 and add it to the value of the box B4. The answer was shown in B5 because that was the current box when the formula was entered. Now the screen looked like:

```
Cursor at: B5    Contents:+B3+B4_

          A                B               C              D
001 EXPENDITURE        1990            1991            TOTAL
002
003 Personnel       $5000.00        $6000.00
004 Equipment       $2000.00        $1000.00
005 TOTAL          [ $7000.00 ]
```

Virgil then continued the process by placing +C3+C4 in box C5, +B3+C3 in D3, and +B4+C4 in D4. Finally, he computed the grand total by placing +B5+C5 in D5 (alternatively, he could have typed +D3+D4 or +B3+B4+C3+C4 or some other ordering of these formulas). At this point, the screen looked like:

```
Cursor at: D5    Contents:+B5+C5_

          A                B               C              D
001 EXPENDITURE        1990            1991            TOTAL
002
003 Personnel       $5000.00        $6000.00      $11000.00
004 Equipment       $2000.00        $1000.00       $3000.00
005 TOTAL           $7000.00        $7000.00     [ $14000.00 ]
```

With the spreadsheet complete, Virgil then hit the / key to get the editing command menu and then pressed X to return to the main menu:

```
The Best of All Possible Spreadsheets
Main Menu

Enter the letter corresponding to the command that you
wish to perform:

C(reate a new spreadsheet at the keyboard)
R(etrieve an existing spreadsheet from disk)
S(ave a spreadsheet to disk)
P(rint a spreadsheet)
X(exit to the operating system)

Choose one:_
```

He pressed an S to save the spreadsheet and responded with the name of a file when a window came up on the screen asking for a file name:

```
Enter the name of the file to save into:
spreadsheet number 1_
```

Virgil proceeded to print out the spreadsheet using the print option on the main menu. Sometime later, additional funds were provided to the department from federal grants, so if Virgil turned in a revised budget rapidly, he could have $3000 for equipment in the 1991 budget instead of only $1000. Virgil grabbed the micro, started up the spreadsheet system, and entered an R when given the main menu. The system responded with a request for the file to be used:

```
Enter the name of the file to retrieve:
spreadsheet number 1_
```

The system went to disk and brought back his spreadsheet data.

```
Cursor at: D5    Contents:+B5+C5

       A               B              C              D
001 EXPENDITURE       1990           1991           TOTAL
002
003 Personnel      $5000.00       $6000.00       $11000.00
004 Equipment      $2000.00       $1000.00        $3000.00
005 TOTAL          $7000.00       $7000.00       $14000.00
```

Virgil changed the current box to C4 by pushing the appropriate arrow keys. He then entered a new value into the box by just typing in the new number, $3000. When he hit the return key, not only was that box changed, but all the other boxes that depended on that value were changed as well: the changes "rippled" through the spreadsheet automatically. The resulting table was:

```
cursor at: C4    Contents:3000

       A               B              C              D
001 EXPENDITURE       1990           1991           TOTAL
002
003 Personnel      $5000.00       $6000.00       $11000.00
004 Equipment      $2000.00       $3000.00        $5000.00
005 TOTAL          $7000.00       $9000.00       $16000.00
```

Virgil then saved the new budget, printed out a copy, and rushed it to the department chairperson. The chair assured Virgil that he would get the additional funds, since he was the first student in with a new budget. Virgil smiled as he passed by the other graduate students who were recalculating and retyping their budgets by hand.

It is true that even experienced computer users might not choose to use a spreadsheet for the simple task just described. However, the true nature of a spreadsheet should be clear. A spreadsheet maintains a table of data. At each spot in the table, the user may place words, numbers, or formulas. It is the formulas that make the spreadsheet truly useful, because any dependencies that exist in the table (e.g., D5 holds the sum of B5 and C5) are automatically maintained as data in the spreadsheet is changed.

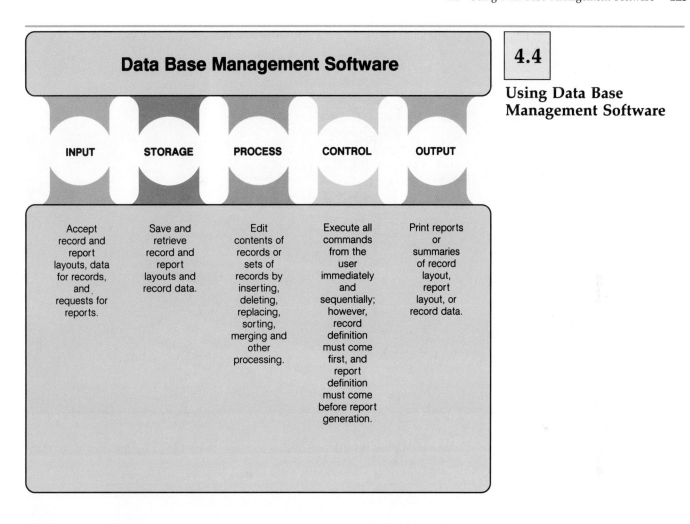

Data Base Management Software

INPUT	STORAGE	PROCESS	CONTROL	OUTPUT
Accept record and report layouts, data for records, and requests for reports.	Save and retrieve record and report layouts and record data.	Edit contents of records or sets of records by inserting, deleting, replacing, sorting, merging and other processing.	Execute all commands from the user immediately and sequentially; however, record definition must come first, and report definition must come before report generation.	Print reports or summaries of record layout, report layout, or record data.

Data base management systems are in many ways very similar to spreadsheets. They can hold labels, numbers, and self-calculating formulas. They extend these capabilities further, however, by providing arbitrary relationships among data that could not be presented in tabular form and by providing substantially better facilities for generating reports.

Case Study

James was a math student at good old MU. To help pay his expenses, he worked for the MU Alumni office. He was in charge of all reporting from the MU alumni file and keeping the file up to date. Of course, he used a data base management system to organize and control his activities. The system he used had two versions, one for the large mainframe computer used by the central administration and one for the microcomputer in his office. The two systems were designed to work in concert to provide a powerful tool for management.

When James arrived at his office, he immediately went over his list of tasks for the day:

1. Add Mr. C. L. Jones to the MU Alumni file.
2. Generate mailing labels for the class of '79.
3. Create a table showing the contributions of alumni from Ohio.

Figure 4-4 Using Data Base
Management Systems

He powered up his IBM microcomputer and then started up the data base management system that was installed on the hard disk drive.

```
The Best of All Possible Data Base Systems
Main Menu

Enter the letter corresponding to the command that you
wish to perform:

C(reate a new data base)
L(oad a data base from disk)
S(ave a data base to disk)
R(etrieve a data base from mainframe)
A(rchive a data base to mainframe)
P(rint a data base report)
X(exit to the operating system)

Choose one:_
```

The first thing James had to do was transfer the alumni file from the mainframe down to the micro, so he pressed the R key. A small window opened up at the bottom of the screen requesting the file to be retrieved. James provided the name of the file: MU ALUMNI.

```
Enter the name of the file to retrieve:
MU ALUMNI_
```

A message flashed onto the screen indicating that a transfer was underway, and James went to get a cup of coffee while he waited. After a few minutes, the micro beeped to signal that the transfer was done. The software assumed that any file transferred down would be the one to be worked on, so the system automatically entered the editing commands menu:

```
The Best of All Possible Data Base Managers
Editing Command Menu

Enter the letter corresponding to the command that you
wish to perform:

A(dd new records)
C(hange records)
D(elete records)
S(earch records)
R(eport on records)
X(exit to Main Menu)

Choose one:_
```

James decided to start with the data entry. The form of the data records in the MU ALUMNI data file had been defined earlier in the year. When he pressed the A, the system displayed an empty data record ready to be filled in. The record contained a number of fields each consisting of a name and a place for data:

```
Last Name:_
First Name:
Street Address:
City:                    State:    Zip:
Year of Graduation:      Major:
Contributions this year:
Contributions past years:
```

With the cursor in the last name field, James entered the name Jones. As he typed, the data appeared on the screen next to the phrase "Last Name:". When James hit the return key, the cursor automatically jumped down to the next field. He continued typing in the data for the rest of the fields. This created the data record for the new alumnus.

```
Last Name:Jones
First Name: Clancy William
Street Address: 100 Main Street
City: Rochester          State:MI  Zip:48833
Year of Graduation: 85   Major: Comp Science
Contributions this year: $    25.00
Contributions past years: $     0.00
```

As James entered the data for the last field, the editing commands menu reappeared:

```
The Best of All Possible Data Base Managers
Editing Command Menu

Enter the letter corresponding to the command that you
wish to perform:

A(dd new records)
C(hange records)
D(elete records)
S(earch records)
R(eport on records)
X(exit to Main Menu)

Choose one:_
```

James was ready to begin generating the mailing list, so he entered an R and responded with the name of the report he wanted generated, namely, the MAILING LABELS report.

```
Enter the name of the report to generate:
MAILING LABELS_
```

The data base management system went into its data files and retrieved the file that specified the form of the MAILING LABELS report, which had been defined earlier in the year. Once the report was found, the system had to be told which records would be included in the report. James wanted mailing labels for the class of 1979 only.

```
Records to be used (enter criteria or ALL):
Graduation = 1979._
```

The data base system took the keyword *Graduation* and found the field name that matched it most closely, *Year of Graduation*. The system then selected from the file all the records in which that field had a value of 1979. The resulting records were then used to generate printed mailing labels.

Now that the mailing labels were complete, James' only remaining task was the generation of the table on contributions. Since this was another type of report, he started from the editing commands menu and responded with the R option again. Now the report to be generated was the CONTRIBUTION TABLE report.

```
Enter the name of the report to generate:
CONTRIBUTION TABLE_
```

The report was to be generated for all alumni contributions from Ohio, so James specified the searching parameter:

```
Records to be used (enter criteria or ALL):
State = Ohio._
```

The report then began to print on the line printer (a printer that prints one complete line at a time), listing the data on all the contributions from Ohio alumni. This particular report form also specified that computations should be performed across certain data in the records of the report. The report that came out on the printer looked something like:

```
Last Name    First Name    Class      Contribution
Azimo        Lou           84         $64.00
Colman       Mark          83         $500.00
Zorba        Tillo         85         $80.00
TOTAL                                 $644.00
```

James looked at the watch. He had only been working for 30 minutes! "Boy!" he thought, "aren't computers great!" With his work finished for the day, his only remaining task was to copy the changed data files containing Jones' record back to the mainframe. He started the process up. It had been in progress for about a minute when suddenly the screen went blank and then began flashing a message:

```
Hardware failure during transmission.
Extended memory failure.
Probable destruction of all files in use.

Next start up time: Unknown
```

James stared at the screen in disbelief. "All the files? My files? ARGHHH!"

The traditional model of a data base management system is a file cabinet. A file cabinet (data base) has a number of folders (records) in it. Each folder contains data on an individual, and the data is identified by type (e.g., first name) and value (e.g., George). A data base system can store, retrieve, and alter the records it manages. It can select some records from the total set based on various criteria, and it can generate reports that summarize the contents of various sets of records. If, as in our example, the form of the data being stored and the layout of reports is complete, the use of a data base system can be

Computer Insights
Proper Care of Floppy Disks

Floppy disks are the primary permanent storage medium for most computer users. The new computer user should be aware of some obvious rules for their proper use:

1. Keep floppy disks away form any magnetic field. Although the user can never be certain about magnetic influences, some of the obvious things to avoid are electric motors, stereo speakers, televisions, airport X-ray machines, and so on. It is true that one might be able to place disks near these devices for years without a problem, because a magnetic field must be rather intense to alter a disk. But an ounce of prevention is worth a pound of cure.

2. Do not use floppy disks that are too cold and never let them get too hot. If the floppy disks sit in a car overnight in subzero temperatures, let them warm up before use. In the summer, never put a floppy disk on the back shelf of a car parked in the hot sun.

3. Never touch any of the exposed parts of a disk. The newer floppy disks have built-in dirt shields that protect the read/write openings to the disk. Older disks, however, do not have such shields and a simple dirty fingerprint on the bare storage medium could cause problems.

4. Do not bend floppy disks. Although floppy disks are, after all, floppy, they should not be creased! Be gentle with them—they are holding your data—and do not abuse them during storage, when inserting them into the drive, or when removing them from the drive.

Following this advice should give the user long service from his or her floppy disks.

quite simple. However, the tasks of designing the form of the data records and creating report layouts are substantially more complex. For those tasks, using a data base management system is more difficult than using word processors or spreadsheets.

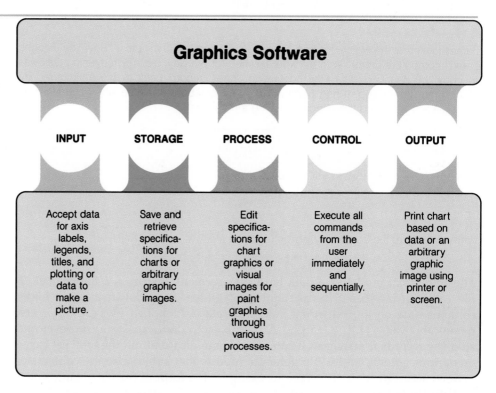

4.5

Using Graphics Software

Graphics software lets users create graphic displays on screens, paper, film, or other media. One example of a graphics applications is presented in the following scenario with the same student, Virgil, in need of a graphic assist.

Case Study

Virgil, the graduate student in psychology, had a problem. The committee in charge of research funds thought the budgets submitted for 1991 were too high in relation to the 1990 budgets. Virgil needed an easy-to-understand presentation showing clearly that his 1991 budget included only very small increases. He immediately thought of a graphic display. After all, wasn't one picture worth a thousand words?

Virgil went to the microcomputer again and called up the new graphics system, which was compatible with the spreadsheet software he had used earlier.

```
The Best of All Possible Graphics systems

Enter the letter corresponding to the command that you
wish to perform:

I(nput data from the keyboard)
L(oad data from a graph file)
T(ransfer data from a spreadsheet file)
S(ave data to a graph file)
G(enerate a graph)
P(rint a graph)
X(exit to operating system)

Choose one:_
```

Virgil typed a T to transfer data from his spreadsheet budget file into the graphics system. When asked for the name of the file, he responded with the name given earlier:

```
Enter the name of the spreadsheet file:
spreadsheet number 1_
```

The graphics system, because it was compatible with the spreadsheet, could transform the spreadsheet table into data that it could use. The system therefore loaded and displayed his budget as:

	A	B	C	D
001	Expenditure	1990	1991	Total
002				
003	Personnel	$5000.00	$6000.00	$11000.00
004	Equipment	$2000.00	$3000.00	$5000.00
005	Total	$7000.00	$9000.00	$16000.00

After this was displayed on the screen for a few seconds, the graphic system automatically returned to its main menu. Virgil wanted a graph with three lines on it: one for personnel, one for equipment, and one for the total. The lines would be constructed by taking the values of the corresponding expenditures and plotting them against the year. Virgil began the creation of a graph by entering the G command to the main menu (generate a graph). The screen then displayed the graph generation menu:

```
The Best of All Possible Graphic Systems
Graph Generation Menu

Enter the letter corresponding to the command
that you wish to perform

G(raph type)
S(elect data)
A(xes definition)
T(itle the graph)
L(abel the axes)
X(exit to Main Menu)
Choose one:_
```

Virgil chose the G (graph type) command from the menu so that he could specify the type of graph to be used. After he typed G, a window opened up at the bottom of the screen and requested the type of graph.

```
Enter the kind of graph desired: (Pie, Bar, or Line)
P, B, or L?_
```

He indicated a line graph by pressing the L key.

Now Virgil had to specify the data to be used. After choosing the S(elect data) option on the menu, he responded to questions concerning how many lines of data were to be plotted and where the data from each would come from. The source of the data were referenced by the row and column designators of the spreadsheet, just as would be done in the spreadsheet program.

Once the data was selected, the positions of the values on each axis had to be specified with the A command. Finally, an overall title had to be given to the graph, and labels were needed for the axes as well. Once Virgil was satisfied that all of the specifications for the graph were correct, he returned to the main menu with the X command.

```
The Best of All Possible Graphics Systems

Enter the letter corresponding to the command that you
wish to perform:

I(nput data from the keyboard)
L(oad data from a graph file)
T(ransfer data from a spreadsheet file)
S(ave data to a graph file)
G(enerate a graph)
P(rint a graph)
x(exit to operating system)

Choose one:_
```

Since the graph was already generated, the only thing that remained was to print it out. From the main menu, the P command was issued to actually print the graph on the printer.

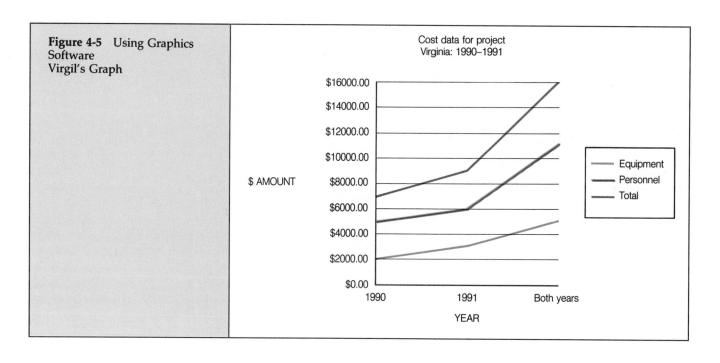

Figure 4-5 Using Graphics Software
Virgil's Graph

"There!" thought Virgil. "That graph shows that my budget increases were only slight from 1990 to 1991." Armed with the graph, Virgil left to defend his budget to the committee.

There are many varieties of graphics systems available today; some, like Virgil's, are used for the creation of business graphs, and some are used for drawing arbitrary pictures. Graphics software gives the user so much precision and control that even the unartistic can create satisfactory graphic images.

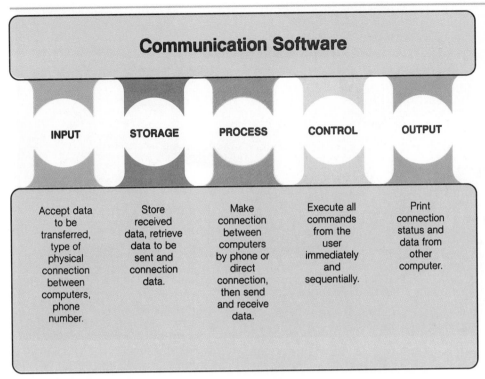

With the growing use of personal computers, communication among computers has become common for most experienced users. Different computers have different resources (software, hardware, data banks, and so forth) that must be transferable from machine to machine. Communications software allows one computer to send data to and receive data from another computer. The following case study presents an example in which a distant computer system is accessed by Michelle, who had big plans for her use of computers.

Case Study

Now that Michelle had finally graduated from business school, she was determined to make her fortune. She just couldn't wait for the day when she'd have enough money to play the stock market! Just to make sure she was ready for that time, she decided to work on developing a good system for predicting stock prices. As a graduation present, her husband had bought her a Compaq microcomputer with a lot of software and a modem. With that modem, Michelle knew she would have access to all of the teleconferencing (electronic communications services using telephone lines) activity in the area. She would be able to use her computer to dial up other computers and transfer data, programs, suggestions, or whatever to her own system. The most obvious use for her modem was accessing the Dow-Jones News Retrieval Service.

For now, Michelle was getting ready to try a new program she had written in Pascal (a highly structured computer programming language) that would predict the stock market. To really test it out, she wanted to get today's closing stock prices. Then she would take the prices predicted by her program and compare them to tomorrow's actual prices. If she could just get a little closer in her predictions, she might be willing to try some hard cash on the program's predictions!

First, Michelle grabbed her communications disk and slapped it into the disk drive. She hit the reset button on the machine, and the computer rebooted itself (restarted its operating system) and called up the communications package:

Figure 4-6 Using
Communication Software

```
The Best of All Possible Communications Packages
Main Menu

Enter the letter corresponding to the command that you
wish to perform

C(all another computer)
H(ang up)
S(et the communications parameters)
L(og all interaction into a disk file)
T(ransfer a disk file)

Choose one:_
```

The first thing that Michelle had to do was to set the parameters for communicating with
the news retrieval service to the proper values. Pressing the letter S, a submenu came
up specifying all of the parameters she could set:

```
The Best of All Possible Communication Packages
Parameter Menu

Enter the letter corresponding to the command that you
wish to perform

B(aud rate (speed).            Current value=1200)
D(ata bits used.              Current value=  7)
S(top bits used.              Current value=  1)
P(arity bits used.            Current value=Even)
X(exit to Main Menu)

Choose one:_
```

Michelle didn't really know what most of these values meant, but she knew how to set them to use the news retrieval service. She would be communicating on the higher speed line, so she selected B to reset the speed of transmission.

```
Enter speed of transmission (300, 1200, or 2400):
2400_
```

She quickly exited the parameter menu with the X command and returned to the main menu. The next requirement was to call up the other computer. From the main menu Michelle pressed the letter C to call the computer. A window appeared requesting the telephone number of the news service:

```
Enter the telephone number:
202-555-1212_
```

The modem was connected to the computer and a standard telephone jack. The computer used the modem to automatically activate the telephone line and dial the number. Michelle sat and waited. The computer at the other end of the phone line finally answered the phone, and the two computers began to talk to each other in that high-pitched whine that Michelle was so used to. Once the communication started, Michelle's communications software performed a very simple task: whatever characters were sent by the other computer, it placed on the screen; whatever characters Michelle typed at the keyboard were sent to the other computer.

With the connection in place, Michelle and the other computer talked to each other. The other computer asked for some identification so that Michelle could be billed properly. Michelle responded with her name and a secret password. The distant computer used a menu to ask what Michelle wanted and she responded by choosing the option to print all of the day's closing stock prices. Just before the other computer began to send data, Michelle issued a special command to her microcomputer (a control-C) that momentarily halted communication and returned her to the main menu of her communication software.

```
The Best of All Possible Communications Packages
Main Menu

Enter the letter corresponding to the command that you
wish to perform

C(all another computer)
H(ang up)
S(et the communications parameters)
L(og all interaction into a disk file)
T(ransfer a disk file)

Choose one:_
```

She pushed the L to turn on the log function. The system responded with a small window at the bottom of the screen:

```
Enter name of file for saving interaction:
dow jones 3/12/90_
```

When the main menu returned, Michelle pressed the C command again to call the other computer. The software responded that a call was already in progress. The connection was reestablished, and communication then continued. The distant computer, which had

Computer Insights
Software Crimes

As in any human endeavor, the ethical treatment of other people is a major concern in computer applications. A wide variety of crimes have occurred in which computers are used to break the law. An all too common example is the illegal copying of proprietary software, whereby a software system costing anywhere from ten to a thousand dollars (or more) is transferred from a licensed user to another unlicensed user just for the price of a floppy disk. Such illegal duplication of software is generally called *software piracy*.

Studies by research firms indicate that at least half of all personal computer software in use in business and government is illegal, pirated copies of copyrighted, proprietary software. Are the "software crackers" who provide copyable disks for programs modern Robin Hoods? Actually, they often rob from the relatively poor (computer software companies that do not get paid for the illicit copy) and give to the enormously rich (e.g., the Federal Government, which would not have to pay for a pirated copy).

Another major type of software crime involves the computer specialist turned criminal. A widely quoted story will serve to illustrate. "Mr. Jones" was the head systems programmer in the central office of a large insurance company. He had direct responsibility for all systems programming and operations, as well as indirect control over data file backup. Jones was well known for his habit of keeping tabs on the system, even on weekends when the insurance company's computer center was on standby operation. One particular weekend, Jones came in and relieved the standby operator. He then assembled copies of the master data tapes for all customer accounts. These tapes contained all the information essential to the daily operation of the company. Next, he electronically erased all the other copies in the tape vault. Finally, he used the operating system to erase all customer data disks and powered down the system to eliminate all other backup. Jones packed the tapes in large aluminum cases, boarded a jet, and flew to Zurich with the cases beside him. In Switzerland he wired the company: "$15 million for the tapes." According to those who tell this story, Jones got his $15 million. Not only that, but the company never attempted to prosecute for fear that their clients and creditors would discover how close the firm had been to total collapse. Without the information on the tapes, the insurance company would have been virtually helpless. It would not even have known the status of its clients' insurance coverage. Rumor has it that Jones is still living in Zurich and, believe it or not, is being paid a retainer by the insurance firm to keep his mouth shut and to help ensure that this never happens again. Whether this story is true or not, the potential for this type of crime is certainly present.

all of the news retrieval data on it, started sending stock names and their closing prices. As Michelle's microcomputer received the data, it displayed it on the screen and simultaneously saved it into the file that Michelle had designated. When the distant computer finished, Michelle interrupted her micro (by typing control-C again), and when the main menu came up on the screen, she gave the H command to hang-up.

Now Michelle was ready to go. She had all of the data, so she started her Pascal program for predicting stock prices. It started to read the news service data from the file and calculate her projections of tomorrow's prices. Suddenly, the system crashed (failed) with a message about arithmetic overflow or something. "Oh well," thought Michelle, "I guess my program blew it. If beating the market were easy, anybody could do it. Maybe I'll get it right tomorrow."

Communication among computers is increasing dramatically now that computers no longer need to be physically near each other to communicate. To accommodate the diverse locations of processing power, telephone linkages between infrequently connected computers and special networking linkages for permanently linked computers will grow in number and capacity. Communication among computers is becoming as common as communication among people.

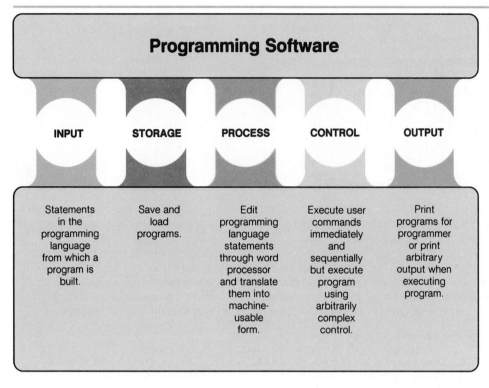

Programming software is designed to help the user create computer programs and manage the large sets of computer programs from which software systems are built. Such software can include a wide variety of helpful computer programs but always has a translator at its core. A translator takes statements from some formal language that people can understand and translates them into instructions that the computer can process. Each of the large number of different formal languages requires a different translator, which is generally named after the formal language it processes. Translators exist for languages like **BASIC, Pascal,** FORTRAN, Ada, C, and COBOL.

Generally, the only people who routinely create software systems are professional computer scientists or avid hobbyists. Thus, the need to make programming software easy to use and understand has been much less urgent than the need for other types of applications software. As we watch Cindy work with her first program in her introductory Pascal class, we can get only the general flavor of programming.

programming software
Software that helps users create and manage computer programs. It usually includes a program preparation system (to help input, edit, save, and execute programs) and a translator (to translate from the user's programming language into a language the computer can process).

BASIC
An easy-to-learn high-level computer programming language (Beginner's All-purpose Symbolic Instruction Code). BASIC has tremendous popularity because it has been included with the hardware of many prominent computer companies.

Pascal
A computer programming language with highly structured data types and control capabilities. It was originally developed for educational purposes but has increasingly been applied to scientific and engineering purposes as well.

Case Study

Cindy entered the terminal room with a feeling of excitement. After using a word processor for a number of years, she had finally decided to take a course in computer programming. Now she was going to find out how to make her own programs!

Taking her Pascal disk from her backpack, Cindy inserted the disk into the IBM PC and turned on the power. In a few moments, the screen cleared and informed her of the current status of her programming task. The screen looked like this:

Figure 4-7 Using Programming Software

```
The Best of All Possible Pascal Programming Systems
Main Menu

Enter the letter corresponding to the command that you
wish to perform:

M(ake a new program)
E(dit an existing program)
S(ave program to disk)
C(ompile the program)
R(un program)
Q(uit)

Choose one:_
```

Since this was her first assignment, Cindy knew that she had to make a new program. Before she pushed the letter M to start that process, she pulled out her class assignment and her notes and went over them.

It seemed that the main purpose of this assignment was to have her type a program written by the teacher into the Pascal system and run it. That way, she would become familiar with the Pascal tools to be used throughout the term without having the pressure of creating her first program at the same time. That sounded good to her!

She ran her finger down the page as she looked over the Pascal program.

```
program one (input, output);
   {The purpose of this program is to introduce INPUT using
    the readln command, STORAGE using variables, PROCESSING
    using addition and multiplication commands, CONTROL via
    normal sequential processing, and OUTPUT using the writeln
    command. It will compute an employee's gross pay given
    hours worked, overtime, payrate, and overtime multiplier
    (like 1 1/2 time)}

var
   payrate:      real;   {storage for employee payrate}
   regularhours: real;   {storage for hours worked}
   overtimehrs:  real;   {storage for overtime worked}
   overmult:     real;   {storage for overtime rate}

begin
 {Print message to screen asking for hours worked}
   writeln ('Enter hours worked:');
 {Read number typed at keyboard and place in storage location
  named "regularhours"}
   readln (regularhours);
 {Similarly for other data}
   writeln ('Enter overtime hours worked:');
   readln (overtimehrs);
   writeln('Enter rate of pay:');
   readln(payrate);
   writeln('Enter overtime multiplier:');
   readln(overmult);

 {Write out message and gross pay formula that uses values
  entered from keyboard and the multiplication operator "*"
  and the addition operator "+"}
   writeln('gross pay should be:',
           payrate*regularhours +
           payrate*overtimehrs*overmult);
end.
```

Cindy reviewed her notes. The teacher had told the class that the first line of the program had to give the program a name and tell the computer that both input from the keyboard and output to the screen would be used. Everything within matching braces—

the symbols { and }—anywhere in the program would be ignored by the computer; this way, people could write comments for themselves and each other about how the program worked. The first large chunk of the program underneath the heading "var" specified what kind of storage the program needed to use. The specifications included names for the storage locations (e.g., payrate) as well as descriptions of the types of values that each would hold (e.g., real—a number with a decimal point). The last major part of the program between the "begin" and the "end." defined the steps the computer was to take. The computer would automatically use sequential control, that is, it would perform the instructions in the order given. As Cindy looked at the steps, she saw that the program asked for four pieces of data from the user and then used this data to figure out and print a new value. The program did, indeed, include input, storage, processing, control, and output.

Turning to the computer, Cindy pushed the M key to make a new program. As soon as she did, a new screen appeared:

```
Insert                        Pg 1 Ln 1  Pos 0
-
```

Cindy found herself inside a word processing system that worked exactly like the one she already knew how to operate! This was going to be easier than she thought. Putting her typing skills to the test, she began quickly. After a few moments, her screen looked like this:

```
Insert                        Pg 1 Ln 14 Pos 55
program one(input, output);
    {The purpose of this program is to introduce INPUT
    using the readln command, STORAGE using variables,
    PROCESSING using addition and multiplication commands,
    CONTROL via normal sequential processing, and OUTPUT
    using the writeln command. It will compute an
    employee's gross pay given hours worked, overtime,
    payrate, and overtime multiplier (like 1 1/2 time)}

var
    pzyrate:       real;   {storage for employee payrate}
    regularhours:  real;   {storage for hours worked}
    overtimehrs:   real;   {storage for overtime worked}
    overmult:      real;   {storage for overtime rate}_
```

Cindy noticed that she had mistyped the word "payrate" as "pzyrate" and quickly moved the cursor back to fix the mistake. Using her word processing experience, she soon had an exact copy of the teacher's program stored in the machine. Now that she was finished, she pressed the escape key to terminate entry of the program (just as she did on her word processing system). The main menu for the programming software then returned to the screen:

```
The Best of All Possible Pascal Programming Systems
Main Menu

Enter the letter corresponding to the command that you
wish to perform:

M(ake a new program)
E(dit an existing program)
S(ave program to disk)
C(ompile the program)
R(un program)
Q(uit)

Choose one:_
```

Playing it safe, Cindy saved the program to disk by pressing the S key. When the computer responded with

```
Enter the name of the file for the save:
-
```

Cindy typed in the name "assignment 1" and pressed the return key. The disk whirred as the program was saved, and the main menu returned. At this point, Cindy's notes said that the compile option had to be invoked. The teacher had said that the computer could not process statements made in Pascal directly—Pascal didn't work with the microprocessor or something like that. The compile option would create a second version of the program that the computer could process. She pressed the C key and the screen quickly returned with some rather cryptic information:

```
COMPILING
   ERROR 524: Unknown Identifier or other Syntax Error in
              Line 21
   PRESS "E" to EDIT
   PRESS "M" for MAIN MENU
-
```

Cindy wasn't sure what ERROR 524 meant, but either she had not typed in the teacher's program exactly as she had thought or the teacher's program was wrong! Cindy wanted to look at the program, so she pressed the E to edit. The computer immediately returned to the word processing program and displayed the Pascal program with the cursor at line 21.

```
 Insert                          Pg 1 Ln 21 Pos 3
program one (input, output);
   {The purpose of this program is to introduce INPUT
    using the readln command, STORAGE using variables,
    PROCESSING using addition and multiplication commands,
    CONTROL via normal sequential processing, and OUTPUT
    using the writeln command. It will compute an
    employee's gross pay given hours worked, overtime,
    payrate, and overtime multiplier (like 1 1/2 time)}

   var
      payrate:        real;    {storage for employee payrate}
      regularhours:   real;    {storage for hours worked}
      overtimehrs:    real;    {storage for overtime worked}
      overmult:       real;    {storage for overtime rate}

   begin
   {Print message to screen asking for hours worked}
      writeln('Enter hours worked:');
   {Read number typed at keyboard and place in storage
    location named "regularhours"}
   qreadln(regularhours);                              ←
   {Similarly for other data}
      writeln('Enter overtime hours worked:');
      readln(overtimehrs);
```

How convenient! The word processor had left the cursor sitting right at the mistake she had made! The mistake was rather obvious. Somehow she had put a letter q at the beginning of the line. Cindy deleted the errant q and exited the word processor. When the main menu appeared on the screen, Cindy pressed C again to see if the compilation would succeed this time. It did! The screen displayed:

```
COMPILING
  No Errors.
  36   lines processed.
  17   statements processed.
   9   comments processed.
```

Since the compilation was successful, Cindy resaved the program when the main menu appeared. Now came the true test: if she ran the program, would it perform as it was supposed to? From the main menu, she pressed the R key to run the program. A message suddenly appeared at the bottom of the screen. It said:

```
Enter hours worked:
-
```

As the cursor flashed under the message, she typed in the number 40 and pressed return. The screen immediately displayed a new message:

```
Enter overtime hours worked:
-
```

Cindy entered 10 and the screen responded again:

```
Enter rate of pay:
-
```

Cindy felt she really understood what the computer was doing: it was going through the list of commands in that "begin" to "end" section and doing them one at a time. When it saw a "writeln" command, it printed something on the screen. When it saw a "readln" command, it expected her to type something at the keyboard. For rate of pay, she entered 3.25 and the screen responded:

```
Enter overtime multiplier:
-
```

Cindy entered 1.5 (the employee got time-and-a-half for overtime) and hit return. The screen then responded with:

```
gross pay should be:   1.787500000E+02
```

The program worked! At least Cindy thought it had. She quickly performed the computation herself

$$40 \times 3.25 + 10 \times 3.25 \times 1.5$$

and got the answer $178.75. She wasn't exactly sure if that was what the computer had printed out, but it looked like it was right. It seemed that the computer used some kind of scientific notation or something, but she wasn't going to worry about it, because she had the answer on the class handout. When the main menu returned, Cindy realized that she had already saved the correct copy of the program to disk, so she pressed the Q key to terminate work with the Pascal system. She packed up and left, feeling pretty good about how simple this first task had been.

Indeed, Cindy had a most pleasant first encounter with computer programming. Because she already possessed word processing skills, it was a straightforward task for her to apply them to this new problem. In addition, Cindy was using supportive and user-friendly program development software. Unfortunately for all beginning computer programmers, there are many problems with programming not suggested by this vignette, for example, (1) copying someone else's program is trivial compared to composing one's own systematic set of instructions for the computer, (2) many software systems are not supportive of the development process, and even simple aids like informative messages about program errors and a word processor that automatically homes in on an error are often lacking, (3) making sure that a complicated program really works is extremely difficult for novices or professionals.

Nonetheless, programming software is of vital importance because it enables professionals to create all the enjoyable and useful software systems for the rest of the computing world. Programming is also a pleasant pastime for any individual who likes to solve problems.

4.8

Summary of Types of Software

The vignettes of this section have described the most commonly used types of applications software. The software has all been presented in a menu-driven form, that is, each system presented the user with a list of options from which the appropriate action could be chosen. Not all systems are menu driven, however. As we will see in the next chapter, some software systems expect the user to type in command words to perform actions, while others use pointing devices and graphic images on the screen. However other versions of operating systems, applications software, and programming software may operate, the examples in this chapter illustrate capabilities and features that are common to many different software systems.

Figure 4–1 summarizes the commonalities of these software systems. Note that the various types of software differ mainly in what type of data they process, e.g., written text, tables, or records. Despite their differences, these systems share many commands, and all share the ISPCO functions. A common sequence of steps is followed when any of these software systems are used. Most interactions with these major software types follow the ISPCO scripts for data input or processing and output.

The first script shows the typical interaction when a person begins an application. The primary activities are inputting information (e.g., a document or table) and saving the information to disk for further processing. For example, one might use a spreadsheet to create a tentative budget and save it for later revision with new data.

DATA INPUT SCRIPT FOR ARBITRARY APPLICATIONS SOFTWARE OR PROGRAMMING LANGUAGE

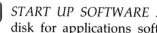 *START UP SOFTWARE AND PREPARE DATA DISK:* Insert software disk for applications software. Have disk ready for storage of data and other results of software use. Issue start-up command.

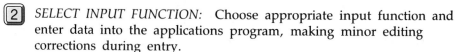 *SELECT INPUT FUNCTION:* Choose appropriate input function and enter data into the applications program, making minor editing corrections during entry.

3 *SELECT STORAGE FUNCTION:* Choose appropriate storage function to transfer the data just entered onto disk or other permanent storage.

Type of Software	Input	Storage	Process	Control	Output
Operating systems	Text for data files.	Save and retrieve arbitrary types of files, using tape, disk, or other media.	Sort, merge, compile and interpret, software libraries.	Schedule jobs to maximize user access and power.	Print data files, file directories, help files, tape data, and so forth.
Word processing applications	Text of document and commands for controlling the printing of the document.	Save and retrieve text and associated commands, usually to and from disk.	Insert, copy, move, delete, change, and replace text and associated commands.	Menus, command lines, or control characters that may or may not be embedded in text.	Printed documents.
Spreadsheet applications	Numbers, labels, and formulas for table.	Save and retrieve table with numbers, labels, and formulas, usually to and from disk.	Insert, copy, move, delete, change and replace numbers, labels and formulas in table.	Menus, command lines, or control characters that may or may not be embedded in table.	Tables with values of formulas calculated and inserted.
Data base management applications	Sets of related data, each one describing a particular entity.	Save and retrieve records of data, usually to and from disk.	Insert, copy, move, delete, change, and replace records of data.	Menus, command lines or control characters that may or may not be embedded in records.	Reports of data record contents and summaries across records.
Graphics applications	Data for graph, titles, legends, axis units, and so forth.	Save and retrieve specifications and data for graph, usually to and from disk.	Insert, copy, move, delete, change, and replace graph data or specifications.	Menus, command lines or control characters that may or may not be embedded in specifications.	Graphic display showing data relationships.
Communication systems	Type of connection, data to be sent to other computer, data received from other computer.	Save data received from other computer and retrieve data to send.	Dial/answer the telephone, send and receive the data.	Menus, command lines or control characters that may or may not be embedded in transmissions.	Status of connection and data from other computer.
Programming languages	Program written in a computer language like Pascal or BASIC.	Save and retrieve files containing programs.	Translate programs into machine language and execute.	Menus, command lines controlling translation and execution.	Listing of programs, files containing translated programs.

Figure 4-8 Comparison of Software Systems

[4] *SELECT OUTPUT FUNCTION:* Choose appropriate output function and print the data just input for checking and archiving.

[5] *SHUTDOWN SOFTWARE AND STORE DISKS:* Issue shutdown command. Remove and store program and data disks.

The second script shows a typical interaction in which a user needs to work with data that has already been saved. In this case, the interaction includes activities such as retrieving a data file, updating the information, processing it for some purpose, outputting a useful report, and resaving the data to disk. For example, one might retrieve an existing spreadsheet, revise the data, print out an up-to-date table, and save the new data to disk.

Once the beginning student is familiar with these underlying ISPCO Scripts, he or she will have a general idea of how to run any piece of software and should be able to avoid feeling utterly helpless when seated at a micro-computer. Once application software is running what must a user do? The answer lies in the script. The user must first learn how to start the applications software and how to enter commands into the system (are menus or command phrases used?). Then he or she should try a few simple examples. The remaining steps in the ISPCO Script can be followed for any type of applications software.

PROCESSING AND OUTPUT SCRIPT FOR ARBITRARY APPLICATIONS SOFTWARE OR PROGRAMMING LANGUAGE

1 *START UP SOFTWARE AND INSERT DATA DISK:* Insert software disk for applications software. Insert data disk with data from previous software use. Issue start-up command.

2 *SELECT STORAGE FUNCTION:* Retrieve data from previous software use from disk.

3 *SELECT PROCESSING FUNCTION:* Alter and repair existing data using any available processing functions.

4 *SELECT INPUT FUNCTION:* Enter new data using any available input functions.

5 *SELECT STORAGE FUNCTION:* Save new and changed data back onto disk or other permanent storage.

6 *SELECT OUTPUT FUNCTION:* Print out the intermediate or final data for archiving and perusal.

7 *SHUTDOWN SOFTWARE AND STORE DISKS:* Issue shutdown command. Remove and store program and data disks.

Chapter 4 Review

Expanded Objectives

The objectives listed below are an expansion of the essential chapter concepts listed at the beginning of the chapter. The review items that follow are based on these expanded objectives. If you master the objectives, you will do better on the review items and on your instructor's examination of the chapter material.

After reading the chapter, you should be able to:

1. distinguish among the seven major types of software.
2. describe the purposes of the seven major types of software.
3. understand the use of menu-driven software.

4. correctly sequence a set of steps for completing a task for any of the seven major types of software.
5. recognize common problems in the use of software.
6. list some of the major similarities and differences in editing processes for the various types of software.
7. explain why different software systems are used together.
8. relate the seven major types of software to the ISPCO model.
9. justify the use of scripts in learning about software.
10. recognize the meaning of major new terms introduced in this chapter.

Review Items

Completing this review will give you a good indication of how well you have mastered the contents of this chapter and prepare you for your instructor's test on this material. To maximize what you learn from this exercise, you should answer each question *before* looking up the answers in the appendix. The number of the corresponding expanded objective is given in parentheses following each question.

Complete the following clusters of items according to the directions heading each set.

A. Match each statement (1–18) with the most appropriate type of software from the list below (a–h). (1,2)

a. word processors
b. graphics software
c. data base systems
d. spreadsheets
e. communications
f. operating systems
g. programming system
h. relevant to all

___ 1. Permits one computer to send data to a second computer.
___ 2. Enables the use of peripheral devices.
___ 3. Enables computer users to write documents.
___ 4. Enables a user to send the same personal letter to several people.
___ 5. A cursor tells the user where on the screen the next character will appear.
___ 6. Makes it possible for a user to interact with applications software.
___ 7. The status line tells the user that he or she is currently working in box B1.
___ 8. When the user changes a number in a table, other related numbers in the table will automatically change.
___ 9. For multiuser computers, this software will require a user to provide an identification code.
___ 10. Assists with the creation of new software.
___ 11. Enables the user to edit data being input.
___ 12. Formulas are applied to numbers in a table.
___ 13. Users can select specific records they are interested in.
___ 14. Requires a modem for its effective use.
___ 15. Must contain a translator.
___ 16. Useful for demonstrating relationships and trends.
___ 17. Enables a user to retrieve data from another computer in a distant city.
___ 18. Useful for generating reports from banks of information.

B. *True or False.*

___ 19. It is not necessary to learn different commands for the same activity when going from one word processing system to another. (5)
___ 20. On a spreadsheet, the width of the columns can be changed, even after all the data has been typed in. (4)
___ 21. The best applications systems for generating budgets are data base management systems. (1)
___ 22. Menu-driven systems require few or no programming skills of the user. (3)
___ 23. Programming software should have access to some type of word processing software for the creation of programs. (7)
___ 24. Accessing remote data bases by computer frequently requires modems. (10)
___ 25. A system crash can result in a loss of data. (5)
___ 26. All applications software is menu-driven. (3)
___ 27. Scripts are designed to help users learn how to use software. (9)

C. *The tasks listed in the numbered items below (28–34) can be completed by following a specific sequence of steps. For each task, choose an appropriate sequence of steps from the lettered items below, e.g., the essential steps to run a previously compiled and saved Pascal program would be a, i, p.*

a. boot the application software system
b. save to data disk or file
c. specify printer options
d. use the spell checker
e. copy rows or columns
f. edit (e.g., copy, replace, insert, delete)
g. enter graph specifications
h. print results
i. load from disk or file
j. type in text or data from keyboard
k. type in labels, numbers, and formulas
l. generate a report
m. search for particular data
n. type phone number at keyboard
o. compile a program
p. run a program

_____28. List the steps required to use a word processor to enter a new hand-written manuscript, print the results, and save it for later use.

_____29. List the steps required to use a word processor to revise and add to a previously input document, print, and save the results.

_____30. List the steps required to use a spreadsheet system to enter a new table and save it for later use.

_____31. List the steps required to revise a previously entered spreadsheet.

_____32. List the steps required to create a bar graph from scratch.

_____33. List the steps required to link up a computer with a computer network.

_____34. List the steps required to enter and run a computer program.

D. *For each numbered ISPCO operation below (35–48), indicate which software system or systems are involved by putting their symbols in the appropriate space. (8)*

SOFTWARE SYSTEM	SYMBOL
word processing	wp
communications	com
spreadsheet	ss
data base management	dbms
graphics	gr
operating system	op
programming software	ps
all types of software	all

SOFTWARE   ITEM

_____ 35. save data to a file.

_____ 36. use a command to change a word throughout a term paper.

_____   37. schedule computer time to do tasks for different users.

_____   38. create a file with an editor.

_____   39. use a formula to calculate values in a table.

_____   40. insert a sentence into a paragraph of a document.

_____   41. convert data to graphic form.

_____   42. compile a computer program.

_____   43. type numbers into a table.

_____   44. print out a graphics display of data.

_____   45. combine records into a new report.

_____   46. retrieve data from a distant computer.

_____   47. print out a table with values calculated from formulas.

_____   48. execute a user-developed program

5

Computer Software: Operating Systems

Essential Chapter Concepts

When you have finished this chapter, you should know:

- The functions of the major component programs of an operating system: the shell and the various parts of the kernel, including the system supervisor, the resource manager, and the file manager.

- The differences among command language, menu, and graphic shells.

- The steps for starting up and shutting down a computer operating system for both single-user and multiuser systems.

- The concepts underlying common ISPCO commands available on operating systems.

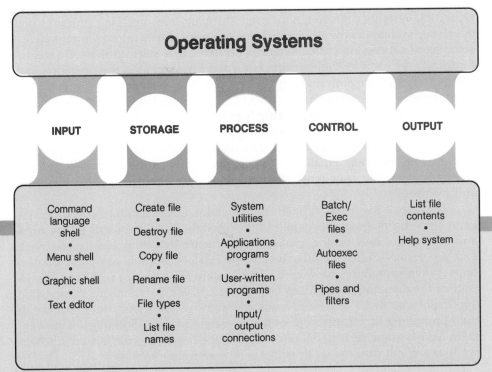

Operating Systems

INPUT	STORAGE	PROCESS	CONTROL	OUTPUT
Command language shell	Create file	System utilities	Batch/ Exec files	List file contents
Menu shell	Destroy file	Applications programs	Autoexec files	Help system
Graphic shell	Copy file	User-written programs	Pipes and filters	
Text editor	Rename file	Input/ output connections		
	File types			
	List file names			

An operating system is a set of programs that initiates and manages the interactions among the hardware and software components of a computer system. The operating system is the most important of all the various types of software, because all the other software depend on it.

The operating system is the software closest to the computer hardware: it contains programs that are necessary to start up the computer hardware, to use a disk drive for storage and retrieval of data, to create a graphic image on the screen, or print text on a printer. These separate programs that perform direct action on the computer hardware are called the **kernel** of the operating system.

All access to system hardware, whether by a user (who wants to access a floppy disk) or by a program (that needs to print a data file on the printer), should be made through the kernel. Using the kernel for all hardware access guarantees that the hardware will be managed in a consistent and coherent manner by all software. The user accesses the kernel through a special operating system program called a **shell**. The shell accepts **commands** directly from the user and then performs the desired action by referencing programs in the kernel. When an applications program accesses the kernel (e.g., to use a hardware device), the program passes control to the kernel programs that actually control the hardware devices. When their job is complete, control returns to the applications program.

Operating systems do not help the user solve many problems directly. Instead, they provide a means to use other software for solving problems. The operating system mainly supervises the use of the computer hardware by users and programs. The operating system determines what software is running, how long it will be allowed to run, and how the hardware on the system is scheduled in conjunction with the various software activities. The software programs that comprise the operating system can be viewed as a set of tools available for any user of the system.

kernel
The part of the operating system that includes the supervisor, the file manager, and the resource manager. The kernel is usually RAM resident, i.e., it stays in RAM as long as the computer is on.

shell
The part of the operating system or applications software that reads user commands and then calls other programs to do what is requested.

command
An instruction that directs a computer to perform a specific task.

5.1

What are Operating Systems For?

Operating systems confuse novice users for many reasons. First, it seems that operating systems come and go. Some software for a microcomputer (e.g., some word processing systems) comes on disks that start up the software automatically as soon as the machine is turned on—where is the operating system? In contrast, mainframe computer operating systems require extensive identification codes and other commands just to start up or end a computer interaction (without even considering how to accomplish anything useful). Second, to the average user, the operating system doesn't really seem to do that much. Besides letting a user look at data on a disk, the purpose of an operating system is not obvious. Finally, to understand many of the concepts of an operating system, the user must already know a lot about computer hardware and software.

Because of the many difficulties involved in understanding operating systems, some users ignore the details of the operating system in which they work and concentrate only on the applications software that they wish to use. Such a choice greatly limits the effectiveness and safety of their computer interactions. When something goes wrong with system hardware or software, knowledge of the operating system can help the user solve the problem. When using applications software, informed users can increase the speed and efficiency of their processing by effective use of the operating system. Both of these advantages have become clear to Bill (who bought the new computer system in chapter 3) as a result of some work with his new computer system.

Case Study

It was late in the evening and Bill's dormitory room was quiet. His roommate, Andy, a computer science major, was gone for the weekend. As Bill worked, the environment of his room seemed rather pleasant—the yellowish glow of his desk lamp, the green characters on his screen, the sound-deadening noise coming from his microcomputer's cooling fan. Quiet. Bill was trying to figure out how to use Freeword, a public domain word processing program that Andy had given him. Public domain software sure was nice: it said right on the disk that it was free and you could give a copy to anybody without worrying about it. That sure made word processing a lot cheaper than having to buy a program at the computer store for a hundred and fifty bucks!

Right now, Bill was trying to find the solution to some problems. He had inserted his Freeword disk into the first disk drive (drive A) and turned on the computer. Everything seemed fine until the screen displayed a troublesome message:

```
Disk is not a system disk or Disk has gone bad.
Replace disk and strike any key to continue
-
```

Not a system disk? What did that mean?

Bill flipped open the manual that Andy had given him with the Freeword software and began scanning it for information. After a half hour had passed with nary a comment about system disks in the index, table of contents, or a quick scan of the text, Bill put the manual aside. Well, maybe it wasn't a problem with Freeword. Good heavens, Bill wondered, is there something wrong with my computer already?

Grabbing the two manuals that came with his computer hardware, Bill looked again for help. On scanning the table of contents, his eyes were immediately drawn to an entry entitled "Error Messages." Bill turned to that section of the manual and was greeted with page after page of error messages. There were thirty pages of error messages! Fortunately, they appeared to be alphabetized. Quickly turning the pages, Bill soon found the exact message that was displayed on his screen. Beneath the message was the following comment:

[Operating System Message]

The ROM Operating System will print this message in two situations: the disk does not have the Ram portion of the operating system on it or the disk has not been formatted. The user should insert the operating system disk to start up the system and press any key to continue.

Bill wasn't sure what formatting was, but he did have an operating system disk that came with his system, so he inserted it into the drive in place of the Freeword disk and hit return. Now he was in business. Soon, the screen had a message on it:

```
Operating System Version 3.1 Installed in RAM
Enter commands at the prompt.

A>_
```

Bill then decided to start up the word processor, so he typed in "freeword," the start-up command Andy had given him, and hit return. The computer did not respond as he had hoped.

```
A>freeword
Improper operating system command

A>_
```

Bill immediately realized his error. He had removed the Freeword disk to insert the operating system disk. He exchanged disks again and reentered the command. This time the word processing system started up properly.

When Andy gave Bill the software, he showed him some of the simple parts of using a word processor, so Bill quickly typed out a short letter to his girlfriend. When the letter was just right, he gave the command to save the letter to his disk so that he'd have a copy of what he sent. After issuing the word processing command to save, the bottom of the screen displayed the message:

```
Disk full. Unable to save. _
```

Even with his limited background, Bill could figure out what that meant. When he had issued the save command, he had seen the light of the second (and empty) disk drive come on momentarily. Then it went out and the disk drive containing the Freeword disk came on. Evidently, that disk was already filled with data and had no room for more. So Bill reached to his bookshelf and tore the cellophane from a new box of disks he had bought at the store. He inserted one of these disks into the second disk drive (drive B) and issued the save command again. Bill was sure there would be room on an empty disk!

Of course, Bill was right—there would be room. But unfortunately he had overlooked something, and a new error message appeared on the screen:

```
Not ready for use of drive B.
Try again, Format disk, or Abort? _
```

Bill was feeling a little exasperated. He was glad that he wasn't under a deadline and was only practicing! He started to type in the phrase "Try again," but as soon as he hit the letter T the drive started again and the same message appeared. After trying again two more times, Bill knew he had to do something else. He was afraid to try the abort option—it just might trash the letter he had written. Not knowing what else to try, he pressed the F for the format disk option, and the system responded with the following message:

```
Insert operating system disk for retrieval of FORMAT.
Press any key when ready.
_
```

Bill swapped disks again, inserting the operating system disk into the first drive in place of the Freeword disk, and pressed return.

```
Insert New Disk in Drive B: and Press Return.
Any other key will abort Format.
Format destroys all data currently on disk.
```

Swap, swap, swap! Bill felt like he was playing musical chairs, but he had already placed the new disk in the second drive, so he pressed return. The second drive turned on and ran and ran and ran. It must have been a full minute or so until it stopped. Bill had been just about ready to give up.

Well, it looked like everything was all set. Freeword was back asking for the name of his document again. Bill entered it again, the second disk drive came on, and the save was successful! Bill then printed out his letter, terminated the Freeword system, and got back to the regular system prompt:

```
A>_
```

He then turned off the computer and went to bed.

It was not until later in the week that Bill had a chance to talk to Andy about what had happened. "Sorry I wasn't around to help," said Andy. "I'm kind of surprised you managed to get as far as you did without help! Let me tell you what happened."

"First, the computer always has to get hold of the operating system when it starts up. That's why you couldn't use the Freeword system directly—the Freeword disk doesn't have a copy of the operating system, while your operating system disk clearly does. Second, there is a lot of extra stuff on the Freeword disk, you know, sample letters and stuff like that, so there was no more room to store anything. You really did need a different disk. Third, anytime you get out a new disk, it has to be set up to work with the operating system by using the operating system 'format' command. You did everything just right, somehow, all without help."

"Well, It was rather exasperating," responded Bill. "Is there any way to make it easier?"

"Sure there is!" was Andy's reply. "Watch over my shoulder while I do a few things for you."

"Let's make a copy of Freeword on a disk with the operating system so that it will start up automatically." Bill watched while Andy worked. Andy first inserted the operating system disk into the computer and turned the system on. When the ordinary system prompt came up on the screen, Andy typed in a special format command:

```
Operating System Version 3.3 Installed in RAM
Enter commands at the prompt.

A>format b: /s
```

"This is a special format command that will prepare a new disk in drive B and put a copy of the operating system on the new disk," Andy explained. The screen responded with the message:

```
Place a new disk in drive B and press the
return key when ready to format.
-
```

Andy placed a new disk into the second drive of the computer and pressed the return key. The drive started up and continued running for almost a minute. Then other messages appeared on the screen:

```
Format of disk is complete.

Now copying operating system to disk.

  362496 bytes of storage on disk
   69632 bytes used for storage of operating system
  292864 bytes remaining

A>_
```

"This new disk is now ready to use," Andy continued. "It has the major routines of the operating system on the disk, but it doesn't have all of them. You see, most operating systems have lots of pieces. Some are called resident, which means that they are always available because they are loaded permanently into the computer's RAM until you turn the machine off. Some are nonresident—that means you have to pull them off the disk every time you need them. The only nonresident one you'll probably want on a word processing disk will be the disk formatter that you used earlier. So let me copy that one to the new disk." Andy typed a new command at the keyboard, the computer carried out the request, and the screen displayed:

```
A>copy  a:format.com  b:format.com  /verify
      1 file copied
A>_
```

"I just told the computer to copy the program named format.com from your first disk drive (a:) to a file called format.com on your second disk drive (b:) and to verify the accuracy of the copy when done," Andy commented. "The next thing to do is to place all of the Freeword software on this same disk." Saying this, Andy removed the operating system disk from the first disk drive and inserted the Freeword disk in its place. The new disk still sat in the second drive. Andy then issued another command to copy the Freeword software, and the system performed as instructed.

```
A>copy  a:freeword.*  b:/verify
   freeword.com
   freeword.hlp
   freeword.ov1
   freeword.ov2
      4 files copied
A>_
```

"Hey, Andy," Bill asked, "how come you could use the copy command that is part of the operating system even though you had removed the operating system disk?"

"Oh, that's what I was talking about when I said that part of the operating system is set permanently into RAM," Andy answered. "As long as the machine is on, the copy command and many other commands will always be available. Incidentally, the form of the command I used is a little different than the one before. Instead of copying only one file, I asked the computer to copy every file that has 'freeword' as the first component of its name. That will copy all of the needed files for the Freeword software. Everything else on the Freeword disk was just related materials. That's why we can now fit everything you need to run the system on one disk: we didn't copy all the unnecessary junk. Your new disk just has the operating system, the formatter, and the word processor."

"Well, I really appreciate your help, Andy. Anything else to do?" Bill asked.

"Only one last thing," Andy responded. "Watch. I'm going to set up a special command file called an autoexec. An autoexec contains commands that are automatically executed when the operating system is loaded. All we have to do is put the command 'freeword' in an autoexec, and your word processor will automatically start up when the computer is turned on. We'll use the text editor that comes with the operating system to create the autoexec since I'm really fast at using it."

Andy replaced the Freeword disk in the first drive with the operating system disk and typed in the command to start the editor. "The text editor is not always available like the copy command is, so we need your operating system disk," explained Andy. Andy's interaction with the screen was very simple. He was creating a special file called "autoexec.bat" on the disk and storing the single command "freeword" in it. During this interaction, the editor printed out an asterisk (*) every time it wanted Andy to type in a command or data, and Andy responded by typing the right phrase after the asterisk. The interaction looked like this (^C means control-C and stops data input):

```
A>edit b:autoexec.bat
  PREPARING NEW FILE
*insert
          1:*freeword
          2:*^C
*end
  WRITING FILE B:AUTOEXEC.BAT TO DISK
A>_
```

"Now I'm done," said Andy. "Anytime you want to use Freeword, just use this new disk we made. It's got the part of the operating system that starts up the computer and stays in RAM, it's got the nonresident disk formatter, and it's got all the needed Freeword programs. Also, it will start up Freeword automatically when you turn the computer on, because of the autoexec we set up. You just put the new disk in the first drive and turn on the computer."

"Thanks a lot, Andy." Bill was truly thankful. He realized how useful it was to have a roommate who was a computer science major!

This case study illustrates a number of facts about operating systems. First, a computer must always have access to operating system software. Some of the operating system software is actually in ROM (just enough to read in the rest from disk), and some of the operating system is loaded into RAM and is available at any time (resident), no matter what disks are in the computer's drives. The remainder of an operating system consists of nonresident routines that must be explicitly loaded from disk whenever used. Second, the operating system controls access to the computer hardware. For example, a new disk cannot be used before a formatter (an operating system program) prepares the disk surface. Finally, the commands available through operating systems are generally diverse and useful; for example, they often provide simple text editors and a means for executing sets of commands automatically. The remainder of this chapter will describe in detail the many resources available in an operating system and how they function.

5.2

The Basics of Operating Systems

From the user's perspective, an operating system is a group of computer programs that accepts commands for operating the computer hardware and software and carries them out within the constraints of policies established by the computer manager or owner. For single-user systems, the operating system will generally carry out any command. For multiuser systems, many decisions have to be made about how the computer resources will be shared, and these decisions may affect the manner in which commands are executed. In both cases, the operating system attempts to maximize the computing power, speed, and security available to each individual user or program within the limits of its operating policies.

Regardless of whether a computer is a micro, mini, or mainframe system, its operating system has a number of components for the management of hardware and software. Unfortunately, there are no standard components for operating systems. From one computer manufacturer to the next, and from one textbook to the next, there are differences in the components' names and in their descriptions. Figure 5–1 shows one example of the organization of the components of an operating system and the manner in which they are interrelated. Each component in the figure has a precise purpose within the operating system's overall function of providing control over system hardware and software:

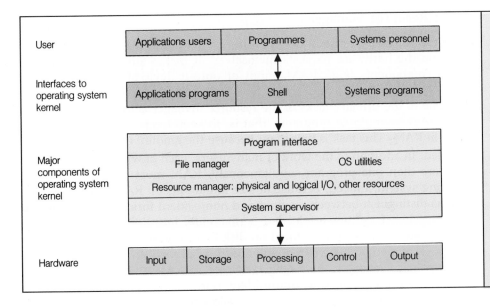

Figure 5–1 The Layers of a Computer Operating System

The System Supervisor

First and foremost, an operating system must oversee turn-taking, that is, it must schedule which software program gets control of a given computer hardware device at any particular time. Turn-taking is necessary because when the computer is running, requests for access to hardware come from different parts of many programs. For example, there could be requests to access the central processing unit or microprocessor, RAM or ROM, disk drives, video screens, or any other hardware components that might exist on a particular system. There will obviously be multiple requests on multiuser machines, where a number of different people ask the computer to perform various tasks at the same time. For example, if there is only one printer on a multiuser system and two different users request a printout at the same time, there must be some method for determining who gets his or her work printed first. In addition, concurrent requests can easily occur on a single-user system as well (e.g., disk drives may transfer data while the video screen is being updated).

Turn-taking or scheduling is enforced by the part of the operating system called the system **supervisor.** The system supervisor is aware of all the different hardware devices on the system, their speeds of operation and other characteristics, and their relative importance. It uses a programmed procedure to combine this information to determine the order in which the hardware requests are completed.

It is interesting to note that when sharing the microprocessor or central processing unit, the operating system itself becomes one of the sharers! For the operating system to work, it must be in control of the processor; however, for any user's program to run, the operating system must turn over control of the processor to the user's program. But if a user's program is running in the processor, how can the operating system ever get control back? What prevents the user currently in control from refusing to relinquish control back to the operating system? Fortunately, the processor does not have total control. There are hardware components in computer systems that can forcibly **interrupt** user programs. These interrupt mechanisms enable the operating system to regain control as needed from a user program that is using the processor.

The Resource Manager

While the supervisor schedules hardware use requests, the **resource manager** works on the hardware requests themselves. It makes sure that requests for system components (e.g., RAM, input or output devices) are of the proper form.

One of the primary tasks of the resource manager is to manage the sharing of RAM by multiple programs, that is, to keep track of which program is where in RAM. This task is important because the amount of RAM in a system is limited. In addition to the work of many users, each of whom might possibly run more than one program simultaneously, RAM must contain part of the operating system. Indeed, because of size limitations on RAM, most operating systems distinguish between resident and nonresident functions. **Resident operating system functions** are loaded permanently into RAM; **nonresident operating system functions** are stored on disk and brought into RAM only when needed. This method allows frequently used programs (the resident portion of the operating system) to be readily available in RAM, while other, less frequently used programs (the nonresident portion) are accessed only when needed (e.g., from disk storage). Besides allowing different programs to share

supervisor
The component of an operating system that controls controls turn taking, i.e., which program is using the hardware devices at any given time.

interrupt
To stop a computer process in such a way that it can be resumed. Interrupts allow the computer to put one process on hold and perform another one.

resource manager
The part of the operating system that insures hardware requests are of the proper form.

resident operating system functions
Operating system functions performed by programs that are transferred into RAM and remain there during all subsequent computer processing until the machine is turned off, e.g., for copying single files.

nonresident operating system functions
Operating system functions performed by programs that are normally stored on disk and transferred into RAM only when requested by a command input by the user, e.g., for copying entire disks.

RAM, a special type of memory management called a **virtual memory system,** is provided in some resource management programs. A virtual memory system allows the user to run programs that are too big to fit into RAM by pretending that part of the disk is really RAM. This system works slowly, but it is quite useful for the occasional large program.

The second major task of the resource manager is to translate hardware requests into the specific instructions necessary to drive the wide variety of input or output devices that may be attached to a system. For example, the specific commands required to make a printer print a line are often different for different printers. Rather than forcing a user to keep track of all of these annoying differences, the resource manager translates from a standard form of input/output request to the specific detailed request for any particular piece of hardware. The parts of the resource manager that contain instructions to make a specific piece of hardware work are called **device drivers.** Device drivers control the physical input/output and are very hardware dependent. For example, the software device driver that controls a printer made by company X may be very different from the device driver that controls a printer made by company Y. Thus, whenever a new piece of hardware is added to a system, it is often necessary to add a device driver specifically designed for that hardware to the operating system.

Above this physical level is the part of the resource manager that processes the standard input/output request forms that come from user programs. This level is called a **logical input/output interface.** It is farther away from hardware and is much less machine dependent.

■ The File Manager

The **file manager** is responsible for mass storage such as disk storage. It manages all access to system mass storage so that each user or program can utilize the variety of available hardware storage mechanisms. The file manager controls (1) the sharing of some kinds of finite storage (like hard disk storage) and (2) the sharing of the hardware that controls indefinitely large storage (like floppy disks or magnetic tape drives). The file manager also provides security so that a user can maintain total control over any data he or she has created, including the ability to specify who, if anyone, can use the data and in what way (e.g., a teacher's storage in which class grades are kept should not be accessible to students).

All access to mass system storage proceeds through the file manager, which guarantees that the storage is managed in a consistent and secure manner. Consistency begins when new storage is added to the system and the file manager **formats** the storage. Formatting a disk means placing a particular structure of sectors on the disk and setting aside a portion of the disk for the **disk allocation table,** which keeps track of where files are placed on the rest of the disk. The file manager then maintains the association of data file names with specific locations on the storage device (e.g., the track and sector numbers on a disk see figure 5-6.).

■ The Shell

Finally, the user must have some method for issuing commands to the operating system. Commands are usually issued through some form of **command language** that must be interpreted and then executed by the other components

---

virtual memory system
A system in which parts of programs not immediately needed are stored externally until needed, thus making it appear that primary storage has more memory capacity than it actually does.

device drivers
The parts of the resource manager program that control the input and output processes of particular pieces of hardware attached to the computer system, e.g., a specific printer or mouse.

logical input/output interface
The part of the resource manager that processes standard input/output requests from user programs and routes them to the appropriate hardware devices.

file manager
The part of the operating system that controls system storage.

format (initialize)
To prepare a storage disk to receive information i.e., bits are written to divide the disk into tracks and sectors and to set up an allocation table.

disk allocation table
A portion of a disk used to associate a file name with the particular set of sectors and tracks where the file contents are stored.

command language
A language consisting primarily of commands, each of which specifies a function to be executed, e.g., copying a file.

of the operating system (e.g., a command like COPY FILE1 TO FILE2 must start up the part of the file manager that makes copies of data). The part of the operating system that reads commands from the user and then activates the proper sections of the operating system to perform the command is called the shell.

■ The Kernel

The supervisor, the resource manager, and the file manager are the core of any operating system and are given a special name, the kernel of the operating system. The user accesses the programs in the kernel through the shell. When the user types in a command to save a file onto the computer disk, the supervisor gives the user a turn, that is, some processing time. During this processing time, the shell accepts the command and requests access to the appropriate portion of the operating system. The resource manager then takes this request and controls the sharing of memory and the requested operating system program. Since a file access is being performed, the file manager oversees all access to the disk to guarantee the consistency and integrity of the file system.

Computer Insights
Common Operating Systems

The concepts described in this chapter are realized in many different operating systems. The choice of operating systems for microcomputers today depends a great deal on the hardware. The most popular ones for microcomputers and minicomputers are:

1. MS-DOS by Microsoft. This operating system and minor variations of it (e.g., PC-DOS sold by IBM) are available on most IBM computers and compatibles.
2. DOS 3.3 by Apple Computer. DOS 3.3 is an extremely primitive operating system that probably would have disappeared by now if it were not for the large base of existing Apple II computers on which it runs.
3. Prodos by Apple Computer. This is the current operating system provided on the Apple II computers.
4. CP/M by Microsoft. CP/M (Control Program for Microcomputers) is one of the first operating systems for microcomputers. Rarely used today.
5. UNIX by AT&T Bell Labs. UNIX may well be the operating system of the future for microcomputers. It provides easy multitasking, made possible by ever-increasing microcomputer power. Many UNIX look-alikes have been created with names like XENIX, PRIMIX, and so on.

6. Apple Macintosh Finder and Multi Finder by Apple Computer. The graphic operating system shell of this computer is modeled after the Smalltalk language developed by the Xerox Palo Alto Research Center. With the mouse as a pointing device, it is revolutionizing the concept of user interfaces.
7. Microsoft Windows. This graphics shell operating system was designed for the more powerful IBM PC and PC-compatible computers. It is so similar to the Macintosh system that Apple Computer initiated a suit against Microsoft for copyright infringement.
8. OS/2, the operating system for the IBM PS/2 family of computers. This system is still under development. It provides a "windows" environment similar to that developed by the Microsoft Corporation.

Unfortunately, the number of existing operating systems is quite large. A user may encounter many systems not listed here, but the concepts described in this chapter and summarized in the ISPCO frame should provide a good understanding of how an operating system functions, no matter which one is used.

In the sections that follow, operating systems' common characteristics and available functions are described. Before we begin this discussion, however, we must emphasize that *although all operating systems are based on the same general concepts, the specific organization and commands for different systems may vary widely.* For example, we will discuss getting the computer to list the names of files. This general process is implemented by the commands CATALOG on an Apple IIe, "dir" on an **IBM PC,** "list" on a Honeywell-Multics, a double click of a mouse on an Apple Macintosh, and so on. Unfortunately, there is no agreement on names or commands for such a basic process. Using different computers is thus very frustrating: a user may understand all the basic concepts and may know exactly what he or she wants the computer to do but may not know the exact command.

◼ Typical Resources Managed by an Operating System

Characterizing the hardware and software resources managed by an operating system is difficult because of the ever-expanding variety of computer systems in use. As noted in Chapter 3, most computer systems include at least the following hardware resources:

1. a central processing unit or microprocessor unit that embodies the control and processing functions,
2. a variety of storage mechanisms including, as a minimum, random access read/write storage (RAM), random access read-only storage (ROM), and disk storage or magnetic tape storage,
3. a set of input and output devices such as terminals (keyboard and screen) and printers

Many other kinds of hardware can be attached to a computing system, for example, additional processors or math coprocessors; or a wide variety of hard, laser, video, and floppy disks. The operating system must know and control the capabilities of each of these physical devices, so that each individual user can have access to all or most of the machine's power.

The operating system must also be able to effectively apportion various software resources at its disposal among the different users. Again, to describe all possible types of software available on a system is not possible, but the most common configuration of software managed by an operating system will include:

1. a set of utility programs for a variety of purposes, such as keeping track of files, copying disks, formatting disks, and so forth.
2. an **editor** for preparing arbitrary character data for entry into the storage system,
3. a number of language translators for computer languages like BASIC or Pascal, and
4. application programs of a variety of types, including word processing systems, spreadsheet systems, and so on.

◼ How Is a Computer Started Up?

Starting up **(booting)** any computer system requires the setup and execution of operating system programs. However, because of the widely varying hard-

IBM PC
The initial entry of IBM into the personal computer field. Replaced by the IBM personal system PS/2 family of more powerful computers.

editor
A computer program included in most operating system software that is able to create, input, and modify the contents of files.

booting
The process of starting up a computer system, usually including the loading of an operating system into memory.

ware and software available on various large and small systems, the start-up procedures may seem quite different.

Single-User systems. Single-user systems are started up by loading the operating system from floppy or hard disk storage:

> User: Inserts any required floppy disks into the disk drives of the system and turns on electrical power for the computer and all attached devices.

operating system loading program
A short program in the ROM of a computer whose purpose is to call up the main operating system from external storage; often referred to as the "booting" or "bootstrapping" program.

> PC: Uses the **operating system loading program,** a special part of the operating system that is built into the computer's ROM. This program has only one purpose—to read the resident portion of the operating system from the disk into RAM (the resident portion of the operating system must already have been stored on the disk). After the resident programs are read in, control is turned over to the shell of the operating system, which will generally begin by printing information that identifies itself on the computer screen. It then starts its cycle of asking for, accepting, and executing commands.

The shell uses some screen symbol (prompt character) to ask for commands, for example, the greater than sign > may be used:

```
The Best Single-User Operating System Ever

Enter Command:
>_
```

The system then waits for the user to enter a command. Once the command is entered, the system executes it and asks for another.

One might wonder why starting up the computer is so complicated. Why isn't the operating system just stored completely in ROM? In principal, it could be and sometimes is. However, it is always possible to improve operating systems by adding new features or correcting any errors. If the operating system were stored in ROM, it could not be easily changed. When it is stored on disk, however, changes can easily be made by altering the disks.

Multiuser Systems. The start-up process can be significantly different on a multiuser computer system. Who controls the system with more than one user? (For example, who turns the computer power on and off?) It is clear that control of the system cannot be given to every individual user. Multiuser systems generally designate one person as the **system operator** or super-user, and that person is responsible for controlling the total system.

system operator
The person who turns a multiuser computer on or off and activates the remote access lines going to the users.

When the system operator starts up the multiuser computer, the interaction with the computer begins just as it does on a single-user system. The operating system is first loaded from disk into RAM. When it takes control, it identifies itself, and then the shell waits for commands. At this point, however: the system operator for a multiuser computer has a special responsibility, activating all of the computer's remote access lines. Once these lines are activated, other users can use the computer through their remote terminals. To make sure that the system operator can still perform any other required tasks while a crowd of other users are accessing the system, the system operator is accorded a higher status than any other user and has a special terminal called the operator's **console,** which is located near the system hardware. For most

console
The special computer terminal connected to a multiuser system through which total control over the system hardware and software can be exercised. The operator seated at the console controls all aspects of the system.

multiuser systems, there is little for the operator to do once the computer is set up, so the computer is left on at all times, even when the operator is away, so that users can access the machine.

While the system operator generally has a key to the room in which the computer is stored and can turn the power on or off, other users can access the computer only from remote sites, for example, at a computer terminal located down the hall. To control access from these remote sites, multiuser operating systems have a **login** procedure that must be performed before any other computer capability is made available to the user.

In multiuser machines, the logging in or signing on process can be critical for maintaining the security of computer storage and accounting for computer use. Through special operating system commands the computer has been given a list of who can use the system and what each legal user is allowed to do. Thus the computer must "know" who is using each remote connection in order to know what the user is allowed to do. The user's identification is generally established by typing in a user name or **ID,** possibly a project name, and a secret **password.** When the user's identity is known, the computer can provide the user with proper access to input, storage, processing, control and output facilities.

On large systems, the identification process has another purpose: billing. Computers cost a lot of money, and the identification process enables the computer to keep track of who is using the computer and, therefore, who should be paying the bills. Many systems control computer use through computer "funny money." A user is given a certain amount of computer "dollars" to spend. Each command that the computer performs for the user gobbles up part of the money. If the user runs out of money, his access to the computer is cut off. At the end of each month, the user is billed for real dollars based in some way on the expenditure of "funny" dollars.

A user of a computer system that requires a password as a means of identification needs to guard his or her password carefully, because it is similar to a signed, blank check. Possession of a user's name and password by another person gives that person access to all of the computer privileges reserved for the legitimate user. Once into the system, an unauthorized user could damage or destroy computer files, use up computer funds, and so on. To protect your computer privileges: (1) never let anyone know your password, and (2) change your password often!

A multiuser system might be started up by the following sequence of action:

Operator: Turns on computer power and activates remote access lines.

User: Turns on power at terminal or microcomputer.

Computer: Completes connection between computer and terminal.

login
Stands for *log in, log on,* or *sign on.* A startup procedure in which users use an identification code and a password to identify themselves to an operating system and establish that they have legitimate access to the system.

ID
An identification code used to identify a user to a computer.

password
A confidential code word or number that enables a user to identify himself/herself to a computer and thus gain access to a computer system. Passwords are most frequently used by operating systems but may be required by any arbitrary software system.

```
Computer: The Best Multiuser Operating System Ever
Computer: Enter Your User Name:
    User: doe, john
Computer: Enter Your Project:
    User: computer class CIS122
Computer: Enter Your Secret Password:
    User: f3loq1/34 (password wouldn't print out)
Computer: Enter Command: _
```

In this example, the computer asks for three pieces of identification to verify the legitimacy of the user. If any of the information typed in by the user does not match the system's records, the operating system will deny further access to its hardware and software. As a security measure, the operating system generally does not print out the user password as it is entered (i.e., the user presses the keys on the keyboard but nothing shows up on the screen or printer). In this way, someone looking over the user's shoulder to try to steal a password would see no visible output.

■ How Is a Computer Shut Down?

For a single-user computer, the system is generally shut down by saving any data of importance that might still reside in RAM into disk files and then turning off the power to the computer and peripherals.

On a multiuser computer, there are two types of shutdown procedures: those for the remote computer user and those for the system operator. As was true for system start-up, the shutdown process for the system operator is essentially the same as that for a single-user system. The system operator must ensure that all needed data has been saved, and then the power switches are turned off.

Remote users shutdown their work in a slightly different way for an obvious reason: when a single user on a multiuser system is finished working, that user does not turn off the computer but just turns off the remote terminal connected to the computer. The remote user must generally use a **logout** procedure to inform the operating system that he or she is leaving the system and that any further commands from the remote terminal will be given by someone else, who will need to be identified by a login or signon process. The signoff procedure frequently informs the user of the amount of computer resources used. An example of a signoff procedure might be:

logout
Stands for *log out, log off,* or *sign off.* A procedure for terminating current use of a multiuser system.

```
     User:  logout
 Computer:  The Best Multiuser Operating System Ever
 Computer:  User DoeJ Leaving
 Computer:  Total Process Time Used:  1.6   seconds
 Computer:  Total Dollar Cost:        $45.34
 Computer:  Remaining Balance:        $874.32
```

5.4

Operating System Input

Operating Systems

INPUT   STORAGE   PROCESS   CONTROL   OUTPUT

Create file • List files • Destroy file • Access file • Copy file • Rename file • File types • File hierarchy

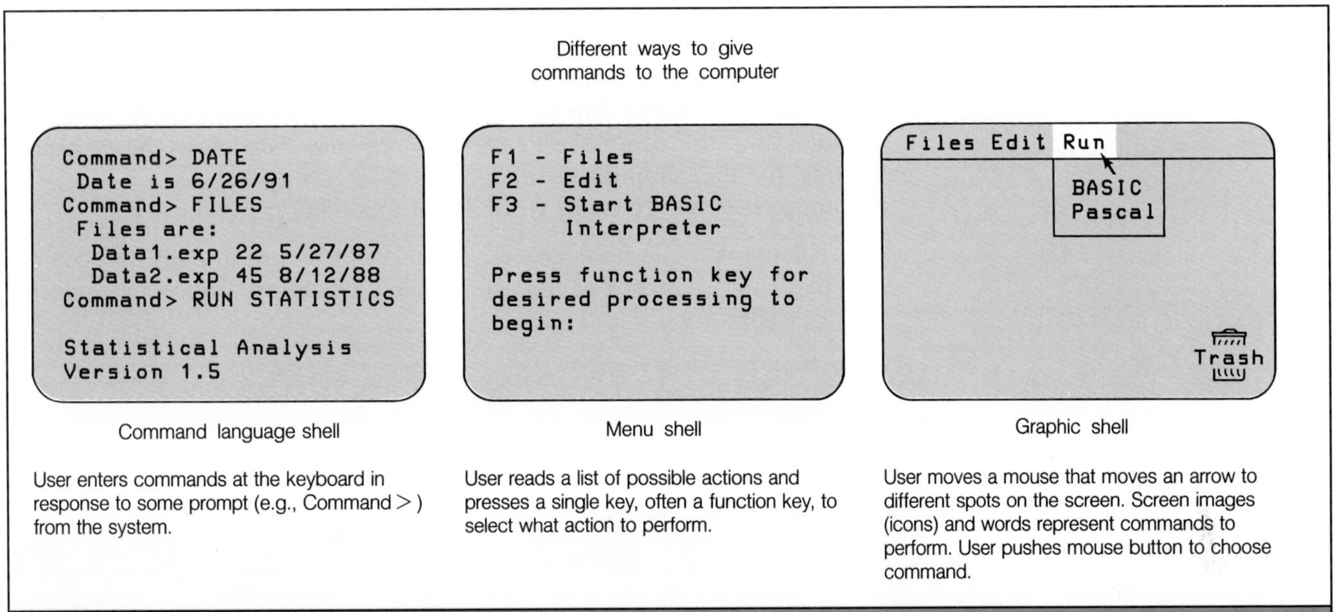

```
Different ways to give
commands to the computer

Command> DATE              F1 - Files          Files Edit Run
  Date is 6/26/91          F2 - Edit                    BASIC
Command> FILES             F3 - Start BASIC             Pascal
  Files are:                      Interpreter
    Data1.exp 22 5/27/87
    Data2.exp 45 8/12/88   Press function key for
Command> RUN STATISTICS    desired processing to
                           begin:                            Trash
Statistical Analysis
Version 1.5
```

Command language shell	Menu shell	Graphic shell
User enters commands at the keyboard in response to some prompt (e.g., Command >) from the system.	User reads a list of possible actions and presses a single key, often a function key, to select what action to perform.	User moves a mouse that moves an arrow to different spots on the screen. Screen images (icons) and words represent commands to perform. User pushes mouse button to choose command.

Figure 5–2 Three Types of Input Shells

The user's most important input to the operating system is the sequence of commands that the computer is to execute. The operating system must perform three tasks during a command input procedure:

1. ask the user for a command,
2. accept the user's specification of the desired command, and
3. perform the designated activity.

This interaction is controlled by the operating system shell, which can have one of three different forms (see Figure 5–2): a command language shell, a menu shell, or a graphic shell. The manner in which commands are requested and entered differs for each type of shell, but commands are generally executed in the same way.

■ The Command Language Shell

In the past, the command language shell was the choice of most operating systems. When the command language shell is used, interactions with the computer resemble interactions in a natural language; its commands are modeled on English. For example, if a user wanted to command the computer to type out the contents of some disk storage named mydata on the computer screen, the computer command would be quite similar to the English statement:

> English: Type out the contents of the disk file name mydata on the screen.

> Command: type mydata

Note, however, that while we can express this command in many other English sentences (Let me see what is in file mydata; I would like to view the contents of the file mydata on the computer screen; or put mydata on the screen for me.), there is only one way to express it in a command language shell. Command language shells generally provide little freedom in the manner in which commands can be expressed, and thus they can be rather traumatic for a beginning computer user to learn. The user may know exactly what task he or she wants the computer to perform but may not know the particular commands that the computer requires.

Command language shells work in the following general manner:

1. The operating system asks for a command by printing on the screen a particular sequence of characters called a prompt. Typical examples of a prompt are:

```
Enter command: _
```

and

```
> _
```

2. The user types in the command in a quasi-English form. The usual form of the command is:

operation parameter1 parameter2 . . . parameterN

operation
The act or processing specified by a computer command, e.g., copying a file.

where the specific **operation** is given first, followed by any number of words that describe the objects that the operation is to work on, for example,

```
COPY DATAFILE1 *PRINTER*
RUN PROGRAM1A
DESTROY DATAFILE4
```

These commands are entered after the system prompt:

```
Enter Command: DESTROY DATAFILE4
```

or

```
>COPY DATAFILE1 *PRINTER*
```

3. Once the command has been entered, the operating system will figure out which of its many component parts is to be used and transfer control to that part. In this way the shell can access the file manager, which can send a request to the resource manager, which would wait for the supervisor to schedule the task and have a file deleted or printed.

Command language shells have one major disadvantage and one major advantage. The disadvantage is that they are generally difficult to learn to use. There is no accepted standard for the languages of shells; they can differ in many irrelevant and annoying ways across various computer systems. Knowing one system does not enable a user to use another system. Even discovering the set of possible commands for a system can be difficult.

Once the language is learned, however, the user can perform virtually any desired action with a brevity and conciseness that are impossible with the other types of shells. The conciseness of the command languages makes them especially well suited to printed explanations; for this reason, command languages have been used in many of the examples in this textbook.

■ The Menu Shell

The **menu shell** derives its name from the menu that one might receive at a restaurant. When dining out, a restaurant patron is not expected to guess what the house offers or memorize its offerings; instead, a document is provided that gives a list of the possibilities. Similarly, a menu shell does not expect the user to remember all of the commands that the operating system can process. Instead, it presents the user with a list of possible commands and asks the user to select which command on the list is to be executed.

It can be more complicated, however. Just as a restaurant patron must choose a dressing after ordering a salad, the user of a menu shell has to specify the objects on which the command is to operate after the command itself is selected. This situation often leads to a set of **nested menus.** Nesting of menus occurs when the choice of an option in the menu must be further clarified and expanded through the use of a **submenu.** The structure of a menu shell is shown in Figure 5–3.

The structure of a menu shell allows the user to make a sequence of choices from successive menus until the action to be taken is clearly defined. The shell will then access the proper part of the operating system to carry out the request. To use a menu shell effectively, the user must know what menu options lead to what specific actions and must keep careful track of where in the nest of menus the processing is.

In the past, the menu shell was not generally favored by operating systems designers, but that is now rapidly changing. However, the menu shell is

menu shell
A user interface with an operating system or applications program that lists available commands on the screen and then allows the user to select from the list. Menus often provide submenus: the selection of one menu item results in the display of and selection from another subordinate menu.

nested menus or submenus
Menus are nested when the selection of an option is one menu must be further clarified and expanded through a selection from another menu.

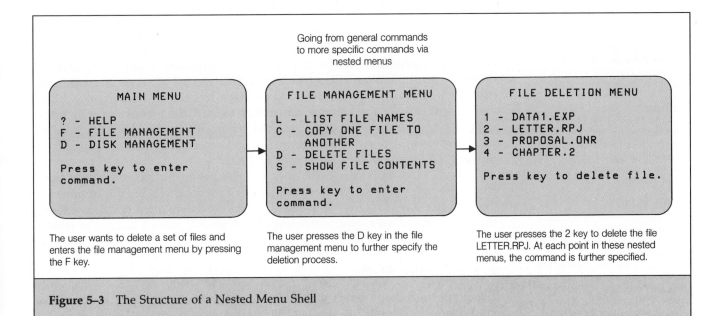

Figure 5–3 The Structure of a Nested Menu Shell

used by many, if not most, applications programs. A menu shell gives the user access to the operating system in the following way:

1. The operating system asks for a command by printing out a list of possible commands on the computer screen and providing a method by which the user can select one.
2. The user follows the selection method and specifies which command is to be executed.
3. The command is executed by having the shell call the appropriate part of the operating system.

A typical menu shell provides an interaction like:

```
The Menu Operating System
Select the command to be performed:
1 = Input a file
2 = Edit a file
3 = Copy a file
4 = Delete a file
5 = Rename a file

Enter option number:_
```

In this menu, five options are listed. Although we have not yet discussed exactly what these commands mean, it should be apparent how the user chooses a command: the user just enters a number between 1 and 5. If the user enters the number 4, a submenu that might look like the following one will appear:

```
File is to be deleted. Choose the file.
1 = Term Paper English 102
2 = Income Tax 1984
3 = Temp Data

Enter number corresponding to file:_
```

reverse video
A switch in the coloring system on a two-color video screen; the lines and spaces using one color are switched to the other color, and vice versa.

scrolling
The vertical movement of text on the display screen, up or down. Scrolling allows the user to see different parts of a document or text, since the screen is usually not large enough to hold all of the text at once.

graphic shell
A user interface with an operating system or applications program that employs a nonverbal language of icons and pull-down menus for giving commands to the computer rather than the more traditional method of typing commands at a keyboard. Graphic shells generally require a mouse or other pointing device.

There are many variations on the general idea of a menu. Instead of entering numbers, the user might be asked to type the first letter of the command or the whole command word. Or one of the commands might be highlighted on the screen in **reverse video** (black on white instead of white on black); the user then presses the up or down arrow keys to choose which item is highlighted and presses the enter or return key to start the processing. Often the entire list of options will not fit onto the screen; then, the user may need to push arrow keys to see more options, or the screen may continuously **scroll** through the list of options as the user watches.

Whatever variation is used, menu shells present a list of options from which the user must select. The advantage of menu shells for the beginner is that they are easy to learn. Conversely, menu shells are often cumbersome for the sophisticated user, who must respond to several menus instead of typing a single line command.

■ The Graphic Shell

The **graphic shell** provides a third kind of user interface that is based on graphic images instead of words. The ideas for these images were originally introduced in the programming language Smalltalk and have since been popularized by the Apple Macintosh computer, the Digital Research GEM product, Microsoft Windows, and other systems.

The purpose of a graphic operating system is to simplify the user-computer interface, that is, to make it easier for the user to tell the computer what tasks are to be performed and for the system to provide feedback as the tasks proceed. The graphic shell eliminates the need to learn the new English-like terms of a command language shell and replaces it with a nonverbal language using graphic **icons,** a mouse, and **pull-down menus** to specify the desired actions. An icon is a small graphic image that appears on the computer screen and corresponds to a real physical object. Recall from chapter 3 that a mouse is a simple pointing device for graphic operating systems. It is about the size of a deck of playing cards, has one or more buttons on it, and is connected to the computer by a cord (its tail!). The user places the mouse on the table and slides it left, right, or in any other direction. The mouse is connected to an arrow on the screen; when the mouse is moved, the arrow on the screen moves in the same direction. Pull-down menus are just another type of menu.

To see how the graphic shell works, let's look at some examples of screens that might appear when a computer with a graphic shell is used (our examples are from the Apple Macintosh computer). The screen in Figure 5–4 contains three items of interest:

1. a **menu bar** at the top (a menu bar is just a menu with the options arranged across the screen in a bar),
2. an arrow or pointer on the screen (its position is controlled by the mouse), and
3. a number of icons.

The screen in Figure 5–4 contains three major icons: two small disk shaped icons that represent disks (RAM disk and paint) and a small trash can icon (Trash) that represents a way for throwing files away.

icon
An image or picture used in graphic shells to represent some physical object in the computer system. For example, a small picture of a disk on the computer screen may be used to represent the physical disk in a disk drive.

pull-down menu
A graphic form of a submenu that is displayed below a menu bar.

menu bar
A list of options arranged across the top of the computer screen in the general shape of a bar.

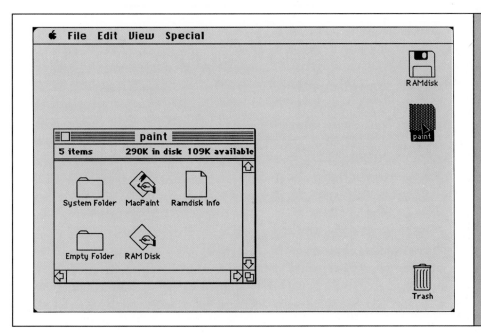

Figure 5–4 A Graphic Menu Shell

Using these elements, computer operations are specified by actions that are similar to actions that would be used with real-world objects. For example, to move a file from one disk to another, the user "goes over" to the first disk (by using the mouse to move the arrow to its picture), "picks up" the file (by pushing buttons on the mouse), "walks to" the second disk (by moving the arrow to the picture of the second disk), and "puts it down" there (again by pushing mouse buttons). It should be obvious that a graphic shell attempts to equate the operations on computer hardware to common everyday activities.

With a command language shell, the procedure for listing the names of all the files on a disk is to type a command like "dir" or "catalog." With a graphic shell, a catalog can be generated by pointing to a picture of the disk and pushing buttons on the mouse. The resulting action resembles opening a book: the system generates a picture of all files on the disk. Figure 5–4 illustrates a graphic directory of the paint disk.

Other uses of a graphic shell are just as straightforward. Across the top of the screen is a list of options (a menu). To perform an action associated with one of the options, the mouse is used to point to the option and then the button is pushed, causing a pull-down menu (a submenu) to appear on the screen. The user holds the mouse button down and moves the mouse pointer down the menu to highlight one option at a time. The button is then released when the desired option is highlighted. Figure 5–5 shows the pull-down menu for the edit option.

To delete a file from the disk, one points at the icon of the desired file, pushes the button on the mouse, and drags the mouse pointer to the trash can icon. Copying a file from one disk to another starts the same way, but the pointer is moved to the second disk drive icon instead of to the trash can icon. Renaming a file or disk is just a matter of pointing to the name on the screen and then retyping a new name. Clearly, this type of operating system seems much easier for a novice user because memorization of commands is not required. However, research has shown that it is difficult for a novice to learn a

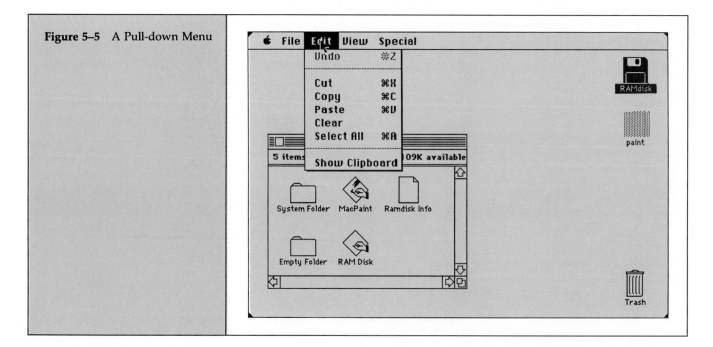

Figure 5–5 A Pull-down Menu

graphic operating system unless someone demonstrates it at least once. This is probably because the connection between the graphic movements on the screen and the underlying operating system functions is difficult to describe in print.

No matter which kind of operating system shell is used, the basic process is the same: the computer asks for a command, the user provides one, and the operating system carries out the command. Note the similarity to communication between humans. Communication through the shell uses (1) a set of terms, (2) a set of rules for combining terms into statements (like the rules of syntax), and (3) an association between the statements and the operating system's actions (meaning). All of these elements are present in any operating system shell, although the differences among operating systems with respect to terms, syntax, and meaning can be extreme.

Of course, none of these three types of approaches needs to stand alone. Many systems use both command language and menus. In future systems, users will probably have a choice of a command language, a menu, or a graphic shell, all for the same operating system kernel.

■ Input through an Editor

Input through a **file editor** or text editor is another primary method of input to a computer system. Editors are programs that are frequently encountered on all types of computers and software. For example, word processors are essentially complex editors used to input and edit documents. In an operating system, the editor allows the user to create a sequence of characters that can be stored in a file and used on the machine. There tend to be three major kinds of editors: (1) character editors, (2) line editors, and (3) screen editors. For the most part, they have evolved in the order in which they were just listed. The screen editor is becoming the standard.

A **character editor** treats the entire file as one long list of characters, no matter what they are, while a **line editor** treats the file as a set of separate lines (each line is separated from the next by some special character like a carriage return), and a **screen editor** treats the file as a visual object displayed on a computer screen (all changes in the file are immediately reflected on the screen; the screen always shows you exactly what you have). Let's see how the three types of editors might display data and accept commands:

file editor
A computer program used to write, enter, and edit files. It allows a user to place arbitrary characters in an arbitrary order.

character editor
A file editor that treats an entire file as one long string of characters.

line editor
A file editor that treats a file as a set of separate lines.

screen editor
A file editor that treats a file as a visual object displayed on the screen, where any changes are immediately reflected on the screen.

Display character editor	Command to delete first two lines:

```
This is data in the file
being edited as a
demonstration of the
differences in editors of
operating systems.
```

```
delete 1-43
No change to display.
(but the first
43 characters are
deleted from RAM)
```

line editor

```
1 This is data in the file
2 being edited as a
3 demonstration of the
4 differences in editors of
5 operating systems.
```

```
delete 1-2
No change to display.
(but lines 1-2 are
actually deleted
from RAM)
```

screen editor

This is data in the file
being edited as a
demonstration of the
differences in editors of
operating systems.

(Move cursor to beginning
of line 1 and press
control-K. Do the same for
line 2). Screen is
immediately updated.

A good screen editor is by far the editor of choice. It provides the user with the most straightforward control over the editing process.

Whatever kind of file editor is being used, the following types of commands are generally included: put data into a file, print the contents of a file onto the screen, delete data from a file, alter data in a file, find a particular phrase in a file, save the current data into a file, bring in data from a particular file, and terminate the editing process. The commands are all aimed at one thing: creating arbitrary data for placement into file storage. *Note that the commands used during editing are not operating system commands, but editing commands.*

As a simple example, consider the creation of a list of addresses using a typical line editor. The uppercase lines are edit commands typed by the user; the others are data.

```
Comp: Enter command:
  User: edit                              Operating system command
Comp: Enter Edit command:
  User: INSERT LINES                      Editor command
  User: Michael J. Spencre               Data for editor
  User: 4123 Main Street                 Data for editor
  User: Ro                                Data for editor
  User: Rochester, MI 48863              Data for editor
  User: STOP INSERT                       Editor command
Comp: Enter Edit command:
  User: PRINT                             Editor command
Comp: 1   Michael J. Spencre
Comp: 2   4123 Main Street
Comp: 3   Ro
Comp: 4   Rochester, MI 48863
Comp: Enter Edit command:
  User: DELETE LINE 3                     Editor command
Comp: Enter Edit command:
  User: ALTER LINE 1 're' TO 'er'         Editor command
Comp: Enter Edit command:
  User: PRINT                             Editor command
Comp: 1   Michael J. Spencer
Comp: 2   4123 Main Street
Comp: 4   Rochester, MI 48863
Comp: Enter Edit command:
  User: SAVE IN FILE "address"            Editor command
Comp: Data saved to 'address'
Comp: Enter Edit command:
  User: STOP                              Editor command
Comp: Enter command:
```

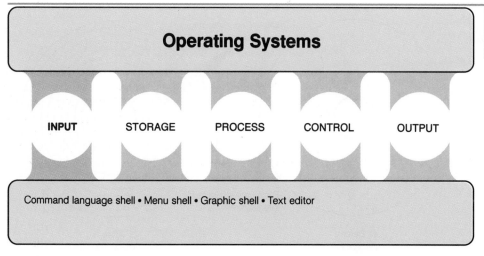

Operating Systems

INPUT   STORAGE   PROCESS   CONTROL   OUTPUT

Command language shell • Menu shell • Graphic shell • Text editor

As we examine the input, storage, processing, control, and output aspects of operating systems, it is important to realize the embedded nature of these functions, that is, an operating system capability which is primarily focused on one of the five ISPCO functions may require the use of the other four functions. For example, this section covers the operating system commands related to system storage. However, from our discussion of shells, it should be clear that the shell must ask for the storage command (output), read in the command (input), and execute it (processing); and all of this must be done in a particular order (control). Embedding of ISPCO functions inside of other ISPCO functions is a natural result of the extreme complexity of software systems and is a correct reflection of actual systems.

In this section we will discuss the operating system commands that manage storage. We will use a command language shell for all the examples, since most present operating systems are of this type and since the command language shell lends itself well to printed explanations. However, the principles we discuss can be applied to any form of operating system shell because they focus on the underlying functions of operating systems, not on the commands by which they are accessed.

■ Creating Files and Volumes

Long-term storage on a system is generally organized in a file system. If the user needs to store some data for a number of days or throughout different computer runs, a place to hold it (a **file**) must be created and given a *file name*. A file is essentially a section of a disk or tape that is given a particular name and set up by a particular user. Files may generally contain anything expressible in bits—names, addresses, computer programs, mail, and so on.

Operating systems generally provide two ways of creating files: implicitly at the request of some operating system command or explicitly at the request of the user. An explicit operating system command for file creation might be:

```
create filename
```

where users insert names of their choosing into the command, e.g., "create mydata" or "create taxrecords1980." Such a command causes the operating

file
A named portion of a disk set aside to hold data, text, commands, or programs.

file name
A sequence of characters that identifies a file. In MS-DOS, 1-8 characters for the name and 0-3 for the extension e.g. COMMAND. COM.

Figure 5–6 Disk Before and After Initialization. a. The magnetic material has no recording on it of any kind. b. Magnetic patterns have been placed on the surface. They are organized into concentric rings called tracks, which are subdivided into arcs called sectors. When data is input to the disk, the magnetic codes for 0's and 1's are recorded onto the disk. Usually, no less than a sector of data can be read from or written to disk at one time.

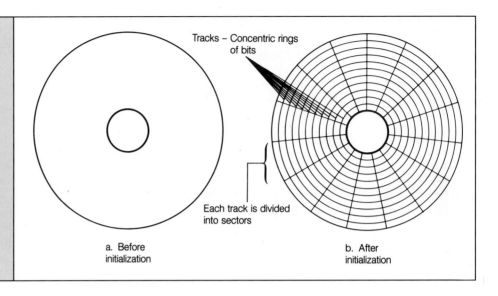

Tracks – Concentric rings of bits

Each track is divided into sectors

a. Before initialization

b. After initialization

initialization (formatting)
Preparing a disk for storing information. Bits are written on the disk to divide it into tracks and sectors and to provide space for a table that links file names to the tracks and sectors allocated to individual files.

system to invoke a particular program in its kernel. This program goes to the disk, finds a chunk of room that is not being used by anyone else, identifies that chunk of storage with the given name, and designates the owner of that file to be the user who created it.

Many variations of this type of command exist on the different operating systems. For example, some operating systems allow different file types; then the user needs to add a parameter like "filetype=type1" to the command. Other systems might require the user to give a maximum size for the file with a parameter like "maxsize=400." In general, then, a file creation command can be substantially more complicated.

For single-user computers, another step must often precede the creation of data files—**initialization** or **formatting** of disk storage. Hard disks and floppy disks come from the manufacturer with their tracks, sectors, and disk allocation tables undefined. Essentially, the formatting process writes circular tracks of bits onto the disk, divides the circular tracks into pieces called sectors, and sets aside part of the disk for a disk allocation table. This table associates a file name with the particular set of tracks and sectors where the file contents are located. The initialization process is illustrated in Figure 5–6.

There is always a specific operating system command for formatting a disk, perhaps something like:

```
format drive = a: volumename = data1
```

This command would format a disk in drive a: and give it the name data1. Note that *initializing a disk generally destroys all data that previously existed on the disk.* Many a beginning student has discovered this fact the hard way by initializing a disk that already had data on it, only to see the data irretrievably lost.

■ Getting a Listing of Existing Files

As the user creates more and more files, their precise names might be forgotten. To help the user in this situation, an operating system usually has a command for listing all the existing files on a disk; this listing is generally called a directory or a catalog. An example of such a command would be:

```
dir
```

This command asks for a directory of all files. When a directory command is given, the operating system will respond with a list of file names, and possibly other data as well, for example,

```
Files for this user are:
   Name          Type Date Created      Size
   addresses     A    10/12/88          35
   data1         R    10/01/87          12
   sortprogram   P    09/09/88          122
```

■ Destroying Files and Volumes

Complementing the ability to set aside storage for a file is the ability to release storage when a file is no longer needed. Typical commands are DELETE, ERASE, DESTROY, and PURGE, for example,

```
delete newdata
```

would destroy the file named newdata and release its storage. It is important to note that most commands of this nature do not actually destroy the data! Instead, they remove the pointers in the disk allocation table that point to the data, releasing that portion of the disk for use in other files. The implications of this fact are two: first, if a file is accidentally deleted, it can often be reconstructed if an attempt is made immediately, because the data itself has not been destroyed yet; second, if a user wishes to keep the contents of a file totally secret, deletion of the file is not adequate, since the data may be reconstructible.

Recall that on a single user system it is also possible to destroy all files on an entire volume or disk through the initialization process.

Safeguards are built in on most operating systems to reduce the likelihood of a file being accidentally destroyed. How could a file be destroyed accidentally? Perhaps the user mistyped the file name, for example, the user might have wanted to destroy a file named newdata1 but accidentally omitted the 1 and deleted newdata—the wrong file. What now? The answer depends on the operating system. Some systems require the user to reaffirm the intention to destroy a file with a message like "Are you sure you want to destroy file 'newdata'?" When such a message comes up, the user has time to rethink and answer no if an error has been made.

Accidental deletion of a file might also occur if the user believed a file was no longer needed, destroyed it, and then realized that it was still needed. What now? The answer again depends on the operating system. An operating system might provide an undelete command to allow the user to recover any file prematurely or accidentally destroyed, provided the user has not yet signed off. On large computing systems, backup copies of all files are automatically saved onto magnetic tape by the computing staff; every night, any file created or altered during the day might be automatically placed onto a magnetic tape for safety. Then if a file is destroyed, it can be recovered up to the point of the previous night by issuing some type of command like "recover."

On a microcomputer, the chances of recovering an accidentally deleted

Computer Insights
Virtual Memory

As any software works, it needs RAM for its programs and for its data, and every computer user eventually runs into the problem of limited RAM. Although the cost of memory is going down, the increase in desktop tools and memory-hungry programs makes the user want more RAM all the time.

A virtual memory system is a concept that was developed many years ago. It is a component of an operating system that allows a program to pretend that the computer has much more memory than it really does and thus allows the computer to handle programs that are too big. It does this by first dividing a program and its data into pieces typically called *pages*. It then loads into RAM as many pages of the program and its data as possible and puts the rest of the pages into auxiliary storage, for example, on a hard disk. The program begins execution, and when it needs one of the pages in the auxiliary storage, the virtual memory system moves some pages currently in RAM out onto the disk and moves the required page from the disk into the free RAM, where it can be used. The choices of what pages are kept in RAM and what pages on disk is generally determined by keeping track of how often pages are used. Whenever a new page must be retrieved from disk, the page in RAM that has been used the least recently is the one moved onto disk to make room.

Virtual memory does not come without a cost. Reading and writing pages to a disk is a slow process compared to the high speeds of RAM. For well-behaved programs where the most commonly used pages stay in RAM for extended time periods, there will be little slowdown. But for programs that rapidly refer to a large number of different pages, reading and writing from and to disk can slow the system tremendously. When this happens, the virtual memory system is said to be *thrashing*.

Virtual memory is memory that is not really there but is just simulated through software techniques. The descriptor *virtual* has been applied to many other software simulations as well. For example, a *virtual machine* is one in which one computer system pretends through software simulation that it is another computer system. As would be expected, simulations run more slowly than a computer in its native mode.

---

backup
A copy of a disk of file that is made as a safeguard against loss or damage of the original.

file permissions
A capability of many operating systems that provides selective access to the files on the system. In general, the creator of a file has the ability to do anything to a file (list it, destroy it, change its contents, and so forth) and can give other users the ability to perform some or all of these same processes on the file.

file are generally not good unless the user routinely creates his or her own **backups**. When working on a microcomputer, it is wise to make a backup copy of any important work on a second disk or tape. After every substantial segment of work, the user should save a copy of the file on the original disk and then insert a second disk or tape and save a second copy in case something goes wrong with the original.

The last concern of the file destruction process is the improper and purposeful deletion of files by another user. An operating system can prevent one user from gaining access to another user's files without explicit permission through the use of **file permissions**. Generally, users are allowed no access whatsoever to a file unless explicitly permitted by the file's owner, that is, unless the file owner gives explicit permission to read from, write into, change contents, destroy, or change permissions on a file, other users will be denied access to it.

■ Protecting Files and Giving Access to Files

There are generally a variety of operations that can be performed on a file, and there is often an explicit form of permission for each operation. The owner of a file can generally control its use through several types of permissions, including:

1. permission to know the name of a file
2. permission to read the contents of a file
3. permission to load in and execute a file containing a program without looking at its contents.

4. permission to append or add data at the end of a file without changing any existing parts
5. permission to modify or change existing parts of a file
6. permission to destroy a file
7. permission to change permissions on a file
8. permission to create a file to be owned by someone else

An example of a command to extend permission might be:

```
permit user=SmithS type=read,destroy file=newdata
```

Once this command is executed, the user SmithS will have the ability to read or destroy the file newdata. If an operating system provides such permission capability, there must also be some method for determining the existing permissions of a file. A command like the following might be used:

```
listpermissions newdata
```

In response to this command, the operating system would list all permissions associated with the designated file for example,

```
file: newdata
R W A M D P
* * * * * *  owner
*            Jones
*        * *  SmithS
```

These permissions indicate that the owner has permission to read, write, append, modify, destroy, and permit; Jones has permission to read only; SmithS has permission to read, destroy, and permit.

Files may be protected in this manner on single-user systems, but they are frequently protected by simpler schemes such as a **lock command**. If only one user is using the storage, protection is required only against accidental deletion. A command like the following one disables the ability to destroy file 1:

```
lock file1
```

If this command has been issued, the command "destroy file1" will not be accepted. If deletion of the file is really desired, the user must first restore the ability to destroy the file with a command like:

```
unlock file1
```

As we noted in the hardware chapter, volumes or disks can also be protected by placing or setting write-protect tabs on the disks; they interfere with the mechanics of the disk drive if an attempt is made to change the contents of the disk.

lock command
A command that prevents the accidental destruction of a file. An unlock command cancels this file protection.

■ Copying Files and Volumes

A user may wish to create copies of files. Copy commands generally require two pieces of information: (1) the name of the file from which the data is to be taken and (2) the name of the file into which the data should be placed. For example, a copy command might look like

```
copy newdata holddata
```

If the operating system expects the first file to be the "from" file and the second one to be the "to" file, the contents of the file newdata would be duplicated in the file called holddata.

Disks or volumes are copied by similar commands on single-user computers. For example, in the command language of one popular operating system,

```
diskcopy a: b:
```

would make the disk in drive b into an exact copy of the disk in drive a. Replacing the total contents of one disk with the contents of another disk (making a disk copy) is usually performed by a nonresident part of the operating system.

■ Renaming/Moving Files

The names of files are generally chosen to reflect something about the files' contents, for example, a name like studentgrades. Most operating systems provide a simple means of changing a file name, usually in the form of a rename or move command, for example

```
rename newdata olddata
```

Although renaming and moving sound like different concepts, on computing systems they are generally the same: one file name and its associated data are deleted from the system and a second is added with a new name but all of the same data. Often a file is renamed to make its name correspond more closely to its contents.

■ File Types

In spite of all the preceding discussion of files, we have not yet considered the structure of a file. A file is one long string of storage bits, which are usually divided into bytes, then words, and sectors. Within these constraints, many operating systems support different **file types**.

A file type is a restriction on the exact form of the data in a file. File types most frequently arise because some system or applications software requires files of a particular form; such software will not process just any file but must have one that is set up in a certain way. For the novice user, the only concern is that computer files created under one applications or system routine might not be usable by another.

Some operating systems support different file types, while other operating systems view all files as of the same type. Two common file types are **sequential** and **random files**; they differ primarily in that the data at the beginning of a sequential file is accessible much more quickly than data at the end of the file, while for a random file, all data can be accessed in approximately the same amount of time. Often there are different commands for using the two kinds of files.

The differences in files created and used by applications software is even more apparent. Data files created by one applications program are usually unique to that program and cannot be reasonably read and understood by any other program.

file type
Although all files are sequences of data, some applications systems expect their data to be organized in some special pattern. Many operating systems and applications programs define a variety of file types that are essentially specifications for some special organization. Common file types in operating systems include sequential and random files.

sequential files
A file form where the data at the beginning of a file is much more rapidly accessed than data at the end.

random files
A file form where all data in a file can be accessed at about the same speed.

UNIX
A sophisticated multiuser operating system developed by Bell Laboratories. Advanced programming skills are necessary for its full use.

MS-DOS
A popular operating system for the IBM PC and similar computers, marketed by Microsoft, Inc.

■ File Hierarchies

When a user accumulates many files on a system, it becomes difficult to keep track of the files—where they are, what they contain, and so on. To provide some organization for the user of many files, some operating systems on both mainframes (e.g., **UNIX**) and microcomputers (e.g., PC-DOS or **MS-DOS**) allow the user to create a file tree or **file hierarchy**. The basic idea is that a file can be either an ordinary file or a file directory that points to another set of files. In a system of this kind, files take on a tree structure like the one in Figure 5–7.

In hierarchical systems, there is always a root to the tree, that is, a directory that can be used to find all the the files. In Figure 5–7, the **root directory,** (named \) contains three files with the names SmithS, Jones, and Block. Each of these three files is itself a directory of files. The Jones directory contains file A and file B. The Block directory contains one file named file2, which is an ordinary file (not a directory). Directory file SmithS contains three files named file1, file2, and file3. File1 is a directory that contains one file named myfile, an ordinary file. File2 is an ordinary data file, and file3 is a directory file containing a data file, data 1.

The figure illustrates several points. First, although computer science types call this structure a tree, anyone can see that it should be called an upside-down tree. Second, any file in the tree that has branches coming out of it must be a directory. Third, one cannot tell by the name of a file whether it is a directory or an ordinary file.

Notice that there appear to be two files with the same name, file2. One might wonder if this is an error, but it is not. When file hierarchies are used, a file is described by the full *path* that one takes from the root of the tree to the file. The path can be described with an **absolute path name** or with a **relative path name.** The absolute path name starts at the root and lists every branch taken to reach the file. In our example, the path for one file goes from the root

file hierarchy or tree
An organizational scheme for files in an operating system, common to many micro, mini, and mainframe computers. In this structure, some files contain data and other files are directories that contain only the names of other files. These directories further point to more files and directories, and so on, resulting in a tree-like file organization.

root directory
The initial file directory in a file hierarchy; it points to all files in the tree, either directly or indirectly through other directories.

absolute path name
In a file hierarchy or file tree, the unambiguous name of a specific file, determined by tracing the path from the root of the tree to the file. Every file in a file tree must have a unique absolute path name.

relative path name
In a file hierarchy or file tree, the name for a specific file determined by tracing the path from wherever the user is working to the file. Since the user can work in different places at different times, relative path names change. Different files can even have identical relative path names at different times.

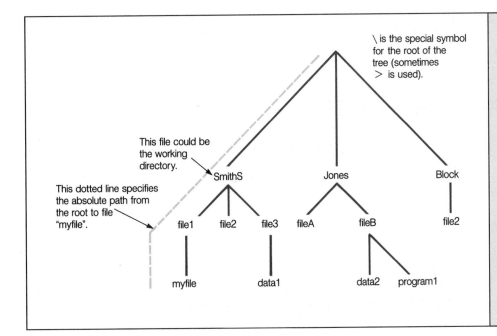

Figure 5–7 File Hierarchies. Any file is completely specified by its absolute path name. The dotted line shows the path followed to reach the file named myfile. Its name is therefore \SmithS\file1\myfile. If a working directory has been set up, say the directory SmithS, then all files are referenced from that point and the relative path name of myfile would be file1\myfile. Absolute names always begin with the root symbol (\); relative names do not.

through SmithS to file2, and the path for the second file goes from the root through Block to file2. The absolute path names for these two files are (1) \SmithS\file2 and (2) \Block\file2.

Relative path names are more convenient to use. If a user is dealing with a number of related files all within one directory, it is tiresome to continually type the entire path that leads to this directory. Hierarchical file systems, therefore, allow the user to set a default beginning for file names. If the path name of a file does not begin with the root symbol (\ in our example), it is assumed that the default beginning should be inserted at the front of the file's path name. In our example, if the default beginning for file names was \SmithS, then the file \SmithS\file2 could be referenced by just file2. Similarly, if the default beginning was \Block, the file \Block\file2 would be referenced as file2. On some systems, the default beginning for file names is called the **working directory.** In such a situation, there is a command to specify which directory in the whole tree will be the assumed directory, unless the user specifies otherwise. For example, the command:

```
change_working_directory \SmithS\f1
```

would assume that the user was "standing" on the directory \SmithS\f1, "looking" further down the tree. If a file name like mydata was given, the system assumes that the user means \SmithS\f1\mydata. The system can tell if the user is trying to use an absolute path name or a relative path name by checking the first letter of the file name used: \ indicates an absolute path name, otherwise it is relative to the current working directory.

working directory
In a file hierarchy or tree, the directory in which the user is currently working. The only purpose of a working directory is to allow the user to use short relative path names rather than longer absolute path names.

■ Other File Operations

There can be many other file operations in operating systems. For example, operating systems might include file commands for verifying the accuracy of file duplication, listing when a file was last modified or accessed, and so on. Almost any command imaginable for controlling the use of files probably exists in some operating system. Although the shells of various operating systems may make file operations seem quite different on different computers, in fact, the concepts underlying file systems are straightforward and common to all systems.

5.6

Operating System Processes

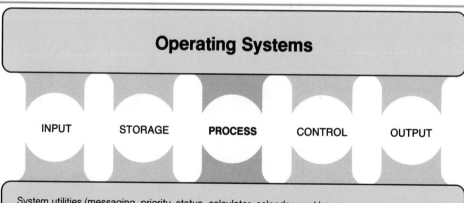

The most important processes provided by the operating system are, of course, those provided in the kernel of the system: the supervisor, the resource manager, and the file manager. These processes are activated by the wide variety of input, storage, process, control, and output functions of an operating system. In this section, we will describe those operating system functions whose main focus is processing. We will briefly describe many types of *system utilities* and programming utilities that are frequently found in computing systems. These software items, although not all part of the resident operating system, are frequently included in what is called *system software* and is viewed by many users as just an extension of the operating system. In addition, running applications software and the process of connecting a user's processing to various nonstandard input/output devices will be described.

■ Executing System Utility Programs

All operating systems come with additional nonresident software called systems programs or **systems utility programs.** These programs, although sometimes not actually considered part of the operating system, are of such universal use that they are **bundled** with the operating system software. Frequently, system utility programs include programs that implement storage commands, e.g., commands for formatting and copying disks. Such utilities have already been discussed under storage. Here, we are concerned with other systems programs; some of particular interest are described in the following paragraphs.

Message Programs   **Message commands** provide a method by which one user can leave a note for another user. On some systems, each user has an **electronic mailbox** to which messages can be sent.

Priority Programs   **Priority commands** allow the user to trade the *cost* of a computer run for the *speed* of a computer run. Users in a great hurry to get something done may be willing to pay a premium for computer time to get their jobs done rapidly. Priority commands allow the user to specify where in the spectrum of speed versus cost he or she wishes to be.

Status Programs   **Status commands** are available to monitor current system load factors such as how many users are on the system, how many tape drives are in use, how much memory is used up, and so on.

Calculator Programs   Having a calculator at hand is a convenience that anyone can appreciate. With all of the computing power available in a computer, an obvious extension is to provide a **calculator program** as a system utility.

Calendar Programs   Given the constant need to keep track of busy schedules, many computer systems provide a software **calendar program** that will keep track of one-time or repetitive events.

Sort/Merge Programs   *Sorting* data in alphabetic or numerical order is a commonly required task, as is the *merging* of two or more sorted sets of data into one large set, still retaining alphabetical or numerical order. Many operating systems provide a **sort/merge program** for these tasks. In such programs, the lines of a data file are generally treated as the unit of analysis, that is, each line is placed in order compared to the other lines.

systems utility programs
Programs often bundled with the operating system because of their frequent use, providing such commands as message, priority, status, calculator, calender, sort/merge, macro/abbreviations, and date/time. Utilities may also include programs to implement some storage commands such as disk copying and formatting.

bundled
Included in the price of the computer, as when computers are sold with software or services or both.

message commands
Commands used to transmit messages among users in multiuser systems.

electronic mailbox
A file used by electronic mail software to hold messages for a user.

priority commands
On multiuser systems, these commands enable a user to select a balance between speed and cost, within an allowed range.

status commands
On time-sharing systems, these commands enable users to determine current conditions pertaining to the computer system, such as the number of users currently logged on and number of tape drives available; then users can estimate the number of devices and amount of time available for completing their tasks.

calculator programs
An operating system utility that allows the user to carry out arithmetic operations.

calendar programs
An operating system utility that maintains scheduling for single and repetitive events.

sort/merge programs
An operating system utility that orders data in an alphabetic or numeric sequence or combines two ordered sets of data.

When using a sort or merge program, the input file(s), the output file, and the ordering need to be specified. A typical interaction with a sort/merge system might look like this:

```
sortmerge
Enter input file(s): DATA-YESTERDAY, DATA-TODAY
Enter output file:   MERGED-DATA
Enter ordering:      COLUMNS 10-15, ASCENDING
```

This sort/merge would read in two data files, DATA-YESTERDAY and DATA-TODAY, and combine them into one data file named MERGED-DATA. In this final data file, the data would be placed in ascending alphabetical order based on the entries in the 10th through 15th columns. Note that "alphabetical order", is not really an adequate description of the sorting process. Sorting generally uses a collating sequence based on the ASCII table, which defines all of the characters that the computer knows and also defines an order. Thus the computer can tell if the characters 5ab&*# comes before or after the characters #@!554, even though people cannot!

Abbreviation Programs Any long-time user of a computer develops patterns of use: certain commands are used frequently and others rarely; particular sets of commands are frequently used in the same order. In such situations, just the typing of the commands seems boringly redundant. Another common system utility called a **abbreviation** facility is designed to alleviate this situation. This facility allows one sequence of characters to stand for another. For example, a user who frequently uses the command "copy" could have the letter c (but only if it occurs as the first letter of the command line) be an abbreviation for "copy." Or a frequently used data file named 1985-ORGANIZATIONAL-DATA-BY-LOCATION could be abbreviated D1985 no matter where it occurred. The interactions to set up these abbreviations might look something like:

abbreviation
A means for combining a set of commonly used commands under one name. When that name is then given as a command, the entire set that it represents is performed.

```
abbrev
Enter input line: C
Enter translation: COPY
Beginning or all: B

Enter input line: D1985
Enter translation: 1985-ORGANIZATIONAL-DATA-BY-LOCATION
Beginning or all: A
```

Thus, the abbreviation facility replaces one set of characters with another. Macros are more sophisticated variations on this idea: the input line contains a macro name and a list of other values, and the translation consists of many lines with places to insert the given values. Macros are discussed more completely in the section on control.

Date/Time Programs Most computer systems provide a built-in clock containing the date and time, which are often useful when generating reports or dating arbitrary computer storage or output. Commands are provided for setting the date and time and for reading the date and time. On multiuser systems,

---

Computer Insights
Desktop Tools and Utilities

The increasing power of computing hardware has made possible many software innovations that were previously infeasible. Desktop tools and utilities are one such innovation. The idea behind desktop tools is relatively simple: a certain set of programs is loaded into the system's memory and kept there for the user to access whenever he or she wants, even in the middle of another program.

Most computer users are familiar with the idea of accessing the operating system through the operating system shell. Sophisticated users are further aware that many accesses are made to the operating system kernel even when an application program is running, for example, whenever a file is used. Desktop tools and utilities go one step further. They allow the user to have small utility programs (that are part of the operating system or an applications program) resident in memory and always available.

The concept of desktop utilities was first widely disseminated by the Apple Macintosh computer. The Macintosh operating system came with a number of built-in desktop utilities including a control panel for managing various computer characteristics, a simple four-function calculator, a little game to play with when a break was needed, and so on. In the middle of word processing, spreadsheeting, game playing, or whatever, the user could pause the current program and place any of the desktop tools on the "desktop" (i.e., the screen). When finished with the desktop tool, the user could remove it from the "desktop" and continue with the applications program wherever it had been interrupted.

---

only the system operator can set the date and time, but anyone can access it. Typical commands to access the date and time might be:

```
date
time
```

These commands read and output the values from the system hardware clock.

◼ Executing Applications Programs

The operating system usually provides access to a variety of applications software, which might include the well-known productivity software systems such as word processors, spreadsheet systems, data base managers, graphics systems, and so on, as well as many other varieties of professional and personal software. On multiuser systems, such software is usually stored in files on hard disk. Commands for activating the software are usually in one of two forms: either just the name of the file or the name of the file preceded by a keyword like RUN, for example,

```
run program1
```

or

```
program1
```

On personal computers, applications systems can often be booted directly at system start-up. The user just inserts the software disk into the booting disk drive and turns the machine on. The operating system loads, followed by automatic loading of the applications program. With a hard disk, the applications program is accessed from the disk directly by turning on the system and then typing in the name of the file containing the software.

◼ Executing Programming Software

When writing a program to carry out a particular process, the programmer must interact with the operating system to prepare and execute the program.

The user must create a file that contains the program, written in some programming language, and then use a language translator to transform the original program into a form that can be processed by the computer.

The program is often prepared through a file editor. While in the editor, the user types in all of the command lines for the particular language and the particular task. Once the file editing process is complete, the new program will reside in a file somewhere on the system. The translation process is then invoked, giving the operating system the name of the file with the program in it and the name of the file to which the converted program should be written, for example,

```
translate programfile newfile
```

In this case, the command "translate" would take the file that contains a program programfile and create a file named newfile that would contain a computer-processible form of the program. Once the program is converted into a form that the computer can process, a command is needed to begin its execution. In some systems, programs are explicitly invoked with a command like:

```
run finalfile
```

There are many variations of these methods, depending on both the operating system and the original language in which the program is written. When the programming process is complete, the user's program becomes a software resource available to the user and, if desired, to other people on the computer system.

■ Connecting Various Input and Output Devices

Since the operating system controls access to system input and output (I/O) hardware, clearly there must be some commands that deal with use of input and output devices. The basic English command for using an arbitrary input device is something like "take the data received by an input device and place it in a file," while the analogous command for an arbitrary output device might be "take the contents of this file and send it to the output device."

In many ways these commands make an arbitrary input or output device look like a file. Many systems provide control over arbitrary input or output devices by providing a mechanism by which such devices are attached to a special file name, for example,

```
attach *tape1* to tape drive tc04
```

and then using this special name in file manipulation commands, such as

```
copy file1 *tape1*
```

The file command programs are designed to know that the "file" is really a tape drive and act accordingly.

Of course, if there is a mechanism for attaching input/output devices to a file name, there must also be a way of disconnecting them later. For example,

```
return *tape1*
```

might be one way to inform the system that the user is no longer using the input/output device attached to the special file named *tape1*.

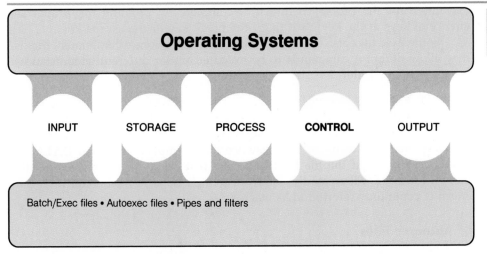

Operating Systems

INPUT   STORAGE   PROCESS   **CONTROL**   OUTPUT

Batch/Exec files • Autoexec files • Pipes and filters

The built-in sequential control of the shell is the primary control mechanism of an operating system. The operating system shell reads one command, executes it, then asks for another. No alternatives are provided, and no repetitions—just one command after another.

At least three common types of control mechanisms have been added to this basic mechanism: **batch** or **exec files, autoexec files,** and **pipes.** All of these devices allow some method of combining more than one operating system command at a time.

■ Batch/Exec Files

In the batch or exec file, a series of operating system commands are entered into a data file and executed as one unit. Once the file has been created, a special operating system command specifies that commands should be obtained from the file rather than from the user at the terminal. For example, suppose the user created the following file using the text editor of the operating system:

```
Filename: DOIT
1. delete file program1.obj
2. pascal input=program1 output=program1.obj
3. run program1.obj
```

Having created this file, the user could issue a command to have the three commands executed in sequence, for example,

```
execute doit
```

or simply:

```
doit
```

Different operating systems, of course, might have different forms for this command, but whatever the syntax, this command tells the shell to read commands from the file named doit rather than from the user. The shell still knows that the user is at the terminal, so if an error occurs in the exec file, a message is printed on the user's screen and the process is halted. In addition, the user

batch file
A file containing a list of separate commands that can all be executed in sequence by referring to the name of the file.

exec file
A batch file.

autoexec file
A special file that contains a set of commands that are to be executed whenever a computer system is booted (restarted). An autoexec file is usually used to customize a computer setup to a particular user's standard routine. The execution of an autoexec file is often invisible to the user, that is, there is no visible indication that anything is happening.

pipes
A special symbol in a command line that allows the user to direct that the output of one command be used as the input to another command.

may interrupt the process before it is complete by pressing the proper sequence of keys at the keyboard (e.g., the break key or the escape key).

Some exec files also allow the conditional execution of commands, that is, they allow different commands to be executed under different circumstances. For example, consider

```
&if exists file DATA1
&then empty DATA1
&else create DATA1
```

This sequence will result in the existence of an empty file named DATA1. It first checks to see if the file DATA1 exists. If it does, then it will empty the file, otherwise it will create the file from scratch. This powerful control mechanism is commonly referred to as macros.

■ Autoexec Files

turnkey system
An applications program whose commands are executed automatically when the computer is turned on so that the user has little more to do than "turn the key" to start the system.

The autoexec file is a special version of an exec file that is of great use in the design of **turnkey systems.** A turnkey system is a computer system that can be started up by the user with little computer knowledge: he or she just "turns the key." i.e., turns the computer on. An autoexec file usually has a predetermined name, for example, "autoexec.bat," "hello," or some other useful mnemonic. The operating system is set up so that when the computer is initially powered up, all of the commands in that special file are executed before the interaction with the user begins. Autoexec files are most frequently used to allow a word processor or other applications program to start up automatically. When the system is turned on, the operating system is loaded and given control. Before it asks the user for the first command, it checks to see if the file with the special name exists. If it exists, it should contain the commands necessary to start up the applications software, and these commands are then executed.

The use of autoexecs has one detrimental result: many users of application software are unaware that an operating system exists or is in use in any computer application.

■ Pipes

Pipes are a special method of executing a sequence of operating system commands. They first achieved popularity with the UNIX operating system but can now be found on simple microcomputer systems. Essentially, a pipe is a special symbol in a command line that allows the user to direct the output of one command to be used as the input to another command. An example of a command sequence using pipes might be:

```
directory | sort ascending | removelines /size<30/ | print
```

In this example, there are four separate commands. The first will generate a directory of all files on the system, but instead of printing the directory on the screen, it will send its output to the sorting routine. The sorting routine will put the directory in ascending alphabetical order. The output of the sorting routine, instead of appearing on the screen, will be read by a special routine that removes all lines in which a size parameter less than 30 is contained. Finally, the output of the removelines command is intercepted by the print routine and printed on the line printer instead of the screen.

This example gives the general idea of pipes: each command can be viewed as a kind of filter that somehow alters the input flow of data before outputting it to the next command.

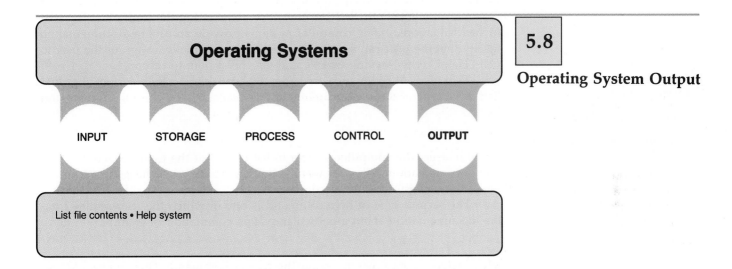

Operating Systems

INPUT   STORAGE   PROCESS   CONTROL   **OUTPUT**

List file contents • Help system

Many kinds of outputs have been described in this chapter, but the commands we will discuss in this section are those whose sole purpose is to output data stored on the computer to the user.

■ Listing the Contents of Files

There must be some mechanism for viewing the contents of a file, whatever they may be. In general, users want to list a file either at the screen or terminal where they are working or on a printer connected to the computer system. There are specific commands for each type of listing. For example, to list the contents of a file on the screen or terminal, one might enter the command:

```
type filename
```

When this command is given, the operating system retrieves the contents of the designated file and displays it on the screen. Because the contents of the file may exceed the size of the screen, most operating systems provide some way for the user to pause the automatic scrolling of the computer screen so that the file contents do not zip by too fast to read. The most common way to do this is to press the keys control-S to stop the listing and control-Q to restart it.

Another command is needed to list the contents of a file to the printer. The command for this task might be:

```
print filename
```

A useful feature on single-user systems is the ability to "log" a computer interaction. By pressing the appropriate keys on the keyboard, all text that appears on the screen will also be printed by the attached printer. The only problem with this feature is that screens and printers often have different display characteristics so that graphic images shown on a screen cannot always be shown on the printer.

■ Help and On-Line Documentation

Every user, from the most experienced and knowledgeable to the newest and most naive, will eventually have questions about using the computer. To assist in such situations, many computer systems provide an on-line documentation facility that the user can access. This facility is essentially a way for the user to yell "Help!" when having trouble and get the system to respond.

help system (on-line documentation)
A facility included in operating systems and many application programs; it displays documentation from the disk about how the system or program should be used.

Two types of commands are generally available in a **help system.** The first lists what type of **on-line documentation** is available. For example, a command like:

```
list_help
```

might instruct the computer system to list out all of the topics covered by on-line documentation. The user would use this facility when he or she does not know the names of particular commands.

The second type of help command is one in which the user requests on-line documentation about a particular system command, for example,

```
help format
```

which requests documentation on the format command. The user would use this facility when the name of the desired command is known, but its precise nature of operation is not.

On-line facilities to help the user generally go no further than these two types of commands. Computer systems in no sense "understand" what a user is trying to do and usually provide little, if any, help without an explicit request.

5.9

Operating System Summary

The operating system controls the use of system hardware and software through a system supervisor, a resource manager, and a file system. The most important point in this chapter is that the *concepts* behind operating systems are straightforward and common to all systems, but the *appearances* of the various operating systems as embodied in their shells can vary dramatically. It is a matter of necessary detail to remember that a list of file names is generated by the command CATALOG for Apple IIe, "dir" for MS-DOS, pointing at an icon and pushing the mouse button for the Macintosh, and so on.

■ The ISPCO Frame for Operating Systems

The important features of operating systems are concisely stated in the ISPCO frame, which should help the reader organize and summarize this chapter's contents.

The frame illustrates a number of points. First, note that the functions provided by operating systems deal primarily with the five functions involved in human and computer thinking, that is, the ISPCO functions.

Second, the primary functions of the operating system shell are *storage* and *input.* Most processing on a computer is done by applications software, whether it is ordinary productivity software like a word processor or very specialized software such as a research scientist might use to simulate the interactions among atoms. In general, applications software packages perform a variety of processing and control steps and output the results to the user. To the extent that operating systems are directly accessed through the shell, they tend to be used mostly for the preparation of data for the applications programs to work on, that is, for input and storage of data.

Finally, notice that the frame comments on few differences between microcomputers and mainframes—that is totally correct, because *few differences remain!* Even the advanced concept of file hierarchies for storage is routinely available on Apples and IBM PCs. There is no question that mainframe computers cost more and provide access to faster processing and a wider range of peripheral devices for many users, but the characteristics of their underlying operating systems are no longer significantly different from those of personal computers. As in the hardware chapter, the ISPCO frame includes a short description of each of the major concepts described in the chapter and a box that can be filled in with the characteristics of the user's own operating system. In this way, the reader can make a concise summary of his or her own computing system in terms of the concepts of the chapter.

Frame for Operating Systems

	Concept	Your System
ON/OFF	COMPUTER ACCESS: Access may require physical access and disks, telephone number, signon command, identifier, password, and signoff command. For this system:	Physical location and disks: Telephone number: Signon command, id, and password: Signoff command:
INPUT	COMMAND ENTRY: Commands are entered through a shell. The command prompt and the means for correcting mistakes varies across systems. For this system:	Shell type: Command prompt: Backspace: Delete line:
INPUT	TEXT EDITOR ACCESS: Input through text editors differs in start-up/shutdown commands and how files are loaded and saved from the editor. For this text editor:	Start-up command: Shutdown command: Load file command: Save file command:
INPUT	TEXT EDITOR COMMANDS: Four crucial commands for editing text are text insert, text delete, text find, and text replace. Commands for this text editor:	Text insert: Text delete: Text find: Text replace:
STORAGE	FORMAT DISK: Storage on disk for micros requires formatting new disks before use. The method for formatting a disk on this system is:	Format procedures:

STORAGE	FILENAMES: File storage in an operating system may differ in terms of legal file names. For this operating system, the file names must be:	Characters in file name: Components of file name: Length of each component: Other constraints:
STORAGE	FILE CREATE AND DESTROY: File creation may expect the user to specify file name, type, size, etcetra. File deletion may require the user to reaffirm. For this operating system:	Creation command: Deletion command:
STORAGE	DIRECTORY AND FILE LIST: Listing the directory of file names or the contents of any specific file (file list) onto the screen is performed in this operating system by:	Directory command: File list command:
STORAGE	FILE COPY AND RENAME: Copying the contents of one file into another or renaming an existing file is accomplished in this operating system by:	Copy command: Rename command:
STORAGE	FILE HIERARCHY: Files may be organized into hierarchies requiring a name separation symbol and commands for working directories. For this system:	Symbol to separate level in names: Change working directory command: View working directory command:
STORAGE	FILE PERMISSIONS: Permissions that one user gives another for file use vary, as do the commands to reference them. For this operating system:	Types of permissions: Command to list permissions: Command to set permissions: Command to change permissions:
STORAGE	FILE BACKUP: Any disk may fail, floppy or hard. Many operating systems provide specific commands to back up a disk with another. For this system:	Command to back up floppy disk: Command to back up hard disk:
PROCESS B = 2 + C	THE BIG FIVE APPLICATIONS: Operating systems give access to applications software. The big five systems are commonly available. To access them on this system:	Word processing: Spreadsheet: Data base: Communications: Graphics:
PROCESS B = 2 + C	OTHER APPLICATIONS: Other applications software may be available, some useless to a given user, some valuable. For this operating system:	Software available: Method for accessing each one:

PROCESS B = 2 + C	PROGRAMMING APPLICATIONS: Programming languages may also be available. Many varieties exist, all with different characteristics. For this operating system:	Assembly languages available: High-level languages available: Method for accessing each one:
PROCESS B = 2 + C	I/O CONNECTIONS: A processing command can connect and disconnect a variety of input/output devices to special file names. For this operating system:	Input/output connections: Connect command: Disconnect command:
CONTROL	EXEC FILES: Exec or batch files control command execution by treating a file of commands as a single unit. Special start-up auto execs may exist. For this system:	Name for exec files: Name for auto start-up exec files: Commands that can be in execs:
CONTROL	PIPES: Pipes allow the output of one command to serve as input for the next; usually a special character is placed between commands. For this system:	Special pipe symbol: Constraints on pipe use:
OUTPUT	OUTPUT TO PRINTER: There are many commands for getting a paper output of a file's contents, of a computer interaction, et cetera. On this operating system:	File print command: Log interaction command: Print screen command: Other paper print commands:
OUTPUT	HELP SYSTEM: Help systems provide access to on-line commentary, possibly with an index into all topics available. For this operating system:	Command to access help index: Command to access help:

▉ The ISPCO Scripts

While operating systems can be used in many ways, most file handling and manipulation is usually performed by programming and applications software. The operating system provides the software environment for various software and hardware systems in two different ways: (1) the operating system can be used to access software and hardware directly, or (2) hardware and software can be installed or set up for easy access. These two methods were illustrated in this chapter's case study.

These two tasks highlight the critical role of the operating system in providing a mechanism for greater hardware and software **compatibility,** that is, the ability to run different brands of software (e.g., Word Perfect versus Microsoft Word) on different hardware configurations (e.g., an IBM with an IBM printer versus an IBM clone with an Epson Printer).

The following scripts summarize these two common and important uses of operating systems.

compatibility
The ability of one device to accept and handle data that have been prepared, processed, or handled by another device, without any data conversion or code modification. Compatibility is of concern for both hardware and software.

The Script for Using Applications Software Turnkey Systems. All but a few computer users use this script. In this type of interaction, often called turnkey execution, all files necessary to use a software package have already been created and stored by someone familiar with the operating system. On a multiuser system, the user simply signs on and enters a command to run the software. On a personal computer system, the user just inserts the start-up diskette and turns on the machine. The script for using a turnkey system shows how turnkey execution works on a personal computer. The user may not even be aware that the operating system is necessary to execute the applications software.

SCRIPT FOR USING A
TURNKEY SYSTEM

1. *BACK UP THE SYSTEM DISK.* Make a copy of the turnkey system disk and put it into a safe place. For copy-protected software this may not be possible.

2. *INSERT DISK AND BOOT SYSTEM.* Insert the turnkey system disk into the computer and start the computer. The computer will first use the disk to load the operating system. It will then find the autoexec file and begin execution of the commands it contains. When the command is reached to start up the applications software, it will begin to operate.

3. *PERFORM ISPCO FUNCTIONS FOR SOFTWARE.* With the application software now in control, interact with the software to perform whatever ISPCO functions are necessary or desired.

4. *EXIT THE SYSTEM.* Terminate the applications software. For some systems this will reboot the computer while others leave the operating system shell in control.

The Script for Creating Applications Software Turnkey Systems. This script summarizes the steps necessary to install an applications program that can be run in the manner illustrated in the turnkey execution script. On multiuser machines, this task is usually performed by professionals. On personal computers, the individual user usually performs the installation. The script for turnkey system creation shows how a turnkey system is created on a personal computer.

As the script shows, new software is installed by: (1) adding the files containing the programs to the files already available to the operating system, and (2) providing a means for the operating system to execute the program files. A similar procedure is followed when adding the programs (the device drivers) needed to operate new hardware devices, e.g., a printer or a mouse.

SCRIPT FOR TURNKEY
SYSTEM CREATION

1. *ASSEMBLE THE NEEDED MATERIALS.* Creation of a turnkey system requires a blank disk, a copy of the operating system including disk formatter, and a copy of the applications software to be automatically started up.

2. *FORMAT THE DISK FOR THE TURNKEY SYSTEM.* Run the operating system disk formatter to prepare the blank disk to accept data.

3. *COPY THE OPERATING SYSTEM ONTO THE DISK.* Place a copy of the operating system onto the just initialized disk. For some

operating system, this is performed by a variation on the formatting command above, while others use a different command.

4 *COPY THE APPLICATIONS SOFTWARE ONTO THE DISK.* The applications software must reside on the same disk as the operating system, so it must now be copied onto the same disk. This may not be possible for some systems that are copy-protected.

5 *SETUP THE AUTOEXEC FILE.* Finally, the operating system autoexec file must be created or amended to issue the appropriate command to start up the applications software. This is usually done by entering the text editor, creating the desired command file, and saving the file to disk so that it will be treated as an autoexec file during start-up. For example, see the case study.

Chapter 5 Review

Expanded Objectives

The objectives listed below are an expansion of the essential chapter concepts listed at the beginning of the chapter. The review items that follow are based on these expanded objectives. If you master the objectives, you will do better on the review items and on your instructor's examination on the chapter material.

After reading the chapter, you should be able to:

1. list the individual components of an operating system and describe their purposes.
2. explain how an operating system relinquishes control to and regains control from other programs.
3. describe the processes of starting up and shutting down the operating system for both single-user and multiuser computer systems.
4. relate the capabilities of an operating system to the major ISPCO functions.
5. differentiate between command language, menu, and graphic shells.
6. differentiate between the commands intrinsic to an operating system (resident DOS) and those for additional utilities that might be included (nonresident DOS).
7. differentiate between four basic control mechanisms for operating systems: sequential control, exec files, autoexec files, and pipes.
8. describe the purposes of the major operating system utilities that are often bundled with operating systems.
9. relate major types of applications software to operating systems.
10. give the meanings of the major new terms introduced in this chapter.

Review Items

Completing this review will give you a good indication of how well you have mastered the contents of this chapter and prepare you for your instructor's test on this material. To maximize what you learn from this exercise, you should answer each question *before* looking up the answers in the appendix. The number of the corresponding expanded objective is given in parentheses following each question.

Complete the following clusters of items according to the directions heading each set.

A. *True or False.*

___ 1. The operating system acts as an interface between the user and the computer hardware and software. (1)
___ 2. Operating systems can connect networks of computer systems. (1)
___ 3. The purpose of the operating system kernel is to read user commands and to call up other programs to be executed. (1)
___ 4. One of the functions of the operating system supervisor is to allocate space in RAM for the various operations. (1)
___ 5. The operating system shell includes the file manager and the resource manager. (1)
___ 6. The utilities of an operating system are stored as external (nonresident) programs. (6,8)
___ 7. A computer mouse enables the user to bypass the keyboard for some operations. (5,10)
___ 8. In contrast to pull-down menus, which can be accessed by the user, nested menus are accessed only by the operating system kernel. (5)
___ 9. Some systems combine the characteristics of command language, graphic, and menu shells. (5)
___ 10. The file editor is the part of an operating system that enables a user to input a sequence of arbitrary characters. (8,10)
___ 11. Commands used during the editing of a file are not operating system commands. (2)
___ 12. Initializing a disk means making the data on the disk secure from unauthorized users. (4,10)
___ 13. Formatting a disk generally destroys all data previously stored on a disk. (4,9)
___ 14. The chance of recovering an accidentally

destroyed file is greater on a mainframe than on a micro. (4)

___ 15. User access to a file is controlled through file permissions. (10)

___ 16. Generally, data in files of the sequential type can be located more swiftly than data in files of the random type assuming equal size. (10)

___ 17. File hierarchies show the relative importance of particular files. (10)

___ 18. Assigning a password is synonymous with locking a file. (10)

___ 19. An electronic mailbox is part of a computer message system. (8)

___ 20. Abbreviation commands enable a user to abbreviate commonly used commands or sequences of commands. (8)

___ 21. The use of an applications program requires the program to interact with an operating system. (9)

___ 22. An undesirable result of using autoexec files is that many users remain unaware of the underlying operating system. (7)

___ 23. On-line documentation is included to provide data needed by the operating system kernel. (8)

___ 24. Help systems can be of assistance only with explicit requests from users. (8)

___ 25. On good operating systems, it is impossible for a user to accidentally destroy a computer file. (4)

___ 26. Backing up computer files is generally done automatically by system personnel on large time-sharing systems. (4)

___ 27. Different computer users may have different sets of permissions for the use of a particular file. (4)

___ 28. The various input and output devices of a computer system can be treated as if they were files by assigning each a special file name. (4)

___ 29. A computer thief cannot access a person's computer account on a time-sharing system, even if the thief has the person's name, project name, and password. (3)

___ 30. On time-sharing systems, computer "funny money" is one method of controlling the amount of resources a person uses. (3)

___ 31. When creating a computer file, the user must immediately give all of the data that will be stored in the file. (4)

___ 32. A directory is a listing of all the hardware devices available on a computing system. (4)

___ 33. An operating system controls the interaction and use of the various ISPCO hardware and software of a computing system. (1)

___ 34. Operating systems on single-user computers are generally simpler than those on time-sharing computers. (1,3)

B. *From the elements listed below, check only those that are major components of the kernel of an operating system.* (6)

___ 35. file manager
___ 36. device driver
___ 37. utility program
___ 38. resource manager

___ 39. formatter
___ 40. system supervisor

C. *For each action on the left write the letter of the component on the right that performs that action.* (1)

___ 41. initializes disks

___ 42. reads commands from the user

___ 43. manages requests for peripheral devices

___ 44. determines the order in which hardware requests are carried out

___ 45. controls the loading and execution of programs

___ 46. controls access to system storage

    a. file manager
    b. device driver
    c. system supervisor
    d. resource manager
    e. shell

D. *Match the characteristics listed on the left with the most appropriate shell on the right.* (5)

___ 47. easiest to learn for the novice

___ 48. closest to natural language

___ 49. text-oriented

___ 50. cumbersome for the sophisticated user

___ 51. eliminates the need for a user to learn keywords

___ 52. uses icons and pull-down menus

    a. graphic shell
    b. command language shell
    c. menu shell

E. *Match the characteristics listed on the left with the most appropriate editor type on the right.* (8)

___ 53. enables users to know continuously what characters have been input

___ 54. treats an entire file as one long list of characters

___ 55. is becoming the standard file editor

___ 56. provides users with the most straightforward control over the editing process

    a. character editor
    b. screen editor
    c. line editor

F. *Match the most appropriate file names in the file organization diagram on the right with the terms on the left.* (4)

___ 57. root directory file

___ 58. directory files

___ 59. possible data files

```
                Smith          Jones
               /     \        /     \
              f1     f2      f3      f4
```

G. *In the following list of commands, check only those that are part of system utility programs.* (6)

___ 60. message system commands
___ 61. status commands
___ 62. file management commands
___ 63. resource commands
___ 64. sort/merge commands

H. *Match each of the characteristics on the left with the most appropriate control mechanism on the right.* (7)

___65. control system that requires little knowledge by the user

___66. allows the user to direct the output of one command to be the input for another

___67. executes a sequence of commands without repetition or alternatives

___68. commands are obtained from a file rather than from a user

___69. used with turnkey systems

a. pipes
b. sequential
c. batch or exec
d. autoexec

I. *Match the sample operating system commands on the left with their descriptions on the right.* (3,4)

___70. SIGNON

___71. SIGNOFF

___72. CATALOG

___73. RUN PAYDATA INPUT = FILE1

___74. EDIT FILE1

___75. ATTACH FILE1 *KEYBOARD*

___76. COPY FILE1 FILE2

___77. COPY PAYFILE TO *PRINTER*

___78. LIST HELP FILEACCESS

___79. SETPERMISSION FILE = FILE1 USER = SMITH ACCESS = NONE

___80. SEND FILE1 TO SMITH

a. provides a means for altering data in a file
b. gives a list of file names
c. limits other users' access to data files
d. provides a check on a user's identity
e. transfers data from one file to another
f. transfers data from a file to an external printer
g. terminates use of a computer
h. executes a user program with a data file
i. allows an external device to be treated as a file
j. communicates with another user
k. provides access to on-line documentation
l. terminates an operating system command

PROJECTS

The best way to understand an operating system is to use it. The following are some interesting ways to investigate your own operating system.

1. TRY OUT THE ISPCO COMMANDS FOR YOUR OPERATING SYSTEM. Regardless of what operating system you are using, it will have commands that correspond to those in this chapter. Obtain the documentation for your operating system and try using it to create files, catalog files, input to files, list files, save files, and so on. Use the ISPCO frames from this chapter as a guide. You can get help from your instructor or from consultants at your college computer center. You can learn a great deal by just playing with the operating system—professionals do it all the time!

2. TRY USING THE TURNKEY USAGE SCRIPT ON YOUR OPERATING SYSTEM: Copy the first script given in this chapter, and use it as a template for executing programs on your computer. First, write down the commands for your operating system that correspond to those in the script. Second, try using those commands to run several programs with your system. A copy of the reference manual for your operating system will give an alphabetical listing of all the commands needed. If you have difficulties, ask your instructor or see a consultant at your computer center. If you have more than one computer available, try the script on several.

3. TRY THE CREATION SCRIPT ON YOUR OPERATING SYSTEM. If you're interested in a somewhat difficult project, try the following: Get a copy of the script from the text, then go to a consultant or to the reference manual for your operating system, and learn which commands correspond to those in the script. If you are working with microcomputers and can get copies of the operating system diskette and a diskette for any public domain application program, you can try using the script to create your own self-booting diskette. As an alternative, try to get your instructor or a consultant to demonstrate the installation procedure for a system like Word Perfect or Lotus 123.

Special Exercise: The Frame for Operating Systems

The ISPCO frame given earlier, provides blank spaces for the user to write down the characteristics of real computer systems. Fill in the frame for the particular system to which you have access so that the concepts of this chapter can be directly applied to your own hardware and software. This frame may also be used to compare different systems by filling in a frame for each system and contrasting the systems on a point-by-point basis.

Your primary source of information for completing this frame should be the documentation available with your software or hardware system.

As a computer user works on more and different systems, each of the boxes in this frame may require expansion into even more detailed descriptions. By then, however, the user will be sophisticated enough to make such expansions easily and without help.

6

Word Processing Software

Essential Chapter Concepts

When you finish this chapter, you should know:

- The steps involved in creating a document with a word processor.

- The differences between the entry mode of operation (when text and commands embedded in the text for later execution are entered) and the command mode of operation (in which commands are executed immediately), and the methods for shifting back and forth between the modes.

- The ISPCO functions available in the command mode of most word processors, including text delete, text move, text copy, text find, text replace, cursor movement, proportional spacing, glossary, spelling correction, windows, and operating system access.

Word Processing Software

INPUT	STORAGE	PROCESS	CONTROL	OUTPUT
Text entry	Load document	Text deletion, movement, and copy	Control for preventing mistakes	Help system
Embedded command entry	Save document	Finding and replacing text	Multifile documents	Page layout
Immediate command entry	Document directory	Using windows	Form letters	Page numbering, headers, and footers
Glossaries	Other file commands	Spelling check	Style sheets	Text size, style, and justification
		Other process functions	Macros	Positioning text on the page
				Indexes and tables of contents
				Other output functions

■ The ISPCO functions that can be embedded in the text to control the final printed document, including margins, tabs, centering, underlining, boldfacing, justification, headers, footers, page eject, keep, float, index, and table of contents.

Word processing software will not make a good writer out of a poor one. To be a good writer, one must have good ideas, clear thinking, and a good command of the language. However, word processing software will help a writer prepare a document that will make any writing appear in its best light. For example, word processing software makes editing easy and thus encourages the writer to rewrite and improve a document. Printing options generate good-looking documents that cause many students to take their writing more seriously. Storing documents by means of a word processor encourages the writer to improve his or her efficiency by including the good passages of earlier documents in new ones. This chapter will describe common word processing features, including both the technical details and the possible uses of this tool.

As is the case for all applications software, *many of the commands and procedures in word processing systems are similar to those in operating systems.* Like operating systems, word processing systems have input, storage, processing, control, and output functions; in this case, they aid in the production of printed documents.

Word processors have two modes of operations:

1. In the **text entry mode**, text and **embedded commands** are inserted into the document for later use. Alteration of the document is limited

text entry mode (or entry mode)
An operational mode in word processing systems that permits written material to be typed into the document.

embedded commands
In word processing systems, commands that are entered into a document while in the text entry mode and used to format a document (e.g., margin justification, centering, line spacing, and page numbering). These commands are always executed when the printing process begins. The results of performing the embedded commands may or may not be shown on the screen, depending upon the design of the word processor.

command mode

In word processing, a mode of operation where commands are to be immediately executed (e.g., input of files, editing and printing options).

to simply moving around the document and inserting and deleting one character at a time.

2. In the **command mode**, commands that are immediately executed are given. These commands deal with input of files, a wider variety of editing options, controlling of the printed form of the document, and other functions.

6.1

How Does a Word Processor Work?

We will begin our examination of word processing with a short vignette of a user working with a traditional word processor. Later in the text we will see how these simple ideas are implemented in the new rapidly improving word processing systems.

In this vignette, we will look in on Roberta, Polly's neice, who is at Mega University and is taking an English composition course. Her assignment is to write a short, short story (one page or less). Since Roberta has read lots of detective stories, she has some good ideas.

Case Study

Roberta sat on the couch while she worked out a draft of her story. Since she was an avid fan of the detective genre, the writing came easily.

After a few minutes of writing, Roberta was ready to start creating her document on the computer. She inserted her word processing system disk into the top drive and turned on her microcomputer. While the computer loaded the operating system and then the word processor, Roberta opened up her word processing manual to the command summary page. After a minute or so, the system was ready and Roberta's computer screen looked like:

```
The Best Word Processing System

Remember:Press the "@" key to enter the immediate command
         menus.

         Press the escape key to leave the immediate
         command menus.

         All other characters will be inserted in the
         document.

Press any key to continue.
```

Roberta needed to set up a disk to hold her short story, so she grabbed a brand new disk, inserted it into the lower drive and began to format it. First, Roberta pressed the @ key to tell the word processor that she wanted to enter a command for immediate execution, rather than text or embedded commands. The top of the screen changed to a menu for specifying immediate commands:

```
Main Menu
D(isk) P(rint) F(ind) R(eplace) B(lock) S(et)
_____

Enter Command:_
_____
```

Roberta pressed the D key because formatting was a disk operation. The disk storage menu then appeared; it allowed a number of options:

```
Disk Menu
L(oad) S(ave) D(irectory) F(ormat) R(emove)
_____

Enter Command:_
_____
```

From this storage menu, Roberta pressed an F for format. The lower disk drive hummed as the disk was formatted. The computer then repeated the main menu screen.

Roberta wanted to prepare a new document, so she pressed the escape key to leave the command mode and enter the text entry mode. Now the word processing program was ready to accept the text of her document. The screen looked like this:

```
ARROWS=cursor DEL=delete character RETURN=new paragraph
@=command prefix @?=online help .=embedded commands
_____

Page 1  Line   1  Character   1
        5   10   15   20   25   30   35   40   45   50
_
```

At the top of the screen was a simple display to remind Roberta of the more important characteristics of the word processor:

1. the use of special keys, e.g., moving the cursor with arrows keys or deleting with the key marked DEL
2. the point of insertion for new text (at the position of the cursor character, _)
3. the method for inserting embedded commands (a period as the first character in a paragraph)
4. the method for entering command mode—in this case, typing a @ followed by the command
5. the ruler that marked column numbers for Roberta's reference and convenience.

Roberta began typing in her story. As she typed, the cursor moved across the screen. Below the constant description at the top of the screen, Roberta's typing looked like this:

```
.justifycenter
The Final Case
.justifyboth

It was a stormy night. A night out of a dime
novel. Peterson _
```

Roberta used the embedded command ".justifycenter" to turn on centering. Embedded commands gave Roberta total control over how the text of the document would appear on the page. The commands would not be printed on the final document; instead, they told the word processor how to print out the rest of the document. In this case, the title that followed the ".justifycenter" command would be centered between the left and right margins when the final document was printed.

Roberta then inserted the ".justifyboth" command after the title to turn off centering and justify (make even) both edges of text. As Roberta typed, she glanced up at the screen and saw that the word "novel" was automatically moved from one line to the next when the computer discovered that it would not fit on the previous line. Roberta knew that the automatic wordwrap option of her word processor was on; it automatically advanced words to the next line so that they would not be broken apart at the boundaries of the screen.

Roberta continued typing until she made an error. She then used the DEL key to delete the erroneous letters and retyped them correctly. For example, when she typed

```
.justifycenter
The Final Case
.justifyboth

It was a stormy night. A night out of a dime
novel. Peterson tailed his suspetc_
```

she misspelled "suspect." She pressed the DEL key twice. The c and t disappeared and the cursor moved two spaces to the left. Roberta then typed ct, the correct letters, and continued with the next words from her manuscript. A few moments later the screen looked like:

```
.justifycenter
The Final Case
.justifyboth

It was a stormy night. A night out of a dime
novel. Peterson tailed his suspect to ann
restaurant._
```

"Whoops," Roberta said, noticing that she had typed "ann" instead of "an" and left out the word "uptown" from her original handwritten document. Roberta could have pressed the DEL key a number of times to erase the word "restaurant," then corrected the word "ann," and finally entered "uptown" and retyped "restaurant," but she decided to use another method. She changed the position of the cursor by pressing the up-arrow key once and the right-arrow key 30 times until the cursor was positioned after the second n in the word "ann".

```
.justifycenter
The Final Case
.justifyboth

It was a stormy night. A night out of a dime
novel. Peterson tailed his suspect to ann_
restaurant.
```

Roberta pressed the DEL key once to delete the second n and then typed "uptown." The word processor automatically moved all of the words to the right and down to the next line to make room for the newly inserted word. Roberta moved the cursor back to the end of the document using the arrow keys and continued to type:

```
.justifycenter
The Final Case
.justifyboth

It was a stormy night. A night out of a dime
novel. Peterson tailed his suspect to an
uptown restaurant. The suspect was_
```

Roberta continued entering more text in this way until the first part of the story was complete.

Roberta ran out of time—she had a class, so she decided to finish later. Leaving the cursor where it was, she pressed the @ key and then a D to reference the disk options. The screen displayed the menu of storage options:

```
Disk Menu
L(oad) S(ave) D(irectory) F(ormat) R(emove)
_____

Enter command:_
_____
```

Roberta checked the menu and chose to save the data to a file. She pressed the S key and then entered a name to identify the document, "English.LastCase." The data disk hummed a while and then the system responded:

```
File 'English.LastCase' has been saved.
```

Roberta shut down the system and headed for her class. After class, Roberta returned to finish her story. She wrote a draft of the conclusion and jotted down some ideas for editing the existing text. Then she booted up her word processor and inserted the data disk for English 101 in drive 2. She called up the disk menu and received the same storage options shown earlier. This time Roberta typed DIRECTORY to ask for the names of the documents on the disk, since she could not remember exactly what name she had used. The system responded with a list:

```
Document List

Name                  Size    Date
English.LastCase      425     9/12
Total storage         425
```

The directory command gave her a list with only one element in it, the file she had created last time. Roberta saw that its name was "English.LastCase," so she then issued the command to load the "English.LastCase" document. Roberta pressed the escape key, and the word processor returned to text entry mode with the same screen it had shown when she had stopped earlier:

```
.justifycenter
The Final Case
.justifyboth

It was a stormy night. A night out of a dime
novel. Peterson tailed his suspect to an
uptown restaurant. The suspect was seated at
a table near a big fireplace. The flames lent
a warm glow to the suspect's face and to the
sumptuous meal he was enjoying. Peterson's wet
trenchcoat felt as heavy as a broken heart._
```

Roberta wanted to replace the word "suspect" with the word "subject" throughout the story. From the main menu, she pressed an R to use a replace command, which replaces one string of text with another. The system asked Roberta for the existing text and Roberta typed it in:

```
Enter current text. Press 'return' when done.
?suspect_
```

After Roberta had entered the word "suspect," the system asked for the string of characters to be put in its place:

```
Enter replacement text. Press 'return' when done.
?subject_
```

Finally, the word processor asked how the replacement should be done:

```
How should replacement be done?
1 Replace all occurrences without asking
2 Replace all occurrences but ask before each one
3 Replace one occurrence only

Enter option: 1_
```

Roberta entered a 1, so the replace command found all instances of "suspect" and replaced it with "subject."

After returning to text entry mode by hitting the escape key, Roberta decided to add a girlfriend for the suspect (now the subject). Moving the cursor to a position after the sentence "The subject was seated at a table near a big fireplace," Roberta typed the additional phrase "with a beautiful girl." As she typed, the old text was automatically shifted to the right and down to accommodate the new text.

Roberta completed her editing and began to add the conclusion to the story. She began a new paragraph by pressing the return key and began typing.

```
It was a stormy night. A night out of a dime
novel. Peterson tailed his subject to an
uptown restaurant. The subject was seated at
a table near a big fireplace with a beautiful
girl. The flames lent a warm glow to the
subject's face and to the sumptuous meal he
was enjoying. Peterson's wet trenchcoat felt
as heavy as a broken heart.

Peterson took stock. He was miserable; as
miserable as a losing gambler._
```

The screen could no longer show Roberta's entire story at one time because it was too large. As Roberta typed new words at the bottom of the screen, lines seemed to disappear off the top of the screen. The lines were not really disappearing, though—they were stored in RAM and were merely being removed from the display.

Roberta continued working until she was finished with the story. The screen at that point looked like:

```
Peterson didn't much care.
.justifycenter
The End
.justifyboth
```

Roberta decided that she wanted to look back at the beginning of the story, so she pressed the up-arrow key a number of times. As the new lines of the story were retrieved from RAM and placed on the top of the screen, the lines at the bottom of the story were removed from the screen. Essentially, the screen was a window that could scroll up and down and look at any part of the story. Roberta scrolled up to the beginning of her story—it was just as she had left it:

```
.justifycenter
The Final Case
.justifyboth

It was a stormy night. A night out of a dime
novel. Peterson tailed his subject to an
uptown restaurant. The subject was seated at
a table near a big fireplace with a beautiful
girl. The flames lent a warm glow to the
subject's face and to the sumptuous meal he
was enjoying. Peterson's wet trenchcoat felt
as heavy as a broken heart.
```

The story was complete. Roberta saved the document to disk, but this time she did not need to give the name of the document. The word processor remembered and used the name of the document Roberta had loaded. Roberta knew that the word processor would remove the old version of the document and replace it with the new one.

With the document saved, Roberta entered the print menu from the main menu. The top of the screen listed many of the printing options available to Roberta through her word processor:

```
Print Menu
L(ayout) P(rinterspecs) S(tart)

_____

Enter command:_
```

Roberta entered the layout command and a description of the page on which the document would be printed was displayed:

```
Initial Justification:     Both
Top Margin (inches):       1
Bottom Margin (inches):    1
Left Margin (inches):      0.5
Right Margin (inches):     0.5
Lines per page:            66
Spacing:                   Double

_____

Enter Command:_
_____
```

Everything looked okay, except that the margins were a bit narrow. Roberta typed in:

    Left Margin=1
    Right Margin=1

so that the margins would be more acceptable.

Roberta knew that the printer specifications had been set up properly during earlier work with her word processor. Since the printer hadn't changed, there was no reason to look at or change them. With everything ready, Roberta issued the start command from the print menu. The document that she had created was sent to the printer attached to her micro. The story would now be printed for the first time. It looked like:

```
                          The Final Case

       It  was  a  stormy  night.   A  night  out  of  a
    dime  novel.   Peterson  tailed  the  subject  to  an
    uptown  restaurant.   The  subject  was  seated  at  a
    table  near  a  big  fireplace  with  a  beautiful  girl.
    The  flames  lent  a  warm  glow  to  the  subject's
    face  and  to  the  sumptuous  meal  he  was  enjoying.
    Peterson's  wet  trenchcoat  felt  as  heavy  as  a
    broken  heart.

       Peterson  took  stock.   He  was  miserable;  as
    miserable  as  a  losing  gambler.   "Private
    investigation  stinks!"  he  shouted.   Taking  off
    his  black  fedora,  he  threw  it  on  the  wet
    concrete  and  jumped  up  and  down  on  it.   Then,
    he  left  to  quit  his  job.   He  never  did  find  out
    how  the  case  turned  out.

       He  didn't  much  care.

                          The End
```

Roberta put the paper with her school books and shut down her computer.

As Roberta created her English paper, she went through a common word processing procedure. She entered text in the text entry mode of the word processor and switched to command mode to save the document to disk. Later, she used command mode to retrieve and edit the document, switched back to text entry mode to enter more new text, and finally switched back to command mode for the final saving and printing of the document. This sequence is all that most users ever need to use with word processors. The only remaining task is to learn the range of commands available in word processing systems.

6.2

Using Word Processing Software

Our case study illustrates a number of concepts that are important to an adequate understanding of word processing systems. The first one we shall consider is the difference between text and commands within a document.

■ Text and Embedded Commands

When typing a document by hand, a number of decisions are made as the text is typed—decisions about such things as the size of the margins, whether to underline a title, whether to capitalize headings, whether to start a new page when a new chapter begins, how to handle footnotes, whether to put the page number at the top of the page or the bottom, and how to format the table of contents. The typist must make all these decisions about the layout of the document, regardless of its contents. A word processor is designed to assist with all of these decisions, and it should give its users a wide range of choices and even allow them to change their choices as they proceed. These decisions have nothing to do with the intended content of the document.

To give the user this flexibility in creating a document, word processing systems require the entry of both text (the content) and embedded commands (the formatting decisions). Since the formatting decisions may be different for

Computer Insights
The Genesis of Word Processing

The mechanical typewriter, the precursor of electronic word processing, was first successfully manufactured in this country in 1873 by E. Remington and Sons, Gunmakers. Its major advantage was that it produced neat, consistently legible output and required a limited amount of skill. By the middle of the twentieth century, the typewriter had been adopted as a regular office fixture. The major problem associated with the typewriter was that changes in a document usually required retyping it.

The electric typewriter that followed operated very much like its predecessor. Once a key was struck, the letter immediately appeared on the paper. Neither the mechanical nor the electric typewriter provided readily for the correction of errors or for making changes in documents.

The Flexowriter, an electric typewriter with a paper tape punch and reader attached, appeared later. As a document was typed, an impulse was also sent to the tape punch to code what was being typed onto a paper tape. If an error was made, the tape could be corrected, and when the typing was completed, the tape could be run through the tape reader to produce a perfect copy. Paragraphs within the document could be deleted or repositioned by physically cutting and rejoining elements of the punched paper tape in the desired sequence. This onerous procedure, coupled with the fact that new information could not be put on a paper tape once it was punched, still left much to be desired.

It was not until 1964, when IBM put its magnetic tape Selectric typewriter on the market, that pervasive use of wordprocessing began. With this machine, form letters and frequently used paragraphs could be typed once and recorded on magnetic tape. These forms or paragraphs could be called up as desired and modified for repetitive letters or reports. Following the introduction of the Selectric, various manufacturers brought out similar devices using magnetic cards, cassettes, and internal belts as recording media.

A confluence of developments, including video display terminals, computer chips, and inexpensive printers, complemented IBM's introduction of the floppy disk in the mid-1970s. The floppy disk permitted individuals to load small operating systems and applications programs into affordable microcomputers, and documents, of course, could also be stored on these disks. Throughout the eighties, these word processing systems have been steadily improved to the point where they have become fixtures in most offices and in an increasing number of homes.

---

different parts of the text, word processing systems must allow the user to intersperse embedded commands throughout the text. Then there must also be some way for the computer to tell the difference between text and commands—for example, is the sentence "Text should be centered" a formatting command to the word processor or a sentence that is supposed to appear in the final document? In general, text and embedded commands are distinguished by using a special form for commands. Anything that is in this special form is considered an embedded command, and everything else is considered text to be printed in the final document.

In the simplest of word processing systems, embedded commands are entered just like text but are identified with some type of special symbol or symbols. In some word processing systems, any line that begins with a period (.) is an embedded command, while any that does not is text. In these systems, the embedded commands and text are entered directly in text entry mode. As an example of this intermixing of commands and text, consider the following:

Source Text Page	Final Text Page

```
This line of text shows
how a period can be
used to identify an
embedded command:
.indent 2
Everything after this
point will be indented
2 spaces.
```

```
This line of text shows
how  a  period  can  be
used  to  identify  an
embedded command:
    Everything after this
    point    will    be
    indented 2 spaces.
```

Note first how the command line ".indent 2" is inserted in the source text along with the rest of the text. When the final document is created, the command ".indent 2" will not be printed, but the text from that point on will be indented an extra two spaces before printing.

Using a period to introduce embedded commands is far from universal. Some systems may use pairs of symbols like ⟨ and ⟩ to designate embedded commands. Anything that comes between the pair of symbols is a command, and everything else is text, for example:

<table>
<tr><td align="center">Source Text Page</td><td align="center">Final Text Page</td></tr>
</table>

```
This is a line of text
that will <capitalize
on>put some things in
<capitalize off>
uppercase
```

```
This is a line of
text that will PUT
SOME THINGS IN
uppercase.
```

In this format, any command can be embedded anywhere in the text by placing them between symbols ⟨ and ⟩.

In most modern word processing systems such as Word Perfect or WORD, the method for entering embedded commands is slightly more complicated: *an embedded command is entered into the text by entering a nonprinting character from the computer's extended alphabet, the ASCII table.* The common choices of characters are the ASCII character codes that correspond to the 10 or 12 function keys (F1, F2, F3, . . .) or the control characters accessed by holding down the control key while pressing ordinary alphabetic characters (control-A, control-B, control-C, . . .). For example, the code control-C might mean begin centering, while the code control-L might mean left-justify. Since these codes have no printing symbol associated with them, their presence indicates a command.

The use of nonprinting ASCII codes for commands, however, presents one problem: since the commands have no printed form, how can the user see where the commands are in the text? This problem is solved by using two different display modes. The ordinary display will be as close as possible to the final output on the printer, for example,

Source Text Page:
Ordinary Mode

```
This is a line of
text that will PUT
SOME THINGS IN
uppercase.
```

In this display the embedded commands are invisible, but their results can be seen. In the alternative mode of screen display, all embedded commands are displayed. By issuing the proper command, the above display would be replaced by:

Source Text Page:
Display Commands Mode

```
This is a line of text
that will <capitalize
on>put some things in
<capitalize off>
uppercase
```

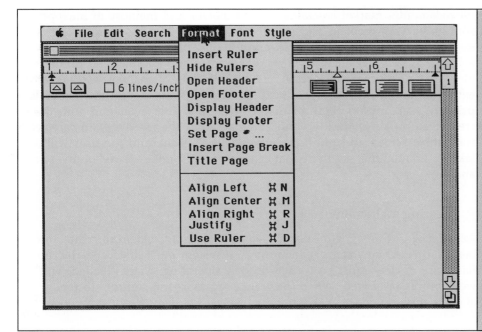

Figure 6–1 Graphic Shell for Word Processing. This example, derived from the Apple Macintosh program named McWrite, shows the essence of a graphic shell for word processing. Note the menu bar across the top, which gives the main menu for the system. The arrow which is controlled by moving the mouse, points to the Format command. When the mouse button is pushed, a submenu containing many formatting options appears.

Systems that work in this way are becoming the most common variety of word processor. In the ordinary display mode, the user gets a good picture of what the final text will look like, yet the embedded commands are accessible for viewing whenever necessary.

As a final example, let's look at embedded command entry using a graphics operating system and a mouse (Figure 6–1). Embedded commands are provided at the top of the screen on pull-down menus that are accessed by the mouse.

No matter what method is used, *all word processing systems must provide a means of intermixing the textual content of the document with the formatting commands that control its final printed form.*

■ WYSIWYG Word Processors

Another closely related issue is the need to see on the computer screen exactly what the final printed document will look like. Since the goal of word processing is a printed page, it is reasonable that the user wants to see the final form of the document on the computer screen.

Unfortunately, with current technology, *the screen at which a user enters a document may have different display characteristics than the printer on which the final paper document will be printed.* For example, it is not uncommon for word processors on microcomputers to use a screen that is incapable of showing an underlined character, yet the system may have a printer that underlines characters with ease. Then the final form of the document can be seen only on the printout, not on the computer screen. Conversely, a screen may be capable of displaying graphic images in many colors yet be connected to a printer that can print only black on white and cannot print graphic images; in this case, the color graphic images on the computer screen cannot be printed in the user's document.

These problems exist because in the past there had not been a push from users for manufacturers to remedy the situation. As the competition within the microcomputer market increases and the power and memory of microprocessors grow, this problem will surely be resolved. Many systems are already designed with totally compatible printers and display screens. A hardware/software system that includes a word processor and a screen and printer with identical display characteristics is called a WYSIWYG (*what you see is what you get*, pronounced "wiz-ee-wig") word processing system. With the ever-falling price of laser printers, both black-and-white and full color, and with the increased emphasis on desktop publishing systems, the trend toward completely compatible screen and printing devices will continue and the user will soon take for granted that anything that can be printed can be viewed on the screen, and vice versa.

Creating a Document

As we saw in the vignette, using a word processing system to create a document can take many steps. Obviously, the system must first be started up: all hardware devices must be turned on, the operating system loaded, and the word processor started. When the word processor is in control, document creation begins.

Initial Entry of Text: Text Entry Mode.   The first step in the creation of a document is the entry of original text and commands. As the text is entered at the computer keyboard, it appears on the computer's video screen and is stored in the computer's RAM.

In the initial part of document creation, the meaning of the text is most important (one nice feature of word processing is that the correctness of spelling, capitalization, and grammar can be checked later). Only minor editing is done during the text entry process. For example, if a word is mistyped, the author can press a key that deletes the last character and erase backwards until the typing error is reached. The author can then repair the problem and continue on with more writing. If the details of the format are known during text entry, the appropriate commands (e.g., skip to the top of a new page for a new chapter) can be embedded in the text.

Automatic wordwrap is a feature of word processors that makes text entry easier because the typist need not use the carriage return to move from one line to the next. When one line is filled up, the word processor automatically moves to the next line without any explicit user command. In general, the return key is used only at the end of a paragraph.

Thus, the entry of original text is a straightforward process much like ordinary typing. The words may be entered from the author's head or from a handwritten document. Only minor typing corrections are made initially as the text and commands are entered.

Saving the Document: Command Mode.   Since most documents are not written at a single sitting, there has to be a procedure for stopping and starting again later, that is, there must be some way to tell the computer, "I am done for now. Save my data to disk. I'll take up where I left off next time I start work."

Thus every word processing system has a command for saving the current text into a system file; the word processing system must access the operating system's kernel to create room for a file and save the current document into it. Notice that saving a document to disk is accomplished by a command that is not part of the text in any way. We do not want to put an embedded command that says "save the text" into the text. Instead, we want to say, "take all of the text and embedded commands that I have entered so far and save them." Such a command is made through the word processing system's second mode of operation, the command mode.

During entry mode, the author enters text and embedded commands into the document. The embedded commands generally focus on how the document is to be printed. During command mode, however, commands are not embedded in the document but are executed immediately. Commands in the command mode generally focus on (1) sophisticated editing, (2) control of files for saving and retrieving documents, (3) starting up or stopping a printout, and (4) interactions between separate documents.

Retrieving the Document: Command Mode.   When the author is ready to resume work on a document that has been saved, the word processor is started up, and in command mode, the author enters a command that says "go and get that document that I was working on yesterday." This *load* command must again access the operating system kernel, this time to read the file created during the previous session. Since an author might be working on several documents simultaneously, the load command always requires the user to specify which document is to be loaded.

Adding to the Document: Text Entry Mode.   Once the appropriate document has been located and loaded, the author is ready to enter more text. Since the author might want to enter new text at any position in the document, word processors provide a simple means for controlling the position of new text entry: new text is always added at the **cursor**, which is usually a flashing symbol that is easily moved. The author moves the cursor to the position in the document for text insertion and begins to type. Usually the user positions the cursor at the end of the previous day's work and continues to enter new text.

cursor
A small blinking box or other character on a computer screen that indicates where the next character typed will appear.

Editing the Document: Command Mode.   Once the rough draft of the document is entered, the user can be more concerned with two other things: polishing the text of the document and selecting a format that will give it a pleasing printed appearance. The user can change text through the text entry mode by positioning the cursor and inserting or deleting and retyping. In command mode, powerful editing tasks can operate on blocks of text. The user can select a block of text (an arbitrary group of consecutive characters) and can then delete, copy, move, center, underline, or boldface the entire block as one unit. There are many formatting options to choose from, but the most common ones are used to set the size of the left, right, top, and bottom margins, to control page numbering, to center titles, and other simple tasks.

Saving and Printing a Document: Command Mode.   When the initial draft of a document has been completed, the author first gives the command to save all of the new work that has been entered and the command to print out the document. The word processor reads through the characters in the text before it sends them to the printer, and it checks to see if any characters happen to be commands. If they are, the command is executed (maybe it changes the margins or skips to the top of a new page), but the characters of the command are not sent to the printer. The characters that are not commands are text and are sent directly to the printer.

Once the author has a printed draft, the real advantages of the word processing system come into play. For example, the user might decide to throw out two or three paragraphs that do not fit, move one section of the document to a new position, copy part of the document to a second location, enter special commands to format the text, tell the system to combine the contents of four separate files, and so on. Major revision and formatting decisions can now be made at the word processor keyboard using the powerful editing, formatting, printing, and file manipulation capabilities of the command mode. Once the editing is finished and the computer file contains a corrected version of the document, the printer is engaged and a final copy is printed.

Computer Insights
Common Word Processing Systems

The major word processing concepts described in this chapter are realized in many different software systems. The most popular word processing systems on microcomputers today include the following:

Wordstar by MicroPro

This was one of the first powerful word processing systems available on an IBM PC and PC compatibles. It is widely used throughout the world. Indeed, many word processing systems mimicked the command structure of Wordstar so that trained word processors did not have to be retrained to switch to a new system. The major problem has been the complexity and confusion of the Wordstar menus.

Multimate by Multimate International

Another word processor for the IBM PC, Multimate copies the command structure of a dedicated word processor made by Wang. Because of the large number of secretarial personnel who know how to use Wang equipment, Multimate provides an easy migration from the dedicated, single-purpose Wangs, to the general-purpose IBM PC.

Word Perfect by the Word Perfect Corporation

One of the major additions to the IBM PC and PC compatibles word processing world, Word Perfect provides an extremely powerful easy-to-use word processor with good on-line help. Now also available on the Apple Macintosh, Word Perfect is one of the two most widely used word processors for personal computers.

Word by Microsoft

One of the few word processing systems available on both the IBM PC and the Apple Macintosh line, Word is well known for its ability to handle arbitrary text fonts and intermix them on the page. Word is the other most widely used word processor, noted for its excellent menuing capabilities.

McWrite by Apple

The Apple Macintosh line of computers was originally packaged with McWrite, a word processing system from Apple. The real power of McWrite was that it allowed the user to take arbitrary graphic images generated by the McPaint software system and embed them into McWrite documents. This capability has been copied in many other word processors.

AppleWriter/Appleworks by Apple

Because of the longstanding popularity of the Apple II microcomputer, Applewriter and later Appleworks have been mainstay word processors for thousands of people. Although not as powerful as most word processing systems (due in part to the lack of power of the Apple II), these systems are adequate for the creation of substantial bodies of text.

Many other word processing systems exist. We do not want to promote those we have mentioned or demote those we have not. A variety of word processing systems with varying degrees of power is available for each type of hardware. The beginning user or the expert can generally find a system appropriate to his or her needs. Reviews of word processors are frequently published in *Info World*, *Byte* magazine, and other periodicals.

Shutting Down the Word Processor. When the user tells the word processor to terminate the session (with a command like QUIT or STOP), the system should check to make sure that all data entered by the user has been saved to disk for permanent storage. If it has, then the system can reasonably return control to the operating system. If all data has not been saved to disk, the word processor should double-check with a statement like CURRENT DOCUMENT HAS NOT BEEN SAVED. DO YOU REALLY WANT TO STOP? and wait for a confirmation before stopping. Such safety checks against accidental loss of work are an absolute requirement for a word processing system. A system without these safety checks built in should be avoided. Of course, the user could always just shut off the power without realizing that completed work had not been saved—in this case, the work would be lost, because the computer cannot do everything.

The Organization of a Word Processor

In all of these interactions with a word processor, it is clear that in many ways it is similar to an operating system. After all, doesn't the word processor just take in commands, execute them, and ask for more? Indeed, *the concept of a kernel of critical functions accessed through a shell applies to any applications software.* Every word processor has a kernel of critical word processing functions that is accessed through a word processing shell. These critical functions include the entry and editing of text, the elemental formatting and printing commands, and access to the underlying operating system kernel for file manipulation. The word processing shell may be a command language, a menu, or a graphic shell. Just as we considered the organization of an operating system in terms of layers (chapter 5), we can visualize a word processing system as a number of interacting layers (see Figure 6–2).

In addition to the word processing kernel, word processing utility functions provide access to a wide variety of other capabilities like counting the number of words in a document, checking spelling, generating tables of contents or indexes, and so on. These utilities are usually stored on disk until needed.

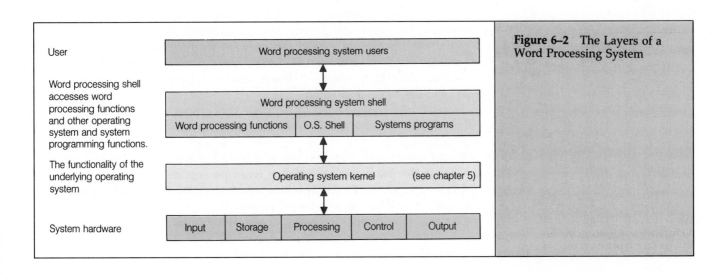

Figure 6–2 The Layers of a Word Processing System

6.3

Word Processing Input

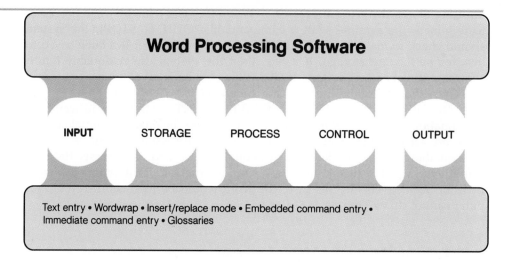

Word Processing Software

INPUT   STORAGE   PROCESS   CONTROL   OUTPUT

Text entry • Wordwrap • Insert/replace mode • Embedded command entry •
Immediate command entry • Glossaries

A word processing system has two different input modes. Text and embedded formatting commands are input in text entry mode, and immediate commands are input in command mode.

■ Text Input

First and foremost, a word processing system must support the entry of text. It should therefore allow the use of any legitimate printable character, including all upper- and lower case letters, all digits, all punctuation marks, special symbols, and so on. Although it has not always been true in the past, all computer manufacturers and word processor designers now make certain that this capability is included.

If the characters on a typical typewriter were the only ones required in human text, there would be few differences among word processors. But even for the simple task of text entry, differences do exist. Is there a method for entering special symbols like those of the Russian alphabet, the Greek alphabet, algebra, or integral calculus? Can superscripted or subscripted symbols be entered? How can underlined or boldfaced characters be entered? Most word processors today allow boldfacing and underlining, but the ability to enter other characters may vary widely. There is no limit to the possibilities—many word processors allow the user to enter a musical note, symbols for the suits in a deck of cards (club, diamond, heart, spade), symbols for male and female, arrows, smiling faces, and so on.

Several other points need to be made concerning the input of text. First, *a space or blank is a character*—it takes up room in memory. Blanks also have a special purpose: extra blanks can generally be inserted next to an existing blank in order to justify both edges of the text (i.e., place the first and last letter of every line in the same columns). Some word processing systems even provide two different kinds of blanks: one kind can have extra blanks added next to it and the other kind (a "sticky" blank) cannot!

Second, most word processing systems provide a **tab** character for the entry of columnar data. Just as on a typewriter, a tab is a special character that says "go to the next tab stop." The word processing system must provide ways

tab
A character analogous to the tab settings on a typewriter, used to align text in tables and other noncontinuous text formats.

to (1) set the columns where the tab stops are to be located, (2) remove the tab stops at a later time, and (3) enter the tab character that causes movement to the next stop. For example, to set up a three-column table, the user would first choose the columns and enter the tab stops; let's say columns 15, 34, and 50 are selected. To enter the data for the table, the user would press the tab key (moving automatically to column 15), type data, press tab (to column 34), type data, press tab (to 50), type data, press tab (to 15 of the next line), type data, and so on. If the user ever decides that the column tabs needs to be changed, changing the tab stops will reposition the table entries automatically.

Third, there are two ways in which text proceeds from one line on the screen to another line. The first and most common way is through an automatic feature called **wordwrap**. Wordwrap starts a new line whenever the old line is filled up. Because the wordwrap feature is automatic, the "carriage return" that caused the start of the new line is called a soft carriage return. A soft carriage return does not exist in the text—it is introduced by the word processor only to allow the proper display and printing of text. The second way to go from one line to another is to use a hard carriage return. A hard return *does* exist in the text and is generally entered by pressing the return or enter key on the keyboard. Hard returns are most frequently used at the end of paragraphs but are appropriate any time the user wants to guarantee that the following text will begin a new line.

Finally, text entry mode is generally subdivided into two other modes: **insert** mode and **replace mode.** If the cursor is somewhere in the middle of the document and new characters are typed in insert mode, all characters past the cursor are moved to the right and the new characters are inserted without affecting the existing characters. In replace mode, new characters that are typed in the middle of the document replace existing characters. It should be obvious that these different modes are for different purposes. Insert mode allows the addition of new text; replace mode changes existing text. Most word processing systems provide a means of switching back and forth between these modes. The choice of text entry modes can be viewed as a **toggle** switch that must be in one position but can easily be switched to the other.

■ Embedded Command Input

In addition to text, the user must be able to enter embedded formatting commands. Earlier in the chapter, we mentioned different ways to enter formatting commands: using a period, using ⟨ and ⟩, using control codes and function keys, and using graphic shells. The key concept is that the system must realize that the commands are not to be printed in the final document, but, instead, are to specify the form in which the text of the document will be printed. For example, most word processors will have one embedded command to start the centering of text and another embedded command to stop centering text. When the word processor reads through the text during output and comes across the start centering command, it does not print out anything; instead it changes its mode of operation to centering. The text following the centering command is processed and is centered as it is output. Finally, the stop centering command terminates the activity.

Since the primary purpose of embedded commands is to format the document, that is, to control its output, typical embedded commands will be described in the section entitled "Word Processing Output."

wordwrap
An automatic feature of word processing systems that causes the computer to advance any word to the next line if it is too long to fit at the end of the current line.

Insert/replace modes
In the insert mode new characters are added to the characters already present. In the replace mode new characters replace those present.

toggle
A single command that permits one to switch from one mode to another and back again, e.g., in word processing, a command that switches from an insert-at-cursor to a replace-at-cursor mode of text entry.

■ Immediate Commands

immediate commands
In word processing and other software, commands which are executed immediately upon being input by the user; in contrast to embedded commands which are input for execution at a later time.

Immediate commands, as their name implies, are performed immediately. Immediate commands are not related to formatting but are used to build up the text and embedded commands that make up the document.

Immediate commands come in two general forms. The first form is the single-keystroke immediate command. Although it may not be obvious at first, such simple activities as cursor movement and simple deletion of text with the backspace or delete key are all immediate commands: they make immediate changes that are not directly related to the formatting or output of the final document. The most common single-keystroke immediate commands are:

1. *Cursor Up One Line, Down One Line, Left One Character, or Right One Character.* These cursor movements are generally performed by pressing **cursor control keys**—the up-arrow, down-arrow, left-arrow, and right-arrow keys, respectively—but they may be accessible through other keystrokes or a mouse.

cursor control keys
Special keyboard keys that move the cursor on the screen, usually including arrow keys to go up, down, left, and right as well as special ones for moving to the "top," or "bottom," of a page or document and to other locations.

2. *Cursor to Beginning of Line or End of Line.* There is no generally defined key choice for this capability, but it is frequently available.
3. *Cursor Up One Page or Down One Page.* These commands are generally performed with special keys labeled PageUp and PageDown, respectively.
4. *Cursor to Top of Document or Bottom of Document.* Cursor control keys labeled Home and End respectively, generally perform these commands, but again, other variations may be found.
5. *Character Delete.* Character deletion is generally performed in one of two ways: a Delete key will usually delete the character at the cursor, while a Backspace key will usually delete the character to the left of the cursor.

Not all computer keyboards have special keys like PageUp, PageDown, Home, and End but as time passes, most new keyboards will have all of these special keys and many more.

Just as important as the single-keystroke immediate commands are the higher-level immediate commands concerned with tasks like: (1) loading documents from disk, (2) saving to disk, (3) sophisticated editing techniques for copying, deleting, moving, inserting, and other operations on text and commands, and (4) controlling the interaction of many documents. These commands are entered through the word processing shell. As in operating systems, the word processing shell may be a command language shell, a menu shell, a graphic shell, or some combination of the three. Whatever type of shell is used, these commands provide the user with a way to manage computerized documents.

Because the higher-level immediate commands are concerned with a variety of system functions, the description of these commands will be spread throughout the sections on word processing storage, processing, and control.

■ Glossaries

glossary
In word processing, a method for increasing data entry speed by allowing the user to type in an abbreviation for a long word or phrase and having the computer automatically replace the abbreviation with the longer word or phrase.

In addition to all of these relatively standard input characteristics, some word processing systems provide a **glossary** which enables a user to type in an abbreviation for a long phrase and have the computer automatically insert the long phrase in place of the abbreviation. Usually a special control character such as a control-G signals the system that a glossary abbreviation is being used. Any time the system finds that character, it takes the word after it as an abbreviation, searches for the proper replacement, and inserts it in place of the abbreviation. For example, if a glossary entry has been created in which "cers" stands for "clinical and epidemiological research study," the full phrase will be inserted into the text whenever the user types the phrase "control-Gcers."

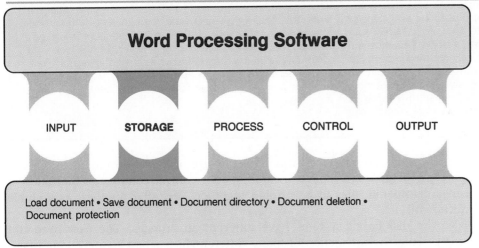

Word processors work on documents using the RAM of a computer. Since RAM must be available for other applications programs and other documents, a word processing system clearly must have some method for transferring data from RAM to permanent file storage and back again.

■ Loading and Saving Documents

Document storage and retrieval are absolutely required in a word processing system, that is, there must be immediate commands for saving and retrieving documents, whatever their state of completeness. These commands are initiated by the user, who must provide the name of the document that is to be loaded into RAM from disk or saved from RAM onto disk.

Word processing systems do not generally provide their own programming to load and save documents. Instead, the word processor accesses the kernel of the operating system. With this access, the word processing system may control the use of the disk in many ways. The user frequently does not even realize that saving a document means creating a disk file via the operating system. The word processor asks the user for a document name, then creates a disk file with approximately the same name and copies the text and embedded commands into it. When the user wants the file back, the word processor will give a list of available documents for the user to choose from. All the talk of documents obscures the fact that documents are operating system files.

Some word processors limit the size of a document to the size of RAM, and some limit the size of a document to the size of a disk. The RAM-based word processors can be much faster to use because they do not require continual access to the disk to get various parts of a document to work on. RAM-

Computer Insights
Document Libraries

Anyone who writes frequently will discover that word processing changes the very way in which writing is done. One of the most important changes involves the use of document libraries.

The central concept behind document libraries is that complete documents are saved on disk to be available for the creation of new documents. As a simple example, suppose a teacher has created a test on a word processor and stored it on a disk. The test can be called up when a similar test is needed another day, modified with a minimum amount of effort, and completed in substantially less time than it would take to write a new one from scratch. A teacher who teaches the same courses many times may

eventually be able to create new tests by simply recombining old ones.

The idea of a document library goes well beyond tests, however. Someone who frequently writes proposals and needs a good description of his or her business facilities can write the description once and then include it time after time in separate proposals. Even a student should word process all documents, because one never knows when the ideas and words generated one day will be useful again. Since one floppy disk can store page after page of text for minimal cost, it is almost silly to throw completed documents away.

based systems do not necessarily limit the size of a *total* document to the size of RAM, because they often include special control commands that allow a series of separate files to be printed together, one after another, as a single document.

The disk-based systems have different advantages. The user need not worry about the interaction of many different files when creating long documents. Furthermore, with good design, access to the disk to retrieve the various parts of document need not be troublesome.

◼ Other Operating System File Functions

Most word processing systems allow access to the full operating system kernel from within the word processing shell. Many operating system commands are clearly of great use to word processing. For example, if a user forgets the precise name of a particular document file, a directory command could determine the name of the file so that it could be loaded into the word processor. Frequently, when the user creates a new file, the command for formatting a new disk to hold that file would be used. Once a file is created, a user might use the ordinary file protection routines to guard against its accidental deletion. And, of course, beyond these commands are all those of the operating system for deleting files, renaming files, and so forth. All should be accessible in a good word processor.

6.5

Word Processing Processes

Word processing systems provide a number of processes for the management of a document. All of these processes are accessed through immediate commands, that is, they are performed when entered, not deferred until the printing of the document.

◼ Editing Functions

The editing features provided by immediate commands are critical to the use of any word processing system. As mentioned earlier, the simplest immediate

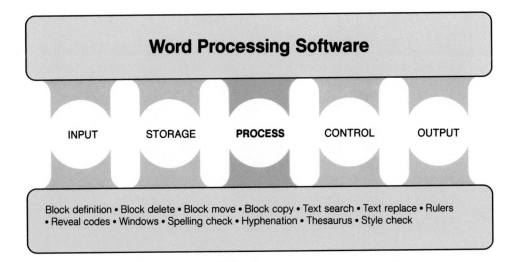

commands for editing are the single-keystroke commands that move the cursor around the document and delete characters at or before the cursor. Besides this simple character-oriented editing ability, there are many immediate commands that process **blocks** of text as a unit. For all **block commands,** the user specifies a portion of the text to be treated as a unit. This specification is usually made by positioning the cursor at the beginning of the desired portion of text, pressing a single-keystroke immediate command that begins block specification, moving the cursor to the end of the block, pressing another key to signal the end of the definition process. As the block is defined, it is generally placed in reverse video or another color so that the user can clearly see which text is included in the block. An example of how a block of text is specified is shown on the next page.

Once the block of text has been defined, a number of things can be done to it—it can be centered, converted to all capital letters, deleted, moved, copied, and so on. On some word processing systems, the block is defined first and the operations on the block second; on others, the operation is specified first and then the block. The two methods are equivalent.

Erasing Text.   Erasing large sections of text (words, sentences, paragraphs, or more) is the simplest block editing function. The use of a text erasure function is simple: tell the computer the starting point for deletion (position the cursor at that point in the text and press some special key), tell the computer the ending point for deletion (again the cursor and a special key), and then tell the computer to go ahead and delete the text. When the command is completed, the designated text will be gone, as illustrated on the next page.

Moving Text.   Moving text around within a document is also a critical function of block editing. Blocks of text are frequently moved from one place in a document to another as an author reorganizes the text that has been written. Again, the steps are simple. The user moves the cursor to specify three points in the document: the starting point of the text to be moved, the ending point of the text, and the point to which the block of text should be moved. When the command is completed, the designated text no longer exists at the original position in the document—it has been moved to the new location. An example of a text move is shown on page 215.

Block
A portion of the text selected for processing as a unit, i.e., copied, deleted, etc.

Block command
An editing command which is applid to a block of text, e.g., delete, move, or copy blocks

The original text as typed into the word processor, with the cursor after the word "zoos".

Down On The Keys

It's peaceful down on the Keys. Everything moves more slowly. The waves, the wind, sun--even the people. You drive down Highway One past the condos and tourists on the big glittering islands. More or less like Miami or any American city.

As you get farther, you begin to see them. Pelicans, gulls, storks,--little ones that run back and forth with the waves like hundreds of Charlie Chaplins--sea birds that you've probably only seen in zoos._

Using arrow keys or a mouse, the cursor is placed at the beginning of the text block. Here, it is before the word "More." Then the BLOCK DEFINE command is given.

Down On The Keys

It's peaceful down on the Keys. Everything moves more slowly. The waves, the wind, sun--even the people. You drive down Highway One past the condos and tourists on the big glittering islands._More or less like Miami or any American city.

As you get farther, you begin to see them. Pelicans, gulls, storks,--little ones that run back and forth with the waves like hundreds of Charlie Chaplins--sea birds that you've probably only seen in zoos.

As the cursor is moved when BLOCK DEFINE is in effect, the text block is highlighted in some way, e.g., reverse video.

Down On The Keys

It's peaceful down on the Keys. Everything moves more slowly. The waves, the wind, sun--even the people. You drive down Highway One past the condos and tourists on the big glittering islands. More or less like Miami or any American city.

As you get farther, you begin to see them. Pelicans, gulls, storks,--little ones that run back and forth with the waves like hundreds of Charlie Chaplins--sea birds that you've probably only seen in zoos.

With the block defined, many commands can be given. Here, a CUT BLOCK command is entered and the text block is removed.

Down On The Keys

It's peaceful down on the Keys. Everything moves more slowly. The waves, the wind, sun--even the people. You drive down Highway One past the condos and tourists on the big glittering islands._As you get farther, you begin to see them. Pelicans, gulls, storks,--little ones that run back and forth with the waves like hundreds of Charlie Chaplins--sea birds that you've probably only seen in zoos.

Block Definition and Deletion

A block of text is defined by marking the beginning, starting the block define process, and marking the end.

```
   Down On The Keys

       It's peaceful down
   on the Keys. Everything
   moves more slowly. The
   waves, the wind, sun--
   even the people. You
   drive down Highway One
   past the condos and
   tourists on the big
   glittering islands. More
   or less like Miami or
   any American city.
```

MOVE

COPY

The text is cut out and the cursor positioned to the new position.

```
   Down On The Keys

       It's peaceful down
   on the Keys. You drive
   down Highway One past the
   condos and tourists on
   the big glittering
   islands. More or less
   like Miami or any
   American city._
```

```
   Down On The Keys

       It's peaceful down
   on the Keys. Everything
   moves more slowly. The
   waves, the wind, sun--
   even the people. You
   drive down Highway One
   past the condos and
   tourists on the big
   glittering islands. More
   or less like Miami or
   any American city._
```

The text is copied instead of cut, so it remains at its current location. The cursor is moved to the goal.

The text is then pasted into this new position. The result of a cut and paste is a text move.

```
   Down On The Keys

       It's peaceful down
   on the Keys. You drive
   down Highway One past the
   condos and tourists on
   the big glittering
   islands. More or less
   like Miami or any
   American city. Everything
   moves more slowly. The
   waves, the wind, sun--
   even the people.
```

```
   Down On The Keys

       It's peaceful down
   on the Keys. Everything
   moves more slowly. The
   waves, the wind, sun--
   even the people. You
   drive down Highway One
   past the condos and
   tourists on the big
   glittering islands. More
   or less like Miami or
   any American city.
   Everything moves more
   slowly. The waves, the
   wind, sun--even the
   people.
```

When the paste operation is given, a text copy has been accomplished.

Block Move and Block Copy of Text

copy
A block command that allows the duplication of a portion of text or graphics. For example, in a word processing system, copy allows the user to duplicate a portion of the document.

string
A sequence of characters drawn from the computer's ASCII code alphabet. Examples of strings include: "hello there," "h39x./12" and "123.23". Note that the string "123.23" is not the same as the number 123.23, just as a typewriter's "123" is different from a calculator's 123.

Search/Replace
Commands which find all instances of a string in text and optionally replace it.

Copying Text. The steps involved in specifying a text **copy** command are exactly the same as those required for a move command. The only difference is that on completion of the command, the original position of the copied text is unchanged. An exact copy has just been placed at the new position in the document. An example of the text copying process is given on the preceding page.

Searching Text. Being able to locate a word or phrase within a text can greatly simplify the management of a large document. To check how a phrase has been used, to find out where the last editing session ended, and for many other purposes, word processors provide an immediate command for searching. A searching function proceeds through a document looking for a particular **string** of characters. In a typical word processor, the user presses some special sequence of keys to initiate a search. The processor then responds by requesting the characters for which to search. If the system finds the specified string in the document, it stops and asks the user if that first occurrence is the one that is desired. If yes, it leaves the cursor there; if no, it searches further in the document for another instance.

The user initiating a search must consider two questions (1) does it matter if the characters in the words are uppercase or lowercase? and (2) must the characters searched for be a full word, or are partial word matches allowed? The point of the first question can be made clear from a simple example: if searching for the characters *hello*, should *hello, Hello, HELLO, HeLLo,* and so on, all be considered successful matches or should just the first one, *hello,* count? Most word processors permit the case of letters to be used or ignored.

The question of full word or partial word matches is also understood best by example: if searching for the characters *man*, should the system match *manifold, remand, salamander,* and all of the other words that contain the three letters *m-a-n,* or should the system only match the word *man*. Both types of searches may be useful, and a word processor should provide both. A simple search is demonstrated on the next page. Pay particular attention to the placement of the cursor before and after the search.

Replacing Text. A replace function is very much like a search function and shares the same concerns of uppercase/lowercase characters and full/partial words. However, instead of just finding a character string, the replace function replaces the old string with a new one specified by the user. As an example, suppose that the word *receive* has been misspelled throughout a document as *recieve*. The system could be directed to automatically search out all instances of *recieve* and replace them with *receive*. Generally, users need to verify the change for each occurrence of the old character string. Note that a replace command can be used to simulate the workings of a glossary. The user could enter an abbreviation for a term throughout the text and then replace the abbreviation by the full term when the text entry is complete. A simple replacement is shown on the next page.

Other Block Commands. Besides the common block editing commands, many other block commands may exist on any given word processing system. Some systems may allow the conversion of a block of text to all uppercase letters, to all lowercase letters, or to the reverse of the current state (upper- to lowercase and lower- to uppercase). A block of text may be underlined, bold-

The cursor is at some arbitrary point in the text before the search or replace is begun. Here, it is at the beginning of the text.

Down On The Keys

_It's peaceful down on the Keys. Everything moves more slowly. The waves, the wind, sun-- even the people. You drive down Highway One past the condos and tourists on the big glittering islands. More or less like Miami or any American city.

SEARCH   REPLACE

The word processor requests the text string to search for, and the user provides it.

Enter search string: Miami

Enter search string: Miami

The word processor requests the text string to search for, and the user provides it.

The word processor finds the first occurrence of the text string and positions the cursor there.

Down On The Keys

It's peaceful down on the Keys. Everything moves more slowly. The waves, the wind, sun-- even the people. You drive down Highway One past the condos and tourists on the big glittering islands. More or less like_Miami or any American city.

Enter replacement: Boston

The word processor requests the new string that is to replace the old one.

Down On The Keys

It's peaceful down on the Keys. Everything moves more slowly. The waves, the wind, sun-- even the people. You drive down Highway One past the condos and tourists on the big glittering islands. More or less like Boston or any American city.

The word processor finds occurrences of the old string and replaces them with occurrences of the new string.

Text Searching and Replacement

faced, changed in size, changed in font, centered, left-justified, right-justified, and so on. Although all of these operations can be performed on blocks of text, an informed user can often enter embedded commands for these functions during text entry. Thus most of these formatting descriptors can be entered in two different ways: during text entry by inserting embedded commands or during editing by the use of immediate block commands. Because each of these commands is most concerned with the output of the final document, the details of these operations are included in the section on word processing output.

■ Screen Display During Editing

All word processors have some variations in the way in which the screen displays the text and embedded commands of a document.

Wordwrap.   Most word processors have a function called wordwrap, which determines whether words may be split in the middle when one line is automatically extended onto the next. Word processors with this facility provide an immediate command for turning the wordwrap on and off. An example of a screen with wordwrap on and off is shown here:

Note that the ends of lines are handled differently in these two displays.

Wordwrap is off

```
In olden times, when the mapmakers reached the limit o
f their knowledge, they would draw a line and pen in a phra
se:"Beyond This Line--There Be Dragons."
```

Wordwrap is on

```
In olden times, when the mapmakers reached the limit
of their knowledge, they would draw a line and pen in
a phrase: "Beyond This Line--There Be Dragons."
```

Wordwrap

ruler
In word processing systems, a line across the top of the display screen that includes tic marks to count off characters and displays the position of tab characters, paragraph indentations, margins, and so forth.

Rulers.   Most word processors also have the option of displaying a **ruler,** a line across the screen that includes tick marks to count off characters (useful for spacing things equally across a line) and also shows the position of tab characters, paragraph indentations, margins, and so forth. An immediate command is generally provided for turning the ruler display on or off. An example of a ruler is given on the next page.

Revealing Codes.   The display of embedded text commands can also be turned on or off in many word processors. For example, if an embedded command to turn on center justification has been given before a title, the user has the choice of viewing the command on the screen (sometimes called **zooming in** or revealing codes) or hiding the command on the screen and seeing its

zooming in
Viewing embedded commands on the display screen along with the rest of the text that is being word processed.

Rulers and Revealed Codes
Rulers are used to position margins, text, tabs and the like although some allow much more than that (see the graphic shell example). The ability to reveal codes is crucial for What-You-See-Is-What-You-Get word processors because all formatting information is purposely hidden from the screen.

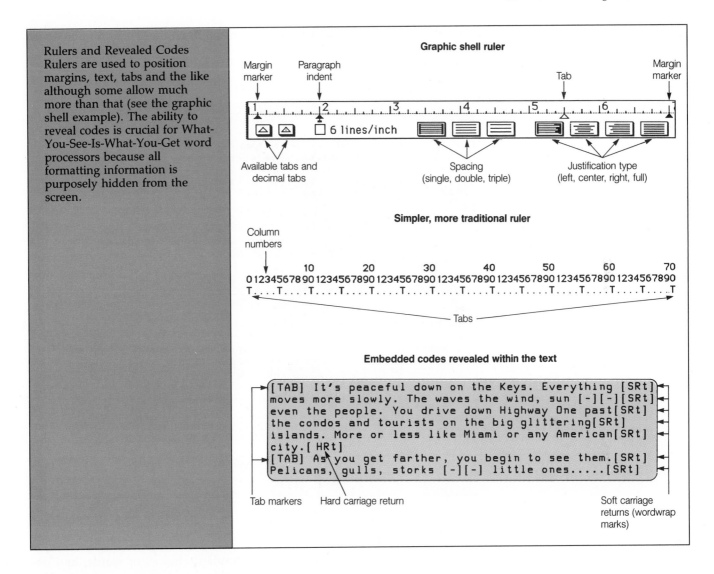

effect instead (sometimes called **zooming out** or hiding codes). Note that regardless of whether the command is visible on the screen, it is operational and will carry out the desired function during document printing. The ability to reveal codes is crucial, especially for what-you-see-is-what-you-get word processors where all formatting information is hidden from the screen. An example of text in which the embedded codes are revealed is shown in the illustration above.

zooming out
Hiding embedded commands so that they do not appear on the display screen with the text that is being word processed, but their effects on the text can be seen.

Windows. Whenever sets of documents are used together or whenever a document is particularly large, the need to **window** the document is strong. Windowing allows the user to split the visual screen on which the editing is being done into more than one part. Each part of the screen can then display different parts of the current document or separate documents altogether, allowing the author to review one part of the text while writing another. There are immediate commands for setting up windows, turning them off, defining what each one will look at, and moving back and forth between them. In the following example, the full computer screen has been allocated to two win-

window
The ability of word processing systems to present data from different documents or files on different areas of the display screen at the same time. Also, operating systems may be able to run separate programs at the same time in different areas of the display screen.

dows. One shows the story that is being written; the other contain notes about the story.

```
                    Down On The Keys

      It's peaceful down on the Keys. Everything moves
more slowly. The waves, the wind, sun--even the
people. You drive down Highway One past the condos
and tourists on the big glittering islands. More or
less like Miami or any American city.

      As you get farther, you begin to see them.
Pelicans, gulls, storks,--little ones that run back
and forth with the waves like hundreds of Charlie
Chaplins--sea birds that you've probably only seen in
zoos._
C:\KEYS.TXT
                                   Doc 1 Pg 1 Ln 13 Pos 6
```

```
_Outline:
 Working title:   Down On The Keys
 Length:          1500 words
 Story:           Start with driving down highway 1. Talk
                  about change in people and life unique
                  in U.S. Flash back to hurricanes and
                  railroads. Life in 40's and 50's. Finish
                  with New Year's Eve.

C:\KEYS.OTL                        Doc 2 Pg 1 Ln 1 Pos 1
```

Language Checking

Errors such as spelling errors, poor or redundant choices of words, and improper or poor grammar are a common problem in human communication. Since errors in books, essays, letters, advertisements, signs, and so on, reflect poorly on the author, many word processing systems have functions to help with these problems.

Spelling Checker.   Spelling is checked through an extensive dictionary available in computer-readable form. On systems with such capabilities, an initial dictionary is provided that includes many of the most common words used in English (usually 40,000 to 200,000 words). To this dictionary can be added an extensive list of other words that are frequently used in the user's own writing but not found in the initial dictionary. For example, a research chemist would need many chemical names and formulas not found in an ordinary dictionary, as well as names of people and organizations frequently referenced in chemistry.

To use the spelling checker, the user first specifies the text to be checked—on most systems it can be an individual word, an arbitrary block of text, or the whole document. The computer then assumes that every sequence of letters in the selected text is a word and runs through the dictionary looking for it. If the word is found, the system just continues with the next word in the text. If the word is not found, the system must then query the user, because one of two things has happened: the word is either misspelled, or it is a word not in the computer's "vocabulary." In either case, the user has many options.

If the word in question is correct but not recognized by the system as so, the user can add it to the dictionary so it will be permanently available for future spelling checks. Another alternative is to add the word only for the duration of the current document; this alternative would be selected when the word is valid for this text but is so special purpose that its addition to the dictionary is undesirable. Finally, the user may choose to accept only the one identified occurrence; for example, this book contains a number of misspelled words as examples—they were accepted at only one spot in the document, but would be not acceptable at any others.

If the identified word is incorrectly spelled, the spelling system must allow correction. Most spelling checkers do this by offering a list of properly spelled words that the user may have meant to use. The user can then select the properly spelled word from the list. Spelling checkers also allow the direct editing of the misspelled word, in case the list does not contain the correctly spelled word.

When the computer provides a list of alternatives for a misspelled word, the list is generated by computer **algorithms** and includes words that are like the misspelled word in many ways. Some of the most common similarities used are: (1) the misspelled word has the same letters as a known word but in a different order (*bouhgt* vs *bought*), (2) the misspelled word has fewer letters than a known word (*bougt*), (3) the misspelled word has more letters than a known word (*boought*) (4) the misspelled word has slightly different letters than a known word (*boughl*) or (5) the misspelled word has similar phonetic sounds to a known word (*bawt*). In each of these examples, the processing that the computer must do is nontrivial: it must somehow find the correctly spelled word based on the incorrectly spelled one. Because of the fuzziness of this task, spelling checkers often cannot come up with the right answer even though it may be listed in the dictionary. Spelling checkers also have the problem of false positives: if the user meant to type *bought* and typed *brought* instead, the mistyped word is a legitimate word and will not be caught by the spelling checker. The example on the following page shows the type of information a spelling checker might provide.

algorithm
Technically, a sequence of steps for the completion of a task that is guaranteed to terminate with either success or an explicit message of failure. Commonly, any sequence of steps for the completion of a task.

Automatic Hyphenation.   The **automatic hyphenation** function uses the same dictionary. Hyphenation maximizes the number of words that can fit on a page, but because people are not always sure where a word should be hyphenated, errors can occur. Often the same dictionary that defines spellings can also identify appropriate hyphenation points within words. The user is generally given the option of whether to allow hyphenation. In addition, there is often a way to explicitly give hyphenating permission for a particular word (regardless of whether it's in the dictionary) by placing a **soft hyphen** in the text. A soft hyphen will not be printed unless it is necessary to divide the word at the end of a line.

automatic hyphenation
A word processing function that uses a computerized dictionary to determine where to automatically hyphenate words at the right margin of the text being processed.

soft hyphen
A word processing command that inserts a hyphen only when a word needs to be broken at the end of a line.

Thesaurus.   Of course, once a dictionary of words is present, it can be used for many other purposes. In some of the more advanced word processing systems, the words in the dictionary are interconnected so that the user in need

The original text is ready to be spelling checked. The user gives the proper command to start the checking.

```
                    Down On The Keys

     It's peaceful down on the Keys. Everything moves
more slowly. The waves, the wind, sun--even the
people. You drive down Highway One past the condos
and tourists on the big glittering ilands. More or
less like Miami or any American city.

     As you get farther, you begin to see them.
Pelicans, gulls, storks,--little ones that run back
and forth with the waves like hundreds of Charlie
Chaplins--sea birds that you've probably only seen in
zoos._
C:\KEYS.TXT                            Doc 1 Pg 1 Ln 13 Pos 6
```

Every word in the document is checked. "ilands" is not in the dictionary, so the speller lists the words it knows that are similar to it. The user may select one of these words, if appropriate, allow the word, add it to the dictionary, or fix the text directly.

```
                    Down On The Keys

     It's peaceful down on the Keys. Everything moves
more slowly. The waves, the wind, sun--even the
people. You drive down Highway One past the condos
and tourists on the big glittering ilands. More or
less like Miami or any American city.
==================================================
A. inland      B. island     C. land       D. alienate
E. aligned     F. aliunde    G. aslant     H. eland
I. eluant      J. eluent
Word not found. Select Word from list or Menu below: ? B
1: Skip once 2: Skip in document 3: Add to dictionary
4: Edit text 5: Phonetic
```

The misspelled word is replaced by word B, the correct word, and the rest of the document is checked with no other errors arising. Note that if the misspelling had been "land" for "island," no error would be detected!

```
                    Down On The Keys

     It's peaceful down on the Keys. Everything moves
more slowly. The waves, the wind, sun--even the
people. You drive down Highway One past the condos
and tourists on the big glittering islands. More or
less like Miami or any American city.

     As you get farther, you begin to see them.
Pelicans, gulls, storks,--little ones that run back
and forth with the waves like hundreds of Charlie
Chaplins--sea birds that you've probably only seen in
zoos._
C:\KEYS.TXT                            Doc 1 Pg 1 Ln 13 Pos 6
```

Spelling Check

of an alternative word for expressing an idea may request a synonym for a word in the document. In the same way that *Roget's Thesaurus* aids the writer in improving the statement of an idea, such facilities in a word processor can improve the quality of an author's writing. Incidentally, an electronic **thesaurus** is so much faster than a manual one that even an author with good language skills might choose to use an electronic thesaurus often! An example of the kind of screen that a thesaurus might generate is shown below:

thesaurus
A book of classified synonyms and antonyms. A thesaurus may be stored on magnetic disk for use by word processors.

The cursor is placed at the word that the author wishes to change, "quiet." Then, the command to access the thesaurus is given.

```
                 Down On The Keys

        It's quiet_down on the Keys. Everything moves
    more slowly. The waves, the wind, sun--even the
    people. You drive down Highway One past the condos
    and tourists on the big glittering ilands. More or
    less like Miami or any American city.

        As you get farther, you begin to see them.
    Pelicans, gulls, storks,--little ones that run back
    and forth with the waves like hundreds of Charlie
    Chaplins--sea birds that you've probably only seen in
    zoos.

    C:\KEYS.TXT                        Doc 1 Pg 1 Ln 2 Pos 20
```

The information in the thesaurus is accessed and all related words are shown on the screen for the user's perusal. Note that the words are grouped by different meanings of the selected word. The user can then select a new word to replace the original, look up other words, or leave the word unchanged.

```
                 Down On The Keys

        It's quiet_down on the Keys. Everything moves

    quiet (adj)       H peaceful     P mile       W mollify
    1 A noiseless     I restful      Q sedate     quiet (n)
      B silent        J untroubled  quiet (v)     8 X calm
      C still      4 K dormant      6 R hush        Y lull
    2 D hushed        L inactive      S muffle    9 Z isolation
      E low           M motionless    T silence   quiet
      F soft          N passive       U stifle      (antonym)
    3 G calm       5 O docile      7 V comfort   10 AA loud

    Enter letters to replace word, 1: look-up word,
    2: quit ? H
```

The designated word has been replaced with the word lettered H, peaceful.

```
                 Down On The Keys

        It's peaceful_down on the Keys. Everything moves
    more slowly. The waves, the wind, sun--even the
    people. You drive down Highway One past the condos
    and tourists on the big glittering islands. More or
    less like Miami or any American city.

        As you get farther, you begin to see them.
    Pelicans, gulls, storks,--little ones that run back
    and forth with the waves like hundreds of Charlie
    Chaplins--sea birds that you've probably only seen in
    zoos.
    C:\KEYS.TXT                        Doc 1 Pg 1 Ln 2 Pos 23
```

Using a Theasurus

Style Checkers. Finally, although just emerging, some word processors are now available that can actually check the style and grammar of writing. They can, for example, detect overly repetitive uses of words or phrases. They might signal that a phrase like "Many of the set of children" should be rewritten as "Many of the children." Any suggestions made by such systems are only suggestions, however, and studies of current style checkers have indicated that strict adherence to their suggestions does not lead to high-quality writing. The complete checking of English syntax and style is not yet available.

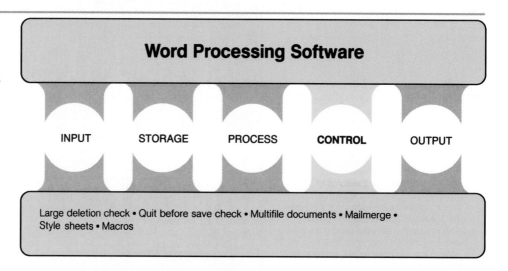

6.6

Word Processing Control

In word processors, control deals with the way sets of word processing commands can be executed—sequentially, alternatively, or repetitively.

▓ Error Prevention

To be both effective and efficient, word processing systems should be very forgiving of the kinds of mistakes that people commonly make. To that end, most word processing systems provide at least rudimentary control over the sequencing of commands so that some simple yet drastic errors do not occur.

Large Deletion Check. The single most important control feature is a safety check that prevents the loss of large volumes of work due to human error. When a user asks to delete a large amount of text, a special check is often inserted into the control sequence to make sure that the user has not accidentally given a command to delete more text than desired. For example, a word processor should *not* have a command that lets the user destroy an entire document with one statement. If the user should happen to issue a command like DESTROY DOCUMENT, the system should always respond with a double-check like ARE YOU SURE YOU WANT TO DESTROY THE WHOLE THING? and await an affirmative reply before taking such a disastrous step.

Quitting-Without-Saving Check. This second safety check has been described earlier. It should be invoked when the text has been altered but not yet saved onto a disk file. If the user attempts to terminate a session and some

Computer Insights
Plagiarism and Term Papers

Plagiarism is a major problem that may arise with the advent of easy word processing. With a society run by paper, it is highly unlikely that someone who copies the work of another for a college term paper or lab report will ever be noticed, much less prosecuted. Ghostwriting and copying have been problems in colleges for years, but with word processing and on-line computer services the problem is compounded.

With on-line services, a computer user could easily access a computerized storehouse of knowledge. For example, various encyclopedias are already stored on computers and are frequently available to the student. A student could easily begin a paper, access the computerized encyclopedia, and copy down an entire article directly into a word processing document. Without writing one word or doing any thinking, the student could have a full completed essay that could, with a little judicious use of the editing capabilities of the word processing system, quickly be reworked and turned in as the student's original thinking.

Fortunately, few students now have the familiarity with both computers and on-line services to make such efforts easier than writing the report from scratch. But as the student population as a whole begins to acquire substantially improved computing skills, one can only hope that students will realize that if they do not do the work, they will not reap the benefits of an intellectual education.

changes have been made to the text but not copied to disk, the system should at least query the user to determine if this loss of work is really desired.

■ Multiple Interacting Documents

For the creation of large or repetitive documents, a word processing system must allow the interaction of different document files to create a total document out of many pieces.

Multifile Documents. In the simplest case, one document is stored in a number of separate files. The reasons for such a split could be many, such as: limitations on RAM for a word processor that allows working documents to be no larger than RAM, limitations on disk space for word processors that can work only on one disk at a time, improved access speed for working on parts of large documents, or the logical organization of a document into many parts. Whatever the reason, a word processing system must allow these separate pieces to be printed as one complete document. On the final printing, the system must allow continuous **pagination** across chapters, the continuation on the same page of the end of one file and the start of another, and so on. These processes are illustrated in Figure 6–3.

pagination
The process of numbering the pages of a document.

Mailmerge. Similarly, if a large number of repetitive documents need to be created (like form letters or proposals on the same material to different organizations), the system should allow one **Template** or **boilerplate file** (a document framework into which specific text can be inserted) to serve as the template of many documents. This type of process is most commonly called mailmerge. The reader should certainly be familiar with the form letter in which the template contains "place markers" or slots for the insertion of specific information for a given letter (e.g., the name and address of the recipient). A special symbol (e.g., &) in the text identifies the slots. For example, the phrases &NAME& and &ADDRESS& in the template letter would serve as a place marker for the insertion of individual names and addresses when the individualized letters are printed.

Template or boilerplate file
A word processing file containing a document framework into which specific text can be inserted.

Mailmerge
Combining a file containing names and addresses with a file containing a form letter to generate a number of individualized letters or documents.

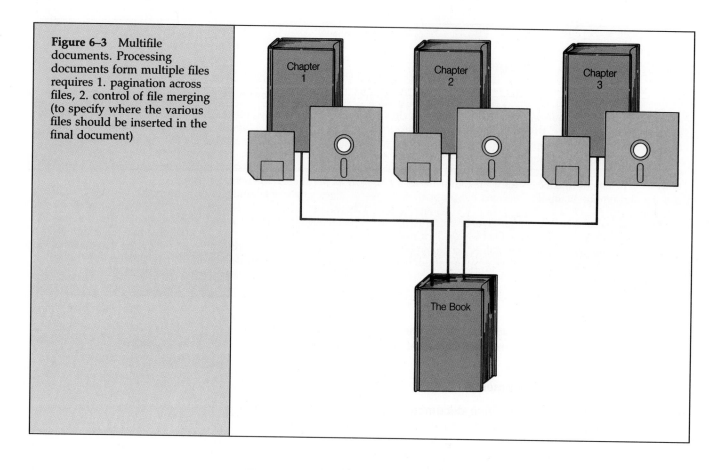

Figure 6–3 Multifile documents. Processing documents form multiple files requires 1. pagination across files, 2. control of file merging (to specify where the various files should be inserted in the final document)

A second file containing many sets of the information required by the template must also be created; for a form letter, the second file would contain many sets of names and addresses. The mailmerge process then continues in a straightforward manner: the word processor reads a set of data from the second file, inserts that data into the document of the first file, and prints the results; it then reads the next set of data from the data file, inserts the data into the document, prints the results. Set after set, each set results in a new printed document. An example of this process is shown in Figure 6–4.

Style Sheets. When a document becomes very large, control over the format becomes ever more difficult. Did the user remember to start every new chapter on a new page, center and underline every chapter title, and always skip down four lines before beginning the text? It is hard to be sure. To help the user remember to do all these things, advanced word processing systems provide style sheets on which the user can specify all such decisions. An example of a style sheet is provided in Figure 6–5.

parameter
A value given to a process that modifies how the process works. For example, the addition process produces one result when given the two parameters 2 and 2 and a different result when given the two parameters 5 and 7.

Macros. All of these control concerns can be addressed by the word processing facility called a macro. A macro is an abbreviation for a set of commands (rather than for just text, as in a glossary). For example, one might create a macro called chapter. Whenever this macro is invoked, all of the standard tasks for beginning a chapter are automatically carried out using the name of the current chapter. The name of the current chapter is a **parameter** of the macro.

A secondary file with data organized into fields is prepared. The fields are generally marked by some special characters and are often given names.

```
<Name          ><Address        ><City       ><St ><Zip>

John Smith      426 Main St.      Lansing      MI    48023
Beth Zuller     1200 Essay Ln.    Okemos       MI    48864
Duncan Padadue  16789 Levan Rd.   Rochester    MI    48063
Jacquelyn Rob   11940 K-Hill      Milford      MI    48824
Candice Knight  30443 Nye         South Lyon   MI    44623
Keith White     3534 Meadowridge  Holly        MI    40223
Pauline Mark    44038 Parkside    Livonia      MI    43324
        •
        •
        •
```

A primary file is created into which the secondary file will be merged. At various places in this text, the data from fields in the secondary file is referenced.

```
May 12, 1991
^<Name>^
^<Address>^
^<City>^, ^<St>^   ^<Zip>^

Dear ^<Name>^:

Don't throw out this letter! Sure, we're asking
for a contribution for public TV. But it's
deductible from your income tax. Now wouldn't you
rather give it to us to spend on Nova programming
than give it to Washington, D.C.? If you agree,
please send us a check. Thanks for listening and
keep watching.

Sincerely,


Bob Martin
```

When the mailmerge command is given, the user must give both the primary and the secondary file names. The word processor puts the two together into a series of completed documents.

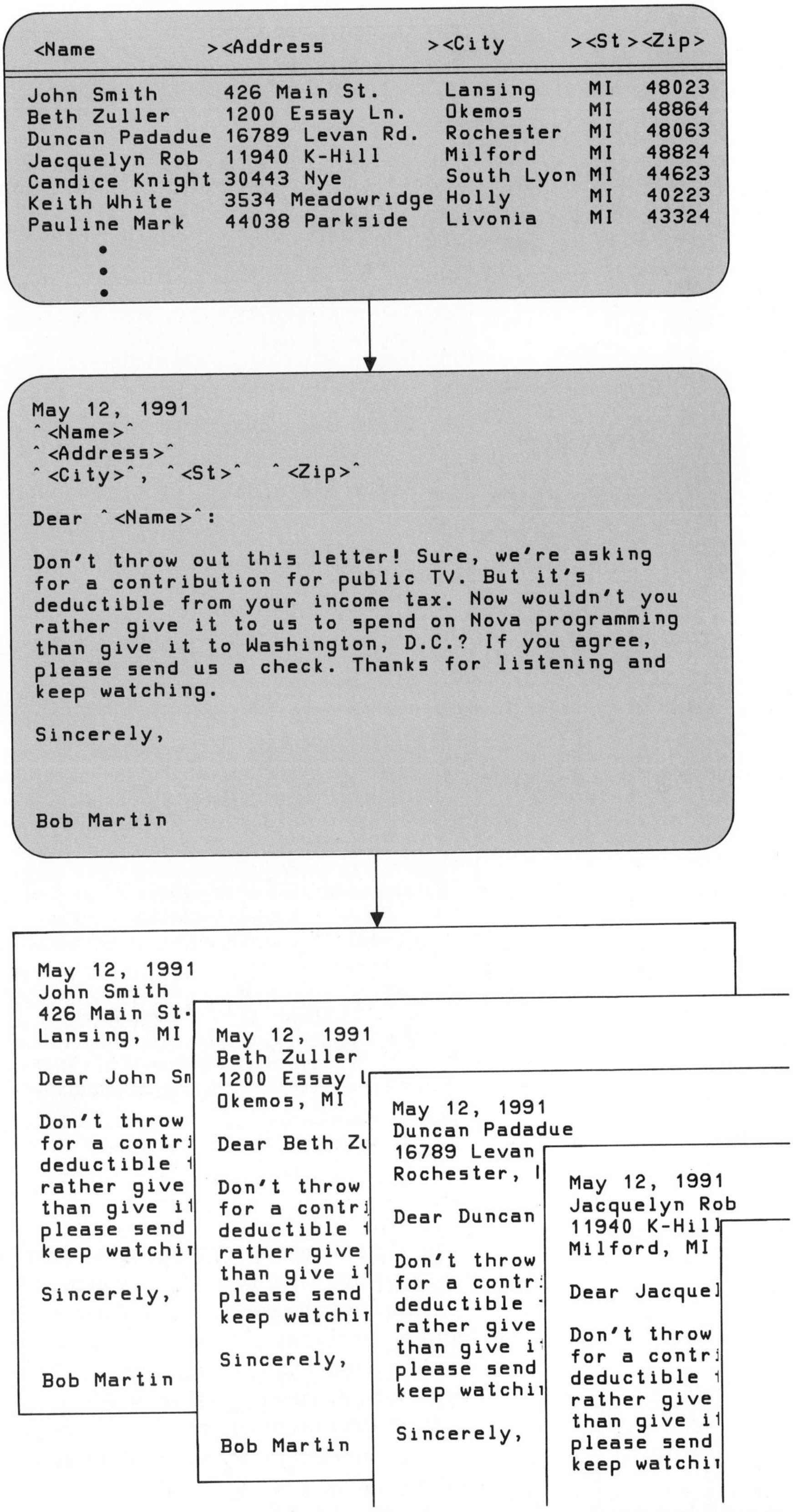

```
May 12, 1991
John Smith
426 Main St.        May 12, 1991
Lansing, MI         Beth Zuller
                    1200 Essay L     May 12, 1991
Dear John Sm        Okemos, MI       Duncan Padadue
                                     16789 Levan      May 12, 1991
Don't throw         Dear Beth Zu     Rochester, I     Jacquelyn Rob
for a contri                                          11940 K-Hill
deductible 1        Don't throw      Dear Duncan      Milford, MI
rather give         for a contri
than give it        deductible 1     Don't throw      Dear Jacquel
please send         rather give      for a contri
keep watchir        than give it     deductible       Don't throw
                    please send      rather give      for a contri
Sincerely,          keep watchir     than give it     deductible 1
                                     please send      rather give
                    Sincerely,       keep watchir     than give it
                                                       please send
Bob Martin                           Sincerely,        keep watchir
                    Bob Martin
                                     Bob Martin
```

Figure 6-4 Mailmerge of documents

```
Style Sheets

NAME              TYPE          DESCRIPTION
Book              Open          Setup of book codes
Chapter           Paired        Chapter setup codes
Section           Paired        Divisions within a chapter
Heading           Paired        Divisions within a section
Subheading        Paired        Divisions within a heading
Screen            Open          Setup for video screen simulation
```

```
Book:
  Style codes:        [PAGESIZE:8.5,11] [MARGINS:1.5,1]
                      [WIDOWS:ON] [ORPHANS:ON]

Chapter:
  Style on codes:     [NEWPAGE] [LINESPACE:2] [UNDERLINE:ON]
                      [CENTER:ON] [BOLD:ON]
                      [TABLEOFCONTENTS:ON,1]
  Style off codes:    [TABLEOFCONTENTS:OFF] [BOLD:OFF]
                      [CENTER:OFF] [UNDERLINE:OFF] [NEWLINE]
                      [NEWLINE]

Section:
  Style on codes:     [NEWLINE] [NEWLINE] [CENTER:ON]
                      [BOLD:ON]
  Style off codes:    [BOLD:OFF] [CENTER:OFF] [NEWLINE]
                      [NEWLINE]
```

Figure 6-5 Style Sheets The purpose of a style sheet is to control the formatting of large documents. Essentially, the user defines a set of named styles within a document along with the particular codes associated with each. The top box shows the names of some styles created for writing a book. The codes are either paired (a beginning set of codes, some text, and a closing set of codes are all inserted) or open (just one set of codes is inserted). The second box shows the definitions of some of these styles. The book style sets the page size, the margin size, and turns widows and orphan controls on. It is an open style, since no text is required to use it. The chapter style goes to the top of a new page, sets line spacing, starts an entry for the table of contents, and turns centering, boldface, and underlining on. It is a paired style, since text is then required (e.g., the name of the chapter) before the underlying paired codes for table of contents marking, centering, boldface, and underlining are turned back off. One of the great advantages of style sheets is that the entire appearance of a document can be changed merely by altering the definition of the various user styles.

Using a macro is like inserting a standard set of commands into the text, and the parameter is the current value being used.

Carrying the concept of a macro to its logical conclusion, there are even word processing systems in which the embedded command languages are general programming languages and include constructs like variables, arrays, loops, case statements, and so on (the meanings of these terms will be clarified in the chapter on programming languages). In these situations, the word processor has all the power of an arbitrary programming language like Pascal or BASIC.

Word Processing Software

INPUT STORAGE PROCESS CONTROL **OUTPUT**

Character size and shape • Embedded graphics • Margins • Page numbering • Headers/footers • Justification • Page breaks • Keep/float • Footnotes • Indexes • Tables of contents

A final printed document is generally the goal of word processing, and there are a myriad of commands for specifying the appearance of the final printed output. These commands are generally available in two forms: (1) immediate commands that specify how the printed page should be set up in the absence of specific embedded commands and (2) embedded commands that declare the type of printing for specific portions of text within a document.

Because there are so many of these commands, good word processing systems provide some type of help system to remind the user what commands are available. Help functions on a word processor acknowledge that many users of word processing systems do not use them often enough to remember all the details of operation. To assist the occasional user, interactive requests for help and information are provided on most word processing systems. For example, the user who forgets the method for underlining a phrase can ask the system what command to use instead of looking the procedure up in the printed documentation

■ Printing Images with Dots

Word processors should allow the user to fully utilize a printer's capability. Printers are generally of two types: those that print full-formed characters like an ordinary typewriter does and those that print each character as a set of closely spaced dots. Printers of the former kind are generally limited to printing text. The user may have the choice between pica or elite spacing, or underlined or boldfaced characters, but little other flexibility is provided. Dot-matrix printers, on the other hand, can print arbitrary characters of any size or shape as well as any graphic image that the word processor allows. This flexibility is possible because the printer can be told which individual dots to print and which not to print for each character or image. In the discussion that follows, most of the capabilities described are available only to printers that print dots, such as dot-matrix, ink jet, and laser printers.

Changing Fonts and Print Sizes. Printed text can vary in three different ways: size, **font,** and typeface. Variation in size is quite obvious. Most standard typewriters allow two different sizes, *elite*, which prints 12 characters to the inch (10/120 inch per character), and *pica*, which prints 10 characters to the

font
A particular style of alphabet that a computer might use during printing. People generally use two different styles: printing and cursive. Computers have many more alternatives, including Gothic, Sans-Serif, and many others.

inch (12/120 inch per character). Advanced word processing systems allow sizes ranging from as small as 5-point type (5/120 inch per character, smaller than elite) up to 72-point type (72/120 inch per character, the size of a newspaper headline).

The font of a printed text may not be as obvious as its size. The font defines the shape of each individual character; for example, in one font the bottom of a lowercase letter t might go straight down, while in another it might curl up to the right. Fonts are generally copyrighted by their developers and have names like Sans-Serif or Times Roman. Word processors may allow the user to interweave a number of different fonts within the same document.

Finally, for any size and any font, the typeface can be altered in many ways. For example, the characters can be underlined, boldfaced, italicized, or shadowed. In each case, there is a procedure for altering any given font to highlight or distinguish certain parts of a text.

All of these variations in the way characters are printed can be used to organize and highlight portions of a document. Examples demonstrating possible variations in size, font, and styles are shown below:

Text Sizes, Fonts, and Styles	
	Text that differs in the SIZE of type
	9 pt type
	10 pt type
	12 pt type
	14 pt type
	18 pt type
	24 pt type
	Text that differs in the FONT used
	Chicago font: abcdefghijklmnopqrstuvwxyz
	Geneva font: abcdefghijklmnopqrstufwxyz
	Monaco font: abcdefghijklmnopqrstuvwxyz
	New York font: abcdefghijklmnopqrstuvwxyz
	Text that differs in the STYLE used
	Boldface text
	Italic text
	Underlined text
	Outlined text
	Shadowed text
	Text with a superscript.
	Text with a subscript.
	Bold, italic, underlined, outlined, and shadowed text.

Computer Insights
Desktop Publishing

Once word processing could be easily performed on micro-computers, it was only a matter of time before computer users wanted more. Word processing systems could do almost anything possible with text: multiple column text, superscripts, subscripts, mathematical formulas, box drawing, indexes or tables of contents, spelling checking, and so forth. If the material to be included on the final document was text, the software existed to create it.

When the Apple Macintosh arrived, however, it had a new capability that everyone wanted: mixing text with arbitrary graphic images. Some of the first advertisements for the Macintosh showed a picture of a tennis shoe in the middle of a letter to a manufacturer. As the authors of this text and so many writers immediately saw, this integration would be extremely useful.

Along with this ability to integrate text and graphics came a new printing technology—laser printers. Before the advent of laser printers, there were only two options for printing on a page: daisy wheel (and similar types of) printers, which created beautiful alphabetic characters but could not easily draw graphic images, and dot-matrix printers, which could create reasonable alphabetic and graphic images but could never quite print text that looked as good as that of the daisy wheel. The laser printers, with a resolution of approximately 300 dots to the inch, were the first readily available printers to provide alphabetic characters and graphic images that were both of excellent quality. (Although 300 dots per inch is a very good resolution, the existing hardware used by publishers has a resolution closer to 3000 dots per inch.) The text of a laser printer is as beautiful as the human eye can perceive, and the graphics are superb as well. Suddenly, the rush began to integrate text and graphics using a laser printer, and desktop publishing was born.

Paul Brainerd, who coined the term *desktop publishing* says that the concept began taking hold in 1985. He led his company, the Aldus Corporation, in the design of Pagemaker, a sophisticated software package designed to use the Macintosh microcomputer and the laser printer to create, merge, and edit text and graphics for the generation of high-quality printed documents. Other software developers have rapidly followed suit. The adoption of desktop publishing is rampant in corporate America, and it is being closely followed by governmental, military, educational, and other institutions. Desktop publishing is now within financial reach of many individuals, enabling them to independently turn out almost any kind and combination of printed and graphic images.

With these new tools, increasingly powerful computers, page scanners to visually scan a picture or photograph and enter it in computer memory, laser printers with increasing resolution, and software systems to control the interaction of all these components, it will soon be easy for a single person to create a text that rivals that of an ordinary publishing house. But we must remember, as we pointed out for word processors, being able to use desktop publishing does nothing to improve a writer's ability to put words together sensibly and communicate effectively.

Graphic Images. Closely associated with the ability to print various fonts in different sizes and typefaces is the ability to store and print general graphic images. Printing graphic images in a document raises two questions: how is the graphic image created? and how is the image integrated into the document? Graphic images are generally created through separate software systems of three kinds: chart graphics systems, paint graphics systems, and draw graphics systems. These systems will be described later in the text; for the present, suffice it to say that arbitrary graphic images can be easily created (e.g., a graph of some data, a drawing of a house or a tiger).

Once a graphic image is created, it must be inserted into the word processing document. Most systems today allow such insertion in only a very primitive way. The data from the image is saved to a disk file and loaded into the middle of the document. The word processor will have a simple embedded command to instruct the printer to treat a portion of the document as commands for printing arbitrary dots on the printer. Because of the way the commands are given, the word processor will generally not allow text to be printed beside graphics. Only in more advanced word processing and **desktop publishing** software is more power available.

desktop publishing
The ability to create large documents of integrated text and graphics with a quality that rivals ordinary published works, but done on a personal computer with appropriate software and high-resolution (laser) printers.

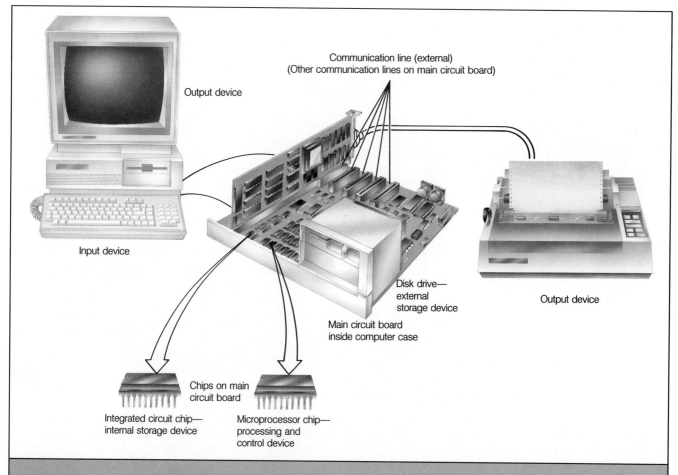

Output device

Communication line (external)
(Other communication lines on main circuit board)

Input device

Disk drive—
external
storage device

Output device

Main circuit board
inside computer case

Chips on main
circuit board

Integrated circuit chip—
internal storage device

Microprocessor chip—
processing and
control device

Merging of Text and Graphics. Many current word processors can insert a graphic image that spreads across the entire page, as in this illustration from chapter 3. More sophisticated interweaving of text and graphics is available in more sophisticated word processors and in desktop publishing systems which allows text to wrap around small figures that do not fill the entire page width and perform other sophisticated tasks.

■ Page Layout

The size of the paper on which the document will be printed and the position of the printing on this paper must also be considered. On most word processing systems, the size of the paper is given in terms of the number of lines of text that can be printed down the page and the number of characters that can be printed across the page. For an elite printer and 8.5-by-11-inch paper, the paper size is generally 66 lines by 102 characters. For a pica printer and the same paper, it would be 66 lines by 85 characters.

Margins. When printing a document, margins of white unprinted paper are left at the top and the bottom and on the left and the right. Therefore, once the size of the paper is given, the word processing system also needs to know the size of the four margins. Top and bottom margins are given in number of lines or inches, left and right margin in number of characters or inches. Some word processing systems may compute things a little differently, for example, some compute the right margin by taking the page width, subtracting the left margin, and then asking for and subtracting the number of characters to be printed across.

Page Numbering. Page numbering is critical for keeping any large document collated properly. Most word processing systems give at least the choice of whether the page number should be printed at the top or the bottom. Some allow the placement of the page number virtually anywhere on the page. Generally, word processors allow the user to specify the starting page number, in case, for some reason, a starting number other than 1 is desired.

Headers and Footers. **Headers** and **footers** are the identifying labels that can appear at the top (headers) or the bottom (footers) of each page. They are generally used to identify the chapter or other topic of the page on which they occur. For example, a user might want REPORT 1 typed at the top of each page of a report.

The various concerns of margins, page numbers, headers and footers are illustrated in Figure 6–6.

header
An identifying label that appears at the top of each page of a document (e.g., REPORT 1).

footer
An identifying label that appears at the bottom of each page of a document.

Header added to appear at top of each page

Margins increased to make column of text narrower

Footer added to each page with embedded page number

```
      Profiles in Computing: John von Neumann

Many of the theoretical foundations of the modern day
computer have been attributed to John von Neumann, a
legendary figure of modern mathematics. One of these
is the "stored program" concept--that the set of
instructions which defines what the computer will do
is stored in the computer's memory and processed just
like any other data. This "stored program" concept was
developed by Arthur Burks, Herman Goldstein and the
mathematician as a solution to the practical problem
of designing the EDVAC computer.
```

```
                        The History of Computing
      Profiles in Computing: John von Neumann

Many of the theoretical foundations of the
modern day computer have been attributed to
John von Neumann, a legendary figure of modern
mathematics. One of these is the "stored
program" concept--that the set of instructions
which defines what the computer will do is
stored in the computer's memory and processed
just like any other data. This "stored
program" concept was developed by Arthur
Burks, Herman Goldstein and the mathematician
as a solution to the practical problem of
designing the EDVAC computer.

                    Page 1 of the essay
```

Figure 6–6 Margins, Headers, Footers, and Page Numbers. The first presentation of text was transformed to the second by a number of embedded commands that would be displayed by a REVEAL CODES command. The embedded commands changed the left and right margins, inserted a header at the top of every page, and inserted a footer (including the proper page number) at the bottom of every page.

■ Text Justification

text justification
A process in word processing for aligning text on a page. The text may be aligned so that it is flush on one or both margins of a page, or it may be centered.

Most word processors allow a choice of **text justification** methods. Text justification generally deals with how the words in a line of text are positioned within the line; if a user tells the computer that there is room for 65 printed characters on a line and the words and spaces for a particular line use up only 62 characters, what does the user do with the extra three spaces? There are generally four alternatives available: left justification, right justification, center justification, and full justification. The four examples below demonstrate each alternative.

Left justification of text

```
Many of the theoretical foundations of the modern day
computer have been attributed to John von Neumann, a
legendary figure of modern mathematics. One of these
is the "stored program"--that the set of
instructions which defines what the computer will
do is stored in the computer's memory and processed
just like any other data.
```

Center justification of text

```
Many of the theoretical foundations of the modern day
computer have been attributed to John von Neumann, a
legendary figure of modern mathematics. One of these
is the "stored program" concept--that the set of
instructions which defines what the computer will
do is stored in the computer's memory and processed
just like any other data.
```

Right justification of text

```
Many of the theoretical foundations of the modern day
computer have been attributed to John von Neumann, a
legendary figure of modern mathematics. One of these
is the "stored program" concept--that the set of
instructions which defines what the computer will
do is stored in the computer's memory and processed
just like any other data.
```

Both left & right justification of text

```
Many of the theoretical foundations of the modern day
computer have been attributed to John von Neumann, a
legendary figure of modern mathematics. One of these
is the "stored program" concept--that the set of
instructions which defines what the computer will
do is stored in the computer's memory and processed
just like any other data.
```

Text Justification

Most word processing systems on microcomputers can handle this level of justification with ease because they assume that all characters are of unit size, e.g., an *i* takes up the same amount of room as an *m* does. For those used to a typewriter, this is no surprise. However, some of the more sophisticated word processors allow proportional spacing, in which the space taken up by the letter *i* is substantially less than the space taken up by the letter *m* (printed books usually use proportional spacing). Unfortunately, this added capability substantially increases the complexity of the justification problem, because the system must keep track of the size of the line and each individual letter, rather than just the number of characters left.

■ Text Placement

The next four commands deal with the placement of **page breaks** (i.e., deciding where to end one page and start the next).

Unconditional Page Break. When the word processor encounters an **unconditional page break** embedded in the text, the system immediately terminates the current page and begins printing the next one. Such a command would be used, for example, before a new chapter to ensure that the new chapter would start printing on a new page.

Conditional Page Break. The **conditional page break** requires an additional piece of information: the amount of room needed on a page. If the word processor encounters a conditional page break command when the amount of room left on the current page is less than the specified amount, a page break will be made; otherwise, the command is ignored. The main purpose of the conditional page break is to prevent one kind of **dangling heading** or **dangling line.** Dangling headings are of two types, **widows** and **orphans,** and result from a computer blindly putting as much text on a page as it can. A widow occurs when the first line of a paragraph becomes the last line of a printed page; an orphan occurs when the last line of a paragraph becomes the first line of the next printed page. Widows can be prevented by putting a conditional page eject before the paragraph with an amount of lines, say ten. If there are ten lines left on the bottom of the page when the new paragraph is encountered, the system just goes ahead and puts it on the page and continues. If there are not ten lines remaining, the system generates a page break and starts the new paragraph at the top of the new page. Some word processing systems provide a preferable method of avoiding widows and orphans: they provide a single command that causes the system to eliminate widows and orphans automatically.

Keep. A **keep** is a section of text that must be kept together on one page. A table of numbers, for example, could include a table title, column headings, and rows of figures, and it would be undesirable to have part of the table printed at the bottom of one page and part at the top of the next. A keep command can be simulated with a conditional page break, but its philosophy is different. Instead of having to count lines as would be required for a conditional page break, a keep has only two commands: a begin keep and an end keep. The system will try to keep everything between those two commands on the same page (see Figure 6-7).

page breaks
In word processing systems, an embedded command that terminates the printing of one page and begins subsequent text at the top of a new page.

unconditional page break
A command that causes a word processor to automatically terminate printing the current page and begin printing the next one.

conditional page break
In word processing, a command that causes a word processor to stop printing on the current page and begin a new page if fewer than a certain number of lines remain on the current page.

dangling heading (or dangling line)
A heading or the first or last line of a paragraph, when printed on a different page from the rest of the paragraph. Conditional page break commands can prevent dangling headings and lines.

widow
The first line of a paragraph appears as the last line on a printed page.

orphan
Last line of a paragraph appears as the first line on a printed page.

keep
A special word processing command that ensures that all of the lines in a given block of text will be printed on the same page

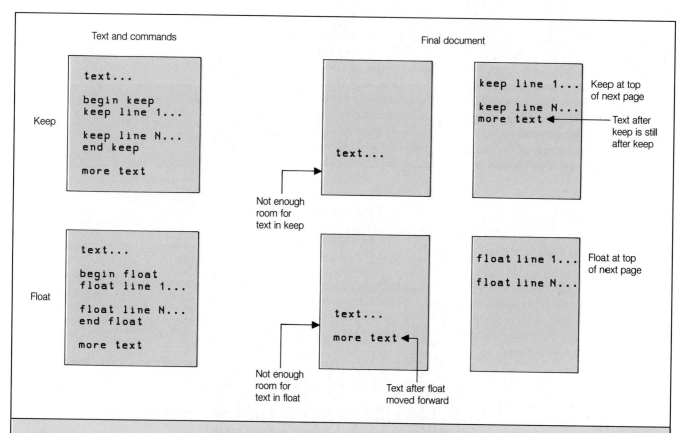

Figure 6–7 Text Keeps and Text Floats. Both keeps and floats ensure that a portion of text stays together on one page. The only difference between the two is way they deal with the lines left blank at the bottom of a page when a portion of text is moved to the top of the next page to keep it together. A keep just leaves the space blank, while a float fills it up with text that originally followed the floated text, thus rearranging the order of the text slightly. Floats are usually used for figures and tables that are referenced as a unit.

float
A special word processing command that ensures that a block of text (e.g., a table) will be kept together on one page but allows text that occurs after the block to be moved before the block to fill out the bottom of a page.

footnoting
In word processing, a special float command that places a footnote reference in the text where the footnote occurs and then floats the footnote to the bottom of the page or end of chapter for printing.

Float. A **float** is similar to a keep, that is, there is a "begin float" command and an "end float" command, and its purpose is to keep text together on one page. However, there is one important difference between a float and a keep. Let us imagine that a user has placed a large table in the middle of some text; the table takes up half of a page. If the table is put in a keep, what happens if the page is three quarters full when the table is encountered? The system would look at the size of the table, see that there is not enough room, and start a new page, leaving one quarter of a page empty. A float acts slightly differently: when the contents of a float do not fit on the page, the system goes to the text after the float, moves it in front of the float to fill up the current page, and then puts the floated material on the top of the next page. With a float, the position of the table within the text can change; in a keep, it cannot.

Footnotes. Once the concept of a float is understood, it is easy to understand another word processing feature of special use for professional and scholarly work: **footnoting** capability. Essentially, a footnote is just a float that is to appear at the bottom of a page. Wherever the quotation or reference is located, the footnote is placed immediately afterwards in a special format. As would be expected, a begin footnote and an end footnote command are required. When the system encounters these commands embedded in the text, it keeps track of the footnote until the end of the page is near and then inserts it. Note that many footnoting systems can be used: numbering from 1 and restarting with 1 for each new page; numbering from 1 and continuing the numbering through the chapter or document; placing all footnotes at the end of the page on which they occur; placing all footnotes at the end of a chapter; and so on. Ideally, a word processor will give the user the method of his or her choice.

■ Indexes and Tables of Contents

Two other capabilities that are built into some word processing systems can automatically generate tables of contents and indexes (See Figure 6-8). Imagine that a large document with many chapters, headings, and subheadings is being written. As the author proceeds through the draft stages of the docu-

An element of text is put in a text block. Then the index or table of contents command is given. This process is repeated throughout the document. Thus many index or table of contents commands are embedded in the text.

```
Augusta Ada Byron was the daughter of Lord Byron, the
poet, and was an excellent mathematician. She
encountered the work of Charles Babbage in a French
paper on his difference and analytic engines. After
contacting Babbage, she translated this paper into
English and added her own notes on the subject.
Included in these notes was the first computer
program, which was intended to compute a mathematical
series of numbers.
```

```
Mark text for 1: Index 2: Table of contents ? 1
Index heading? Computer history
Subheading is: Augusta Ada Byron
```

When the document is complete, a command to generate an index or a table of contents is given. The embedded commands are then used to create the index or table of contents with the proper page numbers.

```
Computer history
     Augusta Ada Byron ............................2
```

Figure 6–8 Generating an Index and a Table of Contents. Tables of contents and indexes are generated by embedding commands in the text to specify what terms will be used in the index or table of contents and then printing the complete list of terms once the document is complete. The major difference between an index and a table of contents is that the index is alphabetically arranged and the table of contents is printed in the order encountered.

ment, tentative tables of contents are made, but whenever a change is made in the document, all of the page numbers in the table of contents must change.

A good word processor can automate this task. All it takes is a special command that tells the system to "put the string 'Chapter 1' into the table of contents and give it the number of the page we happen to be on right now." Every time the computer comes across one of these commands in the text, it remembers the string and the page number. When the system has read through the whole document, it will have remembered the names and page numbers necessary for a table of contents, and it just prints them in the order encountered in the text. Notice that the table of contents is generally printed after the rest of the document. On really fancy systems, the user can even make multiple tables of contents—one for the chapters, one for the figures, and one for the tables.

An index can be automatically generated in exactly the same way. Another special command is needed to store a phrase and associate it with the number of the page on which it was found. The only difference is that the index must be alphabetized before it can be printed. It is also printed at the end of the document. Generating a table of contents and an index is illustrated in Figure 6–8.

6.8

A Final Word Processing Example

Our last example of word processing will demonstrate some of the more sophisticated capabilities available. We return to Roberta, who is helping the local public TV station on their yearly fund-raising drive. She has two jobs before her: to compose a letter for soliciting funds and to finish up a description of upcoming programs to send with the letter.

Case Study

Roberta started up the word processing system and began typing. She had to make sure that this letter was as good as she could make it! She really appreciated the British comedies that the public TV station showed late at night, and she wanted to make sure there were enough funds to continue them. After working for a half an hour, she had the letter finished. It looked, in part, like this:

```
    I'm sure that when you saw this letter, you
were tempted to throw it out. You were right, we
are asking for donations, but please just read a
little farther before you do. The donation you
give to public TV is different in many ways from
any other you will be asked to make because you
benefit from it with programming you like and
extensive tax advantages.

                        .
                        .
                        .

    If I can do anything more to encourage you
to give, please contact me personally. Otherwise,
we look forward to your continued support.
Thank you for listening. And watching.

Sincerely,

Roberta Martin
Fund Raising Committee Member_
```

Now that the text was written, the only thing that Roberta had to do was prepare the text to be used with the mailing list of contributors. This same letter then would be printed out with individual names and addresses ready for her signature. She moved around on the document for a few minutes and inserted the appropriate commands for the mailmerge. When she was finished, the document looked like this:

```
.GF CONTRIBUTORS.LST
.RV NAME,STREET,CITY,STATE,ZIP
.REPEAT

&NAME&
&STREET&
&CITY&, &STATE& &ZIP&

Dear &NAME&:

       I'm sure that when you saw this letter, you
were tempted to throw it out. You were right, we
                         .
                         .
                         .
Thank you for listening. And watching.

Sincerely,

Roberta Martin
Fund Raising Committee Member_
```

The first three commands in the document were embedded commands. The first command was the "get file" command that told the word processor the name of the file that contained the names and addresses of the contributors (CONTRIBUTORS.LST). The second command was the "read variable" command that told the word processor to read one line from the file and to assign the components between commas of that line to the various components listed in the command. For example, if the first line of the contributors file was "John Smith, 426 Main, Lansing, MI, 48063", then "John Smith" would be assigned to NAME, "426 Main" would be assigned to STREET, "Lansing" to CITY, "MI" to STATE, and "48063" to ZIP. The third command causes the system to repeat the letter until all data was read from the contributors file. With these commands, the word processor would print out a series of personalized letters. The first one would look like:

```
John Smith
426 Main
Lansing, MI 48063

Dear John Smith:

       I'm sure that when you saw this letter, you
were tempted to throw it out. You were right, we
                         .
                         .
                         .
Thank you for listening. And watching.

Sincerely,

Roberta Martin
Fund Raising Committee Member_
```

With that done, Roberta issued the commands for the computer to run through all of the contributors and print a personalized letter for each.

Roberta then turned her efforts to the generation of the new program listing. She didn't have all of the text available, but she started the task. As she worked, the second document looked like this:

```
.HEADER                          Program Catalog
.FOOTER              page #
.MARGIN TOP 2
.MARGIN BOTTOM 2
.CENTER
Public Television
Program Catalog
.JUSTIFY LEFT
.FOOTNOTE Supported by Mega University
.PAGE
The station would like to thank the following members of
our fund-raising committee:
.MARGIN LEFT+5
Sarah Miles, Co-Chair
Brain Michaels, Co-Chair
Candice Hurkle
Roberta Martin
Andrew Karras
Jacquelyn Roberts
.MARGIN LEFT-5
.PAGE
The following pages describe the many programs available
to us at the station along with the cost to the station
for their acquisition. It is hoped that each individual
                              .
                              .
                              .
```

Roberta had used many commands in the document. She had specified the layout of the document with the MARGIN commands. The HEADER command would cause the message "Programming Catalog" to appear at the top of each page, and the FOOTER command would print the word "page" followed by the page number at the bottom of each page. Commands like CENTER and JUSTIFY would determine the alignment of the text edges. The PAGE command would cause a new page to begin. The MARGIN LEFT commands were used to temporarily increase the margin by five and then return it to its original value by decreasing it by five.

After working with the document for a little longer, Roberta printed it out. The first few pages looked like this:

```
                              Program Catalog


                         Public Television
                         Program Catalog ¹


_____
¹ Supported by Mega University




                              page 1
```

```
                    Program Catalog
The station would like to thank the
following members of our fund-raising
committee:
     Sarah Miles, Co-Chair
     Brain Michaels, Co-Chair
     Candice Hurkle
     Roberta Martin
     Andrew Karras
     Jacquelyn Robert


                    page 2
```

```
                    Program Catalog

The following pages describe the many
programs available to us at the station
along with the cost to the station for
their acquisition. It is hoped that each
individual
                        .

                        .

                        .

                    page 3
```

Within a few days time, Roberta had fulfilled her commitment to the first part of the fund-raising effort. Her form letter had been printed out for all previous contributors and the catalog of program possibilities was printed, photocopied, and included with each letter. Roberta and the committee had high hopes for the outcome of the drive!

The many ISPCO word processing functions described in this chapter are becoming standard in popular word processing systems for business. In fact, as time passes, the simple (yes, simple!) word processing described in this chapter is being augmented by ever more powerful functions that allow the building of mathematical tables, automatic computation of numeric formulas, multicolumn text, and many other new capabilities. There is a clear move toward word processing systems capable of storing and printing arbitrarily complicated documents.

6.9

Summary of Word Processing Software Usage

▨ The ISPCO Frame for Word Processing

Despite all of these improvements, the main ideas, functions, and commands of word processing can be summarized in terms of the ISPCO functions, as we have done in the ISPCO frame for word processing software. The frame describes word processing concepts and provides blank spaces with questions so that the reader can insert information on particular word processing systems.

This frame illustrates the true nature of word processors. The embedded commands are all described in the output section of the frame. Indeed, the major function of a word processor is to print a document, an output function. All of the formatting commands are therefore described in the output section.

The purpose of the other ISPCO functions is also clear. Input is required for immediate commands, embedded commands, and text. Storage is really only for loading and saving text and embedded commands. Processes are primarily to alter the text and embedded commands that are used for output. Control is used to make the other ISPCO tasks easier by allowing the user to predefine the order in which tasks are to be performed.

Frame for Word Processing Software

	Concept	Your System
ON/OFF	COMPUTER ACCESS: Access to both computer and word processor is needed. May need location, signon, password, telephone number, disk, start-up command. For this system:	Location and disks needed: Telephone, signon, and password: Start-up command for word processor: Shutdown command for word processor:
INPUT	TEXT INPUT: Word processors differ on methods for start and end of text input, character insert and delete, cursor movement, et cetera. For this word processor:	Start and end text input: Character insert and delete: Cursor movement: Other input characteristics:
INPUT	COMMAND INPUT: Word processors differ widely in how commands are interspersed with text input. Function keys, mouse, control keys, etcetera, are used. For this word processor:	Use of function keys: Use of mouse: Use of control keys: Use of other key:
STORAGE	STORAGE ACCESS: Access to underlying operating system commands is mandatory for disk preparation, directories, etcetera. For this word processing system:	Format command: Directory command: Copy command: Other operating system commands:
STORAGE	DOCUMENT ACCESS: Word processors differ on how a document is created, destroyed, loaded, and saved within the operating system files. On this system:	Create document command: Destroy document command: Load document command: Save document command:
PROCESS B = 2 + C	BLOCK COMMANDS: Word processors differ in the way text blocks are defined. Once defined, they may be deleted, copied, or moved. For this word processor:	Block definition command: Block delete command: Block move command: Block copy command:

PROCESS B=2+C	TEXT FIND AND REPLACE: Searching and replacing text require specification of a text pattern to search for and, for replace, a new pattern to replace it. On this system:	Text search command: Text replace command:
PROCESS B=2+C	RULERS AND CODES: Word processors use rulers and reveal embedded command codes in different ways, especially comparing WYSIWYG to other word processors. For this system:	Ruler uses: Ruler access command: Reveal codes command:
PROCESS B=2+C	WINDOWS: Word processors may allow multiple views of one document or simultaneous views of more than one. Many window commands are needed. For this system:	Create window command: Remove window command: Switch window command:
PROCESS B=2+C	SPELLER AND THESAURUS: Word processors may check spelling in a document or provide a thesaurus for finding synonyms during writing. For this word processor:	Spell-check command: Thesaurus command:
CONTROL	MULTIFILE DOCUMENTS: Word processors differ in their ability to merge multifile documents into a single one or to use two files in a mail merge operation. For this system:	Commands to merge files together: Method for mailmerge:
CONTROL	START PRINT: Printing the document is the goal of most word processing. Often the number of copies and other details must be given as well. For this word processing:	Command to start printing:
OUTPUT	TYPEFACE: Word processors differ in the way typeface, typestyle and font are selected. For this word processing system:	Command to change size of type: Command to change font: Commands to boldface underline, et cetera:
OUTPUT	JUSTIFICATION: The four modes of justification are almost universally available in word processors. For this system:	Command for left justification: Command for right justification: Command for center justification: Command for both edge justification:
OUTPUT	PAGE BREAK: Page ejects are used to start text at the top of a new page and can be unconditional or conditional. For this word processing system:	Command for unconditional page eject: Command for conditional page eject:

OUTPUT	PAGE LAYOUT: Page layout describes the position of text on the page including top, bottom, left, and right margins. For this word processing system:	Left margin command: Right margin command: Top margin command: Bottom margin command:
OUTPUT	Header/footer and page number of text are printed on each page to provide organization. For this word processor they are specified by:	Command for header: Command for footer: Command for page number:
OUTPUT	KEEP, FLOAT, AND FOOTNOTE: Keeps, floats, and footnotes keep text together at certain places on a page. The commands for this word processing system are:	Command for keep: Command for float: Command for footnote:
OUTPUT	TABLE OF CONTENTS/INDEX: Table of contents and index commands mark text so that it will appear at document end, alphabetized (index) or not (table of content). For this system:	Command to mark table of contents: Command to generate table of contents: Command to mark index: Command to generate index:
OUTPUT	HELP SYSTEM: Help systems provide access to on-line commentary, possibly with an index into all topics available. For this word processing system:	Command to access help index: Command to access help:

■ The ISPCO Scripts for Word Processing

For most beginning uses of word processing, two separate activities are required. The first is the entry and simple editing of text, while the second is the formatting and final printing of the completed document.

The entry and editing of text is straightforward. The steps involved are writing the document, starting up the word processing system, typing the document with minor editing and formatting commands, and saving the document to permanent disk storage. Although experienced users of word processors frequently compose the text at the computer, beginning users may find it easier to separate the activities. The major steps in the initial creation of a document are described in the new document creation script.

NEW DOCUMENT CREATION SCRIPT FOR WORD PROCESSING SOFTWARE

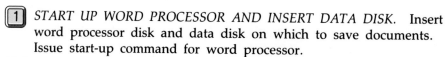

1 *START UP WORD PROCESSOR AND INSERT DATA DISK.* Insert word processor disk and data disk on which to save documents. Issue start-up command for word processor.

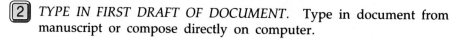

2 *TYPE IN FIRST DRAFT OF DOCUMENT.* Type in document from manuscript or compose directly on computer.

3 *MAKE MINOR CORRECTIONS.* During text entry, make minor corrections by using delete key, cursor keys, and so forth.

4 *ENTER MINOR FORMATTING.* During text entry, enter minor formatting commands like underline or center using appropriate command format for the word processor.

5 *SAVE DOCUMENT TO DISK.* Issue command to save document to permanent storage. Usually save the document to two separate disks, the main data disk and backup.

6 *PRINT OUT DOCUMENT.* Issue print commands for review of current state of document and archiving.

7 *SHUT DOWN SOFTWARE AND STORE DISKS.* Issue shutdown command. Remove and store program and data disks.

Once the data of a document is entered, the user can proceed with the formatting through the entry of embedded commands. The most obvious steps involved in formatting are a repeated sequence of printing the document, deciding on changes in the printed form, entering new embedded commands, saving the document, and printing again. The document revision and completion script describes the major steps in this sequence.

1 *START UP WORD PROCESSOR AND INSERT DATA DISK.* Insert word processor disk and data disk from previous interaction. Issue start-up command for word processor.

2 *RETRIEVE DOCUMENT FROM DISK.* Issue storage retrieval command to obtain document from prior software use.

3 *ENTER NEW TEXT.* Enter any new text including minor corrections and minor formatting.

4 *ENTER MAJOR FORMAT COMMANDS.* Enter commands for titles, section headings, headers, footers, page breaks, keeps, floats, footnotes, table of contents, indexes, and so forth.

5 *SAVE REVISED DOCUMENTS.* Issue the command to save the revised document onto disk.

6 *PRINT OUT DOCUMENT.* Issue command to output document for review of both content and formatting. If corrections remain to be made, loop back to step 3 and repeat.

7 *SHUT DOWN SOFTWARE AND STORE DISKS.* Issue shutdown command. Remove and store program and data disks.

DOCUMENT REVISION AND COMPLETION SCRIPT FOR WORD PROCESSING SOFTWARE

With these scripts and the ISPCO frame, the reader should be able to make use of whatever word processing systems are available. By filling in the ISPCO Frame with the description of the commands of an available word processor, all of the concepts of the chapter will be immediately available to the reader. But only through the use of a real system will the power and effectiveness of word processing software become apparent.

Chapter 6 Review

Expanded Objectives

The objectives listed below are an expansion of the essential chapter concepts listed at the beginning of the chapter. The review items for the chapter are based on these expanded objectives. If you master the objectives, you will do better on the review items and on your instructor's examination on the chapter material.

After reading the chapter, you should be able to:

1. order the general steps involved in creating a document with a word processor.
2. explain the difference between the text entry mode and the immediate command mode in word processing.
3. select appropriate text entry, embedded commands, and immediate commands for specific word processing situations.
4. compare the structure of a word processing system to the structure of an operating system.
5. recognize common editing functions available on a word processor.
6. relate word processing to RAM, ROM, and disk storage.
7. describe the common options available to a word processor for interfacing with printers and monitor screens.
8. match word processing commands with appropriate ISPCO functions.
9. complete a word processing system frame by filling in the commands for your own system.
10. give the meaning of the major new terms introduced in this chapter.

Review Items

Completing this review will give you a good indication of how well you have mastered the contents of this chapter and prepare you for your instructor's test on this material. To maximize what you learn from this exercise, you should answer each question *before* looking up the answers in the appendix. The number of the corresponding expanded objective is given in parentheses following each question.

Complete the following clusters of items according to the directions heading each set.

A. *True or false.*

____ 1. A glossary is a method for replacing an abbreviation throughout the text with a word or phrase. (7,10)
____ 2. Most word processing systems depend on the operating system to access file directories. (4)
____ 3. A float allows a table of contents to move to the beginning of a document. (7,10)
____ 4. A word processing system must interact with an operating system to store and retrieve documents. (6)
____ 5. A header is used to specify the titles of figures in a document. (10)
____ 6. Embedded commands are used for editing (e.g., copying) text in a document. (2,10)
____ 7. A shell is part of a word processor. (4,10)
____ 8. Parts of a word processing system are stored in ROM. (6)
____ 9. There are many similarities between an operating system and a word processing system. (4)
____ 10. In most word processors, it is possible to save a document without leaving the text entry mode. (2)
____ 11. On most computer systems, the characteristics of the monitor screen are exactly matched with those of the printer. (7)
____ 12. Single keystrokes on a word processor can be immediate commands in the command mode. (2)
____ 13. Documents typed on standard typewriters are usually full-justified. (7,10)
____ 14. Embedded commands do not normally appear on the printout of a document. (2)
____ 15. Once the word processing system is in use, the operating system is removed from RAM until the word processor is finished. (4)
____ 16. Immediate commands are included in the text entry mode. (2)
____ 17. A macro is used to split the monitor into two or more sections. (10)
____ 18. Embedded commands are not part of the command mode. (2)
____ 19. For some word processing systems, a user can see the final form of a document only through a printout. (7)
____ 20. To retrieve a document that was worked on the day before, the word processing system must be in the entry mode. (2, 8)
____ 21. The position of the cursor indicates where a user is working on a document. (1,10)
____ 22. Most word processing systems permit a user to destroy a document with a single command. (5)
____ 23. An advantage of word processing systems is that embedded commands can be added at any time, even after the document is completely typed. (1,2)
____ 24. A word processing system can search out all occurrences of a particular word or phrase. (8)
____ 25. In command mode, any command that is entered is executed immediately. (2)
____ 26. All instances of a word that have been consistently misspelled throughout a document can be corrected with a single command. (5)
____ 27. The window function found in some word processing systems permits the user to display different sections of a document on the screen at the same time. (5,10)
____ 28. An unconditional page eject is an embedded

command that causes printing to be terminated at a specific point on a page. (7)

B. *For the following items (29–32), assume that your word processor designates embedded commands with the symbols < and > and uses the set of embedded commands listed below. Your task in items 29–32 will be to give the embedded commands to produce the part of a document described in each item. (1)*

Embedded commands:

\<jc\> = justify center	\<jl\> = justify left
\<jr\> = justify right	\<jb\> = justify both
\<bb\> = boldface begin	\<be\> = boldface end
\<ub\> = underline begin	\<ue\> = underline end
\<kb\> = keep begin	\<ke\> = keep end
\<np\> = new page	\<return\> = new paragraph

\<lm=x\> = set left margin to x inches
\<rm=x\> = set right margin to x inches
\<hd="xxxxx"\> = set header to the designated string
\<ft="xxxxx"\> = set footer to the designated string

29. You want to center the title of your paper on the page. The text following it should be justified on both sides of the page. The title is: "The Impact of Computers," and the text begins: "The major impacts are threefold: social, ..." Place the appropriate text and letters representing specific embedded commands and the text, in the proper sequence (as if you were typing on this word processing system) on the screen below.

30. The beginning of the next section of your paper, "Part I: The Early Years," should start at the top of a new page in boldface and underlined print. Place the appropriate text and letters representing the embedded command in the proper sequence on the screen below.

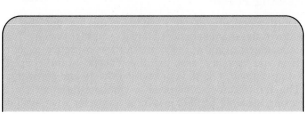

31. You want to include in your paper the following quotation, printed with the left margin indented two inches; at the end of the quotation, the left margin should return to its previous width of one inch.

"The resulting explosion was terrible, according to Rupert: The magnitude of the destruction was close to that of a nuclear bomb. The main reason for the collision of the two trains was probably computer error."

Place the command(s) and text in appropriate sequence on the screen below.

32. You want the phrase "Computer Impacts" to appear at the top of every page of your paper and the phrase "English 101" to appear at the bottom of every page. Place the commands and the text in the appropriate sequence on the screen below.

C. *Assume that your word processing system provides the following immediate commands:*

a. @save
b. @load
c. @directory
d. @delete
e. @rename
f. @home
g. @end
h. @find
i. @replace
j. @new
k. @quit
l. @print
m. @install
n. cursor movement

For each of the items below (33–44), determine which command above (a–n) best completes the task and place its letter next to the item. (3)

___ 33. You have misspelled "Smythe" as "Smith" throughout the whole document.

___ 34. You want a list of the documents previously created with your word processor.

___ 35. You want to revise a previously prepared document called LETTER 10/10.

___ 36. You want to store the document you have been working on as CHAPTER 4.

___ 37. You want to inform the word processor that a new kind of printer has been attached to the computer.

___ 38. You have finished your document and have saved it to disk. Now you wish to stop using the word processor.

___ 39. You want to locate the heading "Section 4.2" in your text so that you can add some new text there.

___ 40. You want to print out the final document.

___ 41. You want to remove the document named DRAFT 1 from the disk.

___ 42. You want to quickly move the cursor to the beginning of the current document.

___ 43. You want to move the cursor to the bottom of the entire document.

___ 44. You want to start a document over from scratch.

D. *Using the ISPCO Frame from this chapter, match the most appropriate function on the right with each command listed on the left. (8)*

___45. save a document on disk

___46. enter text and embedded commands

___47. call up a file directory

___48. move a block of text in a document

___49. print a draft copy of a document

___50. set up a mailmerge job to run later

a. input
b. storage
c. processing
d. control
e. output

E. *Identify the mode (on the right) of each command on the left. (2)*

___51. save a document

___52. add to a document

___53. print a document

___54. type in a document

___55. edit a document

a. entry mode
b. command mode

F. *Check the items below that are commonly available editing function on word processing systems. (5)*

___ 56. erase part of the text in a document.

___ 57. give a command to replace an abbreviation with a phrase, throughout the text.

___ 58. permit automatic hyphenation.

___ 59. move text around within a document.

___ 60. locate specific text in a document on command.

___ 61. call up help function to remind user of available commands.

G. *Without using the ISPCO frame for word processing, see how many command concepts you can recall for each of the following ISPCO functions.*

62. Input Command Concepts: (For example, what keys are used in the text entry mode?)

63. Storage Command Concepts: (For example, what can you do to files?)

64. Processing Command Concepts: (For example, what are the editing commands?)

65. Output Command Concepts: (For example, what are the embedded print commands?)

Projects

Experience shows that doing a project is a great help in understanding a word processor. The following projects are some we have found especially useful. They assume that a word processing system is available.

1. Use your word processor to simulate the first case study of the chapter. Include the correction of plenty of errors. If you have a spell checker program, use it on the story.

2. If you are writing any papers this quarter, consider word processing them. Be sure to: (1) write the outline and much of the paper before you start word processing; (2) practice word processing with something less important first; (3) make backup copies of your disks and files and allow yourself plenty of time.

3. If your word processor has the capability for mailmerge, try simulating the second case study in the chapter. As an alternative, find someone who needs a simple mailmerge for a few letters and try doing it (don't promise that it will work the first time!). Allow yourself three times as much time as you think you will need.

Special Exercise: Completing The Word Processing Frame

The word processing frame includes places for the user to write down the characteristics of a real computer system. You are encouraged to fill in the frame for the particular system to which you have access so that the concepts of this chapter can be directly applied to your own hardware and software.

This frame can also be used to compare different word processing systems by filling in one frame for each system and contrasting the systems on a point-by-point basis.
Your primary source of information for completing this frame should be the documentation available with your software or hardware system.

As a computer user works on more and different systems, each of the boxes in this frame may require expansion into even more detailed descriptions. By then, however, the user will be sophisticated enough to make such expansions easily and without help.

7 Spreadsheet Software

Essential Chapter Concepts

When you finish this chapter, you should know:

- The basic spreadsheet concepts of tables, cells, and cell contents and how spreadsheets are made and used.

- The differences between entry mode (when text and embedded commands are entered) and command mode (when immediate commands are given) for spreadsheet software.

- The ISPCO functions available in command mode, including delete, blank, move, copy, find, replace, and sort.

- The types of labels, values, and formulas that can be placed in tables, including the embedded ISPCO functions for sums, averages, maximums, minimums, and other mathematical, business, and engineering computations.

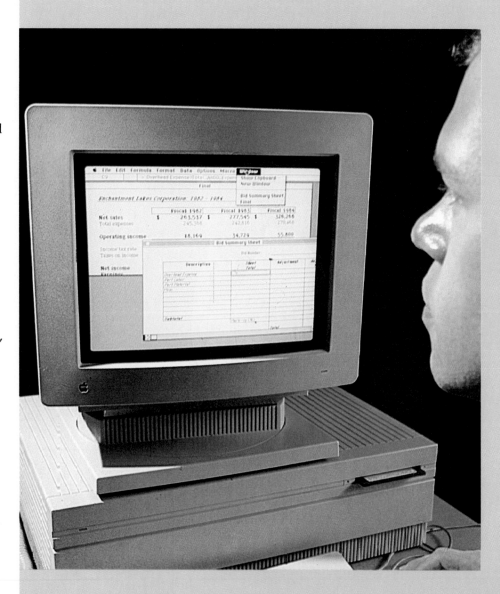

Spreadsheet Software

INPUT	STORAGE	PROCESS	CONTROL	OUTPUT
Embedded command entry • Cell cursor movement • Cell block definition • Cell names • Immediate command entry	Load spreadsheet • Save spreadsheet • Spreadsheet directory • Other file commands	Editing a single cell • Editing a table • Finding cells • Windows • Sorting a table • Protecting cells • Other process functions	Ripple calculation • Automatic recalculation • Manual recalculation • Immediate recalculation • Recalculation order	Table appearance on screen and printer • Mathematical, statistical, business, and other output function

In the last chapter, we discussed the characteristics of common word processing software, whose primary purpose is to perform a variety of ISPCO functions on strings of characters. For example, "Mr. James and Ms. Roberts each ordered 20 IBM's and 30 Apple IIe's!" could be a string created by a word processing system.

Although word processing systems operate on both words and numbers, most word processing ISPCO functions do not treat numbers as numbers. For example, one could enter a table like this one:

	IBM	Apple IIe	Total
Mr. James	20	30	**
Ms. Roberts	20	30	**
Total	**	**	**

into a word processor, but the typical word processor would not be able to add the numbers in the table to give totals by row or column. In this situation, the word processor is analogous to a typewriter with numeric keys: no matter how many numbers one enters on a typewriter, the only thing the typewriter can do with the numbers is print them on the page. The typewriter and the word processor never really view numbers as anything more than a sequence of characters. (Some sophisticated word processing systems now have ISPCO functions for calculations, but typical word processing functions do not include such abilities.)

Spreadsheet software is designed to process more than just textual characters: *electronic spreadsheets can process arbitrary tables of text, numbers, and formulas, using true mathematical operators in the computation of formulas.* For example, a spreadsheet program can accept the table given above and can be instructed to carry out the appropriate mathematical operations to compute the sums in the table automatically, giving

	IBM	Apple IIe	Total
Mr. James	20	30	50
Ms. Roberts	20	30	50
Total	40	60	100

Thus, spreadsheet programs are able to perform the ISPCO functions on *tables* (called spreadsheets), in contrast to word processors, which work with *characters*.

There are, however, many similarities between spreadsheet and word processing software. For example, both have data entry and command modes that are differentiated by a reserved character (e.g., @ or /), function keys, a mouse, or a menu. In spreadsheet software, the data entry mode is dominated by the input and simple modification of table entries called **cells.** Input often consists of embedded commands that are entered into a table and that affect the output that the system generates to the printer and screen. The primary purpose of the entry mode is to establish the contents of each cell and the method by which these contents will be displayed.

In command mode, commands are accepted and executed immediately, acting as built-in processes for the manipulation of tables. The primary purpose of the immediate commands is to develop the spreadsheet—both its organization and its contents.

Spreadsheet software provides many of the specific ISPCO functions that are also found in operating systems. For example, file manipulation, which deals with the storage of tables on disk, plays a critical role in the development process. By now the reader should begin to notice and search for the commonalities of the many software systems we will examine. Spreadsheets use many of the concepts of word processing and operating systems. This repetition will continue across the software systems described in this book, pointing to the larger organizing framework in which all software systems can be placed.

cell
In spreadsheets, a single entry in a table; it may contain either a number, a label, or a formula as its value. Each cell is located at the intersection of a row and column.

Before going into a technical discussion of the ISPCO functions in spreadsheets, let us consider a case study. Beth is a graduate assistant in social science at a small but prestigious college. One of her duties is to help students with their computer-related assignments. Brian is a student in a business class that requires students to use spreadsheet software, and he is having trouble.

7.1

How Does a Spreadsheet System Work?

Case Study

Part One

"Beth, my instructor assigned us a set of problems to solve with a spreadsheet. He gave us these disks. I really don't understand what I'm supposed to do!" said Brian, twisting the system and data disks in his sweaty hands.

Beth rescued the disks and sat Brian at a PC. "Okay. This system disk contains the spreadsheet program, and this other disk is your data disk—it contains already prepared tables for spreadsheets. These tables are sometimes called templates. From the label, it seems that the templates you have are for common business problems. Let me see your assignment."

After perusing the class assignment, Beth continued, "You have to use the various business templates on your data disk to solve the list of problems given in your assignment. Let's begin with your first assignment: calculate the monthly payment on a mortgage. Why don't you start by booting the system disk."

Brian took the system disk, inserted it into the left drive of the PC, and flipped the power switch on. After a few moments the spreadsheet appeared on the screen:

```
CELL A1:

    .---A---..---B---..---C---..---D---..---E---.
01 ┌─────────┐
02 └─────────┘
03
04
05
06
07
```

"What does all that mean?" asked Brian.

"Well," replied Beth, "spreadsheets let you work on tables. Tables have rows and columns. When you start up a spreadsheet system, it presents you with a table all set up with rows labeled 1, 2, 3, and so on, and columns labeled A, B, C, and so forth. Each place in the table is called a cell, and you can put names, numbers, or formulas in any cell. The names and numbers are easy, you just go to the cell you want by using the arrow keys and type in the name or number. The formulas can get pretty complicated."

"You said something about templates," said Brian. "Where do they fit in?"

"Templates are easy, too. They are just tables that someone else already typed in and saved on a disk. That way anybody can load in the table from disk rather than starting from scratch," Beth explained. "Your assignment sheet says that you are supposed to use the template called MORTGAGE.PAYMENT. Let me show you how to load that template into the system."

Brian got up and let Beth sit at the PC, then Beth continued, "First you press the command key that tells the spreadsheet that you want to give an immediate command. On this software system it is a slash. Watch what happens when I press the slash key." As soon as Beth pressed the slash (/), the screen changed to give:

```
B(lank), C(opy), D(elete), E(dit), F(ormat),
G(oto), I(nsert), L(ocate), M(ove), P(rint),
R(ecalculate), S(torage)

Enter Command:
```

"Look at all the commands that you have available. This system is nice because it has a menu shell that can list all your options. The slash gets you into the main menu. From there you go to the submenus. Since we want to get something from disk, I'll press an S for storage."

When Beth pressed the S, the screen changed again. Now the submenu for storage was listed on the screen:

```
D(irectory), L(oad), R(emove), S(ave)

Enter Command:
```

Beth entered the letter L and the screen changed again:

```
Enter name of file to load:
```

She then typed in the name of the file, MORTGAGE.PAYMENT. While the disk drive whirred and read in the template, Beth gave the chair back to Brian. Before he could sit down, the screen showed the selected template. The top line (CELL A1:) indicated the cell where the cursor was currently located.

```
CELL A1:
TEMPLATE FOR:
    .-----------A-----------..----------B----------.
01 │TEMPLATE FOR:                 │
02 MORTGAGE PAYMENTS
03
04 LOAN AMOUNT                              $100,000.00
05 INTEREST RATE (Annual)                          .12
06 INTEREST RATE (Per Month)                       .01
07 TERM (MONTHS)                                   360
08 ------------------------------------------------------
09 MONTHLY PAYMENT                         $    1,028.61
10 TOTAL OF ALL PAYMENTS                   $370,300.53

    ENTER VALUES AND RECALCULATE
```

"Well, Brian," said Beth, "your syllabus says that this example calculates the monthly payment and the total amount paid on a home mortgage. In the example on the screen, a mortgage loan of one hundred thousand dollars at a twelve percent interest rate for thirty years (that's three hundred sixty months) would give a monthly payment of one thousand twenty-eight dollars and sixty-one cents. Over the thirty years of the loan, the total payment would be three hundred seventy thousand three hundred dollars and fifty-three cents.

"Now, this is where the big difference between a spreadsheet table and a table in a word processor becomes apparent. If we go into that table and change any value, we can instruct the computer to automatically recalculate any other values in the table that might need changing. Let me show you how."

Leaning over Brian's shoulder, Beth pressed the arrow keys to change the current cell where the spreadsheet cursor was located. She pressed the right arrow once and the down arrow six times to move the cursor to cell B7. Once there, Beth typed in a new value, 180, just by typing the characters of the number and hitting return. At this point the table was incorrect. It looked like:

```
CELL B7:
180
       .----------A----------..----------B----------.
01 TEMPLATE FOR:
02 MORTGAGE PAYMENTS
03
04 LOAN AMOUNT                      $100,000.00
05 INTEREST RATE (Annual)                  .12
06 INTEREST RATE (Per Month)               .01
07 TERM (MONTHS)             ┌──────180──────────┐
08 ------------------------------------------------
09 MONTHLY PAYMENT                 $   1,028.61
10 TOTAL OF ALL PAYMENTS           $370,300.53

   ENTER VALUES AND RECALCULATE
```

"Wait a minute," responded Brian. "I thought that spreadsheets were supposed to automatically keep these tables up to date. If I still had to pay the same amount for the loan when I'm only keeping the money half as long, I'd want out of the deal right now!"

"Normally, you would be right, Brian," said Beth, "but in this case the template was setup with *automatic recalculation turned off*. This is often done in a template, because if the system recalculates after every change, it can be slow to input new data. Since recalculation was turned off, the table did not automatically recompute all the values when the new term of one hundred eighty months was entered. To manually issue the recalculation command, I just type in /R to invoke the immediate command to recompute."

After recomputation, the table looked like:

```
CELL B7:
180
       .----------A----------..----------B----------.
01 TEMPLATE FOR:
02 MORTGAGE PAYMENTS
03
04 LOAN AMOUNT                      $100,000.00
05 INTEREST RATE (Annual)                  .12
06 INTEREST RATE (Per Month)               .01
07 TERM (MONTHS)             ┌─────────────180─┐
08 ------------------------------------------------
09 MONTHLY PAYMENT                 $   1,200.17
10 TOTAL OF ALL PAYMENTS           $216,030.25

   ENTER VALUES AND RECALCULATE
```

Now that he understood what was going on, Brian quickly entered the various problems from his homework into the computer, read the answers, and recorded them on paper. He was surprised to see how much less the total loan cost was as he decreased the time of the loan.

"Beth," asked Brian, "I have all the answers now, but how does the computer do it?"

Beth explained, "You can find out the formulas that the computer is using just by placing the cursor on the cell containing the mortgage payment—that will display the formula at the top of the screen. Why don't you press the arrow keys so that the cursor is on the monthly payment cell."

Brian did so. Now the screen looked like:

```
CELL B9:
@PMT(B4,B6,B7)
.----------A-----------..----------B-----------.
01 TEMPLATE FOR:
02 MORTGAGE PAYMENTS
03
04 LOAN AMOUNT                        $100,000.00
05 INTEREST RATE (Annual)                    .12
06 INTEREST RATE (Per Month)                 .01
07 TERM (MONTHS)                             180
08 ------------------------------------------------
09 MONTHLY PAYMENT               │   $  1,200.17│
10 TOTAL OF ALL PAYMENTS             $216,030.25

   ENTER VALUES AND RECALCULATE
```

Brian looked with disdain at the second line of the screen where the formula was listed. "Great! What does that mean?" he said.

"It does look complicated," consoled Beth. "B4 is the cell containing the amount of the loan. B6 is the interest rate charged each time period, in this case each month. B7 is the number of months. @PMT is a built-in function that calculates the mortgage payment required.

"But how does the @PMT function work?" Brian asked.

"Brian," replied Beth, "I haven't the slightest idea. The spreadsheet documentation gives an equation, but I haven't bothered to study it—ask your professor."

As Brian left, Beth mused to herself, "That's probably the biggest strength and weakness of spreadsheets—they permit us to do lots of highly complex things without really understanding them?"

Part Two

Later in the term, Brian was back for more help with spreadsheets.

"Beth," he complained, "I can't figure out this assignment. Our instructor told us to set up a spreadsheet 'program' using the example and data given in our class syllabus. I've read this thing ten times and I still don't understand. How can I write a program while I'm putting in data?!"

Beth sighed. She'd given this explanation a hundred times! "Well, Brian, a spreadsheet program is just a template like you used in your earlier assignments. A template is a table that solves the same problem for different sets of data. So, for you to program in a spreadsheet, you must create a table that can be used over and over with different data to solve the same problem. But before you can write a program or template for a spreadsheet, you need to analyze your problem and develop a solution—that's always true whether you use a spreadsheet, data base manager, programming language, or whatever! Let's see the assignment."

Brian pulled the assignment from his backpack and described it to Beth while she read, "We have to develop a template to calculate the tax for any piece of property given the assessed property value, the portion of the property value that is actually taxed, and the tax rate. The formula is tax equals assessed value times proportion taxed times rate."

"Okay Brian," said Beth, "let's get a design by working out a table." After some study and a little help from Beth, Brian created the following table using the sample data from his assignment:

Calculations of Tax

	A	B
1	Assessed Property Value	75,000
2	Proportion of value taxed	50%
3	Tax rate in mils per thousand	.002
4	Total tax	B1*B2*B3*

"Now, Brian," Beth explained, "you can use this table that you've designed as a model and create a spreadsheet table that looks just like it."

Brian booted up the system and entered the following data into the designated cells:

cell A1: the label "assessed property value"
cell A2: the label "proportion of assessed value taxed"
cell A3: the label "tax rate"
cell A4: the label "tax"
cell B1: the number 75000 (the assessed property value)
cell B2: the number 50% (the part that is taxed)
cell B3: the number 0.002 (the tax rate of 2 mils)
cell B4: the formula +(B1 * B2 * B3)

Each of the values was entered by positioning the spreadsheet cell cursor in the specified cell and then typing in the value. Then the body of the spreadsheet looked like this:

```
CELL B4: FORMULA
+(B1*B2*B3)
    .----------A----------..----------B----------.
1   assessed property value                75000
2   proportion of assessed value taxed      50%
3   tax rate                               0.002
4   tax                          [         75.00  ]
```

Beth said to Brian, "All the cells on the spreadsheet appear just as you entered them, except for one: cell B4. This cell doesn't show a formula, it shows a value based on the formula in B4. That formula is B1 times B2 times B3, so the system multiplies the numeric values in cells B1, B2, and B3 and puts the result in cell B4. You can view cells that have formulas in two ways. In the body of the table you see computed value. If you move the cell cursor to the cell, the formula will appear at the top of the screen. Look at the screen right now—the value 75 in cell B4 is highlighted in reverse video. This means that the cell cursor is pointing at B4. At the top of the screen, the formula for B4 is listed."

"Now we'll see the real power of a spreadsheet," Beth continued. "Let's change the value stored in position B3 from 0.002 to 0.003, as if we were asking ourselves how a one mil increase in tax rate would impact the total tax bill." She quickly repositioned the cell cursor to cell B3 and entered the value 0.003. The instant that the new value was typed into B3, the change rippled through the spreadsheet. B4 was updated to its new value of 112.50 automatically, giving a screen that looked like:

```
CELL B3: VALUE
0.003
    .----------A----------..----------B----------.
1   assessed property value                75000
2   proportion of assessed value taxed      50%
3   tax rate                     [         0.003  ]
4   tax                                   112.50
```

"Obviously, if you save your spreadsheet program, other people who don't know much about spreadsheets can use them just by loading in your table and replacing the values in your table with their own values. The system will automatically recalculate the table, and they can record the results of the recalculation." Beth gestured at the screen. "Okay, Brian, that's your template program. It's a general-purpose program that you or other people can use with any set of data. You'd better save it to disk and print it out for your instructor."

Brian placed his data disk in the drive and issued the storage commands he'd learned in class to save the spreadsheet. He typed a / (to enter command mode), followed by an S (the storage command in the main menu), followed by another S (the save command in the storage submenu), followed by the name of the file he wanted to use, "mytemplate."

After the disk drive stopped, Brian input the commands to print out his spreadsheet: / (to enter command mode), P (a print command to get to the printing menu), then A (to specify that he wanted the whole table printed).

Beth ushered Brian out of her office. "Remember," she called after him, "finish your design before you start your spreadsheet on the computer."

Computer Insights
Profiles in Computing: Daniel Bricklin

The tedium of dealing with a company's balance sheet is exemplified by the labor of poor Bob Cratchett in Dicken's *Christmas Carol.* Like monks in their cells, clerks figured their lives away. As late as 1978, business accounting was done primarily through paper balance sheets supported by pencils and calculators. Depending on their complexity, the generation of balance sheets (spreadsheets) might require days, weeks, or even months of effort. With the fluctuations of business, the finished spreadsheet could be soon outdated, requiring continual rounds of painstaking revision. Many firms employed accountants and clerks just for this purpose. Because even the simplest change might require the revision of hundreds or thousands of other numbers in a spreadsheet, managers hesitated to ask for projections based on their speculations. Today, what might have taken a team of accountants weeks to do can be done in a moment by electronic spreadsheets.

The idea of an electronic spreadsheet program originated in 1978 with Daniel Bricklin, a master's candidate in business administration at Harvard University. In 1979, he and a friend, Robert Frankston, a fellow student and skilled computer programmer, developed the first electronic spreadsheet program and named it VisiCalc (*visi*ble *calc*ulator). By incorporating formulas in the program, any numerical change would automatically "ripple" through the spreadsheet, changing the values of all formulas that referenced the changed number. Once a spreadsheet had been created with VisiCalc, modification of the data and recalculation of values became trivial. Bricklin founded a company called Software Arts in Wellesley, Massachusetts, to sell VisiCalc. With the assistance of a gifted marketing manager, Daniel Fylstra, the company was able to sell over four hundred thousand copies of VisiCalc by 1983 and turn Bricklin's invention into sales of several million dollars a year. Not coincidentally, the surge of VisiCalc did much to spur the growth of the Apple Computer Corporation, since the original VisiCalc worked on the Apple II microcomputer.

All good things are eventually replaced by others, and so it was with VisiCalc, which was replaced first by cheaper clones and then by more sophisticated software. The first major leap ahead of VisiCalc was accomplished in 1982 by the Lotus Company's new program, Lotus 1-2-3. This program integrated database management and graphics capabilities with those of the spreadsheet. Lotus 1-2-3 was initially programmed for IBM computers, thus giving IBM the new edge. Despite the fact that VisiCalc has fallen by the wayside, there is no doubt that Bricklin and his colleagues changed the way in which the world does business!

word processing software, these two types of software have many common features, including different input modes (entry and command), similar disk input/output methods, and similar menuing.

When spreadsheet software is started up, the user is immediately shown the basic nature of a spreadsheet: one large table with many rows and many columns is displayed on the screen. The table is composed of a number of individual cells. The location of each cell in the table is given by its **coordinates,** that is, by its column identifier (usually running A, B, C, ..., Z, AA, AB ...) and its row identifier (usually running 1, 2, 3, ...). Typical cell locations might be A1, D211, and AC56. A typical spreadsheet organization is illustrated in Figure 7–1.

Although only one large table is shown, the real use of spreadsheets involves the creation and use of small tables within this larger framework. Spreadsheet systems provide commands for setting up, expanding, contracting, moving, and copying tables and computing a variety of statistics on their contents, all within the framework of the large table. The basic unit of analysis

7.2

Using Spreadsheet Software

coordinates
The position of a cell in the spreadsheet as indicated by row and column identifiers, e.g., A1 is the cell in column A and row 1.

G9: (F2)+F9/F10

	A	B	C	D	E	F	G
1	Grades for CSE125						
2							
3	Name	Prog1	Prog2	Prog3	Final	Total	Percent
4							
5	Brown R	10.00	15.00	15.00	97.00	137.00	0.83
6	Carol M	8.50	15.00	12.00	92.00	127.50	0.77
7	Lacey RC	9.00	11.00	14.00	98.00	132.00	0.80
8							
9	Average	9.17	13.67	13.67	95.67	132.17	0.80
10	Points	10	15	40	100	165	

Figure 7–1 The Organization of a Spreadsheet. A spreadsheet is a large table with many individual cells that extend in both the horizontal and vertical directions. The user can make many small tables within this large one. Each cell in the spreadsheet contains either a number, a label (words), or a formula. In this example, the label "Grades for CSE125" is in cell A1, but because it is so long, it extends into B1. Cell B5 holds a number, the score that R Brown got on assignment Prog1. Cell G9 holds a formula, but you cannot tell this by looking at the reverse-video 0.80. Instead, when we examine cell G9, its formula appears at the top of the screen (+F9/F10). This formula causes cell G9 to display the result of dividing the contents of cell F9 by the contents of the cell F10.

for spreadsheet software is the cells in the table, just as the basic unit for word processing was the characters of a document.

Cells in a table can have several different types of contents. Of course, the first important type is a numeric value, since tables are generally constructed for viewing numeric relationships. The second type is a label, since any tabular summary of data would be useless without words to describe the meanings of the individual rows and columns. Finally, the third type is a function of other cell values called a formula; for example a cell might contain a formula to compute the average of other values in the table.

The first spreadsheet program, Visicalc, was created in 1979 by the Software Arts Company and sold by the Visicorp Company. With the goal of building a user-understandable microcomputer system, Robert Bricklin interviewed a group of accountants and business people to find out exactly what their work was like. The accountants showed one of their work sheets—a large sheet of paper with individual rows and columns marked off to form cells—and explained how they penciled in labels for rows and columns, put in numbers, and then combined the numbers with simple functions (like sums) using pocket calculators. From these paper-and-pencil worksheets came the design for spreadsheet programs that could be used by people trained in disciplines other than computer technology.

At first, spreadsheets were used mainly for budgets and other tabular data. Their most valuable feature was the automatic revision of any cell containing a formula whenever a cell referenced by the formula was changed. Through the years, spreadsheet software has become much more sophisticated, and it is now frequently used for very complicated processes such as maintaining inventory or billing records. Now spreadsheets are often combined in software packages with word processors and graphics programs so that tables can be calculated and directly transferred into documents, either as tables or as graphic displays. Thousands of users continue to use simple spreadsheets for frequently required analysis: calculating taxes, estimating real estate profits based on changing interest rates, and calculating stress resistance of materials in engineering, to name just a few.

■ Tables: The Manual Version of Spreadsheets

All spreadsheet applications begin with the design of a table or a set of tables, a specification of the contents of each cell, and a set of sample data. For example, the user who wants to manage the costs of two pieces of rental property would start with a simple written table that organizes the expenses:

	property1	property2	total
address	223 Main	165 Elm	
rent charged	$625.00	$400.00	$1025.00
mort. payment	$453.00	$355.00	808.00
monthly profit	$172.00	$ 45.00	$ 217.00

This table contains the address, rent, mortgage payment, and profit for each of two properties and sums the last three items for two properties. A person who looks at this table has an immediate understanding of what it means: the first row of the table contains labels describing the items below them and the first column of the table gives descriptions of the items to the right of them. Every element in the table is thus described by the labels of both its row and its column (e.g., "223 Main" is labeled "property1" and "address").

With a computer, however, this intuitive understanding of a table must be replaced by a precise description that the computer is capable of processing. To that end, the table is first rewritten with labels on its rows and columns:

	column A	column B	column C	column D
row 1		property1	property2	total
row 2	address	223 Main	165 Elm	
row 3	rent charged	$625.00	$400.00	$1025.00
row 4	mort. payment	$453.00	$355.00	$808.00
row 5	monthly profit	$172.00	$ 45.00	$217.00

With these labels, we can describe the table precisely as:

A1 = BLANK	B1 = property1	C1 = property2	D1 = total
A2 = address	B2 = 223 Main	C2 = 165 Elm	D2 = BLANK
A3 = rent charged	B3 = $625.00	C3 = $400.00	D3 = +(B3+C3)
A4 = mort. payment	B4 = $453.00	C4 = $355.00	D4 = +(B4+C4)
A5 = monthly profit	B5 = +(B3−B4)	C5 = +(C3−C4)	D5 = +(D3−D4)

Note that the values of many of the cells are formulas that add or subtract values in other cells. For example, consider cell B5, which contains +(B3−B4). Inserting the current values of B3 and B4 into this formula gives B5 = $625 − $453 = $172. Another level of complication arises when a cell containing calculations accesses other cells containing calculations. For example, the contents of cell D5 references the contents of cells D4 and D3, which are both determined by reference to other cells.

These formulas are useful in a special way: their values can be automatically recalculated if any of the cells used by formulas are altered. For example, if the rent for property1 is increased by $25 to $650, the new value in cell B3 can be immediately reflected in a recalculation of B5 to a value of $197, D3 to a value of $1050, and then D5 to a value of $242.

During the creation of any table, four kinds of information are used:

1. *Coordinates*. The coordinates of a cell are its column and row labels, e.g., B5 means column B and row 5.
2. *Labels*. Alphabetic information is used to describe the meaning of rows and columns, e.g., "monthly profit."
3. *Numbers*. Numeric information is used in formulas, e.g., 625.00.
4. *Formulas*. Some cells will contain formulas that specify addition, subtraction, or some other computation involving the values of other cells in the table.

■ Creating a Spreadsheet

Once the table is precisely defined the user enters the information into the computer using the spreadsheet software. As with any applications software system, the user must first start the system up, either by obtaining disks with the spreadsheet programs or by accessing computer files containing the programs. Once a spreadsheet system is started, a very typical display appears on the screen. The display shows a large window containing many table cells and a small window containing data about one particular cell in the larger window. A typical spreadsheet display is shown in Figure 7–2.

An electronic spreadsheet is basically an internally stored table, various parts of which are visible through windows. A window is an electronic process that displays one cluster of information on one section of the video screen. Multiple windows, in which different sections of the spreadsheet are separately displayed on different sections of the screen, are also common.

In addition to the part of the table visible in the window, the screen will generally show some descriptive data on a specific cell of the table designated by the cell cursor. The cell cursor is much like the letter cursor in a word processing or other computing system. Its purpose is to indicate which cell in the spreadsheet is the current one, that is, the one whose value can be changed.

Figure 7–3 illustrates how a spreadsheet display can show only one portion of a larger underlying table of data. The window can be thought of as lying on top of the large spreadsheet stored internally in the computer. In general, a window that fills up the full screen will show about twenty rows of the spreadsheet and between 1 and 20 columns, depending upon their width.

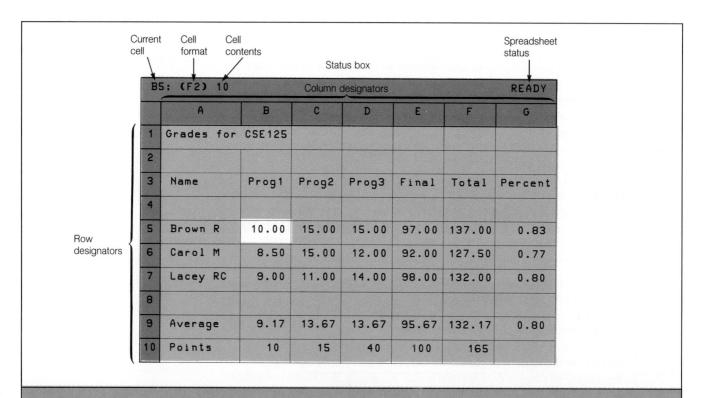

Figure 7–2 Typical Spreadsheet Display. The typical spreadsheet display shows some portion of the spreadsheet table, the current cell (here, B5), which is in reverse video or highlighted in some other manner, and a status box that describes the characteristics of the current cell in detail. Rows are usually numbered, and columns are usually lettered (A–Z, AA–AZ, BA–. . .). The current cell is generally changed by using the arrow keys or a mouse. Sometimes a corner of the status box will be set aside to describe the current state of the spreadsheet (e.g., "ready" or "calculating").

```
B5: (F2) 10
```

	A	B	C	D	E	F	G	H	I	J
1	Grades for CSE125									
2										
3	Name	Prog1	Prog2	Prog3	Final	Total	Percent			
4										
5	Brown R	10.00	15.00	15.00	97.00	137.00	0.83			
6	Carol M	8.50	15.00	12.00	92.00	127.50	0.77			
7	Lacey RC	9.00	11.00	14.00	98.00	132.00	0.80			
8										
9	Average	9.17	13.67	13.67	95.67	132.17	0.80			
10	Points	10	15	40	100	165				
11										
12										
13										
14										
15										

Figure 7–3 The Screen View of a Large Spreadsheet. Although the underlying spreadsheet may be large (some systems allow 1000 rows and 500 columns), only a portion of the spreadsheet can be displayed on the screen at a given time. In this example, the small spreadsheet of grades displayed on the screen is surrounded by the large spreadsheet capacity that still remains to be used. The cursor keys can be used to bring into view a portion of the spreadsheet not currently on the screen. If the current cell is at a screen boundary and the user tries to move off the screen, the window is moved instead, thus allowing more distant portions of the spreadsheet to be viewed.

With the system started up and the window showing a portion of the spreadsheet, the user begins by choosing a cell and entering the data for that cell. Choosing the cell to work on is done by using the arrow keys (or a mouse or other pointing device). The data is then typed at the keyboard, replacing the current cell contents with the newly typed data. As in word processing systems, if the user makes an error during typing, there will be a key that deletes the last character to remove the error (e.g., the backspace key).

Note that on some word processors, there is no distinction between the left-arrow key that moves the cursor to the left and the backspace key that deletes the last character. On such systems the user may become accustomed to using the left-arrow key to back up and correct typing errors. Users of such systems need to be careful when a mistake is made on a spreadsheet: pressing the left arrow will not correct the mistake but may shift the cursor to another cell instead.

In any event, the user enters data in a spreadsheet as follows: move to a cell and enter the cell's contents, then go on to the next cell. In our rental property example, the user would have to place the cursor at B1, C1, D1, A2, B2, C2, A3, B3, C3, D3, A4, B4, C4, D4, A5, B5, C5, and D5, and enter the appropriate information in each cell.

The spreadsheet software computes any calculated cell values automatically. Thus the user can immediately see the computed results as the values and formulas are entered. Sometimes, however, this constant calculation of formulas slows the system down so much that the user will turn the automatic calculation off until all data is entered and then turn it back on to see the computed values in the complete table.

Like word processor documents, spreadsheets are not always completed in one session. Since the data in the spreadsheet is stored in the RAM of the computer, there must be a way to save the cells of the table onto a disk for loading at a future time. Thus the spreadsheet software must be able to access the operating system's kernel programs to find room on the disk and save the current table into it. Again we have the question, how can the spreadsheet tell if the user is entering data for a cell or a command to the spreadsheet system?

The command mode and the entry mode are used in a spreadsheet, just as they are in the word processor. There is usually a single key that signals the introduction of a command—historically, it has often been the / symbol. When this key is pressed, whatever follows is interpreted as a command to be executed immediately rather than as text (labels) or other data to be inserted in a cell. In later interactions with the spreadsheet software, the user may use the command mode to load existing tables into memory from disk, make changes, save them again, and to print out the spreadsheet.

■ Components of Spreadsheet Software

Like word processing software, spreadsheet systems include a set of capabilities in the kernel, a user interface to spreadsheet functions called a shell, and

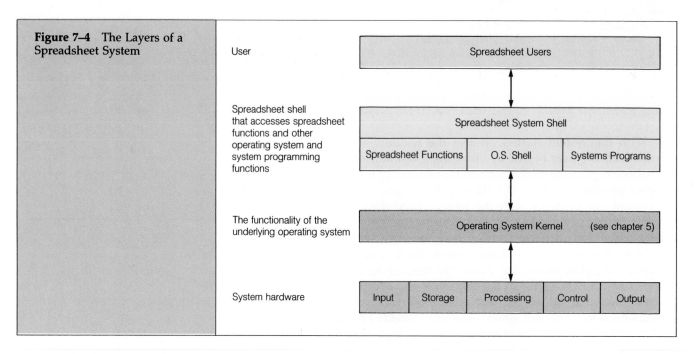

Figure 7–4 The Layers of a Spreadsheet System

User — Spreadsheet Users

Spreadsheet shell that accesses spreadsheet functions and other operating system and system programming functions — Spreadsheet System Shell — Spreadsheet Functions | O.S. Shell | Systems Programs

The functionality of the underlying operating system — Operating System Kernel (see chapter 5)

System hardware — Input | Storage | Processing | Control | Output a set of utility programs. Most spreadsheets use the standard operating system of the computer. The organization of a typical spreadsheet is similar to that of a word processor and is illustrated in Figure 7–4.

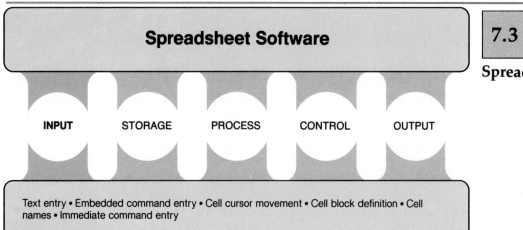

Spreadsheet Software

INPUT   STORAGE   PROCESS   CONTROL   OUTPUT

Text entry • Embedded command entry • Cell cursor movement • Cell block definition • Cell names • Immediate command entry

7.3

Spreadsheet Input

As noted above, spreadsheet software has at least two different input modes: data entry mode and **immediate command** mode. Data entry mode is used for entering the contents of individual cells from the keyboard; the data that is entered can be a label, a number, or a formula that is embedded in the cell. These formula are **embedded commands** that work much like the commands embedded in the text of a word processor document. Immediate command mode is usually concerned with the manipulation of more than one cell at a time and is the manner by which commands are entered for immediate execution. As in word processing systems, the immediate commands for spreadsheets deal with editing, storing, and printing, but in this case the product is a spreadsheet table.

immediate commands
Commands that are always executed immediately when entered, e.g., commands to save, edit, or print. In contrast, formulas (embedded commands) are not always executed when entered, but may be delayed until later.

embedded commands
In spreadsheets, embedded commands are formulas that are entered into cells in the spreadsheet, e.g., a formula like $+B1 * C1$ (multiply the contents of cell B1 times that of C1) could be entered in, say, cell D1.

▪ Input Mode for Text and Numbers

In general, the data entry mode is the default mode in which a spreadsheet system works, since the majority of the work in developing or using a spreadsheet template is entering values into cells. As data is typed during data entry mode, it is placed into the cell pointed to by the cell cursor. Recall from our previous discussions that at any given time, one of the cells is designated as the current cell and is pointed to by the cell cursor. The user can always determine which cell is the current cell by examining the screen: it contains a **status line** (usually at the top of the screen) that shows the user which cell is designated by the cell cursor. For example, the status line on the screen below tells that the cell cursor is pointing to A1. Any characters that are typed while the cursor points to A1 will be entered into that cell and will replace the existing label "Demo."

status line
In applications software systems, a line of text on the video screen that displays the current status of the system, e.g., for spreadsheets it displays the coordinates of the current cell (the position of the cursor), the contents of the cell, and the type of contents. Status lines for other software often display the amount of RAM available, the name of the file in RAM, and so on.

status line
prompt line
edit line

table that follows cursor

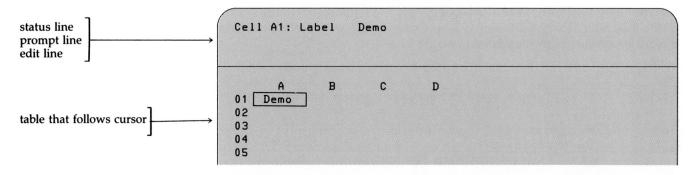

```
Cell A1: Label     Demo



          A        B        C        D
01  ┌──────┐
    │ Demo │
02  └──────┘
03
04
05
```

Data is entered or updated in a cell by first placing the cell cursor on the appropriate cell and then typing the cell's contents, much as one might enter text in a word processor. Typing errors can be immediately corrected with the backspace key to delete the last character.

Since users almost always need to input data for more than one cell, there obviously must be commands for moving the cell cursor. Spreadsheet software is usually set up so that pressing one of the arrow keys (left, right, up, down) moves the cell cursor one row or column in the direction of the arrow.

To illustrate the text entry mode of spreadsheets, let us look at the exact steps required to enter four cells. Suppose that the user wishes to enter:

	A	B	C	D
01	COATS	$34.00	100	$3,400.00

These four values could be entered in any order, but let's consider the most reasonable order, left to right. The user must first press the arrow keys to move the cell cursor so that it points to A1; the cursor position can be verified by looking at the status line of the screen. If the cursor is at A1 and the spreadsheet is initially blank, the status line might look like:

```
Cell: A1
```

The user now presses the keys to enter the word COATS. As soon as the C key is pressed, the status line changes to:

```
Cell: A1     Label   C
```

As the status line shows, the system knows that the letter C cannot be the beginning of a number or a formula, so it must be a label. When the rest of the label has been typed, the user would hit the return key. Hitting the return key terminates this entry but does not change the cell cursor. The status line would then be:

```
Cell: A1     Label   COATS
```

To enter the dollar amount in cell B1 the user must now move the cell cursor by pushing the right arrow key once (or using the mouse to move right one cell). The status line would now be:

```
Cell: B1
```

The user then types in 34. The instant the spreadsheet sees the first character (3), it knows that this entry must be a number and indicates that on the status line:

```
Cell: B1    Number    3
```

When the entry is complete, the user could press the right arrow to enter the value instead of hitting the return key. The spreadsheet software will then do two things: accept the current input for the current cell and move the cell cursor as directed, giving a status line of:

```
Cell: C1
```

The cell cursor is already at C1, but the value in B1 can be verified by looking at the body of the spreadsheet. The user now enters the number of coats in stock by typing 1 0 0 and presses the right arrow. The cursor is now positioned to enter the values in the last cell:

```
Cell: D1
```

■ Input Mode for Embedded Commands

The user now must enter a formula that will multiply B1 times C1 to give the total value of coats. Consider, however, what would happen if the user just types in B1*C1 (the asterisk (*) is the standard computer symbol for multiplication). When the computer sees the first letter, the B, it would assume that a label was being entered, not a formula, and it would treat the entire formula like characters in a word processor—it would not perform the multiplication! Most spreadsheets handle this problem by specifying that formulas must begin with a special symbol, which can be either a number or arithmetic symbol such as a plus (+) or a minus (−) sign. Thus B1*C1 is treated as a label, while +B1*C1 is treated as a formula. This seemingly minor difference is very important to most spreadsheets.

A second way to enter a formula is by using the special symbol that signals an embedded command. Recall from our case study that Brian used the built-in system function @PMT to compute loan payments. The name of this built-in function must be distinguished from the label PMT, which might stand for "prime meridian time." As in word processors, this distinction is made using a special command format. Recall that some word processors use a period in column 1 to designate a command. In spreadsheets, a built-in function is usually indicated by a @ or on some systems by a = in front of the name of the function. Thus, @PMT or =PMT is the name of a built-in function, while PMT is a label.

Getting back to our example, the user would enter +B1*C1 in cell D1. This formula would be shown on the status line, while the body of the spreadsheet would show the result of applying this formula to the data in B1 and C1 is shown:

```
Cell D1: Formula +B1 * C1
          A       B        C        D
  01    Coats   34.00   100.00   3400.00
  02
```

■ Moving the Cell Cursor

Although the cell cursor has been described many times already, several points remain to be made. First, the cell cursor must always be visible on the screen, that is, the cell pointed to by the cell cursor must always be on the visible portion of the spreadsheet. If the cell cursor is pointing to a cell on the far right edge of the screen and the user presses the right arrow, the spreadsheet system will shift the visible portion of the spreadsheet to the right by one column. The column on the far left will disappear from view and a new one will appear on the far right. Similar shifts occur at all of the edges of the screen and simultaneously at that edge of the spreadsheet, no movement beyond that edge will be permitted. The point is that the *window or visible portion of the spreadsheet "follows" the cursor*. To move or "scroll" the window through the spreadsheet one simply moves the cursor with the keys or mouse.

■ Designating Cell Lists in Input Mode

Row/column selection
In spreadsheets specifying a row or column for deleting, moving, or copying by inputing cell coordinates or moving the cursor.

Block selection
In spreadsheets specifying a subtable for deleting, moving, or copying by inputing cell coordinates or by moving the cursor.

Many spreadsheet commands require the **selection** of **rows, columns,** or **blocks** of cells. For example, the built-in system function @SUM, which adds numbers together, expects a set of cells to work on, for example, @SUM (A1,B1,C1). Most systems allow four ways to define a set of cells:

1. as a single cell coordinate (the simplest possible set), e.g., M20
2. as a range of coordinates in one row or one column, specified by giving the first and last elements and separating them by periods, e.g., Z1. . .Z10 would mean the part of column Z that includes Z1, Z2, Z3, Z4, Z5, Z6, Z7, Z8, Z9, Z10
3. as a list of nonconsecutive cell coordinates, e.g., B30, A100, L15
4. as any combination of ranges and lists, e.g., A1. . .A10, B5, K5. . .M5.

On some systems these specifications can be made by moving the cursor with the arrow keys or the mouse to identify rows, columns, or even blocks. Let us consider some examples. Suppose we have a spreadsheet on which we wish to designate the set of cells A1, A2, and A3 for some command, either an immediate command or an embedded command. There are two methods we can use:

1. Type in the cell sequences at the keyboard, either A1, A2, A3 or A1. . .A3.
2. Use the arrow keys, mouse, or other pointing device to enter the data.

Using the arrow keys or mouse is often the best way to enter the data, since the user points directly at the data to be used and can move the pointer to parts of the spreadsheet not currently visible on the screen. For example, to specify the range A1 through A3, the following sequences of actions could be used:

1. *Arrow Keys.* Move the cell cursor to A1 using the arrow keys, press the range indicator (usually a period), press the down arrow two times, and finally press the return key. A1 will first be highlighted on the screen, then as the down arrow is pushed, the other cells will be highlighted as well. When the return key is pressed, the computer knows that the user has finished specifying the cells.

2. *Mouse or Pointing Device.* Move the mouse until the cursor points at A1, press the mouse button, and drag the mouse while holding the button down until the cursor points to A3. Then release the button.

It is only slightly more complicated to specify a block of cells, e.g., the three-by-three table A1, A2, A3, B1, B2, B3, C1, C2, C3, instead of just a row or column. The only difference is that the user must move the cursor (using the arrow keys or mouse) in two directions: down the row 3 and over to column C. The selection of various sets of cells is illustrated in Figure 7–5.

■ Named Cells

Although all spreadsheets can reference any cell or set of cells, the more advanced spreadsheets can give a cell a name other than the one defined by its position in the table. For example, on a spreadsheet program for computing income tax, the cell for adjusted gross income might be F325. Since the adjusted gross income is required at many places throughout the various computations, the user of the spreadsheet program would continually have to remember the cell location F325. If the user can tell the system that cell F325 will be known as AGI (adjusted gross income), then referencing that value from anywhere else in the table will be much easier and more meaningful.

On systems that provide named cells, the name can be entered in many different ways. For example, instead of typing in a formula like +(B3*B4), a name can be entered by using a slightly altered formula e.g., *answer* = +(B3*B4). Once this name is given, other formulas throughout the spreadsheet can reference this value, for example, + (*answer**2).

■ Spreadsheet Shells and Command Mode

All the while that the user is entering text into cells, an array of editing, storage, and output commands are available. These commands are performed immediately when given and are accessed using a command mode of input controlled by the spreadsheet shell. Recall that there are three basic types of shells: command language, menu, and graphic shells. Most spreadsheets use menu-driven shells. The three types of spreadsheets shells are illustrated in Figure 7–6.

Whatever the type of shell, there must be some method to indicate that the shell should process a system command. In many systems, commands are referenced by a reserved character (e.g., a /), while in others, the user points with a mouse or other device to a menu bar. When the command mode is entered, menus and submenus are usually displayed to remind the user of the

Cell selected

	A	B	C	D
1	Grades for CSE125			
2				
3	Name	Prog1	Prog2	Prog3
4				
5	Brown R	10.00	15.00	15.00
6	Carol M	8.50	15.00	12.00
7	Lacey RC	9.00	11.00	14.00
8				
9	Average	9.17	13.67	13.67
10	Points	10	15	40

Row selected

	A	B	C	D
1	Grades for CSE125			
2				
3	Name	Prog1	Prog2	Prog3
4				
5	Brown R	10.00	15.00	15.00
6	Carol M	8.50	15.00	12.00
7	Lacey RC	9.00	11.00	14.00
8				
9	Average	9.17	13.67	13.67
10	Points	10	15	40

Column selected

	A	B	C	D
1	Grades for CSE125			
2				
3	Name	Prog1	Prog2	Prog3
4				
5	Brown R	10.00	15.00	15.00
6	Carol M	8.50	15.00	12.00
7	Lacey RC	9.00	11.00	14.00
8				
9	Average	9.17	13.67	13.67
10	Points	10	15	40

Block selected

	A	B	C	D
1	Grades for CSE125			
2				
3	Name	Prog1	Prog2	Prog3
4				
5	Brown R	10.00	15.00	15.00
6	Carol M	8.50	15.00	12.00
7	Lacey RC	9.00	11.00	14.00
8				
9	Average	9.17	13.67	13.67
10	Points	10	15	40

Figure 7–5 Selection of Cells, Rows, Columns, and Subtables. An individual cell is selected by positioning the cell cursor to that cell. The selection of a compete row or column is unavailable on many systems, but when available, it requires the user to position the cell cursor in the desired row or column and then issue a special "mark row" or "mark column" command. In many systems rows and columns are selected with the block selection command. To select a block, the user must choose one cell as the starting point, issue a "define block" command, and then use the cursor keys to expand the block from this starting cell. The starting cell must generally be a corner of the final block.

a. Command language shell

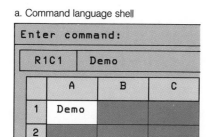

b. Menu shell

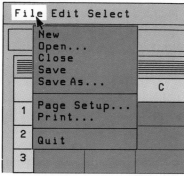

c. Graphic shell

Figure 7–6 Command Input in Spreadsheet Systems.
a. Command language shells present a prompt (e.g., "Enter command:") and wait for the user to respond with a command. They are seldom used with spreadsheets.
b. Most spreadsheets provide nested menus from which the user must select a command. These menus are usually activated by a special key, e.g., a/or ALT key. For example, the user might press arrow keys to change which command is in reverse video and then press return to begin execution of the marked command. Alternatively, the user might press the first letter of the desired command.
c. Graphic shells are available for many spreadsheet systems. On such systems, the user moves a mouse (which in turn moves an arrow on the screen) to select the command to execute. Often menus are an integral part of the graphic shell. In this example, the "File" option in the menu bar was selected using the mouse, and the menu bar is then expanded to give a menu of options concerning file use.

available commands. These menus may contain single characters or entire keywords, or they may be pull-down menus. Once the command mode is entered, the user must generally specify the command and the block of cells or the part of the table on which the command should operate. The subtable is designated in the same manner that the cell cursor is moved, either through arrow keys or pointing devices.

<table>
<tr><td>

7.4

Spreadsheet Storage

</td><td>

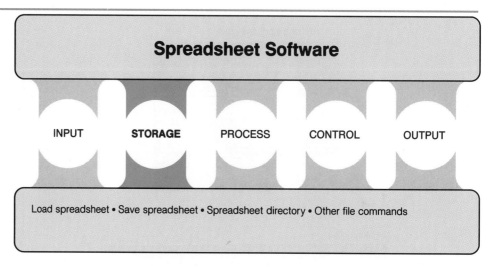

</td></tr>
</table>

As the reader might expect by now, spreadsheets exist primarily in RAM while in use. Therefore, there must be some way to save a spreadsheet from RAM onto a disk and later bring it back from the disk into RAM.

■ Loading and Saving Tables

Loading and saving spreadsheet tables is controlled primarily by the shell. In one form or another, the shell accepts a command to save or load, requests and receives the name of the operating system file, and accesses the ever-present operating system kernel to perform the task. For example, in a command language shell the commands might be something like /SAVE FILENAME1 for storage and /LOAD FILENAME1 for retrieval from disk.

One advanced storage function available on many spreadsheet systems is the ability to **cut** arbitrary tables out of the spreadsheet and save them onto a special system file (a **clipboard**) so that they can be **pasted** into other applications. The desired table within the spreadsheet is first specified, then it is either cut out of the current spreadsheet or copied out (cutting removes it from the spreadsheet,while copying does not). This cut or copied table is then written into a special file on disk. Another applications program can then be started up and can access the special file; for example, a word processor can access the file and paste the spreadsheet table into a word processing document. A specific example of this type of file is the data interchange format (DIF) files, which can be accessed by many varieties of software from many manufacturers. This powerful concept is illustrated in Figure 7–7, which shows the relationship between an original spreadsheet table and its word processing and graphic counterparts.

■ Other Operating System Functions

Just as a good word processing system provides a means to access all disk operating commands, spreadsheets also provide commands like DIRECTORY or DESTROY FILENAME3. The following commands are typical of the storage functions provided by spreadsheets:

- □ FORMAT — to initialize a new disk
- □ CATALOG or DIRECTORY — to get a list of the file names on disk

cut process
A process that allows the user to blank out selected portions of a text, table, or picture and save the erased image to clipboard memory for later use.

clipboard
A special place in memory or on disk where a portion of a text, table, or picture may be stored using a cut operation until the user places it elsewhere using a paste operation. Clipboards are also referred to as temporary storage buffers.

paste process
A process by which text, tables, or graphic images that have been cut at an earlier time are placed back into the document, table, or picture being created.

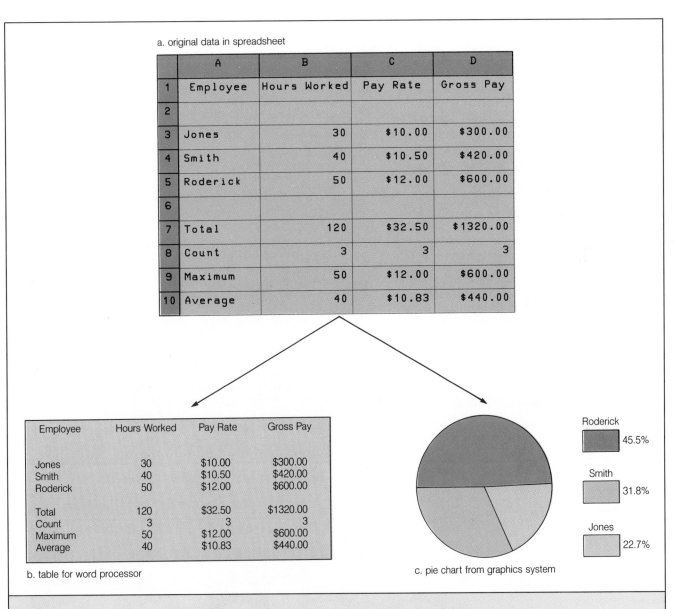

a. original data in spreadsheet

	A	B	C	D
1	Employee	Hours Worked	Pay Rate	Gross Pay
2				
3	Jones	30	$10.00	$300.00
4	Smith	40	$10.50	$420.00
5	Roderick	50	$12.00	$600.00
6				
7	Total	120	$32.50	$1320.00
8	Count	3	3	3
9	Maximum	50	$12.00	$600.00
10	Average	40	$10.83	$440.00

Employee	Hours Worked	Pay Rate	Gross Pay
Jones	30	$10.00	$300.00
Smith	40	$10.50	$420.00
Roderick	50	$12.00	$600.00
Total	120	$32.50	$1320.00
Count	3	3	3
Maximum	50	$12.00	$600.00
Average	40	$10.83	$440.00

b. table for word processor

Roderick 45.5%

Smith 31.8%

Jones 22.7%

c. pie chart from graphics system

Figure 7–7 Transferring Tables to Other Applications Software. a. The original data in the Spreadsheet. b. The original data is converted into text form, which can then be included in an arbitrary word-processed document. In very sophisticated and integrated systems, the table in the document can remain active and changes can be made to it while in the word processor that result in changes to the original spreadsheet. c. Part of the data in the original spreadsheet (the gross pay column) has been input to a graphics system that used the data to create a pie chart showing the relative salaries of the three employees.

□ SAVE — to save the contents of the spreadsheet on disk, either creating a new file or replacing an existing one.
□ LOAD — to bring a spreadsheet previously saved on disk back into RAM for use
□ RENAME — to change the name of a file on disk
□ DELETE — to erase a file from the disk

Computer Insights
Popular Spreadsheet Systems

The concepts described in this chapter are realized in many different spreadsheet systems, but there have been only two dominant spreadsheets: VisiCalc and Lotus 1-2-3. They have spawned many clones and improved versions. Some of the more popular spreadsheets currently available are:

Lotus 1-2-3 by Lotus Development Corporation

Lotus 1-2-3 has been the de facto standard of the IBM and IBM-compatible microcomputer world. The reasons for its popularity were (1) it was the first spreadsheet system to add substantially to the basic functions of the VisiCalc spreadsheet, (2) it was the first system to add easily understood menus, file management, disk management, and print graphics to the basic spreadsheet functions, and (3) it was one of the first spreadsheet systems for the IBM PC. With over 2 million copies sold and, according to Lotus, 70% of the spreadsheet market, Lotus 1-2-3 continues to evolve and add new features. In addition, Lotus Development Corporation has worked hard on the development of an integrated software system that includes spreadsheets.

Supercalc by Computer Associates, Inc.

Whenever a software system sells well, the look-alikes and clones follow rapidly. This has been especially true in the spreadsheet market. Supercalc is one of the few look-alikes that is of high enough quality to command a significant portion of the market itself. Like most clones, Supercalc learned (and continues to learn) from the mistakes and problems of Lotus. Supercalc often contains slightly superior features to Lotus (e.g., lack of complicated copy-protection schemes) at a lower price.

EXCEL by Microsoft

Microsoft is one of the most powerful forces in the microcomputer software industry. EXCEL is an exceptionally powerful spreadsheet system that has an especially attractive feature: it runs in both the Macintosh environment and the IBM PC environments under DOS or WINDOWS.

Ability by Migent

A recent low-cost addition to the computing field, Ability is an integrated system with word processor, spreadsheet, data base, communications, and graphics capabilities. It demonstrates a truism: after the pioneer firms have spent their money determining the important functions for software, other vendors can create systems with equal or better capability at less cost.

7.5

Spreadsheet Processes

Spreadsheet Software

INPUT   STORAGE   **PROCESS**   CONTROL   OUTPUT

Cell contents edit • Subtable blank • Subtable move • Row/column move • Subtable copy • Row/column insertion • Row/column deletion • Windows • Text find • Cell goto • Cell protection

Spreadsheet systems provide a large number of processes for the management of tables. All of these processes are accessed through immediate commands, that is the commands for these processes are performed immediately when entered and do not become part of the spreadsheet.

First, the cell that is to be edited is made the current cell (using the arrow keys or the mouse). In this example, an error was found in the score of Brown on Prog1, so the cell cursor was moved until it pointed to cell B5. Note that the current status of B5 is shown in the status line.

```
B5: (F2) 10
```

	A	B	C	D	E	F
3	Name	Prog1	Prog2	Prog3	Final	Total
4						
5	Brown R	10.00	15.00	15.00	97.00	137.00
6	Carol M	8.50	15.00	12.00	92.00	127.50
7	Lacey RC	9.00	11.00	14.00	98.00	132.00
8						
9	Average	9.17	13.67	13.67	95.67	132.17

Contents of cell duplicated for editing.
Character cursor shows position for editing.

Once the cell has been selected, the user issues an "edit cell" command. Usually the existing contents of the cell are printed on the screen for the user to edit using the backspace and delete keys, the left and right arrow keys, and the rest of the keyboard. In this case, the number 10 is repeated for editing.

```
B5: (F2) 10
  10_
```

	A	B	C	D	E	F
3	Name	Prog1	Prog2	Prog3	Final	Total
4						
5	Brown R	10.00	15.00	15.00	97.00	137.00
6	Carol M	8.50	15.00	12.00	92.00	127.50
7	Lacey RC	9.00	11.00	14.00	98.00	132.00
8						
9	Average	9.17	13.67	13.67	95.67	132.17

After the contents of the cell have been corrected, the user hits the return key. In this example, the correct value (8) has been placed into B5. Since automatic recalculation was active, the table was automatically adjusted so that all computed entries correct.

```
B5: (F2) 8
```

	A	B	C	D	E	F
3	Name	Prog1	Prog2	Prog3	Final	Total
4						
5	Brown R	8.00	15.00	15.00	97.00	135.00
6	Carol M	8.50	15.00	12.00	92.00	127.50
7	Lacey RC	9.00	11.00	14.00	98.00	132.00
8						
9	Average	8.50	13.67	13.67	95.67	131.50

Editing a Cell's Contents

■ Editing Functions

Although spreadsheet systems work on tables instead of characters, many word processing concepts have direct analogues in spreadsheets. Some of the most obvious similarities can be found in the spreadsheet editing process.

Editing Cell Contents.   As the user develops a table, the contents of any given cell may need to be changed. Maybe the user typed an entry incorrectly, or maybe, as the table develops, the user's increased understanding of the problem requires a new solution. Whatever the case, spreadsheet software generally provides an editor (like the editor in a word processor) for altering the contents of a cell.

The cell editor is used by first positioning the cell cursor at the cell to be altered. Then the user enters a special immediate command, for example, /E, where the / designates command mode and the E specifies the edit command. Now the user is in a mini–word processor. The major commands available in this mode are:

1. *Cursor Movement.* The editor will have a character cursor (as opposed to the cell cursor of the total spreadsheet), which can be moved to skip over the parts of the cell contents that the user wishes to retain.
2. *Delete Character.* Some key will delete the character that is at or to the left of the character cursor.
3. *Character Insertion.* Except for the keys with special meanings, all other keys insert their symbols at the cursor in the cell contents.
4. *Termination Character.* Some key, often the return key, is used to signify that the editing is done, the cell contents should be reset, and the editor exited.
5. *Abort Character.* Some key, often the escape key, is used to signify that the editor should be exited immediately without changing the cell contents from its original value.

With these commands, the user can easily make minor alterations in a cell's contents. An example of such an editing process is given on the previous page.

Blanking (Erasing) Cells.   All spreadsheets provide the ability to blank out or erase the contents of cells in the spreadsheet. Note that blanking a cell is *not* the same as deleting a cell. Since a cell occurs at the intersection of a row and column, taking out a single cell without removing the row and column is not possible. Blanking out the contents of a cell, however, is easy to understand: it means erasing what is inside the cell without doing anything to the cell itself.

The blanking function can be requested by a function or control key, by the command mode symbol followed by the blanking command, or by appropriate pointing with a mouse on a system with a graphic shell. Once the command is invoked, the user can specify that a certain cell, certain rows, certain columns, or arbitrary blocks of the spreadsheet should have their contents destroyed, as shown in the figure on the following page.

Clear Spreadsheet.   An extension of the blanking function is the special command that clears the entire spreadsheet. Because this is clearly a drastic action that should be taken with great care, most spreadsheets will ask for verification of the user's intent. Destroying a whole spreadsheet would be a terrible thing to do by accident!

In many systems, the first step is to define the block of cells to be blanked out or erased. This is done by positioning the cursor at a cell, issuing a "define block" command, and moving the cell cursor until the proper block is highlighted. Here, the block D7...E7 has been selected.

D7: (F2) 14					
	A	B	C	D	E	F
3	Name	Prog1	Prog2	Prog3	Final	Total
4						
5	Brown R	10.00	15.00	15.00	97.00	137.00
6	Carol M	8.50	15.00	12.00	92.00	127.50
7	Lacey RC	9.00	11.00	14.00	98.00	132.00
8						
9	Average		9.17	13.67	13.67	95.67	132.17

With the block defined, the user issues an "erase block" command. To avoid mistakes, the system usually asks if erasure is the true intent. Here, the user answered "Y" to the confirmation question, so the system will proceed with the erasure.

D7: (F2) 14					
Erase the specified block? Y					
	A	B	C	D	E	F
3	Name	Prog1	Prog2	Prog3	Final	Total
4						
5	Brown R	10.00	15.00	15.00	97.00	137.00
6	Carol M	8.50	15.00	12.00	92.00	127.50
7	Lacey RC	9.00	11.00	14.00	98.00	132.00
8						
9	Average		9.17	13.67	13.67	95.67	132.17

The contents of the cell block have been erased, the cell cursor was left pointing to the upper left cell in the block, and since automatic recalculation was active, the values of all cells have been recalculated.

D7: (F2)					
	A	B	C	D	E	F
3	Name	Prog1	Prog2	Prog3	Final	Total
4						
5	Brown R	10.00	15.00	15.00	97.00	135.00
6	Carol M	8.50	15.00	12.00	92.00	127.50
7	Lacey RC	9.00	11.00			20.00
8						
9	Average		9.17	13.67	13.50	94.50	94.83

Note: Many systems expect commands for erasure of cell contents in the reverse order. In such cases, first the command to erase is given, then, the user specifies the cell block to be erased. The precise method chosen depends on the spreadsheet system being used.

Moving Cells. The command to move cells in a spreadsheet is specified according to the type of shell the system has—command language, menu, or graphic. Once the move command is given, essentially two pieces of information are required: what is to be moved and where it should be moved. There are generally four possibilities for what to move—an individual cell, one or more rows, one or more columns, or a rectangular block (subtable) of cells. The shape of the block of cells being moved completely determines how the destination of the move will be interpreted. If a row is being moved, it must remain a row and its destination is just a row number. Similarly, a column must remain a column and requires a column position to describe its destination. An individual cell can be moved anywhere in the spreadsheet. A block of cells can only be moved as a block.

Although moving different rows, columns, and tables sounds like the same process, actually there is a difference between moving a row or column and moving a subtable. When a row is moved, the row extends from one edge of the spreadsheet to the other, so the move essentially cuts the row out, moves it elsewhere, and puts it back in. A column move works the same way. For example, if column A is moved to a position after column M, then the old column B becomes column A, the old column C becomes column B, the old column D becomes column C, ..., the old column M becomes column L and the old column A becomes column M. Thus no cell contents are blanked out by the move.

When a block of cells is moved, however, its range does not extend through the entire table in either the horizontal or the vertical direction, and thus the simple moving described above will not suffice. The process of moving a subtable first copies the subtable cells to the new location and then blanks the contents at the old location. Because of this added level of complexity, some spreadsheets allow the movement of full rows or columns but not blocks.

Whatever the variety of move, some interesting questions arise concerning the status of formulas in the spreadsheet. For example, if a cell contained a formula (e.g., $+(A1+A2)$) that referenced two elements in column A, what should happen to the formula if column A has been moved and is now column M? Should the formula still be $+(A1+A2)$ or should it now be $+(M1+M2)$? On most spreadsheets, the formula would automatically change to $+(M1+M2)$. To allow this automatic (and important) adjustment of formulas, spreadsheets place many constraints on how different types of subtables can be moved. An example of a spreadsheet move is given on the following page.

Copy Cells. In a spreadsheet, the copy command is sometimes called a replicate command so that the user does not misinterpret its meaning. In most of its details, the replicate command is identical to the move command, except that the cells that are copied are not blanked out after the copy is made. (Recall that with the move command, the cells that are copied are blanked out after the copy is made.)

The other major difference between a replicate and a move command concerns the way in which formulas that reference other cells are copied. In the move command, the system automatically adjusts all formulas so that values displayed in cells do not change—this is reasonable, because the contents of cells should not change because of a move. In replicating, however, it is not clear whether the formulas should be adjusted automatically. Therefore, as each formula is copied during a replicate, the user can be asked whether each

The first step in moving cells is to specify the block of cells to be moved by positioning the cell cursor at one cell, issuing a "define block" command, and moving the cell cursor so that the desired cells are highlighted. In this example, the cell block to be moved is A6..F6.

A6: 'Carol M						
	A	B	C	D	E	F
3	Name	Prog1	Prog2	Prog3	Final	Total
4						
5	Brown R	10.00	15.00	15.00	97.00	137.00
6	Carol M	8.50	15.00	12.00	92.00	127.50
7	Lacey RC	9.00	11.00	14.00	98.00	132.00
8						
9	Average	9.17	13.67	13.67	95.67	132.17

The next command is a "cut" command, which removes the designated cells but saves their contents internally. Note that the automatic recalculation is performed immediately if it is activated. Also note that cutting out the cells did not remove the cells but just their contents.

A6:						
	A	B	C	D	E	F
3	Name	Prog1	Prog2	Prog3	Final	Total
4						
5	Brown R	10.00	15.00	15.00	97.00	137.00
6						
7	Lacey RC	9.00	11.00	14.00	98.00	132.00
8						
9	Average	9.50	13.00	14.50	97.50	134.50

The user then repositions the cell cursor to another location and issues a "paste" command to return the contents of the cut cells to the spreadsheet.

A10: 'Carol M						
	A	B	C	D	E	F
3	Name	Prog1	Prog2	Prog3	Final	Total
4						
5	Brown R	10.00	15.00	15.00	97.00	137.00
6						
7	Lacey RC	9.00	11.00	14.00	98.00	132.00
8						
9	Average	9.50	13.00	14.50	97.50	134.50
10	Carol M	8.5	15	12	92	127.5

Another common sequence of commands for moving a block of cells is to first issue a "move" command and then, within the move command, specify the block to be moved and the new locations for the moved cells. This second form may be slightly safer because it demands the new locations, while a user might forget to do a paste after a cut is completed.

A copy command is much like a move command, but instead of removing cell values and placing them in another location, it copies the cell contents into the new location. Here, a "define block" command has been issued to set up the cells A6...F6 for the copy.

A6:'Carol M						
	A	B	C	D	E	F
3	Name	Prog1	Prog2	Prog3	Final	Total
4						
5	Brown R	10.00	15.00	15.00	97.00	137.00
6	Carol M	8.50	15.00	12.00	92.00	127.50
7	Lacey RC	9.00	11.00	14.00	98.00	132.00
8						
9	Average	9.17	13.67	13.67	95.67	132.17

The copy command is then issued. Note that it does not remove the contents of the marked cells. After the copy command is given, the cell cursor remains at one cell from the selected set.

A6:'Carol M						
	A	B	C	D	E	F
3	Name	Prog1	Prog2	Prog3	Final	Total
4						
5	Brown R	10.00	15.00	15.00	97.00	137.00
6	Carol M	8.50	15.00	12.00	92.00	127.50
7	Lacey RC	9.00	11.00	14.00	98.00	132.00
8						
9	Average	9.17	13.67	13.67	95.67	132.17

The user then repositions the cell cursor to the desired location and issues a "paste" command to copy the contents of the original cells to the new location in the spreadsheet.

A10:'Carol M						
	A	B	C	D	E	F
3	Name	Prog1	Prog2	Prog3	Final	Total
4						
5	Brown R	10.00	15.00	15.00	97.00	137.00
6	Carol M	8.50	15.00	12.00	92.00	127.50
7	Lacey RC	9.00	11.00	14.00	98.00	132.00
8						
9	Average	9.17	13.67	13.67	95.67	132.17
10	Carol M	8.5	15	12	92	127.5

Copying a Block of Cells

cell reference should remain exactly as it is (an **absolute reference**) or whether the cell reference should be appropriately adjusted (a **relative reference**). Thus the user can have total control over the copying process. Some spreadsheets handle the problem by copying all cell coordinates as relative unless a special symbol (usually a $ or a # sign) is used to mark the coordinates as absolute. Thus, C10 would be copied as a relative reference, while C10 would be copied as an absolute reference. An example of copying is given on the previous page.

Absolute reference
When a formula is copied the coordinates are not changed, i.e., copying (A1+B1) from cell C1 to C10 places (A1+B1) in C10.

Relative reference
When a formula is copied the coordinates are changed, i.e., copying (A1+B1) from cell C1 to C10 places (A10+B10) in cell C10.

Insert Rows or Columns. Inserting rows or columns is conceptually a much easier process than copying or moving, although spreadsheets differ widely in the exact form of the "insert" command. Whatever the form of the command,

A row or column is inserted by positioning the cell cursor into the row or column before the desired location of the insertion. In this example, three new students have been added to the class, all with names that fall alphabetically between Brown and Carol. Hence, the cell cursor is positioned at CarolM, which is highlighted.

A6:'Carol M					
	A	**B**	**C**	**D**	**E**	**F**
3	Name	Prog1	Prog2	Prog3	Final	Total
4						
5	Brown R	10.00	15.00	15.00	97.00	137.00
6	Carol M	8.50	15.00	12.00	92.00	127.50
7	Lacey RC	9.00	11.00	14.00	98.00	132.00
8						
9	Average	9.17	13.67	13.67	95.67	132.17

The "insert" command is given, and the user asks that 3 rows be inserted. The rows are put into place, and any necessary recalculations are done, if automatic recalculation is active. In this case, no change occurs, to any cell displays.

A9:'Carol M					
Enter number of rows to insert: 3					
	A	**B**	**C**	**D**	**E**	**F**
3	Name	Prog1	Prog2	Prog3	Final	Total
4						
5	Brown R	10.00	15.00	15.00	97.00	137.00
6						
7						
8						
9	Carol M	8.50	15.00	12.00	92.00	127.50
10	Lacey RC	9.00	11.00	14.00	98.00	132.00
11						
12	Average	9.17	13.67	13.67	95.67	132.17

Inserting a Row or Column

the user needs to specify only the row or column at which the insertion is to be made and the number of rows or columns that are to be inserted. As the rows or columns are inserted, all formulas are adjusted so that they retain the same meanings they had before the insert. See example on previous page.

Delete Rows or Columns. Directly analogous to the insert, the deletion of rows or columns is also a conceptually simple process (see below). All the user needs to specify is which rows or columns are to be deleted. After the deletion, all references to cells not deleted are adjusted appropriately. Any references to cells that were deleted are replaced with a reference to the built-in system function @ERROR. Thus, if the user accidentally deletes a cell that is explicitly referenced, any formula that referenced that cell and is still in the spreadsheet

A row or column is deleted by first positioning the cell cursor in the row or column to be deleted. In this example, CarolM has dropped the class and is to be deleted form the class list.

A6:'Carol M

	A	B	C	D	E	F
3	Name	Prog1	Prog2	Prog3	Final	Total
4						
5	Brown R	10.00	15.00	15.00	97.00	137.00
6	Carol M	8.50	15.00	12.00	92.00	127.50
7	Lacey RC	9.00	11.00	14.00	98.00	132.00
8						
9	Average	9.17	13.67	13.67	95.67	132.17

The "delete-row" command is given. The entire row is removed from the table and all rows below the deleted ones are moved up. All formulas are updated to retain the desired relations, if possible.

A6: 'Lacey RC

	A	B	C	D	E	F
3	Name	Prog1	Prog2	Prog3	Final	Total
4						
5	Brown R	10.00	15.00	15.00	97.00	137.00
6	Lacey RC	9.00	11.00	14.00	98.00	132.00
7						
8	Average	9.50	13.00	14.50	97.50	134.50
9	Points	10	15	40	100	165

The extension of this example to column deletion is straightforward. When a column is deleted, all columns to the right are collapsed in by one position. Many spreadsheets allow the deletion of more than one column or row at a time.

Deleting a Row or Column

will at least display an error message. (Note that the user could still delete a row included in a range reference and introduce an error without knowing it.)

▇ Screen Display During Editing

Spreadsheet systems can allow hundreds of rows and columns in one table. Since a screen can hold only a small portion of the total table, understanding the relationships among different parts of a large spreadsheet can be difficult. Spreadsheets provide windows to help alleviate this problem.

Windowing essentially allows the user's screen to be broken into parts so that different parts of the spreadsheet can be displayed on different parts of the screen, all at the same time. Windows are used for bringing different parts of a spreadsheet together for simultaneous viewing, and for working on two separate parts of the spreadsheet at the same time. Since in most spreadsheet systems, many separate subtables are built into the single large spreadsheet, having more than one part of the spreadsheet available at a time can be very helpful! Just from the description of windows, the reader can probably guess most of the commands that are required.

Setting Up Windows. Clearly, one command is required to set up the windows initially. The user must specify how much of the screen is to be allotted to each window. The most common setups are (1) a single vertical split where the left side of the screen is one window and the right side another and (2) a single horizontal split where the top part of the screen is one window and the bottom part the other (see figure on the next page). Some systems allow the creation of many windows of arbitrary location and size.

Switching Between Windows. Once windows are created, the user needs to be able to switch from one to another. The user may wish to go to window 1 and insert some data, then move to window 2 and delete some. Therefore, there must be an immediate toggle command for choosing the window to be used.

Synchronizing Windows. Some spreadsheets have another command that is of great use in managing multiple windows that is not as obvious—it is concerned with whether moves in one window affect the display of other windows. Imagine that a large table with 50 columns is set up, and the user wants to visually compare the first column with the last one. It is not possible to get both of these columns on one screen at the same time, so the user creates two vertical windows. The user enters the left window and moves the cursor in it so that column 1 is displayed. The user then enters the right window and moves the cursor in it so that column 50 is displayed.

The question arises, what happens in one window when the user moves *up and down* in the other window? If the goal is to compare the rows in the first column to the rows in the fiftieth column, then as one window moves up or down column 1, the other window should move up or down column 50 along with it, that is, the windows should be synchronized. To allow or disallow this type of coordinated movement, there is usually a command to make moves synchronous or unsynchronous.

Synchronized windows are used primarily to bring distant rows or columns close together. Unsynchronized windows make it possible to work on separate subtables at the same time, where the relative positions of rows or columns are different for the subtables (see figure on page 285).

This screen has been split into two vertical windows showing two views of the same spreadsheet. A toggle command will switch the user from one window to the other. In either window, the user can move around the spreadsheet in the ordinary manner. The windows in this example allow the spreadsheet to display the total points for each student immediately to the right of the student's name.

```
G9:  (F)+F9/F$10
```

	A	F	G	H	I
1	Grades for				
2					
3	Name	Total	Percent		
4					
5	Brown R	137.00	0.83		
6	Carol M	127.50	0.77		
7	Lacey RC	132.00	0.80		
8					
9	Average	132.17	0.80		
10	Points	165			

Horizontal windows are exactly analogous. Here Brown's scores can be directly compared to the average scores.

```
G9:  (F)+F9/F$10
```

	A	B	C	D	E	F	G
1	Grades for	CSE 125					
2							
3	Name	Prog1	Prog2	Prog3	Final	Total	Percent
4							
5	Brown R	10.00	15.00	15.00	97.00	137.00	0.83
9	Average	9.17	13.67	13.67	95.67	132.17	0.80
10	Points	10	15	40	100	165	

Spreadsheet Windows

Removing Windows.   The last command for windowing is expected—a command to remove windows. When windows are no longer needed, the user needs some method to remove them from the screen and allocate their portion of the screen to other windows.

▪ Moving Around the Spreadsheet

With a large spreadsheet and the small window provided by the screen, a user might have trouble keeping track of the location of a particular subtable. Even if the user knows where the cell is, it may take considerable time to scroll the

If a spreadsheet allows the separate windows on the screen to be synchronized or unsynchronized, a second set of row or column designators is required. In this display, the two vertical windows are synchronized: row 1 of the first window is across from row 1 of the second.

G9: (F) +F9/F$10						
	A		F	G	H	I
1	Grades for	1				
2		2				
3	Name	3	Total	Percent		
4		4				
5	Brown R	5	137.00	0.83		
6	Carol M	6	127.40	0.77		
7	Lacey RC	7	132.00	0.80		
8		8				
9	Average	9	132.17	0.80		
10	Points	10	165			

The second column of row designators

The two vertical windows in this example are not synchronized: row 1 in the left window does not correspond to row 1 in right one. The need for the second column of row designators is evident.

G9: (F) +F9/F$10						
	A		F	G	H	I
1	Grades for	5	137.00	0.83		
2		6	127.50	0.77		
3	Name	7	132.00	0.80		
4		8				
5	Brown R	9	132.17	0.80		
6	Carol M	10	165			
7	Lacey RC	11				
8		12				
9	Average	13				
10	Points	14				

Synchronization of Spreadsheet Windows

screen to a cell a few hundred rows or columns away. Two commands assist with these problems.

Text Find. Since most tables have informative labels at the sides and top, a find command can be used to search the table for a particular word or phrase designated by the user. For example, the user could ask the system to search for "payrate." If that phrase exists anywhere in the spreadsheet, the find com-

With the cell cursor in an arbitrary cell, the user issues a "find" command, which will prompt for a string of characters from the user and then try to locate a cell in the spreadsheet that contains these letters. Here the cell cursor was positioned at A2 when the find command was given. The system asked for a string of characters, and the user entered "Lacey". The system then began the search.

```
A2:
FIND What String: Lacey
```

	A	B	C	D	E	F	G
1	Grades for CSE125						
2							
3	Name	Prog1	Prog2	Prog3	Final	Total	Percent
4							
5	Brown R	10.00	15.00	15.00	97.00	137.00	0.83
6	Carol M	8.40	15.00	12.00	92.00	127.50	0.77
7	Lacey RC	9.00	11.00	14.00	98.00	132.00	0.80
8							
9	Average	9.17	13.67	13.67	95.67	132.17	0.80
10	Points	10	15	40	100	165	

This search was successful. The system repositioned the cell cursor at the first cell it found that contained the designated string of characters. If no such cell was found, the cell cursor would not have been moved. The specific order in which the search is done (i.e., by row or by column) can affect the cell that is found when there are many possible matches.

```
A7: 'Lacey RC
```

	A	B	C	D	E	F	G
1	Grades for CSE125						
2							
3	Name	Prog1	Prog2	Prog3	Final	Total	Percent
4							
5	Brown R	10.00	15.00	15.00	97.00	137.00	0.83
6	Carol M	8.40	15.00	12.00	92.00	127.50	0.77
7	Lacey RC	9.00	11.00	14.00	98.00	132.00	0.80
8							
9	Average	9.17	13.67	13.67	95.67	132.17	0.80
10	Points	10	15	40	100	165	

Text Find in a Spreadsheet

mand will locate the cell and center the current window on that portion of the spreadsheet (See figure above).

Cell Goto.   When the user knows the coordinates of the cell to be examined, he or she can generally enter an immediate command called a GOTO (go to). The input to a GOTO can be an arbitrary cell coordinate. If the user is at cell Z1000 and issues the command GOTO A3, the window would immediately refocus on cell A3. A useful variation of this command is the GOTO PRE-VIOUS command, whereby a few simple keystrokes can recenter the window on the cell the user worked at immediately before the current one. This command allows the user to toggle back and forth between two distant cells.

■ Protection

The last important spreadsheet process is the ability to protect cells from alteration. Creating a new spreadsheet template or using a template made by someone else requires a lot of cursor moving and data entry, and a user could easily move the cell cursor to the wrong cell and damage the template or data already entered. To provide some control over this type of error, spreadsheet software often includes cell protection.

Cell protection resembles file protection. The user has full control to protect or not protect arbitrary cells. The types of changes that are allowed for a protected cell can be strictly limited. The most common restrictions are:

1. *No restriction.* Any value may be placed in the cell.
2. *Label restriction.* Only labels may be placed in the cell.
3. *Value restriction.* Only numbers or formulas may be placed in the cell.
4. *Total restriction.* The value in the cell may not be altered.

Commands for locking cells and for unlocking cells generally work on any cell, set of rows, set of columns, or block of cells.

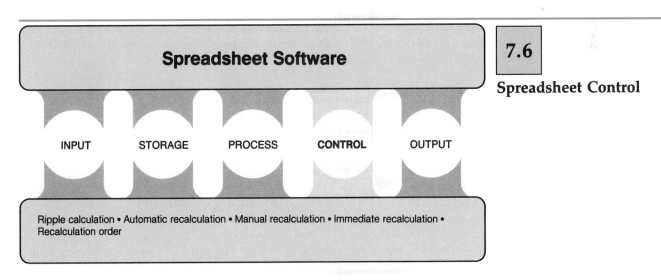

Spreadsheet Software

INPUT   STORAGE   PROCESS   **CONTROL**   OUTPUT

Ripple calculation • Automatic recalculation • Manual recalculation • Immediate recalculation • Recalculation order

7.6
Spreadsheet Control

Like most applications programs, spreadsheets generally provide little programmed control over the inputs, storage, processes, and outputs of the system. The order of tasks tends to be sequential: the user enters a command and the spreadsheet does it, over and over. In this section we shall consider the few control mechanisms available in spreadsheets.

■ Ripple Calculations

Whenever any cell on a spreadsheet is altered, other cells that reference the altered cell may also be changed. And of course, all cells that reference these cells must also be recomputed. Just as a drop of rainwater causes ripples through a pond, so does a change in one spreadsheet cell have the potential to send out ripples (changes) through other cells of the spreadsheet. This automatic recalculation is another feature that sets a spreadsheet apart from simple word processors.

Recalculations, however, brings with it some problems. The first is speed. As the number of cells in the spreadsheet increases, the time it takes to recompute all the formulas increases. The slow speed is noticed as the data is entered, especially on a small microcomputer. When the user enters a new value, the system just sits and waits—the input cursor does not flash, and the cell cursor does not move. After a few moments, all is well—the cell cursor moves and the input cursor flashes. The delay was due to the time it took the computer to perform the recalculations.

Most spreadsheets begin with three recalculation options:

1. Turn on the automatic-recalculation-after-changes mode.
2. Turn off the automatic-recalculation-after-changes mode.
3. No matter what the mode, do a recalculation right now.

These types of commands are essential to any spreadsheet. Recall this chapter's case study, where Brian and Beth used a spreadsheet template that had automatic recalculation turned off. When Beth entered new data in the spreadsheet, the table was not updated. She then issued the command /R to recalculate and update the entire table.

■ Order of Ripple Calculations

Forward reference is another problem that arises in spreadsheet recalculation. It is best demonstrated with a simple example. Imagine that we have a three-cell spreadsheet containing the following values:

□ A1 = the number 10
□ A2 = the formula +A3 * 5 (current value = 100)
□ A3 = the formula +A1 * 2 (current value = 20)

What will happen if the user moves the cell cursor to A1 and resets A1 to hold the number 15?

Let us assume that the recalculation occurs in the order in which the cells are listed. First A1 is reset to 15. Then A2 is set to the current value of A3 (20) multiplied by 5, giving a value of 100. Finally, A3 is computed as the value of A1 multiplied by 2, giving a value of 30. Note the problem: cell A2 was recalculated before A3, when A3 had not yet reflected the change from A1.

Many spreadsheet programs handle this type of forward reference problem automatically by running through repeated recalculations until no more changes occur. On the other hand, one might think that just changing the order of calculation would suffice, but this would complicate the recalculation mode to such an extent that many spreadsheet designers allow only two orders for recalculation:

1. *Row-Major Order.* All of the calculations in row one are done first, starting in column 1, then all the calculations in row two, and so forth.
2. *Column-Major Order.* The calculations are done in exactly the order you would expect: column one first, going from the first row to the last row, then column two, and so forth.

In general, there is little difference between using row-major order and using column-major order. There may be differences in situations where cells reference other cells "ahead" or "forward" of themselves or when a set of cell references is circular (e.g., A1 uses the value of A2, which uses the value of A3, which uses the value of A1). With *circular cell references*, it is possible that no number of iterations will result in stable values. Circular references are generally treated as errors in spreadsheet software.

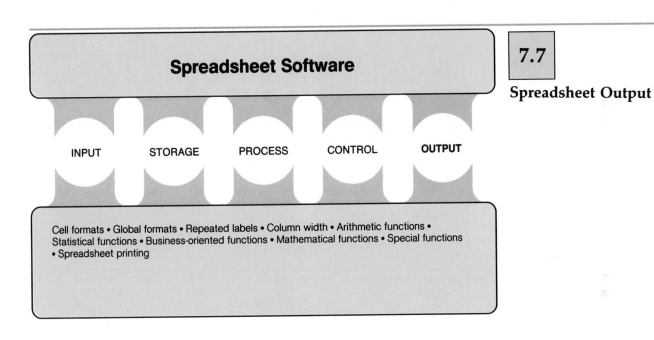

7.7

Spreadsheet Output

The final goal of any spreadsheet is to display a table, either on the screen or on a printer. There are many commands to control the appearance of that display. Many of these commands deal with traditional formatting concerns, but more important are the embedded commands that compute cell values by some mathematical manipulation of the contents of other cells.

■ Display Formats for Screen and Printer

The manner in which the value of a cell is displayed as characters on a screen is a matter of *format*. For example, should the number 5.3 be displayed as 5.3, as 5.30, as 5.300000, rounded off and displayed as 5, or some other variation? Should the characters that will be printed be centered in the column, left-justified, or right-justified?

Formats. Spreadsheets provide a number of formats in which values can be printed: whole numbers, dollars and cents values, arbitrary fractions with a varying number of digits to the right of the decimal point, arbitrary fractions with a fixed number of digits to the right of the decimal point, dates, social security numbers, and so on. Each type of value may then be left-justified, right-justified, or center-justified. Some examples of formatting are shown in Figure 7–8.

Before formatting, all columns on the spreadsheet take up the same number of screen columns, all numbers have only as many digits past the decimal as needed, no decimal points are aligned, and the full table is not visible on one screen.

B2:				
	A	B	C	D	E
1	Grades for CSE125				
2					
3	Name	Prog1	Prog2	Prog3	Final
4					
5	Brown R	10	15	15	97
6	Carol M	8.5	15	12	92
7	Lacey RC	9	11	14	98
8					
9	Average	9.1666667	13.666667	13.666667	95.666667
10	Points	10	15	40	100

Formatting commands reduced the number of screen columns required for columns B through G so that the whole table is visible at one time. The numbers from B5 through G9 have been set to display two positions past the decimal point, and the decimal points are now aligned. These formatting options substantially enhance the appearance of the spreadsheet.

G9: (F)+F9/F$10						
	A	B	C	D	E	F	G
1	Grades for CSE125						
2							
3	Name	Prog1	Prog2	Prog3	Final	Total	Percent
4							
5	Brown R	10.00	15.00	15.00	97.00	137.00	0.83
6	Carol M	8.50	15.00	12.00	92.00	127.50	0.77
7	Lacey RC	9.00	11.00	14.00	98.00	132.00	0.80
8							
9	Average	9.17	13.67	13.67	95.67	132.17	0.80
10	Points	10	15	40	100	165	

Whatever the mechanism for entering format commands, a format specification can generally be attached to a single cell, a row or column, or the entire spreadsheet. As each cell is displayed, the system uses the most specific command applicable. The major format commands include: centering, left or right justification, changing the number of screen columns in a spreadsheet column, establishing the exact format for a number (e.g., dollar, fixed decimal point, floating decimal point, and so on).

Figure 7–8 Spreadsheet Formatting. Whatever the mechanism for entering format commands, a format specification can generally be attached to a single cell, a row or column, or the entire spreadsheet. As each cell is displayed, the system uses the most specific command applicable. The major format commands include: centering, left or right justification, changing the number of screen columns in a spreadsheet column, establishing the exact format for a number (e.g., dollar, fixed decimal point, floating decimal point), and so on.

Repeated Labels. The formats for labels are generally more restricted. The only issue of importance is the justification—left-, right-, or center-. The only variation on this is the so-called repeated label. A user generally can specify that a certain character string be repeated over and over again within a column, no matter how wide the column. For example, a * symbol could be used to draw a line across the top of a column and separate the column label from the column contents:

```
        A
01   NAMES
02   ********
03   JONES
04   ROBERTS
```

Column Widths. One of the common problems associated with spreadsheets is that they rapidly grow too large to display easily on a screen or a printer. Spreadsheet systems provide two basic methods for shrinking the size of the spreadsheet:

1. Reducing the number of screen columns that spreadsheet column occupies (note the potential for confusion here: one spreadsheet column may occupy from 10 to 20 columns of characters on the video screen or printer).
2. Hiding columns.

The user can vary the number of screen columns used to display the columns of the spreadsheet. For example, column 1 of the spreadsheet might require a large number of screen columns because it contains people's full names, while column 2 may need to be only two columns wide because it stores the ages of the people. Allowing the user to vary the size of each spreadsheet column individually provides a means for fitting as much data on the screen or paper as possible.

Hiding does exactly what the name implies: it is a command that prevents a column or row from being displayed on the screen or printer. The cells are still available for holding arbitrary values and referencing by other cells on the spreadsheet, but they are not printed. Besides providing a means to fit more on a page, hiding columns can also be very useful when confidential information (e.g., salary data) is kept on a spreadsheet. The dramatic effects of these formatting capabilities are illustrated by Figure 7–8.

Formatting concerns are manifested in two different sets of commands. One set specifies the format for individual cells, while a second set specifies default formats for the entire table. These global default formats will be used for any cell for which no explicit format is given.

■ Built-in System Functions

One of the cornerstones of spreadsheet processing is the creation of formulas that allow the value displayed in a cell to vary depending on the numbers stored in other cells. The formulas are generally either standard arithmetic computations or system functions for mathematical, business, statistical, or engineering computations.

The arithmetic operations are straightforward and are much like operations in a programming language. Generally, addition is represented by $+$, subtraction by $-$, multiplication by *, division by $/$, and raise to a power by $\wedge$. The unary operations of identity and negation are represented by $+$ and $-$, respectively. Any combination of these arithmetic operators can be used in the formulas for spreadsheet cells. For example, one might enter into cell A4 the formula $+A1+A2*B3/D33$. Then the value displayed in cell A4 would be the number computed using this formula. Parentheses can be used to completely specify the order of operations, e.g., $(A1+A2)*(A3-A4)$.

Similarly, relational operators are provided to answer true/false questions about the relationships between cells. For example, A1<B1 is true if the value in cell B1 is larger than the value in cell A1 and false otherwise. Other relational operators are > (greater than), = (equal to), >= (greater than or equal to), <= (less than or equal to), and <> (not equal to).

The system functions available in most spreadsheet systems include arithmetic and statistical operations on rows, columns, or subtables such as @SUM(B1...B10), as well as mathematical and business-oriented functions. Examples of system functions are:

Arithmetic and statistical computations
1. *@AVERAGE(CELL LIST).* Computes the average of the listed cells
2. *@MAXIMUM(CELL LIST).* Finds the maximum of the listed cells
3. *@MINIMUM(CELL LIST).* Finds the minimum of the listed cells
4. *@NUMBER(CELL LIST).* Counts the number of cells with values
5. *@SUM(CELL LIST).* Adds up the values of the listed cells

Business computations
1. *@PMT(PRINCIPAL, INTEREST RATE, PERIODS).* Computes payments on a loan
2. *@FV(PAYMENT, INTEREST RATE, PERIODS).* Computes future value of an investment

Mathematical functions
1. *@SIN(CELL).* Computes the sine of the value in the cell
2. *@COS(CELL).* Computes the cosine
3. *@TAN(CELL).* Computes the tangent
4. *@ATAN(CELL).* Computes the arctangent
5. *@ABS(CELL).* Computes the absolute values of the cell
6. *@INT(CELL).* Computes the integer portion of the cell

Special Functions
1. *@LOOKUP(VALUE, SUBTABLE RANGE).* Looks up a value in a table defined by the subtable range and returns the corresponding value
2. *@IF(TRUE or FALSE QUESTION, v1, v2).* Returns value *v1* or *v2* depending on the outcome of the question
3. *@AND(v1,v2).* Returns true if *v1* and *v2* are true
4. *@OR(v1,v2).* Returns true if *v1* or *v2* is true
5. *@ERROR.* Propagates the ERROR display
6. *@NA.* Propagates the NA (not available) display

Note that a cell list may be composed of discrete cells separated by commas (e.g., B1, B2, B3, D55) or row and column designators (e.g., B2...B55). Equally important, *in most cases a cell list can be replaced by a reference to another system function!*

The @ERROR and @NA functions have special significance when developing or using templates. @NA stands for "not available," and any computation that uses a cell containing the @NA function will display another @NA message—since the original cell value is not available, neither can any cell based on it be available. The @ERROR function works the same way, but it transmits an @ERROR message to any cell that uses its value. These functions are often inserted into templates so that if the user forgets to enter a vital piece of data, all computations will be flagged as being in error.

■ Printing Spreadsheets

As a minimum, spreadsheets provide for the selection and printing of any subtable in a spreadsheet. A block or subtable is defined and then the print command is issued (in some systems, the print command is given and then the block of cells is defined). It is also possible, of course, to print the entire spreadsheet.

Once the part of the spreadsheet to be printed has been specified, the user can usually control how that printout is positioned on the printed page. Many of the same concerns voiced for word processing arise here again: the size of the margins, the size of the print (pica, elite, or other), headers or footers for the pages of the report, page numbering, whether the printout is upright or sideways, and so on. Examples of some of the output capabilities are given in Figure 7–9. Another option is to print the spreadsheet to a file; this method can be used to insert tables into word-processed documents.

The subtable from A3 through G9 has been selected.

```
A3: 'Name
Print: Enter Range
```

	A	B	C	D	E	F	G
1	Grades for CSE125						
2							
3	Name	Prog1	Prog2	Prog3	Final	Total	Percent
4							
5	Brown R	10.00	15.00	15.00	97.00	137.00	0.83
6	Carol M	8.50	15.00	12.00	92.00	127.50	0.77
7	Lacey RC	9.00	11.00	14.00	98.00	132.00	0.80
8							
9	Average	9.17	13.67	13.67	95.67	132.17	0.80
10	Points	10	15	40	100	165	

Note that the output shows the text only; all formulas, more precise fractions, and so on are lost in this output.

Name	Prog1	Prog2	Prog3	Final	Total	Percent
Brown R	10.00	15.00	15.00	97.00	137.00	0.83
Carol M	8.50	15.00	12.00	92.00	127.50	0.77
Lacey RC	9.00	11.00	14.00	98.00	132.00	0.80
Average	9.17	13.67	13.67	95.67	132.17	0.80

Figure 7–9 Printing a Spreadsheet

7.8

A Final Spreadsheet Example

Case Study

Once the decision is made to use a spreadsheet to solve a problem, the user will find that the spreadsheet system can provide a great deal of help in managing the problem over the long term. Consider the case of Virgil, who is building up a spreadsheet to keep track of the grades of the students in his introductory computer science class.

Virgil started out by typing the title for the spreadsheet, "Grades for CIS 122" in cell A1. The spreadsheet then looked like this:

```
CELL A1: LABEL
Grades for CIS 122

         A          B          C        D        E        F        G
01 | Grades for CIS 122 |
02
   .
   .
   .
19
20
```

Note that although the title was in column 1, the label covered more than one column because nothing else was "in the way."

Virgil was planning to give two programming assignments, two quizzes, and a final in the class, so he placed these in the table next. To compute percentage grades, he also need the weight for each test and the maximum score. This data formed a nice little table all by itself, and he entered it in an empty spot in the spreadsheet by performing the following steps:

1. Set the cursor to A3 and enter the label "Names."
2. Set the cursor to A4 and enter the label "Weight."
3. Set the cursor to A5 and enter the label "Max."
4. Set the cursor to B3 and enter the label showing the name of the graded item, "Prog1."
5. Set the cursor to B4 and enter the weight of Prog1 in determining the final grade, 0.20.
6. Set the cursor to B5 and enter the maximum possible score for Prog1, 15.
7. Repeated steps 4–6 for Prog2 in column C, Quiz1 in D, Quiz2 in E, and Final in F.

Note that the numbers in the table would have no meaning without the labels around them. With the labels in place, it is clear that the weight for Quiz2 was 0.15 and the maximum possible score was 20. The spreadsheet at this point looked like:

```
CELL F5:100
Grades for CIS 122

         A          B          C        D        E        F        G
01 Grades for CIS 122
02
03 Names     Prog1      Prog2     Quiz1    Quiz2    Final
04 Weight    0.20       0.20      0.15     0.15     0.30
05 Max       15         15        20       20      | 100 |
06
   .
   .
   .
19
20
```

In thinking further about the problem, it became clear to Virgil that the major table in the spreadsheet would be the student by score table: a table in which the students were listed on one side and the tests listed on the other. The class list and the list of test names provided the framework for this table. Virgil continued with the following steps:

1. Set the cursor to A8 and put in the label "Student"
2. Set the cursor to B8, C8, D8, E8, F8, and enter the labels "Prog1," "Prog2," "Quiz1," "Quiz2," and "Final," respectively.
3. Set the cursor to A10, A11, A12, A13, and A14, and enter the names of students as labels.

Now the spreadsheet looked like:

```
CELL A14: WarrenM
Grades for CIS 122

         A         B         C         D         E         F         G
01 Grades for CIS 122
02
03 Names     Prog1     Prog2     Quiz1     Quiz2     Final
04 Weight    0.20      0.20      0.15      0.15      0.30
05 Max       15        15        20        20        100
06
07
08 Student   Prog1     Prog2     Quiz1     Quiz2     Final
09
10 BrownR
11 CarolM
12 LacyRC
13 SlackCW
14 WarrenM
 .
 .
 .
20
```

At this point, only the data storage mechanisms of the spreadsheet had been used; nothing had been done that required any calculations. Now Virgil went on to the values that would be based on values stored in other cells. For each of the five tests, he wanted to compute the class average, class maximum, class minimum, and number of students taking the test. In addition, the appropriate total score for each student had to be determined. First, the labels for these new cells had to be entered. Virgil performed the following steps:

1. Set the cursor to A16 and enter the label "Average," to A17 for the label "Maximum," to A18 for the label "Minimum," and to A19 for the label "Number."
2. Set the cursor to G8 and enter the label "total."

Next was the entry of formulas. First, the formulas dealing with average, minimum, maximum and number were added:

1. Set the cursor to B16 (the location for the test average for Prog1) and enter the formula @AVERAGE(B10...B14). This formula tells the system that the value to be displayed in B16 is the average value of the cells from B10 through B14.

2. Set the cursor to B17 (the location for the maximum score on Prog1) and enter the formula @MAX(B10...B14).
3. Set the cursor to B18 (the location for the minimum score on Prog1) and enter the formula @MIN(B10...B14).
4. Set the cursor to B19 (the location for the number of scores for Prog1) and enter the formula @NUM(B10...B14).

Next Virgil entered formulas to compute the percentage score for each student. He performed the following step for the person in row 10:

5. Set the cursor to position G10 (the location for the total percentage score from all the test items for the person in row 10, BrownR) and enter the formula:

(B10/B5 * B4) + (C10/C5 * C4) + (D10/D5 * D4) + (E10/E5 * E4) + (F10/F5 * F4)

This rather complicated formula does one thing five times: it takes a student's test score, divides it by the maximum possible score (to get a fraction correct), and then multiplies it by the weight of that test (to get the fraction of the term total from that score). Each of the five results are then added together to get the weighted percentage score for the term.

Entering the formulas for cells G10 and B16 through B19 took a lot of thinking and typing. One would think that a lot more typing would be required to enter similar formulas for the other students and the other tests. Fortunately, the replicate command makes most of this typing unnecessary.

Virgil did not want to copy the formulas into different locations—he wanted to alter them slightly. He began with the basic form of a replicate command, /REPLICATE B16...B19 at C16...C19, which told the system that he first wanted to copy from the B16 cell (@AVERAGE(B10...B15)) to the C16 cell. But what he really wanted in cell C16, was @AVERAGE(C10...C15). Before the replicate command was finished, it asked whether each cell reference should be used as given (an absolute reference) or whether it should be altered based on its new position (a relative reference). Therefore, when Virgil copied @AVERAGE(B10...B15) to location C16, he specified that B10 was a relative reference, as was B15. The formula in C16 thus became @AVERAGE(C10...C15). The replicate command then copied formulas B17 to C17, B18 to C18, and B19 to C19 and automatically altered them to contain the relative references that Virgil specified.

The rest of the formulas in the table were inserted as follows:

1. Replicate B16 through B19 at D16 through D19, at E16 through E19, at F16 through F19, and at G16 through G19. This set of commands copied over all the formulas for computation of average, maximum, minimum, and number. The cell references in these copies were all specified to be relative.
2. Replicate G10 at G11, at G12, at G13, and at G14. This replication copied the formulas for each student's total score. The cells representing a student's scores (B10, C10, D10, E10, F10) were all relative and changed with each student; the cells that dealt with test score maximums and weights were absolute and remained the same for each student. For example, cell G14 would have the formula

(B14/B5 * B4) + (C14/C5 * C4) + (D14/D5 * D4) + (E14/E5 * E4) + (F14/F5 * F4)

in which all of the row 10 references were replaced by row 14 references, but the row 4 references (B4, C4,...F4) and row 5 references (B5, C5,...F5) remained the same (absolute).

Now that the titles and formulas were inserted, the spreadsheet looked like this:

```
CELL G10:
(B10/B5*B4)+(C10/C5*C4)+(D10/D5*D4)+(E10/E5*E4)+(F10/F5*F4)
Grades for CIS 122

          A         B         C         D         E         F         G
01 Grades for CIS 122
02
03 Names    Prog1     Prog2     Quiz1     Quiz2     Final
04 Weight   0.20      0.20      0.15      0.15      0.30
05 Max      15        15        20        20        100
06
07
08 Student  Prog1     Prog2     Quiz1     Quiz2     Final     Total
09
10 BrownR                                                     0
11 CarolM                                                     0
12 LacyRC                                                     0
13 SlackCW                                                    0
14 WarrenM                                                    0
15
16 Average  0         0         0         0         0         0
17 Maximum  0         0         0         0         0         0
18 Minimum  0         0         0         0         0         0
19 Number   0         0         0         0         0         0
20
```

The test scores were not yet known, so even though there were many formulas in the spreadsheet, they were not yet meaningful. The spreadsheet was now ready for the term's work and would be saved on disk until needed.

After Virgil had graded the first programming assignment, Prog1, he started up the spreadsheet system, loaded in the spreadsheet from disk, and entered the Prog1 scores. The resulting spreadsheet looked like this:

```
CELL B14: 13
Grades for CIS 122

          A         B         C         D         E         F         G
01 Grades for CIS 122
02
03 Names    Prog1     Prog2     Quiz1     Quiz2     Final
04 Weight   0.20      0.20      0.15      0.15      0.30
05 Max      15        15        20        20        100
06
07
08 Student  Prog1     Prog2     Quiz1     Quiz2     Final     Total
09
10 BrownR   10                                                0.133333
11 CarolM   8                                                 0.106667
12 LacyRC   12                                                0.16
13 SlackCW  9                                                 0.12
14 WarrenM  13                                                0.173333
15
16 Average  10.4      0         0         0         0         0.138666
17 Maximum  13        0         0         0         0         0.173333
18 Minimum  8         0         0         0         0         0.106667
19 Number   5         0         0         0         0         5
20
```

Note that the formulas have correctly computed the class average, maximum, minimum, and number of scores for Prog1. Furthermore, the spreadsheet has computed the total percentage of the term's work that each student has completed so far. All of these values were computed from the formulas—none were entered by the instructor. Now that the data entry for Prog1 was complete, Virgil resaved the spreadsheet on disk until he needed it again.

What would happen if a student came in to discuss his or her score for Prog1 and the instructor found that it should be increased? The instructor would simply position the cell cursor on the appropriate cell and enter a new value. What if a new student added the class? An insert row command would be used to insert a row somewhere in the student list—the list could still be maintained alphabetically. If a student dropped, his or her row could be deleted.

This case study shows how the spreadsheet can be used for storing tabular data, computing simple statistics on the tables, and monitoring how changes in the table data change the computed statistics. Variations on spreadsheets generally deal with what built-in functions are available, possibly adding a third dimension to the spreadsheet (so that there are rows, columns, and planes of cells), and integrating the spreadsheet with word processing or other software. Regardless of the variations, the basic concepts remain the same.

Computer Insights
Working Across Spreadsheets

One of the more important features recently added to sophisticated spreadsheets is the ability to reference cells from one spreadsheet while in another spreadsheet. The need for such a capability might arise, for example, if a series of related spreadsheets tracking separate mutual funds is to be integrated into a single spreadsheet.

The general mechanism for making references across spreadsheets is not difficult to imagine. Since spreadsheets are stored in files on disk, the basic problem is to provide a means for giving a file name and a cell location in a cell formula. Although this sounds complex, it really isn't: all that is required is a new syntactic form. For example, a reference to cell A1 in a spreadsheet stored in file FUND1 might be given as FUND1:A1. The system could then be built to look for the cell in the designated file.

When spreadsheets are linked in this way, two types of links are possible, active links and passive links. In an active link, the cell in the second spreadsheet may be referenced *and changed* from the first spreadsheet. Changing a value in the second spreadsheet, of course, requires that the other values in that spreadsheet undergo the typical ripple effect of a change in a value. This process clearly, requires the loading of the second spreadsheet, the ripple calculations, and the resaving of the spreadsheet. With a passive link, the second spreadsheet can be referenced but *not* changed.

Whatever type of link is provided, the ability to link together the results of many different spreadsheets is a useful capability found in most sophisticated spreadsheet systems.

7.9

Summary of Spreadsheet Software Use

Spreadsheet software brought about a revolution in productivity and thus was largely responsible for the rapid growth of microcomputers in their early years. The common *what-if* questions of business could be answered with a speed and precision previously unavailable. Because of their singular importance, spreadsheet software systems are of greater variety than most other productivity software. All spreadsheet systems possess the same basic capabilities for managing tables of data, but the extra functions provided by various software systems are many and diverse. The most common addition is the ability to generate bar graphs of various kinds. Some spreadsheet systems also have an integrated word processing system or a communications system. As these various functions are merged into one system, the reader should understand that the major characteristics of such multicomponent systems can easily be described by combining the descriptions of their individual parts, that is, their graphics, word processing, communications, or other components.

Frame for Spreadsheet Software

	Concept	Your System
ON/OFF	COMPUTER ACCESS: Access to both computer and spreadsheet are needed. May need location, signon, password, telephone number, disk, start-up command. For this system:	Location and disks needed: Telephone, signon, and password: Start-up command for spreadsheet: Shutdown command for spreadsheet:
INPUT	CELL INPUT: Spreadsheets differ in methods for entering numbers, labels, and formulas, moving the cursor, and deleting mistyped characters. For this spreadsheet:	Entering numbers: Entering labels: Entering labels that begin with numbers: Entering formulas: Moving the cell cursor: Deleting characters:
INPUT	COMMAND INPUT: Common methods for the entry of immediate commands include use of the / key, function keys, mouse, et cetera. For this system:	Use of function keys: Use of mouse: Use of control keys: Other key use:
INPUT	CELL LIST INPUT: Many spreadsheet commands require a cell list that is entered by pointing or typing. Cell references may be absolute or relative. For this system:	Single cell: Entire row: Entire column: Rectangular subtable: Combination of the above: Relative reference: Absolute reference:
STORAGE	STORAGE ACCESS: Access to underlying operating system commands is mandatory for disk preparation, directories, et cetera For this spreadsheet system:	Format command: Directory command: Copy command: Other operating system commands:
	SPREADSHEET STORAGE: Spreadsheet's differ on how a spreadsheet is created, destroyed, loaded, and saved within the operating system files. On this system:	Create spreadsheet command: Destroy spreadsheet command: Load spreadsheet command: Save spreadsheet command:

PROCESS B=2+C	ROW/COLUMN COMMANDS: Entire rows or columns of a spreadsheet may be inserted or deleted. Automatic movement of later rows or columns is required. On this system:	Row insert command: Column insert command: Row delete command: Column delete command:
PROCESS B=2+C	SUBTABLE COMMANDS: Subtables may be selected, deleted, copied, or moved, but these operations do not alter the placement of other cells in the spreadsheet. For this spreadsheet system:	Select suitable command: Delete subtable command: Move subtable command: Copy subtable command:
PROCESS B=2+C	WINDOWS: Spreadsheet's may allow multiple views of a single spreadsheet through windowing. Commands exist to create, remove, switch, and synchronize windows. Here:	Create window command: Remove window command: Switch window command: Synchronize window command:
PROCESS B=2+C	GOTO AND TEXT FIND: The cell cursor position is changed by text finds or gotos. The former needs a text string, the latter a cell designator. For this spreadsheet system:	Cell goto command: Text find command:
PROCESS B=2+C	CELL EDIT: Cell contents can be edited using a mini word processor in the spreadsheet. It generally only allows text insertion and deletion. For this system:	Start editing: Exit with changes: Insert character: Overwrite character: Quit without changes: Delete character:
PROCESS B=2+C	SORT: Sorting the rows of a spreadsheet subtable requires specification of the subtable and the column on which sorting is to occur. For this system:	Sort rows command:
CONTROL	PROTECT/RECALC: Cell contents may be protected from change in many ways. Recalculation may be automatic, off, and done in various ways. For this spreadsheet:	Protection on/off: Automatic recalculation on/off: Recalculate now: Change recalculation method:
OUTPUT	PAGE LAYOUT COMMANDS: Page lay out includes margins, type sizes, page size, printer or file used, and so on. For this spreadsheet:	Margins: Page size: Type size: Header/footer: To printer: To file: Cell designator borders:

OUTPUT	FORMAT COMMANDS: Cell format is specified by cell, by row or column, or globally. Format controls screen columns in display and form of display. For this spreadsheet:	Global, row and column specification: Cell and subtable specification: Screen columns per spreadsheet column: Integer: Real: Dollar: Text: Formula:
OUTPUT	PRINT: A print command initiates the printing of some portion of the spreadsheet. For this spreadsheet system:	Specifying portion to print: Beginning the printout: Aborting the printout: Pausing/restarting the printout:
OUTPUT	ARITHMETIC/MATHEMATIC FUNCTIONS: Arithmetic formulas and built-in functions maintain relationships among cells. Some arithmetic and mathematical functions here are:	Addition: Subtraction: Multiplication: Division: Absolute value: Round off value: Integerize value: Square root: Logarithmic: Trigonometric:
OUTPUT	BUSINESS/STATISTICAL FUNCTIONS: Built-in system functions compute many business and statistical values from other cell contents. For this system, some functions are:	Count cells: Sum cells: Average of cells: Minimum of cells: Maximum of cells: Standard deviation of cells: Payment schedule: Net present value:
OUTPUT	HELP SYSTEM: Help systems provide access to on-line commentary, possibly with an index into all topics available. For this spreadsheet system:	Command to access help index: Command to access help:

■ The ISPCO Frame for Spreadsheets

The major functions of spreadsheet software are summarized by the ISPCO frame for spreadsheet software.

The organization of this frame closely matches the organization of the chapter. The major purpose of spreadsheet input is to enter data with embedded formula commands and to enter immediate commands for the editing of data and embedded commands. Storage functions center around the loading and saving of spreadsheet tabular data and, secondarily, allow access to the rest of the operating system kernel. The processing functions are concerned mainly with the manipulation of the data and embedded commands. Control is more important than it was for word processors because the various interdependencies among the data (i.e., some cell values depend on other cell values) must be appropriately managed. Finally, just as in word processing, the embedded formula commands are considered an output function, for the final printed form is the ultimate goal of spreadsheet software.

Spreadsheet software is a simple yet powerful productivity aid that anyone can use. It can be used for balancing checkbooks and budgets, computing taxes, maintaining an address book, and many other practical applications. The spreadsheet frame includes blank spaces so that the user can fill them in to create an easy-to-use summary of his or her own particular spreadsheet system.

■ The ISPCO Script for Spreadsheet Software

Unlike word processing, where beginning users traditionally distinguish between data entry and final formatting, spreadsheet users tend to combine data entry and final printout into a more integrated process, probably because spreadsheet formatting is only a minor part of the more important function of printing out the result of embedded formulas.

Despite this difference, spreadsheet users should begin with a careful analysis of the tables they need to create, just as an author organizes his or her thoughts before writing. Once the spreadsheet user has overall understanding of the required tables, the major steps involved in the use of spreadsheet software are described in the Script for spreadsheet usage. They include entering data and embedded commands, saving data to disk, formatting data, and printing out tables.

With this script and the ISPCO frame for the reader's own system, the reader should find that spreadsheets are quite useful (and even enjoyable to use) in the solution of everyday problems.

SCRIPT FOR SPREADSHEET USE

1. *DETERMINE SPREADSHEET OBJECTIVES.* As in any construction effort, the designer of a spreadsheet must first determine who will use it, the problems they need to solve, how the spreadsheet will help, and so on.

2. *DESIGN THE SPREADSHEET.* Specify the output to be generated by the spreadsheet, then the input needed to compute this output, and finally, the spreadsheet functions that will convert the input to the output. For complex spreadsheets, a plan or model in the form of a handwritten table should be made and a set of test data should be prepared to check spreadsheet construction.

3. *DEVELOP THE SPREADSHEET.* Start-up spreadsheet system. Input numbers, labels, and formulas as defined in the design. Use the copy or replicate command for cells with similar contents. Watch out for circular cell references. Spot-check each formula with data before using it in another formula.

4. *SAVE THE SPREADSHEET.* Save the developed spreadsheet onto disk storage.

5. *EVALUATE THE SPREADSHEET.* Check out the correctness of the spreadsheet using realistic data. Verify the accuracy of all labels. Use protect commands on appropriate cells. Adjust format with format commands. Save the final spreadsheet to disk with its version number or the date.

6. *USE THE SPREADSHEET.* Apply the spreadsheet to the desired problem. If used over and over, expect to modify the spreadsheet to meet new needs and hidden errors.

Chapter 7 Review

Expanded Objectives

The objectives listed below are an expansion of the essential chapter concepts listed at the beginning of the chapter. The review items for the chapter are based on these expanded objectives. If you master the objectives, you will do better on the review items and on your instructor's examination on the chapter material.

After reading the chapter, you should be able to:

1. describe the advantages of electronic spreadsheets over manually implemented spreadsheets.
2. name the parts of a complete spreadsheet table and explain how the parts interact.
3. place the general steps involved in creating a spreadsheet in the appropriate order.
4. give the coordinates of a particular spreadsheet cell, and find the value in a cell, given its coordinates.
5. relate the operation of a spreadsheet to the ISPCO functions.
6. match generalized commands with specific spreadsheet tasks.
7. differentiate between the operations of spreadsheet systems and those of word processing and operating systems.
8. create a simple spreadsheet using labels, numbers, and formulas, including embedded functions for sums, averages, maximums, minimums, and counting.
9. complete a script for using a spreadsheet system and an ISPCO Frame for your own system.
10. give the meanings of the major new terms introduced in this chapter.

Review Items

Completing this review will give you a good indication of how well you have mastered the contents of this chapter and prepare you for your instructor's test on this material. To maximize what you learn from this exercise, you should answer each question *before* looking up the answers in the appendix. The number of the corresponding expanded objective is given in parentheses following each questions.

Complete the following clusters of items according to the directions heading each set.

A. *True or false.*

___ 1. Because the process of automatic recalculation after each entry is so slow, most templates are set up with this function shut off. (10)
___ 2. A template is a stored table that solves the same problem for different sets of data. (2,10)
___ 3. Labels can be either values or numbers. (2,10)
___ 4. The immediate commands for a spreadsheet deal with editing, storing, and printing tables. (5)
___ 5. The cursor determines which cell in a spreadsheet is being operated on currently. (3,10)
___ 6. One limitation of spreadsheets is their inability to scroll from the part of the table currently shown to rows or columns off the screen. (6,7)
___ 7. R1 . . . R6 represents a range of six cells in a table. (1,5,6)
___ 8. Embedded commands are important for the management of tables, e.g., storage or editing. (5,6)
___ 9. In the edit mode, spreadsheets use a character cursor rather than a cell cursor. (5,7,10)
___ 10. Blanking a cell is equivalent to deleting a cell. (6,10)
___ 11. The REPLICATE command and the MOVE command both cause a cell to be blanked out. (6,10)
___ 12. Most spreadsheets are small enough that the rows and columns can be seen in their entirety at the same time. (5,10)
___ 13. *Ripples* in a spreadsheet refers to the automatic recalculation of cell values. (5,10)
___ 14. Designated symbols preceding alphanumeric text are used to differentiate between embedded commands and regular text entry. (7)
___ 15. The text entry and command modes for spreadsheets are very similar in their operation to those of word processing. (7)
___ 16. File manipulation plays a critical role in the development of spreadsheets. (7)
___ 17. It is possible to see arbitrary segments of a spreadsheet on the same screen at the same time. (1,5,10)

B. *Use the spreadsheet frame to match each command on the left with the most appropriate function on the right.* (6)

___ 18. FORMAT

___ 19. FIND

___ 20. CENTER JUSTIFY

___ 21. +(B1 * C1)

___ 22. REMOVE WINDOW

___ 23. LOAD

___ 24. GOTO

___ 25. LOCK

a. input
b. storage
c. processing
d. control
e. output

C. *For the following multiple choice items, place the letter of the best alternative in the space provided.*

___ 26. Which of the following alternatives best describes +A1+A2? (2,6)
   a. label   b. formula   c. value   d. number
   e. coordinate

___ 27. In most spreadsheet programs, which of the following can be copied or replicated? (5,10)
   a. single cells to single   b. rows to rows
   cells   d. all of the above
   c. single cells to rows   e. none of the

___ 28. Which of the alternatives below is the least important storage command for spreadsheet programming? (5)
   a. load files   b. edit files   c. save files
   d. file directory

___ 29. What best describes the cell entry 32?
   a. label   b. value   c. coordinate   d. formula
   e. embedded command

___ 30. To get an exact copy of a row which includes formulas you need:
   a. a replication command   b. a copy command
   c. a copy command and a range of coordinates with teach variable designated as relative
   d. the same as in command (c), with each variable designated as absolute

___ 31. Which of the following is probably not a function of a typical spreadsheet system?
   a. @SUM—adds up a column
   b. @LOOKUP—looks up and returns a table value given the cell coordinates
   c. @STDEV—calculates a standard deviation for a column
   d. @COR—gets correlations of two columns

___ 32. "Cut and paste" refers to copying part of a spreadsheet:
   a. from one place to another in the spreadsheet
   b. from a spreadsheet to a word processor
   c. from one spreadsheet to another
   d. all of the above

___ 33. To save a block of a spreadsheet for copying, you can specify the block to be used by:
   a. pointing at the upper and lower cells with a mouse
   b. pointing at the lower left and the lower right coordinates with a mouse
   c. pointing at the upper left and lower right corners
   d. none of the above

D. *Indicate which commands from the list below are necessary for completing the tasks in items 34–43. (A task may require more than one command.) Place the appropriate letter(s) next to each item.* (6)

a. /BLANK   g. /GOTO
b. /CLEAR   h. /INSERT COLUMN
c. /COPY   i. /INSERT ROW
d. /DELETE COLUMN   j. /LOAD
e. /DELETE ROW   k. /PRINT
f. /EDIT   l. /SAVE

___ 34. Empty all cells in the spreadsheet.
___ 35. Switch the last two rows of the spreadsheet.
___ 36. Get rid of the third column from the right.
___ 37. Add a new column on the extreme left of the spreadsheet table.
___ 38. Eliminate the last row on the bottom spreadsheet table.
___ 39. Make a paper copy of the first two rows of the table.
___ 40. Put the table into disk memory.
___ 41. Retrieve a table previously stored on disk.
___ 42. Move the cursor to another location.
___ 43. Easily modify the contents of one cell.

E. *Consider the cells a–x in the spreadsheet table below*

	A	B	C	D	E	F
01	Item	Year1	Year2	Year3	Total	Average
02	(a)	(b)	(c)	(d)	(e)	
03	(f)	(g)	(h)	(i)	(j)	
04	(k)	(l)	(m)	(n)	(o)	
05	(p)	(q)	(r)	(s)	(t)	
06	Total	(u)	(v)	(w)	(x)	
07	Average					

and determine which cell or cells correspond most closely to the descriptions below. Answer the question by putting a–x in the blank space. (2)

___ 44. A4
___ 45. E5
___ 46. B2...B5
___ 47. +B3+C3+D3
___ 48. @SUM(D2...D5)
___ 49. @SUM(B3,C3,D3)
___ 50. Assume the cursor is on B4. Push right arrow key twice, and up arrow key once. (6)

F. *For questions 51–53, use the previous spreadsheet and select the correct formulas for the cells on the left from the formulas listed on the right. (Labels indicate cell meaning)*

___ 51. E7
___ 52. D6
___ 53. F2

   a. +(C2+C3+C4+C5)/4
   b. @AVERAGE(E2...E5)
   c. +D2+D3+D4+D5
   d. @SUM(D2...D5)
   e. @SUM(B2...D2)/3

G. *Select one or more correct examples from the list on the right for each of the terms on the left.*

___ 54. Coordinate

___ 55. Label entry

___ 56. Value entry (number)

___ 57. Value entry (formula)

   a. 100
   b. +B1*B3
   c. Z1=B1+D2
   d. A3
   e. A1,A2...A10
   f. Z1,A3,B100
   g. 1986
   h. Y1986

___ 58. Range of coordinates

___ 59. List of coordinates

i. @SUM(A1...A10)
j. None of the above
k. COST
l. NAME

H. A set of steps for creating a spreadsheet table is listed in random order below. Put the steps in the most appropriate sequence for creating a table by placing the letters in the correct order in the indicated space. (3)

_____ 60. What is the best sequence for the following steps?

a. move cursor to appropriate cell
b. access spreadsheet program
c. turn on automatic calculation
d. retrieve appropriate template
e. determine table specifications
f. enter values

I. For each of the terms below, specify the most correct definition and one or more correct examples from the lettered definitions and examples below.

Definition	Example	TERM
_____	_____	61. Cell
_____	_____	62. Coordinate
_____	_____	63. Entry
_____	_____	64. Label entry
_____	_____	65. Value entry (number)
_____	_____	66. Value entry (formula)
_____	_____	67. Range of co-ordinates
_____	_____	68. List of coordinates

Definitions

A. An element in the spreadsheet

B. Numbers and/or coordinates separated by +, −, /, or * ...
C. The location or address of a cell in the spreadsheet
D. A set of alphanumeric characters
E. Numbers
F. Values or labels
G. A set of coordinates
H. A set of adjacent coordinates

Examples

a. 100
b. +B1*B3
c. Z1 = B1 + D1
d. A3
e. A4...A10
f. Z1,A3,B100
g. 1986
h. Y1986
i. @SUM(A1...A10)
j. NAME
k. COST
l. the intersection of column 10 and row 20.

Projects

1. PREPARE A TEMPLATE LIKE THE ONE IN THE CASE STUDY. A simple way to become familiar with your spreadsheet software is to go through the case study at the beginning of the chapter and translate the commands into those used in your software. Then check your answers by creating a spreadsheet with your system.

2. PREPARE A TEMPLATE FOR A BUDGET. Find someone who needs a budget or use your own finances to create a monthly budget template. Check the template with estimated values, then enter real values as bills are paid.

3. PREPARE A GRADE BOOK TEMPLATE. One popular use of templates is for grade books, as illustrated in the second case study of the chapter. Find someone who needs a grade book, find out their needs, and create a template for them.

Special Exercise: Completing The Spreadsheet Software Frame

The spreadsheet frame contains special places for the user to write down the characteristics of a real computer system. You are encouraged to fill in the frame for the particular system to which you have access so that the concepts of this chapter can be directly applied to your own hardware and software. This frame can also be used to compare different systems by filling in one frame for each system and contrasting the systems on a point-by-point basis.

Your primary source of information for completing this frame should be the documentation available with your software or hardware system.

As a computer user works on more and different systems, each of the boxes in this frame may require expansion into even more detailed descriptions. By then, however, the user will be sophisticated enough to make such expansions easily and without help.

8

Data Base Management Software

Essential Chapter Concepts

When you finish this chapter, you should know:

- The meaning of important terms, such as: field, record, data base, primary key, secondary key, search, report generation.

- The four modes of operation in data base management systems.

- How to describe and give examples of the ISPCO functions associated with each mode of operation.

- How to describe, in general terms, complex data base management applications.

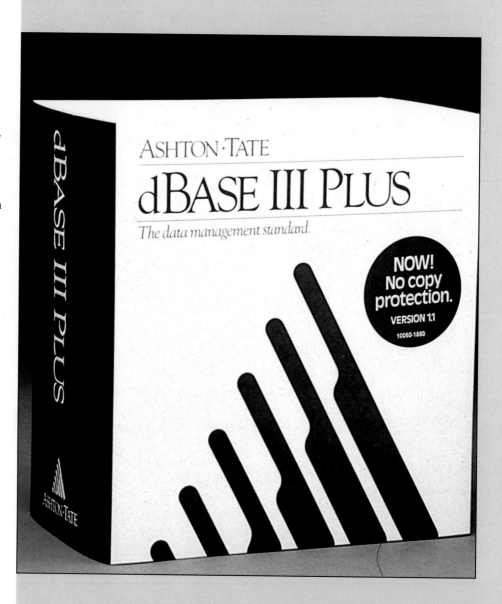

Data Base Management Software

INPUT	STORAGE	PROCESS	CONTROL	OUTPUT

RECORD DEFINITION MODE

INPUT	STORAGE	PROCESS	CONTROL	OUTPUT
Field specifications including name, type, and location	Saving and loading record form	Edit field specifications using insert, delete, copy, and move	—	Summary of record definition

DATA ENTRY/DATA EDIT MODE

INPUT	STORAGE	PROCESS	CONTROL	OUTPUT
Contents of fields and simple editing	Saving and loading data records	Searching and sorting of data base	Defaults for field values	Display of data records

REPORT DEFINITION MODE

INPUT	STORAGE	PROCESS	CONTROL	OUTPUT
Fields to be printed, with formatting for report	Saving and loading report form	Edit report specifications using insert, delete, copy, and move	—	Summary of report definition

REPORT GENERATION MODE

INPUT	STORAGE	PROCESS	CONTROL	OUTPUT
Choice of records and report form	Send report to disk	Searching and sorting of data base	Macros for report generation	Tables, lists, and other summaries in reports

In the last two chapters we have considered two kinds of data: documents and tables. Documents are collections of words or characters that can be input, stored, edited, formatted, and output by a word processor. Tables have cells for holding labels, numbers, or formulas arranged in rows and columns, and they are managed by spreadsheet software.

Data base management software can be similarly described in terms of the data it manipulates. Although data base systems can be viewed from a number of distinct perspectives, the most basic element in a data base is again a table. In a data base system, each row of the table corresponds to information about one particular object, and the columns correspond to characteristics of that object. In addition to this limitation on the meaning of a data base table, there are other differences between the data of a spreadsheet and the data of a data base system. In a spreadsheet system, all subtables are interconnected within the grid of a single large table that allows the deletion of a row or column in one table to possibly affect another table. In a data base, many totally independent tables are connected to each other by more flexible means. Spreadsheets use the single large table for both input of data and output of computations. In contrast, data base management systems provide extensive means for generating new tables and forms just for output purposes. A data base provides a different view of tabular data and makes many kinds of tasks easier to perform than they would be with a spreadsheet but makes other tasks harder.

Before we can continue, some of the basic terms of data base systems must be introduced:

Field:	A label for data (the *field name*) and its value. Example: Field name is "LastName" with a value of "Smith."
Record:	Related fields collected together in one group. Example: Record with three fields: Field "LastName" with value "Brown" Field "FirstName" with value "John" Field "Telephone" with value "555-1234"
Data Base:	Related records collected together in one group. Example: Data Base with two records: Record 1: "LastName" is "Brown" "FirstName" is "John" "Telephone" is "555-1234" Record 2: "LastName" is "Charles" "FirstName" is "Joe" "Telephone" is "555-2233"
Report:	A summary document generated by applying the ISPCO functions to a data base. Example: REPORT: TELEPHONE LIST *Name Telephone Number* *John Brown 555-1234* *Joe Charles 555-2233*

The development of a **data base** requires two basic steps:

1. defining the data **record form,** i.e., specifying the names of all the fields to be used in the records, the kind of data to be stored in each field, how each field will be laid out on a data entry form, et cetera.
2. entering completed data **records** into the data base, i.e., entering data for each field of the record, saving the record, and repeating the process for each record in the data base.

Developing a **report** also requires two basic steps:

1. defining the **report form** for the report, i.e., specifying which fields of the data record should be included in the report, where they should appear in the report, what types of summary statistics should be computed for each field, et cetera.
2. generating the report from a selected and ordered set of records, i.e., choosing some set of records (maybe all of them) to include in the report and inserting the appropriate fields of these records into the report definition.

The actual creation of data bases and generation of reports is not as simple as these steps imply. The details required by each of these steps may be complex. However, data base management software works very much like a powerful spreadsheet system. If one understands how a spreadsheet works, it should be easy to understand data base management systems. Data base management software, like word processors and spreadsheets, has several modes of opera-

---

data base

A logically connected set of data records organized into one or more files used by the data base management system.

record form (or record definition)

A data record description giving the exact specifications for all fields to be used in the data records comprising the data base. Specifications include field names (e.g., Last Name or Telephone Number), the types of data to be entered in each field (e.g., letters or numbers) and other information.

record

A set of data organized into fields which is treated as the basic unit in the data base. Records are generated by entering data into the fields specified by the data record form or definition (e.g., Last Name = Brown and Telephone Number = 555-1234).

report form (or report definition)

A report description giving the specifications for reports. Specifications include the names of fields to be used, where each field should appear, what types of summary statistics should be used with each field (e.g., sums or average), and other information.

report

A report generated by combining a report form or definition with a specific set of data records used in a particular order. To generate a report the user selects a previously defined report form, specifies the data records to be used (e.g., all records), and gives the order (e.g., in alphabetical order of the Last Name field).

tion, and each of the basic ISPCO functions takes on different meanings depending on the mode of operation. For example, the input in the record definition mode specifies the form of the data record. Storage involves saving, deleting, and retrieving these forms. Input in the data entry mode consists of data for the fields of a record, and storage involves saving multiple data records as data base management files. All of these processes will become clear as we examine several examples.

8.1

How Does a Data Base Management System Work?

The power of data base management systems comes primarily from their report generating capabilities. Unlike spreadsheets, which are primarily limited to printing out tables of data, data base management systems provide sophisticated techniques for choosing portions of the data, analyzing the data much as a spreadsheet does, and printing out many types of summaries easily and quickly. Indeed, a data base management system allows the user to store and report on data in any given manner, yet it can quickly adapt to provide new types of reports at any time. Some of these features will become clear as we watch an experienced data base user.

Case Study

Our friend James from chapter 5 is still a student at MU, but now he is earning a lot of money as a consultant for people from small businesses who want to use spreadsheets and data base management software.

Barney, of Barney's Cut Rate Clothes, asked for an appointment, and James went to Barney's office to help with his problem. Barney specialized in only a few sale items but offered very low prices compared to the bigger shops. He was having spreadsheet problems. "You see, James, I have to keep careful checks on my sales so that I can adjust prices immediately on slower moving items. I use a spreadsheet to keep track of sales on a weekly basis. All of my items—coats, pants, and shirts—are color-coordinated, so I only need to keep track of whether coats, pants, and shirts are going fast or slowly.

"But now, I'm adding new items and outlets, and I don't know how to set these up on my spreadsheet!"

"Okay," James said, "Why don't you show me your spreadsheet system on your PC."

Barney had kept his files up-to-date, and he showed James the spreadsheet below. "The problem is, James, I really need better breakdowns of sales, but the spreadsheet gets very cumbersome. I enter my records as rows on a spreadsheet, but I never get around to doing cumulative sales sheets."

```
                BARNEY'S SPREADSHEET SALES SYSTEM
      .---A---..---B---..---C---..---D---..----E----.
   01 Barney's Cutrate Clothes Shop #1        Formulas
   02
   03 Item      Price    Sold     Total
   04 Shirts    $15.00   100      $1500.00    +B4*C4
   05 Pants     $25.00    50      $1250.00    +B5*C5
   06 Coats     $60.00    20      $1200.00    +B6*C6
   07
   08 Barney's Cutrate Clothes Shop #2
   09
   10 Item      Price    Sold     Total
   11 Shirts    $20.00   200      $4000.00    +B11*C11
   12 Pants     $30.00   100      $3000.00    +B12*C12
   13 Coats     $70.00    50      $3500.00    +B13*C13
   14
   14
```

```
15 Barney's Cutrate Clothes Shop #3
16
17 Item      Price     Sold      Total
18 Shirts    $10.00    300       $3000.00        +B18*C18
19 Pants     $20.00    100       $2000.00        +B19*C19
20 Coats     $50.00    100       $5000.00        +B20*C20
21
22 Barney's Shops Sales Report
23 Shop      Sales
24   1       $3,950.00                           @SUM(D4...D6)
25   2       $10,500.00                          @SUM(D11...D13)
26   3       $10,000.00                          @SUM(D18...D20)
27 Total     $24,450.00                          @SUM(B24...B26)
```

James studied the spreadsheet for a while. "Barney," he said, "I think I see your problem. You are using a spreadsheet for a problem that is better suited to a data base system. Properly used, a data base management system can give you your sales reports as well as many other valuable reports. One reason why I think you don't need a spreadsheet is that you are not making use of the recalculation function of the spreadsheet, where you change values and view the results. Another reason is that you are using a large number of tables. In such a case, it is often easier to organize your data into data base records instead of spreadsheet tables."

"But," wailed Barney, "data bases are so complicated and require so much work!"

"Nonsense," said James. "I can set one up right now to do your sales reports. Just let me load my data base system and initialize some data disks on your PC."

James booted up the data base system. On the screen appeared a menu:

```
1.Define Record Form
2.Enter or Edit Data Records
3.Define Report Form
4.Search Records or Generate Report
5.Save Data Base
6.Load Data Base
7.Quit

Enter number of desired option: _
```

"First, Barney, we need to define a form for your data entry." James pressed a 1 to start up the data record definition mode. James then responded to the requests on the screen and specified where each field should appear on the data entry screen, the name for each field, and the type of data that it was to hold. His interaction with the computer began like this:

```
Use arrow keys to move cursor. Press return when cursor is
at desired field position.
```

James's cursor was indicated by a _. He moved it to the position on the screen (row 2, column 1) where he wanted the first field to appear and pressed the return key. He then typed in the name of this field, "Shop," and the screen looked like:

```
Enter name of field at cursor. End with return.


Shop_
```

Now the system needed to know what type of data the field named "Shop" would hold, so it asked for the data type. James entered a C to indicate alphabetic or character data.

```
Data type? Integer Fraction Character $ Date
Enter first letter of desired type: C


Shop
```

The system responded by asking for a maximum number of letters or other characters that would be stored in the field, and James entered 10.

```
Maximum number of characters in field: 10


Shop
```

James continued in this manner for all the fields of the record. After he had finished this process, the system summarized the record definition:

```
F#  Field Name     Field Type          Location
1   Shop           alphabetic (10)      2   1
2   Item           alphabetic (15)      4   1
3   Price          $                    6   1
4   Sold           integer              6  20
5   Sales          calculated(F3*F4)    6  40
```

James had specified five fields of data. The first named "Shop," could hold up to 10 alphabetic characters and would be appear at line 2, column 1 of the screen. "Item" was similarly specified. The field "Price" was restricted to holding dollar values. "Sold" could hold only integers, and "Sales" was a computed field equal to the product of fields 3 and 4, that is, "Price" multiplied by "Sold."

"This sets up a separate record for each item and each shop so that we can generate a better report," James explained to Barney. "Now we switch to the entry or edit mode and enter the data from the spreadsheet."

James pressed the escape key to return to the main menu and chose option 2 (enter or edit data records). A record form using the locations specified by the record definition appeared on the screen:

```
Shop:_                        Record # 1

 Item:

Price:          Sold:          Sales:
```

James entered the data for the first record.

```
Shop:                         Record # 1
NUMBER 1
Item:
SHIRTS
Price:          Sold:          Sales:
$15.00          100            1500
```

Note that James did not (and could not) enter the value for the "Sales" field; as soon as the "Price" and "Sold" fields were defined, the computer automatically computed the "Sales" value and printed it on the screen. With this record complete, the screen displayed another empty form ready for the entry of the next record, and James entered the data for the second record:

```
Shop:                                    Record #2
NUMBER 2
Item:
SHIRTS
Price:              Sold:              Sales:
$20.00              200                4000
```

James continued until all of the data was correctly entered. As he entered the data, he performed whatever minor corrections were required by backspacing and retyping.

"There," he said a few minutes later. "Now that we have the records defined and the initial data entered, we can specify the report you need."

He returned to the main menu and chose option 3 (define report form). His interaction went something like this (his input is shown in uppercase letters):

```
Type of Report: TABLE

Report Title: BARNEY'S SALES REPORT

Fields to be used in desired order:
SHOP, ITEM, PRICE, SOLD, SALES

Do you want column totals? YES

Fields to have column totals:
SOLD, SALES

Do you want subtotals? YES

Fields to define groups for subtotals:
SHOP_
```

Barney looked puzzled. "What's a table report?"

"This system generates two kinds of reports," explained James. "Label reports are used for lists reports like mailing labels. Table reports look more like spreadsheet tables with fields arranged across the top of the table in each row a record."

"So you have chosen a table," interrupted Barney, "with 'Shop', 'Item', 'Price', and so on, across the top?"

"Yes," said James, "and I also asked for column totals for the last two fields, 'Sold' and 'Sales.' "

"And the subtotals?" asked Barney.

"I asked for subtotals to be calculated every time the 'Shop' field changes values, in this case, when it changes from shop number 1 to shop number 2 and from shop number 2 to shop number 3. The only reason that this can work is that the records can be placed in order using any field you choose. We'll put the records in order by 'Shop' so that all the records from shop number 1 come before all of the records from shop number 2, and so on. Let's generate the report so you can see what I mean." James turned back to the keyboard.

Returning to the main menu, James chose the "generate report" option and again responded to the requests of the system:

```
Records to be used? ALL

Order records on fields: SHOP, ITEM_
```

"As you can see," explained James, "I asked that the report contain all of the records and that the records be in alphabetical order based on the contents of the 'Shop' and 'Item' fields."

"Here comes the report!" exclaimed Barney. The report looked like this:

```
Date: 2/25/90                    Barney's Sales Report

Shop                  Item      Sold        Sales

Number 1              Coats       20         1200
Number 1              Pants      100         2500
Number 1              Shirts     100         1500
-----------TOTALS FOR Number 1-----------------------
                                 220         5200
-----------------------------------------------------
Number 2              Coats       60         4200
Number 2              Pants      100         3000
Number 2              Shirts     200         4000
-----------TOTALS FOR Number 2-----------------------
                                 360        11200
-----------------------------------------------------
Number 3              Coats      100         5000
Number 3              Pants      300         6000
Number 3              Shirts     300         3000
-----------TOTALS FOR Number 3-----------------------
                                 700        14000
-----------------------------------------------------
----------------------GRAND TOTALS-------------------
                                1280        30400
-----------------------------------------------------
```

"Well, that's it, Barney. The forms of the records and the report have been defined. When we save the data base to disk, you will be able to input new records to store more data and use the report form to generate reports on your ever-increasing data base," concluded James. "And by the say, here's my bill. I'd appreciate the $200 now."

"No problem—that's a real bargain!" exclaimed Barney. "Thanks for your help. Now I'm all set!"

"Sure you are," thought James, "until you realize how many other reports you really need. Then you'll be back, because now we can easily add all kinds of other reports without any change to the data. That's where data base management systems beat out spreadsheet systems—in the ability to report on the data they have stored!"

James had shown Barney the four major steps involved in the use of data base management systems: *record definition, record entry, report definition,* and *report generation.* Because of the larger number of steps required for the use of data base management systems, such systems may be harder for a novice to understand, but the steps involved are relatively simple and should not deter anyone from using a data base system.

Data base management systems deal with the problem of maintaining and using sets of data. Each set of data consists of a number of records, and each record is divided into fields.

A *record* is a collection of data about some entity. Examples of records include a person's driver's license, checkbook register, and account with the mortgage company or the electric company. Records are kept in address books,

8.2

Using Data Base Management Systems

recipe files, and so on. The contents of a record are limited only by the the creativity of the user. Almost any collection of data can be a record.

A *field* is one of the pieces of data that makes up a record. On a driver's license, the fields might include things like driver's license number, name, address, sex, and date of birth. Note that fields can be composed of other fields that are in turn composed of more fields, and so on. For example, the field "address" might be composed of the subfields "street address," "city," "state," and "zip," while "street address" might itself be composed of "street number" and "street name." In such a chain there will eventually be a field that is not composed of other fields but just contains data; then the type of data that the field will contain must be specified (e.g., "number," "dollar amount," "social security number," or "date"). The type is used to verify that the actual contents of the field correspond to the type expected when the record form was defined.

Finally, a data base is a set of completed records containing information about a real set of objects. The state government has a data base of all driver's licenses. A person's checkbook register is a data base of all of the checks he or she has written. The record form defines the fields for the data; when a number of record forms are filled in, a data base results. A common analogy describes data bases in terms of a filing system: a record is a file folder, a field is a piece of paper with data written on it in the file folder, and the data base is a file cabinet filled with folders.

■ The Shells of Data Base Management Software

As our vignette illustrated, there are four separate activities that must generally be performed in a particular sequence when data bases are established and used: record definition, data entry, report definition, and report generation. Although some variation in order is possible, each activity in this sequence assumes that the ones before it are already complete. This logical ordering of tasks does not prevent the user from commanding the computer to perform tasks in a different sequence. For example, a beginning user might try to enter data before the record is defined—the software would then respond with a message indicating that data cannot be entered until record definition is completed.

In each of these four activities, the user must provide a variety of information and commands. The commands are similar to those used with operating systems, word processors, and spreadsheets, and again, three types of shells are generally available.

Command Language Shells.   In a command language shell, the user must enter commands by typing in the words of the command language. Usually the command name is given first, followed by a set of optional or required parameters that give more information about how the command will be executed. Since there are a number of different modes of operation within a data base management system, some reserved character will probably be used to designate the beginning of a command. For example, a command like the following one might tell the system to save the data base to disk:
@SAVE FILE = CLASS.DATA

In this example, the @ character is the special key that signals the beginning of a command, SAVE is the command to be performed, FILE is a parameter that the save command will use, and CLASS.DATA is the value to be given to the FILE parameter.

Menu Shells. Menu shells are the most frequently used command interface for data base management systems. Many systems use the function keys to select the menu items. For example, each function key might correspond to a menu item as follows:

F1 Define Record
F2 Enter/Edit Data
F3 Define Report
F4 Generate Report
F5 Load Data Base
F6 Save Data Base
F7 Search Data Base
$\vdots$

The user chooses among the major data base modes of operation by pressing a function key and then responds to the submenu that appears.

Graphic Shells. Some data base management systems have carefully structured hierarchies of commands specified in graphic form. In such cases, the user uses a mouse or other pointing device to point at commands on an always visible menu bar. Pull-down menus are usually provided in these environments—when a command on the main menu is selected, a submenu appears below it. For example, when in the record definition mode, selecting ''Field Options'' causes a submenu to appear as shown in the illustration of a graphics shell.

In summary, the commands for controlling a data base management system are closely related to those used in operating systems, word processors, and spreadsheet software.

■ Using the Four Modes of a Data Base Management System

When describing how to use a data base system, we must consider the four modes of operation separately (the major concerns in each mode are the data required from the user and the output provided by the system). Unfortunately, even the four modes of operation may be complex, because different data base

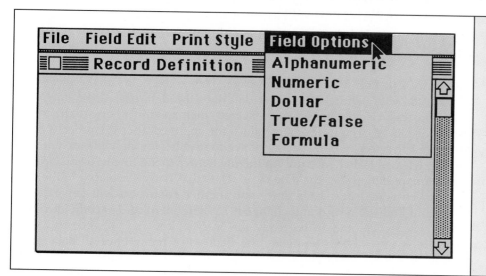

A Graphic Shell for Data Base Design. The graphic shell for a data base system functions like all other graphic shells. Here the record definition mode has been entered, and options for defining and editing record fields are available. In the pull-down menu shown, the user can specify the type of a field as character data, numeric data, dollar amounts, true/false values, or a formula of other fields.

systems work from different underlying models of how data should be organized. In a later section of this chapter, we will describe three models for organizing data: relational, network, and hierarchical data models. In the following short descriptions of the four modes of operation, we will present major characteristics that are true across all models.

record definition mode
The data base management mode in which the record form or definition is created. The first step in using data base software.

Record Definition Mode.   In the **record definition mode,** the user must specify the form of a record, that is, he or she must supply the following data about the fields that make up the record:

1. the field name
2. the type of data to be contained in the field and any additional information required by its type
3. whether the data is required or optional.

In addition to this information, some data base systems require the user to specify the screen location of each field at the same time that the record is defined. This location tells where the field will appear on the computer screen when data is typed in. Such systems require two additional pieces of data:

4. the vertical location of the field on the screen
5. the horizontal location of the field on the screen

Many data base systems allow the user to keep many different kinds of records in one data base; the user then needs to specify this information for each kind of data record.

The method for entering the record definition is straightforward but does vary from system to system. If an explicit **data entry screen** is created during record definition, the record definition process might follow these steps:

data entry screen
A screen display of the data record form provided by many systems to aid the user with data entry and edit.

1. The user is given a blank screen.
2. Cursor controls are used to position the cursor in the desired location on the screen.
3. The user types the desired field name and provides more information about the field, e.g., its type and the number of characters to reserve for data.
4. When all of the fields on the record are defined, the completed form is available for data entry.

In most data base management systems, user prompts make the record definition task quite easy.

record entry and edit mode
The data base management mode in which data records are entered or edited in the data base. This step requires a previously defined record form. Often the second step in using data bases.

Data Entry and Edit Mode and Language.   Once the fields of the record are defined, the user can begin to enter data into the data base. Data entry is a simple process. Usually the screen is cleared, then an empty copy of the record form is displayed. The user enters values for one field after the other. Typing errors are corrected by backspacing. Once the values for all fields are entered, the user has one last chance during the data entry mode to edit or discard the data before placing it into the data base. (Data that has been placed in the data base can be edited at a later time, but another command will generally be required to find the record and change it.) When one record is completed, the system will recycle and to be ready for entry of the next record. A special command is provided to terminate the data entry mode once all data is entered.

As data entry proceeds, most data base systems automatically save the records to disk. Unlike word processing and spreadsheet systems, which tend to work primarily in RAM, data base systems expect that the data will far exceed the capacity of RAM and therefore work more directly with the disk.

Report Definition Mode and Language. The central ideas behind defining a report are straightforward, although the details involved are many. The major steps creating a report definition are:

1. selecting which fields from the original data record will be printed on the report
2. specifing the printing location of each field on the report and the format in which the value will be displayed
3. selecting which statistics will be computed on which fields for inclusion in the report

The first two steps are simple generalizations of the record definition task. The user specifies the names of the fields to be included in the report and then specifies the locations where each field will be printed on the final report, whether the name of each field will be printed with the data, how much room is allocated for each field, and so on.

The statistics to be computed on the fields are simple generalizations of spreadsheet statistics: sums, counts, averages, and so on, can be computed and printed for arbitrary fields in the record. The only question remaining is over what set of records the statistics should be computed—this is usually defined in terms of a set of fields called **break fields.** As the computer reads through record after record, it checks to see if the contents of the break fields change; if they do not change, the records must all "belong together" and the statistics should continue to accumulate. When the contents of the break fields change, however, it is assumed that a new set of records has been encountered—the current values of the statistics are printed, and the computations are restarted for the next set. For example, in our case study all of the records for Shop #1 came before the records for #2, which came before the records for Shop #3. If a report is generated with the "shop" field as a break field, then the current statistics would be printed whenever the "shop" field changed values. Because the records were ordered with all of Shop #1 data first, the statistics summarizing Shop #1 were printed when the break field value changed. Grand totals across all records are routinely provided as well.

Report Generation Mode and Language. The fourth mode of operation is the report generation mode, in which the user must specify three things:

1. the report definition that is to be used
2. the subset of records from the data base that will be summarized by the report
3. the order in which the records should appear.

The report to be used is specified simply by giving the name of a report defined earlier. The subset of records to be used is defined by a **search language.** A search language essentially provides a simple means by which the characteristics of each record in the data base can be used to determine if that record should be included in the report. For example, the user could choose all records in which a certain field has a particular value, or all records in which another field has contents less than (or more than) a particular value. The searching can be specified in a command language or using a menu or a graphic shell; the details of the search specifications will be described later.

report definition mode
The data base management mode in which report forms or definitions are specified. These forms are used as the basis for report generation. Usually the third step in using data bases.

break fields
The fields of a record used to designate what set of records will be treated as a unit during statistical computations. A change in the contents of the break fields will cause current statistical computations to be printed and restarted for the next set of records.

report generation mode
The data base management mode in which printed or screen reports are generated by combining report forms with particular sets of data records. Usually, the fourth step in using data bases.

search language
A formal language through which a set of records having certain characteristic field values can be retrieved from a data base.

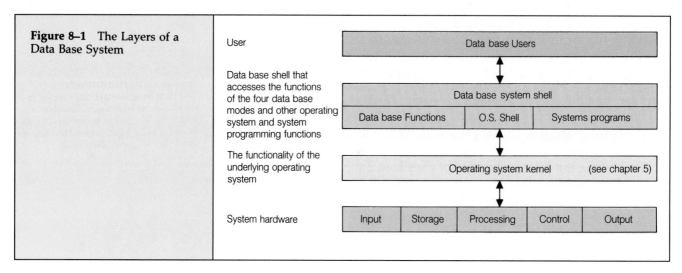

Figure 8–1 The Layers of a Data Base System

Finally, the user can specify the fields to be used to order the selected records in the final report.

▪ The Components of a Data Base Management System

As the reader would probably expect by now, data base software must possess an underlying kernel of data base functions that are accessed through a data base shell. This structure, in turn, sits atop an operating system that manages files and hardware for the computer. The organization of a typical data base management system is shown in Figure 8–1.

8.3

Data Base Inputs

Data Base Management Software

INPUT   STORAGE   PROCESS   CONTROL   OUTPUT

RECORD DEFINITION MODE
Field names, field types, field locations, which fields are required, which fields are keys, and the like

DATA ENTRY/DATA EDIT MODE
Values for fields in records and commands to correct existing records

REPORT DEFINITION MODE
Report name, fields to be used in report, report format

REPORT GENERATION MODE
Choice of records for report, choice of report to use, order of records, and the like

The organizing figure for this section shows the input required in the four modes of a data base management system. In this section we will describe only the most important input associated with the definition and entry of data records. Searching the data base will be described in the processes section and report generation in the output section. This separation is due to the complexity of data base systems: data bases have major components for the input, processing (searching), and output (reporting) of records; although each of these components requires all five ISPCO tasks, their major emphases differ and they are categorized and discussed accordingly.

Record Definition Mode

When a data base is being set up, it is necessary to define what information each record is to contain. Thus, defining the record form is a creative process that requires a clear understanding of the purpose for setting up the data base in the first place.

Once the fields of information have been defined, the creation of the **record structure** is straightforward. On microcomputers, most data base management systems define a record in terms of "screens" of data. With a screen of, say, 24 rows and 80 columns, the user must define where each field should be on the screen, what the limits on the size of the field are, what type of data goes into the field, how the field name should be displayed, what the default value for the field should be (if any), whether the field is required or optional, and so on. As these decisions are made about each field, the evolving form is displayed on the screen. One advantage of a screen definition for a record is that the screen can often be configured to look just like the corresponding paper form, hence simplifying the data entry process. For example, a completed record form might look like:

record structure
The format or arrangement of data elements in a record, e.g., the sequence of the data values entered into the various fields.

```
┌─────────────────────────────────────────────────────────────────┐
│                                                                   │
│  Student Record for Mega University Class CPS111                  │
│                                                                   │
│  Last Name:_ _____  First Name: _____         │
│                                                                   │
│  Street Address: _____        │
│                                                                   │
│  City: _____  State: _____  Zip: _____        │
│                                                                   │
├─────────────────────────────────────────────────────────────────┤
│                                                                   │
│  Midterm Test Score: _____ Midterm Laboratory Score: _____      │
│                                                                   │
│  Final Test Score: _____  Final Laboratory Score: _____       │
│                                                                   │
│  Software Cost: $_____.____  Hardware Cost: $_____.____        │
│                                                                   │
│  Date: _____/_____/_____                                           │
│  RECORD FORM DEFINITION                    (SCREEN 1 OF 1)         │
│                                                                   │
└─────────────────────────────────────────────────────────────────┘
```

This record is designed to contain information about students in a computer course. Both laboratory and classroom scores are recorded at midterm and at the end of the course. Student expenditures are also saved on this form for a study relating hardware and software use to learning. This record will be used throughout the ISPCO sections in this chapter.

If there is more information than can fit on one screen the data record can be continued on a second screen, a third screen, and so on. As the fields are entered, the user must provide all of the information about each field, potentially including:

1. the field name
2. the vertical location of the field on the screen
3. the horizontal location of the field on the screen
4. the type of data, along with the information required by its type. The most common data types and their requirements are:
   a. an arbitrary character string—the maximum size, the default value (if any)
   b. a whole number—the maximum possible value, the minimum possible value, the default value (if any)
   c. an arbitrary number—again, a maximum, minimum, and default (if any)
   d. a dollar amount—maximum, minimum, and default (if any)
   e. a date (month, day, year)—range of values is obvious, defaults might be the current date
   f. a telephone number (area code followed by seven digits and possibly an extension)—the range of values is obvious; possible default area code, default number would generally not make sense
   g. a zip code (only five-digit numbers accepted)—the default value (if any) (One of the problems with the nine-digit zip code is the amount of computer software that will have to be changed)
   h. a state (perhaps only the two-letter postal abbreviations will be allowed)—default state might be curent state
   i. sex—only M or F allowed; default would generally not make sense
   j. a yes/no categorization—possible default
5. whether the data is required or optional
6. whether there is a default value (i.e., an assumed value when none is explicitly given) and the value if used

In summary then, a *record form or record definition includes both the screen containing field names and the specifications for each field*.

Note that some of the information required during record definition is concerned with the data to be stored (e.g., the name and the type of the data), and some is concerned with the input of data (e.g., the horizontal and vertical position). Although many data base systems do not allow the creation of a completely user-defined input form, this capability is clearly desirable so that the computerized record can be made to correspond with the paper version of the same data form.

Once the record definition is complete, many data base systems summarize the information about each field on the screen so that the user can verify the specifications that are not displayed directly on the form. For the data record given above, the user might receive a screen display something like:

```
Field Name                      Type    Size Req? Default
------------------------        -----   ---- ---- ----------
01 Last Name                    alpha    25   Y   -------
02 First Name                   alpha    10   Y   -------
03 Street Address               alpha    35   N   -------
04 City                         alpha    25   N   Rochester
05 State                        alpha     2   N   MI
06 ZIP                          integer   5   N   48063
07 Midterm Test Score           integer   3   N   -------
08 Midterm Laboratory Score     integer   4   N   -------
09 Final Test Score             integer   3   N   -------
10 Final Laboratory Score       integer   3   N   -------
11 Software Cost                $       5.2   N   -------
12 Hardware Cost                $       5.2   N   -------
13 Date                         date      8   Y   today
```

Because the data in spreadsheets and data bases are so similar (see Table 8–1), the commands used in the record definition mode of data base management systems are very similar to those used in setting up a new spreadsheet. There are commands for formatting, for setting the type of value to be stored, for specifying global default values, and so on.

Table 8–1 Comparison of Spreadsheet and Data Base Record

Spreadsheet Concept	Data Base Concept
Table	Data Base
Row of table	Record of data base
Cell of row	Field of record
Cell coordinate	Field name
Cell contents	Field value
Cell contents type	Field value type

Some software systems like LOTUS 123, VP PLANNER PLUS, and EXCEL take advantage of the similarity shown in Table 8-1. They provide special commands for converting spreadsheet tables into data bases. In these cases, the record definition is created by using the contents of the spread sheet cells. These programs automate what was done manually by James in the case study!

■ Data Entry Mode

Record definition is followed by data entry. Values must be placed in all the required fields and possibly in the optional fields to ensure that all necessary information is stored in the data base. The data entry can be done all at once or spread across a number of separate computer sessions. The steps involved in data entry include retrieving the record definition, filling out the record form on the computer screen for as many new records as desired, and then writing all the records back into the existing data base on disk (or creating a new data base in the first data entry session). Two examples of completed records using our sample form are:

```
┌─────────────────────────────────────────────────────────────────┐
│                                                                   │
│   Student Record for Mega University Class CPS111                 │
│                                                                   │
│   Last Name: Anderson_____    First Name: Robert _____  │
│                                                                   │
│   Street Address: 404 Fifth Street_____   │
│                                                                   │
│   City: Lansing_____    State:MI   Zip:48824      │
│                                                                   │
├─────────────────────────────────────────────────────────────────┤
│                                                                   │
│   Midterm Test Score: 50_         Midterm Laboratory Score: 47_   │
│                                                                   │
│   Final Test Score: 50_           Final Laboratory Score: 49_     │
│                                                                   │
│   Software Cost: $_10.00            Hardware Cost: $_30.00         │
│                                                                   │
│   Date: 03/03/86                                                  │
│   RECORD #1                                      (SCREEN 1 OF 1)  │
│                                                                   │
└─────────────────────────────────────────────────────────────────┘
```

```
┌─────────────────────────────────────────────────────────────────┐
│                                                                   │
│   Student Record for Mega University Class CPS111                 │
│                                                                   │
│   Last Name: Green_____    First Name: Moe _____  │
│                                                                   │
│   Street Address: 505 Sixth Street_____   │
│                                                                   │
│   City: Rochester_____    State: MI   Zip: 48063    │
│                                                                   │
├─────────────────────────────────────────────────────────────────┤
│                                                                   │
│   Midterm Test Score: 50_         Midterm Laboratory Score: 50_   │
│                                                                   │
│   Final Test Score: 50_           Final Laboratory Score: 50_     │
│                                                                   │
│   Software Cost: $20.00             Hardware Cost: $_30.00         │
│                                                                   │
│   Date:03/03/86                                                   │
│   RECORD #2                                      (SCREEN 1 OF 1)  │
│                                                                   │
└─────────────────────────────────────────────────────────────────┘
```

Updating a record is obviously similar to entering data initially. The record definition must be accessed, and the records that are to be updated must somehow be identified and extracted from the data base. Then data can be entered in fields where no previous values were entered, and existing field values can be edited. Finally, the altered records must be returned to the data base. For both the initial data entry and the updating of records, most data base management systems provide an automatic **datestamp** whereby the date and time of the last alteration of each record is automatically kept in the record. In this way the user can always be certain of the status of the data base.

As noted before, some software can convert spreadsheets into data bases. These systems input data records by copying the contents of rows in the spreadsheets into records in the data base, as James did manually in the case study.

datestamp
A feature of some data base management systems in which the date and time of the last alteration of a record are automatically kept in the record.

8.4

Data Base Storage

The reader should be able to anticipate the kinds of storage functions available in a data base management system: storing and retrieving the various input required for the data base as well as accessing the underlying operating system functions.

Data Base Management Software

INPUT **STORAGE** PROCESS CONTROL OUTPUT

RECORD DEFINITION MODE
Storage and retrieval of record form • Access to standard storage system commands

DATA ENTRY/DATA EDIT MODE
Storage and retrieval of data in records • Access to standard storage system commands

REPORT DEFINITION MODE
Storage and retrieval of report format • Access to standard storage system commands

REPORT GENERATION MODE
Retrieval of report formats and records • Storage of finished reports •
Access to standard storage system commands

■ Loading and Saving Definitions and Data

There are essentially three types of data that must be saved by a data base management system: the definition of a record form, the data of the many records that use this definition, and the definition of any reports.

Record Form Definition. (In this mode *record forms* are saved and retrieved.) The goal of the data record definition mode is the creation of the empty record. The data base system generally provides capabilities for saving a new record form definition, loading in a form definition created earlier, getting a list of record definitions available, and deleting record definitions. Generally, these tasks are actually accomplished through the use of the underlying operating system and the conventions for file names. For example, if a user created a new record type named "student data" and then asked that this record be saved on disk, the data base management system would generally create a file with a related name (e.g., "record definition student data") and access the operating system kernel to write the data to the disk. During the record definition mode, all disk operations are restricted to files whose names indicate that they are "record definition" files.

Data Record Entry and Editing. (In this mode *data records* are saved and retrieved.) The storage and retrieval of data records would appear to be another case of storing and retrieving files, as in any other application. Again, there will be commands to load, save, delete, and list data bases on disk. (Note that these commands refer to entire data bases including complete files of data records, not individual records within the files.) The storage and retrieval of the data record files, however, is substantially more complex than it is for simple record definition files, primarily because of the relative size of the files. Data record files may contain hundreds or thousands of separate records, and the entire data base will generally not be able to fit into RAM at one time.

Although some simple data base systems are limited to keeping all data in RAM at one time, most systems use special techniques so that the system can "pretend" all of the records are in memory even when they are not. These techniques allow the data base system to keep most of the data records on the disk and only pull into RAM those records that the user is currently accessing. This arrangement is invisible to the user. No commands are given to explicitly reference the disk—the system just does it whenever necessary. Virtually all processing in data base management system uses system storage directly.

There are other constraints on the loading and saving of data records. For example, the records must generally be kept in one particular order (to be described in the next section), otherwise indexes to the data may have to be maintained. All such constraints can be expensive and slow in terms of computing resources.

Computer Insights
The Accuracy and Privacy of Data Bases

In California, a law-abiding man has been arrested repeatedly for felonies committed by another man who bears a slight physical resemblance to him and who has the same last and first names. In Michigan, a judge was arrested several times for stealing his own car when the police computer was not updated with the fact that his stolen car had been returned to him. An honorably discharged ex-serviceman was arrested repeatedly in several states as a deserter because of computer confusion of names. Literally thousands of people have been refused credit on the basis of the credit ratings of other people with similar names.

All of these disturbing events occurred because of human indifference and incompetence in the maintenance and use of national data banks like the National Crime Information Center's Wanted and Warrant Information Systems and the National Credit Information Systems. "Slight mistakes" like failing to input full middle names, update stolen vehicle reports, and so on, led to these outrages. As the use of computers increases, no doubt more and more people will be harmed by careless use of computerized data base systems.

Privacy is also an important issue. From the data base perspective, the right to privacy means the right to control information about oneself by limiting its input into computer data bases and limiting access to such data bases. Privacy is implicit in the Constitution, the Bill of Rights, and English common law, but current laws are woefully deficient in protecting privacy from computers. The most important laws affecting the right to such privacy are:

The Fair Credit Reporting Act of 1979 This federal mandate provides citizens with the right to examine credit records and to change or challenge the contents through litigation.

The Privacy Act of 1974 This law states that citizens have the right to examine their personal data records and to ask federal judges to revise the records if the records are incorrect. It further requires federal agencies to seek the permission of the people who are represented in a data bank before selling federal data banks or using them for purposes not originally intended. This law applies only to government-controlled data banks.

The Fair Information Practice Laws These are laws written by some states to extend the controls of the credit reporting and privacy acts to all data banks, both public and private. These laws allow citizens to examine data bases, correct errors in their personal records, and restrict the use of information about their personal telephone or TV cable use.

With the ever-increasing number and diversity of data bases containing information on ordinary people, privacy is a major concern. The CIA once commissioned a study to provide a description of how the KGB might establish an invisible system of keeping tabs on any person in the United States. The resulting description was almost identical to the Electronic Funds Transfer (EFT) system that is now used with nationally recognized credit cards. The electronic trail left by most people could provide an ideal method for intelligence-gathering activities. If we don't start worrying about personal privacy, it may be that none will exist. Winston Churchill once remarked, "The only thing which saves us from our governments is their ineptitude." Governments with computers may continue to be inept in many areas, but knowledge about individual citizens is probably not one of them.

Report Form Definition and Report Generation. (In the mode *report forms* are stored and retrieved). Like the record definition mode, the report definition and generation modes have provisions for loading, saving, listing, and destroying the various report forms available in system storage. Again, disk access will probably be made through the operating system kernel, using special file names to designate which of the files on the disk are reports. For example, the report named "mailing labels" might be saved on the disk as a file named "report form mailing labels." During the report definition mode, all disk operations will be restricted to files whose names indicate that they are "report" files.

■ Other Operating System Storage Functions

Like both word processing systems and spreadsheet systems, data base management software generally provides a means to access any storage function in the operating system kernel. The most common functions referenced are those for formatting a disk, generating a directory, deleting a file, copying a file, and so on. Such access does not generally use the operating system shell but instead uses part of the data base management system shell to access the operating system kernel directly.

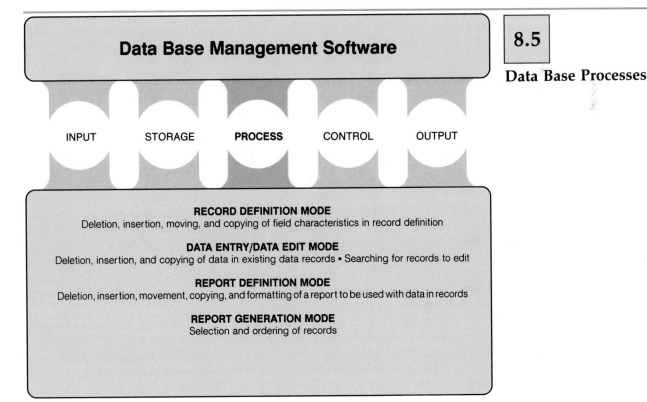

8.5

Data Base Processes

Data Base Management Software

INPUT   STORAGE   **PROCESS**   CONTROL   OUTPUT

RECORD DEFINITION MODE
Deletion, insertion, moving, and copying of field characteristics in record definition

DATA ENTRY/DATA EDIT MODE
Deletion, insertion, and copying of data in existing data records • Searching for records to edit

REPORT DEFINITION MODE
Deletion, insertion, movement, copying, and formatting of a report to be used with data in records

REPORT GENERATION MODE
Selection and ordering of records

The computer processes available to the data base user depend on the mode in which the user is operating.

■ Processing for Record Definition Mode

In the data record definition mode, the primary processes available deal with the insertion, duplication, deletion, modification, and movement of field

field attributes
The characteristics that define the use of a field in a data base management system, including such things as whether the field is part of a primary or secondary key, whether the field data is required, the position of the field on input records, and so forth.

names, field locations, or **field attributes** on the record definition screen. These processes provide a simple method for reorganizing a record form definition without having to retype the whole definition.

Note that attempting to alter the record definition *after* data records have been entered is difficult and may not be allowed on some systems. The data records entered will have been stored on disk with the fields in a certain order and containing certain kinds of data formatted in particular ways. All of this organization uses the current record definition. If the record definition is changed in the record definition mode, either the data base must be started over from scratch or a potentially lengthy adjustment process must be initiated in which the existing data records are reordered, new values inserted, old values deleted or moved, and so forth.

Processing for Data Record Entry or Editing

In data record entry or editing, one might expect to encounter essentially the same commands as are used for data editing on word processors or spreadsheets—deletes, inserts, copies, moves, and so on. However, there is an additional level of complication with data records that did not exist for the characters of a word processor or the tables of a spreadsheet: there are *two levels at which all of these commands could be defined—the record level and the field level.* One could copy records, move records, delete records, and so on and one could also copy field contents, move field contents, and delete field contents.

Editing Commands.   Of the many possible commands for *editing records*, few are generally available. There is usually no command to move records, because the order in which records are stored is defined by alphabetic order on certain fields. Order can be changed only by changing the fields on which order is based. Deleting records is a straightforward task available in all systems; however, specifying which records to delete is a complicated process usually involving the search methods described later in this section. Copying records is rarely allowed, because records that are identical in every entry are not permitted in many data base management systems. The command closest to copying a record is used during data entry, when the user can access the field contents of the last record entered as a starting point for the next record. In this way, if the contents of two consecutive records are almost the same, the user can just modify the values in the old record rather than entering a complete new record. Finally, insertion of records is actually handled in the data entry mode.

Commands for *editing fields* are also limited. Inserting fields is generally not allowed because it would change the definition of the record, something not done without great effort. Deleting fields runs into the same problem. A field's contents may be blanked out, but this process is just an example of the ability to edit or alter a field's *contents.* Every data base system permits the user to edit a field's contents. The problem of choosing which records to edit requires the specification of some subset of records through a search language, just as in record deletion. As far as copying fields is concerned, the fields in a record are generally of such disparate types that copying is not a useful feature.

Although virtually all of the editing commands desired are available in other modes of the data base system, the seeming lack of editing processes in data entry and editing is due to the organization of the data itself. Each record is treated as an individual unit. While entering or editing one record, it is not reasonable to make global changes that affect all other records.

Editing features vary across systems, however, and some systems provide virtually all types of editing commands. In any system, however, searching the data base for records with a particular configuration of data fields is a primary process.

Searching Field Contents. Searching is used in two different parts of the data base management system. It is used in the data entry/editing mode to select records to edit or delete, and it is used in the report generation mode to determine which records are to be included in a report. The searching process can be accessed in either of these modes through the data base management shell. In either mode, there are two aspects to the searching problem:

1. how wide a variety of searches can be made
2. how quickly the searches are made

The variety of searches possible with a particular data base system generally depends on how complex the search statements can be. Search statements are made in a language, and as the reader might expect by now, there are three varieties of languages: those typed in text, those using menus, and those using graphic images.

No matter how the search is defined, **search statements** always reference the fields of a record in conditions such as "the value in the 'age' field must be grater than 30" or "the value in the 'sex' field must be an F." The conditions are generally numeric relations (less than, less than or equal to, greater than, greater than or equal to, equal to, or not equal to) or involve **string matching** (an exact match or some kind of partial match). Separate conditions can be combined or modified using the connective *and, or,* and *not.*

To understand the variety of searches that are possible in typical data base management systems, imagine that we wish to search a data base made up of the student records defined by our sample record form:

search statements
Statements setting the conditions for retrieving data records based upon the contents of fields (e.g., Age > 30 AND Salary < 30000).

string matching
A data base search in which the computer is directed to find all records in which a text field holds a particular set of characters, e.g., Last Name = Jones.

```
Student Record for Mega University Class CPS111

Last Name: _____ First Name: _____

Street Address: _____

City: _____ State: _____ Zip: _____

Midterm Test Score: _____ Midterm Laboratory Score: _____

Final Test Score: _____ Final Laboratory Score: _____

Software Cost: $_____._____ Hardware Cost: $_____._____

Date: _____/_____/_____
RECORD DEFINITION                        (SCREEN 1 OF 1)
```

Furthermore, assume that the data base includes 4,000 records, each containing information on a different student.

The simplest kind of search is a straightforward match. To search for all students with the first name "Robert," the user would call up the record form, position the cursor in the specified field for the match (first name), and then fill in the value to be matched (Robert):

```
Student Record for Mega University Class CPS111

Last Name: _____  First Name: Robert_ _____

Street Address: _____

City: _____  State: _____  Zip: _____

─────────────────────────────────────────────────────────────────

Midterm Test Score: _____  Midterm Laboratory Score: _____

Final Test Score: _____  Final Laboratory Score: _____

Software Cost: $_____._____  Hardware Cost: $_____._____

Date: _____/_____/_____
RECORD SEARCHING                                    (SCREEN 1 OF 1)
```

(In this example and those that follow, the field defining the search is indicated by a screened box on the right side of the form.)

After the data is entered into the field, a special command to initiate the search is given. The search then begins, and all records that have "Robert" in the "First Name" field would be identified for retrieval. Once these records are marked for retrieval, they can be used by the editing or report generation processes without affecting other records in the file. Note how the record form is used: the value to be searched for is entered in the proper field position, and then the form serves as the definition of the search. We will assume that this method is used in all of the search examples that we will discuss, and we will not bother to reproduce the record form for each case.

One kind of search is a *complete* matching—the data in the field must match completely and exactly. For example, when searching for "Robert," a record containing "Rob" or "Roberta" in the First Name field would not be selected. As another example, to find all of the students in the data base who had a grade of 50 on the midterm, the form would be called up and the value "50" would be placed in the "Midterm Test Score" field. Then the search would be initiated and all records in the data base with a "50" in that location would be identified. Finding all Michigan residents or everyone with last name of Smith would be just as simple.

partial string match
A data base search that retrieves all records in which part of the data in the specified field matches a designated string (e.g., a partial string match could find all records in which the field called "last name" begins with "Mc," like McDonald or McPhee).

One can also search for a **partial string match.** For a partial match there are generally two different special characters that can be entered into the search fields:

1. one character that will match (and ignore) any one character in a field and
2. another special character that will match (and ignore) an arbitrary string of zero or more characters.

To show how these characters work, let us use a common pair of characters, a ? to match any character and a * to match an arbitrary string of characters. The following search for a partial string match:

```
┌─────────────────────────────────────────────────────────────────┐
│                                                                   │
│  Student Record for Mega University Class CPS111                  │
│                                                                   │
│  Last Name: Mc?onald_____     First Name: _____        │
│                                                                   │
│  Street Address: _____       │
│                                                                   │
│  City: _____  State: _____  Zip: _____       │
│                                                                   │
│──────────────────────────────────────────────────────────────────│
│                                                                   │
│  Midterm Test Score: _____ Midterm Laboratory Score: _____    │
│                                                                   │
│  Final Test Score: _____  Final Laboratory Score: _____     │
│                                                                   │
│  Software Cost: $_____._____ Hardware Cost: $_____._____    │
│                                                                   │
│  Date: _____/_____/_____                                           │
│  RECORD SEARCHING                        (SCREEN 1 OF 1)           │
│                                                                   │
└─────────────────────────────────────────────────────────────────┘
```

would retrieve the record of any student whose last name began with "Mc," was followed by any one letter, and then ended with "onald." This search is really looking for two different spellings of the same name: McDonald and Mcdonald. Note, however, that names such as McXonald and Mc4onald would also be retrieved in the unlikely event that such records existed in the data base.

The search below uses the second special search character:

```
┌─────────────────────────────────────────────────────────────────┐
│                                                                   │
│  Student Record for Mega University Class CPS111                  │
│                                                                   │
│  Last Name: Mc*_____          First Name: _____        │
│                                                                   │
│  Street Address: _____       │
│                                                                   │
│  City: _____  State: _____  Zip: _____       │
│                                                                   │
│──────────────────────────────────────────────────────────────────│
│                                                                   │
│  Midterm Test Score: _____ Midterm Laboratory Score: _____    │
│                                                                   │
│  Final Test Score: _____  Final Laboratory Score: _____     │
│                                                                   │
│  Software Cost: $_____._____ Hardware Cost: $_____._____    │
│                                                                   │
│  Date: _____/_____/_____                                           │
│  RECORD SEARCHING                        (SCREEN 1 OF 1)           │
│                                                                   │
└─────────────────────────────────────────────────────────────────┘
```

This search would match any record in which the last name began with "Mc" and was followed by zero or more arbitrary characters. It would match names like McDonnel, McCoy, or McIntosh.

Both kinds of partial string matches can be used to identify groups of records or to search for one record when the user is not sure of the exact value to try to match. Matching and partial matching searches can be done on any individual field in the record.

The next type of search concerns numeric comparisons. There are essentially two generally available numeric searches: a **relational search** and a **range search.** Data base systems often do not provide both of these functions, since either one alone can provide both types of searches.

relational search
The use of relational operators ($=$, $>$, $<$, $<=$, $>=$, $<>$) in conjunction with specific data field values to search for and retrieve records in a data base.

range search
A data base search that retrieves all records in which the value of a particular field is between some upper and lower limits (e.g., all records in a personnel data base where the contents of the "age" field is between 40 and 70).

The relational search is the simplest. The user positions the cursor in the desired field and enters one of the six relational operators ($=$, $>$, $<$, $<=$, $>=$, $<>$) followed by a value. The data base is then searched for those records that have the specified relation between their field contents and the value in the search. For example, the following relational search:

```
Student Record for Mega University Class CPS111

Last Name: _____ First Name: _____

Street Address: _____

City: _____ State: _____ Zip: _____

Midterm Test Score: >30_   Midterm Laboratory Score: _____

Final Test Score: _____ Final Laboratory Score: _____

Software Cost: $_____._____ Hardware Cost: $_____._____

Date: _____/_____/_____
RECORD SEARCHING                              (SCREEN 1 OF 1)
```

will cause the system to search for all records that contain a midterm test score greater than 30.

A range search requires some mechanism for specifying a top and bottom limit of a field's value. For example, searching for all students whose midterm laboratory score was between 30 and 50 would require specifying a range search on that field. The range search might be implemented by having the user position the cursor in the field and enter another special symbol such as a #.

```
Student Record for Mega University Class CPS111

Last Name: _____ First Name: _____

Street Address: _____

City: _____ State: _____ Zip: _____

Midterm Test Score: _____   Midterm Laboratory Score: #_____

Final Test Score: _____ Final Laboratory Score: _____

Software Cost: $_____._____ Hardware Cost: $_____._____

Date: _____/_____/_____
RECORD SEARCHING                              (SCREEN 1 OF 1)
```

Then the system would prompt at the bottom of the screen below the form:

```
Enter minimum value:
```

The user would respond with a 30. The data base system would then ask the next question:

```
Enter maximum value:
```

The user would respond with the upper limit of 50. The system would then identify all records where the "Midterm Laboratory Score" field was between 30 and 50. (For any purists who are wondering if the range is inclusive or exclusive, it is generally inclusive, that is, it includes the values 30 and 50).

Users can also identify records based on two or more fields. For example, a user might want to find all the records of students who had a hardware cost of more than $25.00 *and* a final programming score of less than 30 (*both* conditions must be true). Such a search is set up by simply entering data into more than one field of the form. The search just described would be set up as follows:

```
Student Record for Mega University Class CPS111

Last Name: _____  First Name: _____

Street Address: _____

City: _____  State: _____  Zip: _____


Midterm Test Score: _____  Midterm Laboratory Score: _____

Final Test Score: <30       Final Laboratory Score: _____

Software Cost: $_____.____        Hardware Cost: $>25.00_

Date: ____/____/____
RECORD SEARCHING                      (SCREEN 1 OF 1)
```

Whenever two or more fields are defined, the search is an **AND** search in which all conditions must be true for a record to be retrieved.

If a user wanted to retrieve the set of records in which the student had a final test score of more than 30 *or* a software cost less than $10.00, a new method must be used. Two *separate* forms must be filled out, one with the "final laboratory score >30" search, and one with the "software cost < $10.00" search:

AND operator
A logical operator used to combine two true-false values. Given two true-false values, A and B, A AND B asks the question: Is it true that both A and B are true? In data bases, an AND operator can be used to specify a search that will retrieve a record only when two or more requirements are simultaneously met.

```
Student Record for Mega University Class CPS111

Last Name: _____  First Name: _____

Street Address: _____

City: _____  State: _____  Zip: _____


Midterm Test Score: _____  Midterm Laboratory Score: _____

Final Test Score: _____     Final Laboratory Score: >30_

Software Cost: $_____.____   Hardware Cost: $_____.____

Date: ____/____/____
RECORD SEARCHING                      (SCREEN 1 OF 1)
```

```
┌─────────────────────────────────────────────────────────────────────┐
│                                                                       │
│   Student Record for Mega University Class CPS111                     │
│                                                                       │
│   Last Name: _____  First Name: _____      │
│                                                                       │
│   Street Address: _____           │
│                                                                       │
│   City: _____  State: _____ Zip: _____        │
│                                                                       │
├───────────────────────────────────────────────────────────────────────┤
│                                                                       │
│   Midterm Test Score: _____  Midterm Laboratory Score: _____      │
│                                                                       │
│   Final Test Score: _____  Final Laboratory Score: _____        │
│                                                                       │
│   Software Cost: $<10.00_         Hardware Cost: $_____.____        │
│                                                                       │
│   Date: _____/_____/_____                                             │
│   RECORD SEARCHING                            (SCREEN 1 OF 1)          │
└─────────────────────────────────────────────────────────────────────┘
```

OR operator
A logical operator used to combine two true-false values. Given two true-false values, A and B, A OR B asks the question: Is it true that either A or B or both A and B are true? In data bases, an OR operator is used to specify a search that will retrieve a record if any one of the requirements joined by OR is true.

NOT operator
A logical operator used to reverse truth value. If A is true then NOT A is false and visa versa.

primary key
The set of fields on which the records of the data base are ordered for searching.

With these search techniques, virtually any combination of records can be specified, including complete or partial matches, range searches, and a variety of AND, **OR**, and **NOT** requirements.

Searching Theory. The second aspect of searching is the speed at which the searching is done. There is one general truth: the larger the number of records in the data base, the slower the search. What can be done, then, to speed up the search?

Let us consider for a moment the way in which people search. Given an unordered list of numbers, it might take a while to find all the occurrences of a particular number in the set. For example, how many 16's are in the following set of numbers?

```
14  83  12  32  43  65  04  61  23  54  34  16  34  23  12  43  23  11  45  54
39  23  16  23  43  32  99  32  93  87  39  29  19  29  30  36  30  11  00  32
11  22  49  20  99  65  06  55  33  09  23  93  11  14  23  45  43  23  55  35
16  34  44  02  30  40  20  30  48  16  29  34  20  12  59  16  34  33  20  16
```

How much easier the problem is in the following set!

```
00  02  04  06  09  11  11  11  11  12  12  12  14  14  16  16  16  16  16  16
19  20  20  20  20  22  23  23  23  23  23  23  23  23  29  29  29  30  30  30
30  32  32  32  32  33  33  34  34  34  34  34  35  36  39  39  40  43  43  43
43  44  45  45  48  49  54  54  55  55  59  61  65  65  83  87  93  93  99  99
```

Clearly, if one knows the kind of questions that will be asked and arranges the data in a particular way, a search can be made much more quickly. Since the data in a data base has to be in *some* order, why not choose an order that will provide the fastest searching speed?

Records in a data base are stored in alphabetical or numerical order based on a **primary key**. Whenever a user sets up a record, a certain set of fields (one or more, in a particular order) must be specified as the primary key. The data base system will then take the fields in the primary key, pretend each record is one long chunk of data, and store the records in alphabetical or numerical order (if all the primary key parts are numbers), based upon this key. For example, if a data base containing employee records has a primary key of "last name" and "first name," then the records would be stored in alphabetical order based upon the value of the "last name" field, and if duplicate last names occurred, the "first name" field contents would be used to further define the order. For example, a data base of student records stored alphabetically by its primary key of student name, would look something like:

```
Data Base File Contents

Position        Record contents
    1           Brown, Andrew C.    Engineering  22 M 3.42 SR
    2           Calloway, Brian     History      21 M 2.94 JR
    3           Davis, Christine    Chemistry    22 F 3.67 JR
    .               .
    .               .
    .               .
  875           Martin, Deborah A. Nursing       19 F 3.14 SO
    .               .
    .               .
    .               .
```

The choice of primary key should be based on the types of searches that will be conducted most frequently. In addition, it is generally required that every record have a unique primary key. For student records, a logical choice for primary key would be student "name." The primary key would then consist of only one field, and the records would be maintained in alphabetical order using the name field. Note that, because our sample record layout doesn't have a "student number" as part of the "name" field, it would have problems if two students happened to have the same name.

Because the primary key is used to order the data base, it should generally be a stable item that will not change often, if ever. An example of a bad primary key would be the student's class (freshman, sophomore, and so forth), followed by last name: every year or half year, whenever students' classes changed, the entire data base would have to be reordered, a time-consuming and expensive task.

One last comment about searching techniques will complete our discussion. If the user knew that a set of records was stored alphabetically by student name, he or she could be very efficient in finding the record for "Jones, Robert P." The user wouldn't start at the first record and look through to the last but would instead look at the record in the very middle. If the middle record is for "Carter, Richard M," the user need not look at any of the top half of the file; if the middle record is for "Thompson, Susan X," then the bottom half of the file could be ignored. By looking at one record, half of the records have automatically been weeded out. Once the user knows which half the desired record is in, he or she can take this half and look at its middle record, and so on. Thus, to find the record for "Jones, Robert P," only a small number of records need to be looked at.

Since this method of searching works so well when the search is based on the primary key, it would be very useful to be able to make similar searches on a field that is not the primary key. Unfortunately, records can be in only one order, and the searching method described can only work under that condition. However, it is possible to use a **secondary key,** in which a separate copy of some of the fields not in the primary key can be made and placed in their own order (not the primary key order). A user can then search on any of these new fields with the same speed as for a primary key. The disadvantage of secondary keys is that these separate files take up more system memory and must be regenerated whenever any of the secondary key fields are changed.

secondary key
Fields on which secondary index files will be created to speed the searching process for data in fields other than those in the primary key.

◼ Report Definition and Generation Processes

There are few new processes available during report definition and generation. Report definitions must be editable. The editing functions provided for making changes in a report are minimal: deleting a field from a report, adding a field to a report, changing the printing attributes of any field (e.g., where on the paper it will print), and altering break fields. Editing functions across a set of reports provide little more than the ability to delete or copy a report.

Whatever the format of a report, searching plays an important role in report definition and generation. Any report form can be used with any set of records (in any order) retrieved by a data base search. The user must specify both the records to be summarized by the report and the order in which the records should be processed in the report.

8.6

Data Base Control

Data Base Management Software

INPUT   STORAGE   PROCESS   **CONTROL**   OUTPUT

RECORD DEFINITION MODE
None

DATA ENTRY/DATA EDIT MODE
Default values for fields

REPORT DEFINITION MODE
None

REPORT GENERATION MODE
Macros for combining records and reports

Like the other types of software discussed so far, data base management systems seem to have little need for control. A great deal of useful processing can be accomplished without ever having to resort to explicit sequential, alternative, iterative, or procedural control. Instead, the user just enters one command after the other. All control remains with the user.

Although the user can specify any action at any time, the interaction of the four modes of processing results in three simple constraints:

1. Record definition must precede data entry, report definition, and report generation.
2. Data entry must precede report generation.
3. Report definition must precede report generation.

Within these constraints, the user can control the sequence of tasks performed

Computer Insights
Popular Data Base Systems

The major concepts described in this chapter are realized in many different data base management systems. The most advanced ones implement the relational data base model. The dominant data base system using the relational model is Dbase II and its updates Dbase III Plus and Dbase IV. A description of these and other popular currently available systems follows:

DBASE II, III, III Plus, and IV by Ashton-Tate. Dbase II was the first full relational data base system for the IBM PC line of microcomputers. Because of the elegance and power of the relational data model on which Dbase II was constructed, it became a success almost instantly. The successor of Dbase II, Dbase III, and subsequent versions probably have more applications available for them than any other data base system.

Rbase 5000 by Microrim, Inc. As was true for spreadsheets, once a good system is developed, the higher powered or less expensive copies follow. Rbase 5000 is more powerful than Dbase III and includes a wide variety of utilities that may be used in conjunction with the relational data base, including a chart graphics system and a natural language interface.

Reflex by Borland International, Inc. As is generally true in the software domain, the software that runs on the IBM PC is not easily transferable to the Apple Macintosh. Thus the Macintosh often ends up with its own unique software systems. In the data base realm, the Reflex system provides a relational data base that uses the Macintosh operating system environment.

by the system. The most common sequence of activities for data base management will be described at the end of the chapter in the ISPCO Scripts.

Macros are the only other control mechanism frequently available in data base systems. As the reader might infer from previous chapters, macros are a simple method by which frequently performed sequences of commands can be stored and activated by the use of one word or phrase. An example of the use of a macro will be included in the case study at the end of the chapter.

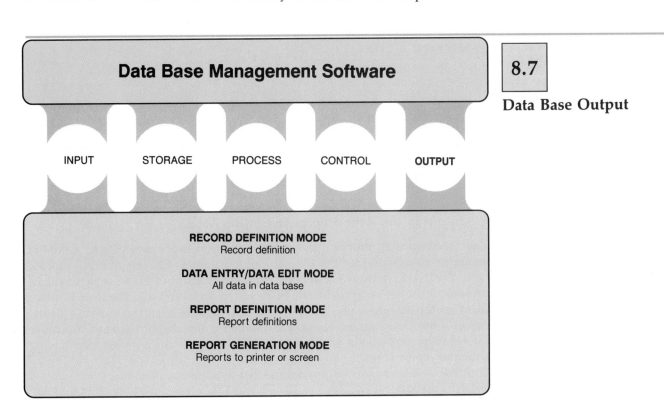

Data Base Management Software

INPUT   STORAGE   PROCESS   CONTROL   **OUTPUT**

RECORD DEFINITION MODE
Record definition

DATA ENTRY/DATA EDIT MODE
All data in data base

REPORT DEFINITION MODE
Report definitions

REPORT GENERATION MODE
Reports to printer or screen

8.7

Data Base Output

Many introductory texts do not try to teach the reader exactly how reports are generated. Instead, they simply gloss over this important operation because of the difficulty of conveying this idea on the printed page. We feel that report generation is so central to data base management that it must be considered in some detail, regardless of the difficulties.

The basic concepts behind the generation of reports can be stated in just a few steps. The user must specify:

1. which fields are to be included in the report (fields can be chosen from those in the original record, and new fields can be created just for the report; the new fields can have constant values, like the current date, or can be computed from the data in existing fields)
2. where each field should appear on the printed page
3. which fields, if any, should be statistically summarized and which fields will be the break fields that define how frequently this summarization should occur.
4. what records should be included in the report
5. the order in which the records should be included

When these steps are completed, the user can print the report.

To understand the steps involved in creating data base reports, let us temporarily put aside our more complicated example of a record in favor of a simpler data record and application. After we complete the analysis of the simple problem, we'll move to a more complex example with sample printouts representative of real data base management software.

Assume that a large number of data records have been entered according to the following data record definition:

```
Last Name:                    First Name:

Address:

City:                     State:     ZIP:

Section Number:

Midterm:    Final:    Project:    Total:
```

and it is now time for the user to define a report.

Output in the Report Form Definition Mode

The user begins by entering the report definition mode and placing fields on an empty screen. (Remember that although we are describing an input process here, the overall purpose of report definition is output!) Some systems might first ask for a list of all fields to be included and then ask the user to place them on the screen. More typically, the user selects from the available fields, one at a time, and places each on the screen using the cursor keys. Consider the following scenario in which the user wishes to define a report form having a **tabular report format.**

The system begins by providing a list of all fields available:

tabular report format
A particular style of data base report in which the data is used to create tables much like spreadsheet tables, with full use of formulas to operate on the data.

```
Field #      Field Name    Field Type
   1         Last Name     character(20)
   2         First Name    character(10)
   3         Address       character(20)
   4         City          character(15)
   5         State         character(2)
   6         ZIP           integer(xxxxx)
   7         Section Num   integer(xx)
   8         Midterm       real(xxx.x)
   9         Final         real(xxx.x)
  10         Project       real(xxx.x)
  11         Total         formula(xxx.x)
Enter field number of field to include in report.
Enter higher number to create a new field.
Enter 0 to quit:_
```

The user enters a 1 because the last name is to appear in the report. The user is then asked to place this field on a report screen with a prompt something like:

```
Position the cursor with the arrow keys and push return
when ready to position field #1.
```

The user must now move the cursor to the desired place on the screen and press return. Having set the position of the field on the final report, the user may then be asked a series of questions concerning the field, for example:

```
Concerning field #1, Last Name

Should the field name be included with every record?
NO
Should the field name head the column?
YES
How many columns should be allocated for the field?
25
```

The original screen listing all the fields will then be displayed again, asking the user to select other fields that should appear on the report. As the user continues to select fields for the report, the report form develops on the screen, often with one or two sample data records to show how the report will eventually look. If the user wanted just a report of total scores by name, report definition might look something like:

```
Last Name   Midterm   Final  TestTot  Project   Total
Abbot          60       70     130       80       210
(example data from record 1 in appropriate columns)
Brown          50       75     125       75       200
(example data from record 2 in appropriate columns)
```

This particular style of report is called a tables or tabular report format. In a tabular report, the data in the data base can be used to create a table much like a spreadsheet table, with labels, numbers, formula fields, and so on. Note that the user has created a new computed field named TestTot (test total). When asked for the field number, the user entered 12 a field number greater than those that actually existed. The system then understood that the user wanted a computed field and asked for a definition of the computed field:

```
Enter the Name for field #12: TESTTOTAL
Enter the Type for field #12: FORMULA
Enter formula for field #12: F8 + F9
```

The F8 + F9 formula indicated that this new field would be defined as the sum of the existing fields, F8 and F9 ("midterm" and "final"). Now that field 12 has been defined, it will be included whenever the list of fields is called up. Field 12 may also be used in the formulas of other new fields.

For any report, but especially for those arranged in columns, the user may wish to compute statistics on all the data in a column (i.e. for all data records) or on some part of a column (i.e. for some of the data records). For example, the report could include the sum of the midterm scores for all students in the class with or without subtotals. Other possible statistics are suggested by the formulas in spreadsheets—average, maximum, minimum, and so forth. The interaction that specifies the statistics might be something like:

```
Are column statistics desired? Yes
Which statistic? AVERAGE
Which fields? MIDTERM, FINAL, TOTAL
Are statistics desired on subsets of records? YES
Which fields are break fields? SECTION NUMBER
```

The specified statistics (the average, in this example) will be printed after all the data in the set of records is printed. By default, the statistics will be printed at the end of all the records included in the report. In addition, break fields can be used to define the subsets of records on which the statistics will be printed. All consecutive records that have the same values in their break fields will be treated as a set. In this example, the average would be computed for every set of consecutive records from the same class section (maybe the user wants to see if students from one section perform better than those from another). The average of all the records would also be computed and printed at the end of the report. Note that it is important to make sure that all records from one class come before all records from another. If the records were in random order with respect to the break fields, the subset statistics would be meaningless.

Once the report form is defined, the user must save the report form onto disk for future reference. The report must be given a name (like TOTAL SCORES REPORT), which will be used during report generation to distinguish it from other report forms stored on the disk.

Report forms do not have to have the tabular format with its columnar arrangement illustrated in the last example. In a **labels format** the user can place the data fields in arbitrary locations on the screen, for example

labels report format
A particular style of data base report in which data is placed on the page in any desired pattern. The name comes from the common use of this format to print address labels.

```
2 First Name      1 Last Name
3 Address
4 City
5 State           6 Zip           14 TOTAL= 10 Total
```

This arrangement is often used to create a mailing label. Notice the new descriptive field, field 14, which contains just the constant character string "TOTAL =". This descriptive data will appear before the contents of field 10, the total score of the student for whom the mailing label is created. When the fields are arranged in this way, some of the system's report capabilities are clearly not applicable; for example, column headings cannot be used because multiple fields appear in the same columns and the individual reports will be used as mailing labels that will be separated from each other.

Once this report form is completed, the user must again save it to disk. A descriptive name like MAILING LABELS would be appropriate.

Output in the Report Generation Mode

The basic tasks in report generation are specifying which records to use, what order to put them in, and what report form to use. If the report forms defined in the last section were available, a user working in the generation mode might have an interaction something like this:

```
Available Report Forms Are:
1. TOTAL SCORES
2. MAILING LABELS
Enter the number of the desired report: 1
```

Note that the report form selected has a tables format. Once the report form is chosen, the user must specify the records that are to be used in the report. The search language described in section 8.5 would be used to select the records in interactions like the following one:

```
Last Name:*                 First Name:

Address:

City:              State:    ZIP:

Section Number:

Midterm:   Final:   Project:   Total:
```

As before, the search is specified on the data entry form. In this case, the * in the "Last Name" field specifies that records with any last name should be used (i.e., all records in the file). When the selection of the data records is complete, the user must specify the order in which the records should be placed for reporting. For example,

```
Enter the fields to be used to define the order of records
in the final report:
SECTION NUMBER
```

Recall that the "section number" field was chosen as the break field when the report was created. The records must therefore be ordered by section number to ensure that the statistics computed on subsets of the selected records are meaningful.

With the report chosen, the records selected, and the order provided, the report could then be printed out; it might look something like

```
Name          Midterm   Final   TestTot   Project   Total
Abbot           60        70       130       80       210
Brown           50        75       125       75       200
    AVERAGES FOR SECTION NUMBER = 1
                55       72.5                          205

Charles         90        90       180       95       275
Douglas         70        85       155       90       245
    AVERAGES FOR SECTION NUMBER = 2
                80       87.5                          260

    AVERAGE FOR ALL SECTION NUMBER
              67.5        80                         232.5
```

Note that when the break field changed, the statistics on the preceding subset of records were computed and printed in the report.

To print out the records using the other report definition (which has a labels format), the interaction would proceed as follows:

```
Available Report Forms Are:
1. TOTAL SCORES REPORT
2. MAILING LABELS

Enter the number of the desired report: 2
```

After the mailing labels report is selected, the user must choose the set of records to print. If, for example, only the records of students living in the city of Rochester were desired, the search request would look like:

```
Last Name:                    First Name:

Address:

City: Rochester               State:      ZIP:

Section Number:

Midterm:    Final:    Project:    Total:
```

The user might want to use bulk mail service, which requires presorting the labels (reports) by zip code and could do this by requesting that the records be ordered by ZIP:

```
Enter the fields to be used to define the order of records
in the final report:
ZIP
```

The report that would be printed would list the names, addresses, and total scores in the order defined previously:

```
Glen Abott
425 Main Street
Rochester
MI 48063                    TOTAL= 210

Robert Brown
31 Cellar Avenue
Rochester
MI 48066                    Total= 220

                  .
                  .
                  .
```

Mainframe data base management systems provide label and table reports much like those above, except that much more elaborate operations can be used in analyzing the data records and huge data bases that would swamp a microcomputer can be accommodated. For example, statistical analysis systems provide a large array of report generators that includes calculation of means, standard deviations, correlations, regression coefficients, and many other statistical analyses.

Many microcomputer data base management systems are parts of integrated systems that provide full-capability word processing, graphics, communication, spreadsheet, and data base management functions for manipulating the same data base.

As in previous chapters, we now include one last case study to illustrate some of the more complex concepts of the chapter.

8.8

A Final Data Base Management Example

Case Study

Polly had set up an independent firm to provide consulting and software for a bank's small business creditors. She had a network of IBM personal computers and paid the bank for computer access to her clients' data files on the bank's IBM mainframe computer. Polly kept her staff small and made maximum use of her small computer network. Polly practiced Tom Peters' and Bob Waterman's *In Search of Excellence* rule of "management by walking about," i.e., backing up her staff, problem solving, and being sure her customers were satisfied, and she was doing well.

As Polly returned from lunch one day, she noticed one of her new customers waiting for help at the customer service desk. "Hi," Polly said. "You must be Art Jones from 'The Artiste of Plumbing,' plumbing shop. Can I help you?"

"I'd appreciate it." Art explained that he was having trouble figuring and mailing out his monthly bills. Since all Art's files had already been stored through the data base management system on some disks he had brought with him, Polly accessed the data base management system through one of the office PCs and loaded his disks. The system displayed a menu of options:

```
 1. Define Record Form
 2. Enter or Edit Data Records
 3. Define Report Form
 4. Search Records or Generate Report
 5. Macro Manipulation
 6. Save Data Base
 7. Load Data Base
 8. Quit

Enter number of desired option:_
```

Polly entered a 7 and proceeded to load in Art's data base. Then she entered a 2 to update the records in his data base with the new data from his fistful of receipts. The screen displayed a record form to initiate a search:

```
Customer ID:
Last Name:              First Name:
Street:
City:                   State:        Zip:

Date of last entry:
previous balance:
New charges:
New payments:
New balance:
```

"Okay, Art, let's begin with all those payments and new charges you've brought with you. Let's see, the first is a check for fifty dollars from C. C. Roberts," To retrieve the Roberts records, Polly entered "Roberts" into the last name field and then pressed the function key to start a search. Soon the Roberts record appeared on the screen. "The first thing we have to do is move the data in 'New balance' to 'Previous balance.' I guess it's obvious that last month's new balance becomes this month's previous balance." She reset the 'Previous balance' field to be the same as the current value of the 'New balance' field. "Now we'll enter fifty dollars in the new payment field, and since there are no new charges, we have to put a zero there," Polly said. After entering the new amount, Polly saw the 'New balance' correctly updated from the two changes. She pressed the function key to save the record. The system then displayed another empty form for another search update.

"Next? New charges for Fred Brown for twenty-five dollars. All right, we'll access his record and enter that in the new charges field." Polly again entered a search command, retrieved the record, updated the data, and saved the changed record. This procedure continued until the month's bills and payments had been entered: accessing a record, entering new charges or new payments, and saving the results.

Once the posting was finished, Polly asked Art about the reports he needed and found that he needed two kinds of reports:

1. an accounts receivable report, i.e., a table listing the name of each customer and the amount owed to the plumbing shop
2. an address label for each customer for billing, i.e., name and address for all customers who owed him money.

Polly began by accessing existing data base reports that her office kept on file and quickly set up similar reports for Art and saved them on Art's disks under the names "ART RECEIVABLES" and "ART MAILING." The general form of the first report she created was:

Accounts Receivable Report

CUSTOMER NAME	ADDRESS	BALANCE OWED
Fred Brown	77 Cynthia St.	$ 25.00
Claudia Knash	11 B. Baker St.	50.00
Victor Sands	300 Market	100.00

The second report had the following form:

Mail Label Report

Fred Brown
77 Cynthia St.
Lansing, MI 48823

Claudia Knash
120 Fair View St.
Lake George, IL 10057

Victor Sands
800 Market St.
Lake George, IL 10057

Of course, Polly had to specify the fields to be printed, their locations, and so forth, as is necessary for any report definition, but since these were such standard reports, it was simple to create them by modifying existing ones.

"Well, Art," Polly said, "from now on, whenever you want to bring your accounts up to date, follow this list:

1. Load the data base programs.
2. Enter your receipts and new bills using the data editing option.
3. Return to the main menu and ask for the report generator option.
4. Give the program these names: ART RECEIVABLES (to generate your accounts receivable report) and ART MAILING (to generate the mailing labels).

"If you have any problems, call me or one of my staff." Later, Polly noticed that Art had returned with more bills. He was working at one of the PCs, busily posting bills, calling up reports, and chortling happily at the results.

Because Polly had a few minutes to spare, she sat down at another machine and decided to spend some time working out another procedure for Art. The system Art had now would do the job, but she knew that his work could be simpler with a special kind of record updating that was possible with her data base system. She would create a macro that would do much of the moving and adjusting of data automatically for Art.

Polly entered the macro manipulation mode from the main menu. She then entered a series of command language statements. Although her data base was generally menu-driven, she had to enter the list of commands that made up the macro in a command language. The statements in the macro looked like this:

```
 1. Begin.
 2. Next record.
 3. If done goto finish.
 4. Field 'previous balance' = field 'new balance'.
 5. Field 'new charges' = keyboard input.
 6. Field 'new payment' = keyboard input.
 7. Field 'new balance' = field 'previous balance' +
                          field 'new charges' -
                          field 'new payment'.
 8. Save record.
 9. Repeat from begin.
10. Finish.
11. Generate ART RECEIVABLES.
12. Generate ART MAILING.
```

Polly reviewed the macro. The first line was a label used by line 9. Everything between these lines would be repeated over and over. Line 2 would read the data from the next record, but if all records had been processed, line 3 would cause a jump to line 10 to generate the final reports on lines 11 and 12. Lines 4, 5, 6, and 7 (in that order) would make changes to the data in certain fields. Line 8 would save the new record. It all looked good.

Polly saved the macro on disk. She knew it was only a matter of time before Art would come back. Then she could give him this macro to make his tasks a little easier.

What Polly did in a few minutes was an extremely complicated task that at one time required weeks of effort by an expensive computer programming staff. Now, using a data base management system selling for as little as two hundred dollars, such tasks can be performed not only by people like Polly, but by ordinary business people who can create their own programs and save them for repeated use. This case study illustrates the profound effects that computer resources now have and will continue to have on the world of commerce.

8.9

Advanced Topic: Data Base Models

Throughout our discussion, we have conceptualized data bases in terms of the computerization of manual files. Although this simple conceptualization makes it easier for the reader to understand most of the important concepts of data base management systems, it does leave out one critical aspect of data base theory: the variety of competing models around which computerized data bases can be structured. The major purpose of these models is to describe how data records of different types are supposed to interact. For example, if an employer had a data base that contained records of an employee's pay history and separate records of an employee's demographic data, the manner in which these two types of records interact must be carefully defined.

In modern data base systems, there are three different models that describe how the various record types in a data base can be tied together: the hierarchical model, the network model, and the relational model. Any real data base system must choose one of these models as its foundation and build from there. Each model has its own advantages and disadvantages and thus commercial systems of all three types can be found.

■ The Hierarchical Model

data hierarchy
A method of organizing a data base that establishes a top-down relationship among the data records. Searches begin at the top and proceed downward.

As the name implies, a hierarchical data base model establishes a **data hierarchy** of the different record types that exist within a data base. A treelike structure is set up in which one record type is defined as the *root record type*. All other record types are connected to this root record type by pointers that designate what records are associated with the root. Thus all data, no matter what type of record it actually lies in, must be accessed by starting at a record of the root type.

An example of a hierarchical data model is shown in Figure 8–2. The root record is the employee's personnel record, and it includes pointers to other record types for medical history and pay history.

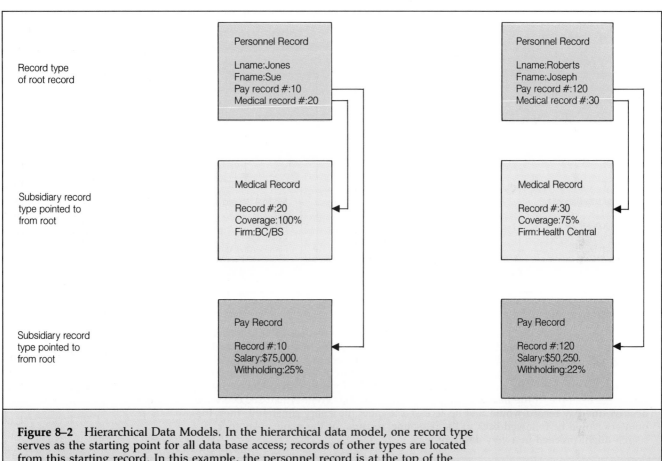

Figure 8–2 Hierarchical Data Models. In the hierarchical data model, one record type serves as the starting point for all data base access; records of other types are located from this starting record. In this example, the personnel record is at the top of the hierarchy. All data about an employee, whether demographic, salary, or medical, is found by starting at the personnel record and working down from there. For example, to find Sue Jones' salary, the first step is to find her personnel record, where the pointer to the pay record is located. The proper pay record is then retrieved, and the salary amount is accessed in the appropriate field of that record.

With a model of this form, the data entered for each individual in the data base would start with a root type record; other records could then be reached from this root using the pointers.

◼ The Network Model

The network data base model is essentially an extension of the hierarchical model. In a network model, any record type may point to any other record type. There is no "root" and no data base "tree." The information in the data base may be examined starting at any record of any kind and following pointers from one data record type to another.

An example of a network data base is shown in Figure 8–3.

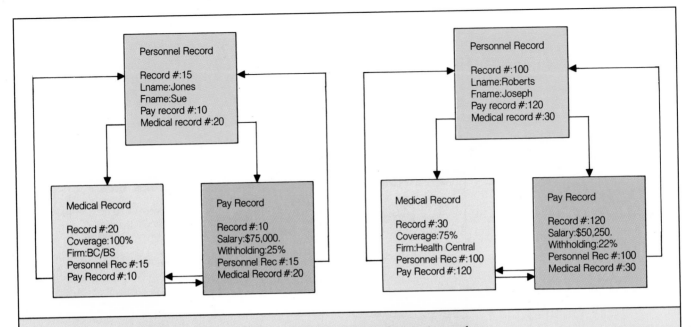

Figure 8–3 Network Data Models. In a network model, the records exist in a rather amorphous and unorganized form. Any record type may point to any other record type. Access to data in the data base can thus start anywhere and proceed in any direction. Although this example shows all records pointing to all other records, this need not be the case. Any particular piece of data can be found in many different ways. For example, if the names of all persons with salaries greater than $60,000 were desired, the pay record would first be accessed to meet the salary constraint, then the pointers would be followed back to the personnel records for the names. Another search might proceed in a very different way.

■ The Relational Model

Of the three models, the relational data base model is the most mathematically complete system, and it is thus becoming the most respected model. In addition, relational data bases are simple and obvious extensions of spreadsheet systems.

The basic element in a relational data base is a *relation*. Surprisingly, a relation is just a table of rows and columns in which each row represents a record while each column represents a field of the record. In the relational model, the record and field are given different names: the record is called a *tuple* (rhymes with couple), while the field is called an *attribute*.

The true power of the relational model comes into play with three simple operations. The SELECT operation is a search of a data base; it creates a new table from an old one by removing some rows. The PROJECT (long "o" sound) operation is used to throw out unneeded fields. Project creates a new table from an old one by removing some columns. The JOIN operation joins two separate tables into one by means of a field common to both tables.

The concepts of a relational data base and these three basic operations are illustrated in Figure 8–4.

General Concepts

Relations, much like spreadsheet tables, are defined. Each row is called a tuple.

Relation 1

Field 1	Field 2	Field 3
Data 1-1	Data 1-2	Data 1-3
Data 2-1	Data 2-2	Data 2-3
Data 3-1	Data 3-2	Data 3-3

Relation 2

Field 4	Field 2
Data 1-4	Data 1-2
Data 2-4	Data 2-2
Data 3-4	Data 3-2

Operation SELECT creates a new temporary table by copying some rows from another table. Here, Relation 1 and some comparison (e.g., Field #1 > 34) give a new table.

Field 1	Field 2	Field 3
Data 1-1	Data 1-2	Data 1-3
Data 3-1	Data 3-2	Data 3-3

Operation PROJECT creates a new temporary table by copying some columns from another table. Here, Relation 1 and a specification of what fields to keep give a new table.

Field 1	Field 3
Data 1-1	Data 1-3
Data 2-1	Data 2-3
Data 3-1	Data 3-3

Operation JOIN creates a new temporary table by combining two tables into one using a field they have in common to control the combination. Here, Field 2 is used to combine Relation 1 and Relation 2 into a single new table.

Field 1	Field 2	Field 3	Field 4
Data 1-1	Data 1-2	Data 1-3	Data 1-4
Data 2-1	Data 2-2	Data 2-3	Data 2-4
Data 3-1	Data 3-2	Data 3-3	Data 3-4

Specific Example

Personnel relation

Lname	Fname	Emp.#
Holmes	Sam	023
Jones	Sue	015
Roberts	Joseph	100
Victor	Ellen	093

Pay relation

Emp.#	Salary	Withhold.
015	75,000	25%
023	75,000	25%
093	41,700	20%
100	50,250	22%

Medical relation

Emp.#	Coverage	Firm
015	100%	BC/BS
023	100%	Health Central
093	70%	BC/BS
100	75%	Health Central

To find out what health firms are used by employees with salaries greater than $60,000:

1. SELECT from Pay relation where salary > $60,000, giving:

Emp.#	Salary	Withhold.
015	75,000	25%
023	75,000	25%

2. JOIN with Medical relation using employee number as the common field, giving:

Emp.#	Salary	Withhold.	Coverage	Firm
015	75,000	25%	100%	BC/BS
023	75,000	25%	100%	Health Central

3. PROJECT from this relation to retain the firm field giving:

Firm
BC/BS
Health Central

Figure 8-4 In relational models, a set of records is represented by a table with the columns representing fields and the rows representing records. Because a record cannot have more than one valve for each field, (e.g. a field named "children" could not contain more than one name), relational data bases usually contain many types of records. The three operations of select, project, and join are then used to manipulate the various tables to give the desired result as in the specific example above.

8.10

Summary of Data Base Management System Use

The differences between a data base management system (DBMS) and a spreadsheet system lessen or grow depending upon the direction from which the two are examined. A spreadsheet keeps data in tabular form and can contain either character data, numeric data, or formulas based on other data. Yet a data base management system also keeps track of data, which is usually character data, numeric data, or formulas based on other data. A data base is often viewed as a table in which each row of the table is a record and each column of the table represents a field within the record (in fact, the most common model for data base systems, the relational model, views a record in exactly that way!). It seems that spreadsheets and data bases are not very different.

If data base systems stopped there, the differences would indeed be minimal. However, there are three areas in which data base systems provide extensive features not routinely found in spreadsheets: (1) the selection of subsets of data, (2) the manipulation of different types of records, and (3) the definition and generation of a variety of report forms.

Data base management systems have sophisticated procedures for selecting a subset of records from the total set that is stored. A wide variety of searching techniques are provided for selecting records, including text matches of many types, numeric comparisons, and logical combinations of these. Through these search methods, virtually any subset of records can be identified for further processing.

Data base systems can store many different kinds of records at once, e.g., one record type might hold driver's license information while another might hold license plate data. Matching data across these two types of records (e.g., locating all drivers of a given car or all cars used by a given driver) is far easier with data base software than with a spreadsheet. Thus, data base systems are usually preferred when many types of data records must be used together.

Finally, from the perspective of summarizing and reporting on the stored data, data base systems provide much greater flexibility and power than do spreadsheet systems. Data base systems allow existing fields and newly created fields to be placed in arbitrary positions on pages of arbitrary size. Summary statistics of many types can be computed on a multitude of break fields. All this reporting power can be used in combination with the record selection and record integration power already described.

In spite of all the increased capabilities of a data base system over a spreadsheet system, there is one negative aspect of data base use: it is more complicated than using a spreadsheet. Data base systems have multiple modes of operation (record definition, data entry, report definition, report generation), which enforce an ordering on the tasks the user must perform. Data base systems keep data stored away in records that are not as visible to the user as a constantly displayed spreadsheet screen. Each individual user must thus decide between data base systems and spreadsheet systems for managing data. If the data management is simple, spreadsheets will be enough. As the tasks become more complex, the greater power of data base systems will be required.

■ The ISPCO Frame for Data Base systems

As should be expected by now, the major functions of data base software can be summarized by ISPCO frames; the following four frames for data base software provide that summary .

The organization of these frames closely matches the organization of the chapter. The four modes of operation of data base systems are readily apparent. In the record definition mode, the user creates a form which contains fields giving a name to each type of data to be stored and which also restricts the type of values allowed. Once it has been created, the record form definition can be stored, retrieved, or edited. The record form definition is followed by data entry, in which the values for a particular record are entered into the corresponding fields of the record form and stored onto system disk files. Storage of entered data is usually automatic, and data stored in the records may be edited or deleted.

After the record form has been defined, and usually after some data has been entered, the report form definition specifies a mapping from the record definition to the printed page. Since the record form may not contain all the information desired for the printed page, the report definition usually allows the creation of new, temporary fields. The user defines the report form by positioning the original fields of the record and any newly created ones on the final output page. With the report definition in place, the user can generate reports on data in the data base by using search commands to select a subset of records; the summary of this data is then printed according to the report definition.

The ISPCO frames provide a basis for the description of data base software. By filling in the boxes on the right side of the frames, the user will have an easy-to-use summary of his or her own data base system organized in the framework of this text.

Frame for Data Base Software: Record Form Definition

	Concept	Your System
ON/OFF	COMPUTER ACCESS: Access to computer and DBMS are needed. May need location, signon, password, telephone number, disk, start-up command. For this system:	Location and disks needed: Telephone, signon, and password: Start-up command for DBMS record definition: Shutdown command for DBMS record definition:
INPUT	COMMAND INPUT: DBMSs differ in how commands and other input are distinguished, how characters are inserted and deleted, cursor movement, etc. Here:	How to specify commands: Character insert and delete: Cursor movement: Other input characteristics:
INPUT	RECORD DEFINITION: Records are composed of fields. The features of a field are its name, its data type, and its default. Use in a key is optional. For this DBMS:	Field name entry: Data type entry: Default value entry: Search key use entry:

INPUT	COMPUTED FIELDS: An important data type for a field is a computed field derived by calculation from other field values. Entry of calculated fields is done here via:	Arithmetic manipulation: Built-in function manipulation:
INPUT	SCREEN ENTRY FORM: Although not always available, many DBMSs require specification of a screen position, typeface, etc., for field value entry. For this DBMS:	Screen position entry: Typeface entry:
STORAGE	STORAGE ACCESS: Access to underlying operating system commands is mandatory for disk preparation, directories, etc. For this DBMS:	Format command: Directory command: Copy command: Other operating system commands:
STORAGE	DEFINITION ACCESS: DBMSs differ on how record definitions are created, destroyed, loaded, and saved in operating system fields. On this system:	Create record definition file: Destroy record definition file: Load record definition file: Save record definition file:
PROCESS B = 2 + C	DEFINITION EDITING: Editing the definition of a record involves deleting fields, changing field characteristics, and inserting fields. For this DBMS:	Add new field command: Delete existing field command: Alter existing field command:
CONTROL	CONTROL CONSTRAINTS: DBMSs are usually menu-driven with little built-in control. Record definition must logically precede all other activities. On this system:	Method to guarantee record definition is done first:
OUTPUT	RECORD DEFINITION OUTPUT: DBMSs provide some mechanism for printing out record definitions for archival and verification purposes. For this DBMS:	List all records defined command: List individual record definition command:

Frame for Data Base Software: Data Entry and Editing

	Concept	Your System
ON/OFF ON OFF	COMPUTER ACCESS: Access to computer and DBMS are needed. Usually done the same way as in Record Definition but occasionally different. For this system:	Location and disks needed: Telephone, signon, and password: Start-up command for DBMS data entry/edit: Shutdown command for DBMS data entry/edit:

INPUT	**RECORD ENTRY:** DBMSs differ in how values of various types are input. Simple line editing is usually allowed. If an input form is defined, it is used. Here:	Field value input method: Character insert and delete: Cursor movement: Use of input forms:
INPUT	**DEFAULT FIELD ENTRY:** DMBSs provide some means for designating that the default value is to be used, usually, just by hitting return. For this DBMS:	Method for entering default:
INPUT	**CORRECTING INPUT:** After an entire record has been entered but before it is stored, the DBMS usually allows a correction pass. For this DBMS:	Method for starting correction: Method for specifying bad field: Method for changing Field:
STORAGE	**DATA BASE ACCESS:** DBMSs differ on how a data base is created, destroyed, loaded, and saved within the operating system files. On this system:	Create data base command: Destroy data base command: Load data base command: Save data base command:
PROCESS B = 2 + C	**RECORD SEARCHING:** The DBMS may be searched for records to delete or alter. Many search options are available. For this system (more under report generation):	Start search command: String match command: Partial string match command: Numeric range match command:
PROCESS B = 2 + C	**ALTER/DELETE RECORD:** After a record has been located by searching, it may be either deleted or altered. For this DBMS:	Record deletion command: Record alteration command:
PROCESS B = 2 + C	**RECORD RESTRUCTURE:** Restructuring records (adding, deleting, or changing fields after entry of records) is done infrequently on developed data bases. For this DBMS:	Method for restructuring record:
CONTROL	**CONTROL CONSTRAINTS:** Obviously, data entry cannot occur until record definition is complete. It may be possible to aid entry of new records with macros. For this system:	Method for macro use to aid data entry of records:
OUTPUT	**DATA BASE PRINTOUT:** Printout of all records in a data base for archival and verification purposes is necessary. To do so on this data base system:	Data base printout command:

Frame for Data Base Software: Report Form Definition

	Concept	Your System
ON/OFF [ON OFF]	COMPUTER ACCESS: Access to computer and DBMS are needed. Usually done the same way as other modes but occasionally different. For this system:	Location and disks needed: Telephone, signon, and password: Start-up command for DBMS report definition: Shutdown command for DBMS report definition:
INPUT	REPORT ENTRY: DBMSs differ in how the various parameters for report definition are entered. For this system:	Character insert and delete: Cursor movement: Function and control keys: Mouse operation:
INPUT	FIELD SELECTION: The user must specify which fields of the various records are to be included in a report. The method for field selection for this system is:	Method for selecting a field for inclusion in a report:
INPUT	COMPUTED FIELDS: The value of a computed field is a function of values in other fields of the same record. The requirements for computed fields in this system:	Arithmetic manipulation: Built-in function use: Built-in functions available: Text label fields:
INPUT	BREAK FIELDS: Break fields are used to provide summary statistics whenever the value of the break field changes in a set of records. For this system:	Statistics available: Methods for ordering record sets: Method for specifying break field:
INPUT	FIELD PLACEMENT: Whether an ordinary field, a break field, or a computed field, the data from the field must be placed in position. For this DBMS:	Method for field placement on report page:
STORAGE	REPORT ACCESS: DBMSs differ in how the report definitions are created, destroyed, loaded, and saved in operating system files. On this system:	Create report definition: Destroy report definition: Load report definition: Save report definition:
PROCESS B = 2 + C	REPORT EDITING: Once a report is finished, it may be edited in many ways to change the fields used, their locations, and so on. On this DBMS:	Method for editing a report definition:

CONTROL	**CONTROL CONSTRAINTS:** Record definition must precede report definition, since field names must be known. No other constraint exists logically. For this system:	Method to guarantee record definition precedes report definition:
OUTPUT	**RECORD DEFINITION OUTPUT:** DBMSs provide some mechanism for printing out report definitions for archival and verification purposes. For this DBMS:	List all reports command: List specific report command:

Frame for Data Base Software: Report Generation

	Concept	Your System
ON/OFF	**COMPUTER ACCESS:** Access to computer and DBMS are needed. Usually done the same way as other modes but occasionally different. For this DBMS:	Location and disks needed: Telephone, signon, and password: Start-up command for DBMS report generation: Shutdown command for DBMS report generation:
INPUT	**COMMAND ENTRY:** DMBSs differ in how the commands for report generation are input. For this system:	Character insert and delete: Cursor movement: Function and control keys: Mouse operation:
STORAGE	**REPORT ACCESS:** To generate a report, the user must be able to access the report definition created earlier. To do so in this DBMS:	Method for accessing report definition:
STORAGE	**DATA BASE ACCESS:** To generate a report, the user must be able to access the records of a data base created earlier. To do so in this DBMS:	Method for accessing data base:
PROCESS $B = 2 + C$	**RECORD SEARCHING:** The DBMS may be searched for records to be included in the report. Many options are available. For this system (more in data entry/edit):	AND search criteria command: OR search criteria command: SELECT, PROJECT, JOIN commands (for relational data base only):
PROCESS $B = 2 + C$	**RECORD ORDERING:** The order of the retrieved records will affect summary statistics of break fields. To specify the order in which records should be placed:	Method for specifying order of retrieved records:

CONTROL	CONTROL CONSTRAINTS: Record definition must clearly precede all three other modes. To aid with report generation, macros are often used. For this system:	Method for macro use to aid report generation:
OUTPUT	PAGE LAYOUT: DBMSs may allow the specification of margins, headers, footers, et cetera to give a visually pleasing report. The format options available here:	Margin commands: Header/footer commands: Other format commands:
OUTPUT	PRINTER/FILE OUTPUT: The final report may be sent to file or printer. If sent to a file, it can be combined with other documents using a word processor. For this DBMS:	Report to printer command: Report to file command:
OUTPUT	GENERATE REPORT: After all the specifications have been given, the user must be able to initiate the report generation task. For this DBMS:	Command to initiate report generation:

▪ The ISPCO Scripts for Data Base Software

The four modes of data base operation center around two basic problems: entering data and reporting data. The ISPCO scripts for data base software thus focus on these two separate issues.

The first script describes the major steps in the creation of a record form definition and the entry of data. Obviously, the most important prerequisite to the use of a data base system is knowledge of what data is to be managed. The script begins at this point and then proceeds to the creation of the record definition and the entry of data. Following is the script for data base record definition and data entry.

SCRIPT FOR DATA BASE RECORD DEFINITION AND DATA ENTRY AND EDITING

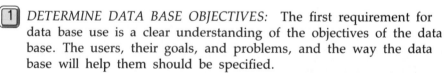

[1] *DETERMINE DATA BASE OBJECTIVES:* The first requirement for data base use is a clear understanding of the objectives of the data base. The users, their goals, and problems, and the way the data base will help them should be specified.

[2] *DESIGN DATA BASE:* Given the description of how the data base will help the user, the data base designer must consider what types of records with what varieties of fields should be created to provide the needed assistance. The designer should make a list of all record types, all fields in each record, and all the characteristics of each field. A set of prototypical records should be created for testing purposes.

3 *DEVELOP DATA BASE:* The data base should be started up, the record definition mode entered, and all information regarding the form of all records should be entered. After being reviewed for correctness, the record definitions should be saved to disk.

4 *ENTER AND EDIT DATA BASE RECORDS:* The data base should be started up and the appropriate record definitions loaded. The user must then start the data entry/edit mode and begin entering data into the system. Minor typographical errors are corrected during initial entry. Save changes to disk.

5 *RETRIEVE RECORDS FOR DELETION OR ALTERATION:* If records have already been entered, the user can retrieve any records that need to be deleted or altered by using appropriate search commands. Once the records are retrieved, appropriate actions can be taken. Save changes to disk.

6 *EVALUATE THE DATA BASE:* Early during data base development, the data base should be evaluated to ensure that it can meet the objectives of the system. This can be done initially with the test records developed during design. Large data bases can be difficult to develop, so frequent evaluation during the initial stages is critical.

The second script focuses on the definition and use of reports. Although one of the primary advantages of data base systems is that new and varied reports can be created with ease, the user should have at least some basic reports clearly in mind before beginning to use a data base system. (After all, it makes little sense to put data into a system if one doesn't know how it will be taken out later!) The script assumes that a particular type of data summary is required and helps the reader work through the steps involved in the creation and use of reports. Following is the script for data base report definition and generation.

SCRIPT FOR DATA BASE REPORT DEFINITION AND REPORT GENERATION

1 *DETERMINE THE OBJECTIVES OF THE REPORT:* Since many reports may be generated from the same data base, the report designer must clearly determine the purpose of any particular report, including the user of the report, their problems and goals, and how the report will help them achieve desired tasks.

2 *DESIGN THE REPORT:* With knowledge of the report's purpose, the report designer must determine (1) the data base of records to use, (2) the appearance of the report, including what existing fields, computed fields, break fields, and text labels should appear, and (3) the order in which the records should be placed for report generation. Producing a sample report by hand is quite useful in designing a good report.

3 *DEVELOP THE REPORT:* The data base must be started, the report definition mode entered, and all appropriate information entered regarding the form of the report, the fields to be included in the report, and all other details decided on during report design. The report definition should be saved to disk.

4. *GENERATE THE REPORT:* The report should be generated by (1) accessing the proper data base, (2) retrieving the desired set of records, (3) sorting the records into the desired order, (4) accessing the proper report definition, and (5) starting the report process. The report may be sent to either printer or disk file.

5. *EVALUATE THE REPORT:* The generated report should be reviewed by its users for form and content. If not acceptable, the report form can be edited until the users are satisfied. If changes in the report form cannot alleviate problems, the data base itself may be in error and may need restructuring to add or delete various types of data.

6. *EVALUATE THE DATA BASE:* With the entire data base process completed for the first time, the entire system, from record definition and data entry to report definition and generation can be evaluated. Keeping a log of user reactions to the reports available through the system is a good method for continued maintenance, evaluation, and improvement of the data base system.

With these scripts and the ISPCO frame, the reader should be able to use a data base system to solve data base problems. Data base systems are complicated software programs that provide a power that is quite necessary to many businesses and also fill some personal/professional needs.

Chapter 8 Review

Expanded Objectives

The objectives listed below are an expansion of the essential chapter concepts listed at the beginning of the chapter. The review items for the chapter are based on these expanded objectives. If you master the objectives, you will do better on the review items and on your instructor's examination on the chapter material.

After reading the chapter, you should be able to:

1. discriminate among the activities of the four data base management modes (record definition, data entry, report definition, and report generation).
2. sequence the steps involved in record definition, data entry, report definition, and report generation.

3. compare the structure of a data base management system to that of word processing and spreadsheet systems.
4. describe the command structure employed in data base management systems.
5. relate the operations of data base management systems to the ISPCO functions.
6. explain the major advantages and disadvantages of using data base management systems.
7. describe the major strategies for searching a data base.
8. summarize the scripts for developing and using a data base management system.
9. complete the last column in the data base management system frame for the specific system to which you have access.
10. recognize the meanings of the major new terms introduced in this chapter.

Review Items

Completing this review will give you a good indication of how well you have mastered the contents of this chapter and prepare you for your instructor's test on this material. To maximize what you learn from this exercise, you should answer each question *before* looking up the answers in the appendix. The number of the corresponding expanded objective is given in parentheses following each question.

Complete the following clusters of items according to the directions heading each set.

A. *True or false*

___ 1. A data base will accept data before a record is defined. (2)
___ 2. Unlike operating systems, data base management systems are limited to control by command language shells. (4)
___ 3. Many of the commands for data base management systems are closely related to those used in word processing and spreadsheet systems. (4)

___ 4. Typing errors that occur during data entry in a data base management system can be corrected by backspacing and retyping. (1,2)

___ 5. Break fields are used to indicate which fields will be subject to statistical treatment. (5,10)

___ 6. A datestamp automatically records the date when a record is altered. (10)

___ 7. In order for a data base management system to operate effectively, all of the data in the data base must be in RAM at the same time. (1,5,6)

___ 8. It is a relatively simple task to alter the definition of a record, even after data has been entered into the data base. (2,6)

___ 9. In a data base management system, data bases are constructed from sets of fields, which in turn are constructed from sets of records. (3,5,10)

___ 10. Unlike spreadsheet systems, data base management systems cannot use formulas to automatically compute elements in a record. (3)

___ 11. Most data base management systems are able to generate two kinds of reports: label reports and table reports. (1,5,6)

___ 12. A record is the name for pieces of data that are collected into fields. (10)

___ 13. Fields of data can be composed of other fields. (3,10)

___ 14. The selection of statistics to be computed is done in the report generation mode. (2)

___ 15. In the record entry and edit mode, commands for storage apply to complete files of data records rather than to individual records. (4)

___ 16. The commands for editing data in a data base management system are essentially the same as those used with spreadsheet and word processing systems. (3)

___ 17. Searching a data base for all records with football scores between 21 and 50 is an example of a relational search. (7)

___ 18. Once a set of fields is designated as the primary key, it is seldom changed. (2,10)

___ 19. Most data base management systems make considerable use of explicit sequential, alternative, iterative, and procedural control. (4)

___ 20. Because empty records and empty fields are used as basic units for data base design, macros can't be set up for frequently performed sequences of commands. (10)

___ 21. Part of report form definition is selecting the fields that are to be included in the report. (1)

___ 22. A tabular data base management system report format can use formulas to automatically calculate field contents. (5,10)

___ 23. During report definition, the user can arbitrarily position the cursor to place fields wherever he or she desires on the screen. (1)

___ 24. Specifying which records are to be deleted from a file is difficult in most data base management systems. (6)

___ 25. Inserting a record into a file is executed in the data entry and edit mode. 91)

___ 26. Inserting new fields into records at any time is generally not allowed, since it would change the definition of the record. (1,2)

___ 27. A user can search a data base on any field common to a set of records. (7)

___ 28. The two types of numeric searches for a data base are relational and range searches. (7)

___ 29. Whenever two or more fields are defined in a search, the search is an *or* search. 97)

___ 30. Generally, the larger the number of records in a data base, the faster the search time. (7)

___ 31. When searching a data base on the last name field, the computer is slowed because it must search through every name in the data base. (7)

B. *Match each of the search objectives on the left with the most appropriate search type from the list on the right.* (7)

___ 32. Find all records with the First Name "Robert."

___ 33. Find all records containing either "Score<100" or "Age>20."

a. relational
b. range
c. AND
d. OR
e. matching

___ 34. Find all records containing Scores less than 30.

___ 35. Find all records containing IQ Scores of 100 for sex-male.

___ 36. Find all records containing Scores between 160 and 170.

___ 37. Find all records with Last Names beginning with "La."

C. *Match the data base management system concepts on the right with the equivalent spreadsheet concepts on the left.* (3)

___ 38. cell contents

___ 39. cell coordinate

___ 40. row

a. record
b. data base
c. field name
d. field value
e. field value type

___ 41. cell contents type

___ 42. table

D. *Match the most appropriate data base management system component on the right with its manual equivalent on the left.* (10)

___ 43. contents of a file cabinet

___ 44. pieces of paper in file folder

a. field
b. record
c. report
d. data base
e. primary key

___ 45. a file folder

E. *Respond to each of the following items.*

___ 46. In the record definition mode, which of the following alternatives must the user usually specify? (1)
a. whether the data is required or optional
b. the names of the fields
c. the vertical and horizontal locations of the fields

d. the type of field contents
e. all of the above
___ 47. The steps for establishing and using a data base management system are randomly ordered in the list below. Show the correct sequence of steps by writing their letters in order on the line above. (2)
a. report definition
b. report generation
c. data entry
d. record definition
e. data editing

Projects

1. Create a data base for the first case study. The initial case study in the chapter is simple enough to provide a good learning experience for an initial project. First translate the commands and activities of this case study into the corresponding ones for your data base software. You will probably need a reference manual or the completed frame for your software. Second, use the scripts from this chapter to develop and test the data base.

2. Create your own simple data base. Creating a data base for a collection of high fidelity recordings or video cassette tapes is a very popular exercise for students. You will need to create a data base record for each element (e.g., cassette) in your collection. Each record must have an identification number so you can locate the element physically in your library. Once the data base is complete, you can search it by inputting questions to your micro or you can produce a printed listing that you can search manually. If you want some ideas, go to a well-run video store and check out their system.

3. Other data base projects. Data base system are remarkably useful. Once you become experienced in using data base software, you will probably find many people interested in working on a data base with you. Some examples of student projects from the authors' courses include: college library search and retrieval systems, inventory control systems for small businesses, student records systems for large undergraduate courses, science data bases for high school and college teachers, and many others.

Special Exercise: The Data Base Software Frames

The data base software frames contain special boxes where the user can write down the characteristics of a real computer system. You are encouraged to fill in the frame for the particular system to which you have access so that the concepts of this chapter can be directly applied to your own hardware and software. These frames can also be used to compare different systems by filling in one frame for each system and contrasting the systems on a point-by-point basis.

Your primary source of information for completing these frames should be the system documentation available with your software or hardware system.

As a computer user works on more and different systems, each of the boxes in these frames may require expansion into even more detailed descriptions. By then, however, the user will be sophisticated enough to make such expansions easily and without help.

Graphics Software

Essential Chapter Concepts

When you finish this chapter, you should know:

- The ISPCO activities in using a typical system for painting pictures.

- The ISPCO activities in using a typical system for creating charts.

- The commonalities and differences between these two types of graphics systems.

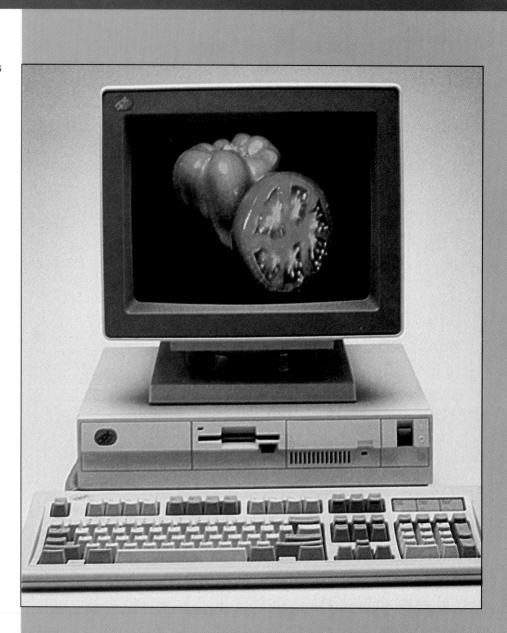

Graphics Software

INPUT	STORAGE	PROCESS	CONTROL	OUTPUT
Input graphic elements	Save/load pictures and clip-art	**PAINT** Edit picture using processes to copy, move, delete, and so forth.	No control in most systems	Print out the picture
Input data for chart	Save/load charts or data and commands	**CHART** Generate pie, bar, or line charts	No control in most systems	Print chart with format, size, labels, titles

Computers were first used for numeric processing. They were initially created to do complex mathematical and logical computations that would have been impossible by hand. As computers became less expensive yet more powerful, the focus of computing began to shift from numeric processing to include symbolic processing as well. Word processing is now one of the major uses of computing systems, and with still more powerful and less expensive computers coming, graphic design is becoming another major use for computers.

Different types of computer graphics systems exist for the creation of different types of graphic images. Some systems are designed to create graphic images from tables of numeric data: they can generate pie charts, bar graphs, scatter plots, and so on, using numeric data that might come from business operations, a scientific experiment, or many other sources. Other graphics systems allow the creation of arbitrary graphic images like architectural drawings or cartoons. With these systems the user can create visual images in multiple colors to show the latest design of a tennis shoe for an advertisement or an image of the human eye for an anatomy class. Still other graphics systems have a wide variety of purposes such as designing bridges, buildings, and electronic circuits, composing music, and animating moving pictures.

The general ideas behind all these systems are the same. First, each system is designed to handle only a given type of graphic image. Second, these graphic images are built from a particular set of primitive or elementary images in the same way that words and sentences are built from the letters of the alphabet. Finally, there is a set of operations that combine these images according to a precise rules. This chapter will examine these ideas more closely in terms of two types of computer graphics systems: (1) systems for generating graphs from data and (2) systems for generating arbitrary and unstructured visual images (so-called picture painting systems).

9.1

A Graphics System Case Study

As computerized graphics capabilities become accessible to more and more people, they will eventually provide the standard against which any graphic image will be compared. Vic, the subject of our current case study, is about to make this discovery.

Case Study

Vic was sitting at a large table in the university library with graph paper, colored pens, rulers, and other drawing paraphernalia spread out around him. He's was tired. He had been working on his lab report all night and had just laid his head down on the table for a brief rest.

After a few moments, Vic raised his head and resumed his work. As he surveyed what he had already done, he realized that the scale of his chart was wrong—there wouldn't be enough room for the data on the high end! Vic took out a large gum eraser and began gently erasing part of his graph while loudly swearing.

As if in response to his discordant remarks, one of Vic's roommates walked up.

"Hey, what's all this about?" asked Steve.

"What? Oh, hi, Steve." Vic looked embarrassed. "Sorry, I didn't mean to be so loud. It's just that I'm getting so darn tired of having to redo these graphs for my lab report. It's due tomorrow. I have to present the results of the chem experiment with 'professional quality graphs and images.' At least that's what the assignment says. I need to make some charts of the data and pictures of the apparatus I used. I think the chance of my doing anything of professional quality when it comes to drawing is about the same as my chance of becoming president."

"Would you like some help with your graphs?" asked Steve. "I've got a free hour now."

"You can do all this in an hour?" Vic was doubtful, but willing to try anything.

"Sure, just bring your stuff and follow me!" Steve commanded.

A few minutes later Steve was seated in front of an IBM PC in the microcomputer lab with Vic perched next to him. Steve checked out a couple of disks from the lab assistant, inserted them into the disk drive, and started the machine up. "First, let's concentrate on generating those charts you wanted," he said.

"Okay," said Vic. "The chart is supposed to be a plot of the atmospheric pressure versus the temperature of the gas in an experiment we did. We're supposed to verify Charles' law experimentally. Here are the numbers we got."

Vic pulled out a sheet containing two columns of numbers: one column with pressure measurements and one column with temperature measurements.

Steve looked over the data and turned to the PC. "I don't remember much about chemistry, but from the data, I think that the graph will be really simple to run off. I'm using the school software called Graph-It. It'll do simple scatter plots like nobody's business."

"What do you mean, scatter plots?" asked Vic.

"Don't worry," replied Steve. "It's just the name for the kind of plot that you want. To create one, we just set up a kind of computerized graph paper with an X and a Y axis. We'll let the X axis of the graph represent the temperature and the Y axis represent pressure. Then we just plot all these pairs of numbers that you have. Watch."

Vic watched over Steve's shoulder as the Graph-It system took control. A main menu appeared on the screen:

```
Graph-It System: Main Menu

L(oad data from disk)
S(ave data to disk)
E(nter data from keyboard)
D(efine graph characteristics)
G(enerate graph)
Q(uit)

Enter letter corresponding to desired option:_
```

Steve entered an E to enter data from the keyboard. Upon inputing the E, the system responded with a number of questions that Steve answered in succession.

```
Enter the number of values for each point: 2

Enter the values of each point on a separate line.
Separate the 2 values with commas.
When finished entering data, enter the phrase 'end'.

point 1: 298, 760.0
point 2: 300, 765.1
       .
       .
       .
point 50: 398, 1015.0
point 51: end
```

"What I just did," explained Steve, "was to create a kind of data base that the Graph-It system can work with. We can then use the system to create many different kinds of graphs from this data."

"Well, I don't want anything fancy," said Vic. "All I want is a simple chart with the points plotted and axes labeled—just the basics."

"No problem," Steve assured him. "Now we specify the graph's characteristics."

The software had returned to its main menu when Steve entered "end" after finishing the data entry.

```
Graph-It System: Main Menu

L(oad data from disk)
S(ave data to disk)
E(nter data from keyboard)
D(efine graph characteristics)
G(enerate graph)
Q(uit)

Enter letter corresponding to desired option:_
```

This time Steve entered the letter D to define the characteristics of the graph. The interaction that followed went like this:

```
Which type of graph do you wish to generate with the data?

P(ie Chart)
S(catter Plot)
B(ar Graph)

Enter letter corresponding to desired option:_
```

Steve entered the letter S because Vic needed to generate a scatter plot.

'Since I told the system that we wanted to generate a scatter plot,'' explained Steve, 'it will now ask us lots of questions about what we want the scatter plot to look like.''

Vic watched the screen closely as Steve entered more commands:

```
What is the label for the first variable (the X axis) ?
TEMPERATURE

What are the units for the first variable (TEMPERATURE) ?
K

What minimum value should be allowed for TEMPERATURE?
Enter a number or DATA to get from data: 200

What maximum value should be allowed for TEMPERATURE?
Enter a number or DATA to get from data: 400

With TEMPERATURE between 200 and 400, how many divisions
do you want on the TEMPERATURE axis? 20
```

Steve then responded to similar questions concerning the second axis:

```
What is the label for the second variable (the Y axis) ?
PRESSURE

What are the units for the second variable (PRESSURE) ?
MM

What minimum value should be allowed for PRESSURE?
Enter a number or DATA to get from data: DATA
Lowest value in data is 760

What maximum value should be allowed for PRESSURE?
Enter a number or DATA to get from data: DATA
Highest value in data is 1015

With PRESSURE between 760 and 1015, how many divisions do
you want on the PRESSURE axis? 20
```

The Graph-It system continued to direct the interaction by asking for the remaining specifications needed to create the graph.

```
What is the title of the graph? (terminate with 'END')
EXPERIMENTAL VERIFICATION OF CHARLES' LAW
CHEMISTRY 133
VIC J. SUNDANCE
END

Do you want the title centered? (Y or N): Y
```

"There," said Steve. "All of the data is set. The system knows the coordinates of all the points to plot and it has a description of the graph to be plotted. Ready to do it?"

"Sure." Vic's reply was immediate.

From the main menu, Steve issued the command G to generate the graph.

The printer connected to the PC started chattering. It was a dot matrix printer, so it could print graphic material. After about two minutes, the chart was complete. It looked like this:

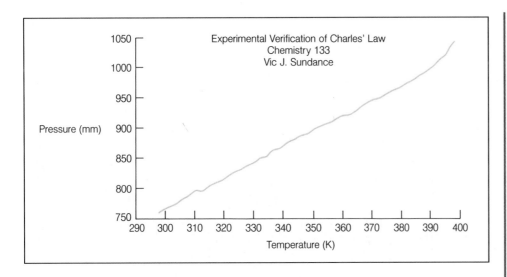

"Okay, Vic, your graph is complete. I won't save the data on disk because I don't have any disks with me, but this is so quick that even if you want to regenerate it later on, it won't take long. What else is there?" Steve asked.

"I do have to make some kind of drawing of the experimental setup," Vic replied, "but I guess we can't do anything like that on your PC. It isn't any kind of graph."

Steve smiled. "It's true that drawings aren't graphs, but that's where other graphics software comes in. Let me switch to another computer and insert the other disk I got. It has a 'paint' program on it that will let you create really fine pictures of just about anything."

As Steve moved to an Apple Macintosh computer and started the next program, Vic grabbed a chair, pulled it next to Steve's, and sat down. Maybe he should change his major to computer science. It seemed like Steve knew about software that could do just about anything!

What appeared on the screen looked very complicated to Vic:

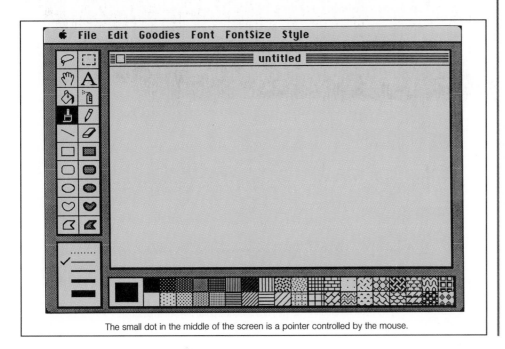

The small dot in the middle of the screen is a pointer controlled by the mouse.

Across the top of the screen was a set of words. On the left side of the screen were two columns of strange symbols, and the bottom of the screen was filled by two rows of other odd symbols. Vic realized that the screen display contained some kind of graphic menu, but he couldn't figure out what was what.

Steve began, "The Apple computer company looked far and wide for an easy way for people to interact with computers. They settled on a graphic operating system shell that was first marketed on the Macintosh/Lisa line of computers. Once they decided to go with a graphic shell, one of their first pieces of software was a figure-drawing system named MacPaint." Vic appreciated the background that Steve was giving him.

"The row of words across the top is a menu of options. The two columns of little pictures on the left side represent different tools that are available. The two rows across the bottom show different patterns that can be used by the tools. The open part of the screen is where we can draw a picture. The whole thing is controlled with a mouse."

Steve reached over and grabbed the mouse. As he moved the mouse around on the table, an arrow on the screen moved in a similar way. When Steve moved the mouse away from him, the arrow on the screen went up; when the mouse was moved toward him, the arrow went down. Any movement of the mouse on the table—circles, figure eights, or whatever—was mirrored by the arrow on the screen.

"Now," asked Steve, "what did your experimental setup look like?"

"Well," Vic said, "here are the original drawings I was working on." He pushed a paper toward Steve. "We had a sealed flask that had a thermometer suspended in the center through a rubber stopper, a pressure gauge attached to the side, and an electric burner that we used to slowly raise the temperature."

"Okay, let's start drawing the flask." Steve was getting down to business! He moved the mouse until the arrow on the screen pointed to the open rectangle with rounded corners in one of the columns on the left side of the screen. Then he clicked the button on the mouse. The little picture of the rectangle changed to reverse video: everything that had been white turned black and vice versa. When he moved the arrow back onto the drawing portion of a screen, it was replaced by cross hairs like those in a gun sight.

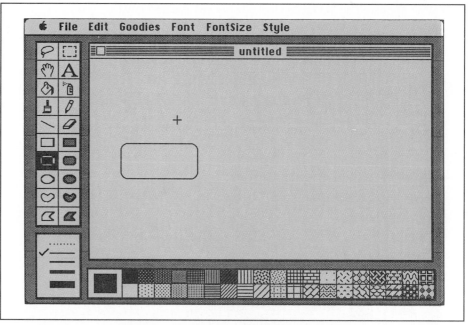

The box with rounded edges has been added to the evolving figure.
The graphic pointer controlled by the mouse is now represented
by the cross hairs.

"First, we'll draw the bottom of the flask. I decided to make it from a rounded rectangle. When I push the mouse button in now, I will define one boundary of the rectangle. Then as I move the mouse around, I can make a rounded rectangle as big or as small as I like. When I have just the rectangle I want, I release the mouse button and the image will stay."

Vic just watched silently as Steve worked. In a moment, Steve had drawn a base for the flask on the screen.

"Now, I'll adjust that rectangle. I'll click on the eraser and erase its top, then I'll go into line mode and draw the neck of the flask." Steve worked quickly as he talked and continued drawing Vic's experimental setup.

Vic and Steve then began to discuss the diagram. Vic didn't like the looks of the stopper in the flask, so Steve made it slimmer and longer. The electric burner seemed to be too large, so Steve reduced its size. The figure wasn't centered on the screen, so Steve moved it. After about ten minutes of work, Steve had the screen just the way Vic wanted it.

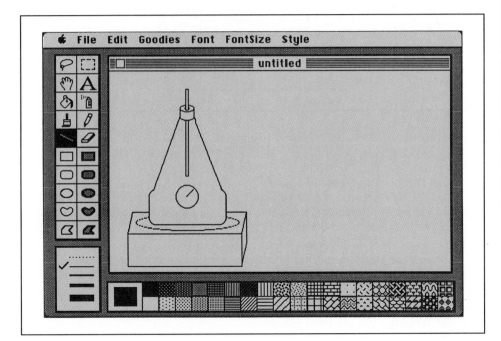

"That's a great picture!" exclaimed Vic. "Print it out now, so I can label things and get it ready to turn in."

"Hold on!" was Steve's reply. "We can do any labeling you want right here. One of the options in a paint program is to put text anywhere you want on the screen. So just tell me what text you want and where you want it, and we can do it right here."

When the last label was finished, Steve issued the necessary commands to print the picture on the screen onto paper. It looked like this:

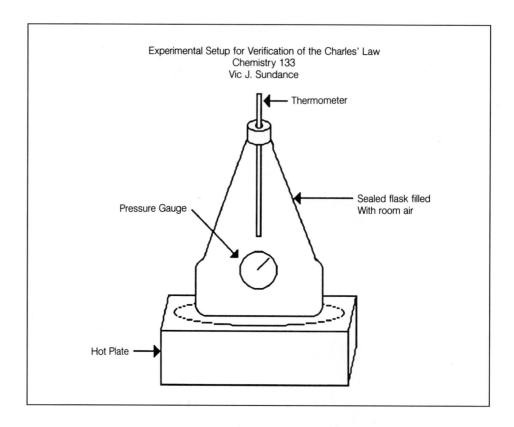

Experimental Setup for Verification of the Charles' Law
Chemistry 133
Vic J. Sundance

Thermometer

Sealed flask filled
With room air

Pressure Gauge

Hot Plate

Vic was delighted. Using the right software, Steve had been able to rapidly turn out high-quality graphics. Vic knew that he would probably get a slightly better grade just because his diagrams looked so good.

"Well, Vic, I'm glad you like the results. These systems are really easy to use, and I can give you some pointers on using them if you want to learn them yourself. I've got to run now, my free hour is almost up."

As our case study demonstrated, two types of graphics systems are commonly available. One type is for the creation of charts, the other is for the creation of pictures. Both are relatively simple to use, although the picture systems require a certain level of artistic ability and patience and thus some users get far better results than others.

paint system
One of the two major types of computer graphics systems, used to create arbitrary graphic images.

9.2

Using Graphics Software

chart system
One of the two major types of computer graphics systems, designed to create pie charts, bar charts, and other clearly defined types of graphics.

Although there are many types of graphics software for many different applications, only two types are of interest to most users: **paint systems** and **chart systems**. The major focus of painting systems is the creation of arbitrary graphic images such as the famous image of a tennis shoe that was used in the initial advertising campaign for the Apple Macintosh computer systems.

The way a paint system works is quite simple. Paint software essentially provides a computerized piece of graph paper that contains 50–300 (or more) rows and columns *per inch* and is displayed on the computer screen. Each cell on this graph paper can be set to one color from a group of allowed colors. The size of the cells is obviously quite small, so that even the smallest image on the screen is composed of many cells. A paint system provides the user with a number of drawing tools and some kind of pointing device for creating an arbitrary image within this framework of cells. Many paint systems have low resolution (i.e., the number of cells in a given area on the screen is small), and thus the images have a grainy look (diagonal lines look like a series of separate dots) and other less-than-ideal characteristics. Paint systems with high resolution (e.g., 300 or more cells per inch) have greater density than the human eye can see, so that arbitrary shapes can be drawn with clarity and precision. A graphic image created by a paint system is shown in Figure 9–1.

The second major type of graphics system is the chart system. A chart system is used to create graphical representations of numeric data. For example, given data listing the population of various groups, a chart system could be used to create a **pie chart** that showed the relative proportion of the population in each group. In addition to pie charts, chart systems commonly include the ability to create **line graphs** (plot points on an X–Y coordinate frame) and **bar graphs** of many varieties. An example of each type of chart is shown in Figure 9–2.

pie chart
A type of graph in which data is represented by wedges of a circle. The total area within the circle represents the sum (100%) of the data, and the wedges represent percentages of the total.

line graph
A type of graph in which data points are plotted and connected by smoothed lines.

bar graph
A type of graph in which data is represented by a series of bars or rectangles of varying height. The height of each bar corresponds directly to the value of the data.

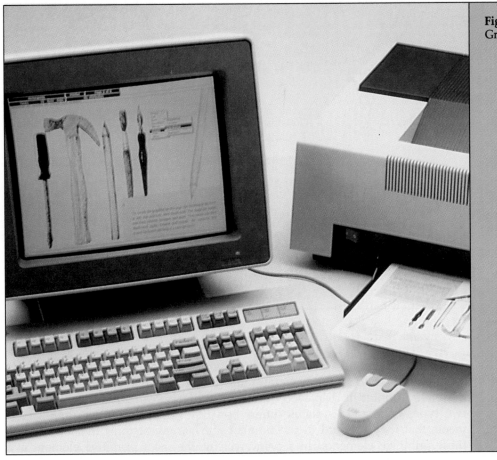

Figure 9–1 Simple Paint Graphics Output

Figure 9–2 Chart Systems Capabilities

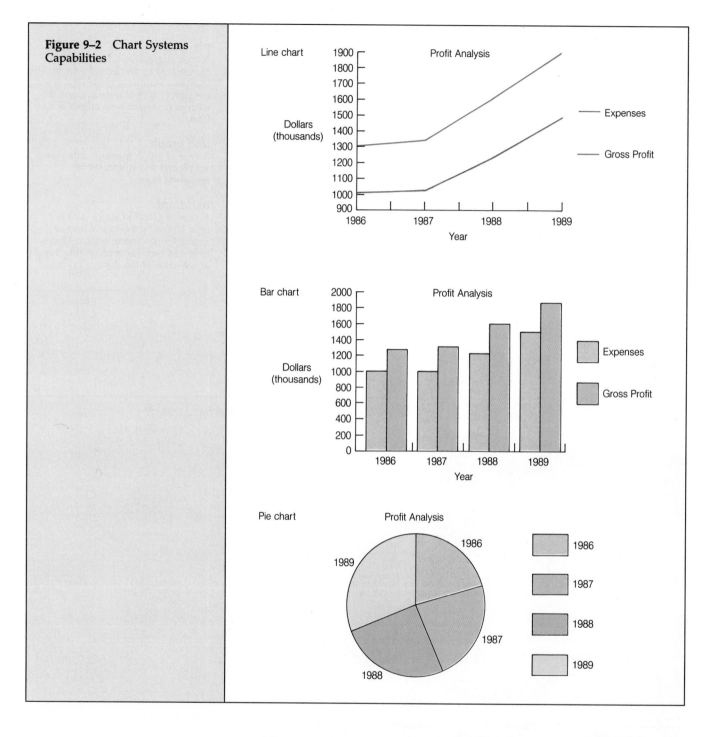

When considered abstractly, the differences between a paint system and a charting system may seem slight. Their graphic images are displayed on the same output devices—the bar graph and the tennis shoe can be printed on a dot matrix printer or displayed on the computer screen with equal ease. The two types of graphic systems differ, however, in the primitive graphic elements that they use and in the number and variety of tools that manipulate these primitive elements. In a paint system, the most primitive element is a

Computer Insights
CAD/CAM Software

Computer-aided design (CAD) is an important engineering tool in which graphics and simulation programs aid engineers in the design of products. Suppose the task is to design a really good beer mug. A design engineer might begin by sitting down at a computer and calling up past designs. In the process, it might be decided that the mug should be easily stacked, hard to tip over, and should not dribble. Graphics pointers on the screen are used to select operators that draw lines or arcs, rotate the developing image in any way, shade in various areas of the image, and so on. Finally, the computer sends schematics for the finished mug to the attached printer. Beautiful! A beer drinkers dream! Next, the engineer creates a second mug and tries to stack them—everything's fine. The computer is then asked to estimate how easily the mugs can be overturned. If the mugs tip too easily, the engineer can ask that the height-to-width ratio of the mug be reduced to produce a squatter mug. Finally, the engineer can request hard copies of various perspectives of the mug and statistics on stability and include them in a proposal for a new product.

Computer-aided manufacturing (CAM) follows computer-aided design. In CAM, computers are used to produce dies and to control the process of production. Once a design for

a beer mug or any other CAD-designed product is accepted, a CAM system can be used to create the production molds based on the CAD data files. Then a CAM production-control computer can be programmed to control the work of nonmobile industrial robots that inject hot liquid glass into the mold, test the resulting glass, and then send it on down the assembly line for packaging and delivery to all the customers eagerly awaiting their new untippable beer mugs.

The final step is flexible manufacturing, in which CAD/CAM is integrated with a factory of industrial robots operated by a computer network that is ultimately controlled by humans. An example is the Hitachi Limited Flexible Manufacturing Cell (FMC) method, in which the factory consists of networks of computers that are programmed to control specific parts of the design and operating tasks. One FMC might control the design of a particular component, while another controls the actual production of that component. The overall control of this subprocess is provided by a Local Area Network (LAN) computer-person system. Total factory coordination across all subprocesses is provided by ever higher level computer-based systems. Regardless of level, each FMC, LAN, or higher-level system is composed of humans, computers, and programmable industrial robots.

cell on the computerized graph paper. Each cell can be colored in different ways, and a number of tools are available to create dots, lines, squares, circles, rectangles, letters, numbers, and so on, from sets of these cells. The primitive elements of chart systems are much more complicated, consisting of full graphs with labeled axes, legends, titles, data points, and so forth. The tools that are provided in chart systems manipulate these elements to change titles, plot points, and perform other manipulations. Note that a chart can be created in a paint system, but an arbitrary picture cannot be created in a chart system. Also note that the number of steps required to create and modify a chart in a chart system are far fewer than those required to produce a picture in a paint system.

There are many other kinds of graphics systems in the computing world, such as **computer-aided design** and **computer-aided manufacturing** systems that can hold graphic images of an entire aircraft carrier, electronic circuit systems that can graphically display complex circuit chips, and animation systems for creating cartoons. The major differences in their software are in the primitive elements and the ways for combining them. Thus, although the discussion that follows is concerned only with paint and chart systems, the basic ideas presented there could be generalized to arbitrary graphics systems.

computer-aided design and computer-aided manufacturing (CAD/CAM)
An applications software system using graphics to partially automate design and manufacturing in industry.

■ Using Paint Systems

The hardware requirements of a paint system include some kind of drawing device. By far, the device of choice is a computer mouse. As the mouse is moved along a table, up, down, left, or right, its changes in position are re-layed to the computer and a pointer on the screen makes similar moves. The mouse is used to position the tools on the evolving picture and the mouse buttons are used to select and operate the tools used to perform most of the painting actions.

The paint system is started up like any other software system, by loading in the software and turning control of the computer over to the software. Once the system is running, the user begins to paint.

Painting a picture with a paint graphics system is in many ways analogous to painting a real picture. The user begins by staring at a blank "canvas" (the screen). Many "brushes" and other tools and an assortment of colors are available for the artist to use. The artist chooses a brush or tool and a color and draws an image. The picture is then only partially done. The user continues to choose a brush or tool and a color and apply them to the painting. There is frequently no variation from this traditional artistic method.

At times the user may want to end the paint session before the picture is complete. The picture exists only in the computer's RAM at this point, but paint systems always provide a way of saving the painted image onto disk. The user can return at a later time, reload the saved image from disk, and continue painting the picture. When the picture is complete, the user saves the final copy onto disk and issues the commands that will print the picture on the black-and-white or color printer or **plotter.**

There are two variations on this scheme. The first is provided by **clip art.** Since graphic images are somehow stored as strings of bits inside the computer, paint systems provide a way of selecting a portion of a painting and making a copy of it. This copy can be saved independently of the rest of the painting and then inserted into other paintings. Thus, an artist could create a catalogue of images that could be selectively chosen and merged with arbitrary paintings in the future. Because of the utility of such collections of images, many software packages of clip art are available for commercial paint systems.

The second important variation involving paint systems is their frequent integration with word processing systems. Although images cannot be altered within word processors, many paint systems provide a mechanism whereby a figure created in a paint system can be electronically clipped out and inserted into a word-processed document. This capability provides a substantial amount of power for the creation of arbitrarily complicated documents and is already leading to desktop publishing software. With the introduction of high-quality, inexpensive laser printers and good software, it is possible that in the future many books will be created and typeset by an author seated at a home word processor.

plotter
A computer output device capable of presenting data in graphic form on paper by drawing lines much as a person would with pen and ink.

clip art
In a paint graphics system, a catalogue of stored images that can be selectively chosen and merged with other graphic images as the user wishes.

■ Using Chart Systems

Because the creation of charts appears to be a complicated task, it may seem surprising that no mouse or other pointing device is generally needed. The creation of charts is actually very constrained; the forms of graphs are already well established. In a bar graph, bars can be stacked on top of each other, clustered next to each other, or placed one in front of the other. For any graph, axes must be labeled, titles inserted, and legends provided. In a chart system, the user only needs to specify the type of chart, the data to be used in the chart, and the labels for the chart.

Using a chart system begins with the loading and execution of system software. From that point on, a chart system looks much more like traditional applications software than does the paint system. Chart systems can have any type of shell: command language, menu, or graphic. Whatever the type, the user must specify three things: (1) the type of chart desired, (2) the data to use, and (3) the labels for the chart.

Only three basic types of charts seem to be made with any degree of frequency: line graphs, bar graphs, and pie charts. In order to completely specify the remainder of the charting process, the choice of graph type must be made first.

Specifying the data for a chart is really a data base management or spreadsheet kind of task. The user needs to have some mechanism for entering the data into the chart system; the input is done either at the keyboard or through a file created by other means. The file mode of input is especially important, because data generated by other software can be output to a file and automatically fed into the chart system without human intervention.

Given the data and the type of chart, defining the characteristics of a particular chart is a straightforward task. Once the type of chart has been selected, the user will be asked to enter more specifications depending upon the type. For example, the sets of bars in a bar chart may be stacked on top of each other, placed one in front of the other leaving only parts of each bar visible, or placed next to each other in a cluster, so the user who selects a bar chart will be asked to specify one of these styles.

Once the three parts of a chart specification are completed, users often proceed in one of two ways. In the first case, a standard graphic output is to be generated repeatedly for more than one set of data. Then the specification of the chart form must be saved to serve as a template for each new set of data. Thus the user can apply the same chart parameters to each set of data to produce a new chart in a very short time.

The second way in which chart systems are frequently used is to create a variety of graphic representations for one set of data. Different presentations of the same data can give widely varying impressions: some representations can be purposely deceiving, while others can be clear and accurate. When uncertain which type of graph would best display some data, a user might create a variety of different graphs from the same data. In this case, the data needs to be saved and used repeatedly with different graphics specifications.

It should be clear that chart graphics are substantially different from paint graphics. Chart graphics systems generate only a few kinds of graphic images, but they do it with speed and ease. Paint graphics systems allow the user to create arbitrary images but would be much slower and less accurate for creating a chart. Across the gamut of graphics software in the professions, there will always be a trade-off between greater variability in the images that can be created and greater ease in creating particular images. It is not yet possible to have both variability and ease in a single graphics system.

The inputs to graphics systems are essentially those of traditional software systems augmented by a variety of graphic or pointing devices. In the discussion that follows, we will consider paint graphics first and chart graphics second, as we did in the previous section.

9.3

Graphics Input

■ Paint Graphics Input

Input to paint graphics systems generally consists of mouse movements made in one of twenty or more drawing modes using one of twenty or more patterns of color. Mouse movements are also used to specify all commands to the sys-

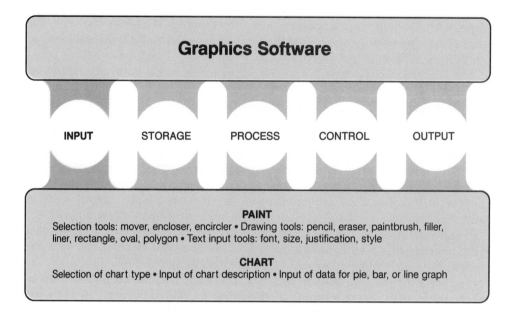

Graphics Software

INPUT   STORAGE   PROCESS   CONTROL   OUTPUT

PAINT
Selection tools: mover, encloser, encircler • Drawing tools: pencil, eraser, paintbrush, filler,
liner, rectangle, oval, polygon • Text input tools: font, size, justification, style

CHART
Selection of chart type • Input of chart description • Input of data for pie, bar, or line graph

tem through a graphic shell. Only occasional input of labels and words comes
from the keyboard.

With the large number of drawing modes and color patterns, the first
concern is how the modes and colors are selected. The typical paint program
screen shown in Figure 9–3 demonstrates several features of mode selection.
Twenty different input modes are represented in the two columns on the left
side of the screen; each mode has its own little graphic symbol called an icon.
Note that all of the twenty icons except one are shown with dark writing on a
light background, while one square in the first column contains a light square

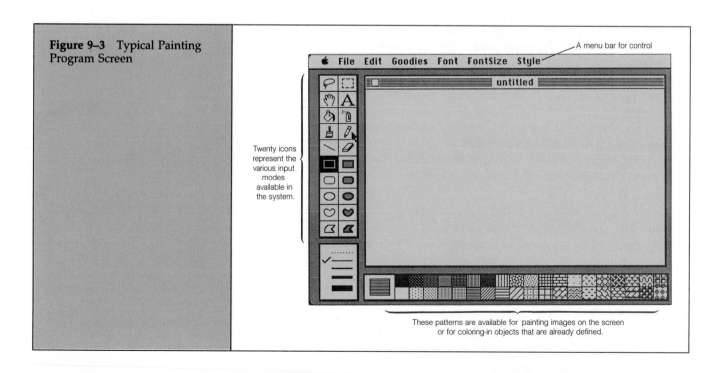

Figure 9–3 Typical Painting
Program Screen

Twenty icons
represent the
various input
modes
available in
the system.

A menu bar for control

These patterns are available for painting images on the screen
or for coloring-in objects that are already defined.

on a dark background. In general, one of the twenty modes will be active at any particular time, and that one will be displayed in reverse video (i.e., with a light icon on a dark background). The user can easily tell what the input mode is by scanning the columns on the left for the reverse video image of one of the icons.

The method for changing from one input mode to another is also demonstrated in Figure 9–3. Notice the dark arrow pointing to the icon shaped like a pencil. This dark arrow can be moved around on the screen by moving the mouse. If the user wants to change the input mode, he or she must move the mouse around on the table until the black arrow on the screen points to the icon for the desired new mode. Once the arrow is in the proper location, the user presses a button on the mouse to change the input mode from the old mode to the new one pointed to by the arrow. This change is immediately apparent, because the reverse video image of the old mode is converted back to its ordinary form and the ordinary image of the new mode is converted to reverse video.

Now that we know how to change input modes, we will illustrate the types of graphic images that can be created in each of these modes and show how the mouse is used in each mode to create these images. The twenty different modes and the images that can be created by them are shown in Figure 9–4.

As we consider each input mode in turn, the reader should remember that the modes described here represent types that are generally available in paint systems. Slight variations are to be expected in any particular software system.

The Mover. A paint system generally allows the user to create an image that fills an entire page (or maybe more). Only a small portion of this large image can be displayed on the video screen at one time. The purpose of the **mover** is to adjust the portion of the full page that is displayed on the screen. The mover itself does not generate new graphic images but just moves the visual screen around on images created by other input modes. The mover works when the user positions the cursor on the picture part of the screen and presses a mouse button. While the button is depressed and as the mouse is moved up, down, left, or right, so will the picture be moved. In Figure 9–4, the mover icon is a tiny human hand.

mover
A paint system input mode that enables the user to adjust the portion of the full page that can be seen on the screen at one time.

The Encloser Selector. Paint systems allow a number of processes to be performed on portions of the graphic image, for example, rotating an image, changing it to reverse video, and many other processes described in subsequent sections. The input option called the **encloser** allows the user to create a rectangle on the screen to designate which portion of the video screen can be operated on by these processes. The user implements this option by placing the cursor at one spot on the screen and pressing one of the mouse buttons down. The cursor is then moved (by means of the mouse) to a new location that acts as the diagonally opposite corner of a rectangle. When the mouse button is released, two points have been defined—one when the button was pressed and the second when the button was released. These points form the opposite corners of a rectangle, and everything within this rectangle can then be operated on by system processes. Again, this input mode does not add anything to the visual image. The icon often used for the encloser is a dashed line rectangle.

encloser selector
A paint system input mode that lets the user create a rectangle on the video screen. Paint system processes can then be used to operate on graphic images within this rectangle, e.g., to delete or copy the images.

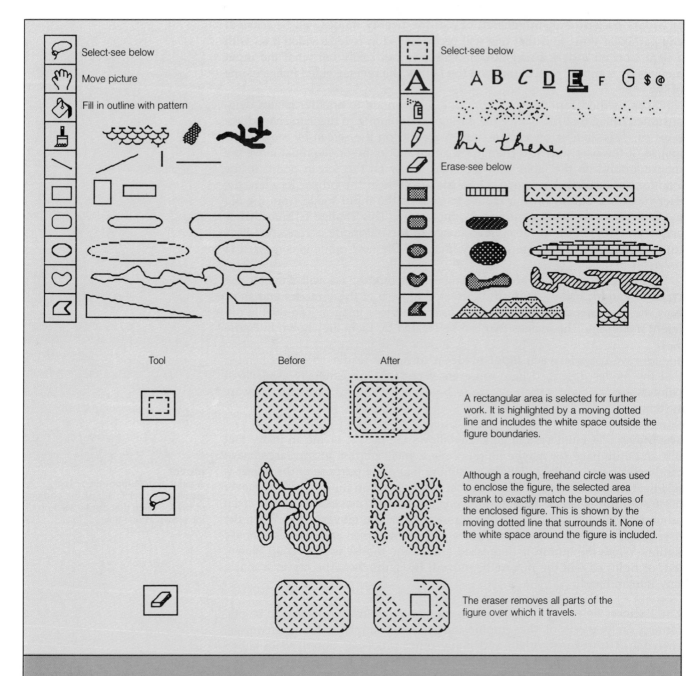

Figure 9–4 In the Apple MacPaint system, twenty basic input modes are available. The top two deal with selecting a portion of the figure for copying, deletion, and so forth. The move picture mode allows the screen to display various portions of a large picture. The *A* indicates the text input mode, used for labeling or other alphabetic input. The various painting tools allow the user to choose one of many available patterns. The eraser removes the portions of the picture it touches. The pencil draws free form lines, while the line drawer is restricted to straight lines. The lower ten input modes draw a variety of shapes that can be either filled with a pattern or left empty.

The Encircler Selector.   This input mode is essentially a generalization of the encloser. The only difference is that instead of defining a rectangular portion of a figure, the **encircler** allows the selection of an arbitrarily shaped part of the screen. The user moves the cursor to a starting point on the screen, presses the mouse button, and while holding the mouse button down, traces a path that encircles the desired portion of the screen. Note that the path must start and stop at the same point. Like the encloser, this input does not create any new visual image but instead selects the portion of the image that can be transformed by paint processes. The icon often used is a lasso.

encircler selecter
A paint system input mode similar to the encloser; it allows the user to draw around an arbitrarily shaped part of the screen that can then be operated on by system processes, e.g., copied or moved.

The Pencil.   This input mode provides a mechanism for drawing lines on the screen as if drawing with a **pencil.** In this input mode, a line is drawn on the screen if the mouse button is held down as the mouse is moved. The user can move the cursor to an arbitrary position on the screen (while not pressing the button) and then press the button to draw any line desired. The icon is usually a pencil or pen.

pencil
A paint system input mode that lets the user draw arbitrary lines on the screen, as if drawing with a pencil.

The Eraser.   This input mode provides a mechanism for erasing portions of the screen. Again, the button on the mouse must be held down to operate the **eraser.** While the button is held down, all portions of the screen over which the cursor is moved are erased. Note that the icon for the eraser is a small box that looks something like a blackboard eraser.

eraser
A paint system input mode that lets the user remove (erase) portions of a graphic image from the screen.

The Paintbrush.   This mode of input is similar to the pencil mode, except that the lines drawn can be wider and can use a variety of colors or textures. In the **paintbrush** operation, the user can select (1) the size and type of paintbrush and (2) one of the colored patterns shown in the bottom two rows of the screen. Once these selections are made, use of the paintbrush mirrors that of the pencil. If the button is held down as the mouse is moved, a swath of paint is left behind; if the button is not held down, only the cursor moves. A paintbrush icon is usually used for this tool.

paintbrush
A paint system input mode that lets the user draw arbitrary lines of varying width, color, and texture on the screen.

The Filler.   The **filler** mode allows an enclosed area to be colored with an arbitrary colored pattern. The user specifies the colored pattern that will be used for the fill operation by positioning the cursor on a pattern in the bottom two rows of the screen and pressing the button on the mouse. The user than moves the cursor to a place on the screen and momentarily presses the mouse button. Starting from the cursor and emanating outward, the designated pattern is painted in place until a boundary is reached. The icon is often a can of paint.

filler
A paint system input mode by which an enclosed area of a graphic image can be arbitrarily colored.

The Liner.   The **liner** mode allows the user to create arbitrary straight lines. For paint systems, the two points that define a straight line are the location of the cursor when the mouse button was pressed down and the location of the cursor when the mouse button was released. The liner allows the user to create any number of arbitrary straight lines. A line is a common icon for the liner.

liner
A paint system input mode that allows the user to create arbitrary straight lines in whatever colors are available in the system.

Alphabet/Numeric Input.   In the **alphabet/numeric input mode,** the keyboard is used to enter labels or other arbitrary text. The mouse is first used to position the cursor to an arbitrary point on the screen, then the button is pushed to mark the chosen spot. Then any characters typed at the keyboard

alphabet/numeric input mode
A paint system input mode in which the computer keyboard is used to enter labels and other arbitrary text into the graphic being designed.

rectangle
A paint system input mode that enables the user to form a rectangle on a graphic screen. The rectangle may be filled with a solid color or a colored pattern or left empty, as the user chooses.

rounded rectangle
A paint system input mode identical to the rectangle mode, except the corners of the rectangles are rounded.

oval
A paint system input mode that allows the user to generate arbitrary oval or circular figures.

will appear on the screen, beginning at that spot. The user generally has control over the font, size, centering, and other characteristics of the characters. The icon commonly used is a letter.

The Rectangle: Filled or Empty.   **Rectangles** are defined by two points—the diagonally opposite corners of a rectangle whose sides are oriented with the sides of the screen. The two points that define the rectangle are the point at which the mouse button is pushed down and the point at which it is later released. The difference between a filled and an empty rectangle is that when the filled rectangle is completed, it is painted with the current pattern, while the empty rectangle is not.

The Rounded Rectangle: Filled or Empty.   The **rounded rectangle** mode is identical in concept to the rectangle mode described above, except that the corners of the rectangles are rounded. For small rectangles, it is possible that no rounding will occur due to inadequate resolution of the screen (i.e., the dots of the screen are not small enough to allow the system to draw a smooth rounded edge).

The Ovals: Filled or Empty.   The **ovals** mode is conceptually like the rectangle and rounded rectangle modes. The only difference is the shape of the image being created. The image is again defined by the two points where the mouse button is pressed and later released. The first point (when the button is pressed) is considered to be the center of the oval. The second point gives two pieces of information: the second point will lie on the oval itself, and the relative changes in the X and Y directions tell how much like a circle the oval will be. For example, if the second point lies on a 45° diagonal from the initial point, a circle will be drawn, because the change in the X direction is the same as the change in the Y direction.

The Arbitrary Enclosed Shape: Filled or Empty.   The input mode for arbitrary enclosed shapes is very much like the encircler mode, except that instead of selecting a portion of the screen, the path traced by the mouse becomes part of the image. This input mode differs from the pencil mode in that the first and last points in the shape must be connected. If they are not connected by the user, the system will connect them. Like most input modes dealing with paths, the path defined by the mouse while the button is depressed defines the image.

The Arbitrary Enclosed Polygon: Filled or Empty.   The arbitrary enclosed polygon input mode is exactly like the arbitrary enclosed shape mode, except that the shape is defined by a series of separate points connected by straight lines. Instead of tracing a path with the mouse, the user momentarily presses the mouse button to mark the points that will define a series of lines. The lines are added, one after the other with each new button press, until the user brings the mouse back to the initial starting point. Obviously, the only difference between the filled enclosed polygon and the empty one is whether the current pattern is painted into the newly defined enclosure.

There are often still more variations on the input modes described here. The user of any particular paint system should learn the general concepts described here first and later learn the idiosyncrasies of his or her particular paint software.

■ Chart Graphics Input

In comparison to the inputs possible for paint systems, the input for chart systems is trivial: it is essentially all done from the keyboard or from files generated by other software systems. Recall that there are three essential items that must be specified to create a chart: the type of chart, the data to be charted, and descriptive items such as labels.

Commands are input to a chart graphics system through one of the three shell types (a command shell, a menu shell, or a graphic shell). Commands are used to specify the type of chart and describe its characteristics. As each command is entered, the system does little more than remember the command to use later when generating the final graph.

Data can be input in one of two ways, either at the keyboard or from a system file. Entering data from the keyboard is straightforward once data entry is initiated. Inputting data from a file is generally far more important, because data from spreadsheet, data base management, statistical analysis, or other applications software packages can be written into a file and analyzed visually through the chart system. To enter data from files, one usually loads the file on the screen and simply uses the cursor keys or the mouse pointer to select (mark with reverse video) the cells containing the data to be charted.

There are no consistently followed sets of modes in chart systems because the task is so simple: specify all of the parameters, then generate the graph.

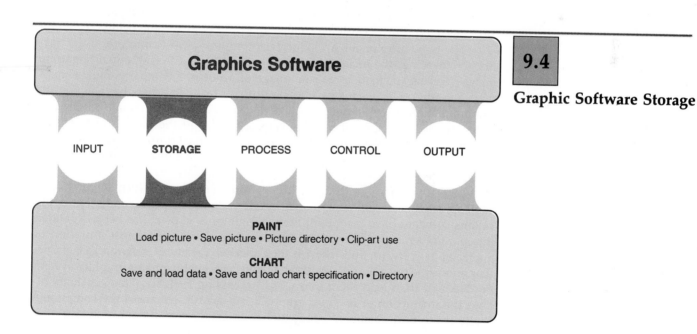

9.4

Graphic Software Storage

Both types of graphics systems described in this chapter must use system storage to store and retrieve the graphic images that they create. Storage for paint systems involves a special kind of file that holds the visual image itself. This type of storage is required because there is no structure to a paint graphics image other than the colors assigned to the small squares of which the image is built. The storage for chart systems generally contains the parameters from which chart graphics can be created—the chart graphics themselves are not stored. Let us consider the storage for these two types of graphics software in greater detail.

■ Storage for Paint Graphics

Obviously, paint graphics systems sit atop an operating system that controls the use of the computer hardware and software. The user may wish to call on the ordinary capabilities of the operating system to perform activities like getting a directory of files, deleting a file, changing directories or disks, and other file system activities; the paint software should allow access to these functions. The paint system should also allow tasks that are more specific to graphics, such as the loading, saving, and merging of paint graphic images.

Loading and saving the graphic images made in a paint system are exactly analogous to the loading and saving activities performed in word processors, spreadsheets, or data base managements systems. The unit that is loaded and saved is an arbitrary figure instead of words, tables, or sets of tables, but no other differences exist. The user gives a command through the system shell to capture the graphic image on disk. A second command is given later for reloading the image.

The other major aspect of storage in paint graphics systems is the clip art function mentioned earlier in the chapter. The clip art function allows the user to take a figure stored in one disk file and merge it with another figure by placing the image from the disk on top of the image currently being created in memory. The picture that is being retrieved from storage and added into the working figure must clearly be smaller than the new graphic being created.

The popularity of clip art is increasing rapidly. Most computer users have neither the time, the inclination, nor the ability to create high-quality graphic images. Trying to create a realistic image of a horse, a company logo, a trademark, or any other desired object is a difficult task, so artists have joined the computer market by creating catalogues containing many small pictures. A user who needs a particular image can look through the pages of the picture catalogue, find the desired image, select it with an enclosing input, clip it out (this process will be described in the next section), and insert it into the picture being created.

Now that there are integrated software systems in which word processors, spreadsheets, data base management systems, graphics, and other applications software have been built into a single unit, clip art has been expanded into a number of variations. A user can take data from almost any kind of applications software and insert it into another variety of software. Of particular interest is the ability to store the images created by a paint graphics system on disk and then load them into word processing systems. This capability allows the interaction of text and graphics and greatly enhances the computer's ability to support document production.

■ Storage for Chart Graphics

Storage for chart graphics systems is even simpler than that of paint graphics systems. A good chart system will of course allow access to underlying operating system functions such as directories, file deletion, and so on. The only other important storage function is loading and saving the data and description of charts.

Some systems provide no way to save chart data or descriptions but only a way to load commands from an ordinary system file. On such systems the user must use a text editor or word processor to create the set of commands to generate a chart and then place these commands into a file. Once the file is created, the chart system is started and a special command is given to read and execute the commands in the file. If the user wishes to alter the chart generation procedure in any way, the chart system is exited, the editor is used to alter the ordinary system file, and then the chart system is restarted and the chart generation process is tried again. This procedure is often adequate because the generation of charts is primarily a noninteractive procedure.

Other more sophisticated systems allow the user to save data and chart specifications at arbitrary times and and also allow sets of charts to be merged into one. Either system is capable of creating high-quality chart graphics.

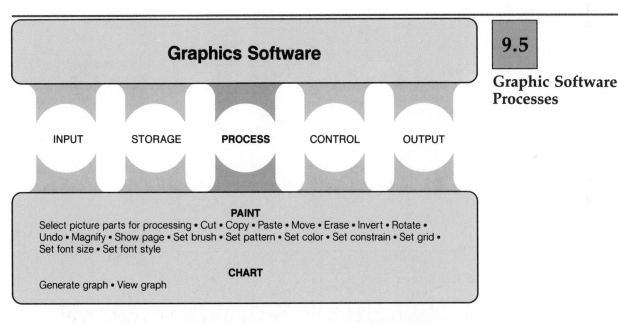

9.5

Graphic Software Processes

The processes available in graphics systems are highly dependent on the type of images being created. With paint graphics, the image is created by coloring in dots on the computer equivalent of a large piece of paper, thus the processes available deal with the manipulation of arbitrary pieces of the picture. Chart graphics, on the other hand, involve a constrained task (defining charts), so the processes available deal with the manipulation of chart concepts and not with graphic images.

■ Paint Graphics Processes

The first set of processes deals with the subparts of the picture that were selected in the encloser or encircler input mode. Recall that when the paint graphics system is in the encloser mode, the mouse is used to draw a rectangle around part of the picture. Similarly, in the encircler mode, the mouse is moved along a path that encircles an arbitrary part of the picture. However the portion of the screen is selected, there are a number of graphic processes that can be performed on the selected portion.

Cut, Copy, and Paste. a. To perform a cut from the original figure, an area of the figure is first selected using one of the available selection tools. The cut command is then issued, and the selected portion of the figure is removed and stored in memory for future use, but only until the next cut or copy command is issued. b. A copy starts in the same manner as a cut. A portion of the figure is selected, and then a copy command is given. A copy of that portion of the figure is made in memory for future use, but there is no visible change on the screen to indicate that the copy has occurred. c. Both a cut and a copy leave a clip art figure ready for use. The paste command brings up the clipped figure, which floats above the underlying image. Once the clipped figure is positioned correctly, pressing the mouse button makes its position permanent.

a. Original figure

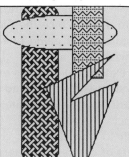

Figure with selected area

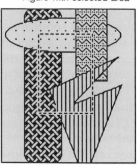

Selected area cut

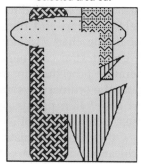

b. Original figure

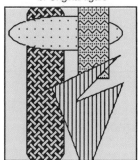

Figure with selected area

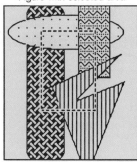

Selected area copied

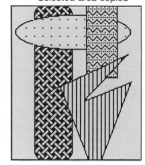

c. Original figure

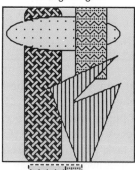

Figure with floating clip art

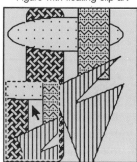

Figure after paste

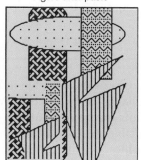

Clip Art figure from
the last cut or copy command.

Cut. The purpose of the cut process is twofold. The cut first blanks out the selected portion of the screen, then it saves the image that has just been erased to a special place in memory or on disk called a clipboard. The selected portion of the picture is removed from its original position, but it is saved for reinsertion in a different location at a later time.

Copy. The purpose of the copy process is to make a copy of some portion of the user's picture and place it on the clipboard so that it can be added into the picture at a later time. The copy process is just like the cut process, except that no erasing occurs. With the copy process, the user can easily create many duplicate images in one picture.

Paste. The paste process is the ultimate goal of the copy and cut processes. The paste process retrieves the portion of the picture held on the clipboard and inserts it into the picture that the user is currently developing. When a paste request is issued, the image retrieved from the clipboard is first placed right in the middle of the screen, on top of the image the user was creating. By using the mouse to place the pointer on the image to be pasted and then holding the mouse button down, the user can move the pasted picture to any point on the screen without disturbing the underlying picture. Once the image to be pasted is in the proper position on the user's picture, the user releases the mouse button, moves the pointer off the pasted image, and presses the mouse button once. The position of the pasted image is now permanent, and the pasted image now covers up whatever image was originally behind it.

Examples of the cut, copy, and paste processes are shown on the previous page.

Erase or Delete. The **erase process** is similar to the cut process, except that the image removed is permanently lost—it is not copied onto the clipboard. An example of an image before and after erasing is given below:

erase or delete process
A process for removing a portion of text or graphics from the graphic image being created. The removed portion is lost permanently.

Original figure	Figure with selected area	Selected area deleted
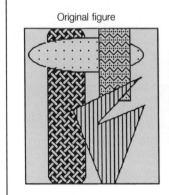	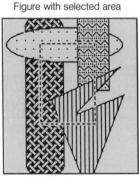	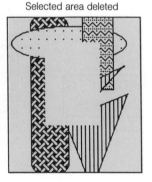

To perform a delete with the selection tools, an area of the figure is first highlighted using one of the available tools. In this example, the encloser was used to highlight a rectangular portion of the image. When the delete command is given, the selected area is removed, but it is not possible to paste the deleted portion.

Invert. On black-and-white paint systems, the **invert process** replaces all white cells with black ones and all black cells with white ones in the selected portion of the picture. With color paint systems, it is not necessarily obvious what colors should be switched to what other colors. There is usually a background color and a current color being used for drawing, and an inversion switches these colors. An example of an image before and after inversion is given below:

invert process
A paint graphics process in which the colors of cells are switched among themselves, e.g., all black cells replaced by white cells, and all white cells replaced by black cells.

Inverting the Colors. On black-and-white graphics systems, inversion is well defined. On color systems, the user must be careful to specify exactly how the color changes should occur.

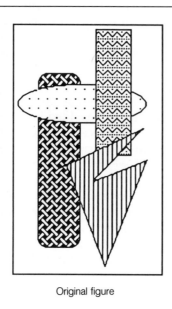

Original figure

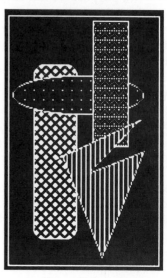

Figure after inversion

rotate process

A paint graphics process that permits the user to change the position of a portion of a graphic by rotating it on an axis perpendicular to the screen.

flip process

A paint system process for reversing a portion of an image from left to right or top to bottom. The portion reversed must have been selected by the encloser or encircler.

Rotate and Flip: Horizontal or Vertical.   The **rotate process** and **flip process** are just a matter of rotating the image on an axis. Rotation spins the image around a point that lies in the center of the image. For a vertical flip, the image is rotated (or flipped) around a line that goes from the left side of the screen to the right side through the center of the image. For a horizontal flip, the line around which the rotation occurs is a line from the top of the screen to the bottom. Examples of rotation, horizontal flip, and vertical flip are given below:

Flipping and Rotating Images. A selected portion of a figure may be rotated, flipped horizontally or flipped vertically. These processes aid in the creation of mirror images and other figures that are derivatives of the original.

ABCDEFG HIJKL	ABCDEFG HIJKL	ꟻƎꓷƆꓭA HIJKL	HIJKL ABCDEFG
Original figure	Rotated figure	Figure flipped horizontally	Figure flipped vertically

undo process

A process that allows the user to remove the effect of a process performed in error. In a paint graphics system, the undo process enables the user to correct mistaken inputs or processes made while developing a graphic.

The next set of processes deals with the manipulation of the entire picture and the use of some of the tools. These processes do not require the selection of any portion of the current painting.

Undo.   A critical feature of any good paint system, the **undo process** allows the user to repair the damage done by a mistaken input or process. For example, if the user switches to the erase mode and accidentally sends the eraser over part of the picture that should not have been erased, the undo process would allow the user to start the erase over again. For most systems, *the undo can undo only the last process or input.* For example, if the user presses the mouse button, erases some of the picture, and releases the button, then presses the button again, erases more, and releases the button again, the undo would be able to recover the picture only from the second erase. It is important to note that not all processes and inputs are undoable. A user must be quite careful when performing an action that cannot be undone. An example of an erase and an undo is shown below:

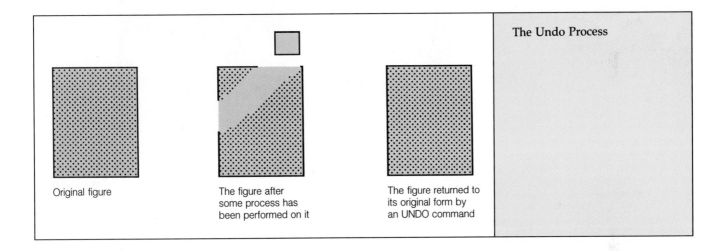

The Undo Process

Original figure | The figure after some process has been performed on it | The figure returned to its original form by an UNDO command

Magnify (Fat Bits). For very fine control over the graphic image, many systems provide a **magnify process** which allows the user to examine the picture under magnification so strong that each individual cell can be easily distinguished. Under this high level of magnification, the user can polish any portion of the picture that was difficult to handle using the normal display. When magnification is on, the user can see only a small portion of the total page of graphics. After the detailed work has been completed, magnification must be turned off to continue with normal processing. Note that most input modes work normally during magnification. Often a small inset figure will appear on the magnified screen to show what the current area of the picture would look like in unmagnified form. An example of an image in regular and magnified form is given on the next page.

magnify process
A paint graphics process that allows the user to enlarge a portion of an image to the point where individual cells can be distinguished. It is used to make more precise refinements of an image.

Show Page. Paint systems cannot generally display a full 8.5-by-11-inch figure on one screen, so the screen shows only a small window of the whole page. The window can be moved around on the page using the mover input mode described earlier. The **show page process** acts as an inverse of the magnify process and allows the user to see the entire page containing the complete picture on the screen. The page cannot be seen in clear detail—the purpose of the show page mode is to let the user see the relative layout of the page and move the working window to different portions of the picture. An example of

show page process
A paint graphics process that enables a user to reduce the size of a graphic so that the entire page containing the complete picture can be seen on the screen. Its purpose is to let the user see the layout of the entire page, but fine detail cannot be seen.

The Magnification Process

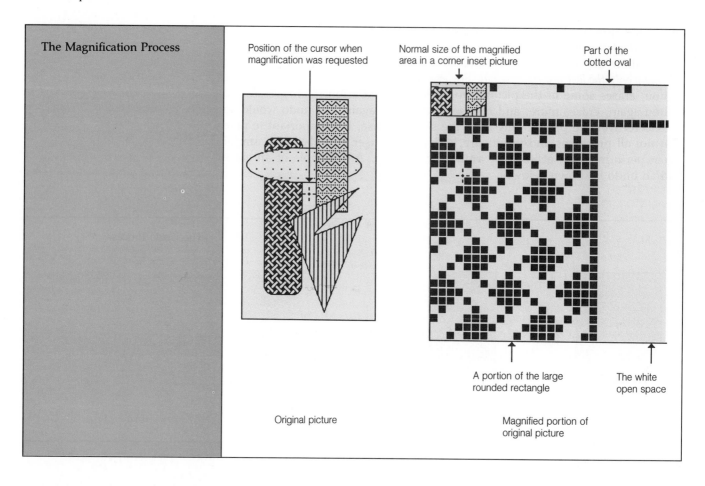

Position of the cursor when magnification was requested

Normal size of the magnified area in a corner inset picture

Part of the dotted oval

A portion of the large rounded rectangle

The white open space

Original picture

Magnified portion of original picture

The Show Page Process.

Moving the mouse when inside the dotted border changes the portion of the total figure that is displayed on the screen. Moving the mouse when outside the dotted border but on the page repositions the entire figure on the underlying page.

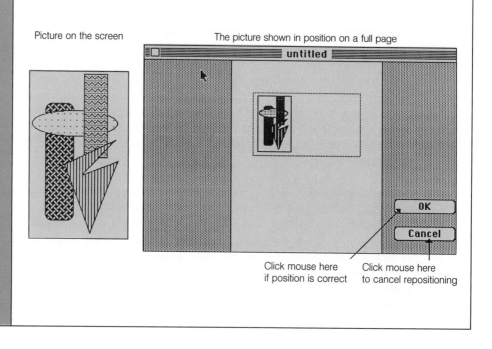

Picture on the screen

The picture shown in position on a full page

untitled

OK

Cancel

Click mouse here if position is correct

Click mouse here to cancel repositioning

an original picture and its entire page as shown by the show page process given on page 386.

Erase Picture. The **erase picture process** throws out the entire picture being worked on. This command must be used with care since it is one of the processes that usually cannot be undone.

Set Brush. The **set brush process** allows the user to set the size and shape of brushes used in the paintbrush input mode.

Set Patterns. The user also has control over the pattern that the paintbrush leaves behind as it paints. The **set pattern process** is used to select a pattern from a set of twenty or so patterns shown in the rows at the bottom of the screen; the paint system may allow other possibilities or may allow the creation of user-specific patterns. Some typical patterns and brush types are shown below:

erase picture process
A paint graphics process that erases the whole picture.

set brush process
A paint graphics process that determines the size and shape of the brushes used in the paintbrush input mode.

set pattern process
A paint graphics process that selects the pattern that will be painted by paintbrush.

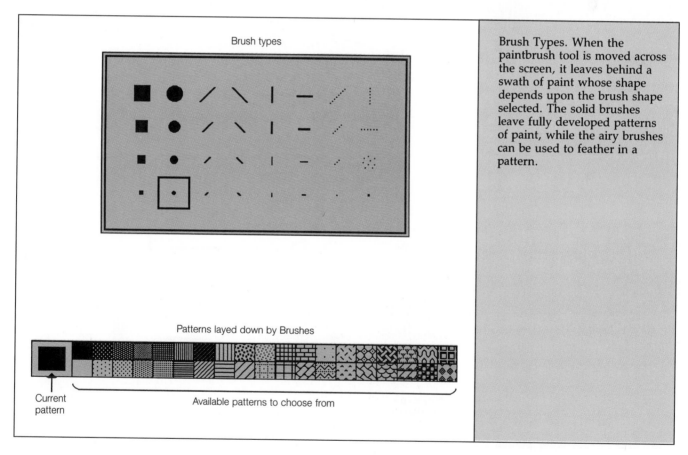

Brush types

Brush Types. When the paintbrush tool is moved across the screen, it leaves behind a swath of paint whose shape depends upon the brush shape selected. The solid brushes leave fully developed patterns of paint, while the airy brushes can be used to feather in a pattern.

Patterns layed down by Brushes

Current pattern

Available patterns to choose from

Set Colors. For color paint systems, the **set color process** allows the user to choose the background color and the painting color. Some paint systems will allow only these two colors to be used in any given painting. Other systems may allow four or more colors to be used in the display. Obviously, the more colors used in the painting, the more specialized the output device will have to be to capture all of the colors.

set color process
A paint graphics process that lets the user choose the background and paint colors used in a graphic.

constrain process
A paint graphics process that restricts the manner in which other parts of the paint system (usually the input modes) operate.

Set Constrain: On or Off. The **constrain process** restricts the manner in which other parts of the paint system operate. The constrain option is typically used to force special cases for the input modes. For example, if constrain is on, the oval input mode will draw only circles, the rectangle input mode will draw only squares, and the mover input mode will allow movements in only the vertical or the horizontal direction (whichever is chosen first, but not both).

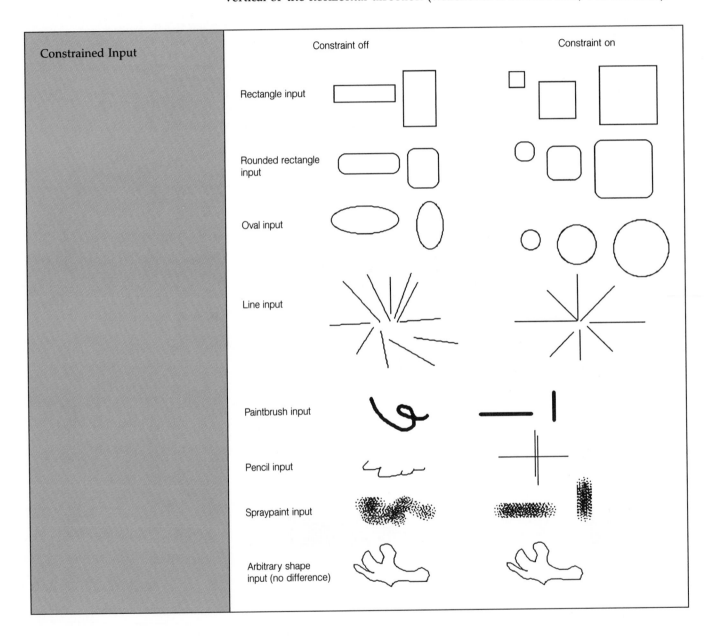

grid process
A paint graphics process in which a grid helps the user align various portions of a graphic and maintain correct size relationships.

Set Grid: On or Off. One problem with the freedom provided by paint systems is that it is difficult to align different portions of the picture or to guarantee that different images are of the same size. When the **grid process** is on, the user is restricted to making geometric shapes of only certain sizes (e.g., rectangles must have sides whose lengths are multiple of a quarter of an inch) and placing images only on certain spots in the picture. The grid process essentially constrains the placement of graphic elements to positions that can be easily lined up visually. The effects of the grid process are illustrated below:

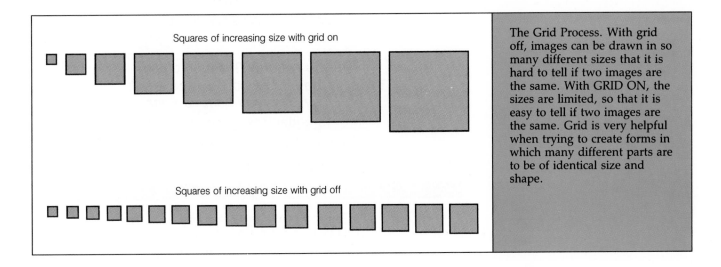

Squares of increasing size with grid on

Squares of increasing size with grid off

The Grid Process. With grid off, images can be drawn in so many different sizes that it is hard to tell if two images are the same. With GRID ON, the sizes are limited, so that it is easy to tell if two images are the same. Grid is very helpful when trying to create forms in which many different parts are to be of identical size and shape.

The last set of processes deals with the manner in which character input is added to a painting. These processes are generally similar to those of word processing systems, but because most figures require some type of labeling or explanation, paint systems must provide a mechanism for entering textual information.

Choose Font.   The font process specifies the particular typographic font that will be used when letters are printed. Many fonts are well known, and many are quite esoteric.

Choose Style: Underline, Italic, Boldface, and so forth.   Whatever font is selected, the user may wish to have the letters in the font underlined, italicized, boldfaced, and so forth.

Choose Size.   Each font in a paint system is available in numerous sizes ranging from as small as 8-point type to as large as 48-point type.

An assortment of different fonts, styles, and sizes is shown on the next page.

Choose Alignment.   The last facet of text use is whether the text is to be aligned on the left, aligned on the right, or centered. Examples of each type of alignment are given on the next page.

Paint systems thus provide a wide variety of processes that can be used to alter portions of the picture that the user is painting. Some processes deal with the alteration of particular parts of the picture, while others are concerned with the use of system input modes and text generation. With all of these processes available, the user can create many paint images with considerable ease and speed.

Varying Fonts, Styles, and Sizes of Text

This is in Chicago Font
This is in Geneva Font
This is in Monaco Font
This is in New York Font

This is regular Geneva Font
This is bold-faced Geneva Font
This is italicized Geneva Font
<u>This is underlined Geneva Font</u>
This is outlined Geneva Font
This is shadowed Geneva Font
This is everything-ed Geneva Font!!

This is 9 point plain Geneva Font
This is 10 point plain Geneva Font
This is 12 point plain Geneva Font
This is 14 point plain Geneva Font
This is 18 point plain Geneva Font
This is 24 point plain Geneva
This is 36 point
This is 48
This is 72

Alignment of Text

THIS TEXT IS ALIGNED WITH THE LEFT SIDE	THIS TEXT IS ALIGNED WITH THE RIGHT SIDE	THIS TEXT IS ALIGNED ALONG BOTH EDGES	THIS TEXT IS ALIGNED WITH THE CENTER
Left alignment	Right alignment	Full alignment	Center alignment
←	→	↔	↔

■ **Chart Graphics Processes**

Because of the nature of the charting process, there are essentially no processes beyond graph generation for a typical chart graphics system. The user inputs a variety of information that tells the system what the graph should look like whenever it is generated. Then the user issues some kind of command that tells the system to generate the graph. When this command is issued, the system generates a graph that is determined by the information that the user input. Little if any processing is done! Usually the graph is automatically displayed on the screen for modification and regeneration by the user; otherwise a view-the-graph command is available.

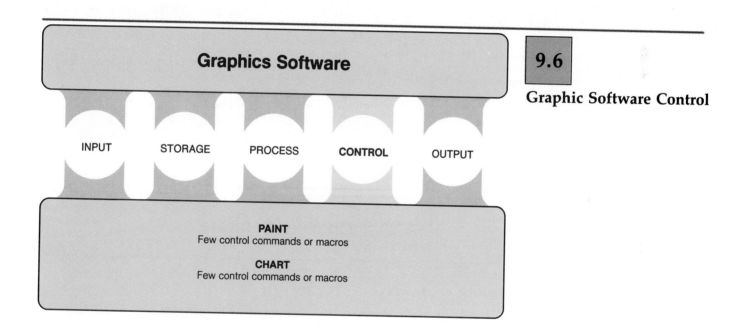

9.6

Graphic Software Control

With all of the verbiage describing the input and processing features of graphic systems, the brevity of the section on control may be surprising. *In most paint and chart graphics systems, there are essentially no control mechanisms other than sequential control.*

Recall that control deals with determining the order of the tasks performed by a computer system. In a paint graphics systems, the user paints by selecting an action and performing it immediately. There is no mechanism that chooses one task over another or repeats a task a certain number of times.

This lack of control features seems to be common to most of the chart graphics systems. Some chart systems do allow the user to apply a sequence of chart descriptors to different sets of data. This ability could be viewed as a kind of procedural control, but that is stretching the point.

Our perspective is that present graphics systems generally do not use control to any extensive degree, probably because of the nature of graphics tasks. Graphics systems create visual images, which are notoriously difficult to describe in words. Control is always specified in words, so it may be that graphics systems lack control mechanisms because of our inherent difficulty in describing the output of such systems.

Computer Insights
Popular Graphics Systems

Paint graphics systems were introduced and developed in the graphics environment of the Apple Macintosh computer. The IBM environment has only recently been able to produce systems that approach the graphics capabilities of the Macintosh. Some major paint graphics systems available for microcomputers are:

MacPaint by Apple Computer Corporation. Most of this chapter's discussion of paint graphics was based on the MacPaint system. As the first paint graphics system, MacPaint's look and feel have established a standard that many software companies want to copy. The Apple Corporation has been the graphics pioneer and still maintains a leadership position in the field.

PC Paint Plus by Mouse Systems Corporation, Microtex Industries, Inc. PC Paint is a MacPaint look-alike for the IBM PC family of computers. Although it differs in some minor ways from the MacPaint system, it

provides most of the essential characteristics of the MacPaint system.

Freelance by Lotus Development Corporation. In a relatively recent development, Lotus has come forth with an IBM PC paint system. Although the system is more menu-driven and text-based than the MacPaint system, many of MacPaint's major drawing tools, selection tools, and manipulation tools are provided.

Another important item in the graphics field is the new operating system and hardware for the IBM PS/2 microcomputer systems. The hardware capabilities of the new IBM PC line have advanced graphics capabilities and the look and feel of the IBM operating system is similar to that of the MacIntosh. Although different from the Apple system, the new IBM operating system is substantially graphic in its orientation. Many industry observers expect all future computers to make much greater use of graphics.

9.7

Graphic Software Output

Graphics Software

| INPUT | STORAGE | PROCESS | CONTROL | **OUTPUT** |

PAINT
Print picture

CHART
Pie charts: center, size, labels, legend, title • Bar charts: size, bar root, bar width, crosshatching, stacked bars, labels, legend, title • Line charts: type, size, line appearance, labels, legend, title

The output mechanisms provided in graphics systems turn out to vary greatly among the different types of systems, so we will again consider the paint and chart systems separately.

■ Paint Graphics Output

The only output feature of a paint system is a command that says "Print it!" This command essentially requests that the visual image developed earlier by a set of processes and inputs be transferred to some output device.

Note that output in a paint graphics system is different from output in a word processing system, where many of the commands are not actually executed until the output command is given (in such cases, the formatting commands were viewed as output controls). On a paint systems, however, the painting is already complete when output is requested. It has been displayed on the screen during its development and is not altered in any way as it is transferred to the output device. Thus, output for paint systems consists of nothing more than the command to initiate the printout to a printer or to a disk file for later use with a word processor.

■ Chart Systems Output

Chart systems are more analogous to word processing systems in terms of the control of output. In a chart system, the user specifies a number of commands that tell how the image will look when it is generated. These commands, however, do not generate the image, and it will not be generated until the output command is received. Thus we consider most of the commands for controlling the creation of a chart to be commands for output.

The commands that describe the characteristics of chart system output are largely specific to the type of chart being generated. In the following paragraphs, the output commands are organized according to the three types of charts.

Pie Charts. The pie chart consists of a large circle divided into pielike wedges. The data that the user provides determines the size of each wedge in the pie. The primary purpose of a pie chart is to give a feeling for what portion of the whole pie any wedge occupies. The data for a pie chart is simply a set of single numbers, each of which has an associated label.

The total pie represents the sum of all of the numbers, and the size of any wedge is the ratio of that data item to the total of all the data. The important parameters in the creation a pie chart are:

- □ *Pie Center.* The user must be able to position the chart in an arbitrary position on the page where it will be printed. For pie charts, the user must first specify the position of the center of the pie. The position is generally specified as an X and a Y value, where both values are in inches, the X value gives the distance between the center and the left side of the page, and the Y value gives the distance between the center and the top of the page.
- □ *Pie Size.* Once the center of the pie is defined, the user must specify the size of the pie. The size is usually defined in terms of the radius of a circle around the pie center. Pie charts in different positions and with different radii are shown on the next page:
- □ *Data:* a set of numbers, one for each wedge in the pie chart.
- □ *Data Labels: Values, Sizes, Locations, Style, and Font.* Each wedge of a pie chart must be labeled, and the user must provide these labels before a chart can be made. Many chart systems allow the user to specify the size, font, style, and location of the data labels. Labeling is exactly analogous to the textual processes described earlier and will not be illustrated further.
- □ *Legends: Values, Sizes, Locations, Style, and Font.* A graph may require a legend in which certain abbreviations or symbols are defined. A

Pie Chart Positioning and Size. The actual pie chart always lies against the background of a larger figure that includes titles, legends, and so on. The user can generally determine the position and size of the pie chart circle with respect to the underlying background and the page on which the pie chart will be.

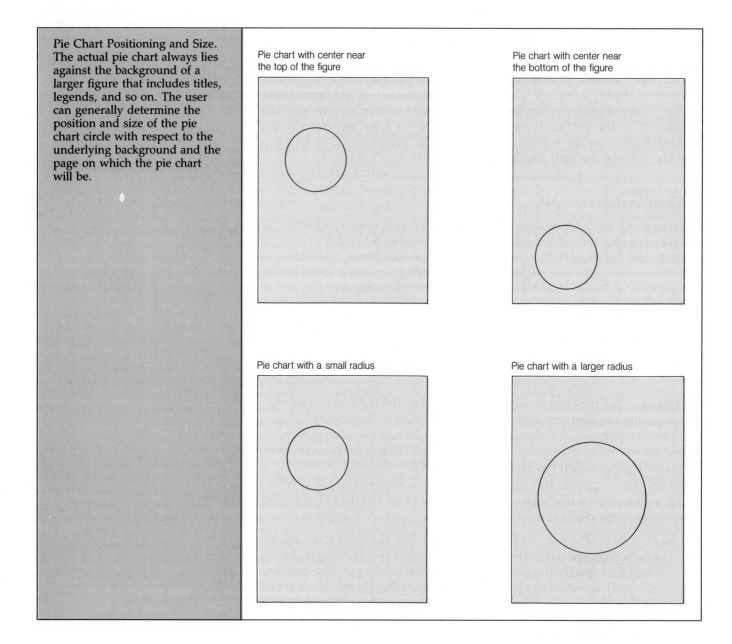

Pie chart with center near the top of the figure

Pie chart with center near the bottom of the figure

Pie chart with a small radius

Pie chart with a larger radius

good chart system will allow the user to define such legends and select the size, style, character font, and location on the page.

□ *Title: Values, Sizes, Location, Style, and Font.* Finally, a pie chart should have a title, and again the user must specify the size, style, font, location, and text (value).

An example of a completed pie chart is shown on the next page. Note that it contains a title, a legend, and a pie with various labeled wedges.

Bar Graphs.   Bar graphs have a different purpose from pie charts. They are intended to show the *distribution* of data, that is, the way that a set of data varies across a set of parameters. Users frequently wish to compare a number

a.

Company spreadsheet
data on car sales
in January serves
as the source of
data for the pie chart

	A	B
1	Salesman	Sales
2	Batke	23694
3	Foster	48761
4	Gaines	159323
5	Judd	87432
6	VanTil	8730

b.

Title ⟶ Car sales for January by salesperson

Legend

Batke
Foster
Gaines
Judd
VanTil

A Finished Pie Chart. a. Appropriate commands are given to use the first column, rows 2–6, as the data labels and the second column, rows 2–6, as the corresponding data. This input, together with formatting commands describing the chart's titles, legends, style, and so forth, yield the result shown in b.

of different distributions, and bar charts often display more than one set of numbers at a time; in such cases, multiple bars from different sets of numbers are combined together for comparison.

In creating bar charts, there are again a large number of characteristics that must be specified before the chart can be generated.

- □ *Chart Location.* As for pie charts, the user may wish to control the position of the final chart on the page. A mechanism may be provided to allow the user to specify the location of the lower left corner of the bar chart.
- □ *Chart Size.* The size of the chart is defined in terms of the lengths of its X- and Y-axes. These lengths are usually defined with the specification of the axes, which will be described shortly.
- □ *Bar Root.* The bars in a bar chart generally rise from the bottom of the chart. Some systems, however, allow bars to have positive or negative values. In such cases, the **bar root** (the Y value from which the bars will be extended) may be defined as different from the bottom of the

bar root
The Y value at which the bars of a bar graph begin; usually 0, but occasionally some other positive or negative value.

graph. The example below shows a graph with a normal bar root and one with a root in the center of the chart, allowing both positive and negative values.

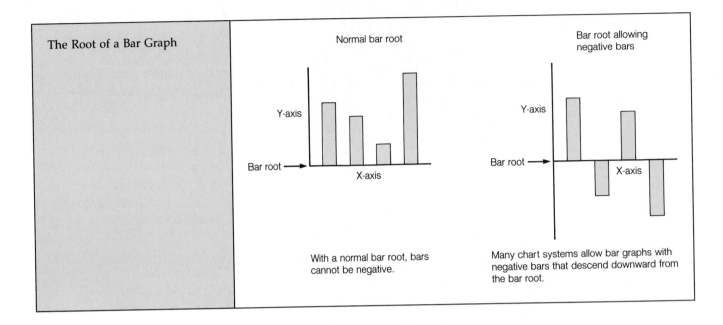

The Root of a Bar Graph

Normal bar root

Y-axis

Bar root →

X-axis

With a normal bar root, bars cannot be negative.

Bar root allowing negative bars

Y-axis

Bar root →

X-axis

Many chart systems allow bar graphs with negative bars that descend downward from the bar root.

□ *Bar Width.* The width of the bars on a bar graph must clearly be limited, and the user may have control over how wide the bars will be.

□ *Multiple Bar Visual Difference.* If distributions between different sets of data are to be compared, there will be more than one set of bars on the same chart, and the user must be able to make these sets distinguishable. Usually different crosshatching is used to distinguish the sets of bars, although simple color differences may be used on color systems.

□ *Multiple Bar Comparison: Stacked, Hidden, or Clustered.* Once multiple sets of bars have been visually distinguished, there still remains the problem of how to arrange the bars next to each other. Three possible variations are generally available. With **stacked bars,** the bars are placed one on top of the other, with each bar of the proper length. This presentation is most reasonable when the sum of the bars is some constant value. Using **hidden bars** is the most concise way of comparing data; it places the longest bar in back, the next longest bar in front of that, and so on, with the shortest bar in front. Such a display can be confusing, because the order can change from one bar set to the next. However, all bars are simultaneously visible for all values. Finally, clustering the bars just places the related bars next to each other, leaving a gap between the groups of data. **Clustered bars** may well provide the most intuitively satisfying representation. Examples of these multiple bar methods are given in the figure on the next page.

stacked bars
In a chart graphics system bars that are placed on top of each other in a bar graph, generally used when the sum of the bars represents a constant.

hidden bars
In a chart graphics system, a method of combining multiple bar charts into one chart by placing the related bars before or behind each other, leaving the taller bars partially hidden by the shorter bars.

clustered bars
In a chart graphics system, a method of combining multiple bar charts into one chart by grouping the related bars of the various bar graphs.

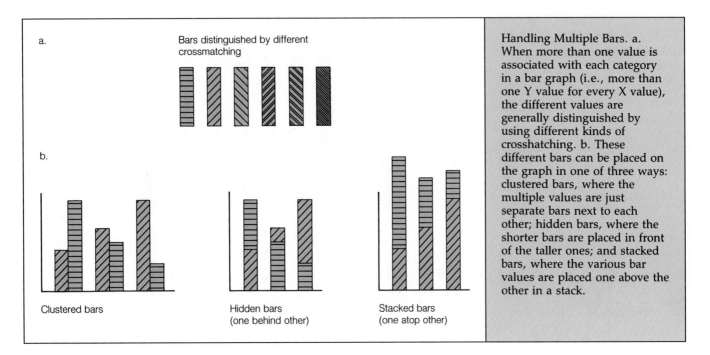

a. Bars distinguished by different crossmatching

b.

Clustered bars

Hidden bars
(one behind other)

Stacked bars
(one atop other)

Handling Multiple Bars. a. When more than one value is associated with each category in a bar graph (i.e., more than one Y value for every X value), the different values are generally distinguished by using different kinds of crosshatching. b. These different bars can be placed on the graph in one of three ways: clustered bars, where the multiple values are just separate bars next to each other; hidden bars, where the shorter bars are placed in front of the taller ones; and stacked bars, where the various bar values are placed one above the other in a stack.

- □ *X-Axis: Label, Division, Maximum, Minimum, Step, Length* The X-axis of a bar graph is generally numeric or categorical. If numeric, the user must specify the smallest value, the maximum value, and what increment to use to separate one bar from the next. For categorical data, the user must specify the labels for each value on the X-axis. In either case, the user may also be able to specify a label for the X-axis and the length of the X-axis.

- □ *Y-Axis: Label, Division, Maximum, Minimum, Step, Length.* The same types of information required for the X-axis must be specified for the Y-axis. The only difference is that the Y-axis is virtually always numeric. The only label required is a label that gives the meaning of the axis.

- □ *Data.* Obviously, the most important part of the bar graph is the data. If the data consists of just one distribution (or data set, i.e., one set of numbers), the graph is easy to generate. If there is more than one distribution, the user will need special ways to identify each data set.

- □ *Legends: Values, Sizes, Locations, Style, and Font.* A legend is most critical when multiple distributions are displayed in a bar graph. The legend must associate the visual differences that identify the data of different sets with the names of the different data sets.

- □ *Title: Values, Sizes, Location, Style, and Font.* As in a pie chart, the title of a bar graph and its location must be specified.

To illustrate the complexities of a bar graph, a completed bar graph with multiple bars, legend, title, and labels is shown on the next page. It contains three sets of data and uses clustered bars.

A Finished Bar Chart. a. Again, the data in a spreadsheet serves as input for the chart system. Here data for five salesmen over three months will be plotted in a bar graph. b. This example shows a clustered bar chart. The multiple sales values for each salesperson have been clustered next to each other. The crosshatching distinguishes the bars for each month.

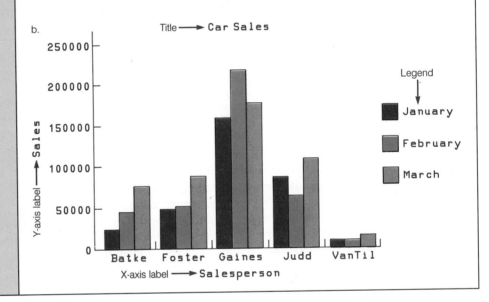

a.

	A	B	C	D
1		January	February	March
2	Batke	23694	45334	76234
3	Foster	48761	52970	89920
4	Gaines	159323	217654	175420
5	Judd	87432	63228	110334
6	VanTil	8730	9135	11965

b. Title → Car Sales

Line Graphs. Line graphs are the last type of chart commonly encountered. There tend to be three variations on the line graph: the **connected line,** the **scatter plot,** and the **linear approximation.** The first variety just connects the points with a series of straight lines; the second just plots the points without any connecting lines; and the third performs a statistical analysis to determine what line is the best approximation of the data points and then plots that line, usually along with the data points.

The characteristics that must be specified to generate a line graph are generally like those of a bar graph.

- □ *Chart Location.* As for the previous types of charts, the user may be able to specify where the chart will appear on the page.
- □ *Chart Size.* The size is usually specified by giving the lengths of the X- and Y-axes, as is done for the bar charts.
- □ *Multiple Line Visual Difference.* Like bar graphs, line graphs can be used to compare different sets of data. In such cases, there are generally two methods of distinguishing the various sets of data

connected line
A type of line graph generated by a chart graphics system in which the points of the graph are connected by a series of straight lines.

scatter plot
In chart graphics systems, a variation of the line graph, in which the data points are plotted but are not connected by lines.

linear approximation
A variation of the line graph in which a statistical analysis is performed to determine the straight line that best approximates the data points.

visually: (1) the points in the different data sets can be represented by different symbols, and (2) the lines for the different data sets can be shown in different colors or by different types of dashed lines. Some of the varieties of points and lines are shown below:

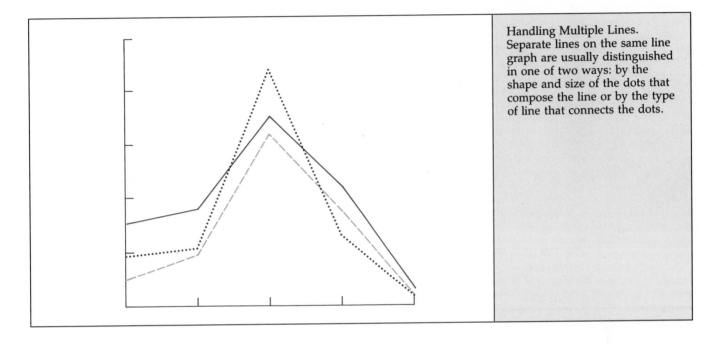

Handling Multiple Lines. Separate lines on the same line graph are usually distinguished in one of two ways: by the shape and size of the dots that compose the line or by the type of line that connects the dots.

- *X-Axis: Label, Division, Maximum, Minimum, Step, and Length.* Again, the user must specify the maximum and minimum values that will be plotted on the graph, as well as the length of the axis. The user must also specify the steps on the axis that will be represented by tick marks and the divisions that will be labeled. Once the axis is defined, the user also needs to provide a general label describing the axis.
- *Y-Axis: Label, Division, Maximum, Minimum, Step, and Length.* The specifications required for the Y-axis are exactly analogous to those for the X-axis.
- *Data.* As in any chart, the data is the most important part. For line graphs, the data set is defined as a series of points, each point having an X value and a Y value. More than one data set may be used. If different sets of data are being compared on the same chart, the user must be able to identify which data points belong to which data set.
- *Legends: Values, Sizes, Locations, Style, and Font.* Legends for line graphs are most important when multiple sets of data are shown. The visual differences that distinguish the data sets must be identified in the legend. The user often has control over the exact content, location, and style of the legend.
- *Title: Values, Size, Location, Style, and Font.* The title of a line graph is exactly like the title of any other type of graph.

The line graph on the next page shows two data sets:

A Finished Line Chart	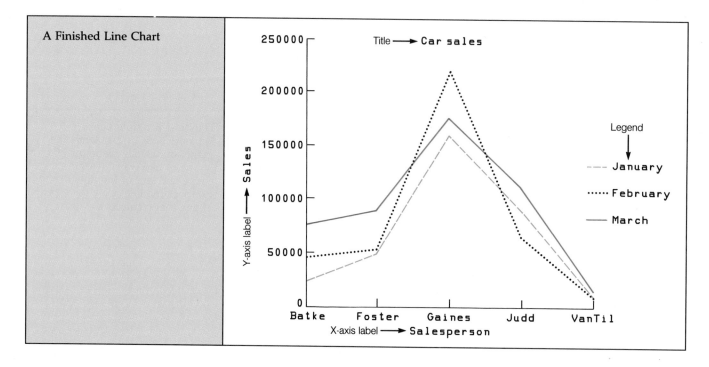

9.8

A Final Graphics Example

Creating complex graphic images has become so much simpler with modern software that graphics libraries are becoming common and different graphics systems are being designed to communicate with each other. Vic is back again, this time preparing a report for his economics class on the annual profits of major United States corporations over the last twenty years.

Case Study

Vic realized that to create the final graphic image he had in mind, he would need to use both a chart and a paint graphics system. He would use the chart system to generate the basic bar graph he wanted and then enhance the final printed form using the paint graphics system and a clip art catalogue he had. Vic started up the chart graphics system and entered the profit data for GM, Ford, Chrysler, and AMC. He chose a clustered bar scheme and placed appropriate labels on all of the axes. The resulting chart was quite nice. It is shown on the next page.

But Vic wasn't yet satisfied with the chart, even though it already looked good. From the menu bar, he chose the cut option followed by the paste option to a special file called the scrapbook. This procedure saved the entire graphic image from the chart system, but it did not interfere with and was separate from the ordinary disk file created by a save command. This special file was the mechanism for transporting the chart created in the chart graphics system to the paint graphics system. Once the cut and paste operations were finished, Vic quit the chart system and started up his paint graphics system.

The first thing that Vic did in the new system was load in a file of clip art. He had a number of files to choose from, and he selected a file containing corporate logos. After the file was loaded, a visual catalogue of small figures appeared on the screen as illustrated on the next page.

One at a time, Vic enclosed the various car producers' logos and copied them to the scrapbook file. When he had pulled out the logos for all four car producers, he

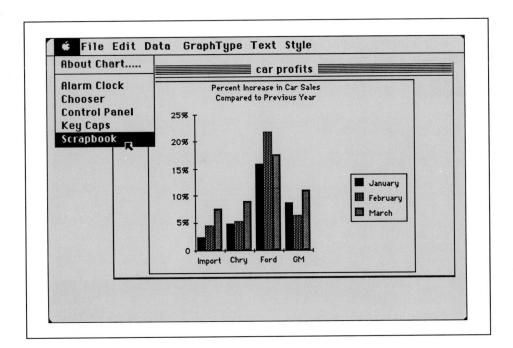

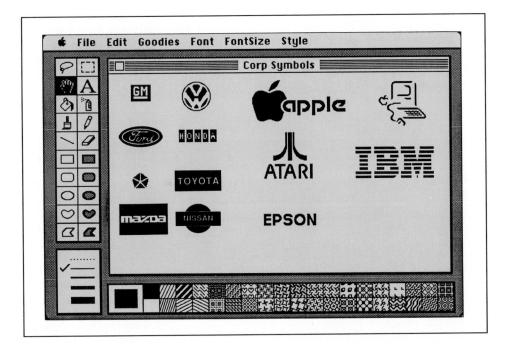

cleared the graphics system and began anew. With a clear screen, he started pulling things out of the scrapbook. First he pulled out the chart he had pasted into the scrapbook from the chart graphics system. Then, one after the other, Vic cut the company logos out of the scrapbook and placed them in the appropriate places on his chart's legend. When he was finished, he had a beautiful chart that had required the use of both a chart and a paint system. The final graphic is shown on the next page. He was glad that his roommate had bought that clip-art catalogue.

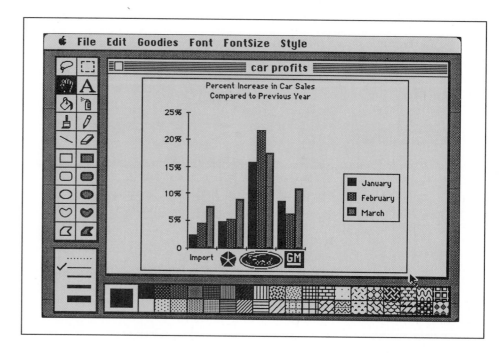

It is true, as Vic has discovered, that paint and chart graphics systems can complement each other. He used the chart graphics system because it created the bar graph and did the mathematical computations to figure out exactly how long to make each bar. The paint graphics system helped make a good chart even better by adding pictorial images to the legend.

Computer Insights
The Two Types of Paint Systems

Although the text presents paint graphics systems as identical in concept, there is one dimension in which paint graphics systems do vary. Some systems, like the Apple MacPaint program, do not keep track of the steps required to create a picture. Instead, they continuously retain the current version of the picture. This method is quite similar to the ordinary picture-painting process—the steps required to create a painting are irrelevant, only the final product is important. The picture data is stored by keeping track of the color of each dot in the picture, but there is one problem with this storage method. When hardware advances improve the resolution of the output devices and allow smaller dots, there is no straightforward way to improve the quality of the picture. Each big dot is just composed of a set of smaller ones.

Another approach to picture data storage is to keep track of the steps required to make the picture rather than the final product. This method is used in the paint graphics system called MacDraw. For example, MacDraw keeps track of the series of steps used to draw the picture, such as drawing a circle of radius 4.325 inches with center at the point 4,5, drawing a square circumscribing this circle with its sides parallel to the edges of the screen, and so on. The advantage of this approach is that when devices of higher resolution are available, they can immediately be used to improve the appearance of the picture because the commands (like draw a circle) can be duplicated in the higher-resolution environment.

Either approach can be used with excellent results. The MacPaint-like systems are easier to use because the steps used to create a picture are forgotten by the system and ignored by the user—only the current picture is significant. The MacDraw-like systems, although harder to use, can use output devices with a wide variety of resolutions.

In the previous chapters on applications software, we saw a clear progression in complexity from word processing to spreadsheets to data bases. In all three systems, manipulations were performed primarily on symbols. This progression does not continue into graphics systems, where the objects being created are visual, not symbolic, in nature.

Despite the change to visual images, the similarity of many of the processes involved should not surprise the reader. Just as symbolic applications systems have various input methods for symbols, so do graphics systems provide various ways to input visual images. In the same way that word processors, spreadsheets, and data bases have storage processes to save and retrieve information from disks, so do graphics systems load and save visual information from disks. Processes in graphics systems deal with deleting, inserting, copying, and moving visual images in much the same way that the other applications software systems provide for deleting, inserting, copying, and moving their types of data.

Indeed, across all applications software, it seems that systems *differ primarily in terms of the primitive elements they employ and the methods by which they build structures from these primitive elements*. Once the structures are in place, many editing methods exist for modifying or supplementing them. Whether the systems are those described in this text, systems for the construction of music, pinball games, or adventure games, many of the concepts remain the same.

■ The ISPCO Frame for Graphic Systems

The major functions of graphics software are summarized by the ISPCO frame for paint graphic software and the frame for chart graphics software. The reader should fill in the boxes on the right side of the frames to create an easy-to-use summary of his or her own graphics system described in the framework of this text.

The frames point out the basic differences between chart and paint graphics systems. Chart graphics systems build little if any intermediate structure. The only thing the user does is enter the data from which the output is to be generated and then direct that the output be generated. The user cannot perceive the effect of most chart graphics commands until the system generates the final chart. Because of this output orientation, most of the commands for chart graphics are described as output functions.

Paint graphics systems, on the other hand, do not postpone the generation of visual images. Instead, they maintain a current graphic image and provide a number of ways to alter this image. Thus we have described most of the paint graphics commands as processes that input and edit an existing picture.

No matter how the functions in paint and chart graphics systems are organized, both systems provide new capabilities for generating high-quality documents. The graphics frames are given on the next several pages.

■ The ISPCO Scripts for Graphic Software

By now, the reader could probably generate a basic ISPCO script for graphics systems. The steps that were first given for operating systems have been repeated frequently. As new varieties of applications software have been dis-

Frame for Paint Graphic Software

	Concept	Your System
ON/OFF	COMPUTER ACCESS. Access to computer/paint system is needed. May need location, sign-on, password, telephone number, disk, start-up command. For this system:	Location and disks needed: Telephone, sign-on, and password: Start-up command for paint system: Shutdown command for paint system:
INPUT	COMMAND INPUT: Paint systems generally use menus and pointing for input. Pointing is best done by mouse, but cursor keys can suffice. To start a new picture:	Use of mouse: Use of cursor keys: Use of function/control keys: Command to start new picture:
INPUT	DRAWING TOOLS: Many drawing tools are available. Most are selected from menus and then used with the mouse. For this paint system:	Pencil: Straight line: Paintbrush: Filler: Set brush shape: Set pattern: Eraser:
INPUT	SHAPE TOOLS: A wide variety of tools are used to create enclosed shapes, either filled with color or pattern or left empty. For this paint system:	Rectangle/Square: Oval/Circle: Arbitrary polygon: Arbitrary shape:
INPUT	EDITING TOOLS: Many editing tools allow selection and editing of only one small portion of a picture. The editing tools for this paint system are:	Encloser: Encircler: Cut: Copy: Paste: Flip: Invert: Rotate:
INPUT	ALPHABETIC TOOLS: Alphabetic information is a critical part of many figures and is provided in many ways in a paint system. For this particular system:	Font specification: For alphabetic input: Size specification: Style specification: Justification:
STORAGE	FIGURE ACCESS: Paint figures require storage and retrieval from disk storage. Clip art also requires access to other disk figures. For this system:	Load paint figure command: Save paint figure command: Load clip art figure: Save clip art figure:
PROCESS B = 2 + C	GLOBAL PARAMETERS: Many global parameters affect the manner in which the various painting tools perform. Included in this paint system are:	Set color: Set constraint: Set grid: Undo command:

PROCESS $B=2+C$	CHANGING PERSPECTIVE: A large paint image may not fit on a small computer screen, and the normal screen perspective may not be good for detail work. On this system:	Show full page on screen: Enter fat bits close-up mode:
OUTPUT	PICTURE PRINTING: When the final image is complete, the user must print out the image to printer or screen. With this paint system:	Print command:

Frame for Chart Graphic Software

	Concept	**Your System**
ON/OFF	COMPUTER ACCESS: Access to computer/chart system is needed. May need location, sign-on, password, telephone number, disk, start-up command. For this system:	Location and disks needed: Telephone, sign-on, and password: Start-up command for chart system: Shutdown command for chart system:
INPUT	COMMAND INPUT: Chart systems generally use menus and textual input, since few graphic images are directly drawn. For this particular chart system:	Use of mouse: Use of cursor keys: Use of function/control keys: Command to start new picture:
INPUT	DATA INPUT: Charts are representations of data. Methods must exist for entering sets of data directly from files or spreadsheets. Here:	Direct entry of data: Entry of data from file: Entry of data from spreadsheet:
INPUT	CHART TYPE: Three types of charts are generally available: bar, line, and pie. To specify the type of chart on this system:	Pie chart: Bar chart: Line chart:
INPUT	CHART LABELING: Charts are labeled on the axes (bar and line charts), with legends and with titles. To enter these labels for this chart system:	X-axis: Y-axis: Legends: Title:
INPUT	PIE CHART CHARACTER: Pie charts differ in their center location, size, and subtle variations involving pie chart style, labeling, and so on. For this system:	Pie center location: Pie size: Pie style: Pie labeling:

INPUT	BAR CHART CHARACTER: Bar charts differ in their location, size, bar root, bar width, method for bar comparison, and stylistic variations. For this system:	Chart size: Chart location: Bar root: Bar width: Method of bar comparison: Bar chart style:
INPUT	LINE CHART CHARACTER: Line charts also differ in many ways, including the type of chart (scatter, regression, and connected), size, location, style, and so on. For this system:	Chart size: Chart location: Line chart type: Method of line comparison: Line chart style:
STORAGE	CHART ACCESS: The user must be able to save and load the specifications for a chart from disk. For this system:	Loading chart specifications: Saving chart specifications:
OUTPUT	CHART PRINTING: When the specifications are finished, the user must print out the image to printer or screen. With this chart system:	Print command:

cussed, many of the steps have remained the same. Following is the script for paint graphics systems.

SCRIPT FOR PAINT
GRAPHICS IMAGE
CREATION

1. *PREPARE HAND-DRAWN SKETCH OF FIGURE.* Even for a simple figure, think first before wasting time on the computer. Draw the image approximately the size that the finished figure should be.

2. *START UP PAINT GRAPHICS SYSTEM.* The system should be started up. If not already prepared, a disk should be initialized to hold any figures that will be created during the painting session.

3. *USE PAINT INPUT TOOLS TO CREATE FIGURE.* The figure creation begins by using the constructive tools for drawing lines and shapes, and the keyboard for alphanumeric characters. During this phase the small screen may have to be moved around frequently on the larger figure being developed.

4. *USE PAINT PROCESSES TO ALTER FIGURE.* As painting proceeds, some portions of the figure may be selected for processing that can copy the portion to another spot, move it to another spot, invert colors, stretch or collapse it, and so on.

5. *SAVE THE FIGURE TO DISK.* When painting is complete, the figure is saved to disk for later use. Saving should always be done before printing.

6. *PRINT OUT FIGURE.* The last step is to print out the newly created figure on the printer or to disk. From disk it can often be transferred into a word-processed document.

The next script on the creation of chart graphics is also simple.

1 *PREPARE THE DATA FOR THE CHART.* The data for the chart includes the data to be plotted in the chart (from files, spreadsheets, or whatever), titles, legends, labels for axes, and so on. Note that pie charts plot single numbers, while bar and line charts plot pairs of numbers.

2 *START UP THE CHART GRAPHICS SYSTEM.* The system should be started up. If not already prepared, a disk should be initialized to hold any figures that will be created during the chart graphics session.

3 *SELECT THE TYPE OF CHART TO BE CREATED.* Generally, a chart system can create pie, bar, and line charts. The first specification is thus the type of chart to be displayed. Many systems allow the user to change this on the fly so that the same data can be viewed using different types of charts.

4 *INPUT THE DATA AND CHART SPECIFICATIONS.* The next requirement is the data to be graphed. More than one set of data can be charted at a time on bar and line graphs. Many other characteristics of the chart must be specified including titles, legends, axes labels, and so on. Specific style characteristics that depend on the type of chart must also be entered. At this point, generate the chart and view it on the screen. Revise the specifications and regenerate as needed.

5 *SAVE THE DATA AND SPECIFICATIONS TO DISK.* When the data entry and chart specifications are complete, the user should save the information to disk for future use.

6 *PRINT OUT THE CHART.* The last step is to print out the newly created chart on the printer or to disk. From disk it can often be transferred into a word-processed document.

SCRIPT FOR CHART GRAPHIC IMAGE CREATION

With these scripts and frames, the reader should be able to use graphics systems to generate arbitrary graphics. Although these systems are easy to use, a new user might discover that special hardware is required to make full use of both kinds of graphics systems.

Chapter 9 Review

Expanded Objectives

The objectives listed below are an expansion of the essential chapter concepts listed at the beginning of the chapter. The review items for the chapter are based on these expanded objectives. If you master the objectives, you will do better on the review items and on your instructor's examination on the chapter material.

After reading the chapter, you should be able to:

1. compare and contrast the general characteristics of paint and chart systems.

2. discriminate among the main types of charts and pictures produced on computer graphics systems.
3. explain the use of clip art in the generation of charts and pictures.
4. describe the command structure employed in computer graphics systems.
5. relate the operations of computer graphics systems to the ISPCO functions.
6. correctly sequence a set of tasks for creating a chart or picture on a computer graphics system.
7. create a simple chart and picture using a computer graphics system.

8. complete a script for one or more of the generic processes of a computer graphics system.
9. complete the last column in the graphics system frame for the specific computer graphics system to which you have access.

10. recognize the meanings of the major new terms introduced in this chapter.

Review Items

Completing this review will give you a good indication of how well you have mastered the contents of this chapter and prepare you for your instructor's test on this material. To maximize what you learn from this exercise, you should answer each question *before* looking up the answers in the appendix. The number of the corresponding expanded objective is given in parentheses following each question.

Complete the following clusters of items according to the directions heading each set.

A. True or false.

___ 1. A critically important chart system input device is a pointer called a mouse. (5)
___ 2. In paint systems, mouse movements specify commands through a graphic shell. (4)
___ 3. In chart systems, data is primarily input through the keyboard. (5)
___ 4. A chart can be created in a paint system, but an arbitrary picture can't be created in a chart system. (1)
___ 5. Chart systems depend to a large extent on files generated by other software systems for their input. (5)
___ 6. Clip art is an important source of images for paint graphics systems. (1,3)
___ 7. There is no consistently followed set of input modes for chart systems, because the input task is so simple. (5)
___ 8. The print command is the only major output feature used by a paint system. (5)
___ 9. The bar root of a bar chart determines whether the bars of a chart extend up, down, or in both directions. (2)
___ 10. Input for paint systems comes from either the keyboard or a file created by other means. (1,5)
___ 11. The "encircler tool" is used to draw circles of various sizes. (4,5)
___ 12. Sequential control is essentially the only control mechanism used in paint and chart systems. (1,5)
___ 13. Paint systems use embedded commands that cause the final hard copy of an image to differ from the screen image. (4,5)
___ 14. Generally, far fewer steps are required to paint a picture than to produce a chart. (1)
___ 15. To fill up the inside of a rectangle you would use the paintbrush tool. (4,5)
___ 16. Paint systems use icons to reference specific input modes. (1,5,10)
___ 17. To see a part of your picture not on your screen you can use the mover tool. (4,5)

___ 18. Input for chart systems is entered through one of the three shell types (command, menu, or graphic). (1,4)
___ 19. Neither paint nor chart systems can operate effectively without using system storage to store and retrieve images. (1,5)
___ 20. Before you can cut and paste in paint graphics you must use either the encloser or the encircler tools. (4,5)
___ 21. A scatter plot is a type of line graph. (2,10)
___ 22. Stored images from different files can be merged by graphic systems. (3)

B. Match the most appropriate system on the right with each of the characteristics listed on the left. (1)

___ 23. uses a mouse as the primary input device
___ 24. faster production of a graphic
___ 25. less accurate or precise
___ 26. used to produce bar graphs
___ 27. can produce arbitrary images
___ 28. usually has higher resolution
___ 29. uses the pencil tool

a. chart system
b. paint system

C. Give a short description of the function of the following:

30. undo

31. filler

32. clipboard

33. scatter plot

34. Y-Axis

35. legend

36. title

37. paintbrush

38. invert

39. X-Axis

D. *Match each of the descriptions on the left with the most appropriate type of graph from the column on the right. (2)*

___ 40. the most concise way of comparing data

    a. stacked bars
    b. line graph
    c. clustered bars

___ 41. used when the sum of the bars is a constant

    d. hidden bars

___ 42. groups of related bars

___ 43. places shorter bars in front of taller bars

___ 44. points are plotted

E. *Choose the one best mode on the right for performing each of the tasks on the left. (5)*

___ 45. delineates the area in which paint system processes can operate

    a. cut
    b. mover
    c. encircler
    d. set brush

___ 46. erases a portion of an image and saves it for later use

    e. copy
    f. erase picture

___ 47. fixes the width of a paint stroke

___ 48. adjusts the portion of a graphic page that is viewed on the screen

___ 49. can save but does not erase

F. *Below is a list of randomly ordered steps that could be used in the process of creating a graphic. Determine the most appropriate sequence for these steps, and place the letter of each step in order in the space provided. (6)*

_____ 50. What is the best sequence for the following steps?
a. go to show page mode
b. draw the desired image on the screen
c. determine the purpose of the graphic
d. refine the picture
e. augment the drawing with an image from the clipboard
f. go to pencil mode

Special Exercise: Completing the Frames for Paint Graphics and Chart Graphics Software

The paint graphics and chart graphics frames contain empty boxes where the user can write down the characteristics of his or her own computer systems. You are encouraged to fill in the frame for the particular system to which you have access so that the concepts of this chapter can be directly applied to your own hardware and software. The frame can also be used to compare different systems by filling in one frame for each system and contrasting the systems on a point-by-point basis.

Your primary source of information for completing this frame should be the documentation available with your software or hardware system.

As a computer user works on more and different systems, each of the boxes in this frame may require expansion into even more detailed descriptions. By then, however, the user will be sophisticated enough to make such expansions easily and without help.

Communications Software

Essential Chapter Concepts

When you finish this chapter, you should know:

- The hardware components required for communication between computers, including communications cards and modems.

- The characteristics of a communications line, including speed, data bits, stop bits, parity, duplex, mode, and handshaking.

- The characteristics of typical communications systems, including messaging, file transfer, file and print captures, and macros.

- The characteristics of network systems, including mail systems and conference systems.

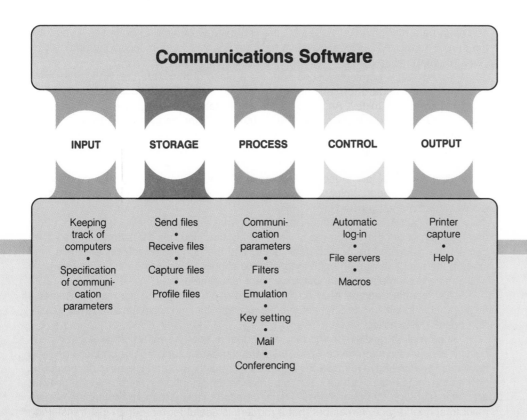

Communications Software

INPUT	STORAGE	PROCESS	CONTROL	OUTPUT
Keeping track of computers • Specification of communication parameters	Send files • Receive files • Capture files • Profile files	Communication parameters • Filters • Emulation • Key setting • Mail • Conferencing	Automatic log-in • File servers • Macros	Printer capture • Help

With the ever-growing use of computers throughout the world, communications software, which allows two computers to talk to each other, is becoming an increasingly important type of applications software. Communications between computers can vary in many ways and can include sending and receiving alphabetic characters, computer programs, data files, messages, pictures, and any other type of information that can be encoded on a computer. Like people, computers can "speak" different languages, and communicate at various speeds. Thus, for two computers to communicate, they must generally use a shared language at an agreed-upon speed.

In the following case study we will meet Anne, a computer science teacher, and Mike, an English teacher. They are working on a joint project to help the students in Mike's English class learn how to use word processors for their writing assignments. Their offices are in different buildings, and Mike has an Apple Macintosh, while Anne has an IBM PC. Anne is seated at her PC and is in the middle of a phone call to Mike.

10.1

Computer Communications

Case Study

"Mike, I just wrote that introduction for you on my IBM. Do you want me to print it out and bring it over with me when we get together?"

"Well, Anne," Mike replied, "I was hoping to be able to insert what you wrote into the rest of the course materials that I've generated. I'd really like to have all of the materials on one machine. Is there some way I can get my Apple to read your introduction and then put it with the rest of my course materials?"

"In theory we should be able to," said Anne, "but getting computers to talk together can often be a real pain. Let's see . . . the first thing we'll need to do is see if you have the proper hardware. Does your system have an RS–232C communications port?''

"A what?'' Mike asked, the puzzlement in his voice very obvious.

"An RS–232C communications port. It's a piece of hardware that works according to a published standard for sending and receiving data. We would need it to get your computer to talk to mine.'' Anne continued to explain, "The hardware is just a circuit board that knows how to take data from your computer and translate to and from a standard form. Just look at the back of your machine. Is there any unused plug that is long and skinny and has thirteen holes in one row and twelve holes in the row below that?''

"Just a minute, let me look,'' Mike replied. Anne could hear him moving his computer in the background. "Well, I think I have one. Does the plug look like a long rectangle with the top ends pushed in?''

"Yes,'' said Anne, "that could be it. That means we can probably get the data from one machine to another if you really want to. My machine has the same plug, so if we can set the machines up next to each other, find the right cable to connect them, and start up the right software on each machine, we should be able to do it. I hope you have a little more equipment, though, because there is a simpler way.''

"It's sounding complicated enough already—I'll sure go for something simpler. I might be able to talk the department into buying that 'little more equipment.' What exactly do I need?'' Mike asked.

Anne replied quickly, "A modem. A modem is another collection of electronic circuits; it translates data from the RS–232C data standard to and from a phone line. If you have one, we don't have to move the computers or anything. I can just have my computer go through my modem, call up your computer on the telephone, wait for you to answer, and then send the data right across. That's a better solution. If you try to get the department to spring for one, remember that a modem is useful for more than just transferring files. You can use it to access arbitrary computer systems that have dial-in telephone lines set up.''

"Whew,'' said Mike, "now it sounds more complicated to me. How many different kinds of translations are needed?''

"Well, Mike,'' Anne answered, "there are often three different types of signals needed for communication. The first type is the internal signals that your computer uses inside itself. The second type of signal is the kind that can be sent back and forth across this special kind of plug that works according to the RS–232C standards. The third kind of signal can go across telephone lines. With three varieties of electrical signals, there must be ways to translate from one type of signal to another. There is generally an electronic circuit board that translates between the computer's internal signals and the RS–232C connector. The modem translates from RS–232C to your phone and back.''

"I'll be happy to take your word for it,'' was Mike's reply. "I don't know if I can find a modem. Let me check around the office here, and I'll call you back in a few minutes.''

True to his word, Mike called back seven minutes later.

"I didn't have one,'' said Mike, "but I borrowed one from George. We're all set then, right?'' Mike was getting enthusiastic. The thought of having all the data on his Apple was exciting.

"Super,'' said Anne. "Now all we have to do is make sure you have the right software, too.''

"I think I'm all set there,'' said Mike. "George gave me a disk with a program called Comm-it. Is that okay?''

"Yep, Mike, we're in business. Let me set up my machine and I'll be right over. Then we can copy the data over and be done with it.'' Anne turned to her computer and inserted a disk in each drive. The disk in the first drive was labeled "communications software''; the one in the second drive was labeled "English intro.'' She started the software, entered a few commands, and left for Mike's office, leaving her computer on and running.

At Mike's office, Anne knocked and entered. In her typical no-nonsense style, she said, "Let's get going here. I have a class in a half hour. Where's your modem?''

Taking the small, boxlike modem from Mike, Anne reached to the back of the machine and connected the modem to the RS–232C plug on the back of the computer. Then she connected the modem to the phone line. It was a good thing George had given Mike the right plugs! As she sat down, she saw the communications software disk lying next to the machine, picked it up, inserted it in the disk drive, and booted the system up. Mike peered curiously over Anne's shoulder as the first screen appeared:

```
COMM-IT COMMUNICATIONS PROGRAM INTERFACE
Enter Command:_
```

"I might as well tell you what we're doing as we go along," said Anne. "Then we can do this anytime we want without having to leave our offices. First I had to take the modem and the plugs that George gave you and connect them all up. If they're the right plugs, it's pretty hard to do that wrong. When they're in place, we can send data from the computer to the phone line and back again."

"Then I just started up the software, and it's waiting for a command now. In general, the first set of commands you have to give any communications system specifies how messages will be sent across the communications line. There are four parameters that are almost universally needed: the speed, the number of data bits, the number of stop bits, and the type of parity. All of these things need to be set so that your computer on one end of the line knows how to talk to the computer at the other end."

"I'll take your word for it. It all sounds like gobbedygook to me," was Mike's reply.

"Well, it's really not hard." Anne was sympathetic. She had seen the trouble that beginning users have too many times. "The speed is just how many bits of data are sent per second. Normal rates across telephone lines are 300 bits per second, 1,200, or 2,400 but they can be much higher.

"The data that is sent across the line is just the on-off values that make up codes. For example, to send an *A* across the line using the ASCII code, a 01000001 is sent. You can generally ask for the full ASCII code with eight data bits, or you can reduce the variety of characters sent and only use seven data bits. If you don't need the full range of characters, the speed increases a little. The number of stop bits generally runs from 0 to 1 or 2. That tells how much of a buffer is between each character. Parity is just a special way to check on whether the data transmissions is okay."

Anne typed as she talked. She entered the command to set the speed:

```
COMM-IT COMMUNICATIONS PROGRAM INTERFACE
Enter Command: set speed =1200
```

She then proceeded to enter the rest of the commands:

```
Enter Command: set data=7
Enter Command: set step =1
Enter Command: set parity=off
```

"For us, I set the communication speed to 1200 bits per second. I had to use that speed because both this modem and the one in my office are set to run at that speed. We have to pick some speed that both machines can use, and of course, we pick the fastest speed common to both. The other parameters just have to be the same on both machines. Now that all of the parameters are set, it's time to make the call," Anne said.

"Okay. What number do I dial?" Mike asked. "Your office?"

"Yes," Anne replied, "but don't do it—the computer will do it."

"Wait a minute! How can a computer dial the telephone? It can't even lift up the receiver!" Mike couldn't believe it was possible.

"Oh, come on, Mike," was Anne's firm response. "I've gotten hold of your answering machine at home so many times, I can repeat your message by heart. You really should change that message! Anyway, you know perfectly well that your answering machine doesn't have to lift up the phone—it just has to be connected to your phone line. The electronic circuits that are built into the modem can connect to the phone line, too. Not only can they translate to and from the RS–232C plug and the phone line plug, but they also let me dial the phone right here at the keyboard. Watch."

Mike watched as she typed her office number at the computer keyboard. As she punched the numbers on the keyboard, he heard a dial tone come out of the modem. Then he heard the touch tones that dialed her office. The phone rang a couple times and was answered with a high-pitched whining sound that lasted for a moment and then disappeared. Communication between the two computers had been established!

"That's my computer answering my phone," Anne explained. "I have a similar kind of hardware and software set up as we have here, except that my computer is an IBM. Before I came over, I started up the software on my machine and set it to expect a call. Whenever two computers talk to each other, one is designated as the originator of the call and the other as the answerer. I set mine to answer, and yours is originating the call."

Anne turned away from the screen. "One of the problems with communications is a matter of control. We have two separate machines at two different sites and possibly a person at each machine. Who is supposed to get control and when? Can I give your machine a command to be executed or can your machine give mine a command? All of that has to be set up and defined through software. I set up my system to accept commands from the other computer, in this case, your computer. It can be dangerous to do that, because if somebody else called my computer while it's in that mode, they could erase my disks or do other damage. I wasn't too worried, though, since I was coming right over and the software requires my secret password."

"So," asked Mike, "what do we do now?"

"Well, first I need to know what you want to call the file on your computer that we will put my introduction into. How about 'English intro from Anne'?"

"No," said Mike, "just call it 'intro.' I don't type as fast as you do, so I like to keep things short."

"Okay." Anne entered another command at the keyboard.

```
COMM-IT COMMUNICATIONS PROGRAM INTERFACE
Enter Command: receive intro
```

"Now all I have to do is tell my machine to start sending the data." Anne gave the machine one more command.

```
COMM-IT COMMUNICATIONS PROGRAM INTERFACE
Enter Command: !send intro.for.Mike
```

"Anne," Mike asked, "why did you put an exclamation point in front of the send command but not in front of any of the other commands?"

"That's just the way that this particular piece of software works. Any command with an exclamation point in front of it is sent on to my computer as a command for it to perform. All other commands are assumed to be commands to your computer. I just gave my computer the command to send the data."

As Anne sat back, the screen of the computer came to life. Line after line of data that Mike had never seen before came zipping across his screen. The disk drive on Mike's computer would occasionally turn on for a moment. Mike and Anne sat discussing their future research plans for about 15 minutes until finally the computer beeped at them twice and the screen came to a rest. The screen looked like this:

```
COMM-IT COMMUNICATIONS PROGRAM INTERFACE
Transfer Summary:
     File name:          intro
     Bytes transferred:  108,524

Enter Command:_
```

"That's it," Anne said. "The file is transferred to your machine and is on your disk under the name 'intro.' I transferred it just as a text file, so you should be all set."

"Super, Anne!" Mike replied. "But I was wondering, as long as you have the connection, you know that great adventure game that you have on your machine? Could you transfer it over here so that I can run it on mine?"

"No, I can't, Mike." Anne chided Mike, "First, you know what I think about software piracy—I write software myself, and let me tell you, I think it's theft! I work long and hard to create a good system and don't think anybody should get it free!"

"But ignoring that, I couldn't do the transfer even if I wanted to. You can generally transfer information to and from computers only if the data is meaningful to each computer. Since I just transferred a written document stored in standard ASCII code between our machines, there was no problem. A program, however, does not contain ASCII characters but instead contains commands to the particular computer you are using, and let me assure you that the processor commands for an Apple and an IBM are so different that it would not be possible for one of them to run a program written for the other directly."

"Well, it was just a thought," Mike lamented.

"I'll tell you what," laughed Anne. "Let me connect you up to my bulletin board service and let you try some games there. That should give you more than enough relaxation for now!"

Anne gave the commands to hang up the phone line to her computer and then started up another call. She called off-campus to the telephone number of the computer network she subscribed to and gave her special identification codes so that her account would be charged for the computer access. Then she switched to the games section of the service and started up the help system. She stood up and started toward the door.

"Have fun playing," she said. "Just be sure to turn the computer off for a few moments when you are done so that the call is hung up. See you at our regular meeting tomorrow."

Mike just waved at her over his shoulder. He was already intrigued by an adventure game described on the screen. Someday, he really would have to do something about his addiction to these silly adventure games! Oh, well, that would have to wait until he rescued this princess from the evil wizard!

Communicating data and programs between different computers is generally a task of great complexity. A large number of hardware and software components on each of two or more separate computers must be compatible and all work together.

■ Communications Hardware

The first level at which two computer systems must be compatible is the hardware level. The communications process requires a transmitter of data, a communication line over which the data is transferred, and a receiver of data. Two-way communication must take place in two directions at once. A typical communications process is illustrated in Figure 10–1.

Figure 10–1 shows two personal computers (the transmitters and receiv-

10.2

Using Communications Software and Hardware

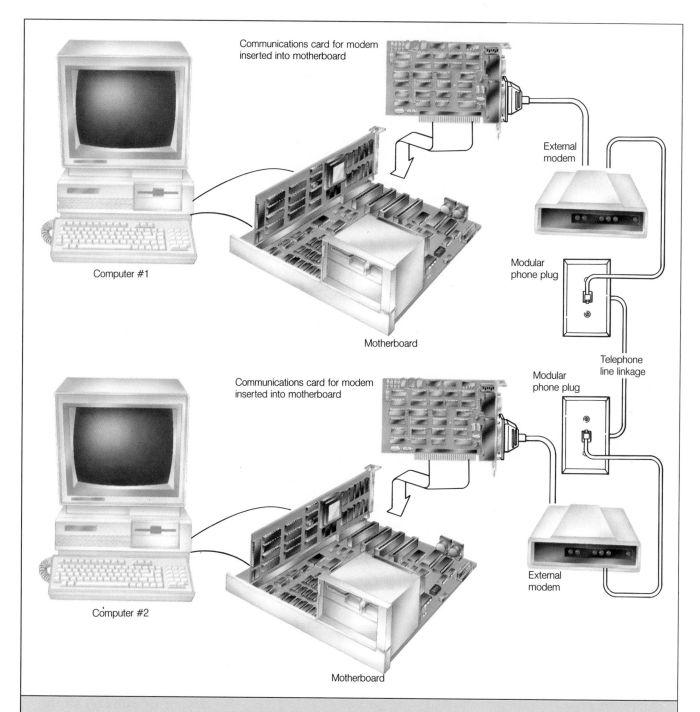

Figure 10–1   A Typical Communications Setup. Communication requires two computers. Each must possess the proper circuitry and software to allow the connection to take place. In this figure, two microcomputers are connected by a telephone line. Signals on one computer are sent into a communications card that converts them to a standard form. These signals enter a modem, where they are converted to an audible form that can be transmitted through telephone lines. When they arrive at their destination, the message coding is reversed. Although the figure shows two microcomputers, the same principle applies no matter how large or small the computer.

ers) and the three major types of communication hardware: communication cards, modems, and the telephone network communication line. These hardware devices are necessary to solve the two main problems of intercomputer communications: the signal standardization problem and the transmission distance problem.

The signal standardization problem is caused by the lack of hardware compatibility. Machines made by different computer manufacturers do not use the same types of electrical signals in the electronic circuits of their computer chips and motherboards. For example, the Apple Macintosh is built around a microprocessor chip from the Motorola 68000 family and uses different electrical signals from those of the IBM PS/2 Model 50 computer, which is based on the Intel 80286 microprocessor. Direct communication between these pieces of hardware that use different kinds of electrical signals is impossible.

The transmission distance problem concerns the problem of transmitting messages between computers over long distances. The electrical power inside most computer systems is not great enough to send any electrical signal over a very long distance. The voltage and current levels used inside the body of a computer are generally low and cannot be transmitted across wires for more than short distances. Thus even if one had two identical computers, the ability to transmit data from one computer to the other would be limited by distance.

Communications standards and communications cards provide the solution to the standard signals problem. The **communications card** is a **circuit board** that translates electrical signals from the motherboard and chip to and from a standard form that can be used across computers. Communications standards are agreements within the computing industry on a standard form for electrical signals between computers. Many different standards with names like RS–232C, RS328, and RS422, have been established. Each name stands for a written document that specifies what types of signals are to be used and how the signals will be used to communicate data.

These standards for communication differ in many ways. For example:

1. A standard may specify **parallel communication** or **serial communication.** In serial communication, only one bit of data is sent at a time and only one communication line is used. In parallel communication, many bits of data are sent at the same time, each down its own communication line.

2. A standard may specify a selection of **simplex, half-duplex,** or **full-duplex communication.** Simplex allows communication in one direction only; half-duplex allows communication in both directions, but only one direction at a time; full-duplex allows communication in both directions at the same time.

3. A standard may specify **asynchronous** or **synchronous communication.** Asynchronous communication can occur at any time and requires special start and stop signals surrounding the communication, while synchronous communication occurs at time intervals defined by a system clock.

Standards can differ in various other ways, but as long as they are well established, manufacturers across the electronics and communications industries can create communications hardware devices that can be linked with those of other hardware vendors to permit communication between computers and other devices such as printers.

Probably the best known standard is the one mentioned in the case

---

communications card
A special set of circuits that translates a computer's internal signals to an external standard (e.g., RS–232C), thus allowing a computer to communicate with peripheral devices or with other computer systems.

circuit board
A thin card, usually made of resinous or laminated material, containing an electrical circuit of etched copper; used in digital computers to perform various functions. Also called a circuit card. A communications card is a special type of circuit board.

parallel communication
Communication between two computing devices in which many bits of data are sent at the same time, each down its own communication line. *See also* serial communication.

serial communication
A standard for communication in which only one bit of data at a time can be sent down a single communication line. *See also* parallel communication.

simplex communication
Communication in which data is transmitted in only one direction.

half-duplex communication
Communication in which data can be transmitted in only one direction at a time.

full-duplex communication
Communication in which data is transmitted in both directions at the same time.

asynchronous communication
A standard for communications between two computing devices in which data can be sent at any time, but the characters must be coded so that the receiving computer is signaled when they are being sent and when the communication is completed.

synchronous communication
A standard for communication in which data transmission occurs at time intervals defined by a system clock.

study, the RS–232C standard (*R*ecommended *S*tandard number *232*, revision *C*, of the Electronic Industries Association, accepted in August, 1969, for the interface between data terminal equipment and data communication, equipment using serial, binary data interchange). The RS-232C standard describes how a particular kind of plug that can hold up to 25 wires (called a DB–25 plug) is to be connected for communication. Each wire used has a particular label, purpose, and voltage. An RS–232C connector is shown in Figure 10–2.

Once a communications standard such as the RS–232C is selected, computer manufacturers create a set of special circuits, usually called a communications card, that will translate from their own internal electrical signals to the external standard and back again. Since communication among computers is a communication of bits, the wires in the RS–232C connector that are used must have a value of zero or a value of one at any time. The translation process thus translates from the internal bit representation of the computer to the external bit representation of an RS–232C line. If an RS–232C connector is available in two different computers, then the only communications hardware required over short distances is to connect the back of one machine to the back of the other with the proper wires. Figure 10–3 shows how a direct connection can be set up between two computers using only a cable and a simple communication adapter called a null modem.

The transmission distance problem is usually solved by the use of modems attached to public telephone lines. The problem of communicating across distances can also be solved by another type of electronic circuit. For example, many computer users with extensive computer facilities create **repeater circuits** that allow them to directly connect many of their computer systems with standardized connections. At points in the communications line where the signal is becoming weak, they insert an electrical circuit that reads the weak signal, amplifies it, and sends it on its way using electrical power from an ordinary wall socket. While this system works for connecting different computers in one or more adjacent buildings (e.g., as in Local Area Networks), it would generally not be adequate for connecting computers that are hundreds of miles apart. In principle, the repeater circuits could be used, but the cost of laying cables for hundreds of miles is well beyond the financial capabilities of most users. Besides, there is already a large communications network that stretches throughout the entire nation to virtually every home and office: the telephone network.

Given the existence of the telephone network, the obvious method for communicating across long distances is to somehow use the telephone lines. To that end, another special circuit board was created, one that could translate

repeater circuits
Circuits that amplify signals that are weakened by distance as they are transmitted between computer systems connected by their own private transmission lines (as opposed to telephone lines).

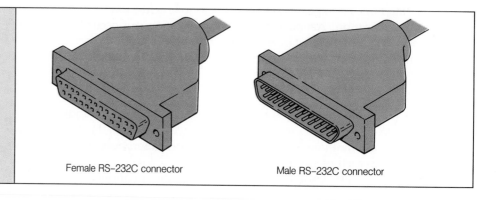

Figure 10–2 The RS–232C Connector. The standard RS–232C connection has 25 pins in a plug shaped like this one.

Female RS–232C connector   Male RS–232C connector

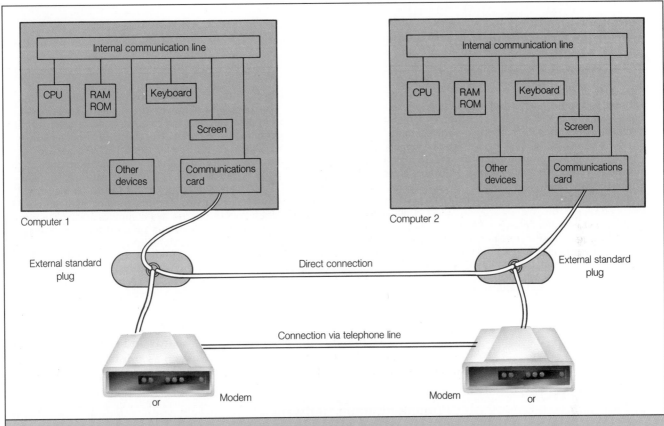

Figure 10–3   Pathways of Data Between Computers. Generally, two computers can be connected directly or connected by some other communications link. If connected directly, they must be close together for the computers to have enough power to send signals between them and have a cable called a null modem that interchanges some wires in the connections. Using another communications link (e.g., via modems) transfers this burden to the external communications system.

a standard signal like the RS–232C to and from an audio signal (a signal a person can hear) that could be carried over a telephone line. The technical name for this process is **modulation-demodulation.** The electrical signal is modulated and demodulated, and the circuit that performs this *mo*dulate-*de*modulate function is known as a **modem.** Since the modem circuitry goes back and forth between phone lines and a standard like RS–232C, the circuitry must clearly have two connections, one to a phone line and the other to an RS–232C plug on the computer.

In summary, with the existence of RS–232C connections and modems, the communications problem has largely been solved at the hardware level. For long distances, electrical signals in one computer are converted to RS–232C form, then converted to audio signals on a telephone line, sent across the telephone line to a second computer, translated back to RS–232C form, and finally translated to the electrical signals for the second computer. If the distance between the two machines is short, the modem link can be ignored and the two RS–232C connectors wired directly together. Figure 10–3 shows both of the two possible paths that data can take in its journey from one machine to an-

modulation-demodulation
The process of converting digital signals into analog signals and back again to permit computer systems to communicate via telephone lines. *Modem* is a contraction of the two terms.

modem
A device that connects a computer to a telephone line and through which two computers may communicate. A modem translates from the electronic signals of a computer to the auditory (acoustic) signals of a telephone line and vice versa. Modems require a standard signal usually provided by a communication card.

Computer Insights
A Popular Communications System: Kermit

The concepts described in this chapter are realized in many different software systems. Unfortunately, the types of communications links that are made between computers are so varied and the software so special-purpose that few standards have been developed. Even the exact timing of when a computer fetches an instruction to execute may affect the software. Hence, communications software is extremely hardware-dependent.

In this difficult software environment, the academic world has been one of the few sources of widely applicable software. The communications system named Kermit was developed in the academic community and has been written for virtually every combination of hardware and software systems commonly in use today. The IBM PC version of Kermit

cannot be run on the Apple Macintosh or the Digital Equipment VAX or the Tandy. However, these different versions of the Kermit system can be used to allow each of these computers to communicate together because all versions follow the same protocol in the use of the RS–232C standard for sending messages, data files, and commands. Whenever any two computer systems need to communicate, each of the two users can find a version of Kermit to run on his or her computer system. With two Kermits running and the connection complete between the two computer systems, either of the two versions of Kermit can be used to control interactive communication or noninteractive file transfer. Users of many different computer systems are thankful for this useful tool.

other. It may be noted that communication standards and cards are often used for communication with input-output devices such as printers, as well as with other computers.

■ Communications Software

Because the tasks performed by most communications systems are very limited, communications software is, by far, the easiest software to use of all the types described in this text. Essentially, there are only two communications tasks: sending messages back and forth between two computer systems and sending files back and forth between two computer systems.

Once the necessary hardware is correctly connected, the task of communicating is straightforward. The user must perform the following steps:

1. start up the communications software
2. specify the communications parameters
3. complete the connection between the computers
4. interact with the other computer system to transfer messages or files back and forth
5. terminate the communication link

Starting up communications software is no different from starting any other applications software system. Generally, a disk containing the communications program is inserted in the disk drive, and appropriate commands are given to begin the software execution (note that some communications cards or modems come with such programs built into a ROM chip in the hardware, thus making other software unnecessary). Once the software takes control, the user interacts with the computer through a shell, just as in any other system. The communications shell may be a command language shell, a menu shell, or a graphic shell. In any case, the user's next task is to specify a number of communications parameters.

Even after the hardware standards are set (e.g., the RS-232 standard and compatible hardware is properly connected, there are many minor variations in the way two computers communicate. These minor variations (i.e., parameters) must all be specified before the final connection can be made. The most important variations are discussed in the following paragraphs.

Speed. The communication of data, whether across standard plugs, communications boards, or across telephone lines, occurs at a given rate of speed that is generally specified in terms of the number of bits per second that can be transmitted. Very old systems were designed to transfer at 110 **baud** (110 bits per second); this slow speed was used because many of the computer printers were mechanical devices that printed slowly. Other limits on communication speed were originally based on the quality of telephone lines. Since telephone lines were not originally intended to carry data, the **noise** resulting from high-speed communications would often distort the messages, altering the data. This problem kept speeds low, and the available speeds on telephone lines were usually 110 or 300 baud. With advances in electronic hardware, current phone rates are more typically 1200 and 2400 baud and can reach 9600 baud. As telephone networks are upgraded with newer and more sophisticated transmission equipment, phone lines will be capable of handling higher and higher rates.

When computer equipment is connected directly, the transmission rate can increase dramatically. On typical RS–232C connectors, rates can easily be as high as 19,200 baud. With other standards for connectors, communication rates can even reach **megabits** per second (millions of bits per second). Other technologies such a satellites and **fiber optics** allow even greater speeds. The obvious prediction is that the speed and reliability of communications will continue to increase.

Data Bits. The ASCII table provides an important translation between computer bit patterns and human symbols. Because it is based on a byte of data (eight bits), there are 256 possible patterns, but usually only half of the possibilities are actually used. Even 128 bit patterns are more than enough for the frequently used human symbols (uppercase and lowercase letters, digits, and special symbols) and many computer symbols as well (control-A, . . . , control-Z, and so forth). Because 128 patterns are usually adequate, most systems allow the transmission of either seven or eight data bits per character.

If seven bits of data can be sent instead of eight, there is a savings of one eighth (12.5%) in the amount of data sent. Since this difference significantly increases the speed of transmission, users generally send only seven data bits instead of eight. The only time seven digits are not adequate is when the information being transferred is not an ASCII **text file**. For example, a program of instructions could be transferred between two identical machines; in this case, all eight bits would be needed for transmission, and the transfer rate would be slower.

Stop Bits. In asynchronous communication, in which signals are sent and received at arbitrary times, special signals called **start bits** and **stop bits** are used to indicate when a signal is coming and when the signal is finished. Recall that the communications line has a value of 0 or 1 on each of its wires. By convention, the line has a value of 1. (That is, when the line has a positive voltage, e.g., 5 volts, that is read as a 1-signal. When the voltage drops, e.g., 0 volts, that is read as a 0-signal.) When the data starts coming across, the line

baud
In data communication, a measure of the speed at which communication occurs. Typical rate for personal computers are 300, 1200, 2400 or 9600 baud (bits per second) across ordinary telephone lines and significantly higher across more controlled communication lines.

noise
Anything causing distortion or interference during communication.

megabit
Roughly equivalent to one million binary digits.

fiber optics
A technology in which glass fibers carry information using laser light at an extremely high rate of speed.

text file
A file that contains an unspecified sequence of text data (arbitrary characters, e.g., ASCII codes) that cannot be interpreted as a directly executable program by the operating system. ASCII text files are widely used for computer communications, e.g., between applications programs such as two different word processors.

start bit
In asynchronous communication, a bit that precedes the code of a character to indicate to the receiving computer that a character is about to be received.

stop bit
In asynchronous communication, a bit that follows the code for a character to indicate to the receiving computer that the character has been completed.

Computer Insights
Unauthorized Computer Access

With the advent of extensive data communications networks has come the modern equivalent of the western stagecoach robber: the hacker. Computer hackers are people who use telecommunications to obtain illegal access to computer resources.

Physical security is the most tamperproof method of guaranteeing the integrity of a computer operation. If access to a computer is limited to those who can physically enter the facility, then elaborate security procedures such as physical or electronic barriers, armed guards, and special identification badges can be used. Unauthorized persons trying to access a computer system would then have to get by all of these safeguards, and hacking would be possible only from the inside (by people already working for the institution that owns the computer system).

Once access to a system through telephones or other communications devices is permitted, security drops significantly. If a communications network is accessed through a public telephone number, security then depends on controlling who knows the telephone number, the account sign-ons, and the passwords. The problem with software security is that it depends heavily on the security consciousness of its owners and legitimate users. People whose accounts are illegally accessed often cooperate unknowingly by being careless and unimaginative about passwords. Using obvious passwords such as names, social security numbers, and famous dates is an invitation to hackers, as is using the same password over a long period of time. Determining passwords from a random list of characters and periodically switching from one password to another would probably defeat the majority of hackers.

To illustrate how a hacker works, let's imagine that a computer hacker, for whatever motivation, would like to help young widow Jones save her farm, which will be subject to foreclosure unless she can meet the $1,000 payment due by December 25. The hacker thinks he can solve this problem if he can gain access to the bank's records on the widow Jones, but how can he gain access?

To begin with, the Hacker's electronic bulletin board has already provided him with the telephone number of the computer system for the bank's loan department (it hasn't been changed in the last five years). The hacker uses his modem-equipped personal microcomputer to dial up and

connect. At this point the bank computer begins its interrogation. "Account No.?" Widow Jones has some helpful information. In her visits with the bank loan officer, Matthew James Braddock, Jr., she has noticed that he generally begins computer sessions by typing in 5891. Sure enough, that causes the computer to ask for the sign on.

Knowing that most people use their names for sign ons, the hacker tries several variations on the loan officer's name. When he tries MATT, it works. The next step, determining the password, is more difficult, since most people are more careful about passwords. The hacker tries various combinations of Matt's names, birthdate, and social security number (the latter obtained by the widow in polite conversation with Matt). The bank computer cooperates by providing multiple opportunities to try different combinations, without canceling access. Finally Mrs. Jones suggests that they may be overestimating Matt's intellectual capabilities and suggests they type in his initials, MJB. Sure enough, this gives access to the files. Since the bank computer loan system is user friendly and menu-driven, the hacker easily locates the widow's account. After a few minor changes, the monitor shows that not only does the widow not owe $1000 on her farm, but she has, in fact, overpaid the bank by $5000.

A security system can detect hacker activity by keeping data on sign-on attempts and counteracting it by rejecting a user after too many attempts on a single contact. It can also monitor changes in the amount of use (such as a significant increase), maintain a use log for each account, and request verifications periodically from the person in charge of the account. Any business, no matter how small, should have at least a part-time security officer to check over attempted accesses, account use charges, and new and old files. An occasional in-house test of security by someone using hackers' methods can also keep employees alert.

Society can control hacking by treating it seriously. Under British and United States law, hacking can be treated either as the relatively minor crime of petty larceny (stealing electronic service) or as the major crime of forgery (stealing by forging access passwords) or harmful access (destroying records, e.g., by means of a virus program). Britain has turned hard-line recently by prosecuting hackers as forgers while some states in the U. S. are prosecuting hackers for harmful access.

parity
A means of detecting errors during communication by adding an extra bit to each character sent and thus establishing an even number (for even parity) or odd number (for odd parity) of 1's in each character. If the receiving computer reads a number of 1's that differs from the parity, the transmission is suspect.

has a start bit of 0, which signals the receiving computer that a character is coming. After this start bit come the 7 or eight data bits, followed by one or two stop bits that have values of 1.

Parity. The purpose of **parity** is to aid in the detection of errors in transmission. Because of the possibility of distortion, noise, and other line problems, it is possible that any given 0 or 1 sent down the line could be incorrectly received. To provide some level of detection for such errors, a **parity bit** is added as an extra bit in each **character set.** Parity can be even, odd, or ignored. If the parity is even, then the parity bit is given a value so that the data bits plus the parity bit contain an even number of ones. If the parity is odd, then the parity bit is given a value so that the data bits plus the parity bit contain an odd number of ones. For example, imagine that the following single character is to be sent

parity bit
The extra bit added when using parity.

character set
A group of characters that is distinct and designed for a specific purpose, such as a group of characters that forms a message to be transmitted through a communications systems.

0 1 0 0 1 0 1 1

and that parity is even. This character has an even number of 1's (four). The parity bit that is added must keep the parity (the number of 1's) even, so the added (ninth) bit will be a 0:

0 1 0 0 1 0 1 1 0

This expanded character representation has an even number of ones. The error correction occurs as follows:

Character sent:	0 1 0 1 1 1 0 0
Parity:	odd
Parity bit:	1
Bits sent:	0 1 0 1 1 1 0 0 1
Bits received by second computer:	0 1 1 1 1 1 0 0 1
Error:	The third bit was switched from 0 to 1 by line noise.
Detection:	The number of one bits received was six, an even number, but parity was odd. Therefore, there was an error in transmission, so 'resend' is requested.

Table 10–1 gives some more examples of parity bits given a character to be sent and a particular parity. The parity bit, then, is just one method for checking the integrity of the data transmission. There are obvious limitations to this method. For example, if two bits are received incorrectly, the parity would remain correct and the error would not be detected. Suffice it to say that there is no error detection procedure that guarantees that there will be no errors, but parity and other error-detection methods can be used to keep the integrity of communications at a very acceptable level.

Duplex. There are essentially three kinds of communications lines: simplex, which can send data in one direction only (and are rarely used); half-duplex,

Table 10–1 Sending Parity Bits

Character to Send	Parity	Parity Bit	Bits Actually Sent
0 1 0 0 0 0 1 1	even	1	0 1 0 0 0 0 1 1 1
0 1 0 0 0 0 1 1	odd	0	0 1 0 0 0 0 1 1 0
0 1 1 1 1 1 0 1	even	0	0 1 1 1 1 1 0 1 0
0 1 1 1 1 1 0 1	odd	1	0 1 1 1 1 1 0 1 1

which can send data in either direction, but only one direction at a time; and full-duplex, which can send data in both directions at the same time. Today, most computer connections are made in full-duplex mode, but occasionally half-duplex is used.

The duplex is usually important only in determining whether characters sent from one computer to another are printed on the first computer's screen by the first computer or the second. Two simple problems can occur during communication with another computer: nothing the user types at the computer appears on his or her computer screen, or two copies of everything the user types appear on his or her screen. For example, if the user types the word *elephant*, the screen can sometimes show

```
(nothing)
```

or

```
eelleepphhaanntt
```

The first problem is probably caused by setting the computer to full-duplex when it should be set to half-duplex. In half-duplex operation, each computer is expected to print any characters it sends down the communication line onto the screen as well. If the computer doesn't do this, it looks like nothing that the user types is really being sent.

The second problem is usually caused by setting the computer to half-duplex when it should be set to full-duplex. In full-duplex communication, each computer assumes that the other computer will "echo" back each character it receives, and these echoed-back characters will be printed on the screen automatically. If the sending computer is also printing them on the screen itself, double characters will occur.

origin mode
In computer communications over telephone lines, a condition in which a computer can initiate a connection. *See also* answer mode.

answer mode
In computer communications across telephone lines, a condition in which a computer waits for the other to originate a connection. For two computers to send messages at the same time, two different pitches of sound are used, one for each computer. One computer must be in answer mode, identifying it as taking one of the two pitches. The other must be in originate mode, identifying it as taking the other pitch.

handshaking
A means of coordinating the timing of messages between different computers by using reserved characters passed back and forth to indicate whether or not a message may be sent.

Originate and Answer Mode.   Whenever two systems communicate, one system must initiate the connection and the other must be ready to respond when a communication request is encountered. These two modes are called the **originate mode** and the **answer mode.** Most computer users keep their computer in the originate mode so that they can choose the time and method of access to other computer systems. For any communication to occur, one computer must be in originate mode and one in answer mode.

Handshake.   When two computer systems communicate, it is possible for one system to be sending data down the communications line when the system that is supposed to receive it is busy doing something else (e.g., writing data on a disk) and cannot "listen." If this were to happen, the data being sent would be lost to the receiving system, and the receiving system might not even be aware that it had missed anything. To avoid this problem, most systems use a **handshaking** convention. Two separate characters in the ASCII table are set aside for this special use: one character means "I'm busy now, so don't send any messages to me," while the other means "I'm ready for any message you can send." The most common handshake is called the XOn/XOff handshake; the "I'm busy" character is usually a CONTROL-S, and the "I'm ready" character, CONTROL-Q. When both systems are set to utilize a handshaking method, the chances of errors in transmission are reduced.

When all of these parameters are set to appropriate values on *both* computers, the user must initiate the communication. If the computers are to be connected directly via their standard communications boards, initiation is often nothing more than connecting the machines with the appropriate cable and telling the software to begin communications. With telephone lines, the only extra step is that the telephone must be dialed to call from one computer to the other. Some old modems required the user to dial the number on the telephone itself, but virtually all modern modems possess dialing capabilities that can be referenced by software.

Once the connection is established between the two computers, two separate kinds of transfers can take place: an **interactive transfer** of messages and a **noninteractive transfer** of files. For example, suppose a user has called up a network service to play some type of computer game. The network computer actually controls the game, with the user's computer merely acting as an intelligent interface between the network computer and the user. If the network computer wants to send the user a message (e.g., "You win!" or "Game over."), that message must appear on the user's screen. Similarly, when the user specifies the next move in the game by typing at the keyboard, that move must be sent to the network computer. This communication is interactive, that is, neither the user nor the network computer can send lots of data at once, because each communication depends upon the immediately preceding one.

Contrast this type of interaction to the interaction in our case study. Mike did not want to look at the introduction typed by Anne while it was being transferred. In fact, there was no interaction going on at all. Once Anne had initiated the file transfer, they sat back and discussed future research plans without paying any attention to the data being sent from Anne's computer to Mike's. This type of transfer is noninteractive and clearly of different character than game playing interactions.

Once two computers are connected, the user can perform either or both types of communication for as long as he or she desires. Only when all messages and files have been transferred will the user close down the communications link either by giving a software command to do so or by physically turning off the machine.

interactive transfer
A transfer of messages between computers in which the response of each computer depends on the message. *See also* noninteractive transfer.

noninteractive transfer
In computer communications, a transfer of data between two computers in which no further input is required during the transfer process.

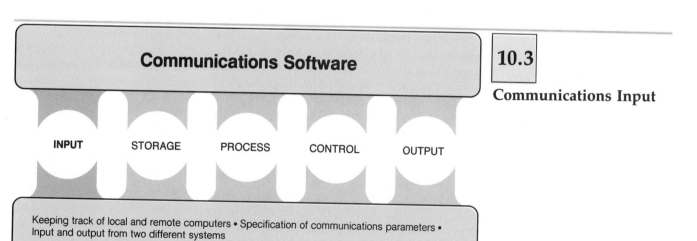

Communications Software

INPUT   STORAGE   PROCESS   CONTROL   OUTPUT

Keeping track of local and remote computers • Specification of communications parameters • Input and output from two different systems

10.3

Communications Input

The input to communications systems can be described relatively briefly because communications systems are primarily used to access many of the other kinds of software described in this text. For example, a communications system might be used to access an operating system, start up a data base management system, or access a spreadsheet. The primary complexity of communications systems lies in the fact that the user can control more than one computer at a time, and thus the software system must be able to distinguish between input to be given to one computer system and input to be given to another computer system. We must also consider an interesting question that arises from the use of communications systems: if two computers are connected, is the output generated by the second computer really output, or is it just input to the first computer?

Keeping Track of Computers

The user of a communicating computer has only one input keyboard and one output screen but has potentially more than one computer that needs input or generates output. The user keeps track of which computer is getting input and which computer is generating output through **modes of operation** much like the modes described in many of the other applications software systems. There are three modes of operation in communications software: **local mode, remote mode,** and **file transfer mode.** In the local mode, any input is directed to the local computer and any output is generated by the local computer. In remote mode, the input is directed to the distant computer and the output is generated by the distant computer to which the user has connected. In file transfer mode, the two computers work together to transfer data from one machine to the other without displaying the data directly to the user.

In many communications systems, standard messages printed by the software identify which mode is in operation. Since either the user's local system or the remote system can generate any kind of display on the user's screen, there is generally no continuous indication of which computer is in charge. Instead, whenever the mode is switched, a special onetime message appears on the screen, so it is up to the user to keep track of which system is responding. Although this may sound like a less-than-ideal solution, the operating characteristics of the local and the remote system are frequently distinct enough that it is easy for the user to tell which system is which just by watching what is being done.

When communications software starts up, the system is normally in local mode, that is, the local computer is ready to read and perform commands typed in at the keyboard. Thus the system is ready to establish the communication parameters specified in the user's initial interaction. Figure 10–4 is an example of how parameters might be set in a graphics shell; a communications system can have any of the three kinds of shells.

Once the parameters are set, the user issues the appropriate commands to connect the local computer to the remote computer. This action automatically puts the system in remote mode, in which the user interacts with the remote computer, with the local computer serving merely as a conduit through which messages flow. The user then has many possible courses of action. One is to just remain in remote mode and interact with the remote computer. Another possibility is to press the command key that switches the machine to local mode to process any local commands desired. The user's remaining option is to issue a remote command and a related local command to cause the

modes of operation
In general, distinct and conceptually different manners in which one piece of software can operate. Different modes are usually characterized by different screen displays and different ISPCO commands. Example are the text entry and command modes used in word processing software. In communications software, local, remote, and file transfer modes are used for different purposes and act in different ways.

local mode
In communications software, a mode of operation in which input and output are associated with the user's local computer.

remote mode
In communications software, a mode of operation in which the input and output are associated with the remote computer to which the user has connected.

file transfer mode
In communications software, a mode of operation in which the local and remote computer systems work together to transfer data from a file on one machine to a file on the other without displaying the data directly to the user.

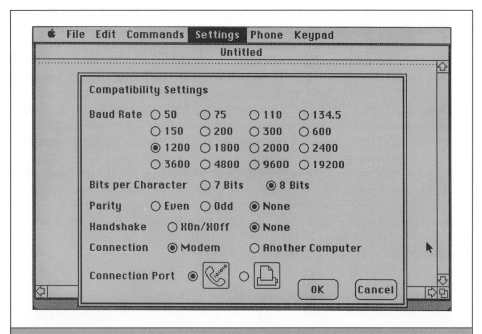

Figure 10–4 Setting Communication Parameters. In this example of a graphic shell for a communications system, the user can set the speed of communication (50–19,200 baud), the number of bits required for each character, the use of parity for checking transmitted characters, handshaking (a way for the computers to tell if the receiving computer is momentarily busy and unable to accept more data), and whether the connection is through a modem or a direction connection. Setting the connection port simply specifies which of the serial ports on the back of the machine will be used for communication. All settings are made by moving a mouse so that an arrow is inside a button. When all parameters are set, the OK button is clicked.

remote computer to send a file of data to the local computer or to cause the local computer to send a file of data to the remote computer. When all processing is complete, the user is responsible for terminating interaction with the remote computer, terminating the communication link, and then shutting down the local computer.

▪ The Difference Between Input and Output

As mentioned earlier, it may seem like a difficult task to determine what is input and what is output when dealing with multiple computer systems simultaneously. The ISPCO definitions provide the most useful solution.

Input was originally defined as information that was being transferred from outside the computer system to inside the computer system. In terms of the user's local computer system, is the data being received from the remote computer input or output? Clearly, it is input to the user's local computer. It is coming from a device, not the keyboard, it is true, but a device that is external to the user's computer.

The data coming from the remote computer to the user's local computer must also be considered input to the local computer because the local computer has total control over what happens to it. The communications software can cause all messages from the remote computer to be displayed on the user's screen, or it can send all messages to a disk file and show nothing on the screen. In fact, communications software also provides a way to totally ignore any messages from the remote computer. Thus, the user's computer is in control of input it receives, whether from the keyboard or from a communication line.

Remember, though, that the remote computer is also processing and controlling itself. Just as the user's local computer decides what to do with messages it receives, the remote computer has the same options. For example, the remote computer might keep a record of the entire interaction it has with everyone who calls, or it might ignore all messages from the local user and permit no use of its resources. The most instructive model for computer communication is human communication: two people may communicate freely, record conversations, ignore each other, tell other people about what is said in the conversation, and so forth. In theory, all of these possibilities exist in the communication between two computers.

10.4

Communications Storage

Communications Software

| INPUT | **STORAGE** | PROCESS | CONTROL | OUTPUT |

Send files • Receive files • Capture files • Profile files

Like all types of applications software systems, communications software sits atop the operating system. Therefore, any requests for storage functions made through the communications system will almost inevitably be transferred to the underlying operating system routines for processing. Thus it is clear that virtually all the storage functions of the operating system are available in communications software packages. Tasks like getting the directory of a disk, initializing a disk, copying files, and so on, are frequently available, but they are not of primary concern. The important interactions between system storage and communications software are in four communication-specific storage tasks: sending data files to remote systems, receiving files from remote systems, capturing an interaction between a local and a remote system, and saving and loading **profiles** of the communication process.

Sending Files. Sending files from the local system to the remote system is a relatively straightforward task. The user must first inform the remote system that a file with a particular name is coming, then he or she switches back to local mode and tells the local computer the name of the file whose contents is to be sent.

Receiving Files.   File transfer in the other direction is just as simple. First, in local mode, the user tells the local system that a file with a given name will be transmitted from the remote computer. Then the user tells the remote computer the name of the file to be transferred.

Whatever the direction of the data transfer, the two computers continue sending and receiving the file contents, generally ignoring other uses of the communication line, until the entire contents of the file has been sent. At this point the software systems use some compatible way to indicate that the transfer is complete.

An additional concern in file transfer is the method by which the file contents are sent (called the *protocol* for file transfer). Whenever possible and especially when files containing programs are being transferred, the user should try to use special error-checking protocols. One popular file transfer protocol is the XModem protocol created by Ward Christensen. It sends a file across the communications line in separate "blocks" and encloses each block with data for double-checking the accuracy of transmission. If all of the double checks in each block indicate accurate transfer, the probability of correct transfer is quite high. File serving is another type of file transfer which is discussed in the section on control.

capture
During communications, the process of recording to a file and/or printer the exact sequence of messages that flows back and forth between the local and the remote computers.

Capture.   At times a user may want to record the exact sequence of messages that flows back and forth between the remote and the local computer. This process is clearly not a file transfer, since neither system contains a file from which data is sent. However, communications systems allow a user to **capture** everything that appears on the user's screen during the interaction into a disk file. For example, a user may wish to list out the most recent Dow-Jones averages on the screen and also retain them to review later. To do this, the communications system provides a pair of commands that turn the recording of the interaction on and off. When the recording is turned on, the user must specify the name of the disk file into which the recorded data will be placed. When recording is turned off, the system terminates the capture and performs any appropriate end-of-file processing.

profiles
A specific configuration of parameters commonly used by a particular user and saved for easy reference. For example, communications parameters can be saved into a file and called up as needed, thus sparing the user from having to re-enter the parameters one at a time each time a connection is made.

Profiles.   Most users communicate with a particular set of computer systems that does not change frequently. As long as the same communications links are used, most of the communications parameters (speed, data bits, and so on) do not change. To relieve the user from having to re-enter such information every time a linkup is made, most communications systems can save a specific configuration of communications parameters into a file called a profile. The profile can then be called up every time a connection is made, thus removing the need to continually re-enter parameters.

Communications systems generally provide only a minimal number of processes because the primary process—communication—has few variations. A number of processes are universal to virtually every communications software package, but some generally exist only on large systems that serve as centers for computerized conferences, data bases, and large information sources.

10.5

Communications Processes

■ Universal Processes

The first set of processes available in virtually all communications systems deals with setting the parameters described in the previous section. Commu-

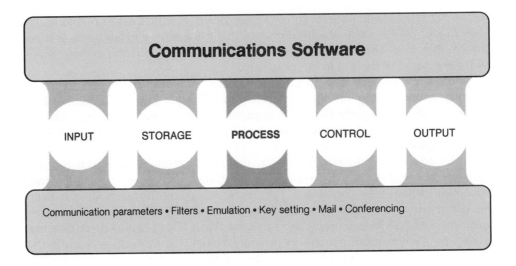

Communications Software

INPUT   STORAGE   **PROCESS**   CONTROL   OUTPUT

Communication parameters • Filters • Emulation • Key setting • Mail • Conferencing

nications software must set the speed of communication, the number of data bits, the number of stop bits, the parity, the mode, and handshaking. In addition to these parameters, which deal with the physical use of the communications line, another set of processes specifies how the local computer operates in the communications process.

Port.   With the ever-increasing power of computer hardware, it is common for a computer to have more than one **communications** card. The user must then have some means of specifying which communications card is to be accessed by the software. To accomplish this, each card in the system is assigned a logical name referred to as its **communications port,** which also identifies which plug on the back of the computer is to be used to connect a cable to the communications card. It is possible for a system to have more than one communications link active at the same time and switch between the two by changing which communications port the software is using.

communication port
The logical device name used by software to identify a communications card which is built-in or attached via an expansion slot to the motherboard. The port identifies the plug on the back of the machine to which the card is attached.

Filters.   Once the data is traveling as it should from one computer system to another, other questions remain concerning the representation of the data once it reaches the receiving computer. For example, should a carriage return character (usually a Control-M) be inserted at the end of each line as the data is sent? If a carriage return character is received, should it be removed? Should it be appended to a line-feed character? Because these issues are often of concern, many communications systems provide filters that take in a line of data and send it out with slight modifications. Thus the various "lines of data" produced by different computers can be accommodated. There are many such variations across computer systems; they involve the differences in how computer systems store data in files, not how the data is communicated.

Emulation.   There are many popular computer terminals in the business world. These terminals may or may not be intelligent and are generally connected to large mainframe computers. The manner in which these terminals interact with the mainframe is generally built into the terminal and is not subject to much change. To accommodate people and computer systems that are used to a particular kind of computer terminal, many communications programs have modes that allow them to emulate (mimic) the behavior of commonly used computer terminals. **Emulation** alleviates the need for retraining users and alterating system software; the local computer modifies its own behavior to behave like a particular computer terminal.

Key Settings. Just as there is a need for emulation, a user may wish to control which keyboard command keys are used to switch from the local computer to the remote computer and back again, send an interrupt to a computer, or perform other functions. Many communications systems allow the user to define which keyboard keys access which functions.

Connections. The connection between computers is generally made in one of three ways. If the computers are to be connected directly by an RS–232C connector, the only thing that the user must do is activate the circuits that control the connection, usually by issuing a command like GO or CONNECT. However, if a telephone link is to be used, there must be some method for dialing the appropriate telephone number. The user will generally be given one or two methods for dialing numbers. The simplest method is to enter a command like DIAL and then type the telephone number at the local keyboard. When the carriage return is pressed, the computer will connect to the phone line and dial the number. A nicer method, available on some systems, is to enter the name of the person, computer, or network that one wishes to access. Such systems maintain a data base that associates telephone numbers with names and given just the name, can look up the number and then do the dialing.

■ Conferencing and Electronic Mail Processes

In addition to all of the commonly available processes described above, there are many software systems through which a user can run a network or **bulletin board service** from an arbitrary computer. Anyone who wishes to perform such an activity clearly has many concerns beyond those of the ordinary computer communicator. For example, allowing more than one user to access the system at the same time requires many communication ports, a method for the different concurrent users to share access to system files, and so on. Although full coverage of these topics is beyond what the authors feel is important in this text, a few of the important capabilities of such systems are described below.

Mail. Computer networks have begun to serve as a new kind of **electronic mail** service. In such networks, each user is given a special file on the system disk to serve as his or her **mailbox.** This mailbox is accessible for input from other users through a mail program but is totally private to everyone otherwise. (The system is analogous to the postal service: anyone can send mail to an individual's home via the postal service, but people are not allowed to deliver mail to an individual's mailbox otherwise.) The nice part about electronic mail service is that the user need not be logged into the computer system for mail to be sent. Any mail that comes while the user is away from the computer is just saved in the appropriate computerized mailbox until the user checks the box. There are obvious concerns about privacy: can users read mail not addressed to them? Can users be assured that even the owner of the hardware system cannot invade their mailboxes? Such concerns are quite legitimate and are mirrored in the postal service (did the mail carrier really deliver all my mail?). In principle, there is always the possibility of privacy violations, but if

emulation
The imitation of one computer system by another. The system performing the imitation must be capable of accepting the same data and programs and achieving the same results as the original system.

bulletin board service
An on-line computing service that can be accessed by a personal computer with communications software. Bulletin board services generally provide means for posting notices, responding to notices, and sending and receiving mail.

electronic mail
Communications or operating system software that enables users of multi-user systems to send messages to other users on the system.

mailboxes
Special disk files that are assigned to individual members of a computer network and to which other members may send messages.

they occur frequently, the mail service as a whole will not last long. Whatever problems exist with computerized mail systems, they are used extensively in many business, industrial, and academic settings with mainframe computing resources.

conferencing
An extension of electronic mail services in which participants interact usually with one person establishing the purpose and rules of the interaction.

Conferencing. **Computer conferencing** is in some ways an extension of mail services. A conference is essentially a focused set of discussions on particular topics. A conference has an organizer who is responsible for setting the purpose and tone of the conference, checking the items submitted for discussion, and so on. Aside from the organizer, the conference also has participants who can do many things: post a message item for public review and comment, react to public messages posted by others with either a public response or a private message, or just watch the interactions among other conference participants.

Conferences can be a lot of work for the participants because they seem to inevitably expand past their original focus into the world of computing or

Computer Insights
On-Line With the Information Revolution

The information revolution is the view that the western world is moving from a predominantly industrial society into what is popularly called the Information Society. John Naisbitt in his book *Megatrends* (Warner Books, 1984) states the principle this way: "The new source of power is not money in the hands of a few, but information in the hands of many."

Perhaps as a response to the need, the ordinary person's access to useful and usable information is increasing in an almost geometric rate, facilitated by information utilities. Information utilities are companies that sell time on time-shared mainframe computers with windows to a wide range of information services. Commercially, they have been available since 1972. Examples of major information-vending services are Compuserve, the Source, Bibliographical Research Service (BRS), DIALOG, and the Dow Jones News Retrieval Service. Each of these vendors has a large number of different data bases available for their customers. DIALOG, for example, has over two hundred data bases. By subscribing to an information utility, users have access through a modem to all of the data bases provided by the vendor. The subscriber's costs for on-line time vary from $6 to over $100 per hour.

The offerings of these vendors are extensive. BRS, for example, includes among its over one hundred databases: MEDLINE (covering all aspects of biomedicine and the health sciences), PsycINFO, Catalyst Resources for Women, SSCI (social sciences information), ERIC (information for educators), DISS (dissertation abstracts on-line), HBRO (Harvard Business Review on-line service to business and management), AAED (multi-disciplinary encyclopedia), PETE (profiles of national colleges and universities), SOFT (microcomputer software directory), IVDA (investment information), BANK (editorial content of American Banker daily newspaper), and many, many more.

Data bases like these exist for all major professions and are proliferating almost daily. There are now well over a thousand data bases. Electronic data bases, in contrast to other information storage and retrieval systems, have two unique features. First, subscribers can query the data bases from literally anywhere, as long as they have a computer and a modem attached to a telephone line. Secondly, the methods for searching the data bases are very powerful. For example, suppose an engineer wants to know the stress effects for carbon steel in a suspension bridge in arctic temperatures. Instead of getting a list of all documents in the data base dealing with bridges, he or she can enter the four search terms *bridge, suspension, carbon steel,* and *arctic* and get a list of documents dealing with the combination of those four specific terms. If desired, the search can also be limited to documents from a particular period of time.

Beyond professional databases are a whole plethora of information services including tax assistance, record keeping, selected daily news, travel information, electronic shopping, games, bulletin board services, videotext, electronic mail, computer conferencing, electronic funds transfer, courses, biorhythms, jobs available, and information on college financial aid, to name just a few.

We are approaching the moment when we can have in our homes access to information far superior to that found in the old style public libraries, with our own automated reference librarian built into the system. It is not yet clear what the social consequences of such utilities will be. Examples of issues as yet unresolved include effects on privacy, copyright, computer crime, reduced social interaction, and life style. Whatever the consequences, electronic information services are changing the shape of our society and the way its members spend their lives.

life in general. Sifting through the masses of items and responses for those that are reasonable and useful can be quite time-consuming. A good conference organizer can help rein in superfluous public items and keep the conference on track.

Connections within Connections. No computer network reaches everyone, but almost everyone can be reached by some computer network. Many networks allow a user to access one computer for the express purpose of attaching to another computer. It is not uncommon for sophisticated computer users to go through three or four networks before they arrive at their final destination. For example, a user in California could reference the CAD/CAM system at Oakland University's School of Engineering and Computer Science in Michigan by first accessing **TELENET,** from TELENET accessing the Merit Network, from the Merit Network accessing Oakland University's local area network, and from that local area network accessing the Prime Computer System. Although relatively straightforward, such electronic journeys can become expensive, as a user is charged for the time used on *each* computer system.

TELENET
A widely used national network of computers with access to many data base and computer services.

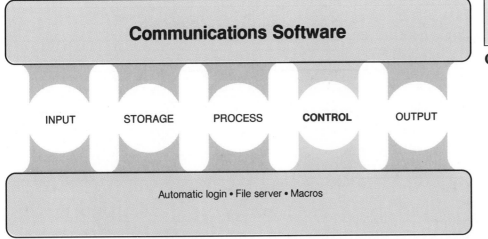

10.6

Communications Control

There are relatively few control structures in communications systems at this time, probably because the range of activities performed by communications systems is still relatively small.

Automatic Login. Frequent users of network services generally choose communications systems that contain automatic login procedures. Logging into a network service requires the user to dial a number, wait until a connection is made, and enter identification data like a user ID and a password. Computers are ideal for this repetitive task, so some communications systems provide an automatic login method in which the user can specify the login steps in a file and then command the system to perform them in order. One nice feature of this process is that such software systems generally allow automatic redialing of the same telephone number if a busy signal is encountered.

File Server. If a user wishes to transfer a number of files, many systems offer a method for controlling the transfer of multiple files in the user's absence.

Such systems offer some type of file server mode in which the user can create a file containing a list of file names. On appropriate command, the system then begins the transfer of the named files from one system to the other. As soon as one file is transferred, the system goes to the next file name in the list and begins to transfer it, too.

Macros. As the most general extension of the other control mechanisms found in communications systems, macros provide the user with a simple way of storing and later executing sequences of actions. A macro is essentially an abbreviation for a set of commands. For example, one might create a macro called "dow-jones-news." Whenever this macro is invoked, all of the standard steps that make up the communications process are performed automatically, including waiting until the middle of the night when rates are cheap, dialing the network service, entering an ID and a password, transferring files that have standard names and contain daily stock market data, and logging out. Macros enable the user to perform extremely complex sequences of activities with only a few keystrokes.

10.7
Communications Output

Communications Software

| INPUT | STORAGE | PROCESS | CONTROL | OUTPUT |

Printer capture • Help

There remains little to be said about the output of communications software. Since one of the main purposes of communications software is to allow the transfer of messages to and from another computer, the output that is sent from the local computer to the remote computer is of critical importance, as is the corresponding transfer of data in the other direction. These operations, however, have already been covered in sufficient detail, so that only two output functions remain to be described: the capture of an interaction on a printer and help systems.

Printer Capture. Just as a communications interaction can be captured in a file, most communications systems provide some means by which everything that appears on the user's screen can be printed on an attached paper printer. Such a print capture is not concerned with whether the screen data was put there by the local computer or by the remote computer—whatever its origin, the data that is shown on the screen also appears on the printer. Many users of communications software use printer capture routinely so that nothing that transpires disappears from the computer screen and is lost—it is all recorded on the printer.

Help. Like any complicated software system, communications systems can provide a variety of help levels for experienced or novice users. Everyone forgets something sometime, and the existence of on-line reminders can be very useful.

In our final case study, Mike has taken a major step by connecting his home computer to a communications service. He has connected a modem to his computer and purchased a software communications system. Then he bought a subscription to the service, Information-On-Line.

10.8

A Final Communications Example
Case Study

Mike opened up the package from the software store. His "subscription" to Information-On-Line looked more like a book than anything else. He opened the book and started reading. It told about the concepts behind on-line services, the hardware and software that he would need, the services available, and so on. Two pages of the book were glued together and labeled, "Secret ID and password enclosed: If opened, product cannot be returned." He ripped it open and saw a page that looked like this:

```
Signup User ID Number:   100431,304
Signup Password:         LAKE*RABBIT
AGREEMENT TYPE:          CM4432KRDSDK4
SERIAL NUMBER:           143323
```

He knew what an ID and password were. He wasn't sure what the other items were for. He saw a section in the book entitled "Getting Started" and flipped to it. It contained a list of telephone numbers all over the world! Scanning through the list, he found a number for his metropolitan area. "Well, here goes nothing!" he thought.

He started up his hardware and the software communications program. His manual said that the telephone lines were set up as "seven-bit ASCII even parity or eight-bit ASCII no parity, one stop bit, full duplex, 300 or 1200 baud (1200 with higher costs)."

"Ah, yes," he remembered, "nothing in life is free! Well, let's set those options." Quickly typing, Mike set up his communications software in the prescribed way and issued the command to have his computer dial the telephone. "Hey, everybody!" he yelled to his wife and children, "Don't use the phone! I've got the computer connected to it!"

Within a few minutes, his computer was successfully connected to the remote computer and he was staring at a request for a sign-on ID. He entered the code number. The remote computer asked for a password, and he gave it. Then, before he could do anything else, he found himself having to answer a whole slew of questions. What were his name, address, and telephone number? What kind of computer was he calling from? What were the characteristics of the software he was using? Did he wish to pay by check or have his Mastercard or Visa billed? He chose Visa, since there would be a minimum monthly charge if he paid by check but there would be none with Visa. He typed in his Visa number and the expiration date with intrepidation. He did not like giving a strange computer the ability to charge his credit card account!

Once all of the questions were answered and his responses verified, the system gave Mike a new code number for his ID and a new password. "Well, I guess that's just being safe," he thought.

Now Mike was ready to explore. A menu of options appeared on the screen. The system seemed pretty easy to use: just read a menu and choose an option. The initial menu looked like this:

```
Information-On-Line

   1. Bulletin Boards
   2. News/Weather/Sports
   3. Electronic Mail
   4. Electronic Shopping
   5. Entertainment and Games
   6. Health
   7. Travel
   8. Business and Money Matters
   9. Data Bases for Reference
  10. Conferences
  11. Finding What You Want
  12. Subscriber Assistance

Enter number corresponding to choice:_
```

Mike really didn't know what he wanted to do. "Oh well, why not the news," he said to himself. He pressed a 2. The screen immediately changed to another menu.

```
News/Weather/Sports

   1. World
   2. Local
   3. Sports
   4. Weather
   5. Business
   6. AP Wire Service
   7. Hollywood
   8. Rock & Roll

Enter number corresponding to choice or M:_
```

He pressed a 4 to get weather. The screen changed to another menu.

```
Public Weather Information

1 Local forecasts        2 State Forecasts
3 Extended Forecasts     4 Weather Warnings
5 Marine Forecasts       6 Precipitation
7 What's New             8 Help

Enter number corresponding to choice or M:_
```

Mike decided to see what the local forecast was, so he typed a 1 and received a request for the city name:

```
Enter city name:_
```

He typed in "Detroit," and the system responded with:

```
Detroit Metropolitan Area Forecast
National Weather Service, Detroit, MI

Today:    Sunny, High upper 50s, light northeast winds.
Tonight:  Clear, Low near 30, light variable winds.
Tomorrow: Sunny, High upper 50s.

Enter city name:_
```

After checking a few more cities, Mike decided to leave the local forecasting, but he wasn't sure how to do that! He pressed the return key. . . . "Whew, it got me out and back to the main weather menu. But how do I get out of here?" The prompt suggested typing an M, so he did. He was immediately returned to the next higher level, the one on news, weather and sports. He typed an M again and returned to the original main menu where the whole session had started. "How many menus deep was I, anyway?" he asked himself.

Two hours passed without Mike noticing it. He had been exploring and enjoying his newfound friend, that Information-On-Line computer! Here are just some of the things that he did:

- *Entered a new car showroom in the electronic shopping mall.* There Mike scanned through all the cars offered by the various manufacturers, looked at the details of one particular car, priced it, and directly compared two different cars at the same time. Unfortunately, it cost ninety cents to ask for the price of a new car! Mike had been right—nothing is free.
- *Scanned through the inventory of a sporting goods store in the electronic shopping mall.* Mike checked to see what price he could get on a new down sleeping bag.
- *Joined a conference (bulletin board) on the use of Apple Macintosh computers.* Mike knew that this service would be useful. The conference consisted of notes and comments placed into files so that anyone could read them and respond to them. Even he could enter a new note. Mike realized that if he ever had a question about his hardware or software, he could post a message and wait for someone to give him an answer. The bulletin board also included programs that he could copy onto his own computer and use. There were lots of other conferences available. Mike planned to check into them later.
- *Made plane reservations for his family to visit Disney World.* Mike's family was planning to take the trip at the end of the next month, and Mike discovered that he could access the airlines' computers himself. When he told the on-line service to make a plane reservation, a message that said connection made appeared. Evidently the remote computer connected to his computer had actually called a third computer to process his request. Unfortunately, he was charged extra as he browsed the listings!
- *Checked the current Dow Jones Average using the business data bases.* Although Mike was not yet involved in the stock market, he was thinking of starting a self-directed IRA. He had actually been able to watch the running ticker tape that he had always seen in the movies.
- *Performed a short literature search on computer uses in the teaching of English.* This service cost more money, but having the computer search through journals was a lot faster than doing it himself! Now he had a list of five recent articles that looked like what he wanted.
- *Sent electronic mail to Anne.* Since she was the one who had introduced him to on-line systems, he couldn't resist telling her, so he composed a message and sent it to her. Evidently the computer would keep the message on disk storage somewhere until she read it.
- *Started participating in an adventure game.* The game that Mike had tried in Anne's office had been so much fun, he couldn't forget it, so he had started an adventure already. This one was supposedly the original classic adventure with an underground cave to be explored. He had successfully mapped out the route to enter the underground cave, but he knew there would be much more to do!

After all of this fun and time, Mike was ready to leave the system. As he logged out, the computer printed out a message saying that he had been charged $14.55. "Hmmmm," he thought, "the charges are less late at night and on weekends. Maybe I'll have to do more of my on-line work then. On the other hand, I've already got a phone bill, an electric bill, a gas bill, and who-knows-what-other-kind-of bill. I should probably just get used to another bill each month, an *information utility* bill."

Mike turned the machine off and sat down to read the book that came with the subscription. Now that he had tried the system, the book would probably make a lot more sense to him.

As Mike has discovered, on-line services have many uses. One cannot yet pretend that they are indispensable, but as the use of computing increases and more and more people have business and personal computers available, the number of consumers using an information utility will increase, and this increase will spur competition and further improve the services available to the user.

10.9

Summary of Communications Software Usage

Communications systems are the easiest to use of all the systems described in this text because in a way, they do the least. Communications systems do only one thing—connect one computer to another—and the connection process is actually much simpler than the many coordination tasks that must be performed to make the communication meaningful. For example, as Mike worked with his on-line service, all his communications software did was send the messages that Mike typed to the service's computer and print messages that the service's computer sent Mike onto the screen. The complicated part of managing the on-line service was performed by a totally separate software system on the service's computer.

■ The ISPCO Frame for Communications Software

Despite their simplicity, the functions of communications systems can be described, as usual, by ISPCO frames. Following is the frame for communications systems.

Frame for Communications Software

	Concept	Your System
ON/OFF [ON/OFF]	COMPUTER #1 ACCESS: Access to communications package and computer is needed, including location, sign ons, disks, commands, and so on. For this system:	Location and disks needed: Telephone, sign on, and password: Start-up command for communications system: Shutdown command for communications system:
ON/OFF [ON/OFF]	COMPUTER #2 ACCESS: Access to a second computer is required (and often a third or fourth computer as well, one at a time). In this case, for the second system:	Location and disks needed: Telephone, sign on, and password: Start-up command for communications system: Shutdown command for communications system:

INPUT	COMMAND INPUT: The precise method for command input must be specified. Often each computer has a different system. Here:	Use of function and control keys: Insert and delete characters: Mouse use: Other key use:
STORAGE	STORAGE ACCESS: Access to underlying operating system commands is mandatory for disk preparation, directories, and so forth. For this communication system:	Format command: Directory command: Copy command: Other operating system commands:
STORAGE	PROFILE FILES: Communications systems generally allow storage of communications parameter profiles in system files. For this system:	Load parameter profile: Save parameter profile:
STORAGE	FILE TRANSFER: Communications systems allow file transfer in either direction: user to remote or remote to user. For this system:	Local-to-remote file transfer: Remote-to-local file transfer:
STORAGE	LOG SESSION: Communications system allow a full file log of an interactive session (all input/output is saved in a file). For this communication system:	Log session on command: Log session off command:
PROCESS B = 2 + C	PARAMETER SETTING: Communication requires the setting of many parameters describing line conditions, computer types, and so on. For this system:	Speed: Parity: Start bits: Stop bits: Duplex: Handshaking protocol: Data bits: Originate/answer mode:
CONTROL	AUTOMATED CONTROL: Control in communications systems is embodied in automatic logins, automatic file transfers, and macros. For this computer system:	Automatic login: Automatic file transfer: Macros:
OUTPUT	PRINT SESSION: Communications systems can print an entire interactive session to the printer during the session. For this system:	Print session on command: Print session off command:

■ The ISPCO Scripts for Communications Software

The two ISPCO scripts for communications software follow. The first script (script for communication software interactive session) describes the steps involved in ordinary communication with distant systems; note that two computers must be set up for such communication.

SCRIPT FOR
COMMUNICATION
SOFTWARE INTERACTIVE
SESSION

1 *START UP COMMUNICATIONS SOFTWARE.* The communications package on the local computer must be started first. The user should have documentation on both systems available as well as any disks needed for file transfer or session log.

2 *SET COMMUNICATIONS PARAMETERS.* The speed, parity, number of data, start, and stop bits, duplex, and many other communications parameters must be set to match those of the remote computer to be accessed.

3 *SET TELEPHONE NUMBER OR DIRECT CONNECT.* The two computers can be connected by a telephone line or a direct cable. The software must be told which method is used and for a phone link the number for the software to dial.

4 *CONNECT WITH REMOTE COMPUTER.* The software is told to make the connection. It dials the telephone number (if not directly connected) and tries to establish communication. If it is successful, a message from the remote computer should appear on the screen. If not, some parameter may be set incorrectly, or the remote computer may be unavailable.

5 *SAVE COMMUNICATIONS SETTINGS TO DISK.* Once the communications parameters have been successfully determined, they should be saved to disk as a profile file for future use.

6 *INTERACT WITH REMOTE SYSTEM.* The remote computer begins by treating the local computer as a dumb terminal. The remote computer sends messages it expects to be printed and accepts messages it assumes came from a keyboard. However, the local computer can also print out the interactive session or log the session into a disk file. Interactive file transfer is also available.

7 *TERMINATE CONNECTIONS AND SHUTDOWN.* When the interaction is complete, the user must be certain to terminate interaction with both computers. First the user terminates the session with the remote computer and only then shuts down the local computer.

The second script (script for communication software file transfer) deals with the transfer of files. In the first case study, Anne transferred a file from her computer to Mike's. In the final example, Mike's conference on Mcintosh computers provided program files that could be transferred to his computer. The ability to transfer files of data directly from one computer to another is of ever-increasing importance.

With these scripts and the completed ISPCO frame, the user should be able to use a communications software system and organize the details of its operation in terms of the concepts learned in this chapter.

1. START UP COMMUNICATIONS SOFTWARE. As before, the interaction begins by starting up the communications software so that the two computer systems can communicate.

2. PREPARE FILES FOR SENDING OR RECEIVING. The files that are to be transferred must be prepared, whether on the local computer or on the remote computer.

3. SET COMMUNICATIONS PARAMETERS AND CONNECT. As for any communications session, the parameters must be properly set, and then the communication is initiated.

4. START UP FILE TRANSFER SOFTWARE ON REMOTE SYSTEM. File transfer requires communications software to be running on the remote system. Once that software is begun, the two software packages, one on each machine, will talk directly to each other about the file transfer.

5. TRANSFER FILES. Commands are given to the local software to initiate file transfer. The local software communicates with the remote software to perform the desired tasks. Usually, whole sets of files can be transferred in batches.

6. SHUT DOWN BOTH SYSTEMS. When file transfer is complete, both systems are shut down as before.

*SCRIPT FOR
COMMUNICATION
SOFTWARE FILE TRANSFER*

Chapter 10 Review

Expanded Objectives

The objectives listed below are an expansion of the essential chapter concepts listed at the beginning of the chapter. The review items for the chapter are based on these expanded objectives. If you master the objectives, you will do better on the review items that follow and on your instructor's examination on the chapter material.

After reading the chapter, you should be able to:

1. list and describe the setting of common parameters for connecting remote computers.
2. sequence in appropriate order a set of written general procedures (steps) for connecting remote computers through a communications system.
3. list and explain some common limitations of communications systems for transferring data between remote computers.
4. differentiate among common standards adopted for the use of computer communications systems.
5. explain the relationships among the following computer communications system elements: software, communications card, port, and modem.
6. relate the activities involved in operating a computer communications system to the ISPCO functions.
7. describe the command structure employed in computer communications systems.
8. complete a script for one or more of the generic processes of a computer communications system.
9. complete a computer communications system frame for the specific system to which you have access.
10. demonstrate understanding of the major terms introduced in this chapter.

Review Items

Completing this review will give you a good indication of how well you have mastered the contents of this chapter and prepare you for your instructor's test on this material. To maximize what you learn from this exercise, you should answer each question *before* looking up the answers in the appendix. The number of the corresponding expanded objective is given in parentheses following each question.

Complete the following clusters of items according to the directions heading each set.

A. *True or false.*

___ 1. The electronic signals output from all RS–232C communication cards are the same. (4)

___ 2. The electronic signals inside computer systems

from different manufacturers are generally not the same. (4)

___ 3. There is an agreed-on standard for electrical signals between computers. (4)

___ 4. Serial communication allows for the simultaneous transfer of more than one bit of data at a time. (1)

___ 5. Synchronous communication requires a start bit and one or two stop bits. (10)

___ 6. The name *modem* comes from the abbreviation of *modulate-demodulate*. (10)

___ 7. Modems are connected to telephone lines. (5)

___ 8. Even parity is used for the communication of characters containing an even number of ones, while odd parity is used for characters containing an odd number of ones. (1)

___ 9. During communication between two computers, both computers must be set to the originate mode or both to the answer mode. (1)

___ 10. When two computers are connected, the user's computer is called the *local* computer. (10)

___ 11. Specific messages sent between two computers can be captured either on disk or by a printer. (6)

___ 12. Emulation is a software technique in which communications software can act like a word processor, spreadsheet, or other software system. (6,10)

___ 13. Computer communications systems permit a user to dial telephone numbers directly through the keyboard. (2)

___ 14. Privacy of communication can be guaranteed in computer mail systems. (3)

___ 15. Computer conferences provide for the creation, viewing, and answering of public announcements. (10)

___ 16. One computer network can connect a user to other networks. (2)

___ 17. Macros allow some communications software systems to increase the size of the data files being transferred. (10)

___ 18. It is now possible for one computer to send data at 1200 bits per second, while a second, remote computer receives it at 300 bits per second. (1,3,4,6)

___ 19. A computer receiving data from a remote computer must be turned on and have a communications program called into RAM. (2,6)

___ 20. One advantage of transferring computer programs through a modem is the automatic translation to fit different computer systems. (3)

___ 21. A number of standards have been set up across different computer systems to specify the form of electrical signals used to transfer data between remote computers. (4)

___ 22. The maximum rate at which data can now be transferred by common telephone lines is 2400 bits per second. (1,3)

___ 23. Parity is a means for ensuring that there will be no errors in a transmission. (1)

___ 24. In the interactive transfer of data, each

communication depends on the immediately preceding one. (6,10)

___ 25. A user can, on command, switch among local, remote, and file transfer modes. (1)

___ 26. Data received from a remote computer is considered output. (6)

___ 27. Profiles of communication relieve the user from having to re-enter the same parameters each time a linkup is made with a remote computer. (10)

___ 28. It is sometimes necessary to go through several networks before accessing the desired computer system. (2,6)

___ 29. *Macros* and *profiles of communication* mean the same thing. (10)

B. *For the section below, match the descriptions on the left with the appropriate terms on the right. (10)*

___ 30. a device for translating between a computer's internal signals and an RS–232C signal

___ 31. a device for translating between an RS–232C signal and an audio telephone line signal

___ 32. a method for detecting errors in data transmission

___ 33. a transmission method in which many bits of data are sent down many wires at the same time

___ 34. a serial communication standard

___ 35. a communication line with data moving in both directions at the same time

a. half-duplex
b. parity
c. serial
d. communications card
e. RS–232C
f. full-duplex
g. parallel
h. modem

C. *The randomly ordered list below contains steps for setting up a communications link through a modem. Indicate the correct sequence of these steps by placing their letters in the correct order, in the space provided. (2)*

_____36.

a. complete the connection between computers
b. terminate communications link
c. start up communications software
d. specify parameters
e. transfer messages or file

D. *Match each description on the left with the appropriate standard for communication on the right. (4)*

___ 37. one bit of data at a time sent on one communication line

___ 38. requires special start and stop signals

___ 39. data travels in one direction only

    a. asynchronous
    b. simplex
    c. macro
    d. serial

E. *Match the communications activities on the left with the hardware on the right. (10)*

___ 40. translates signals so that data can be carried by telephone lines

___ 41. translates the computer's internal electrical signals into another form and back again

___ 42. permits the user to specify the communications parameters

___ 43. the logical name of the connection for attaching a modem to a communication card

    a. communications port
    b. communications card
    c. telephone line
    d. communication software
    e. modem

F. *Use the communication software Frame to match each of the activities on the left with its appropriate ISPCO function. (6)*

___ 44. capturing an interaction between two computers on a disk

___ 45. setting parameters for transfer of data between remote computers

___ 46. automatic login

    a. input
    b. storage
    c. processing
    d. control
    e. output

___ 47. transferring a file

___ 48. providing help information

___ 49. saving a profile

G. *Match each specification for communication on the left with the appropriate description on the right. (1,10)*

___ 50. number of data bits

___ 51. number of stop bits

___ 52. speed of communication

___ 53. type of parity

___ 54. type of mode

___ 55. start bit

    a. bits of data per second
    b. a check to determine how correctly data was transmitted
    c. determines how much of the ASCII code will be available
    d. choice of programming language
    e. indicates when a signal is coming
    f. establishes which computer initiates and which responds
    g. indicates when a signal is complete

Special Exercise: The Frame for Communications Software

The ISPCO frame for communications software contains boxes in which the user can write down the characteristics of a real computer system. You are encouraged to fill in the frame for the particular system to which you have access so that the concepts of this chapter can be directly applied to your own hardware and software. This frame may also be used to compare different systems by filling in a frame for each system and contrasting the systems on a point-by-point basis.

Your primary source of information for completing this frame should be the documentation available with your software or hardware system.

As a computer user works on more and different systems, each of the boxes in this frame may require expansion into even more detailed descriptions. By then, however, the user will be sophisticated enough to make such expansions easily and without help.

Programs, Programming Languages, and Programming Software

Essential Chapter Concepts

When you finish this chapter, you should know:

- The meanings of the terms *computer program*, *programming software*, and *programming language*.

- How professionals use the basic types of programming software tools.

- The characteristics of machine languages, assembly languages, high-level languages, very high level languages, and fourth-generation languages.

- The common programming languages used today and the areas in which they are most frequently used.

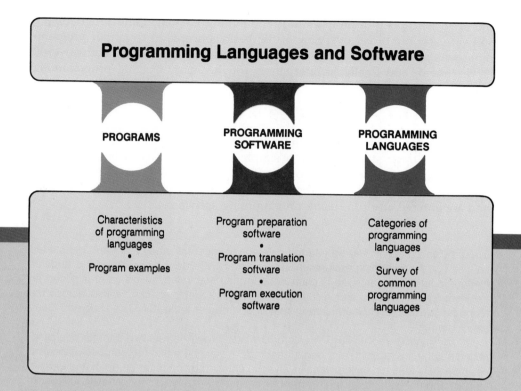

Programming Languages and Software

PROGRAMS

- Characteristics of programming languages
- Program examples

PROGRAMMING SOFTWARE

- Program preparation software
- Program translation software
- Program execution software

PROGRAMMING LANGUAGES

- Categories of programming languages
- Survey of common programming languages

So far, two types of computer software have been described in this text: operating systems software and applications software (i.e., word processors, spreadsheets, data base management systems, communication packages, and graphics systems). Yet in none of these discussions have we considered how such software is created! But why is it important to study computer programming?

Most professional people, whether they are in business, law, science, teaching, medicine, engineering or other fields, are increasingly involved with computer software. They are involved as consumers, as users, as evaluators, and sometimes as supervisors of software training or development. These roles do not require people to be programmers, but such roles do require them to have an accurate perception of the programming process. Chapters 11 and 12 provide the reader with such a necessary general understanding of programming. Thus, the purpose of these chapters is not to teach the reader how to program, but rather to teach about (1) the fundamental ideas underlying programming, (2) the basic tools available for programming, and (3) the methods and techniques used by skilled programmers. This knowledge should help dispel the mystery surrounding programming and provide the reader with an important understanding of what is involved in creating applications software and what a programmer can be realistically expected to accomplish. Perhaps no less important, the knowledge will also provide the reader with the basis for learning more about the fascinating field of programming and system development. This chapter concentrates on the fundamental ideas of programming, software tools, and languages. Chapter 12 describes methods and techniques of software engineering.

Because the use of operating systems and applications software differs substantially from the task of programming, a new organizational scheme will be used in the last two chapters. In this chapter, a case study will introduce the basic concepts of a program, a programming language, and programming software. Then a broad overview of the basic concepts of computer programming will be presented. Third, the major types of programming software will be discussed, and finally, a brief survey of the many existing programming languages will be given.

11.1

How Is Computer Programming Done?

This case study will introduce the reader to computer programming. In our case study, three students have a simple problem that is to be solved by a previously written computer program. The goal of this case study is to help the reader understand that programs are written in programming languages and are entered and run, using programming software.

Case Study

Jim, a business major, walked into the cafeteria to meet his study team and get started on their first programming assignment. The instructor, Dr. Jones, had asked the students to work together in teams, as is often done in the "real world." Jim's team included an engineering major, Sue, and Gouri, an exchange student. As Jim walked across the room, he saw Sue and Gouri already seated at a corner table. "Hi, Jim," Sue and Gouri said together.

Jim grinned and replied, "Hi, sorry I'm late." Then he reached into his briefcase, pulled out the assignment, and began reading, "It says here that the purpose of this first assignment is to teach us the steps involved in entering a computer program and to have us read and understand a simple computer program written in a programming language. The program is the one that Dr. Jones gave us in our lab handout."

"Yes, I have looked closely at the assignment and feel that it is indeed simple," Gouri responded.

"Okay, everybody," said Sue, "since we need a micro, let's go over to the lab."

A few minutes later, the team entered one of the school's microcomputer labs. From the lab assistant, Jim got a disk with the programming software on it. Then he sat down at a machine, inserted the disk into the drive, and turned the machine on. After a few moments, the operating system had finished booting and sat waiting for his commands.

"Starting up the system, at least, is easy," Jim commented. The screen looked like this:

```
CSE125 Introduction to Programming.
Press the number corresponding to the language you wish to
use:
     1.BASIC
     2.PASCAL
Number?_
```

Sue volunteered to enter the program. "With my piano training, I'm the fastest typist that you'll ever see!" she said.

As Sue sat down at the micro, Jim asked, "Anybody know anything about entering the program into the computer?"

"Yes, most certainly," Gouri replied. "The computer program is entered by using a word processor or by using programming software that works like a word processor. A program is typed in, in much the same way that one would type a term paper or a letter. Sue, would you be good enough to start the programming system?"

Sue pressed a 1 to enter the BASIC language system and was confronted with a typical word processing screen:

```
Super-Basic Programming System
                        Page 1   Line 1 Pos 0
  ▬



F1 Load    F2 Save    F3 Search F4 Block   F5 Delete
F6 Copy    F7 Move    F8 Format F9 Print   F10 Run
```

"Okay," said Sue, "now what?"

"Well," Gouri replied, "the menu at the bottom explains the use of the function keys on the keyboard. There is no special command for entering the program. You just start typing."

"Yeah, I guess that's obvious," Sue mused. "Well, give me the program and I'll start."

"Wait a minute!" Jim interrupted. "I've got two programs!"

Sure enough, the lab handout had one program on the front and one on the back. The one on the front began:

```
 10 REM BASIC EXAMPLE, PROGRAM #1, CSE 125.
100 REM The first thing that the programmer must do is
110 REM ask for the number of coats that were sold.
120 PRINT "How many coats were sold?"
130 REM
140 REM The second step is to read the number that the
150 REM user types in at the keyboard and place it
160 REM into a named storage location in RAM.
170 REM INPUT NUMBER_COATS
```

The program on the back began in a different way:

```
/*Set-up for Pascal Program #1 for CSE 125*/
program p1(input,output);
 var number_coats, price, sales: real;
 begin;

/* The first thing that the programmer must do is
   ask for the number of coats that were sold.   */
writeln("How many coats were sold?");

/* The second step is to read the number that the
   user types in at the keyboard and place it
   into a named storage location in RAM.      */
readln(number_coats);
```

"You dope!" said Sue. "It's the same program, written in two different programming languages, BASIC and Pascal. You can see that they do the same thing. We need the front side, the BASIC example."

"Now, now," said Gouri, "please, let us continue. Dr. Jones suggested that if we wanted to see what the program really does, we should look only at the lines that do not begin with REM. She said that the REM lines are only comments that the computer will ignore. I have already marked my handout. The program must truly be simple, because it contains only six BASIC statements."

Gouri placed his handout in front of Sue. It looked like this:

```
100 REM The first thing that the program must do is
110 REM ask for the number of coats that were sold.
120 PRINT "How many coats were sold?"              ←
130 REM
140 REM The second step is to read the number that the
150 REM user types in at the keyboard and place it
160 REM into a named storage location in RAM.
170 INPUT NUMBER_COATS                             ←
180 REM
190 REM The third step is to do the same process of
200 REM printing and inputting for the price of
210 REM each coat.
220 PRINT "What was the price of each coat?"       ←
230 INPUT PRICE                                    ←
240 REM
250 REM Compute the sales for the coats
260 REM using multiplication (*) and store
270 REM the answer in a place named SALES.
280 LET SALES = NUMBER_COATS * PRICE               ←
290 REM
300 REM Print out the answer using a character string
310 REM in double quotes and a reference to the
320 REM SALES variable to retrieve the answer from RAM.
330 PRINT "Sales for coats are:" ;SALES            ←
```

"Well, I'll type it in," said Sue. Despite her excellent typing skills, Sue made many mistakes as she typed. She quickly corrected them, as any user of a word processing system would, by using the arrow keys, the delete key, the backspace key, and so on. The software that supported the entry of the computer program seemed to be easy to use. After a few minutes of typing, the BASIC language version of the program was in the computer. Sue saved the program by pressing the F2 (save) key and giving the name of the file in which to save the program (PROGRAM1).

"So far, so good. What are we supposed to do next, Jim?" asked Sue.

Jim glanced over Sue's notes. "Well, now we're supposed to use the programming software to execute the program that you just typed in. To execute the program, the programming software reads each line of the program and does what it says. We have to give the program any data that it asks for by typing it in at the keyboard. The program will talk to us through messages on the screen."

"The F10 key is supposed to run the program, so when I press it, the program should start up," interrupted Sue. She pressed the F10 function key, and the program began to execute. The interaction proceeded as follows, with Sue typing in the two numbers requested by the computer:

```
How many coats were sold?
?10
What was the price of each coat?
?50.00

Sales for coats are: 500.

Ready
_
```

"Most certainly," said Gouri, "the program we have just run was quite simple. Perhaps we should run the program again and use another set of test data."

"Okay," said Jim, "but while we're doing it, why don't we follow along on the lab sheet to see how each statement in the program is working?"

Sue pressed the F10 key to start the program again, and the interaction proceeded as follows:

```
How many coats were sold?
?_
```

Looking back at the printed copy of the program, Jim pointed to line 120. "That's from line 120, which is:

```
120 PRINT "How many coats were sold?"
```

I guess that PRINT is the command for the output function in BASIC."

"Okay," said Sue, "but where did the second question mark come from? There's only one question mark on line 120!"

"Obviously ," smirked Jim, "it came from the next line

```
170 INPUT NUMBER_COATS.
```

I read the text, and it said that an INPUT command prints out a question mark so that you know when the computer is waiting for you to type something at the keyboard."

Sue input the number 15 and responded to the next request for the price of coats by typing in 13.25. Finally, the screen looked like this:

```
How many coats were sold?
15
What was the price of each coat?
13.25

Sales for coats are: 198.75

Ready

-
```

Gouri summarized the interaction. "Yes, the program is now clear. The commands in line 220 and 230

```
220 PRINT "What was the price of each coat?"
```

```
230 INPUT PRICE
```

operated in the same way as the first two commands. The first line, 220, printed a message, while the second line, 230, printed a question mark and waited for a number to be typed in at the keyboard. After the number was typed in, it was stored in a place called PRICE. Finally, line 280

```
280 LET SALES = NUMBER_COATS * PRICE
```

multiplied together 15, the number of coats, and 13.25, the price of each coat, and stored the result in a place called SALES. The last line, 330

```
330 PRINT "Sales for coats are:" ;SALES
```

merely printed out a message with the answer!"

"Okay," said Sue, "I see input, storage, processing, and output. Obviously, the numbers we typed in were the input. The micro stored the numbers in RAM—that's storage. The multiplication was processing, and the $198.75 was the output. I see all of the ISPCO functions except control. Was there any control?"

"Most assuredly, yes," replied Gouri. "Control is concerned with the order in which the functions are performed. As we read the lines in the program, we assumed that the lines would be done in order. The computer was exercising control by doing the lines in the order of their line numbers.

"Well, I sure hope that all of our assignments are this easy!" Jim said vehemently. "Now we've got time for partying!"

"You sound like the type who always has time for partying," complained Sue.

"Oh my," said Gouri, rolling his eyes. "This could be a long term!"

It is true that the task assigned to these three students was simple. Nonetheless, they discovered that a computer program is nothing more than a list of statements in a language that the computer can understand and perform in the prescribed order. They also practiced using programming software to enter and run a program that was written by someone else. Finally, they saw that the standard ISPCO functions were present in even a small program.

11.2

The Concepts of Computer Programming and Programming Languages

Programming Languages and Software

PROGRAMS   PROGRAMMING SOFTWARE   PROGRAMMING LANGUAGES

Characteristics of programming languages: vocabulary, grammar, meaning, pragmatics • Program examples: Psuedo-code, BASIC, Pascal, LISP

program
A set of programming language instructions that direct the computer to perform ISPCO functions needed by the user.

programming language
An artificial language used to write instructions directing a computer to perform ISPCO functions. Traditional programming languages include commands for the explicit control of the order in which instructions are executed.

Programming Software
Computer programs designed to help programmers correctly input, translate, and execute other programs.

Programming begins when a potential computer user finds that his or her problem cannot be solved by available application software. The user must either be able to program or turn to a programmer for assistance. Once the needs of the user are identified and the design of the program is completed the **program** can be written. Since the computer does not speak English, a programmer must learn to speak in a language that the computer can process, a **programming language.** The programmer uses the programming language to write a set of instructions or statements called a program. Next the programmer uses **programming software** to input and translate the program into a language the computer can execute. Finally, the user tests the program and uses it to process his or her data in order to solve the original problem. Several definitions are critical to understanding this process.

- □ *Computer Program.* A computer program is a set of instructions written in a programming language that directs a computer to perform certain input, storage, processing, control, and output functions which fulfill the user's needs. Programs usually include explicit mechanisms of control that specify the order in which instructions are to be performed (for example, the line numbers in the BASIC program for the case study).
- □ *Computer Programming.* Computer programming consists of a set of activities, which a person must perform in order to successfully create a computer program. These activities generally include four major stages: 1) determining the goals of the user(s), 2) designing a program to meet those goals, 3) using a programming language to write the designed program for a computer, and 4) evaluating and maintaining the final, completed program.

□ *Programming Language.* A programming language is an artificial language that a computer can process in which instructions requesting ISPCO operations are written. Traditional programming languages (like BASIC or Pascal) include control statements for specifying the order of control, i.e., sequence (do in the order given), selection (do one of two sets of instructions) and iteration (repeat a set of instructions).

□ *Programming Software.* Programming software consists of programs that help people with the various activities of computer programming. Generally, programming software aids with: 1) entering and editing a computer program written in a programming language, 2) translating the statements of the computer program into a form that the computer can directly execute, and 3) executing the final program to accomplish its purpose.

Although these definitions may seem complicated, the activities they involve are similar to some everyday human activities. How many times has the average person left a list of requests for a spouse or friend? "Please pick up the tickets for the show. Get gas in the car. Make the reservations for 6 P.M. Put a bottle of champagne in the fridge." No great mental effort is required in leaving this simple list of instructions. The originator of the note had a series of goals concerning a night on the town and enlisted the help of a friend by jotting down a set of instructions for the friend to perform. Presumably, this person will receive the list, read it, and execute each request in turn.

Programming the computer also begins with a person who has goals to be met, but instead of writing down a list of instructions for another person, the programmer writes down a list of instructions for the computer. This is a little more difficult because the computer doesn't speak English, so the programmer must speak in an artificial programming language that the computer can understand. Once the list of instructions is written, the programmer can use programming software to enter, translate, and execute the instructions. These steps are further illustrated in the figure on the next page.

■ What are the Characteristics of Programming Languages?

The purpose of any language is communication. There are many natural languages (e.g., English, French, and German). Linguists have analyzed the structure of natural languages and how they are used in order to determine many of the characteristics of natural language interaction. All natural language communication requires:

1. a *vocabulary* of words that corresponds to the common events of human experience (e.g., words for objects that people can see, hear, touch, taste, or smell and words that describe how people reason and remember)
2. a *grammar* or **syntax,** whose primary purpose is to define how words in a sentence are related to each other (e.g., in "the red book and tall man," the rules of syntax tell us that *red* modifies *book* and *tall* modifies *man,* not the other way around)
3. a *semantics* or meaning that comes from combining the vocabulary with the grammar (e.g., in "Bob threw the ball to Mary," the syntax and vocabulary combine to give an image of Bob initiating the action that transfers a ball from his possession to Mary's)

syntax
The structure of expressions in a language, or the rules governing the structure.

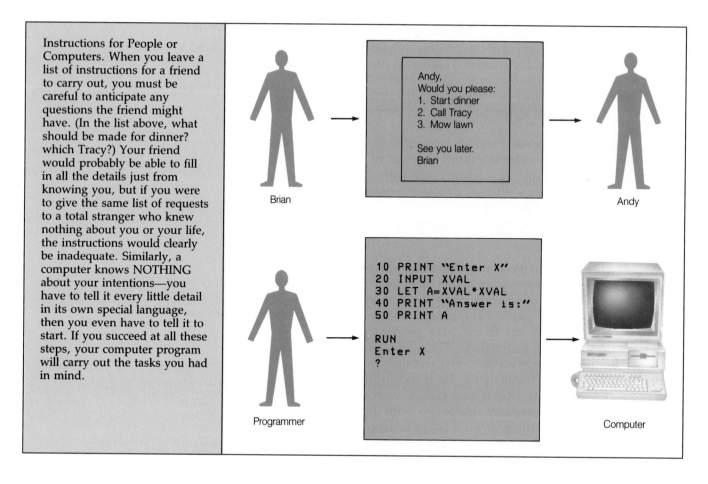

Instructions for People or Computers. When you leave a list of instructions for a friend to carry out, you must be careful to anticipate any questions the friend might have. (In the list above, what should be made for dinner? which Tracy?) Your friend would probably be able to fill in all the details just from knowing you, but if you were to give the same list of requests to a total stranger who knew nothing about you or your life, the instructions would clearly be inadequate. Similarly, a computer knows NOTHING about your intentions—you have to tell it every little detail in its own special language, then you even have to tell it to start. If you succeed at all these steps, your computer program will carry out the tasks you had in mind.

4. a *pragmatics* or real-world component that verifies what is said against the known possibilities of the real world (e.g., "Bob swam across the Atlantic Ocean without stopping" is not reasonable, given knowledge of the real world)

As technology has progressed, *artificial languages* have been created to concisely express ideas that would be difficult to express in a natural language. The most obvious example is the language of mathematics. Imagine the difficulty of stating and working with complex mathematical functions in the words of an ordinary natural language!

Most important for us, however, is the class of artificial languages known as *programming languages*. Like natural languages, programming languages are designed for communication, but the communication is from humans to computers. Such languages have vocabulary, syntactic, semantic, and pragmatic characteristics that allow a programmer to give instructions to a computer.

Vocabulary.   The vocabulary of programming languages consists of keywords that refer to a computer's ISPCO functions and data on which these functions will operate. In this chapter's case study, for example, the microcomputer had devices for input (the keyboard), storage (RAM), output (the screen), and processing and control (the microprocessor chip); and the BASIC language had keywords that controlled each device and the flow of information among them. Only three BASIC language keywords (INPUT, LET, and PRINT) were used in the case study:

INPUT PRICE

Input a number from the keyboard and store it in RAM at a location labeled PRICE.

LET SALES = NUMBER_COATS * PRICE

Process by multiplying the value in NUMBER_COATS by the value in PRICE and storing the result in SALES.

PRINT SALES

Output the value in the storage location SALES to the screen.

The BASIC language contains many other keywords and statements that correspond to ISPCO functions.

Syntax. The syntax of a programming language consists of the rules that determine how the keywords are combined to specify commands. For example, BASIC syntax specifies that commands must generally consist of a line number followed by a keyword, followed by some type of argument or piece of data for the keyword to operate on. Thus some combinations of words are legitimate in BASIC, and others are not. For example,

120 LET SALES = NUMBER_COATS * PRICE

is legitimate, while

SALES NUMBER_COATS PRICE 120 LET = *

contains the same vocabulary but is not legitimate.

The computer needs rules of syntax in the same way that humans need similar rules in natural languages. For example, rules specify the order of words in English, and "the the the one boy ball other side from to hit" has no meaning because it does not follow the rules of English syntax. But the same words do make sense when properly ordered: "the boy hit the ball from one side to the other." An example of syntax in BASIC is the rule that the two terms on each side of an asterisk (*) must specify the RAM locations containing data that will be multiplied together.

Semantics. The semantics of a programming language specifies the meaning of a sentence that is syntactically correct. The meaning is determined in part by the keywords and data specified in the programming language statement, but there can be other considerations. For example, let's look at the simple BASIC statement:

LET X = 2 + 3 * 4

Although this statement is syntactically correct, it has two possible interpretations, or meanings. The first interpretation is to multiply the 3 and 4 together to get 12 and then add 2 to get a total of 14. The second interpretation is to add the 2 and 3 together to get 5 and then multiply 5 times 4 to give a value of 20. Because of the possibility of multiple interpretations, anyone using a programming language to communicate with the computer must understand the semantics of the programming language as well as its keywords and syntax.

Pragmatics.   Finally, pragmatics is concerned with what is possible in the real world. The best example of a pragmatic concern would probably be another mathematical example:

```
LET  X  =1483329212234457677843345546632873486849454 8   *
14009882366647389255678789876545456677665545556
```

Even though the vocabulary of this BASIC statement is correct, the syntax is correct, and even the meaning is well defined, most computer systems are incapable of giving an exactly correct answer to this equation because their microprocessors are not built to handle numbers containing so many nonzero digits.

Programming languages are thus artificial languages through which a programmer can communicate instructions to a computer. Programming languages have the same components as natural languages, namely, vocabulary, syntax, semantics, and pragmatics. A good programmer must have a thorough command of each aspect of a programming language.

■ What Do Programming Languages Look Like?

Programming languages look a great deal like some of the command languages that are used with the application software shells, which were described in the various chapters on operating systems, word processors, spreadsheets, and the like. In fact, the major difference in traditional programming languages is the importance of statements for control. Recall that the command languages for the applications programs described in the previous chapters all provided many commands for ISPO (e.g., SAVE FILE1 to save a file), but very few commands for control (graphics software for example had none). In contrast, traditional programming languages always include at least a minimum number of powerful commands that provide *explicit control* over the order in which the ISPCO statements are executed. Generally, programming languages provide at least three types of control: *sequence* (executing a set of statements in the order given), *selection* (executing one of two different sets of statements), and *iteration* (repeating a set of instructions). All three will be seen in use with the programs that follow.

To illustrate some of the concepts of programming languages in more detail, we will now look at an expanded version of the program from the case study. Our program again deals with the problem of determining sales for a clothing store. This time, however, there will be two separate items to sell and more than one store for which a report is requested. The program will first be given in **pseudo-code** and then in three different programming languages (BASIC, Pascal, and LISP). As the examples in these computer languages are presented, note their similarities in vocabulary, syntax, and semantics.

Pseudo-code contains natural English statements written in an indented style that makes the translation of the statements into computer instructions easier. Pseudo-code is very important in the design of a computer program because it is easy for the programmer to write, read, and understand. Hence, without needing to think like a computer, the programmer can concentrate on what the instructions should say. After a careful analysis of these structured English instructions, the programmer can be relatively certain that the program will work and can begin translating the pseudo-code into the chosen programming language.

pseudo-code
A technique used by program designers to describe a program in short, concise, English language phrases structured by keywords, such as *if-then-else, while-do,* and *end.*

Assuming that a careful analysis of the problem has already been completed, a pseudo-code description of the program might look something like this:

Sample Program in Pseudo-Code
1. ASK for the number of stores to be processed.
2. READ the answer and SAVE it in a storage location named NUMBER_STORES.
3. FOR each STORE from number 1 to NUMBER_STORES:
    a. ASK for the number of coats sold.
    b. READ the answer and SAVE in NUMBER_COATS.
    c. ASK for the price of each coat.
    d. READ the answer and SAVE in PRICE_COATS.
    e. ASK for the number of hats sold.
    f. READ the answer and SAVE in NUMBER_HATS.
    g. ASK for the price of each hat.
    h. READ the answer and SAVE in PRICE_HATS.
    i. COMPUTE COAT_SALES as NUMBER_COATS * PRICE
    j. COMPUTE HAT_SALES as NUMBER_HATS * PRICE.
    k. COMPUTE TOTAL SALES as COAT_SALES + HAT_SALES.
    l. PRINT messages giving SALES.
4. PRINT message saying "DONE."

There is no magic to pseudo-code. No doubt an experienced programmer would directly program such a simple problem without even considering the use of pseudo-code. Yet every programmer is at times faced with problems of sufficient difficulty that writing down the intended solution in such quasi-English is an important aid in the development of the program.

Once the pseudo-code description is complete, the programmer translates this description into a computer program. The details of this process will be discussed in the next chapter. For the present, we will look at the following examples of the finished program in three different programming languages (i.e., BASIC, Pascal, and LISP).

Sample Program in BASIC
```
100 REM Get the number of stores.
110 PRINT "How many stores will be processed?"
120 INPUT NUMBER_STORES

130 REM Set up the repeated processing for each store.
140 FOR STORES = 1 TO NUMBER_STORES

150     REM Start processing for coats.
160     PRINT "How many coats were sold?"
170     INPUT NUMBER_COATS
180     PRINT "What was the price of each coat?"
190     INPUT PRICE_COATS

200     REM Repeat for hats.
210     PRINT "How many hats were sold?"
220     INPUT NUMBER_HATS
230     PRINT "What was the price of each hat?"
240     INPUT PRICE_HATS

250     REM Compute sales.
260     LET SALES_COATS = NUMBER_COATS * PRICE_COATS
270     LET SALES_HATS  = NUMBER_HATS  * PRICE_HATS
```

```
280     REM Compute total sales.
290     LET TOTAL = SALES_COATS + SALES_HATS

300     REM PRINT the report.
305     PRINT "Total Sales for Store ";STORE
310     PRINT "Sales for coats are ";SALES_COATS
320     PRINT "Sales for hats are ";SALES_HATS
330     PRINT "Total Sales are      ";TOTAL
340 REM Mark end of repetition and go back and do
350 REM the next store.
360 NEXT STORE
```

Sample Program in Pascal

```
/*Set up for Pascal program */
program p2 (input,output); label 1,2;
 var number_coats, price_coats, number_hats, price_hats,
     sales_coats, sales_hats, total:    real;
     store, number_stores:              integer;
 begin;

/* Get number of stores */
writeln('How many stores will be processed?');
readln(number_stores);

/* Set up repetition for each store */
for store := 1 to number_stores
   /* Get coats data */
   writeln('How many coats were sold?');
   readln(number_coats);
   writeln('What was the price of each coat?');
   readln(price_coats);

   /* Repeat for hats */
   writeln('How many hats were sold?');
   readln(number_hats);
   writeln('What was the price of each hat?');
   readln(price_hats);

   /* COMPUTE SALES */
   sales_coats := number_coats * price_coats;
   sales_hats  := number_hats * price_hats;
   total  := sales_coats+sales__hats;

   /* PRINT REPORT */
   writeln( 'Total Sales for Store',store);
   writeln( 'Sales for coats are ',sales_coats);
   writeln('Sales for hats are ',sales_hats);
   writeln('Total Sales are    ',total);

/* end of repeated commands */
end;
/* Pascal end matter */
 end.
```

Sample Program in LISP

```
(defun exampleprogram ()
   (prog (number_stores store
      number_coats price_coats number_hats price_hats
      sales_coats sales_hats total)

      ;Get the number of stores
      (print "How many stores will be processed?")
      (setq number_stores (read))
      ;Setup the repeated processing for each store
      (do ((store 1 (+ 1 store)))
           ;check for end of processing
           ((>store number_stores))
```

```
    ;Start processing for coats
    (print "How many coats were sold?")
    (setq number_coats (read))
    (print "What was the price of each coat?")
    (setq price_coats (read))

    ;Repeat for hats
    (print "How many hats were sold?")
    (setq number_hats (read))
    (print "What was the price of each hat?")
    (setq price_hats (read))

    ;Compute Sales
    (setq sales_coats (* number_coats price_coats))
    (setq sales_hats  (* number_hats price_hats))

    ;Compute Total Sales
    (setq total sales (+ sales_coats sales_hats))

    ;PRINT REPORT
    (print (list "Total Sales for Store " store))
    (print (list "Sales for coats is " sales_coats))
    (print (list "Sales for hats is  " sales_hats))
    (print (list "Total Sales is     " total))

  ;Mark end of repetition and program
)))
```

From these examples, it is evident that a program written in one language has a different form from the same program written in another language. Differences exist in vocabulary and syntax, at the very least. Yet, these programs also demonstrate that despite the differences in form, the various languages can convey identical (or almost identical) meanings.

Programming Languages and Software

PROGRAMS   PROGRAMMING   PROGRAMMING
                SOFTWARE   LANGUAGES

Program preparation software: word processor, syntax-directed editor • Program translation software: interpreters, compilers • Program execution software: debug aids, program trace, program break

11.3

What Is Programming Software?

program preparation software
Software that aids in the entry of newly designed computer programs into the computer; program preparation software has editing functions similar to those of a word processor.

program translation software
The software that translates from the programming language used by the programmer into machine language that can be executed by the computer.

program execution software
The software that executes a translated program on data for the programmer and user.

As shown in Figure 11–1, developing a program for a computer application requires three types of computer software tools. The first tool, **program preparation software,** assists with the entry and editing of the programming language statements. The second tool, **program translation software,** transforms the statements of the programming language into a form that the computer can execute. The third tool, **program execution software,** actually executes the prepared programs and may also include other aids to determine the correctness of the program being run.

Figure 11–1. Programmer Users and Their Software. The programmer uses two pieces of software to prepare an applications program for a user. The first is the program preparation software that allows the enter of program statements, and the second is the translation software that prepares the statements for computer execution. The user also uses two types of software. The execution software loads in the applications program, which the user then interacts with to obtain the desired results.

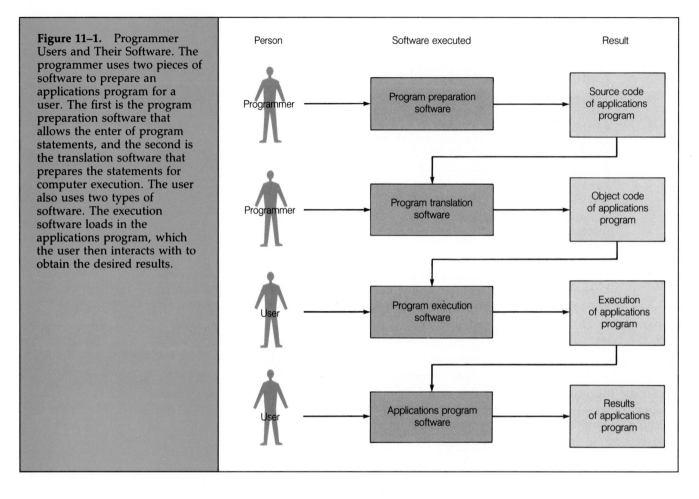

■ Program Preparation Software

Program preparation software must be able to accept program statements from the user at the keyboard and store these statements on disk for access by the program translation and program execution software. Program preparation software contains most of the text editing functions of a text editor or word processor, including correction of errors (by deleting, inserting, copying, or moving blocks of text) and string substitution. Obviously, the program preparation software must also be able to save a program on disk and reload it later for further editing. Because these functions are so similar to the functions provided by a word processing system, *many programming software systems do not provide any explicit program preparation software* but expect the user to use a text editor (e.g., from an operating system) or word processor (e.g., Word Perfect) to enter programming language statements into the computer.

For any professional programmer, the ability to maintain and use a library of completed computer programs is critical to effective and efficient work. To provide ready access to such programs, some program preparation software systems provide "include" directives. The "include" function (e.g., "include my-graphic-routines") allows the user to enter a special command into a computer program. This command essentially says, "when this program is run, go to the program library and get the program or file named 'my-graphic-routines' and include it right here, just as if it had been retyped at this point."

With this capability, a programmer does not need two copies of a program to include it in two systems. Instead, the program is kept in only one place and referenced by placing the "include" function in each system. Many programming software systems include a "Programmers Toolbox," containing useful programs or parts of programs which can be accessed with the "include" function in each system.

Some programming language systems provide a **syntax-directed editor,** which is essentially a word processing system with a special added capability: it knows the proper syntax of the programming language being used. A syntax-directed editor watches the statements that the programmer enters and does not permit the entry of any statement that is not syntactically correct. This function is very useful, because many hours of a programmer's time can be spent just in searching for and correcting small typing errors or improper uses of the programming language. Unfortunately, at this time few programming systems provide sophisticated syntax-directed editors.

■ Program Translation Software

Once a program has been created and entered into the computer, the user must access program translation software, which translates the original program (the **source program**) from the language used by the programmer (the **source language**) into the language used by the machine. This new form of the program is called the **object program.** The need for this step may confuse the novice programmer. Hasn't the programmer already learned the computer's language? Isn't a program written in a programming language ready for a computer to execute? The answer to both questions is no. Recall from chapter 3 that computers work only on strings of 0's and 1's, (so-called **machine language**). Generally, a programming language statement is not a string of zeros and ones. Instead, the programming language statements represent other computer commands that also exist in machine language form; program translation software transforms the statements of the programming language into the 0's and 1's of machine language.

There are two primary ways of implementing the translation between the programming language and machine language; they are based on two different kinds of software, a **compiler** and an **interpreter.** A compiler is a program that translates the user's program statements into a form that can be directly executed. Compiled programming languages are often very fast, because the translation needs to be done only once. After that, the translated form is used whenever the program is run and the first form is ignored.

An interpreter works differently. Instead of translating from the user's language to a form that the computer can use, an interpreter looks at each statement in the program, figures out what it means, and executes it. Interpreters are usually slower, because they must interpret each statement every time they are executed.

The difference between a compiler and an interpreter is frequently confusing for beginning programmers, but a simple analogy makes the difference quite clear: Imagine that two people who speak different languages (e.g., English and German) wish to communicate. One way for them to communicate would be to have the English speaker write down everything he or she wanted to say in a book. Then a translator would be called in. The translator would painstakingly go through the English book and create a corresponding German book. The translator could then leave, and the German speaker could read the

syntax-directed editor
A program preparation software function that does not permit the entry of statements that are syntactically incorrect.

source program
The initial form of a program written in a source language and entered through an input device for translation into machine language.

source language
The programming language used to generate the instructions of a source program. The source program must be translated into an object program before it can be executed by a computer.

object program
A machine language program resulting from the translation of a source program (written in the source language) into a form that can be directly executed.

machine language
A programming language whose code is in a binary (0's and 1's) form that can be executed directly by a computer without translation. Also called an object language.

compiler
A computer program that translates a source program (written in a programming language, like BASIC) into an object program (in machine language). Computers translate the entire program before any part of the program is executed.

interpreter
A program that translates statements from a source programming language (e.g., BASIC) into a machine language equivalent. Interpreters translate and execute each line of a computer program before proceeding to the next one.

German version of the book while the English speaker kept the English version.

A compiler does exactly what this translator did. The English speaker and the computer want to communicate. The English speaker creates a program. A translator (compiler) is called in to make a second copy of the program in a language that the computer understands. The compiler can then be dismissed, and two versions of the program exist, one in English and one in "computerese."

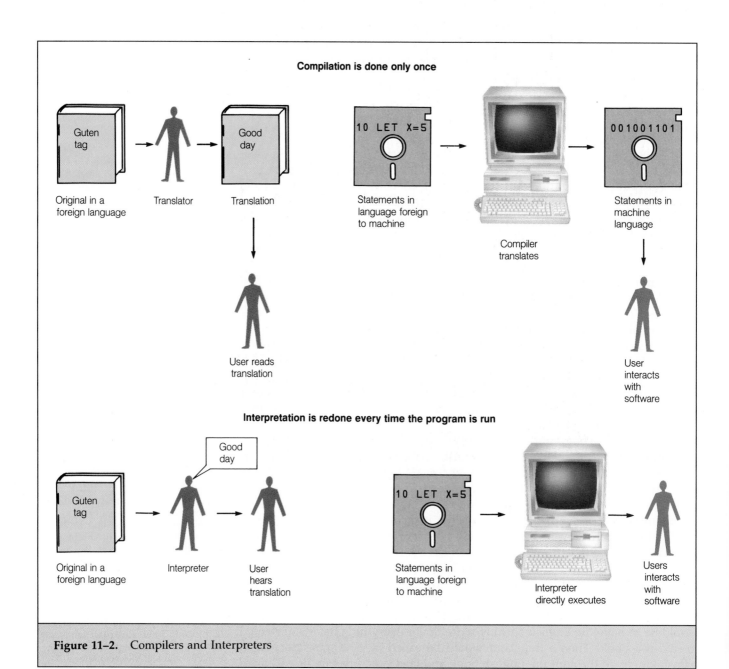

Figure 11–2.   Compilers and Interpreters

The second way for the English and German speakers to communicate is through an interpreter. In this case, instead of doing a static, one-shot translation, the interpreter must always be present. Each time the English speaker makes a statement, the interpreter immediately gives that statement to the German speaker in German. There is no permanent storage of the translation, so the German speaker must comprehend and act on the statement immediately. In an interpreter the program translation and program execution functions are interwoven together.

This is exactly how an interpreter between a human programmer and a computer works. The interpreter is always present. It reads one line from the computer program, translates it, and gives it to the computer. The computer must immediately perform any required action, because another line will be coming momentarily. These differences are illustrated further in Figure 11–2.

After the programmer has written the statements in a programming language and entered them into the computer, the computer must verify that the statements are in the proper form before the program can be executed. Although human communication is sometimes fuzzy, ambiguous, or unclear, instructions to a computer in a programming language must be unambiguous and quite precise. This required precision is difficult for even an experienced programmer to maintain, especially since typing errors are always possible. Thus, one of the tasks of the program translation software is to check the programming language statements for proper syntax. A **syntax checker** reads through a proposed program and identifies those statements in the program that are in improper form. The programmer can re-enter the text editor or word processor (the program preparation software) and correct the problems. After all the incorrect statements have been corrected, the program translation software prepares the special form of the program that can be directly executed.

syntax checker
A mechanism that applies syntax rules to determine whether statements in a computer program are in the proper form.

■ Program Execution Software

Since the primary function of program execution software is to execute the computer program, access to the translated version of the program is required. The translated version is loaded into the computer's RAM and linked up to any other required programs on the system, then control is given to the new program by setting the instruction counter in the system's microprocessor to the first command in the new program. As the microprocessor continues its operation, the new program is executed. In interpreters this whole process occurs on a program statement by statement basis.

In addition to this fundamental task, program execution software can also provide assistance during program development, including

1. detecting improper uses of operations (e.g., trying to numerically add letters instead of numbers);
2. tracing the processing of the program at every step, so that all of the "invisible" processing becomes apparent
3. suspending program execution at any point, looking at or changing values of **variables,** and then continuing execution.

variable
A portion of computer memory that has been given a name and is intended for the storage of a particular type of value, e.g., NUMBER_COATS (the name) = 10 (the value).

The detection of improper operations is the simplest aid available in program execution software. If the programmer asks the computer to perform an operation that is impossible (e.g., "What is the sum of 'George' and 'Robert'?''), the computer cannot carry out the request. At the rudest level, program execution software might respond with a simple message that an impossible operation was tried and then abort execution. At a much friendlier level, a message identifying the problem statement would be given to the programmer, and then the system would allow the programmer to examine the variables and their values to see what might have caused the problem.

program trace
A troubleshooting technique in which an output device makes a record of the execution of each step of a program to permit an analysis of the program.

Some systems provide a **program trace** which helps the programmer examine what each step of the program does when executed. A program trace prints out a message to the programmer as each statement in the program is performed. The message identifies the statement being executed and often includes the values of data being processed. One of the most common mistakes in programming is performing operations out of order, and a program trace helps to detect such errors.

program break (or breakpoint)
A specified point in a computer program where the program can be interrupted for checking and debugging.

Placing a **program break** at specified point in a program is another useful tool for detecting errors. A program break allows the programmer to see the status of a program as it is executing. If the programmer specifies a number of points to examine in a program, execution of the program is suspended at each of these points and control is transferred back to the programmer. The programmer then can request the values of any variables in the program to see if they are correct at that point.

Program execution software has generally lagged far behind its potential. Although program trace and break options are frequently available, they are generally difficult to use and thus require extra effort on the part of the programmer. Because of this lack of user-friendliness, these effective aids are often not used.

11.4

Categories of Programming Languages

Programming Languages and Software

PROGRAMS   PROGRAMMING   PROGRAMMING
            SOFTWARE   LANGUAGES

CATEGORIES OF PROGRAMMING LANGUAGES
Application command, procedural and nonprocedural languages • First-generation: machine language • Second-generation: assembly language • Third-generation: high-level languages • Fourth generation: very high level languages

There are many descriptive categories which may be applied to computer languages. In the section, we will describe only the most commonly recognized categories: application languages, procedural and non-procedural programming languages, and machine, assembly, compiled, and interpreted programming languages.

■ Application Software Languages

These are the languages used with the shells of application software, e.g. word processors, spreadsheets, and data base managers. Included in this type are *command languages* (with statements like "Save myletter" or "delete database1"), ordinary *command menus* (with statements like: "Type your choice: 1-save 2-delete"), and *graphics command menus* (with such things as a mouse, icons, and a menu bar). As we noted in earlier chapters, these languages provide very few commands involving the control function. Generally, control is provided directly by the user who gives commands for ISPO in whatever order is required by the problem. Thus, *most application software languages lack commands for explicit control of the ISPCO functions*. However, as users of application programs become more and more sophisticated, application languages are starting to introduce mechanisms for the control functions. Macros are an example of this trend. Throughout the descriptions of word processing, spreadsheets, data bases, and so on, the concept of a *macro* was introduced. A macro was defined as a control mechanism for abbreviating a sequence of commands and causing the sequence to be automatically executed by one command.

application software languages
The command, menu, and graphics menu languages used to operate application software, such as word processors, spreadsheets, graphics programs and the like. Control is mainly provided by the order in which users request ISPCO functions.

■ Procedural Programming Languages

These languages include the vast majority of the programming languages in use today, including all such major languages as FORTRAN, COBOL, BASIC, Pascal, Algol, Ada, and many others. *Procedural programming languages are characterized by a powerful set of commands for explicit control of the ISPCO functions*. The control commands, at a minimum, include *sequence* (executing a predefined set of commands in the order given), *selection* (executing one of two or more sets of predefined commands), and *iteration* (repeatedly executing the same set of predefined commands). Control commands make procedural programming fundamentally different from simply using an application software system.

When using the word processors, spreadsheets, and the like, the user inputs a command and the software reads the command and executes it. The user views the results and, if problems arise, responds reactively to the problems as they occur. In procedural computer programming, in contrast, the computer program includes an ordered sequence of statements *with control instructions that are all defined before any are executed*. Because of this, the computer programmer *must anticipate* what will happen and prepare instructions for any outcome. The major conceptual differences between using applications and procedural programming languages are summarized in the figure on the next page.

Because of the need to anticipate possible decisions and to program control instructions for handling them, computer programming is generally a more difficult task than the use of application systems. Computer users who have used application software for years might still avoid computer programming. There is no need to do that, however, once the differences between application programs and programming are made clear. If the user can lay out a sequence of steps that should be carried out and, at each point in the sequence, anticipate any problems that might arise and plan for them, then the user can program.

procedural programming languages
Traditional programming languages like BASIC and Pascal. Control is mainly written into the program by means of control commands for sequence, selection, and iteration which are provided by the programmer.

Command Languages and Procedural Programming Languages. In procedural programming languages, the user must anticipate possible situations and plan ahead on how they will be handled. In applications settings, the user is not required to plan ahead as much but can view the situation and then decide what actions are to be performed.

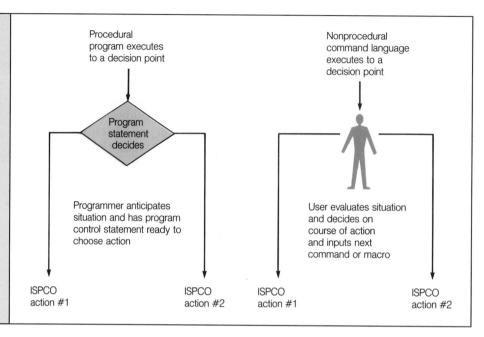

nonprocedural programming languages
New programming languages like PROLOG and VP EXPERT designed primarily for artificial intelligence. Control is shared between the programmer and the computer.

■ Nonprocedural Programming Languages

A relatively new type of language called a nonprocedural language, is becoming increasingly important. The difference between a nonprocedural and a procedural language is usually defined as follows: if you need only tell the computer *what to do* then the language is nonprocedural; if you must tell the computer *what to do and how to do it* the language is procedural. For example, if one tells a taxi driver, "Take me to the baseball stadium," that is much more nonprocedural than when another person, who also wants to go to the baseball stadium, tells the driver, "Get on I-75 going south. When you get to Jefferson Avenue turn off . . . and so on." In the first case, the passenger said *"what,"* not *"how"* to procede, and the taxi driver had to supply the remaining details for the passenger. In the second case, the passenger specified *"how"* to procede to the stadium. Unfortunately, such distinctions seem difficult to maintain in the real world. For instance, in the taxi example above, how is saying, "Get on I-75," any more procedural than, "Take me to the baseball stadium."? To get on the I-75 interstate freeway, the taxi driver must still have knowledge of the highway system, albeit, slightly less knowledge than that required to get to the stadium. In either case, the passenger is assuming that the taxi driver can understand some simple level of instructions.

In short, nonprocedural programming is not very precisely defined, but is a label applied to a wide variety of ideas. Among the languages that seem to clearly fall in this category, such as Expert System Shells and PROLOG, the main difference between procedural and nonprocedural seems to rest in the manner in which control statements are stated. In *procedural languages the control is explicit and under the direct control of the programmer:* the programmer must state the exact conditions under which one of two specific sequences of operations is to be performed. In *nonprocedural programming, much more of the control seems to be left to the computer:* the programmer can state a goal and let the computer decide what sequence of which operations to perform to reach that goal. For example, in the medical field, an expert systems language could allow one to tell the computer to find all relevant diseases given a set of symptoms and a medical knowledge base. The computer itself is left to determine the method it will employ to achieve this goal.

■ First-Generation Languages: Machine Language

Computer instructions at the most primitive level are defined by the strings of 0's and 1's that correspond to instructions for the control and processing unit; this language is called machine language. The name is appropriate because the sequences of 0's and 1's that define a particular computer program do so only for a particular control and processing unit (i.e., machine) made by a particular manufacturer. For example, a video game program written in machine language for an Apple microcomputer would not be recognizable to an IBM microcomputer. The sequences of 0's and 1's that define a program for one computer are generally meaningless to computers produced by other manufacturers. In fact, the coding of 0's and 1's used with any particular computer has been rather arbitrarily selected by the manufacturer of the integrated circuit chip from which the computer is built.

To create a computer program in machine language, the programmer would have to perform the following steps:

1. After a pseudo-code version of the program has been finished and the design of the program is certain, carefully write down on paper the sequences of 0's and 1's that represent the instructions that make up the new computer program.
2. Turn the computer on and start up a special program for entering machine language programs. This program is often stored in the ROM, but it may also be read from an external storage device.
3. Laboriously (and probably with frequent errors), enter the sequences of 0's and 1's that define the new program.
4. Transfer control of the computer from the machine language entry program to the new program and test the new program.
5. Check the program for any errors, and locate the instructions responsible among the 0's and 1's.
6. Correct the errors by rewriting potentially every line of the program.
7. Repeat the cycle, starting at step 2.

Only through a special machine language entry program can a programmer enter a machine language program into a computer. This program requires two types of data from the programmer: the locations in the computer memory where the instructions are to be stored and the instructions to be stored in the specified locations. Both the locations and the instructions are typed as strings of 0's and 1's (or alternatively as base 8 or base 16 numbers). As the programmer types in the numbers, the entry program places the instructions in the specified locations, and this process is repeated until the entire program is entered.

After the machine language program is stored, the machine language entry program must recognize at least one more command: a command to transfer control to the location where the first instruction of the new machine language program has been stored. Thus, control of the computer is transferred from the machine language entry program to the program written by the programmer, allowing the new program to take control of the computer and complete its task. This process is illustrated below:

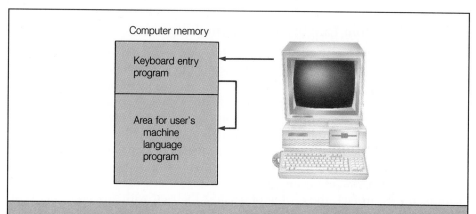

Entry and Execution of Machine Language Programs. Although rarely used, most systems provide some mechanism for the direct entry of machine language codes. A software creation program is started up and the user enters the exact binary codes of the program. No translation software is needed, since the user is directly entering machine code. Execution software can directly start up such a program.

assembly language
A low-level programming language that uses mnemonic abbreviations to represent the 0's and 1's used in machine language. Before a computer program written in assembly language can be used, it must be translated into machine language by a special computer program called an *assembler*.

assembly language programs
A program written in assembly language.

■ Second-Generation Languages: Assembly Language

A complex program called an assembler has been devised to make machine language programming easier. An assembler translates assembly language, a more English-like language for locations and instructions, into the 0's and 1's of machine language. In assembly language, sets of letters from the English alphabet correspond to patterns of 0's and 1's. Whenever a particular set of letters is entered, the assembler translates it into (i.e., replaces it with) the proper bit patterns of 0's and 1's that the computer is able to recognize. Using an assembler thus allows the programmer to program in a more humanlike language and lets the computer translate this language into the 0's and 1's that the computer can work with.

The computer does not directly execute the **assembly language program**. It first treats the letters of the assembly language program as if they were English text and then translates the letters into the patterns of 0's and 1's that it understands. This translation is performed as follows:

1. As each letter is entered at the keyboard, the corresponding ASCII code is stored somewhere in the computer memory.
2. Once the entry of the English-like code is complete, the translation process is begun, that is, the ASCII code, which is stored in memory, is translated by the assembler into strings of 0's and 1's that are then stored at another location in memory.
3. The machine language program created by the assembler can now be executed by transferring control of the computer to the first location in the program.

The entry and translation processes are illustrated in the figure below.

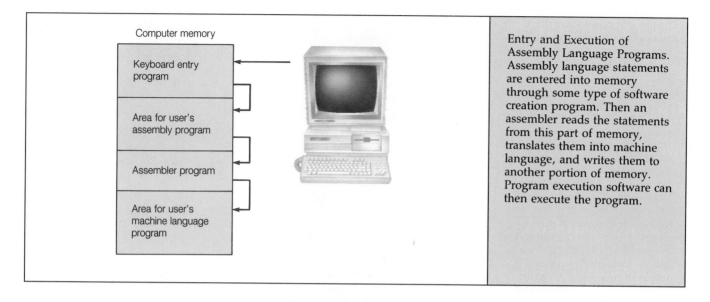

Computer memory

Keyboard entry program

Area for user's assembly program

Assembler program

Area for user's machine language program

Entry and Execution of Assembly Language Programs. Assembly language statements are entered into memory through some type of software creation program. Then an assembler reads the statements from this part of memory, translates them into machine language, and writes them to another portion of memory. Program execution software can then execute the program.

■ Third-Generation Languages: High-Level Languages

The hierarchy of computer languages has another level above assembly languages, but the characteristics of the languages at this level are extremely varied. These languages are generally called **high-level languages,** and they are usually more complex than assembly languages. BASIC and Pascal are familiar examples of high-level languages. These languages are one step closer to human communication, but again, they cannot be directly executed by the computer. Instead, they must be translated into machine language.

As mentioned earlier, one standard method for translating a high-level language into strings of binary digits is to use a translating program called a compiler. The compiler translates each statement of the high-level language into a sequence of assembly language statements. Once this step is complete, the assembler (which already exists) is called upon to finish the job of translating into machine language. When the compilation process is finished, the original high-level program that was stored somewhere in memory has been translated into a second form that consists of the 0's and 1's of machine language. These steps are illustrated in the figure for compiled languages on the next page.

Another method for executing a program written in a high-level language is to write a program that can read through the high-level language and carry out its instructions without bothering to translate it into machine language. This type of program is called an interpreter. The concept behind an interpreter is that each statement in the high-level language has one or more corresponding machine language programs that can do whatever the statement instructs. An interpreter will thus have one or more machine language programs for each of the high-level statements that a programmer might write. The high-level program is executed by invoking these machine language programs in the proper order.

The general technique of using interpreted high-level languages is illustrated in the figure for interpreted languages on the next page. When a state-

high-level language
A computer programming language that uses English-like commands, in contrast to the more cryptic assembly language or machine language.

Entry and Execution of Compiled High-Level Languages. Compilers often work directly with assemblers rather than redoing all the processing available there. The user of a compiled language uses some type of software creation program to enter the language statements into the computer's memory. Then a translation program, the compiler, is started. It reads in the program statements and writes out assembly language statements. These statements are then processed by an assembler that writes out machine code for execution. Of course, both of these processes can be combined into one software program. Once the compilation and assembly are complete, they need not be performed again unless the program is changed.

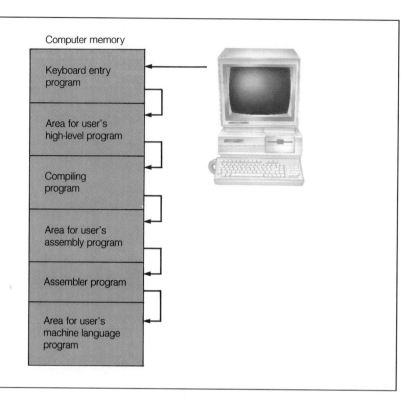

Entry and Execution of Interpreted High-Level Languages. Like a compiler, an interpreter works with program statements that have been entered using some type of software creation program. Once these statements are in memory, the interpreter reads the program statements and directly executes them. There is nothing inherent in a language that dictates a compiled or an interpreted form. Many languages are available in both compiled and interpreted versions.

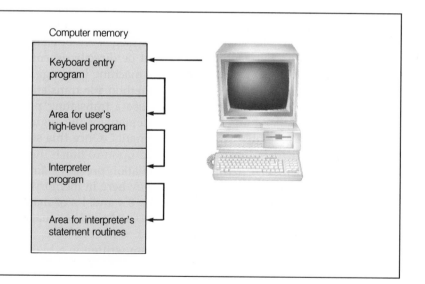

ment in the high-level language is encountered, it is not translated into machine-level instructions; instead, the interpreter calls up a previously written machine language subprocedure to perform the desired action.

We will conclude our comparison of machine language, assembly language, and high-level languages with the table below, in which instructions for the same task are given in each of the three language levels.

Clearly, programming this task in machine language would be subject to error. A programmer would need to memorize many bit patterns and their

---

Programming Across the Language Hierarchy

Common Task: Add two numbers stored in different memory locations and put the result in a third memory location.

Machine Language	Assembly Language	High-Level Language
0100 1 0000001	LOADP 0,V1	LET V3 := V1 + V2
0110 0 0000010	ADDP 0,V2	
0101 1 0000011	STOREP 0,V3	

---

corresponding computer instructions. If a programmer ever needed to change a machine language program, it would probably be necessary to reprogram a large number of the machine language statements.

In contrast, the assembly language program is much easier to use. The programmer does need not to remember such difficult bit patterns but instead needs to remember only simple English-like instructions. For example, LOADP might stand for "load processing register" and STOREP for "store processing register." An English symbol like V1 or V2 can be used if a memory location is needed, then the computer finds an unused spot in its memory and equates the chosen symbol with the bit pattern for that address.

High-level language programs, however, are the easiest to use. They require fewer statements, because any high-level statement can be translated into hundreds of machine language statements. The English-like high-level language constructs for storage definition, control, processing, input, and output are powerful because of their relative ease of use. When these high-level languages are used, the computer assumes responsibility for a great deal of the detail that previously had to be attended to by the human partner. Use of such languages frees programmers to concentrate on the more important task of solving problems.

The development of programming languages has continued to advance into a fourth generation which will be discussed in detail in the next section.

Programming Languages and Software

11.5

A Brief Survey of Programming Languages

PROGRAMS   PROGRAMMING SOFTWARE   PROGRAMMING LANGUAGES

SURVEY OF PROGRAMMING LANGUAGES
FORTRAN • COBOL • APL • LISP • BASIC • PASCAL • C • ADA • Logo • PROLOG • Modula-2

The purpose of this section is to acquaint the reader with a number of the more important programming languages. From the previous discussion, one might expect this section to begin with machine language, then continue with assembly language, and finally go on to high-level languages. However, consider the characteristics of machine language and assembly language.

Every computer has a machine language—placing a pattern of bits into any computer's instruction decoder will cause some input, storage, processing, control, or output function to occur. Unfortunately, computers that have different processors generally have different machine languages. Across the large number of microcomputers, minicomputers, and mainframe computers that have been created by dozens of different vendors, few identical hardware systems can be found, and thus there is no standard machine language that can be presented here. Although comments could be made about IBM's choice of the 8086/80286/80386/80486 chip family or Apple's choice of the 68000 family, little would be gained from presenting long lists of computers and their corresponding machine languages.

Assembly languages present the same problem. Although they are far easier to use than machine languages, assembly languages are closely modeled after machine languages. Again, little would be gained by tallying the possible assembly languages in which one can program.

Only for high-level languages is there enough consistency across computer systems to provide a meaningful discussion. In fact, the **portability** of programs in high-level languages is one of their major advantages. Portability allows programmers to apply their efforts to a variety of machines, that is, a program written in high-level language X for machine Y can probably be run in the same high-level language on machine Z. Thus, portability helps to standardize programming languages. Our survey, therefore, focuses on traditional, high-level, programming languages.

portability
The ease with which a program written for one particular hardware/software system can be transported to another hardware/software system.

■ High-Level Programming Languages

There are a wide variety of high-level programming languages in the world of computing. No one has yet created a language that is ideal for all situations, probably because the language requirements in one setting are frequently very different from those of another. As an introduction, a few of the high-level languages that are of historical and current interest are described below:

- □ *FORTRAN.* FORTRAN (*formula trans*lation) was the first widely accepted scientific language available on computers. It remains the most widely used language in scientific and engineering applications.
- □ *COBOL.* COBOL (*common business oriented language*) is by far the most widely used business language because, for many years, all federal programming contracts required programs to be written in COBOL.
- □ *APL.* APL (*a programming language*) is an interpretive language that is very elegantly designed for handling matrix manipulation problems. (A matrix is an **array** of numbers much like a table.) APL is one of the few languages that has developed an entirely new alphabet for its use, thus an APL program is almost totally incomprehensible to the uninitiated.
- □ *LISP.* LISP (*list processing language*) is another elegant interpretive language. It is one of the primary tools of researchers in the field of

array
A set of related data, all of the same type, stored together and referenced as a single unit. Arrays can have a number of *dimensions*. For example, an array of one dimension is a list, an array of two dimensions is a table, an array of three dimensions is a stack of tables (a cube), and so forth.

artificial intelligence. Some of its major advantages include the easy way in which one piece of data can be made to point to other pieces of data and the fact that the form of data and program statements are identical.

☐ *BASIC.* BASIC (*b*eginner's *a*ll-purpose *s*ymbolic *i*nstruction *c*ode) is currently the most common interpreted language for microcomputers. Historically, the standard BASIC language provided with most early computers was not well designed, but newer, more sophisticated versions are now available, and BASIC continues to be generally easy to use and adequate for many programming needs.

☐ *Pascal.* Pascal, named after the mathematician Blaise Pascal, is the new compiled, **structured programming language** that is becoming popular on microcomputers. Pascal may replace BASIC as the language of choice for micros in the future.

☐ *C.* C is the compiled language developed by Bell Laboratories in which the UNIX operating system is written. As UNIX becomes more popular, the popularity of C is also increasing.

☐ *Ada.* Ada, named after Augusta Ada Byron (see chapter 2), is the new standard language for all work done for the U.S. Department of Defense (DOD). Ada may become as significant as the previous DOD standard language, COBOL.

☐ *Logo.* Logo is essentially a variation of LISP that has a nicer syntactic form for statements and a graphics ability centered around a tiny image called a turtle. The turtle can be used to draw a line as it "walks" around a screen. Logo has frequently been used to teach computer programming to elementary school children.

☐ *PROLOG.* PROLOG is a new language that focuses on telling the computer *what* to do, not *how* to do it. Proponents of PROLOG look forward to solving the problem of knowing whether a program is really correct and to having the computer write programs automatically.

☐ *Modula-2.* Modula-2 is a replacement for Pascal that includes many very useful features that were left out of Pascal.

This list of high-level programming languages is in no way complete, but it does contain many of the most commonly used languages. New languages are being developed rapidly as computers become more powerful. As we might expect, each time the computer gains some new capability, a new or modified language must be created so that the programmer can utilize that new ability.

■ Very High Level Programming Languages

The highest level programming languages are not easily defined or explained, partly because of their rapid development. However, several aspects of these **very high level languages** (VHLLs) need to be considered.

VHLLs are often described as nonprocedural languages. Indeed, many VHLLs do allow programming without the requiring that explicit program control be provided. When using ordinary high-level languages such as Pascal, the programmer proceeds through four steps in creating a program: (1) determination of what is needed (**goal analysis**), (2) determination of how the goal is to be accomplished (**program design),** (3) **program development**, and (4)

structured programming language
A programming language that emphasizes organizing a program into logical pieces or modules for ease of programming, testing, and maintenance.

very high-level languages (VHLLs)
Nonprocedural programming languages that are problem specific, in which programmers deal primarily with goal analysis and program design, with the translation program performing the remaining tasks of development and evaluation.

goal analysis
A procedure of interview, data collection, and review for determining the users, goals, resources, and constraints involved in the creation and use of a program or system. Its purpose is to generate a well-defined statement of system requirements.

program design
The translation of the goal analysis results into a design or plan for the development of a program.

program development
The implementation of a computer program design, including the selection of a programming language and the actual programming.

program evaluation
Testing a computer program to see if it performs as intended; its principal concerns are verification (does the program's performance match its design?) and validation (does the program solve the user's problem?).

applications generators
Interpreter-translators that convert VHLL programs into the ISPCO activities defining word processing, spread sheet or data base management applications.

program generators
Programs that interact with a user through an interview process to complete goal analysis and program design and then independently compile the new program using a lower-level language.

program evaluation. The use of VHLLs requires only the first step (goal analysis) or, at most, the first step and part of the second. A powerful translation program then performs the remaining programming tasks, including specification of the control function. Several different approaches to VHLLs are presently in use.

Applications Generators.   Word processors, spreadsheets, data base systems, and graphics software are tailored to perform certain types of processing. For example, if a user needs to store a lot of data on a variety of objects and generate many types of reports, a data base management system seems appropriate. Similarly, budgets requiring constant revisions and automatic updating suggest the use of spreadsheets. These applications software packages are often considered **applications generators**.

For example, when a new data base is needed, the user does not need to write a program in an ordinary programming language. Instead, a data base system is started up and the knowledgeable user uses the general functions of the data base system to create a data base design, data base search mechanisms, and data base reports. The result of this preparation is a complete software system. With the record format, searching methods, and reports defined, the system is ready for use by clerks, data entry personnel, and others who will be working with the data base. Without using one line of a "programming language," the user has developed a complete working applications system. The development of finished applications with such applications generators will undoubtedly continue to grow as a major technique for using computers to solve real problems.

Program Generators.   Programs that write other programs are called **program generators**. Such programs interact with a user to determine his or her goals and to design software to meet those goals. The program generator creates and compiles a finished program, using a lower-level language to meet the design specifications. The domain of a program generator might be quite small, e.g., a program generator might write only programs for the display of a form on a computer screen and the entry of data into this form. Yet the programs created by such program generators will generally be totally correct and virtually guaranteed to work. Such systems are not in wide use as yet, because much of the theory of how they should work is poorly understood. However, some major corporations now use program generators as the only approved tool for corporate software development.

Fourth-Generation Languages.   *Fourth generation languages* is a widely-used and ambiguous term. At the very least, fourth-generation languages might include applications generators and program generators, or a fourth-generation language might be an ordinary programming language, like BASIC or Pascal, augmented by a wide variety of programming aids. Such aids might include:

1. Screen design aids that automatically display the BASIC or Pascal statements and use a particular screen layout on a video screen.
2. Interfaces to data base management systems that allow ordinary programming languages to carry out complex data base processing (storage, retrieval, and report generation) by passing such processing to an underlying data base system.
3. Similar interfaces to underlying spreadsheet systems, chart graphics, systems, paint graphics systems, mathematical analysis tools, and so on.

Other possibilities for fourth-generation languages have no relation to ordinary programming languages. They process statements in their own much higher level language, using statements that concern entire data bases, screens, graphic images, et cetera. Fourth-generation languages of this type may be misnamed because they generally do not allow the user to create an arbitrary application but can create only selected applications (e.g., they might be very good at creating data management programs but be unable to create a video game of any variety). Thus, languages of this design should perhaps be termed applications programs rather than fourth-generation languages.

Fourth-generation languages have one aim: to simplify the task of programming a computer. Most fourth-generation languages are therefore non-procedural. They generally provide an easy-to-use interface that pays careful attention to the human factors involved in program creation. Some of these languages are designed primarily for use by skilled professionals and assume a high level of training for their users, while others are equally accessible to both skilled and unskilled users.

Perhaps the most important point about fourth-generation languages is that the novice user can take heart. Although the mechanics of typical programming languages like BASIC or Pascal should be understood, other varieties of computer software provide substantially easier ways to get a computer to do what is needed.

The purpose of programming languages is to provide a way to give commands to a computer. Any of the languages described in this chapter (i.e., machine languages, assembly languages, high-level languages, or very high level languages) can be used to give instructions to a computer, but they differ in such features as ease of use, portability, and speed of the finished product. When comparing these programming languages to the applications software examined earlier in the text, differences appear in two distinct dimensions.

11.6

Programming Languages Summary

Dimension 1: Storage and Processing Complexity. Programming languages (e.g., Pascal or BASIC) support general-purpose, simple storage structures (e.g., places to store numbers or names) and processes (e.g., addition and subtraction). Programmers can create any kind of complex storage structure (e.g., an income tax table) or process (e.g., balancing a checkbook) using the elemental structures and control functions.

In contrast, applications software, (e.g., spreadsheet systems) provide complex storage (e.g., a spreadsheet table) and processing (e.g., ripple calculation after a change), but they are very specific and not general-purpose (e.g., the spreadsheet cannot be used to make a video game).

Dimension 2: Control Complexity. Programming languages (e.g., BASIC or Pascal), provide a large number of commands for control, including sequence, selection, and iteration. It is through these three control commands that complex processing and storage can be built out of sequences of simple processes and storage commands.

In comparison, applications software (e.g., spreadsheet systems) already have complex data structures and processing commands, so there is less need for control complexity and therefore *few control commands* are provided.

In summary programming languages provide simple, general-purpose data structures, many simple, general-purpose processing commands, and complex control capabilities, while applications software languages provide complex, special-purpose data structures, complex, special-purpose processing commands, and very limited control capabilities. The various software systems examined in this text can be compared graphically in terms of these two dimensions:

Dimensions of Software Systems

Complex storage and processes	data base systems	(new software may develop here)
	spreadsheets	programming languages
	word processors	
Simple storage and processes		programming languages

| Simple control | . . . | Complex control |

If present trends continue, new systems will be developed along specific lines that merge programming and applications software. Already, applications software is moving to support more general-purpose data structures and more complex commands for control, including programs with sequence, selection, and iteration. Similarly, programming languages are providing interfaces to complete applications packages that can be treated as subsystems of an arbitrary software system. The two types of software will no doubt continue to converge.

Chapter 11 Review

Expanded Objectives

The objectives listed below are an expansion of the essential chapter concepts listed at the beginning of the chapter. The review items that follow are based on these expanded objectives. If you master the objectives, you will do better on the review items and on your instructor's examination on the chapter.

After reading the chapter, you should be able to:

1. understand the simple BASIC commands REM, INPUT, LET, and PRINT.
2. relate the concepts of vocabulary, syntax, semantics, and pragmatics to programming languages.
3. discriminate among program preparation, translation, and execution software.
4. distinguish between procedural and nonprocedural programming languages.
5. discriminate among assemblers, compilers, and interpreters in terms of their functions and operations.
6. recognize the characteristics of selected high-level languages.
7. discriminate among the four generations of computer programming languages.
8. relate ISPCO functions to computer programming.
9. discriminate among machine, assembly, and high-level languages.
10. recognize the meanings of major new terms introduced in this chapter.

Review Items

Completing this review will give you a good indication of how well you have mastered the contents of this chapter and prepare you for your instructor's test on this material. To maximize what you learn from this exercise, you should answer each question *before* looking up the answers in the appendix. The number of the corresponding expanded objective is given in parentheses following each question.

Complete the following sets of items according to the directions heading each set.

A. True or False.

___ 1. Programs used to run high-level language programs are called program execution software. (3)

___ 2. There are statements in programming languages that are not executed by the computer. (1)

___ 3. A program trace helps programmers detect incorrect control statements in a program. (3)

___ 4. When a computer program executes a command, it deletes it from the program. (3)

___ 5. One way a computer demonstrates control is by causing functions to be performed in an appropriate sequence. (8)

___ 6. Programming languages are natural languages used to write instructions that computers can process. (2)

___ 7. The rules of syntax of a programming language determine how key words are arranged to specify commands. (2)

___ 8. Pseudo-code is a form of machine language that can be interpreted directly by the computer. (6, 7)

___ 9. A compiler immediately translates each program line as it is entered. (5)

___ 10. The use of nonprocedural programming languages does not require the programmer to provide explicit statements of control. (4)

___ 11. In general, using applications software requires many control instructions. (4)

___ 12. One advantage of a machine language program is that it can be executed on all makes of computers. (7)

___ 13. A major source of error in procedural language programming is incorrect sequencing of 0's and 1's (5,7)

___ 14. In BASIC, LET statements are used for the input function, while PRINT statements are used for the output function. (1)

___ 15. Assemblers are programs that assist programmers in writing machine language programs. (5)

___ 16. High-level languages can now be directly executed by computers without interpretation or translation. (6)

___ 17. Instead of translating a computer program from one computer language into another, an interpreter calls up equivalent, existing subprocedures. (5)

___ 18. Assembly language programs are much easier to change than machine language programs. (5)

___ 19. "C" is an example of a high-level language. (6)

___ 20. While programs that write other programs do not yet exist, their invention is predicted for the near future. (8)

___ 21. *Portability* refers to how widely a particular programming language may be used across various hardware and software systems. (7)

___ 22. Lower-level programming languages require greater translation than higher-level ones. (7)

___ 23. Programming in machine language is more prone to error than is programming in either assembly or high-level languages. (5,7)

___ 24. A word processing program written for the IBM PS/2 will probably work directly on the Apple Macintosh II. (7)

___ 25. Computers cannot directly execute commands in assembly language. (5)

___ 26. High-level languages are closer to the form of human communication than are assembly languages. (7)

___ 27. The portability of higher-level languages is greater than that of lower-level languages. (7)

___ 28. Any one high-level language statement might translate into hundreds of machine level statements. (7)

___ 29. In very high level languages, translation programs may actually perform development tasks, in addition to performing the evaluation steps of program design.(7)

B. *For each of the following matching questions, select the best alternatives on the right for each item on the left.*

Matching—set I (3)

___ 30. enables programmers to edit

___ 31. enables programmers to save and load programs

___ 32. uses a compiler to carry out its function

___ 33. permits use of a program trace

___ 34. identifies improper syntax

___ 35. detects improper operations

___ 36. allows program breaks at specified points to check for errors

a. program execution software
b. program translation software
c. program preparation software

Matching—set II (7)

___ 37. the easiest language in which to program

___ 38. requires the programmer to remember bit patterns

___ 39. one of its statements may translate to hundreds in another language

___ 40. requires the computer to be responsible for more details than do the other languages

___ 41. translates one language into another

___ 42. most portable between hardware systems.

a. assembly language
b. high-level language
c. machine language

Matching—set III (6)

___ 43. used mainly in the field of artificial intelligence

___ 44. the most commonly used language on microcomputers

___ 45. used to teach programming to elementary school children

___ 46. tells the computer *what* to do rather than *how* to do it

___ 47. the most widely used language in business

a. COBOL
b. BASIC
c. Ada
d. Logo
e. PROLOG
f. LISP
g. Pascal

Matching—set IV (7)

___ 48. assembly language

___ 49. machine language

___ 50. high-level language

a. first-generation language
b. second-generation language
c. third-generation language
d. fourth-generation language
e. fifth-generation language

Matching—set V (6,8)

Study the graph below and determine the proper position of each system in the right-hand column. Place the letter of each system at the appropriate number on the graph.

Complex storage and processes

___ 51.   ___ 52.

.

___ 53.

.

.

___ 54.   ___ 55.

Simple storage and processes

a. data base systems
b. programming languages
c. word processors
d. new software types
e. spreadsheets

Simple control   ···   Complex control

Computer Programming and Systems Design

Essential Chapter Concepts

When you finish this chapter, you should know:

■ The four stages in the Program Development Life Cycle.

■ How each step in the Program Development Life Cycle should be carried out.

■ The basic concepts of structured programming.

■ The commonly used methods of creating good, well-structured programs.

■ The relationship between program and system development.

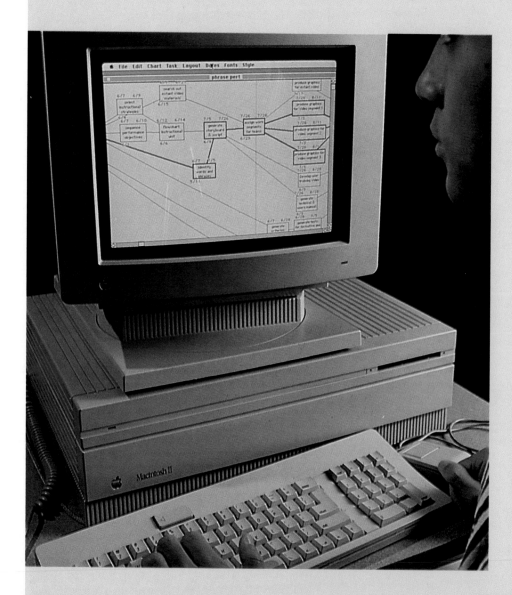

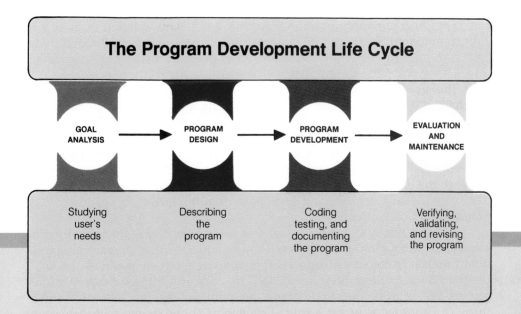

The Program Development Life Cycle

GOAL ANALYSIS	PROGRAM DESIGN	PROGRAM DEVELOPMENT	EVALUATION AND MAINTENANCE
Studying user's needs	Describing the program	Coding testing, and documenting the program	Verifying, validating, and revising the program

This chapter will introduce the process of **computer programming**, describing the four stages of programming and the methods used in each stage. To make our discussion of programming more meaningful, we will first take a brief look at ordinary problem solving, because computer programming is a special kind of problem solving.

In the nineteenth century, psychologists studied gifted problem solvers and found that they share many common characteristics. Two of these traits have counterpoints in modern programming. The *first characteristic* is that effective problem solvers attack problems in four steps by:

1. studying the problem carefully and restating it in a clear and concise form,
2. developing and clarifying a potential solution,
3. applying the solution to the problem, and
4. evaluating the results.

If the results are satisfactory, the solution is used as long as it is needed and continues to work. If the results are not satisfactory, the problem solver restudies the problem or tries a different potential solution. The programming equivalent of the four-step problem-solving process is the *Program Development Life Cycle (PDLC)*. The four stages of the **PDLC** are:

1. *Goal analysis.* The problem is studied carefully and restated in a clear form.
2. *Program design.* A plan for using the computer and other resources to solve the problem is developed.
3. *Program development.* The plan for solving the problem is carried out.
4. *Program evaluation and program maintenance.* The results of using the plan are examined to see if the problem has been successfully solved or if the process must be initiated anew. Once the problem is successfully solved, the program is continuously evaluated and maintained as long as it remains useful.

This chapter was written with Jeane C. Vinsonhaler, Ph.D.

computer programming
The process of designing and writing computer programs.

PDLC
The Program Development Life Cycle is the set of steps taken in creating and operating a computer program: goal analyses, design, development, evaluation and maintenance.

The programming process is a difficult one. In the solution of most real programming problems, the programmer moves back and forth through these four stages during the entire useful life of the program, usually understanding and solving one part of the problem at a time.

The *second characteristic* of effective problem solvers is that they break problems down into subproblems. Restructuring a problem into subproblems simplifies the task by breaking it into parts which may be more easily understood and solved separately. For example, suppose the problem is to drive from Wall Street in New York City to Geary Street in San Francisco. This large problem can be broken down into three subproblems: (1) getting from Wall Street to the interstate freeway, (2) following the interstate freeway from New York City to San Francisco, and (3) getting from the interstate freeway in San Francisco to Geary Street.

The programming equivalent of this second problem-solving method is **structured programming.** In structured programming, the original programming problem is separated into subprograms or **program modules.** (A subprogram is a set of computer instructions that perform a specific task, e.g., inputting data values). The subprograms are combined together by control structures. (A **control structure** is a way of combining subprograms so that they are executed in the correct order). The control structures used in structured programming include *sequence* (executing a set of instructions one after the other), *selection* (executing only one of many separate sets of instructions), and *iteration* (repeating a set of instructions). As we proceed through this chapter, our understanding of the program development life cycle and structured programming will be developed and refined. A number of important terms related to these ideas will be used frequently throughout this chapter:

- □ *Program.* A set of instructions written in a computer programming language, designed to achieve a specific objective.
- □ **Subprogram** or *program module.* A part of a program that performs a specific, well-defined operation. Subprograms include procedures, **subroutines,** and functions.
- □ **Program Product.** A software package that includes a tested program and **documentation** on the program.

structured programming
A method of designing and constructing programs by breaking the program into logical modules and coherently combining the modules using a few well understood control structures, thus improving program clarity, reducing testing time and increasing productivity.

program module or **subprogram**
A part of a computer program designed to perform a specific task for the program.

control structures
Syntactic structures in a programming language that control the order in which statements are executed. Types of control structures include sequencing, selection (alternation), iteration (repetition or looping), and procedure calls.

program product
A software package that includes program modules, installation data, and documentation.

documentation
The collection of information that describes the exact procedures for working with computer software and/ or hardware, including manuals, reference guides, and tutorial instruction.

12.1

The Program Development Life Cycle

We will begin our examination of the programming process with a case study that focuses on the stages of the Program Development Life Cycle and the problem-solving nature of programming.

Case Study

It was a bright, warm day, so Gouri, Jim, and Sue decided to work outside. As Gouri approached the appointed meeting site, he spotted Jim and Sue seated comfortably on the grass with their backs against a huge oak. They were arguing, as usual. A large brown squirrel and a small duck were watching them attentively.

"That's a mallard, I tell you!" said Sue. "Oh! Hi, Gouri. did you bring the assignment?"

"Yes, indeed," Gouri replied. "And I brought extra copies for you two."

The three studied the assignment for a few minutes in silence. It included an interview with their imaginary user, Barney, the clothing company magnate. Gouri spoke first,

"From this interview, we are supposed to create a suitable program by going through the four programming stages that Dr. Jones described in class."

"Oh, yeah," interjected Jim, "goal analysis, design, development, and evaluation and maintenance."

"Okay," said Sue. "Let's start the goal analysis. Let's see. We're working with several different clothing types sold by each of Barney's stores. Hmmm . . . we know some things about the program. First, the output should show the total dollar amount of the sales for each type of clothing and the sales for all clothing for each store. Second, the dollar amount of sales for each type of clothing is computed by multiplying the number sold by the selling price. Finally, total dollar sales for each store is the sum of the sales for each type of clothing." Sue looked quite pleased with herself.

"In addition," Jim pointed out, "the program has to do all that for as many stores as Barney wants reports for."

"Yes," said Gouri, "and our program must process data for three types of clothing: coats, hats, and shirts."

Sue started writing on a piece of paper. "I'll write all this down and make up some test data, as Dr. Jones suggested," she said. Sue wrote:

Store: No. 1, 123 West Main Street

Type	Number	Price	Sales
COATS	10	50	500
HATS	20	20	400
SHIRTS	30	25	750
TOTAL			1650

After the team had finished analyzing the sample data, they felt that they truly understood the problem and the requirements of the program. They were now ready to proceed to the next stage of the programming process, program design.

Gouri started the discussion. "As I understand it, program design is basically a description of the program that we will write to solve the problem. According to Dr. Jones, it should have three basic parts. The first part is a description of the data elements that the program will use, like 'number of items sold' or 'selling price.' Then, there are the processing elements—that's where we define the sales for each type of clothing as a function of the number sold and the selling price. Finally, there must be a *control structure* that specifies the order in which the processing will occur."

Sue interrupted, "You know, there is a match here between the program design and the ISPCO functions. The data elements will be *input, stored,* and *output*—that's the simplest level. Then they will be *processed* by the processing elements, and the whole thing will be *controlled* by various control structures."

"I think that you are correct, Sue," Gouri replied, "but please let me continue. The design that I would use would look like this." Taking paper from his briefcase, Gouri wrote:

Data elements.
1. TYPE   = the name of each type of clothing
2. NUMBER = the number sold of each type of clothing
3. PRICE   = the selling price of each type of clothing
4. SALES   = the sales for each type of clothing

Processing elements.

1. Let SALES hold the value NUMBER * PRICE (the formula for computing the sales for each type of clothing)

Control structure.

1. For each type of clothing, do steps 2–3
2. Input data for each type of clothing (TYPE, NUMBER, PRICE)
3. Compute SALES for each type of clothing (see process element #1)
4. For each type of clothing, do step 5
5. Output SALES for each type of clothing

"Well," said Jim, "that looks okay to me."

"Hold on a minute," Sue interrupted. "Let's do a walk through—you know, simulate what the program will do, so that we can check out these ideas with our test data."

They all looked at the data and tried to envision how the procedure that Gouri had written would work. Jim frowned.

"I see a problem. The design that Gouri wrote forgot about the store name and the calculation of the total sales for each store."

"Also," admitted Gouri, "I forgot to repeat the process for more than one store."

Jim then revised the design specifications (each new specification is indicated by an arrow):

Data elements.

$\rightarrow$ 1. STORE   = the name of each store.
    2. TYPE   = the name of each type of clothing.
    3. NUMBER = the number sold of each type of clothing.
    4. PRICE   = the selling price of each type of clothing.
    5. SALES   = the sales for each type of clothing.
$\rightarrow$ 6. TOTAL   = the total sales for each store.

Processing elements.

    1. Let SALES hold the value NUMBER * PRICE (the formula for computing the sales for each type of clothing).
$\rightarrow$ 2. Let TOTAL hold the sum of all the sales for each store.
$\rightarrow$ 3. Compare the STORE name to the phrase "DONE" (to see if any more stores are to be processed).

Control structure.

$\rightarrow$ 1. Input STORE, the name of each store.
$\rightarrow$ 2. If STORE = "DONE" (process element #3), then end.
    3. For each type of clothing, do Steps 4–5.
    4. Input data for a type of clothing (TYPE, NUMBER, PRICE).
    5. Compute SALES for each type of clothing (process element #1).
    6. For each type of clothing, do step 7.
    7. Output SALES for each type of clothing.
$\rightarrow$ 8. Compute and output TOTAL for each store (process element #2).
$\rightarrow$ 9. Continue for the next store, starting at step 1

Having completed the design in pseudo-code, the team adjourned to the Micro Lab and began the program development stage.

The first step in the program development stage was the translation of the pseudo-code description of the program into BASIC, the programming language that was being used in the course. They used the same programming software they had used in their last assignment (i.e., software for entering program statements into the computer).

After coding and inputting, the program looked like this:

```
100 REM Give starting message.
110 PRINT "Barney's Clothing Store Sales Report."
120 REM
130 REM Get which store.
140 PRINT "Enter which store:"
150 INPUT STORE$
160 REM
170 REM Stop (END) if the store name is "DONE."
180 IF STORE$ = "DONE" THEN END
190 REM
200 REM Get coat data.
210 PRINT "How many coats were sold?"
220 INPUT NUMBER_COATS
230 PRINT "What was the price of each coat?"
240 INPUT PRICE_COATS
250 REM Compute sales.
260 LET SALES_COATS = NUMBER_COATS * PRICE_COATS
270 REM
280 REM Repeat for other types of clothing.
290 PRINT "How many hats were sold?"
300 INPUT NUMBER_HATS
310 PRINT "What was the price of each hat?"
320 INPUT PRICE_HATS
330 LET SALES_HATS = NUMBER_HATS * PRICE_HATS
340 PRINT "How many shirts were sold?"
350 INPUT NUMBER_SHIRTS
360 PRINT "What was the price of each shirt?"
370 INPUT PRICE_SHIRTS
380 LET SALES_SHIRTS = NUMBER_SHIRTS * PRICE_SHIRTS
390 REM
400 REM Print name of store.
410 PRINT "Store: ";STORE
420 REM Print sales by type of clothing.
430 PRINT "Sales for coats are ";SALES_COATS
440 PRINT "Sales for hats are ";SALES_HATS
450 PRINT "Sales for shirts are ";SALES_SHIRTS
460 REM
470 REM Compute and print the total sales for each store.
480 LET TOTAL = SALES_COATS+SALES_HATS+SALES_SHIRTS
490 PRINT "Total Sales are "TOTAL
500 GO TO 130
```

Next, the team used the programming software to translate and execute the program. Because the BASIC language they were using was an interpreted language, this step consisted of merely telling the programming software to "run" their BASIC program. No major problems occurred, so the team proceeded to the next programming stage, program evaluation.

"In the program evaluation stage, we must test the program carefully with our test data and ask ourselves if it truly solves the original problem," said Gouri as he began to run the test. At the end of the test, the team looked over their output:

```
Barney's Clothing Store Sales Report.
Enter which store:No. 1, 325 Main Street
How many coats were sold?10
What was the price of each coat?50
How many hats were sold?20
What was the price of each hat?20
How many shirts were sold?30
What was the price of each shirt?25
Sales for Store: No. 1, 325 Main Street
Sales for coats is 500
Sales for hats is 400
Sales for shirts is 750
Total Sales are 1650
Enter which store:DONE

Program Execution Terminated Normally
```

The team spent another fifteen minutes printing out the program so that they could turn it in. Then they ran the program a few more times with mock data (data they made up from several stores), feeling rather smug about the ease with which they had created their first program. They agreed to meet later to talk about program maintenance.

When the team reconvened a few days later, Jim was excited. "I translated our program into Pascal, so now we can run it on the mainframe computer, too! That's part of program maintenance, right?"

"Well, that's really great, Jim," Sue said, somewhat sarcastically, "but your Pascal program has real problems, if it runs like our BASIC program did!"

"What do you mean?" Jim replied.

"I decided to run our program with a real user, like Dr. Jones suggested," responded Sue, "So I had my roommate sit down and pretend that she was Barney. The first thing that she did was type some data in wrong! Instead of typing in $20 as the cost of a hat, she typed in $2000. So her work got all muddled up and she had to start over. Then, she complained about the way the program ended, kind of in the middle of things. We didn't provide any message for the program to say that it was finished!"

"Oh, my," said Gouri. "Does this mean that we must rework our program before turning it in?"

"No," replied Sue. "I talked to Dr. Jones about it. She said that I had discovered a real-world fact of computing—programs are never finished, and evaluation of a program should continue as long as it is used, implementing improvements or replacements whenever needed. She said we didn't have to work anymore on this one, though, thank goodness!"

Even in this simple example, the programming team went through the standard steps for solving a problem. Although real-world programs are of substantially greater complexity than this one, the program development life cycle remains the same.

12.2

What Happened in the Case Study? An Overview of the Program Development Life Cycle

To emphasize the concepts just demonstrated, we will review each of the four stages of the program development life cycle illustrating our discussion with the programming task from the case study.

■ The Four Stages of the Program Development Life Cycle

Goal analysis. Goal analysis is the process of obtaining a clear idea of what the program should do, i.e., determining the objectives of the program. Goal analysis includes a description of the user, the tasks that the user wants to

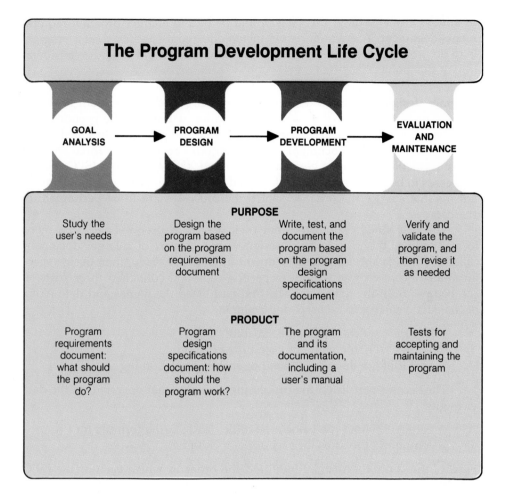

accomplish, and the constraints on the program and development process. In our case study, the problem was to produce a sales report for Barney's clothing company, but that description alone did not sufficiently define the problem. The team also needed to know what data would be input to the computer, how sales would be calculated, how the results would be displayed, and what data values might be used. As these questions point out, even the simplest programming problem requires considerable explication before the design of a program is begun.

In the case study, the team described the results of their analysis primarily through a sample set of input data and output results:

Store: No. 1, 123 West Main Street			
Type	**Number**	**Price**	**Sales**
COATS	10	50	500
HATS	20	20	400
SHIRTS	30	25	750
TOTAL			1650

program requirements document
Documentation that specifies what a proposed program is supposed to do; a cohesive, integrated description of a problem and its context, drawn from the data generated by goal analysis.

subroutine
A subprogram referred to as a routine or subroutine in some languages (e.g., BASIC and FORTRAN) and as procedures in others (e.g. Pascal).

design specifications document
A description of a computer program that is intended to solve the problem described in a program requirements document; the output of the program design stage.

In a more formal setting, this table would be part of a larger **program requirements document.** A program requirements document specifies *what* a program is to do, not how to do it. Structured programming would not be a consideration at this point.

Program design. Program design is the process used by the team to define the component parts of the computer program in English-like pseudo-code. Program design describes *how* the program is to do what was specified in the program requirements document. The design process consists of three separate steps: (1) defining the data elements to be used, (2) defining the ISPO (not C) processes to be performed on the data, and (3) describing the control (C) mechanisms that specify the order in which the processes are to be performed on the data.

The case study team wrote out their design in pseudo-code. In a more formal setting, the pseudo-code design would be part of a larger document called the **design specifications document.** In our case study, their design specifications document was written in pseudo-code and contained three parts as can be seen from the following. The first part listed the names and definitions of the data elements to be used, for example,

- □ STORE   = the name of each store.
- □ TYPE   = the name of each type of clothing.
- □ NUMBER = the number sold of each type of clothing.

The second part listed the processing elements that operated on the data elements:

- □ Let SALES hold the value NUMBER * PRICE (the formula for computing the sales for each type of clothing).

Finally, the control structures indicated the order in which each of the ISPO activities was to be performed:

- □ Input STORE, the name of each store.
- □ If STORE = "DONE" then end.

The problem in the case study was so simple that the programming team did not have to use structured programming techniques. In a more complex task, structured programming would have been introduced at this point in the design, and the program would be broken into subprograms or modules.

Program development. Program development is the process of creating the computer program from the design description and consists of four steps. The first is the *restatement of the pseudo-code design in a language that the computer can process.* In the case study, the pseudo-code was restated as BASIC language instructions:

```
100 REM Give starting message.
110 PRINT "Barney's Clothing Store Sales Report."
120 REM
130 REM Get which store.
140 PRINT "Enter which store:"
150 INPUT STORE$
160 REM
170 REM Stop (END) if the store name is "DONE."
180 IF STORE$ = "DONE" THEN END
190 REM
```

```
200 REM Get coat data.
210 PRINT "How many coats were sold?"
220 INPUT NUMBER_COATS
```

.
.
.

The second step in program development is *entering the programming language instructions into the computer*. The case study team had to start up the program preparation software, enter their BASIC program into the computer, and save the program to disk.

The third step in program development is *testing the program* by starting up the program translation software and the program execution software to run the program. For the BASIC program in our example, an interpreter that both translated and ran the program was used. As the interpreter processed the simple program, the team began testing the program by inputting data with known answers:

```
Barney's Clothing Store Sales Report.
Enter which store:No. 1, 325 Main Street
How many coats were sold?10
What was the price of each coat?50
   .
   .
   .
Sales for Store:No. 1, 325 Main Street
Sales for coats is 500
   .
   .
Total Sales are 1650
Enter which store:DONE

Program Execution Terminated Normally
```

The team verified that the sums were correct. Then they retested the program with other data and concluded that the program was probably correct.

The fourth step in program development is the *creation of documentation* that includes both comments built into the program for the programming staff and external documents for the users of the program. (Little documentation was needed for the simple program in our case study.) At the end of the program development stage, the program should be completed, tested for obvious errors, documented, and ready for evaluation.

Program evaluation and maintenance. Program evaluation is concerned with two types of evaluation: **verification** (determining whether the program's performance matches the specifications in the program design) and **validation** (determining whether the program solves the user's original problem). Program verification is done by running the program with a variety of sample data and confirming that accurate results are obtained. Program validation is more difficult. It is done by having actual users work with the completed program. If program validation is successful, it becomes program maintenance, i.e., as changes occur in the organization using the program, the program is modified and adapted. In our case study, the program failed the validation test; if this program had been prepared for a real-world user, the programming team

program maintenance
The process of modifying and adapting a computer program to fit with changes in hardware, other software and users needs.

verification
The process of ensuring that the computer program meets the objectives stated in the program design specifications.

validation
The process of determining the extent to which a program meets the needs of a user.

would have had to return to one of the previous steps of the program development process.

The steps of the program development process are summarized graphically below.

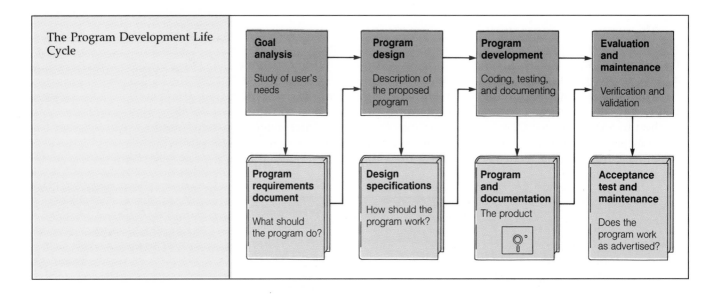

The Program Development Life Cycle

The Role of Structured Programming in the Program Development Life Cycle

The problem in the case study was so simple that there was no need to use structured programming. Nevertheless, the problem can be used to illustrate the concept. First, let us consider a more complete definition of structured programming (adapted from Anthony Ralston and Edwin Reilly, Jr., *The Encyclopedia of Computer Science and Engineering* [New York, Second Edition Van Nostrand Reinhold Co., 1983]): Structured programming is a methodological style of designing and constructing programs by (1) coherently concatenating logical subprograms and (2) using only a small number of well-understood control structures both within and between the subprograms.

Concatenating means linking together. **Logical subprograms** (or modules) are parts of a program that are independent but can be combined together to perform the functions required of the program. "Well-understood control structures" refers to sequence, selection, and interation.

Thus, structured programs have two characteristics: (1) they are composed of subprograms that independently perform the functions required of the program, and (2) they usually use only three types of control statements: sequence, selection, and iteration. These three types of control structures are summarized in Figure 12–1.

In Figure 12–1, a task can be a single action (or step), for example, task 1 might be: compute SALES = PRICE ∗ NUMBER and task 2 might be: output SALES. A task can also be a logical segment of a program (consisting of several steps), for example: input TYPE, input NUMBER, input PRICE. The condition C in the figure refers to a relationship (such as: Variable STORE has value "DONE") which can be true or false.

Now, let us use the program in the case study to illustrate structured

concatenation
The linking together of the elements of a system (e.g., linking subprograms to form a structured program).

logical subprograms
Independent parts of a program that when combined perform the functions required of the program.

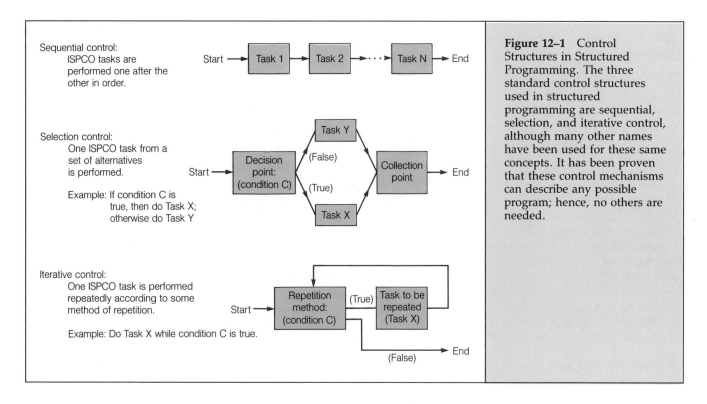

Figure 12–1 Control Structures in Structured Programming. The three standard control structures used in structured programming are sequential, selection, and iterative control, although many other names have been used for these same concepts. It has been proven that these control mechanisms can describe any possible program; hence, no others are needed.

programming. First, we can examine the program in terms of its logical sub-units (these subunits would be subprograms in a more complex problem). The following control structure has the same control specifications as in the case study, but the pseudo-code has been changed slightly and indentation has been added to show the logical structure of the problem.

The case study control structure.
1. Input STORE name.
2. If STORE = "DONE" then end. Else continue.
3.   For each type of clothing: COATS, HATS, SHIRTS, repeat steps 3, 4, 5, and 6
4.   Input data for a type of clothing (TYPE, NUMBER, PRICE).
5.   Compute & output SALES: SALES = NUMBER * PRICE.
6.   Repeat for the next type of clothing (from step 3).
7. Compute and print TOTAL Sales for each store: TOTAL = Sum of SALES for all types of clothing.
8. Continue for the next store (from step 1).

From this pseudo-code design, it can be seen that the program has two logical subunits: (1) repeating everything until STORE = "DONE" (i.e., steps 1 through 8) and (2) repeating the input and sales calculation for each of the three types of clothing (i.e., steps 3 through 6). During the program design stage, structured programming methods are used to uncover such logical subunits and form them into subprograms.

Second we can also re-examine the program in terms of the three control structures that characterize structured programming. Sequence is used throughout the pseudo-code design (i.e., step 1 is executed before step 2, and step 2 before step 3). Selection is used to continue execution of steps 1–8 until STORE = "DONE," and iteration was used to repeat steps 3 through 6. Thus, the program used only the three control structures to order both the individual steps and the segments of the pseudo-code program.

The reader may wonder why these three control structures are so important. Part of the answer is that programs are much easier to read and understand if only a few types of control structures are used. The other part of the answer is that these structures permit programs to be written without **unconditional branches** (i.e., instructions that transfer control from one place in a program to some other arbitrary place). Unconditional branching instructions interfere with a person's ability to read and understand a program, because the reader's thought process is continuously interrupted with detours. The problem is similar to the one that occurs when you read the front page of a newspaper. As you read a story, you are suddenly directed to section C, page 10, for the rest of the story. By the time you have found and read section C, page 10, you have forgotten where you left off on the front page. Structured programming involves more than simply not using unconditional branches, but this is a very important aspect.

In a real-world program design, the subprogram and control structure aspects of structured programming would first be considered in the program design stage and would continue on into the program development stage. The total programming task would be broken down into subprograms. Specifications would be written for each subprogram, using only sequence, selection, and iteration (if possible). The total program design would include a description of how the subprograms should be combined to form the larger program. Only the three types of control structures would be used to combine subprograms in the total design. The reader's understanding of structured programming will be expanded later, when the characteristics of modules are considered in more detail.

▇ People in the Program Development Life Cycle

In our case study and in the process of creating any computer program, many roles must be filled by members of the programming team. To understand programming, one must be aware of these roles.

The **analyst** is usually responsible for overseeing the total process of goal analysis, program design, program development, and program evaluation and maintenance. The analyst's most important tasks are the completion of an adequate goal analysis and a reasonable program design.

The programmer is responsible for writing the program in the computer's language, based on the given program design. The programmer performs the specific tasks of writing, testing, correcting, and documenting the program.

The user is responsible for applying the completed program to the processing of the data and for validating the usefulness of the program.

One person might perform more than one role, as in our case study. For example, person A (the analyst) might be responsible for analyzing the current tax law and designing (in pseudo-code) a procedure for computing income tax. Person B (the programmer) might have the task of translating the solution into a particular programming language and preparing it for a user. Finally, person C (the user) might input tax data into the program to calculate the appropriate income tax. Could A, B, and C be the same person? Of course, but the roles of analyst, programmer, and user would still be present and distinct.

---

unconditional branch
A computer programming instruction that transfers control from the current statement to any other arbitrary statement in a program; also called a GOTO statement.

analyst
A person responsible for the processes of goal analysis and program design; this person may also supervise program development, and program evaluation and maintenance.

The rapid pace at which new hardware and software systems are introduced to the computing community demands that any program or system designer keep in constant touch with new technologies, companies, and products. Advances in available computing resources may make designs and programs that are impossible to achieve one day feasible the next day. Just a few of the "cutting edge" products are described below.

The NeXT Machine

In October 1988, Steve Jobs, one of the founders of the Apple Computer Corporation introduced the NeXT computer, the first product of his new corporation, NeXT, Inc. Hoping to duplicate the success of the Apple II and the Apple Macintosh, Jobs and his company have created a new personal computer that has exceptional power and is designed initially for academic use.

The heart of the NeXT machine is the Motorola 68030 microprocessor chip, running at a speed of 25 MHz (megahertz). The supporting hardware for this processor includes (1) a 25-MHz mathematical coprocessor that is designed specifically for fast arithmetic computations, (2) a 10-MIPS (million instructions per second) digital signal processor (a processor for arrays of numbers) that can be harnessed for voice input, sound, and other real-world input/output, (3) twelve DMA (direct memory access) channels that allow peripheral devices to rapidly access memory without slowing down the processor, (4) a minimum of 8 megabytes of RAM, expandable to 16 megabytes, (5) a removable 256-megabyte read/write/erasable magneto-optical disk, and (6) a built-in Ethernet network connection. The monochrome screen attached to this processing power has 1,120 by 832 pixel resolution, and an optional 400-dot-per-inch laser printer can be added at an extremely low price.

Bundled with this hardware is a large body of software that includes (1) a Unix-like operating system named Mach, (2) the renowned Adobe Postscript system, with drivers for both the screen and the optional laser printer, (3) a word processor (WriteNow), (4) two programming languages, Allegro Common LISP and Objective-C, (5) a data base server (Sybase SQL Server), (6) a network file system (by Sun), (7) a Unix-like mail system, (8) NeXT's sound and music generation software, and (9) a digital library that includes *Webster's Ninth New Collegiate Dictionary, Webster's Collegiate Dictionary, Webster's Collegiate Thesaurus,* the *Oxford Dictionary of Quotations,* and the Oxford Press' *William Shakespeare: The Complete Works.* The voice recognition system that Jobs had hoped to deliver with the NeXT computer is not yet available.

Although the NeXT computer is not available to the public yet, it provides a complete platform for most academic uses and a good value for its price compared to machines of similar capability from other vendors. Because it provides so much, the current price (over six thousand dollars) is high for the average user. Thus, it is not clear that Jobs' goal of defining a new minimum standard for computing will be achieved.

The Macintosh IIx

The Apple Macintosh IIx is another machine based on the Motorola 68030 microprocessor chip. The IIx is now driven by a relatively slow clock of 16 MHz and is standardly equipped with 4 megabytes of main memory, expandable to 8 megabytes. It is supported by a math coprocessor chip (the Motorola 68882) and a proprietary, paged memory management unit that allows advanced multitasking under its operating system, A/UX (another Unix-like operating system). An 80-megabyte hard disk is available as well as a special "superdrive" floppy disk that is capable of reading and writing both Apple and IBM floppy disks. The price for a IIx with a hard disk drive was initially over nine thousand dollars; the IIx is now available to the public.

The IIx does not yet begin to use the power and speed available in the 68030 microprocessor, but it does provide an easy path for upward migration to more powerful Macintosh II's to come. In comparison, the NeXT computer appears to provide substantially more performance at a substantially lower price.

The IBM PS2 Model 70-A21

The fastest of the IBM personal computer line is currently the IBM Model 70-A21. It is driven by the powerful Intel 80386 chip (the major competition to the Motorola 68030) at a speed of 25 MHz. The microprocessor is supported by its version of a numeric coprocessor (the 80387) and includes a 64K-byte RAM cache that speeds memory access. A 120-megabyte hard disk is standard, as is a 2-megabyte main memory that can be expanded to 8 megabytes. A major advantage of the 70-A21 is that its microprocessor is not directly on the computer's motherboard but is instead on a small card of its own. With this design, it may be possible to add future, more powerful members of the 80x86 family of microprocessors, without losing the money invested in all the other components of the 70-A21 system. The price for the 70-A21 was initially over eleven thousand dollars, again making the price/performance ratio of the NeXT computer look very good.

The Intel 80486 Microprocessor

The October 31, 1988, issue of the news weekly *Info World* quoted a member of the 486 (the Intel 80486 microprocessor) standards committee as saying that the 486 generation of PCs is only a year away. The 486 microprocessor will retain the same basic architecture as the 386 but will operate at substantially higher speeds. With speeds for the 386 already in the 25-MHz range, speeds in the 40-MHz range have

(continued)

been predicted for the 486. With 486 systems available so soon, the IBM 70-A21 design, which will allow the system to utilize the power and speed of new chips, seems well considered.

Magneto-optical disks

Magneto-optical (M-O) disk drives are just one of the new disk technologies aimed at providing massive amounts (e.g., in the thousand megabyte range) of rapid, random access, read/write storage for personal computers. This technology merges optics with magnetic storage by using a laser to heat small portions of a disk to very high temperatures (572 degrees Fahrenheit) and then writing data with a weak magnetic field. As the disk storage of a personal computer be-

comes virtually unlimited, the basic principles of how disk storage is used may well change.

Summary

The effects of these advances on the computing field are unknown. With the always-present demand for more raw computing power, easier, friendlier interfaces, and special-purpose hardware and software, the system designer must always keep one eye on the changing marketplace, where new hardware and software are promised and (one hopes) delivered. Because some resources are promised and never delivered (so-called vaporware) the designer must keep the other eye on present, and well-established technologies that cannot disappear before one's eyes.

12.3

The Goal Analysis Stage

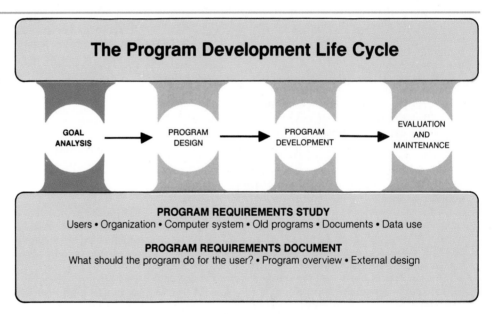

Developing a program generally occurs in one of two settings: (1) a new application is created from scratch or (2) an existing program is modified, either because of perceived problems with it or because of new needs. In either case, a goal analysis must be performed to uncover the true problem for which the new or modified program is being designed and the context in which the program must be developed. Goal analysis is thus primarily investigative in nature; it is an attempt to bring to light all of the organizational and computing factors that affect the program design. Our discussion of goal analysis, as well as the other three stages, will be in terms of inputs, outputs and methods.

▉ Goal Analysis Inputs

user/initiator
Person or persons primarily responsible for stimulating the development of a computer programming project.

This information comes from many different sources, the most important of which probably is people. The **user/initiator** is the person (or people) who initiated the development of the computer programming project. The user/initiator serves as a focus for information about the perceived problem for which the program is being developed.

The other potential users of the program are another important source of information. Everyone who will be affected by the new program is in some sense a user, including people whose decisions and information are used in the creation of the program, people who will enter the data or generate the reports, and people who will receive the reports. All of these users will play a role in the success of the program and should be consulted.

People, of course, are not the only sources of information. A wide variety of work activities and written documents characterize the operation of any organization. These activities and documents can be a concrete referent on what the program should do. Other observable objects and events can also serve as information input; for example, the specific hardware and software environment available to the program's users affects the potential design and must be identified and studied in detail. Any program is designed to solve a problem in a particular environment. This environment constrains the range of possible solutions to the problem and must be investigated in the goal analysis stage.

Another important input for goal analysis is the analyst's knowledge of the application area of the program. For example, if a program for retail accounting is to be developed, the analyst's knowledge in this field is critical to understanding and communicating with the user. Since it is impossible for a single analyst to be expert in all application areas, a team of analysts with diverse backgrounds often performs the goal analysis.

■ Goal Analysis Outputs

The various inputs of the goal analysis stage should clearly define the specific problem to be solved and the context in which the solution will be used. Once this information is collected, those involved in goal analysis must integrate the information into a cohesive description of the problem and its context. This description is generally in a written form called the *program requirements document*. A sample format is given below:

Format for a Program Requirements Document

1. *Program overview and summary.* A general statement of the problem to be solved or the tasks to be performed by the program.
2. *Program environment.*
   a. Potential users of the program.
   b. Hardware and software to be used.
   c. Other factors, and constraints (such as operational procedures, cost limitations, and so on).
3. *Functional requirements.*
   a. Data input sources, diagrams showing how data is communicated and used, and data output for the program.
   b. Sample input/output sequences that the program should produce, e.g., data entry prompts and reports to be generated.
   c. Data processing activities that the program should perform (e.g., sorting data).
4. *Preliminary design.*
   a. Suggested solutions or designs, e.g., a logical (abstract) program and a proposed (real) program.

b. Feasibility studies for the suggested solutions e.g., of the proposed program.

c. Acceptance criteria for the program.

Once the program requirements document is complete, the program design stage begins. During this stage, a particular program is designed to solve the problem described in the program requirements document. If errors exist in the program requirements document, they will be reflected in the design of the finished program. Therefore, great care must be taken to ensure that the program requirements document adequately describes the functions and the context of the proposed program.

■ Goal Analysis Methods

The methods most commonly used in the investigation just described are systematic interviews, questionnaires, direct observation of work activities, work product sampling, direct observation of communications, and document collection and analysis.

Beyond basic data collection, there are two significant methodological issues: the conceptual nature of the requirements description and the language used in it.

The Program Requirements Description.   After the necessary information has been obtained in the investigation, the analyst's task is to model the problem to be solved and the context in which it exists. The analytic process is often conceptualized in terms of three systems:

1. The present program (if one exists). What is its purpose, what are its subprograms, and how are they interrelated?
2. The logical program. A general description of the new program (which is derived from the present program, if it exists). What does the program do (not how does it do it)?
3. The proposed program (which is derived from the logical program). What changes should be made in the existing program, or what are the requirements for a new program?

The description of the proposed program (item 3) is sometimes included in the program design stage, where it is called the *external design*. Once a good model has been developed of what the proposed program is supposed to do, the constraints imposed by the context must be taken into account and the results packaged into a program requirements document.

The Requirements Specification Language (RSL).   The program requirements document is a description of what the program is expected to do. Program requirements documents are usually written in ordinary languages such as English. The problem with ordinary languages is that they contain ambiguities; for example, English terms such as *suitable* or *flexible* may mean different things to the analyst, the programmer, and the user. One partial solution to the problem of ambiguity is to use more formal methods of description such as **data dictionaries** or **data flow diagrams** in the program design process. Data dictionaries identify and describe the data elements (e.g., PRICE and SALES in the case study) that appear to be necessary for the new program. Dictionary contents include the name of the data item, its purpose, its source, etcetera. Data flow diagrams summarize data sources, data stores, transformations of

data dictionary
A list of the data elements used in a program, including their names, uses, and any assumptions made about their entry and exit from the system.

data flow diagram
A device for summarizing sources, stores, transformations, and transfer of information among data elements of a present or proposed program.

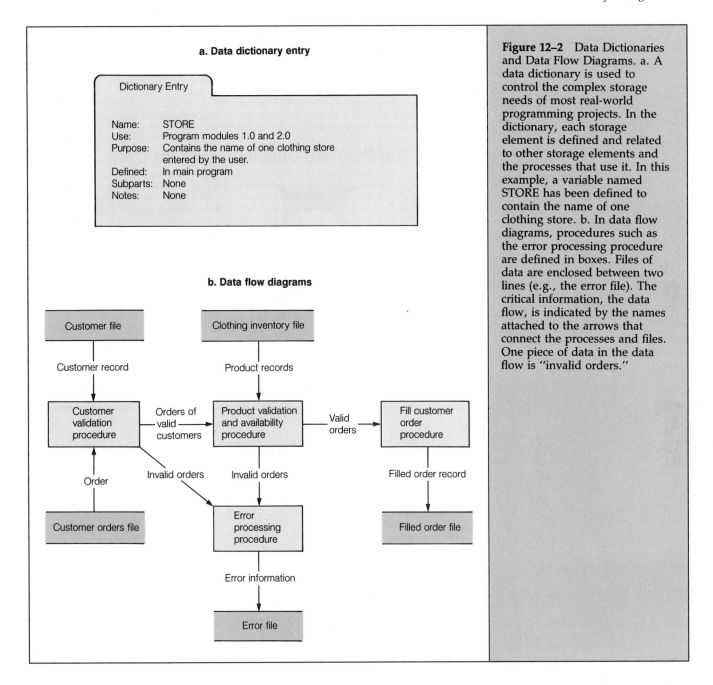

a. Data dictionary entry

Dictionary Entry

Name: STORE
Use: Program modules 1.0 and 2.0
Purpose: Contains the name of one clothing store
entered by the user.
Defined: In main program
Subparts: None
Notes: None

b. Data flow diagrams

Customer file

Customer record

Clothing inventory file

Product records

Customer validation procedure

Orders of valid customers

Product validation and availability procedure

Valid orders

Fill customer order procedure

Order

Invalid orders

Invalid orders

Filled order record

Customer orders file

Error processing procedure

Filled order file

Error information

Error file

Figure 12–2 Data Dictionaries and Data Flow Diagrams. a. A data dictionary is used to control the complex storage needs of most real-world programming projects. In the dictionary, each storage element is defined and related to other storage elements and the processes that use it. In this example, a variable named STORE has been defined to contain the name of one clothing store. b. In data flow diagrams, procedures such as the error processing procedure are defined in boxes. Files of data are enclosed between two lines (e.g., the error file). The critical information, the data flow, is indicated by the names attached to the arrows that connect the processes and files. One piece of data in the data flow is "invalid orders."

data, and the exchange of information among the data elements in the present or proposed program.

Another more complete solution to the problem of language ambiguity is to use a **requirements specification language** (RSL). An RSL is a formal, computer-readable language with a restricted vocabulary and syntax, used for writing program requirements. When an RSL is used, the computer can be used to check the program description for consistency, omissions, or errors in structural control, and it can also generate simulations of programs that match the requirements definition. In short, the computer can help ensure that the program requirements document is clear and unambiguous enough to be used to

requirements specifications language
A formal computer-readable language with a restricted vocabulary and syntax, used for writing program requirements.

create the program design and is a valid reflection of the users' needs. Such languages may also have features that assist with the process of program design.

12.4

The Program Design Stage

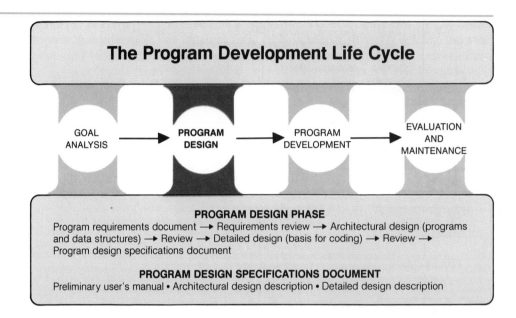

The Program Development Life Cycle

GOAL ANALYSIS → PROGRAM DESIGN → PROGRAM DEVELOPMENT → EVALUATION AND MAINTENANCE

PROGRAM DESIGN PHASE
Program requirements document → Requirements review → Architectural design (programs and data structures) → Review → Detailed design (basis for coding) → Review → Program design specifications document

PROGRAM DESIGN SPECIFICATIONS DOCUMENT
Preliminary user's manual • Architectural design description • Detailed design description

The computer program design is a model of a proposed solution to a user's problem. The solution is constrained to being a computer program that operates on the hardware and software systems available to the user. This section will describe sound program design and the process by which such design is created.

▢ Program Design Inputs

There are two primary inputs to the program design stage: one is the output of the goal analysis stage (the program requirements document), and the second is human expertise in solving problems with computers. The program designer must bring a wide variety of expertise to the program design task.

One type of expertise involves knowledge of standard methods for solving programming problems. For example, given a data structure containing a list of student names, the program designer should know how to alphabetize the names in the list.

data structure
The types of data elements and the relationships among the data elements in a program or design.

A second type of expertise is knowledge of the **data structures** of computer programs. Computer programs model data from the real world and, thus, the program designer must have a good understanding of how to use the data structures of a programming language to create a computer model of objects such as checking accounts, checkerboards, or golf courses.

Knowledge of the hardware and software environment in which a program will operate is a third type of expertise. The designer must understand how the hardware and software environment will affect any programs that are to be developed.

A fourth type of expertise is knowledge of the domain or application area in which a program will function. Obviously, knowledge of the banking business will help a designer create a better banking program.

■ Program Design Outputs

The major output of the program design stage is the design specifications document, a description of a computer program that is intended to solve the problem described in the program requirements document. Later, the computer programmer will use this description to develop the actual computer program. A sample format is given below.

Format for a Design Specifications Document

1. *Program overview and summary*
2. *Preliminary user's manual*
   a. User display and report formats.
   b. User command summary.
3. *Data structures*
   a. Data input, data flow diagrams, data storage, and data output.
   b. Data dictionary (names and attributes of data elements).
   c. Formats for data storage and retrieval.
4. *Program structure*
   a. Name and functional description of each module in the program.
   b. Interface specifications for each module, e.g., which modules are used by other modules.
   c. Interconnections among data and program modules, e.g., which programs use what data.
5. *Development plans and suggestions.*

Types of program designs.   For complex programming problems, three types of program designs are created and used in the design specifications document: the *external design*, the *architectural design*, and the *detailed design*. The external design results from a careful study of the program requirements document. It attempts to refine the program requirements and to describe, at a very abstract level, a program that will meet the requirements. The distinction between the program requirements document and the external design is not sharp. For simple programming problems, an informal external design may be created as part of the program requirements document. For complex programming problems, a formal external design is generally created during the design process; a successful review of the requirements document must then be completed before work is continued on the design.

The architectural design is developed from the external design. The architectural design shows the basic structure of the program, that is, it

1. breaks down the complex data sets and data processing functions into smaller, less complex segments or modules;
2. identifies data sources; and
3. establishes communications links between the modules.

An example of an architectural design is given on the next page. The detailed design is developed from the architectural design. It is concerned with the particular algorithms to be used for processing, specific data structures, actual connections among program and data modules, program packaging, and so forth. The detailed design will be considered when the program development stage is discussed.

AN EXAMPLE OF PROGRAM DESIGN OUTPUT

To make our explanation of design output more concrete, we will discuss a highly simplified example of architectural design. As the basis of any design one finds the concepts of program and data structures. In essence an architectural design is a description of (1) the program modules and data elements and (2) the structure or interconnection of the program modules and data elements. **Structures** are anything constructed in an orderly way from components. Obviously, structures can be created from segments of programs or pieces of data—the question is *how*.

structure
The arrangement or relationship of the component parts of a system.

The Concept of program and data structure.   We have already discussed creating structured programs from modules linked together by sequence, selection, and iteration. However, we have not yet described *how to create structures or what modules to use*. One way to create structure is to use a hierarchy. Everyone uses hierarchies: in business, there are management hierarchies (managers direct supervisors, who direct workers); in geography, there are political hierarchies (countries include states, which include counties, which include cities). Computer program designers also use hierarchies for both program and data structures.

program structure
The arrangement of program elements that result from joining logical subprograms using sequence, selection, and iteration.

Program structure refers to the fact that well-written programs have a definite organization or structure. That is, they are assembled from logical subprograms using sequence, selection, and iteration. Let's look again at our clothing store sales problem. The problem whose program structure is shown below is identical to the problem from the case study, except that the data is stored on disks and more than one kind of sales report is produced. The program is designed to input a set of data for storage, save the data, retrieve the data, and generate sales reports. The **program structure chart** could look like this:

program structure chart
A diagram of the hierarchy of programs and subprograms.

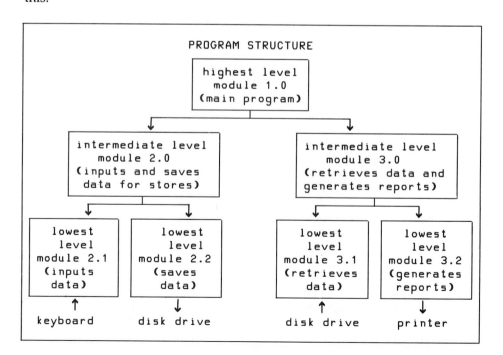

The program for the clothing company has been broken down here into a three-level hierarchy with seven program modules. The main program (module 1.0 at the highest level of the hierarchy) uses two subprograms (modules 2.0 and 3.0 at the intermediate level). Each of the two intermediate level subprograms uses two of the lowest level subprograms; for example, module 2.0 uses module 2.1 (at the lowest level) to input data and module 2.2 (also at the lowest level) to save data. The arrows at the very bottom of the figure indicate the movement of data into and out of the set of program modules.

Note that each of the modules is organized to achieve one of the objectives of the program: module 2.1 inputs data from a keyboard, module 2.2 saves the data on a disk, and so on. Note also that the modules are separated in such a manner that many modifications can be accomplished by changing single modules; for example, if a new type of report is needed, probably only the report generator (module 3.2) would have to be changed or replaced.

Data structure refers to the fact that data elements such as NUMBER, PRICE, and SALES can also be combined in an orderly way. The data elements needed in a particular program design have to be organized for searching and retrieval. Data hierarchies are a very common method of combining individual data elements into a coherent structure to clarify how they must be stored and retrieved. For example, dictionaries use a hierarchy: the data elements are words and definitions; the words are alphabetized, and the definitions for each word are ordered by part of speech (noun, verb, and so forth). An example of a hierarchical data structure is presented below.

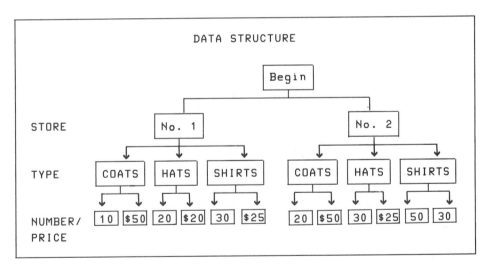

This example shows the data structure containing the data elements (with data values) used by the program. For the sake of simplicity, relatively little information about the data is specified here. More detail will be given later when the program is coded in BASIC. Like the program structure, the data structure is hierarchical. STORE (the name of the store) is at the highest level, TYPE (COATS, HATS, and SHIRTS) is next, and finally, the values of NUMBER and PRICE are stored at the bottom for each type of clothing.

The data structure tells the programmer how data is to be stored and retrieved. In this example, the design specifies that the entire data set would be saved so that, given the name of the STORE (e.g., NO.1) and the TYPE of clothing (e.g., COATS), the program module could retrieve the correct values for NUMBER and PRICE (e.g., 10 and $50). The design does not, however, specify exactly which of the many possible methods should be used to program the data structure.

The interaction of the programs and the data structures. Two very important ideas are implicit in the program and data structures: the *call-and-return* process and *data sharing*. The call-and-return process enables one program module to use another. In order for the main program (module 1.0) in the program structure example, to use its subprogram (module 2.0) to input and save data, the main program must "call" the subprogram, i.e., turn control of the computer over to the subprogram. Once the subprogram has finished its task, it must "return" control of the computer back to the main program. A line connecting two modules in a hierarchical structure chart shows that the higher-level module calls the lower-level module and the lower-level module then returns control to the higher-level module.

Data sharing is also implicit in the structure charts. In order for two modules to operate on the same data, the data must be communicated between the modules. Thus, in order for module 2.1 to input data and module 2.2 to store the same data, the data structure must be accessed by both modules. As another example, suppose the main program inputs the name of the store (STORE) and the number of clothing types (NT) to be entered by the user. The values of STORE and NT would then have to be passed from the main program to the subprograms. Similarly, the subprograms would pass information back to the main program, e.g., a message indicating that the data have been successfully processed. Generally, most modules need access to the data structure. All programming languages have mechanisms that allow modules to be called from other programs and that permit modules to share data through **parameter passing,** common data structures, and other means.

parameter passing
The sending of data from one program to another.

Program Design Methods

Hierarchical charts and free-form English are often used to describe the program design for simple programming problems. For example, hierarchical structure charts and English were used in the example of an architectural design which was just discussed above. However, computer science and software engineering professionals have developed a wide variety of other design representation techniques such as HIPO diagrams, flowcharts, pseudo-code, and Warnier-Orr diagrams. These techniques provide "languages" in which a designer can easily detail the ISPCO functions of a proposed computer program with maximum accuracy and minimal ambiguity. Some of these techniques are described briefly in the following paragraphs.

Program Design representation techniques.

top-down program design
A hierarchial design process in which major operations are first determined, then simpler operations within each major operation, and so on, until the operations are simple enough to be written as program language commands.

1. *Hierarchical input/process/output (HIPO) diagrams.* HIPO diagrams are used to represent a hierarchy of program modules by their inputs, outputs, and processing functions. They are designed specifically to be used in **top-down program design** (in top-down design, only the upper levels of the program design are completed in the architectural design; the lower levels are completed as the detailed design progresses). Three types of HIPO diagrams are commonly used. A visual *table-of-contents* is a two-directional graphic description of the tasks the system performs. *Overview HIPO diagrams* list the inputs, processes, and outputs for each of the elements in the program's

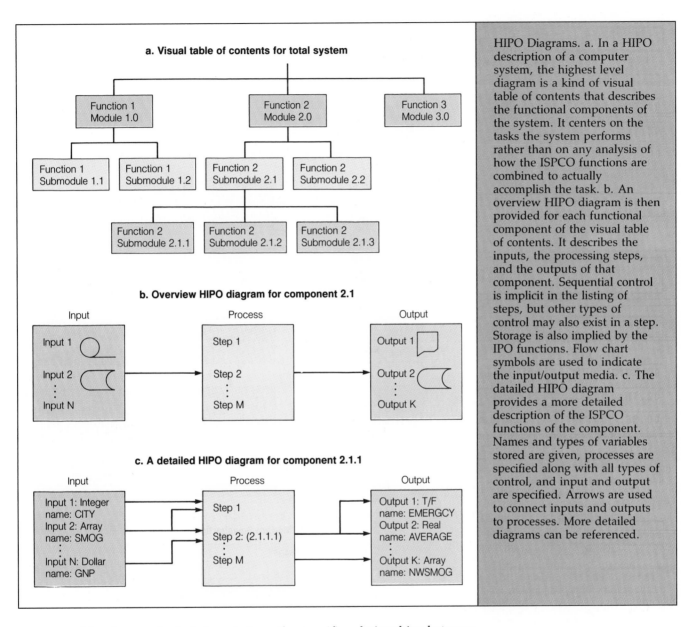

a. Visual table of contents for total system

Function 1 Module 1.0 — Function 2 Module 2.0 — Function 3 Module 3.0

Function 1 Submodule 1.1 — Function 1 Submodule 1.2 — Function 2 Submodule 2.1 — Function 2 Submodule 2.2

Function 2 Submodule 2.1.1 — Function 2 Submodule 2.1.2 — Function 2 Submodule 2.1.3

b. Overview HIPO diagram for component 2.1

Input: Input 1, Input 2, ⋮, Input N

Process: Step 1, Step 2, ⋮, Step M

Output: Output 1, Output 2, ⋮, Output K

c. A detailed HIPO diagram for component 2.1.1

Input: Input 1: Integer name: CITY; Input 2: Array name: SMOG; ⋮; Input N: Dollar name: GNP

Process: Step 1; Step 2: (2.1.1.1); ⋮; Step M

Output: Output 1: T/F name: EMERGCY; Output 2: Real name: AVERAGE; ⋮; Output K: Array name: NWSMOG

HIPO Diagrams. a. In a HIPO description of a computer system, the highest level diagram is a kind of visual table of contents that describes the functional components of the system. It centers on the tasks the system performs rather than on any analysis of how the ISPCO functions are combined to actually accomplish the task. b. An overview HIPO diagram is then provided for each functional component of the visual table of contents. It describes the inputs, the processing steps, and the outputs of that component. Sequential control is implicit in the listing of steps, but other types of control may also exist in a step. Storage is also implied by the IPO functions. Flow chart symbols are used to indicate the input/output media. c. The datailed HIPO diagram provides a more detailed description of the ISPCO functions of the component. Names and types of variables stored are given, processes are specified along with all types of control, and input and output are specified. Arrows are used to connect inputs and outputs to processes. More detailed diagrams can be referenced.

table-of-contents, but do not show the specific relationships between the input, processes, and output. *Detailed HIPO diagrams* describe what particular input goes into subprocesses and what output is generated. The hierarchical decomposition can continue through as many levels as desired. Examples of HIPO diagrams are given above.

2. *Flowcharting.* Flowcharting is the oldest formal representation technique in programming. Special symbols are used to represent the various components of a computer program (e.g., files, disks, tapes, inputs, outputs, processes, control decisions). These symbols are then connected with lines and arrows to describe how a particular program functions. Two examples of flowcharts are given on the next page. The upper one is a traditional flowchart. The lower one is a structured flowchart, a variation of the traditional flowchart suggested by Isaac Nassi and Ben Shneiderman.

3. *Pseudo-code.* As we have noted, pseudo-code (sometimes called

Flowcharts. a. There are many varying conventions for flowchart symbols. Symbols represent keyboards, disks, magnetic tapes, screens, communication lines, sorting and merging processes, and many other things. Arrows connect symbols to indicate sequences. A decision point (the diamond shape above) asks a yes/no question and performs different actions according to what the answer is. Flowcharts like these are not widely promoted because they do not correspond well to structured programming concepts, but they are often used. b. Modern flowcharts like the charts proposed by Nassi and Shneiderman have a more compact form and provide special symbols for all the structured programming control structures. In this example sequential control is clearly indicated as the steps progress down the page. Repetition of a sequence of tasks until a condition is met (e.g., calculating across each store's sales until DONE is entered as a store name) is represented by a DO WHILE. The statements included in the DO WHILE are clearly delimited by the indented style.

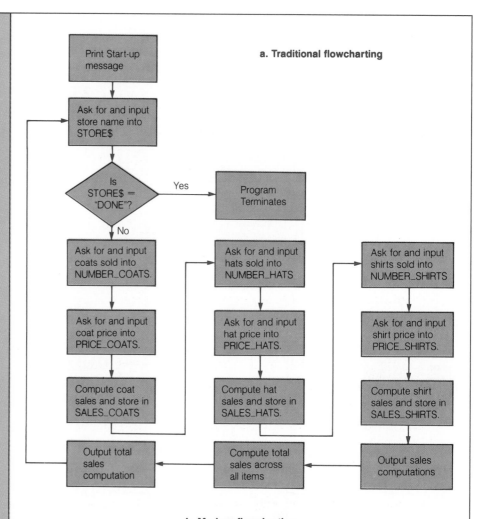

a. Traditional flowcharting

b. Modern flowcharting

Print startup message
Set STORE$ = ""
Ask for and input store name into STORE$
DO WHILE STORE$ <> "Done"
Ask for and input coats sold into NUMBER_COATS
Ask for and input coat price into PRICE_COATS
Compute coat sales and store into SALES_COATS
Ask for and input hats sold into NUMBER_HATS
Ask for and input hat price into PRICE_HATS
Compute hat sales and store into SALES_HATS
Ask for and input shirts sold into NUMBER_SHIRTS
Ask for and input shirt price into PRICE_SHIRTS
Compute shirt sales and store into SALES_SHIRTS
Print computed sales data
Compute total sales
Print total sales
Ask for and input store name into STORE$

```
CLOTHING-STORE-PROCESSING:

    Write out start-up messages
    Ask for and input store name into STORE$
    REPEAT WHILE STORE$ is not equal to "DONE"
        Ask for and input coats sold into NUMBER_COATS
        Ask for and input coat price into PRICE_COATS
        Compute coat sales and store into SALES_COATS
        Ask for and input hats sold into NUMBER_HATS
        Ask for and input hat price into PRICE_HATS
        Compute hat sales and store into SALES_HATS
        Ask for and input shirts sold into NUMBER_SHIRTS
        Ask for and input shirt price into PRICE_SHIRTS
        Compute shirt sales and store into SALES_SHIRTS
        Print to screen all computed sales
        Compute total sales
        Print to screen total sales
        Ask for and input store name into STORE$
```

Pseudo-Code

structured English) is used by program designers to describe programs in short, concise, English phrases. Key words such as IF-THEN-ELSE, DO-WHILE and END describe the flow of control and the other English phrases describe the processing actions. Design in pseudo-code usually proceeds from the top down. Many researchers in computer science and cognitive psychology believe that pseudo-code is quite useful. Different rules and different degrees of formalism established by various computer professionals have resulted in a number of versions of pseudo-code; all connect well with programmers' natural language ability. Pseudo-code can replace traditional flowcharting and it also reduces the amount of external program documentation required. An example of pseudo-code is given above.

4. *Warnier-Orr diagrams.* Warnier-Orr diagrams are still another technique for graphically showing the structure of a computer program. They can be applied equally well to both the steps of a program and the data structures that it uses. Some of the basic ideas behind such diagrams are illustrated below. Brackets indicate the general hierarchical structure, and special symbols represent the three control constructs of structured programming.

```
Clothing Store    { BEGIN
Program (1)
                    Output start-up message

                    Ask for and input store
                    name

                    Process data for store
                    (1, N)
                    END
```

```
{ BEGIN
  Ask for and input coats sold into NUMBER_COATS
  Ask for and input coat price into PRICE_COATS
  Compute coat sales into SALES_COATS
  Ask for and input hats sold into NUMBER_HATS
  Ask for and input hat price into PRICE_HATS
  Compute hat sales into SALES_HATS
  Ask for and input shirts sold into NUMBER_SHIRTS
  Ask for and input shirt price into PRICE_SHIRTS
  Compute shirt sales into SALES_SHIRTS
  Print out sales computation
  Compute total sales
  Print out total sales
  Ask for and input store name
  END
```

Warnier-Orr Diagrams. Here the processing of data for a store is performed between 1 and N times, while the entire process is performed once.

Program design languages (PDL). A more complete method for representing designs is provided by computer-readable formal languages and associated computer software. For example, Daniel Teichroew's Problem Statement Language can be used in the development of both the program requirements document and the design specifications document. PDLs often accept constructs that have the form of hierarchically structured programs, but they do not contain programs. Instead, they contain English text descriptions of what the module is supposed to do. The software associated with these languages can be used to generate highly detailed specification documentation, including structural diagrams. It can also analyze the design descriptions and perform consistency and completeness checks.

The purpose of all of these representation techniques (as well as many others such as decision tables, decision trees, and action diagrams) is to more effectively communicate the design of a computer program from the designer to the programmer. No one technique is universally accepted. Many large computing organizations make policy decisions on the method(s) to be used within the organization.

Principles of structured program design. A top-down or hierarchical structure was used in the program design example. The results of the design process were shown, but no explanation of the process was given, nor were other methods of design mentioned. In the following summary, the general idea of structured program design and brief descriptions of some specific techniques are presented.

modularity
The organization of a large system so that small parts with related functions are gathered together into modules; the resulting modules are internally cohesive but highly independent of one another.

debug
To find and remove mistakes in a computer program. Said to have been coined when Grace Hopper found a moth which had shorted out the circuits of an early mainframe computer.

1. *Modularity or reductionism.* The fundamental principle of good structured program design is **modularity**. The total program is broken into many interconnected modules called subprograms, subroutines, functions, or procedures. Each subprogram is itself a program with a particular processing capability. The subprogram is accessed (called) when another program needs that capability. The subprograms are the building blocks from which the complete program is constructed. One of the great advantages of modular design is that programmers can test and **debug** each module separately before assembling the modules into the program. Specification of the modules and how they can be assembled to form the complete program is a key aspect of program design.

2. *Modular independence.* One of the principles of modularity is that to the greatest degree possible, pieces of programs and data that are used together should be placed in the same module, while those that do not share data or subprograms should be kept apart. Following this principle creates modules that are independent of each other. Stating this more formally, *the number and complexity of communications among program modules should be minimized.* The cohesion (communication within the module) should be maximized, and the coupling (communication between modules) should be minimized. Thus, there should be a lot of data sharing, common processing, and common functions within the modules, but there should as little as possible between the modules. As part of the program design stage, a chart may be drawn to examine the dependencies among the various program modules. Designs that have high degrees of dependency are undesirable because change in one module may

cause ripples throughout many other modules, requiring extensive redesign.

3. *Top-down design.* Top-down design was illustrated by the structures in the clothing company examples. It is one of the principal methods for determining the organization of modules in a design. The organization of a business firm also reflects top-down design: an executive at an upper level assigns a task to a subordinate, who performs it and passes the results back up to the executive. Similarly, a program can be designed so that the higher-level subprograms call successively lower-level (and less complex) subprograms. The design proceeds from a definition of the tasks performed by the higher-level programs to the tasks assigned to lower-level subprograms. Each subprogram task can then be further broken into still lower level subprograms. Such designs are represented by program structure charts that show the hierarchy of programs and subprograms.

The top-down approach is used with **successive refinement.** As the module description proceeds from the top downward, the ISPCO task to be performed becomes more and more specific and well-defined until the description is sufficiently clear that it can be directly coded into a programming language.

4. *One-entry/one-exit design.* Formal mathematical proofs show that all conceivable program sequences can be expressed with the three control structures of sequence, selection, and iteration, provided the program has only one entry (beginning) and one exit (end). Hence, the one-entry/one exit design rule is an important principle of program design, because it ensures that structured programming can be used during program development.

5. *Data encapsulation/data abstraction.* As the independence of modules is increased, the ultimate independence is eventually reached: the programmer-users of a module know only what a module does, not *how* it works. As various data structures are designed for a program, they are accompanied by the definitions of all of the legal operations that can be performed on the data, hidden or encapsulated in a module. Precisely how the data and internal operations are implemented is no longer important to the programmer-user, as long as the method of referencing the operations is known.

6. *Black box analysis.* All of the methods so far mentioned assume that the designer has a clear idea of what the program does, that is, that the basic ISPCO functions are clear from the program requirements document. In the real world, however, this is often not the case (the requirements may not be sufficiently specific). In this situation, the black box method becomes useful.

A black box view of a program can give an end-means analysis, that is, the program can be viewed as a **blackbox** from which outputs are generated. The outputs can generally be inferred from the program requirements document or at least be identified as suitable or unsuitable by the users. One can then infer the input needed to generate the output. Finally, from the input-output description, one can infer enough of the required processing to get the design underway.

successive refinement
A process in which a program is decomposed hierarchically; major features are described first, followed by successively more detailed layers of descriptions. Top down design.

data abstraction (or encapsulation)
The practice of encapsulating data structures and routines to manipulate the data in single independent packages that hide implementation details. These "objects" are then used in all the programs of a software product.

blackbox
a device that produces a specific output from known input but whose detailed internal operation is either unknown or unspecified.

end-means (blackbox) Analysis
A system design technique in which the system is treated as a blackbox. First, output is inferred from the system requirements. Second, input is inferred from output. Finally, processing is inferred from both.

walkthrough
A manual simulation of a program design using real data.

In a complex programming problem, the designer may use more than one of these techniques, since most of them are not mutually exclusive.

The Design Walkthrough and Execution Simulation. Program designs can be evaluated by a variety of simulation methods. One of the most common is the design **walkthrough,** in which the programmer traces the operations specified in the program design for a group of colleagues, using a sample input for which the output is known. Many other methods are used for complex programs, including computer *execution simulation,* in which a design defined in a program design language is simulated by computer.

In summary, the program design stage is primarily concerned with: (1) the reformulation of the program requirements document into an abstract description of the program and (2) the conversion of this abstract description into a more concrete form. Design is a human, creative task that is only partly understood. Techniques exist to help designers think through the process and new languages aid in the description of problems and solutions; but in the end, program designers, like all other professionals, bring their own experience and expertise to a particular problem and to the search for a solution.

12.5

The Program Development Stage

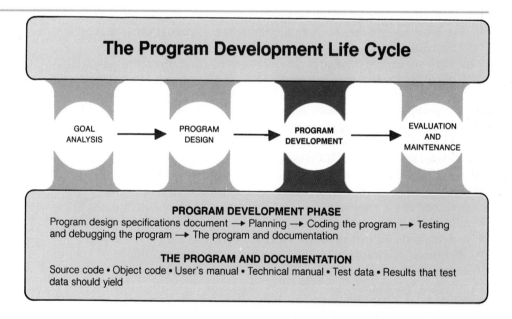

The Program Development Life Cycle

GOAL ANALYSIS → PROGRAM DESIGN → PROGRAM DEVELOPMENT → EVALUATION AND MAINTENANCE

PROGRAM DEVELOPMENT PHASE
Program design specifications document → Planning → Coding the program → Testing and debugging the program → The program and documentation

THE PROGRAM AND DOCUMENTATION
Source code • Object code • User's manual • Technical manual • Test data • Results that test data should yield

program coding
The process of translating design specifications into a computer program written in a specific computer programming language.

Three major activities are performed in the program development stage: **program coding,** program testing, and program documentation. These activities are much easier to describe and specify than those of the program design stage, because program development is primarily a translation task in which the solution stated in the design specifications document is transformed into statements in a particular programming language.

▪ Program Development Inputs

There are two major inputs to the program development stage: (1) the design specifications document and (2) the hardware and software environment (including the programming language) available to the user.

The design specifications document, which was created during the design stage, describes how the computer will be used to reach a solution to the original problem. The programmer studies the design specifications document before beginning the task of translating the design into the selected programming language.

The architectural design, which describes the program and the data structures, is the most important part of the design specifications document for planning and organizing the program development activities. The program structure defines the function and organization of the program modules (from the highest to the lowest levels), and the data structure defines each data element, describes how the data elements should be stored and retrieved, and shows the flow of data through the programming modules.

The *detailed design, which is also part of the design specifications document, is used for the actual coding of the program*, that is, the translation of the design into a computer language. As we have noted, the detailed design proceeds from the architectural design to specific designs of the individual modules, data record formats, and so forth. The detailed design should be so specific that program instructions can be written directly from the design. An example of a detailed design for Barney's Clothing Company will be presented shortly, when the coding process is demonstrated.

The proposed program must operate within a hardware and software environment that includes computers, operating systems, programming languages, and the training resources available to the user. The programmer generally has little control over any of these environmental factors but may have some say in the choice of language for implementing the design.

There are many different reasons for choosing a particular language. One factor is the application area. Many languages have been designed for specific types of applications. For microcomputer applications, the language of choice has been BASIC, although Pascal has recently become another viable alternative. For business organizations, however, COBOL remains the probable language of choice. FORTRAN is the language in which most engineering applications are written. Artificial intelligence applications are developed in the pointer languages LISP and PROLOG.

A second reason for choosing one language over another is psychological—different languages establish different mind-sets and make some things easy to do and other things difficult. Virtually all computing languages can do anything from video games to data base management systems, but different languages have different "personalities" that make the creation of some types of programs easier with one language than with another.

The most common reason for choosing a language, however, is probably an economic one: some languages are far more popular than others, and popularity means portability. If a language is popular, then it can be used on a wide variety of computer hardware systems, and a program written in that language can be more easily transported from one hardware system to another.

Finally, it should be noted that languages have unique operating environments, that is, they may provide program creation or program execution software, and this software is of varying usefulness. For example, interpretive languages, such as LISP or APL, usually have a language specific editor for entering, editing, and checking programs.

Program Development Outputs

There are three major outputs associated with program development: (1) the computer program, written in the chosen language, (2) the program documentation, and (3) the test data and the results for all verification studies performed during the development of the program.

The Computer Program.   The computer program usually includes both a source program written in the programming language and an object program written in machine language. The program must be in a form suitable for installation in the user's hardware and software environment as specified in the program requirements document. Commercial products are often delivered with an installation program to help the user set up the program for use with particular operating systems and hardware configurations.

user's manual
Documentation that describes how to use a program. Often includes installation instructions, a tutorial, and a list of all commands with instructions and examples of usage.

technical manual
Documentation that describes the details of the implementation choices made during computer program development, for use by programmers and technicians for repairing and upgrading the program.

The Program Documentation.   Two types of program documentation are generally prepared for a complex program: a **user's manual** and a **technical manual.** The user's manual is designed to be used by people with limited technical background. A sample format for a user's manual is shown below.

Format for a User's Manual

1. *Introduction.* Product overview: objectives of the software, modes of operation, types of input and output, and how to use the manual.
2. *Getting started.* Instructions for installing the program with operating systems. Sign-on and sign-off procedures. Review of ISPCO functions available. Help features.
3. *Tutorial.* An example of the use of the program, showing important functions and using a simple, representative data set.
4. *Command reference.* An organized list of all commands, including a description of the purpose and use of each command, with examples.
5. *Glossary* and *subject index.*

Computer programs are not static. They evolve over time as the users' needs and problems change. To help programmers make these changes, a *technical manual* for the program is usually prepared. The technical manual is designed to be used by computer programmers and technicians. It describes the details of the implementation choices made during program development. With this document, the original programmer (or another programmer) can rediscover the workings of the program and repair problems with the existing program or enhance its features.

The Test Data and Results.   The results of the initial program testing should be given to the users of the program to demonstrate that the program works successfully. Nothing is worse for the user of a new computer program than to have it work incorrectly. Providing users with information on testing serves as one last check that the program was designed and implemented properly. We refer here mainly to verification testing, which ensures that the program meets the objectives stated in the design specifications document.

■ Program Development Methods

The three major activities of the program development stage (coding, testing, and documenting) usually interact in actual practice, but we will discuss them separately in this section. First, however, we must take a brief look at a program development plan.

The Program Development Plan. A *program development plan* specifies the major activities in the development of the program and schedules the program milestones. The plan can be informal (as in the case study) or formal (for a more complex programming task). When a plan is not developed, the project is often very costly, wasteful of effort, and seldom finished on time. The following example shows activities that might be included in a plan for a complex programming project.

Program Development Plan

1. *Design specifications document review.* The programming team reviews the design specifications document with the designers to be sure that the design and testing methods are correctly understood.
2. *Programming language decision.* The programming team decides on the programming language to be used and reviews the hardware and software available to the user.
3. *Procedures for coding the program modules.* Choices are made on the order and manner in which the program modules are to be coded.
4. *Procedures for testing the program and modules.* A basic plan for program testing is created and test data are obtained.
5. *Procedures for documentation development.* Documentation outlines, guidelines, and schedules are created.
6. *Methods for management of the programming task.* If there are several programmers on the team, a particular management approach may be selected. Milestones such as source code reviews by other programmers, completion and review of coding and testing, and completion and review of documentation are established and scheduled.

Coding the Program. Program coding is the process of translating the design specifications document into a computer program or set of programs in a particular computer programming language. The architectural design provides the skeleton for planning and understanding program coding, but the detailed design is the real basis for coding. Given architectural and detailed designs, there are at least three major coding methods that can be used:

1. *Bottom-up coding.* In this method, coding proceeds from the lowest-level modules in the design structure to the highest-level modules. First, the lowest-level modules are coded and tested. Then, the next-highest modules are coded and tested, with the low-level programs in place. Finally, the highest-level modules are coded and tested, with all of the other level modules in place. In our design example in section 12.4, coding would begin with modules 3.2, 3.1, etcetera and finish with the main program (module 1.0). The problem with this approach is that testing the lower level modules requires the preparation of *test harness programs* (dummy programs that replace higher level programs during testing). For example, a test harness program would be needed to replace the main program (module 1.0).
2. *Top-down coding.* In this method, the highest-level modules are coded first, followed by the next-highest level modules, and so on until the lowest-level modules are coded. In our example, coding would begin with the main program (module 1.0) and finish with modules 3.1 and 3.2. The problem with this approach is that *stub programs* (dummy programs that replace lower-level programs during testing) must be

created. In our example, stub programs should be needed for modules 2.0 and 3.0 in order to test the main program. In general, stub programs are cheaper to develop than test harness programs, and thus the top-down coding is usually preferred to bottom-up coding.

3. *Sandwich coding.* This approach uses more than one coding method. For example, top-down and bottom-up methods might be used simultaneously, or the bottom-up method might be used for the data handling modules and the top-down for the other program modules.

EXAMPLE OF PROGRAM CODING

Coding the Program Structure.   The detailed design is the primary input for program coding. If structured programming is used, the detailed design specifications would include structure designs for each program module. Then the design could simply be translated into its programming language equivalent, followed by the assembly of the program modules and testing.

We will illustrate this process by showing how a program module from a detailed design might be translated into BASIC language code. This module is from the architectural design specified for Barney's Clothing Company given in Section 12.4 of this chapter. The following shows (1) a detailed design for the main program (module 1.0) and (2) how this detailed design might be coded in BASIC. The detailed design for the main program is:

Detailed Design for the Main Program (module 1.0)

Purpose: Input sales data for a store and generate a report.
Begin program.
Print Start-up message to the user.
Input the value of STORE$—the name of the store.
Input NT—the number of clothing types to be input.

Call module 2.0—the input and save module.
Call module 3.0—the retrieve and report module.
Print shutdown message to user.
End program.

During coding, this description might be transformed into the following programming language statements:

BASIC Language code for the Main Program (module 1.0)

```
10 REM Main Program coded in BASIC.
20 PRINT"This is Barney's Program."
30 PRINT"Please type in the name of the store."
40 INPUT STORE$
50 PRINT "Please type in the number of types of clothing sold by the
   store."
60 INPUT NT
70 REM Call MODULES 2.0 and 3.0
80 GOSUB 200
90 GOSUB 300
100 PRINT"Processing is Finished."
110 END
```

Lines 80 and 90 call modules 2.0 and 3.0, which begin at lines 200 and 300, respectively.

The coding process would then be repeated using detailed designs for the other modules in the program. This example should give the reader a general idea of how the program structure is coded. Note that this is not a complete program, but only a highly simplified example of a coded module.

The Data Structure. The detailed design is also the primary input for coding the data structure; it provides specific information about the data elements, including names, definitions, and structures. This information is needed by the subprograms that input, save, and retrieve data. A detailed design is presented below for the data structure example used for Barney's Clothing Company in section 12.4 of this chapter. For simplicity, not all the information relating to data structure (e.g., information on how the program modules should share common data) is included.

Detailed Design of the Data Structure

General Specifications on Data Storage
The programs do not update the data files. All data for the entire period must be input at one session. STORE is the name of the store for which data is stored or retrieved. NT is the number of different types of clothing sold by the store. The example data uses "NO. 1" for the store name and NT = 3 for the number of types of clothing.

The Data Storage Hierarchy
STORE—Name of the store.
     NT—Number of types of clothing sold.
          TYPE—Name of each type of clothing.
               PRICE—Price of each type of clothing.
               NUMBER—Number sold of each type of clothing.

Example Data Set for One Store
STORE—NO.1 Barney's Downtown Store
     NT—3
          TYPE—Coats
               PRICE—$50
               NUMBER—10
          TYPE—Hats

       .
       .
       .

The coding for the data structure involves the use of BASIC commands to read and write disk files, so it is not shown here. Any reasonable coding that fulfills the detailed design specifications would be appropriate.

Structured Programming and Coding. It should be clear from our discussion that structured design can translate into structured coding. However, well-structured design can be translated into poorly structured code, if a structured coding style is not used.

The purpose of structured coding is to linearize the flow of control through a program, so that the execution of statements follows the sequence

Computer Insights
System Development Tools

Fourth generation languages have already been introduced, and we will now see how they can be used in the creation of information systems.

Application Factory, by Cortex Corporation. Application Factory is designed to help build on-line transaction systems through the use of a high-level procedural language (BUILDER), a nonprocedural language, a procedure diagramming system, and an automatic documentation generator. The key to Application Factory's power is that well-understood simple tasks like screen design, file design, data entry and editing, menu definition, and report definition can be developed easily using special nonprocedural languages, while arbitrarily complicated procedures can be developed in BUILDER.

When creating a procedure, the systems developer can see its steps in a quasi-graphic form by using the procedure diagrammer to show the control structure. In addition, the documentation generator can take the descriptions of the system provided during the development process and create a complete set of correct and up-to-date documentation. The resulting systems can be run interpretively during prototyping and development and then compiled for the finished system.

The specific operating details of Application Factory cannot be easily demonstrated, because much of the development process involves the nonprocedural interaction of the user with the screen. This system has sufficient power and speed to serve as a total replacement for third generation languages like COBOL in many situations. Application Factory is close to a true fourth-generation language.

FOCUS by Application Builders, Inc. FOCUS is a full-function language that can do everything a conventional language can do and can be used by both experienced and novice users. At the center of a FOCUS information system is a data base manager. The information maintained there can then be accessed through an ordinary search language and

reported through a typical report generator. Additional capabilities in FOCUS include a chart graphics system, financial analysis tools, decision support functions, natural English language commands through a system named Intellect, fully security to protect data from unauthorized use, an interactive data entry system for the generating screen formats, and control of distributed processing across many users. Programs written in third generation languages can directly access the FOCUS system and its capabilities, and FOCUS can directly reference other routines written in third generation languages. The data base manager is designed to work with its own files as well as files created by many other varieties of applications software. Small FOCUS programs would be something like the following examples:

```
Get a Report

LIST STUD-NUM AND
  PERCENT AND GRADE
  IF CLASS IS "CSE125'
```

```
Generate a Graph

SET HAXIS-6, VAXIS-4
GRAPH FILE GRADES
HEADING CENTER
 "Grades by Class"
SUM GRADE ACROSS
    CLASS
```

The FOCUS system is powerful and easy to use. It appears to be more like an integrated set of separate processing functions than a new generation of languages, but this approach is at least as significant as that of Application Factory.

Many other fourth generation languages exist (e.g., NATURAL, NOMAD2, RAMIS II). They are generally based on combining the management of a data base with many of the well-understood and common problems from business (data entry and editing, choosing options from menus, and so on). As the power of personal computers increases, such systems may become part of the ordinary software of ordinary users. If so, then the real explosion in software will begin.

in which the code is written. A linear flow of control enhances the readability of the code, facilitating understanding, debugging, testing, documentation, and modification of the program.

Program Testing and Debugging Methods.   Program testing will be discussed in the next section—only those methods specifically related to program coding and debugging will be discussed here.

Verification testing is performed during program development to test whether the program meets the specifications stated in the design specifications document. Verification testing is composed of two parts: unit testing and integration testing. *Unit testing* is the independent testing of single program modules. *Integration testing* is the testing of the entire set of program modules with all modules in place (i.e., integrated into a program).

Verification testing can be accomplished by analytic methods or by program execution. *Static formal testing* uses mathematical methods to formally prove the correctness of the program. *Data testing* uses sample data sets to test the program.

Structured programming is the most important aid to program debugging. Structure helps to locate errors in the code by isolating them within a single module. Once the module containing the error has been identified, the following steps are typically used:

1. Information is collected about the bug. For example, the programmer determines when, where, and under what conditions the bug occurs.
2. The programmer looks for patterns. What differentiates the failures from the successes? Can the error be isolated in the code?
3. The programmer generates an hypothesis as to what might be wrong by examining the code that is probably responsible for the error.
4. The hypothesis is tested by running the program with extra output statements or diagnostic data. If the hypothesis is proved wrong, another hypothesis is generated.
5. A correction is implemented to eliminate the bug.
6. The programmer verifies that the error has been corrected.

Success in debugging often depends on step 3. The ability to generate good hypotheses comes mainly from experience, usually bitter experience!

Documenting the Program.   Drafts of the user's manual and the technical manual can be created in the program design stage or as an early step in the program development stage. The manuals can then be used as guides during programming and as a place to write down details about the program as it is coded, tested, and debugged. The technical manual is often assembled from programmers' notebooks and technical memoranda generated during program development and testing. Sometimes a librarian is appointed to systematically collect these materials for later use.

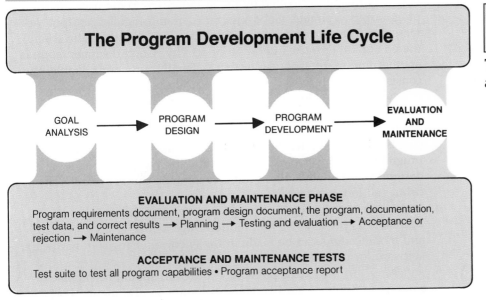

12.6

The Program Evaluation and Maintenance Stage

Like the three earlier programming stages, the program evaluation and maintenance stage can be described in terms of its inputs, outputs, and methods. Two types of program evaluation will be discussed in this section. *Verification* asks if the program product was built correctly, referring to the match between the program and the design specifications document. *Validation* asks if the correct program product was built, referring to the match between the program, the program requirements document, and the users' true needs.

Inputs for Program Evaluation and Maintenance

There are a number of major inputs for program evaluation. First, both the computer program and the program documentation must be available as inputs, since they must be evaluated together. Second, the products of the goal analysis and design stages must be available in order to perform verification and validation testing. Third, the major results of the testing performed in the program development stage must be available, along with the data used and the expected results. Fourth, there must be an evaluation site or user group where evaluation can take place; this step may necessitate the installation of the program on the user's computer.

In addition to these four inputs, a formal *program acceptance testing plan* may also be used. Such a plan may be developed in the design stage, but if it is not and if the program is complex, the plan should be prepared later and should specify a formal procedure for acceptance testing of the program.

The final important input for program evaluation is a set of criteria for good programs, for example:

1. *Reliability and correctness.* A program should always work correctly for valid data. A program should also be able to function with a wide range of nonvalid data. Incorrect input should not crash the system (cause the operating system to terminate abnormally), but should generate suitable error messages and leave the system in control, allowing the user to correct the errors.
2. *Usability.* Good programs should be easy to use. User-friendly aids, such as menus and prompts, should be available. In addition, on-line help (information provided by the system to help the user run the program), is desirable. Good programs should regularly output messages to help users monitor what is going on, especially when there is no other overt indication of activity. Good documentation is another important aspect of usability. Finally, programs should be consistent in their use of notation, techniques, and style so that the user will not have to adapt to a wide variety of user interfaces in the same program.
3. *Testability.* A program should be delivered with benchmark **test data** (sometimes called a **test suite**) so that the user can verify that the program functions correctly. If possible, the program should be designed so that any subprograms it contains can be tested and debugged independently.
4. *Maintainability.* A program should be as well structured and as adaptable as possible, so that hidden **bugs** can be easily corrected and modifications can be made in the event of changes in hardware, software, or user needs.
5. *Portability.* To the extent possible, a program should be capable of running in different hardware and software environments. Portability

test data
Data generated or acquired to determine whether a newly designed program works and how well it works.

test suite
A set of data that tests all of the critical capabilities of a program.

bug
An error in a computer program.

depends in part on modularity and the programming language used. Compatibility is related to portability; in this situation, *compatibility* refers to whether the program is compatible with programs already in use by the program user.

6. *Generalizability.* A program should have **generalizability,** that is, it should solve as general a problem as possible so that the same program can be used for a wider variety of situations than was originally intended, thus obviating the need for many similar programs.

7. *Efficiency.* Program efficiency refers to the speed with which a program runs and the amount of storage it requires. With the greatly reduced cost of modern computer hardware and RAM, efficiency has become less important. However, programs that "hog" memory or keep the user waiting for long periods of time should be avoided. A program can be made more efficient by writing it in a compiled language or by coding frequently used subprograms in assembly language.

generalizability
The degree to which a single process can solve a large number of similar problems, thus obviating the need for many processes.

A programmer should keep these characteristics of a good program clearly in mind as the design is developed. If the final program does not meet most of these criteria, the programming effort has failed.

■ Program Evaluation and Maintenance Outputs

The major output of the program evaluation and maintenance stage is the program acceptance testing report, which summarizes the results of the evaluation of the program. It should summarize each of the various requirements and specifications given in the goal analysis and design documents. Even if the program is not accepted, the report is valuable for revising the program (or possibly as legal evidence). A sample format for a program acceptance testing report is presented below. The same format could also have been used for the program acceptance testing plan.

Acceptance Testing Report

1. *Requirements to be verified or validated.* Name and description of each major requirement stated in the program requirements and the design specifications documents.
2. *Test cases for each requirement.* Description of the test case to be used for each requirement, including the expected outcomes of the tests and the capabilities to be demonstrated by the tests.
3. *Results of testing already completed.* As tests are completed, the results should be compiled in a verification/validation report.

The second major output of this stage, assuming that the program has been accepted by the user, is the material for the maintenance of the program. This material includes a test suite and a maintenance plan. The test suite consists of a set of data that tests all of the critical capabilities of the program. Also included in the test suite are the expected results for the test data. In a sense, the test suite is an extension of the program acceptance testing process. The maintenance plan summarizes the procedures for periodic maintenance testing, program revision and debugging, development of new versions of the system, etcetera. For complex, widely used programs, the cost of maintenance may exceed the total cost of creating the program in the first place.

◼ Methods of Program Verification

Verification of the accuracy of a program usually includes three major types of program tests: empirical data tests, static formal tests, and self-evident program tests.

Empirical data tests can be conducted in a number of different ways. Usually, however, the first test is to run the program on a problem with a known solution. The programmer begins the execution of the completed program and provides data when it is required. When the program completes the task, the results are compared to the known solution. If the known and test solutions are the same, testing continues.

Other empirical data tests based on the nature of the program are then run. Clearly, empirical data tests can be more useful for some purposes than for others. Four types of tests are commonly used. *Functional tests* test whether the program can process ordinary data, including maximum and minimum values. *Stress tests* try to crash the program by using unreasonable or erroneous data. *Structural tests* use data that exercises all possible pathways through the program (e.g., all options available to the user). *Performance tests* use standard benchmark data to examine the execution time of the program.

Even if no errors are found in any of the empirical data tests, it cannot be concluded that no errors exist. Professional programmers sometimes express this dilemma by noting that if all the tests have found no error, it only means that the program has not been tested enough! Thus, the impossibility of ever totally verifying the accuracy of a program with empirical data has led to the implementation of other alternatives.

Static formal tests are a second method of verifying the accuracy of a program. In this method, the programmer defines statements about the program that are expected to be true as the program executes (e.g., "At this point in the program, all of the names in the list have been placed in alphabetical order."). Unfortunately, English statements cannot be used. Instead, the statements must be made in a special mathematical language called *predicate calculus*. It is possible to express virtually all of the conditions that might ever be needed in predicate calculus, but it is not an easy language to use. For example,

FORALL X (THERE-EXISTS Y (IMPLIES (PERSON X) (MOTHER X Y)))

expresses the idea that all people have mothers. Verifying the correctness of a simple ten-line program might take an entire page of equations in predicate calculus; thus, it is rarely used for program verification. However, new methods that use computers to verify the code are considered promising.

Self-evident tests, which are based on structured programming, are the final method for verifying the accuracy of a program. The idea behind this method is to make the computer program so simple to understand that the correctness of the program is self-evident (obvious) to the user. People can generally handle only a limited amount of complexity (three to seven pieces or chunks of information) at any one time. Thus, if the program can be broken down into information chunks or subprograms that are small enough to be clearly understandable, the user can have reasonable confidence that the entire program is correct.

◼ Methods of Program Validation and Maintenance

Program validation concerns the extent to which the program meets the present needs of the users as well as potentially different future needs. Program validation methods are too complex and extensive for detailed study here. The fundamental idea behind them is that the program must be studied under operational conditions by regular users. Thus, the program validation process begins with on-site acceptance testing by the users before the program is completed and released. Acceptance testing becomes maintenance testing after the program has been released and is operational.

Program maintenance is primarily concerned with keeping the program valid and operational as new programming errors appear, as changes occur in hardware and software, and as users' needs change over time. Program validity is usually maintained by releasing new versions of the program from time to time. For highly successful commercial programs, the new versions may involve a repetition of the entire program development process. Eventually, most programs "die" and are replaced by entirely new programs; some, like old soldiers, just fade away.

An in-depth discussion of systems development is beyond the scope of this book. However, we can explain the fundamentals by relating them to our discussion of programming. System development can be viewed as a generalization of program development in which concern is given to people, data and hardware—as well as to software. Solving problems for people requires more than programs. Whenever a real-world problem is solved, consideration must be given to all four components of the computer system: (1) people and their procedures, (2) data and data acquisition, (3) programs and documentation, and (4) hardware and hardware-related devices. Thus, the programming process is only one part of creating a useful computer system. The other part, **systems development,** will be discussed in terms of its relationship to the simpler task of programming.

◼ What is Systems Development?

Formally a people-computer system, called an **information system,** is defined by the *Encyclopedia of Computer Science and Engineering* (Van Nostrand Reinhold Co., New York, 1983) as an organized collection of people, data, hardware, and software designed to process information as needed by the users of the system. Information systems are also called data processing systems in business, but are most frequently simply called systems. Systems are thus defined in much the same way as programs and program products, but they are concerned with the total problem, not just the software. Examples of information systems include: personal computer workstations for students, engineers, researchers, and other professionals; local area networks for small businesses or departments in large businesses; and mainframe computer facilities and networks that support large businesses, industrial plants, communications services, and **data processing** service centers.

The following are three important characteristics of information systems:

1. Like programs, systems are characterized by structure. A system has four components—people, data, software, and hardware—and like program modules, these components must interact with each other and must be organized into well-defined structures. Often, the same forms of **hierarchical structure** used in programming are used in

12.7

Programming and Systems Development

systems development
The process of creating and operating an information system by executing the four steps in the System Development Life Cycle (SDLC), including goal analysis, design, development, evaluation and maintenance.

information system
An organized collection of people, data, software, and hardware that interact to achieve specific information processing goals. Often referred to as simply a "system."

data processing
The manipulation of large amounts of data to form useful knowledge for business, government, and other organizations.

hierarchical structure
A set of elements arranged in a top-down hierarchical manner according to a common property, e.g., an organization chart for a business.

creating systems—top-down design, successive refinement, modularity, and so forth. The following hierarchical structure shows **subsystems** commonly used in systems development:

subsystem
A component or element of an information system, e.g., the people, data, software, and hardware subsystems.

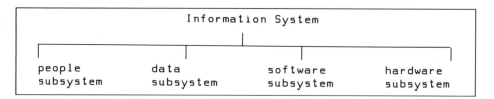

SDLC
The System Development Life Cycle (SDLC) is the process of applying the four steps (goal analysis, design, development, evaluation and maintenance) to an information system consisting of people, data, software, and hardware.

2. Systems are developed using a life cycle model like that used in programming. The **Systems Development Life Cycle (SDLC)** includes the same four stages—goal analysis, design, development, and evaluation and maintenance—as does the PDLC. As before, the description of the system becomes progressively more and more concrete during these four stages, until the system can actually be created, i.e., people can be trained, programs written, hardware purchased, data collected and so forth.

3. Systems developers address all aspects of creating a computer system. Thus, the systems approach is characterized by equal concern for all components of the system and the proper interface of components, i.e., the communication necessary to make the components work together.

■ How Does Systems Development Differ from Programming?

Systems development is much more complicated than program product development, since all four components of the system (people, data, software, hardware) are given equal importance. Furthermore, the systems approach not only requires each component to function properly and independently but it also requires all components to function properly together so that the total system will work. An overview of a common method of organizing the SDLC is given in the figure on page 519.

The figure shows how the task of systems development can be broken into five parts: the total system, the people component, the data component, the software component, and the hardware component. The four stages of development are applied to the total system and to each component of the system. In practice, systems development usually proceeds as follows: a goal analysis is performed (1) for the system, then (2) for the people component, (3) for the data component, (4) for the software component, and finally (5) for the hardware component. When that is completed, the process of design is then undertaken for the total system and then for the five subsystems. In practice, the stages affect each other and are often repeated. For example, the requirements of the total system might be re-examined in the light of the requirements identified for each component. Organizing the task into people, data, software, and hardware is obviously a way of restructuring the problem into simpler, more easily solved subproblems. The total system problem then deals with the integration of the components into a functioning system.

The concept of structure is much more complex in systems development than in program development. Each of the system components is often treated as a subsystem and organized hierarchically into modules. For example, recall that in the program design stage, the program specifications were organized

System Component	Goal Analysis	Design Phase	Development Phase	Evaluation and Maintenance	An Overview of the Systems Development Life Cycle
System	*System Requirements.* What will the system do? what components will be needed?	*System Design Specifications.* How will the system work? How will the components work?	*Planning and development of the system.* Complete and test system components and completed system.	*Evaluation and maintenance of the system.* Testing components. Testing system.	
People	*People Subsystem Requirements.* What types of people are needed?	*People specifications.* What must each type of person do? What procedures are needed?	*Plan for people.* Hiring and training people. Testing procedures with data base and software.	*Evaluation of procedures and interface with system.* Maintain people, components, and procedures.	
Data	*Data Subsystem Requirements.* What types of data are needed?	*Data Specifications.* How will data be obtained? How will data be stored?	*Data base development.* Data collection. Data storage with software.	*Evaluation of data base and interface.* Maintain data base.	
Software	*Program Requirements.* What types of data processing will be needed?	*Program Design Specifications.* What program modules are needed? What must each module do to the data?	*Development or acquisition of software.* Software tests with data base and hardware.	*Evaluation of software and interface.* Maintain software.	
Hardware	*Hardware Requirements.* What types of hardware will be needed?	*Hardware Design Specifications.* What hardware components are needed? What must each component do?	*Acquire hardware components.* Test with software and data base.	*Evaluating hardware and interface with software and system.* Maintain hardware.	

into functional modules connected by control structures. In **systems design,** this approach is often applied to the design of the non-software components. For example, in the hardware design, hardware specifications might be organized by function, e.g., input devices, storage devices, control and processing devices, and output devices.

Although the Systems Development Life Cycle includes the same steps as the Program Development Life Cycle, there are major differences. We shall now look at SDLC in more detail, comparing each step with the corresponding step of the PDLC. Some points in this discussion will be especially important to readers who may wish to develop their own personal computer system.

systems design
The process of producing a set of valid, unambiguous design specifications for a proposed system. System design incorporates both the breaking of the system into modules (system, analysis) and the combination of the modules to form the system (system synthesis).

The Systems Goal Analysis Stage

The inputs and outputs of the systems goal analysis stage are much the same as in programming. The first task is to determine the users' needs and the second is to document them in the system requirements document, which must include the requirements for the people and their procedures, the data and the data structures, the software, and the hardware. Procedures are essentially programs for people and must be tested in the same manner as computer programs.

The greater emphasis on people is one of the major differences in the systems approach and also one of the major sources of problems for the **systems analyst.** The study of the people and the procedures that will be an important component of the new system must be carried out carefully with attention to potential people problems. For example, when there is an existing system, one frequently encounters **upstream problems:** some of the people important to the new system do not cooperate, and the system fails. ("Upstream" refers to the principle that one should never build a waterwheel on a stream unless one is sure that the upstream owners are not planning a dam.) The systems analyst must realize that people will make or break the system and that these people must perceive the new system as offering them significant advantages over the existing one.

The **invisible system** is another common people-related problem: the formal procedures that people report using may not, in fact, be the ones actually used. For example, some systems studies have uncovered elaborate, document-oriented communications procedures that serve no function, since short informal personal communications are actually used. The paper system is simply seen as an unnecessary evil required by the head office.

Other "people problems" are especially important to an individual PC system developer. In **ivory tower design,** the analyst (e.g., a computer salesperson) fails to perform a requirements study and simply "designs the system you really need," that is, the one the designer personally likes. In the **hidden**

systems analyst
The person responsible for the goal analysis and design phase of the SDLC; may also supervise development and evaluation as well.

upstream problem
Resistance to some aspect of a proposed information system by its intended users.

invisible system
A problem in systems goal analysis, in which people use procedures other than those they report using.

ivory tower design
A situation in which an analyst designs a system based on a personal view rather than on a systems requirement study.

hidden agenda problem
A problem that occurs during systems analysis when irrational factors, such as prestige, underlie the user's overtly stated system requirements.

Computer Insights
Ben Franklins' Technology Trap

The technology trap is the tendency of systems designers to place too much emphases on complex hardware when simpler methods exist.

One of the best commentaries on the technology trap was written over two-hundred years ago by Benjamin Franklin. His incisive comments on the need to consider the true value of a system in terms of its actual goals are found in "Poor Richard's Remarkable Striking Sundial Project"

How to make a STRIKING SUNDIAL, by which not only a Man's own Family, but all his Neighbors for ten Miles round, may know what a Clock it is, when the Sun shines, without seeing the Dial.

Chuse an open Place in your Yard or Garden, on which the Sun may shine all Day without any Impediment from Trees or Buildings. On the Ground mark out your Hour lines, as for a horizontal Dial, according to Art, taking Room enough for the Guns on the Line and so of the rest. The Guns must all be charged with Powder, but Ball is unnecessary. Your Gnomon or Style must have twelve burning Glasses annex't to it, and be so placed that the Sun shining through the Glasses, one after the other, shall cause the Focus or burning Spot to fall on the Hour Line of One, for Example, at One a Clock, and there kindle a

Train of Gunpowder that shall fire one Gun. At Two a Clock, a Focus shall fall on the Hour Line of Two, and kindle another Train that shall discharge two Guns successively; and so of the rest.

Note, There must be 78 Guns in all. Thirty-two Pounders will be best for this Use; but 18 pounders may do, and will cost less, as well as use less Powder, for nine Pounds of Powder will do for one Charge of each eighteen Pounder where as the Thirty-two Pounders would require for each Gun 16 Pounds. Note also, That the chief Expense will be the Powder, for the Cannon once bought, will with Care, last 100 Years.

Note moreover, that there will be a great Saving of Powder in Cloudy Days.

Kind Reader, Methinks I hear thee say, That is indeed a good Thing to know how the Time passes, but this Kind of Dial notwithstanding the mentioned Savings, would be very Expensive; and the cost greater than the Advantage, Thou art wise, my Friend, to be so considerate beforehand; some Fools would not have found out so much, till they had make the Dial and try'd it.

. . . Let all such learn that many a private and many a publick Project, are like this Striking Dial, great Cost for little Profit.

agenda problem, the users have hidden goals that are not brought to light but which will ultimately determine user satisfaction with the finished system (e.g., an executive wants a more powerful PC than the other executives have). In the **hardware syndrome,** the analyst is so intent on the hardware component that he or she fails to closely examine the software and other needs of the users and the actual value of the hardware for the users of the system.

The Systems Design Stage

Many of our descriptions of program design also apply to the systems design stage. Inputs and outputs for systems design are fundamentally the same. The systems design stage begins with a study of the systems requirements document and ends with the approval of a systems *design specifications document.* The difference between systems and program design is in the complexity of the task. The systems design must provide specifications for the people, data, hardware, and software subsystems, and these specifications must be checked for compatibility with each other and with the system requirements. These checks frequently reveal errors that must be corrected. For this reason, the systems designer often shuttles back and forth between the goal analysis and the design stages as problems are uncovered and corrected. Hence, the distinction between these two stages is often not precise, and they end only when satisfactory working documents are completed. Sometimes the analysis/design takes so long that groups of users purchase personal computers to meet their immediate needs and eventually cancel the corporate systems development contract entirely.

The same techniques used to handle complexity in program design are also used in systems design. Thus, systems design makes maximum use of modularity, hierarchical design, top-down structure, and the other related techniques. For example, each component can be designed to be as independent as possible of the other components, so that changes required in the design of one component will not affect the designs of the others. Compatibility between independent components is maintained by using a fixed set of rules to limit communication between components. Another goal of systems design is to keep the initial system as simple as possible, but provide for later additions and modifications. An **open-ended system** makes specific provisions for adding new components, such as programs and data structures, after the system is built. Like program designers, systems designers frequently use computer software for the statement, simulation, and testing of designs.

There are many problems common to systems design. One is the **technology trap** where the design is overcomplicated by too much emphasis on the hardware and software components. In large systems, the technology trap yields a system in which computer technology is used for tasks that people could do more effectively. *A balance must be maintained between automation and human effort, in order to yield a workable design.* In small systems, the technology trap results in the purchase of powerful hardware that is seldom fully used. This problem is very common when individuals develop personal computer systems for professional or small business use. One way of avoiding this problem is to use the **NASH** method. The acronym NASH (*needs assessment, ap-plication decisions, software selection, and hardware selection) specifies the correct order in which to design a personal computer system:

1. *Needs assessment.* The initial step in acquiring any computer system is a clear statement of the users' needs. A novice designing his or her

---

hardware syndrome
Systems analysis problem in which the analyst is so intent on the hardware component that the actual needs of the user are poorly examined.

open-ended system
A system in which specific provisions have been made to add new components (e.g., new software, hardware, and data structures) after the system is built.

technology trap
The tendency to build unneeded computer systems or subsystems simply because the technology is available, without regard to actual value to the user.

NASH
An acronym (*Needs assessment. Application decisions, Software selection, and Hardware selection); used in systems design, to describe the correct procedure for selecting hardware.

own personal computer system often insists that this is impossible, usually because he or she is not familiar with the capabilities of personal computers. The first step should be to take a course or read a textbook like this one and get some firsthand experience. Then, the individual can study his or her own information uses and collect work samples to serve as a basis for design.

2. *Applications decisions.* Once the individual's needs are carefully stated, decisions must be made on what applications can help meet those needs. Priorities should be assigned to applications in word processing, spreadsheets, data bases, graphics, statistical analysis, etc.

3. *Software selection.* Once the desired applications are known, specific software for those applications can be selected. Several applications systems may adequately meet the designer's needs, and these systems can be determined by work samples. In choosing among PC software, the key factor to remember is that PC hardware changes significantly over any three-year period. Thus, one should select software widely enough used to ensure that it will remain available.

4. *Hardware selection.* Only after all of these steps are complete should one consider selecting hardware; clearly, any hardware that will execute the selected software will be acceptable. At this point, cost, manufacturer's reputation, quality of local service, and other criteria can be used to make a final decision on hardware components.

People new to the computing game often perform these steps in reverse order, HSAN. They start by purchasing hardware, basing their decisions on price, power, and technological wonders. Then they purchase whatever popular software is available for their PC. Next, they see what applications the software will support, and finally they try to find some needs that the resulting system meets. The major result of the HSAN method is the accumulation of vast amounts of elegant but seldom-used computer hardware.

The Systems Development Stage

The major input for this stage is the systems design specifications document, which is subject to formal review and updating. Again, development begins with the preparation of plans for the development, evaluation, and testing. The outputs of this stage are: (1) an operational system in which the people, data, software, and hardware components are in place and functioning; (2) system documentation; and (3) a testing and maintenance suite that provides users with test data and results for system maintenance.

The methods used in systems development are similar to those in programming, but in systems development they are applied to all four components. Further, in system work the sharp distinction between the development and the evaluation phases frequently does not exist for the four components of the system. For example, the people component is often developed and evaluated first to allow the users of the system to participate in the final design and development planning for the other components. Similarly, the hardware may be installed and subjected to verification testing before the software component is completed.

Another major difference in systems development is that there are usually three software options. Purchasing an existing software package is the major option for most personal computer users. Packaged software includes very high-quality single-application and multi-application systems. Examples of single-application software include Word Perfect and Microsoft Word for word processing, Lotus 1–2–3 and Excel for spreadsheets, and DBase III or IV and many others for data base applications. Multi-application or *integrated* systems usually support the big five (word processing, spreadsheets, data bases, graphics, and communication); examples include Appleworks and Microsoft Works. There is a vast array of other software for small systems users. Many software packages exist for the larger system as well, including extremely powerful text and data base products capable of operating on huge banks of data.

The second software option is to develop new software tailored to the specific system under development. The high costs of software development make this a less viable option. The third option is to purchase a software package and modify it for the special needs of the system. Many system software products are specifically designed for this purpose.

Another important aspect of systems development is the replacement of an existing system with a new system. Four methods are commonly used. In the **cold turkey** method, the entire old system is completely replaced by the new system at one time. The obvious difficulty with this method is that new systems seldom work exactly right the first time. The **parallel systems** approach keeps both the old and the new systems operating simultaneously until the new system has been debugged; the problem here is cost and practicality. The **phase-in/phase-out** method replaces parts of the old system separately so that total failure is avoided; as the new parts are proven, the old parts are dropped. Finally, a **pilot system** approach tests the new system on part of the information load of the old system to try to uncover the most serious bugs before the new system is put into operation.

Systems development projects are plagued by many problems, including inadequate provisions for training and for software and software maintenance. The latter problem is common to both large and small projects. A common assumption is that the cost of computer hardware is the major factor to be considered in developing and operating computer facilities. However government and industry studies indicate that software and training costs are much greater than hardware costs over the life of a system. Wise designers expect that for each dollar spent on hardware, at least two dollars must be spent on software and software support, especially training. When this money is available up-front in the design phase, the developer can provide adequate documentation, continuing in-house on-the-job training, on-staff system expertise, and so on.

Another major problem in large systems development is upper-management indifference. "Letting the departments buy what they want" can result in real headaches because of the **redundancy principle.** More is not better if it means acquiring different brands of hardware and software. The cost of maintaining, using, and learning about computer hardware and software is directly related not to the number of systems purchased but to the number of different systems purchased. The cost of maintaining and using two identical computers is much less than the cost of maintaining and using two machines made by different manufacturers, and adding systems that are compatible with existing ones increases costs only marginally. Furthermore, compatible systems can be interchanged to provide a backup when any single unit must be repaired or replaced. The redundancy principle holds as well for small systems development, where there may be a temptation to acquire many different brands to "cut costs."

cold turkey method
A procedure for replacing one information system with another without any phase-out time for the system being replaced.

parallel systems method
A method of converting from one information system to another in which the old and the new systems are temporarily operated side by side to protect the client organization in case the new system fails during the shakedown period.

phase-in/phase-out method
A method of converting from one information system to another by allowing the old system to expire gradually while the new one is moved into full operation one stage at a time.

pilot system method
A method for converting from one information system to another by testing the new system on only a small part of the old system's information load.

redundancy principle
The cost of operating and maintaining a system is related not so much to the number of identical systems purchased as to the number of different systems purchased, e.g. training costs can double if two different word processors are used in an organization.

The Systems Evaluation and Maintenance Stage

As in programming, the inputs to the **systems evaluation** and maintenance stage include the system components, the documentation, the test suite, and the evaluation plan. The outputs include the evaluation report and the system maintenance plan.

The same basic testing and evaluation procedures are used in both programming and systems development. However, testing four components generates some additional concerns. For example, the evaluation and maintenance plan must include provisions for inside and outside testing for each of the subsystems. **Inside testing** is like unit testing of programs; it tests each subsystem individually by verifying that it meets the design specifications. **Outside testing** is like integration testing; it determines whether the subsystems function properly together. Both evaluative and diagnostic tests are important. Evaluative tests are used in the decision to accept or reject the system, but they may be too limited or too general to be used to maintain the system or identify more specific problems with it. Diagnostic tests are used to identify specific problems in components or component interaction.

The systems maintenance plan is of critical importance. Once the system developer leaves, the users are often largely on their own. Neither a small nor a large system can be maintained properly without a sound maintenance plan and trained personnel. Especially in PC systems developed by individuals, the retailer or manufacturer is the main source of assistance with problems and for maintenance. The reputation of these firms for service is an important consideration. PC software packages have two ''magic numbers'': the serial number of the original software diskette and the telephone number for technical assistance where a trained specialist can be reached (provided the user has the first number). One of the big advantages of purchasing software from established software houses is the availability and quality of the technical assistance provided.

Another special problem for the small computer system developer is providing good operational procedures for the system after it has been installed and is operating. The acronym **PEARLS** is sometimes used as a reminder of the characteristics of a well-run system, whether small or large. PEARLS stands for:

☐ *Purpose.* Formalizing a specific statement as to who will use the system and how it will help them.
☐ *Evaluation.* Systematically collecting data on how well the system is meeting its objectives.
☐ *Access.* Providing documents, software, hardware, data, training, and procedures for people with access to the facility.
☐ *Repair and maintenance.* Keeping all of the data, documents, software, and hardware operating and properly backed-up.
☐ *Location.* Providing a location maximally convenient for users.
☐ *Security.* Protecting the system from accidental or intentional physical loss.

The evaluative criteria summarized for programs can also be applied to systems, that is, systems should be general, usable, modular, easily modified, etc. In systems work, however, the key criteria is happy, productive users. Underlying all the methods of systems development is a common principle: the system is supposed to help the user.

This principle is the general basis for systems development as long as the following three assumptions about the users' needs are true. First, the intended users of the system must perform certain information processing tasks in order to achieve given objectives. Second, the users suffer at least some information overload: they cannot easily perform all the tasks required of them. Third, the information system is specifically intended to help users with their objectives. Given these assumptions, we can state the principles of maximum system use:

- **The relevance rule.** The tasks performed by the system must be relevant to the users' needs. The system will have value, if and only if, the set of tasks performed by the system overlaps the set of tasks that the users must perform.
- **The simplification rule.** The system must reduce information overload. It will have value, if and only if, it significantly reduces the information-processing load of its users.
- **The knowledgeable user.** The users must have a valid understanding of the new computer system and a correct perception of their own needs. Studies of systems development suggest that good systems with poorly trained users have about the same success rate as poor systems with well-trained users.

Most small PC system developers can probably at least avoid total failure if these simple principles are kept in mind, from the goal analysis to the maintenance stage.

relevance rule
A principle of maximum system use that states that the value of a system depends on the overlap of its tasks and the tasks that the user must perform.

simplification rule
A principle of maximum system use that states that system effectiveness depends on the degree to which it reduces the information processing load of its users.

knowledgeable user rule
A principle of maximum system use that states that the effectiveness of a system depends on how well people have been trained to use it.

The key to understanding modern programming is the *Program Development Life Cycle (PDLC)*, which consists of four interrelated programming stages: goal analysis, program design, program development, and program evaluation and maintenance. The PDLC emphasizes the critical tasks and products of each stage.

In the goal analysis stage, the programming problem is defined by studying the user's needs. The major product of this stage is the program requirements document, which describes what should be done by the program. This document is often formally reviewed before the next stage is undertaken.

In the program design stage, a program that is expected to satisfy the user's needs is described. The proposed solution is documented in the design specifications, which describes how the program should work. Included in the specifications are the major products of this stage: the external design is a highly general, abstract description of the program; the architectural design is a more concrete description of the program that includes summaries of all of the subprograms and data to be used; the detailed design is a highly specific description of the program that is suitable for coding into a programming language. Often the architectural and detailed designs are formally reviewed before work proceeds.

In the program development stage, a working program is developed from the detailed design by: (1) coding (translating) the detailed design into a programming language, (2) testing and debugging the resulting program, and (3) documenting the program. The products of this stage are the computer program, the documentation (including a user's manual), and the test data and results that partially verify the program.

12.8

Summary of Computer Programming and Systems Development

The evaluation and maintenance stage verifies, validates, and maintains the program. Verification deals with whether the program was built correctly (does the program do what it was designed to do?). Validation deals with whether the correct program was built (does the program meet the user's needs?). Maintenance ensures the continuing value of the program in the face of change. The products of this stage may include an acceptance testing report, a test suite (data and results for maintenance testing), and a maintenance plan. Programs are frequently accepted or rejected on the basis of the acceptance testing results.

Systems development is essentially a generalization of program development. Like program development, systems development restructures problems into subproblems (people, data, software, and hardware problems) that are then further broken down. As in programming, the solution is divided into stages—goal analysis, design, development, and evaluation and maintenance. Because of its complexity, systems development is much more difficult than program development, and serious failures in systems development are not uncommon.

This chapter has taken a software engineering approach to the programming and systems development process. The development process can also be viewed less formally as an artistic, creative, or personal endeavor. The software engineering perspective was chosen for several reasons. These reasons will serve as the conclusions to this chapter.

First, although this disciplined, systematic approach to software and systems was created for large complex tasks, it can be used in a simpler form for any but the most trivial systems or programming tasks. In our experience, this approach will almost invariably produce better programs, systems, and decisions regardless of the level of skill of the person or the level of complexity of the problem.

Second, systems errors are very costly, in both dollars and tears. Research studies of systems development projects show that the later an error is discovered, the greater the cost and effort required for its correction. One way of attacking this problem is to use a method that establishes discrete steps in programming and systems development and systematically evaluates the products of each step. (This method is reflected in the programmers' maxim: "The sooner you start coding, the longer it will take.") Thus, we have stressed structured systems, structured programming, and the importance of formal reviews, especially in the goal analysis and design stages.

Finally, even people who are not computer professionals need to know the rudiments of a systematic approach to computer programming and systems development. Computer software is a major and growing economic factor in any organization. In 1980, the U.S. automotive industry contributed about 2.3 percent to the gross national product. In the same year, the contribution of the computer industry was about 5 percent. It jumped to 8 percent in 1985, and it is still increasing. Further, it is estimated that in these years more than twice as much was spent on software systems and software systems maintenance as was spent on computer hardware. Thus, computer software is an important and growing cost to most organizations. You may not need to know how to program to use a computer, but being able to recognize good software and competent software and systems development is becoming a survival skill even for ordinary people.

Always remember that, in the final analysis, programming is problem solving. Regardless of the powerful techniques and tools of software engineering, either existing or yet to come, the basic problem-solving paradigm of programming remains unchanged: analyze the user's problem, design a solution, implement the design, and validate and update the solution as the user's needs change.

Chapter 12 Review

Expanded Objectives

The objectives listed below are an expansion of the essential chapter concepts listed at the beginning of the chapter. The review items that follow are based on these expanded objectives. If you master the objectives, you will do better on the review items and on your instructor's examination on the chapter material.

After reading the chapter, you should be able to:

1. explain the purpose and characteristics of structured programming.
2. Indicate the logical subunits and the specific control structures used.
3. differentiate among the roles of analyst, programmer, and user.
4. list four major areas of expertise needed by a designer of computer programs.
5. differentiate among external, architectural, and detailed program design.
6. sequence the documents produced during the Program Development Life Cycle in their order of development.

7. contrast the functions of the various documents generated in the Program Development Life Cycle.
8. Arrange a list of program elements or data elements into their logical hierarchical structure.
9. describe the relationships of the elements in a program or a data hierarchy.
10. compare and contrast the following techniques for design representation: flow charting, pseudo-code, Warnier-Orr diagrams, and HIPO.
11. match major programming activities with the appropriate stages of the Program Development Life Cycle.
12. list four main criteria that programmers use in choosing among programming languages.
13. match the names of the major criteria for judging computer programs with their descriptions.
14. describe the similarities and the differences between the Program and System Development Life Cycles.
15. explain the use of the NASH and PEARLS principles.
16. define the new terms and concepts introduced in the chapter.

Review Items

Completing this review will give you a good indication of how well you have mastered the contents of this chapter and prepare you for your instructor's test on this material. To maximize what you learn from this exercise, you should answer each question *before* looking up the answers in the appendix. The number of the corresponding expanded objective is given in parentheses following each question.

Complete the following clusters of items according to the directions heading each set.

A. Match each step on the left with the most appropriate stage on the right. (11)

____ 1. determines program requirements

____ 2. implements a system design

____ 3. determies the needs of the client

____ 4. determines the effectiveness of a solution

a. goal analysis
b. program design
c. program development
d. program evaluation

____ 5. restates the problem in a clear form

____ 6. determines the structure of a program

____ 7. devises a plan for solving a problem

____ 8. produces an application to solve a problem

B. The documents below are developed during the various stages of the Program Development Process Life Cycle. Indicate the sequence in which these documents are produced by marking the first one with the letter a, the second one with the letter b, etcera. If a document can be developed in more than one stage, use the first possible stage. Use an x for documents not mentioned in the text. (7)

____ 9. global design plan review

____ 10. program development plan

___ 11. preliminary structure document

___ 12. design specifications document

___ 13. program requirements document

___ 14. program acceptance testing report

___ 15. program evaluation structure charts

___ 16. technical manual

___ 17. user's manual

C. *Match the roles on the right with the responsibilities on the left.* (4)

___ 18. validate program effectiveness

___ 19. carry out goal analysis

___ 20. translate design into computer instructions

___ 21. document the computer program

___ 22. design the computer program

    a. user
    b. programmer
    c. analyst

D. *Match the roles on the right with the tasks on the left, which might be carried out in developing a computer income tax program.* (3)

___ 23. translate a procedure for computing income tax into a computer language

___ 24. input data to calculate income tax

___ 25. design a procedure for computing income tax.

___ 26. include current income tax law in the program design

___ 27. document the new income tax computer program

___ 28. determine program effectiveness for computing income tax

    a. programmer
    b. user
    c. analyst

E. *True or False.*

___ 29. Computer systems depend upon compatibility among software and hardware elements. (16)

___ 30. Technical manuals describe the use of computer hardware. (16)

___ 31. The primary purpose of the goal analysis stage is to clarify the appropriate output of a proposed computer program. (11)

___ 32. The black box or end-means method focuses on goal analysis. (16)

___ 33. Goal analysis provides the basic data needed to design an information system. (11)

___ 34. The expected constraints on a new computer program are determined during the goal analysis stage. (11)

___ 35. Structured programming requires that a complex computer program be broken down into subprograms. (1)

___ 36. Structured programming doesn't use unconditional branching instructions. (12)

___ 37. Program structures are the elements resulting from goal analysis. (11)

___ 38. Data elements can be combined into a data structure. (16)

___ 39. It is difficult to make program modifications when a hierarchial program structure is used. (1)

___ 40. The use of a data hierarchy helps clarify how data elements are stored and retrieved. (16)

___ 41. Data must be communicated within and across the modules of a program hierarchy. (1)

___ 42. It is common in structured program design to combine modules that do not share data. (1)

___ 43. It is desirable to have a high degree of dependence among the modules of a structured program. (1)

___ 44. Structured programming uses a wide variety of control structures. (1)

___ 45. An architectural design described both program structures and data structures. (5)

___ 46. The major activities performed in the program maintenance stage are coding, testing, and documentation. (11)

___ 47. Program documentation is an output of the program evaluation stage. (11)

___ 48. Sandwich coding uses more than one computer program coding method. (16)

___ 49. The type of testing done during the program development stage is called *validation*. (11, 16)

___ 50. Unit testing determines how well the modules of a structured program work together. (11, 16)

___ 51. A common means of verification is to run a problem whose solution is known through an untested computer program. (11,16)

___ 52. The accuracy of a program can be totally verified only through empirical data. (16)

___ 53. Effective program validation requires that data be collected from regular users under operational conditions. (11, 16)

___ 54. The programmer rather than the designer must have knowledge of data structures. (4)

___ 55. An important area if expertise for the user is a knowledge of the domain in which a program will function. (4)

___ 56. HIPO is a technique for describing program design specifications. (10)

___ 57. Warnier-Orr diagrams are a means of detailing the ISPCO functions of a proposed computer program. (10)

___ 58. Pseudo-code can be used in place of flowcharting to describe program design specifications. (10)

___ 59. Economics is one of the most common reasons for choosing one particular programming language over another. (12)

___ 60. Knowledge of standard programming methods for solving simple problems is important to program development. (4)

___ 61. Documentation of a computer program is the first step in design. (11)

___ 62. Data abstraction is a method of program design. (1, 11)

___ 63. In developing an information system, goal analysis clarifies the system's outputs. (11)

___ 64. Abruptly replacing one information system with another is called cold turkey. (11)

___ 65. Software and software support for an information system are more costly than hardware support (16)

G. *Match the description on the left with the program design types on the right. (5)*

___ 66. used in the actual coding of a program

a. architectural
b. external
c. detailed

___ 67. program instructions are written directly from this design

___ 68. describes the data structures of a program

___ 69. describes the program structures of a program

___ 70. describes, at an abstract level, a program that will meet specified requirements.

H. *Indicate which of the criteria for effective computer programs on the right best match the descriptions on the left. (13)*

___ 71. A program should be able to run in different software environments.

a. reliability
b. generalizability
c. portability
d. modularity
e. usability
f. efficiency
g. testability
h. maintainability

___ 72. A program should not consume too much memory.

___ 73. A program should not crash because of incorrect input.

___ 74. Subprograms should be designed so that they can be debugged independently.

___ 75. The larger processes of a computer program should be logically divided into smaller processes.

___ 76. A program should be as adaptable as possible.

___ 77. A program should have good documentation.

___ 79. Program processing should not keep users waiting.

___ 80. The program should have a high degree of compatibility with various hardware environments.

I. *Match the tasks on the left with the stages of the system development process on the right. (11)*

___ 81. determine system requirements

a. goal analysis
b. systems design
c. systems development
d. systems evaluation

___ 82. prepare a plan for systems development

___ 83. determine the needs of the client

___ 84. determine the effectiveness of the new system

___ 85. validate the information system

___ 86. specify the structure of the system

J. *Match each item on the left with the most appropriate principle on the right. (16)*

___ 87. help determine how well a new system meets client needs

A. NASH
B. PEARLS

___ 88. determines actual system needs of client

___ 89. protects system from accidental or deliberate loss

___ 90. selection of hardware

___ 91. determines applications required to meet client needs

___ 92. maintains the information system

K. *Logically arrange the following program elements into the correct hierarchy by placing the letters of the proper element in the blank spaces. (8)*

___ 93. highest level program

a. Program 3: employee payroll program
b. Program 2: inputs hours worked and calculates pay for all employees
c. Program 1: Prints a paycheck for a single employee.

___ 94. intermediate level subprogram

___ 95. lowest level subprogram

Appendix

The keys for the tests found in the review sections at the end of the chapters are presented in this appendix. As mentioned in the review section these tests should be viewed as practice tests. Research has demonstrated that they are best used when the user:

1) completes the test before looking at the correct answers, 2) keeps track of the items missed, and 3) studies the relevant sections of the text to determine why responses were incorrect.

Chapter One Key

1. T 2. F 3. F 4. F 5. T 6. T 7. F 8. T
9. F 10. F 11. F 12. f 13. g 14. b 15. a
16. d 17. d 18. b 19. e 20. c 21. a 22. d
23. f 24. a 25. c 26. b 27. e

Chapter Two Key

1. F 2. T 3. T 4. T 5. T 6. F 7. T 8. T
9. F 10. T 11. T 12. T 13. T 14. T 15. F
16. T 17. T 18. T 19. F 20. a 21. d 22. c
23. e 24. b 25. b 26. c 27. a 28. e 29. e
30. bc 31. abcd 32. be 33. abcde 34. c 35. b
36. a 37. e 38. a 39. b 40. d

Chapter Three Key

1. T 2. T 3. F 4. T 5. T 6. F 7. T 8. T
9. T 10. T 11. F 12. T 13. F 14. T 15. F
16. F 17. F 18. F 19. T 20. T 21. F 22. F
23. F 24. F 25. T 26. F 27. T 28. T 29. F
30. F 31. T 32. T 33. T 34. T 35. T 36. T
37. T 38. F 39. T 40. F 41. F 42. T 43. T
44. T 45. T 46. T 47. T 48. F 49. T 50. F
51. F 52. T 53. T 54. T 55. F 56. T 57. T
58. F 59. d 60. a 61. b 62. b 63. f 64. d
65. a 66. e 67. g 68. b 69. a 70. c 71. a
72. b 73. c

Chapter Four Key

1. e 2. f 3. a 4. c 5. h 6. f 7. d 8. d 9. f
10. g 11. h 12. d 13. c 14. e 15. g 16. b
17. e 18. c 19. F 20. T 21. F 22. T 23. F
24. T 25. T 26. F 27. T 28. ajfbdh 29. aifbdh
30. akfbh 31. aikefb 32. aimefgdh 33. ani
34. ajop 35. all 36. wp 37. op 38. all 39. ss,
dbm 40. wp 41. gr 42. ps 43. wp ss dbm
44. gr 45. dbm 46. com 47. ss dbm 48. os ps

Chapter Five Key

1. T 2. T 3. F 4. F 5. F 6. T 7. T 8. F
9. T 10. T 11. T 12. F 13. T 14. T 15. T
16. F 17. F 18. F 19. T 20. T 21. T 22. T
23. F 24. T 25. F 26. T 27. T 28. T 29. F
30. T 31. F 32. F 33. T 34. F 35. X 36. 0
37. 0 38. X 39. 0 40. X 41. A 42. E 43. D
44. C 45. C 46. A 47. C 48. B 49. B 50. C
51. A 52. A 53. B 54. A 55. B 56. B 57. \
58. SMITH 59. JONES 60. X 61. X 62. 0 63. 0
64. X 65. D 66. A 67. B 68. C 69. D 70. D
71. G 72. B 73. H 74. A 75. I 76. E 77. F
78. K 79. C 80. J

Chapter Six Key

1. T 2. T 3. F 4. T 5. F
6. F 7. T 8. F 9. T 10. F

11. F 12. T 13. F 14. T 15. F
16. F 17. F 18. F 19. T 20. F
21. T 22. T 23. T 24. T 25. T
26. T 27. T 28. T 33. i 34. c
35. b 36. a 37. m 38. k 39. h
40. l 41. d 42. f 43. g 44. j
45. b 46. b 47. b 48. c 49. d
50. d 51. b 52. a 53. b 54. a
55. b 56. X 57. 0 58. 0 59. X
60. X 61. 0
29. <jc>
The impact of computers
<jb>
The major impacts are are threefold: social, . .
30. <np>
<bb><ub>
I. The Early Years
<be><ue>
31. <1m = 2>
"Theresultingexplosion. . . . .computererror."
<1m = 1>
32. <hd = "Computer Impacts">
<ft = "English 101">
62. Start and end text input, character insert and delete, cursor movement, other input characteristics; use of: function keys, mouse, control keys and other keys
63. Commands: format, directory, copy (and other operating system commands). Create, destroy, load, and save documents.
64. Block definition, delete, move, copy commands. Text search and replace command. Ruler use and access and reveal codes commands. Create, remove,and switch window commands. Spell-check and thesaurus commands.
65. Type size, font, bold face, underline, etc. Left, right, center, and edge justification commands. Unconditional and conditional page eject commands. Left, right, top and bottom margin commands. Header, footer, and page number commands. Keep, float, and footnote commands. Commands for marking and generating table of contents and indexes. Access help index and help.

Chapter Seven Key

1. T 2. T 3. F 4. T 5. T 6. F 7. T
8. F 9. T 10. F 11. F 12. F 13. T 14. T
15. T 16. T 17. T 18. B 19. C 20. E 21. A
22. D 23. B 24. C 25. C 26. B 27. D 28. B
29. B 30. D 31. D 32. D 33. C 34. A,B

35. C,I 36. D 37. H 38. D 39. K 40. L 41. J
42. G 43. F 44. M 45. W 46. B,H,N,T 47. E
48. D7 49. K 50. D 51. B 52. D 53. E
54. D 55. J 56. A,G 57. C 58. C 59. F
60. E,B,D,A,F,C 61. A,e 62. C,d 63. F,abhijk
64. D,hjk 65. E,ag 66. B,bc 67. H,e 68. G,f

Chapter Eight Key

1. F 2. F 3. T 4. T 5. T 6. T 7. F 8. F
9. F 10. F 11. T 12. F 13. T 14. T 15. T
16. T 17. F 18. T 19. F 20. F 21. T 22. T
23. T 24. T 25. T 26. T 27. T 28. T 29. F
30. F 31. F 32. E 33. D 34. A 35. C 36. B
37. E 38. D 39. C 40. A 41. B 42. A 43. D
44. A 45. B 46. E 47. D,C,E,A,B

Chapter Nine Key

1. F 2. T 3. T 4. T 5. T 6. F 7. T 8. T
9. T 10. F 11. F 12. T 13. F 14. F 15. F
16. T 17. T 18. T 19. F 20. T 21. T 22. T
23. B 24. A 25. B 26. A 27. B 28. A 29. B
40. D 41. A 42. C 43. D 44. B 45. C 46. A
47. D 48. B 49. C 50. C,D,A,F,B,E
30. A process that allows the user to remove the effect of a process performed in error.
31. A paint system input mode by which an enclosed area of a graphic image can be arbitrarily colored.
32. A special place in memory where a portion of text or picture can be stored until the user chooses to place it elsewhere.
33. A chart graphic system in which the data points are plotted, but are not connected by lines.
34. A vertical line on a chart graphic that defines its height, used with the X-axis to fix points on a graph.
35. A key accompanying a graphic, that identifies the visual differences that distinguishes different data sets presented.
36. It is a characteristic of all graphic chart outputs, which describes the figure as required by the user.
37. A paint system input mode that lets the user draw arbitrary lines of varying width, color, and texture.
38. A paint graphics process in which the colors of cells are switched among themselves.
39. A horizontal line on a chart graphic that defines its width, used with the Y-axis to fix points on a graph.

Chapter Ten Key

1. F **2.** T **3.** F **4.** F **5.** F **6.** T **7.** T **8.** T
9. F **10.** F **11.** T **12.** F **13.** T **14.** F **15.** F
16. T **17.** F **18.** F **19.** T **20.** F **21.** T **22.** F
23. F **24.** T **25.** T **26.** T **27.** T **28.** T **29.** F
30. D **31.** H **32.** B **33.** F **34.** A **35.** G
36. CDAEB **37.** D **38.** A **39.** B **40.** E **41.** B
42. D **43.** A **44.** B **45.** C **46.** D **47.** C **48.** E
49. C **50.** C **51.** G **52.** A **53.** B **54.** F **55.** E

Chapter Eleven Key

1. T **2.** T **3.** T **4.** F **5.** T **6.** F **7.** T **8.** F
9. F **10.** T **11.** T **12.** F **13.** F **14.** T **15.** T
16. F **17.** T **18.** T **19.** T **20.** F **21.** T **22.** F
23. T **24.** F **25.** T **26.** T **27.** T **28.** T **29.** T
30. C **31.** C **32.** B **33.** A **34.** C **35.** A **36.** A
37. B **38.** C **39.** B **40.** B **41.** A **42.** B **43.** F

44. B **45.** D **46.** E **47.** A **48.** B **49.** A **50.** C
51. A **52.** D **53.** E **54.** C **55.** B

Chapter Twelve Key

1. a **2.** c **3.** a **4.** d **5.** a **6.** b **7.** b **8.** c **9.** x
10. d **11.** x **12.** b **13.** a **14.** g **15.** c **16.** e or f
17. f or e **18.** a **19.** c **20.** b **21.** b **22.** C **23.** a
24. b **25.** c **26.** c **27.** a **28.** b **29.** T **30.** F
31. T **32.** F **33.** T **34.** T **35.** T **36.** T **37.** F
38. T **39.** F **40.** T **41.** T **42.** F **43.** F **44.** F
45. T **46.** T **47.** F **48.** T **49.** F **50.** F **51.** T
52. F **53.** T **54.** F **55.** F **56.** T **57.** T **58.** T
59. T **60.** F **61.** F **62.** F **63.** T **64.** T **65.** T
66. c **67.** c **68.** a **69.** a **70.** b **71.** c **72.** f
73. a **74.** g **75.** d **76.** h **77.** b **78.** e **79.** f
80. c **81.** a **82.** b **83.** a **84.** d **85.** d **86.** b
87. B **88.** A **89.** B **90.** A **91.** A **92.** B **93.** a
94. b **95.** c

Glossary

abacus A primitive computer used for storing numbers according to the location of counters that slide back and forth in groves or on rods.

abbreviation A means for combining a set of commonly used commands under one name. When that name is then given as a command, the entire set that it represents is performed.

absolute path name In a file hierarchy or file tree, the unambiguous name of a specific file, determined by tracing the path from the root of the tree to the file. Every file in a file tree must have a unique absolute path name.

absolute reference When a formula is copied the coordinates are not changed, i.e., copying (A1 + B1) from cell C1 to C10 places (A1 + B1) in C10.

address The part of a computer instruction code that specifies a particular storage location for data in memory; in other instances, the location of a particular input, storage, processing, control, or output device of a computer.

algorithm Technically, a sequence of steps for the completion of a task that is guaranteed to terminate with either success or an explicit message of failure. Commonly, any sequence of steps for the completion of a task.

allocation table *See* disk allocation table

alphabet/numeric input mode A paint system input mode in which the computer keyboard is used to enter labels and other arbitrary text into the graphic being designed.

AND operator A logical operator used to combine two true-false values. Given two true-false values, A and B, A AND B asks the question: Is it true that both A and B are true? In data bases, an AND operator can

be used to specify a search that will retrieve a record only when two or more requirements are simultaneously met.

analog computer a computer that directly uses voltage and current levels to represent information. Voltage and current can take on many different values, compared to digital computers, which use only two different values, on and off. Most modern computers are digital computers, which can easily model the characteristics of analog computers.

analyst A person responsible for the processes of goal analysis and program design; this person may also supervise program development, and program evaluation and maintenance.

analytic engine A mechanical computer proposed by Charles Babbage but never completed by him. It was to be the first true computer capable of all five ISPCO functions.

answer mode In computer communications across telephone lines, a condition in which a computer waits for the other to originate a connection. For two computers to send messages at the same time, two different pitches of sound are used, one for each computer. One computer must be in answer mode, identifying it as taking one of the two pitches. The other must be in originate mode, identifying it as taking the other pitch.

application software languages The command, menu, and graphics menu languages used to operate application software, such as word processors, spreadsheets, graphics programs and the like. Control is mainly provided by the order in which users request ISPCO functions.

application software software for common applications such as word processing, spreadsheet processing, data base management, graphics, and communications; also called productivity software.

applications generators Interpreter-translators that convert VHLL programs into the ISPCO activities defining word processing, spread sheet or data base management applications.

arithmetic/logical unit (ALU) the portion of a central processing unit or microprocessor in which arithmetic and logical processes are performed. The ALU does not include the instruction counter and instruction-decoding circ uitry.

array A set of related data, all of the same type, stored together and referenced as a single unit. Arrays can have a number of *dimensions*. For example, an array of one dimension is a list, an array of two dimensions is a table, an array of three dimensions is a stack of tables (a cube), and so forth.

artificial intelligence A field of study whose goal is to create computer systems that exhibit intelligent behavior (possess problem-solving skills, understand natural language, and so on). It draws eclectically upon the fields of computer science, psychology, education, linguistics, brain physiology, and other disciplines concerned with human reasoning and intelligence.

ASCII code An individual element in the ASCII table; a standardized code for representing alphabetic, numeric, and other characters as bit patterns.

ASCII table A table that lists the 128 possible patterns of seven bits (0000000, 0000001, . . . , 1111110, 1111111) and the corresponding characters of an extended alphabet that includes the full human alphabet and some additional computer characters.

assembler A computer program that reads an assembly language program and creates a corresponding machine language program that can be processed by the computer hardware.

assembly language A low-level programming language that uses mnemonic abbreviations to represent the 0's and 1's used in machine language. Before a computer program written in assembly language can be used, it must be translated into machine language by a special computer program called an *assembler*.

assembly language programs A program written in assembly language.

asynchronous communication A standard for communications between two computing devices in which data can be sent at any time, but the characters must be coded so that the receiving computer is signaled when they are being sent and when the communication is completed.

autoexec file A special file that contains a set of commands that are to be executed whenever a computer system is booted (restarted). An autoexec file is usually used to customize a computer setup to a particular user's standard routine. The execution of an autoexec file is often invisible to the user, that is, there is no visible indication that anything is happening.

automatic hyphenation A word processing function that uses a computerized dictionary to determine where to automatically hyphenate words at the right margin of the text being processed.

backup A copy of a disk of file that is made as a safeguard against loss or damage of the original.

bar graph A type of graph in which data is represented by a series of bars or rectangles of varying height. The height of each bar corresponds directly to the value of the data.

bar root The Y value at which the bars of a bar graph begin; usually 0, but occasionally some other positive or negative value.

base 2 number A number represented by powers of 2, e.g., in base 2, $101 = 1 \times 2^2 + 0 \times 2^1 + 1 \times 2^0 = 4 + 0 + 1 = 5$ in base 10.

BASIC An easy-to-learn high-level computer programming language (Beginner's All-purpose Symbolic Instruction Code). BASIC has tremendous popularity because it has been included with the hardware of many prominent computer companies.

BASIC language translator software that translates programs written in the BASIC language into machine language.

batch file A file containing a list of separate commands that can all be executed in sequence by referring to the name of the file.

batch operating system An operating system able to manage the processing of a sequence of computer users' jobs, *one at a time*, without human intervention.

baud In data communication, a measure of the speed at which communication occurs. Typical rate for personal computers are 300, 1200, 2400 or 9600 baud (bits per second) across ordinary telephone lines and significantly higher across more controlled communication lines.

benchmark a standardized set of data processing tasks designed to test the relative performance of different hardware or software systems.

binary code a method of representing letters, numbers and other characters using only the binary digits 0 and 1.

binary digit a single on/off switch in computer storage; the values 0 or 1.

binary number system The representation of numbers using only zeros and ones. The binary number system is discussed in chapter 3.

binary operation an arithmetic process in which two operands are taken in and one result is given back.

bit An abbreviation for *bi*nary dig*it*.

blackbox a device that produces a specific output from known input but whose detailed internal operation is either unknown or unspecified.

block A portion of the text selected for processing as a unit, i.e., copied, deleted, etc.

block command An editing command which is applid to a block of text, e.g., delete, move, or copy blocks

block selection In spreadsheets specifying a subtable for deleting, moving, or copying by inputing cell coordinates or by moving the cursor.

booting The process of starting up a computer system, usually including the loading of an operating system into memory.

break fields The fields of a record used to designate what set of records will be treated as a unit during statistical computations. A change in the contents of the break fields will cause current statistical computations to be printed and restarted for the next set of records.

bug An error in a computer program.

bulletin board service An on-line computing service that can be accessed by a personal computer with communications software. Bulletin board services generally provide means for posting notices, responding to notices, and sending and receiving mail.

bundled Included in the price of the computer, as when computers are sold with software or services or both.

bus a communications line shared by computer hardware; e.g., a group of circuits over which ISPCO devices can exchange data and control signals; also an industrial standard architecture for personal computer bus design, e.g. the Micro Channel Architecture (MCA) used in IBM PS/2 or the Nubus used in the MCintosh II.

byte A set of eight consecutive bits.

calculator programs An operating system utility that allows the user to carry out arithmetic operations.

calendar programs An operating system utility that maintains scheduling for single and repetitive events.

capture During communications, the process of recording to a file and/or printer the exact sequence of messages that flows back and forth between the local and the remote computers.

card reader a computer input device that reads the patterns of holes on punched cards and transfers the information into a computer.

cell In spreadsheets, a single entry in a table; it may contain either a number, a label, or a formula as its value. Each cell is located at the intersection of a row and column.

central processing unit (CPU) The computer's "brain"; it consists of an instruction counter, an instruction decoder, and the arithmetic/logical unit for performing the various processes of arithmetic and logic. Often a single microprocessor chip.

character editor A file editor that treats an entire file as one long string of characters.

character set A group of characters that is distinct and designed for a specific purpose, such as a group of characters that forms a message to be transmitted through a communications systems.

chart system One of the two major types of computer graphics systems, designed to create pie charts, bar charts, and other clearly defined types of graphics.

circuit board A thin card, usually made of resinous or laminated material, containing an electrical circuit of etched copper; used in digital computers to perform various functions. Also called a circuit card. A communications card is a special type of circuit board.

clip art In a paint graphics system, a catalogue of stored images that can be selectively chosen and merged with other graphic images as the user wishes.

clipboard A special place in memory or on disk where a portion of a text, table, or picture may be stored using a cut operation until the user places it elsewhere using a paste operation. Clipboards are also referred to as temporary storage buffers.

clustered bars In a chart graphics system, a method of combining multiple bar charts into one chart by grouping the related bars of the various bar graphs.

cogged wheel A gear used in early calculators to automatically carry place value from units to tens, from tens to hundreds, and so on.

cold turkey method A procedure for replacing one information system with another without any phase-out time for the system being replaced.

command An instruction that directs a computer to perform a specific task.

command delimiter a symbol that separates a command from the parameters or data on which the command operates.

command language A language for controlling the ISPCO tasks performed by applications software such as word processing or spreadsheet systems. These languages are usually simpler and easier to use than computer programming languages. Often they are nothing more than a simple set of responses to alternatives presented on the screen.

command mode In word processing, a mode of operation where commands are to be immediately executed (e.g., input of files, editing and printing options).

command summary a listing or brief glossary of the commands used with a given software system (e.g., word processor). Found in hard copy documentation and sometimes in on-line help systems.

communication line or bus A hardware device shared by the storage, input/output and control/processing hardware. It is used to transfer information among the ISPCO hardware.

communication port The logical device name used by software to identify a communications card which is built-in or attached via an expansion slot to the motherboard. The port identifies the plug on the back of the machine to which the card is attached.

communications card A special set of circuits that translates a computer's internal signals to an external standard (e.g., RS–232C), thus allowing a computer to communicate with peripheral devices or with other computer systems.

communications software Applications programs that enable two or more computers to interact with one another.

compatibility The ability of one device to accept and handle data that have been prepared, processed, or handled by another device, without any data conversion or code modification. Compatibility is of concern for both hardware and software.

compiler A computer program that translates a source program (written in a programming language, like BASIC) into an object program (in machine language). Computers translate the entire program before any part of the program is executed.

component compatibility the ability of various hardware or software system components to exchange data properly, without conversion or code modification. Based on a shared set of rules for communication.

computer A tool that can input, store, process, and output information and control the sequence of these actions. A modern electronic computer is adaptable to a wide variety of uses because the instructions that control the computer's actions are stored in memory and can be altered to meet changing needs.

computer-aided design and computer-aided manufacturing (CAD/CAM) An applications software system using graphics to partially automate design and manufacturing in industry.

computer communications network The linking of two or more computers so that files or messages can be shared among them; a computer network.

computer facility the combination of hardware, software, documents, and people that can be used to apply computer software to real problems.

computer literacy a level of knowledge and skill that enables a person to function in a world increasingly dependent on computer-based information systems.

computer network A linking of two or more computers so that information can be shared among them.

computer program A procedure for solving a problem with a computer; a list of instructions that directs the computer to perform certain tasks to produce the desired results.

computer programming The process of designing and writing computer programs.

computer programming systems software systems that help programmers create new programs by aiding with program entry, translation and execution.

computer terminal *see* terminal.

concatenation The linking together of the elements of a system (e.g., linking subprograms to form a structured program).

conditional page break In word processing, a command that causes a word processor to stop printing on the current page and begin a new page if fewer than a certain number of lines remain on the current page.

conferencing An extension of electronic mail services in which participants interact usually with one person establishing the purpose and rules of the interaction.

connected line A type of line graph generated by a chart graphics system in which the points of the graph are connected by a series of straight lines.

console The special computer terminal connected to a multiuser system through which total control over the system hardware and software can be exercised. The operator seated at the console controls all aspects of the system.

constrain process A paint graphics process that restricts the manner in which other parts of the paint system (usually the input modes) operate.

control character A letter from the computer's expanded alphabet, typed by holding down the designated control key and pressing an ordinary key. The computer's alphabet includes a control-A, a control-B, and so forth.

control key A specially designated keyboard key that

acts like a shift key in that it changes the meaning of the ordinary alphabetic keys. The *A* key becomes a control-A, the *B* key becomes a control-B, and so forth.

control structures Syntactic structures in a programming language that control the order in which statements are executed. Types of control structures include sequencing, selection (alternation), iteration (repetition or looping), and procedure calls.

conversational interaction the free interaction between the computer and a user on a multi-user system; the user gives commands and the computer obeys them, allowing the user to behave as though in complete control of the computer, even though the computer is serving a number of users, concurrently. *See* time-sharing.

coordinates The position of a cell in the spreadsheet as indicated by row and column identifiers, e.g., A1 is the cell in column A and row 1.

copy A block command that allows the duplication of a portion of text or graphics. For example, in a word processing system, copy allows the user to duplicate a portion of the document.

core *see* magnetic core storage.

crash or system crash an unintentional halt in the execution of the operating system so that the system must be restarted. Usually accompanied by a loss of data; also any severe hardware or software failure.

CRT an abbreviation for cathode ray tube, the video screen used with most personal computers.

cursor A small blinking box or other character on a computer screen that indicates where the next character typed will appear.

cursor control keys Special keyboard keys that move the cursor on the screen, usually including arrow keys to go up, down, left, and right as well as special ones for moving to the "top," or "bottom," of a page or document and to other locations.

cut process A process that allows the user to blank out selected portions of a text, table, or picture and save the erased image to clipboard memory for later use.

daisy wheel printer an impact printer that prints full-formed characters much as an ordinary typewriter does, using a circular plastic or metal wheel as the source of the character impressions.

dangling heading (or dangling line) A heading or the first or last line of a paragraph, when printed on a different page from the rest of the paragraph. Conditional page break commands can prevent dangling headings and lines.

data Information provided to the computer for processing or returned to the user after processing.

data abstraction (or encapsulation) The practice of encapsulating data structures and routines to manipulate the data in single independent packages that hide implementation details. These "objects" are then used in all the programs of a software product.

data base A logically connected set of data records organized into one or more files used by the data base management system.

data base management system (DBMS) A set of programs designed to store an interrelated collection of data and allow it to be accessed for a variety of purposes and by a variety of users within an organization.

data base manager *see* data base management system.

data dictionary A list of the data elements used in a program, including their names, uses, and any assumptions made about their entry and exit from the system.

data encryption the process of transforming data into a code that cannot be understood by anyone without the code. Often a means of securing data from unauthorized access.

data entry screen A screen display of the data record form provided by many systems to aid the user with data entry and edit.

data flow diagram A device for summarizing sources, stores, transformations, and transfer of information among data elements of a present or proposed program.

data hierarchy A method of organizing a data base that establishes a top-down relationship among the data records. Searches begin at the top and proceed downward.

data processing The manipulation of large amounts of data to form useful knowledge for business, government, and other organizations.

data structure The types of data elements and the relationships among the data elements in a program or design.

datestamp A feature of some data base management systems in which the date and time of the last alteration of a record are automatically kept in the record.

DBMS *see* data base management system.

debug To find and remove mistakes in a computer program. Said to have been coined when Grace Hopper found a moth which had shorted out the circuits of an early mainframe computer.

default A value or operation that is automatically used by a program if none is specified by the user.

design documentation a written description of the design for a computer program or system which is used as the basis for development.

design specifications document A description of a computer program that is intended to solve the problem described in a program requirements document; the output of the program design stage.

desktop publishing The ability to create large documents of integrated text and graphics with a quality that rivals ordinary published works, but done on a personal computer with appropriate software and high-resolution (laser) printers.

device drivers The parts of the resource manager program that control the input and output processes of particular pieces of hardware attached to the computer system, e.g., a specific printer or mouse.

difference engine A mechanical computer envisioned by Charles Babbage; it would perform mathematical computations using the method of differences.

digital computer A computer that uses only two separate values of voltage and current levels to represent information (e.g., ''on'' might be represented by the value 5 volts and ''off'' by 0 volts). On analog computers, in contrast, virtually every continuous value between on and off may be used (e.g., 5 volts, 4.264 volts, 3.5 volts, 3.43 volts). Most modern computers are digital computers because they can easily model the characteristics of analog computers.

direct access *see* random access.

directory In an operating system, a list of file names (displayed through text or graphic images) to show the data or program files stored on a disk or tape.

disk A random access circular magnetic storage medium that is divided into a series of concentric rings called tracks. The tracks are further divided into parts called sectors. Information is read from and written to the disk by rotating the disk so that various portions travel under a magnetic read/write head. The most common varieties of disks are magnetic 5.25" floppy disks, 3.5" disks, and hard disks. Recent developments include optical disks of much larger capacity.

disk allocation table A portion of a disk used to associate a file name with the particular set of sectors and tracks where the file contents are stored.

disk drive A device that reads data from magnetic disks and writes data on them.

diskette a removable magnetic storage media disk for a personal computer. ''Floppy'' or flexible disks include 5.25 and 3.5 inch versions.

distributed processing A network mechanism in which the tasks making up a particular activity are divided among a set of separate computers.

documentation The collection of information that describes the exact procedures for working with computer software and/or hardware, including manuals, reference guides, and tutorial instruction.

dot matrix printer A printer in which the images are created by a series of small pins impacting an inked ribbon. Different images are created by different patterns of pin strikes, that is, by having some pins impact the ribbon and others hold back as each character is printed.

editor A computer program included in most operating system software that is able to create, input, and modify the contents of files.

electronic computer A computer in which data is handled electronically, that is, by electrical currents, thus permitting rapid performance of input, storage, processing, control, and output, especially compared to earlier mechanical computers.

electromechanical computer A type of early computer in which data was represented by cogged wheels and processing was performed by altering the positions of the wheels using small, electrically driven motors.

electronic mailbox A file used by electronic mail software to hold messages for a user.

electronic mail Communications or operating system software that enables users of multi-user systems to send messages to other users on the system.

embedded commands In spreadsheets, embedded commands are formulas that are entered into cells in the spreadsheet, e.g., a formula like + B1 * C1 (multiply the contents of cell B1 times that of C1) could be entered in, say, cell D1.

embedded commands In word processing systems, commands that are entered into a document while in the text entry mode and used to format a document (e.g., margin justification, centering, line spacing, and page numbering). These commands are always executed when the printing process begins. The results of performing the embedded commands may or may not be shown on the screen, depending upon the design of the word processor.

embedding of computer systems Embedding of computer systems occurs when one computer system becomes a part of a more complex system. For example, a word processing system might be placed on a silicon chip and become part of computer hardware.

empty directory file In a file hierarchy or tree, a subdirectory intended to point to other files but pointing to no other files at the current time.

emulation The imitation of one computer system by another. The system performing the imitation must be capable of accepting the same data and programs and achieving the same results as the original system.

encircler selecter A paint system input mode similar to the encloser; it allows the user to draw around an arbitrarily shaped part of the screen that can then be operated on by system processes, e.g., copied or moved.

encloser selector A paint system input mode that lets the user create a rectangle on the video screen. Paint system processes can then be used to operate on graphic images within this rectangle, e.g., to delete or copy the images.

end-means (blackbox) Analysis A system design technique in which the system is treated as a blackbox. First, output is inferred from the system requirements. Second, input is inferred from output. Finally, processing is inferred from both.

enter key the key used to terminate a typed set of characters and enter them on the communication line to the computer; sometimes labeled as a return key.

erase or delete process A process for removing a portion of text or graphics from the graphic image being created. The removed portion is lost permanently.

erase picture process A paint graphics process that erases the whole picture.

eraser A paint system input mode that lets the user remove (erase) portions of a graphic image from the screen.

escape key a special key on the keyboard that generates an nonprinting ASCII code that is often used to get out of an on-going process (e.g., to stop printing a document in a word processor).

exec file A batch file.

executive workstation a personal computer designed to support the activities of the typical executive with capabilities such as forecasting using spreadsheet software, accessing data through telecommunication networks, and writing with word processors.

expansion slots Places on the motherboard in which other circuit boards may be inserted to expand the capabilities of the computer, e.g., to increase the size of memory, to add a printer, and so on.

external storage Magnetic disk or tape storage attached through controller devices to the motherboard.

fiber optics A technology in which glass fibers carry information using laser light at an extremely high rate of speed.

field attributes The characteristics that define the use of a field in a data base management system, including such things as whether the field is part of a primary or secondary key, whether the field data is re-

quired, the position of the field on input records, and so forth.

file A named portion of a disk set aside to hold data, text, commands, or programs.

file editor A computer program used to write, enter, and edit files. It allows a user to place arbitrary characters in an arbitrary order.

file hierarchy or tree An organizational scheme for files in an operating system, common to many micro, mini, and mainframe computers. In this structure, some files contain data and other files are directories that contain only the names of other files. These directories further point to more files and directories, and so on, resulting in a tree-like file organization.

file manager The part of the operating system that controls system storage.

file name A sequence of characters that identifies a file. In MS-DOS, 1-8 characters for the name and 0-3 for the extension e.g. COMMAND. COM.

file permissions A capability of many operating systems that provides selective access to the files on the system. In general, the creator of a file has the ability to do anything to a file (list it, destroy it, change its contents, and so forth) and can give other users the ability to perform some or all of these same processes on the file.

file transfer mode In communications software, a mode of operation in which the local and remote computer systems work together to transfer data from a file on one machine to a file on the other without displaying the data directly to the user.

file tree *see* file hierarchy.

file type Although all files are sequences of data, some applications systems expect their data to be organized in some special pattern. Many operating systems and applications programs define a variety of file types that are essentially specifications for some special organization. Common file types in operating systems include sequential and random files.

filler A paint system input mode by which an enclosed area of a graphic image can be arbitrarily colored.

first generation computers The first computers to handle data electronically through the use of vacuum tubes. If a vacuum tube was conducting electricity, it represented a 1 and if it was not conducting, a 0.

flip process A paint system process for reversing a portion of an image from left to right or top to bottom. The portion reversed must have been selected by the encloser or encircler.

float A special word processing command that ensures that a block of text (e.g., a table) will be kept together on one page but allows text that occurs after the block to be moved before the block to fill out the bottom of a page.

floppy disk A low-cost, random access plastic disk that stores data magnetically. Most commonly used with personal computers.

font A particular style of alphabet that a computer might use during printing. People generally use two different styles: printing and cursive. Computers have many more alternatives, including Gothic, Sans-Serif, and many others.

footnoting In word processing, a special float command that places a footnote reference in the text where the footnote occurs and then floats the footnote to the bottom of the page or end of chapter for printing.

footer An identifying label that appears at the bottom of each page of a document.

format 1. to initialize a disk, i.e., using a command in the operating system to prepare a disk to store information. 2. the specification of how text is to be arranged on a page for output, e.g. by a word processor. 3. In programming the specification of how characters are to be input to or output from a set of variables.

format (initialize) To prepare a storage disk to receive information i.e., bits are written to divide the disk into tracks and sectors and to set up an allocation table.

fourth generation computers Modern electronic computers using large scale integrated (LSI) circuits or very large scale integrated (VLSI) circuits as the technological base for their computations.

frame (ISPCO frame) An illustration that summarizes the generic or general input, storage, processing, control, and output capabilities of hardware or software systems; frames provide places for the reader to enter information on his or her specific system.

full-duplex communication Communication in which data is transmitted in both directions at the same time.

function a basic computer operation or capability (e.g., input, storage, processing, control, output).

function a basic computer operation or capability (e.g., input, storage, processing, control, output).

function keys Special keys on a computer keyboard that generate codes in the computer's extended alphabet (not in the human alphabet). There are usually 10–12 function keys labeled F1, F2, F3, . . . , F12. Any software system can then use these special keys to represent commands, e.g., F6 might mean "delete line of text" in a word processing system.

generalizability The degree to which a single process can solve a large number of similar problems, thus obviating the need for many processes.

general-purpose computer a computer whose programs can be readily changed, enabling it to serve many widely different purposes.

general-purpose programming language a programming language not dedicated to a particular application or class of problems but useful for virtually any programming tasks.

gigabit approximately one billion bits.

gigabyte approximately one billion bytes.

glossary In word processing, a method for increasing data entry speed by allowing the user to type in an abbreviation for a long word or phrase and having the computer automatically replace the abbreviation with the longer word or phrase.

goal analysis A procedure of interview, data collection, and review for determining the users, goals, resources, and constraints involved in the creation and use of a program or system. Its purpose is to generate a well-defined statement of system requirements.

graphic shell A user interface with an operating system or applications program that employs a nonverbal language of icons and pull-down menus for giving commands to the computer rather than the more traditional method of typing commands at a keyboard. Graphic shells generally require a mouse or other pointing device.

graphic software *see* graphic application systems.

graphics software Programs that enable users to create visual displays on screen, paper, film, or other media. The visual displays are generally of two types: business graphs like bar charts or pie charts and arbitrary graphic images like pictures of space shuttles or tennis shoes.

grid process A paint graphics process in which a grid helps the user align various portions of a graphic and maintain correct size relationships.

half-duplex communication Communication in which data can be transmitted in only one direction at a time.

handshaking A means of coordinating the timing of messages between different computers by using reserved characters passed back and forth to indicate whether or not a message may be sent.

hard disk A rigid disk of metal coated with a magnetizable substance which is permanently mounted in a disk drive. Hard disks are faster and hold more data than floppy disks.

hardware The physical devices making up a computer system.

hardware compatibility The ability of hardware devices to function correctly together i.e., the ability of one device to accept and handle information processed by another device without any conversion or recoding.

hardware syndrome Systems analysis problem in which the analyst is so intent on the hardware component that the actual needs of the user are poorly examined.

header An identifying label that appears at the top of each page of a document (e.g. , REPORT 1).

help system (on-line documentation) A facility included in operating systems and many application programs; it displays documentation from the disk about how the system or program should be used.

hidden agenda problem A problem that occurs during systems analysis when irrational factors, such as prestige, underlie the user's overtly stated system requirements.

hidden bars In a chart graphics system, a method of combining multiple bar charts into one chart by placing the related bars before or behind each other, leaving the taller bars partially hidden by the shorter bars.

hierarchical structure A set of elements arranged in a top-down hierarchical manner according to a common property, e.g., an organization chart for a business.

high-level language A computer programming language that uses English-like commands, in contrast to the more cryptic assembly language or machine language.

IBM PC The initial entry of IBM into the personal computer field. Replaced by the IBM personal system PS/2 family of more powerful computers.

icon An image or picture used in graphic shells to represent some physical object in the computer system. For example, a small picture of a disk on the computer screen may be used to represent the physical disk in a disk drive.

icon-driven menu system a graphics menu that uses icons (small stylistic drawings) and other graphic images instead of key words for the entry of commands. *See also* graphic shell.

ID An identification code used to identify a user to a computer.

immediate commands In word processing and other software, commands which are executed immediately upon being input by the user; in contrast to embedded commands which are input for execution at a later time.

impact printer A printer that creates images by causing a letter or pin to impact an inked ribbons. Impact printers are generally of two types: dot matrix printers and daisy-wheel printers.

information society A society characterized by (1) a shift from jobs in production to jobs in information processing, (2) a growing need for a better educated work force with computer skills, and (3) greater productivity (more goods for less cost) due to better use of information in the production process.

information system An organized collection of people, data, software, and hardware that interact to achieve specific information processing goals. Often referred to as simply a "system."

ink jet printer a printer that creates images by spraying ink from small ink jets to form characters made up of patterns of dots on the paper.

initialization (formatting) Preparing a disk for storing information. Bits are written on the disk to divide it into tracks and sectors and to provide space for a table that links file names to the tracks and sectors allocated to individual files.

input Accepting information from the environment, e.g., when a human sees or when a computer detects the keys pressed at its keyboard.

insert/replace modes In the insert mode new characters are added to the characters already present. In the replace mode new characters replace those present.

inside testing Verifying the validity of the individual components of a system as part of the systems evaluation stage.

instruction counter A register in the microcomputer or central processing unit that gives a memory location for the next instruction to be used.

instruction decoder A register in the CPU that interprets bit patterns as instructions to perform built-in processes on data.

instruction register A set of circuits inside a computer where instructions to the computer are placed for decoding and execution. Instructions include operation codes and addresses for data to be processed.

integrated circuit an electronic circuit etched on a small silicon chip. *See also* chip.

integrated circuit chip A complete circuit containing a large number of transistors imprinted on a small piece of silicon. Used for virtually all aspects of computer hardware fabrication.

integrated circuit memory The fastest type of storage built from integrated circuit chips.

integrated circuit technology The fabrication of entire circuits with many transistors using the same material from which transistors are made. With this technology, large circuit boards can be replaced by tiny pieces of semiconductor material.

interactive mode the mode of operation in which the user gives a commands and waits to see the results of the command before giving another; the most common mode for operating systems and applications programs.

interactive transfer A transfer of messages between computers in which the response of each computer depends on the message. *See also* noninteractive transfer.

intercomputer communication Communication between separate computers via an external communication bus.

internal storage Storage composed of integrated circuit chips directly attached to the motherboard.

interpreter A program that translates statements from a source programming language (e.g., BASIC) into a machine language equivalent. Interpreters translate and execute each line of a computer program before proceeding to the next one.

interrupt To stop a computer process in such a way that it can be resumed. Interrupts allow the computer to put one process on hold and perform another one.

intracomputer communication Internal communication among the ISPCO hardware devices that comprise a single computer via the internal communication bus on the motherboard.

invert process A paint graphics process in which the colors of cells are switched among themselves, e.g., all black cells replaced by white cells, and all white cells replaced by black cells.

invisible system A problem in systems goal analysis, in which people use procedures other than those they report using.

ISPCO model The organizing framework for this text; it shows the most significant aspects of any computer hardware or software in terms of five functions: input, storage, processing, control, and output.

ivory tower design A situation in which an analyst designs a system based on a personal view rather than on a systems requirement study.

k approximately 1000 (actually 1024, which is the value of 2 raised to the tenth power).

keep A special word processing command that ensures that all of the lines in a given block of text will be printed on the same page

kernel The part of the operating system that includes the supervisor, the file manager, and the resource manager. The kernel is usually RAM resident, i.e., it stays in RAM as long as the computer is on.

kilobyte Approximately one thousand bytes of information. (1024 bytes)

knowledgeable user rule A principle of maximum system use that states that the effectiveness of a system depends on how well people have been trained to use it.

labels report format A particular style of data base report in which data is placed on the page in any desired pattern. The name comes from the common use of this format to print address labels.

large scale integrated (LSI) circuits Single chips containing 100–1,000 gates (basic functional units like transistors) per chip.

laser printer A type of printer that uses an electrostatic process to place characters on paper. Laser printers provide speed, quality, and flexibility that are currently unmatched by other printers and are the basis for the growth of desktop publishing.

linear approximation A variation of the line graph in which a statistical analysis is performed to determine the straight line that best approximates the data points.

line editor A file editor that treats a file as a set of separate lines.

line graph A type of graph in which data points are plotted and connected by smoothed lines.

line printer A printer that prints an entire line of characters as a unit rather than printing one character at a time.

liner A paint system input mode that allows the user to create arbitrary straight lines in whatever colors are available in the system.

Local Area Network (LAN) A private communications network connecting several computers by cable within a limited area such as a building or a group of building.

local mode In communications software, a mode of operation in which input and output are associated with the user's local computer.

lock command A command that prevents the accidental destruction of a file. An unlock command cancels this file protection.

logical input/output interface The part of the resource manager that processes standard input/output requests from user programs and routes them to the appropriate hardware devices.

logical operators Processes that accept true/false values as input and give back true/false answers according to particular patterns. The most commonly used logical operators are AND, OR, and NOT.

logical subprograms Independent parts of a program that when combined perform the functions required of the program.

login Stands for *log in, log on,* or *sign on.* A startup procedure in which users use an identification code and a password to identify themselves to an operating system and establish that they have legitimate access to the system.

logout Stands for *log out, log off,* or *sign off.* A procedure for terminating current use of a multiuser system.

machine dependent some aspect of software or hardware that requires a particular make of machine.

machine language A programming language whose code is in a binary (0's and 1's) form that can be executed directly by a computer without translation. Also called an object language.

machine language programming The most primitive computer programming language, in which all instructions are made from strings of 0's and 1's. Machine language is the only language the computer processes directly. Any other programming language must be translated into machine language before it can be used.

magnetic core memory Internal computer memory using tiny rings of metal, each able to store a single bit of data; used for many years until replaced by semiconductor devices.

magnetic storage Storage that is random or sequential access, nonvolatile (data retention does not require electricity), read-writable (contents can be changed), and uses either fixed or removable media (floppy disks and tape are removable while hard disks are fixed).

magnify process A paint graphics process that allows the user to enlarge a portion of an image to the point where individual cells can be distinguished. It is used to make more precise refinements of an image.

magnitude the absolute value of a number or quantity.

mailboxes Special disk files that are assigned to individual members of a computer network and to which other members may send messages.

mailmerge Combining a file containing names and addresses with a file containing a form letter to generate a number of individualized letters or documents.

main circuit board (motherboard) An electronic circuit board containing the power source, communication line, microprocessor and internal storage chips and expansion board slots (places in which to plug other circuit boards). The main circuit board provides the basis for the combination of other hardware to form a computer.

mainframe computer A large computer with powerful peripheral devices able to store huge amounts of data and serve many users at the same time.

main memory the portion of computer storage made up of the electronic circuits that can be addressed most rapidly.

math coprocessor An integrated circuit chip used to perform arithmetic processes at higher speeds than are possible with the microprocessor chip alone.

mechanical computer A computer that operates through levers and cogged wheel gears rather than through electrical means. Also referred to as mechanical calculators.

megabit Roughly equivalent to one million binary digits.

megabyte Approximately one million bytes of information. (1,048,576 bytes)

menu bar A list of options arranged across the top of the computer screen in the general shape of a bar.

menu-driven software software that uses a menu shell, i.e., commands are chosen from a list presented by the computer.

menu shell A user interface with an operating system or applications program that lists available commands on the screen and then allows the user to select from the list. Menus often provide submenus: the selection of one menu item results in the display of and selection from another subordinate menu.

message commands Commands used to transmit messages among users in multiuser systems.

microcomputer A small personal computer in which control and processing are performed by a single silicon chip called a microprocessor. Microcomputers typically cost less than $10,000.

microprocessor A single silicon chip that performs the control and processing functions of a small personal computer.

miniaturization the continuing process of reducing the size of computer hardware components by using more and more advanced technology.

minicomputer A small computer that can service more than one user at a time through ten or fewer terminals. The cost of a minicomputer is typically less than $100,000.

MIPS million information processes per second; a measure of computing power. Currently the most powerful microcomputers are capable of about 3 or 4 mips (eg. the Intel 80 386 operating at 25 megaherty runs at 3.5 MIPS).

mock data data that is representative of real data and is created for checking whether all aspects of a new program are working correctly.

model A representation of a process, concept, or device that is less complex than the real thing, e.g., a scale model of an airplane represents only the physical dimensions of the plane. See also ISPCO model.

modem A device that connects a computer to a telephone line and through which two computers may communicate. A modem translates from the electronic signals of a computer to the auditory (acoustic) signals of a telephone line and vice versa. Modems require a standard signal usually provided by a communication card.

modes of operation In general, distinct and conceptually different manners in which one piece of software can operate. Different modes are usually characterized by different screen displays and different ISPCO commands. Example are the text entry and command modes used in word processing software. In communications software, local, remote, and file transfer modes are used for different purposes and act in different ways.

modularity The organization of a large system so that small parts with related functions are gathered together into modules; the resulting modules are internally cohesive but highly independent of one another.

modulation-demodulation The process of converting digital signals into analog signals and back again to permit computer systems to communicate via telephone lines. *Modem* is a contraction of the two terms.

mouse A hand-held pointing mechanism that controls cursor/pointer movement on a computer screen. Buttons on the mouse are used for input.

mover A paint system input mode that enables the user to adjust the portion of the full page that can be seen on the screen at one time.

MS-DOS A popular operating system for the IBM PC and similar computers, marketed by Microsoft, Inc.

multimate a popular word processing program that operates much like the Wang dedicated word processing system.

multi-tasking systems computer systems that allow the user to perform many separate tasks simultaneously.

multi-user system a system that gives many users simultaneous access to hardware and software. *See also* time sharing.

NASH An acronym (*N*eeds assessment. *A*pplication decisions, *S*oftware selection, and *H*ardware selection); used in systems design, to describe the correct procedure for selecting hardware.

nested menus menus are nested when the selection of an option in one menu must be further clarified and expanded through sub-menus.

nested menus or submenus Menus are nested when the selection of an option is one menu must be further clarified and expanded through a selection from another menu.

noise Anything causing distortion or interference during communication.

noncommercial electronic computers Computers developed between 1945 and 1951, when computers were not sold commercially. To acquire a computer during this period, an organization had to build one.

noninteractive transfer In computer communications, a transfer of data between two computers in which no further input is required during the transfer process.

nonprocedural programming languages New programming languages like PROLOG and VP EXPERT designed primarily for artificial intelligence. Control is shared between the programmer and the computer.

nonresident operating system functions Operating system functions performed by programs that are normally stored on disk and transferred into RAM only when requested by a command input by the user, e.g., for copying entire disks.

NOT operator A logical operator used to reverse truth value. If A is true then NOT A is false and visa versa.

object language machine language.

object program A machine language program resulting from the translation of a source program (written in th e source language) into a form that can be directly executed.

open-ended system A system in which specific provisions have been made to add new components (e.g., new software, hardware, and data structures) after the system is built.

operand the data on which a process or operation is to be performed.

operating system A set of programs that manages the hardware and software resources of a computer system and enables the user to interface with application programs and peripheral devices. It controls the execution of computer programs and may provide scheduling, debugging, input/output control, accounting, compilation, storage assignment, data management, and related services.

operating system loading program A short program in the ROM of a computer whose purpose is to call up the main operating system from external storage; often referred to as the "booting" or "bootstrapping" program.

operating system software Programs designed to operate computers with minimal human supervision; discussed in chapter 5.

operation The act or processing specified by a computer command, e.g. , copying a file.

operation code The part of a computer instruction that indicates what operation (e.g., addition or subtraction) is to be performed on the data.

OR operator A logical operator used to combine two true-false values. Given two true-false values, A and B, A OR B asks the question: Is it true that either A or B or both A and B are true? In data bases, an OR operator is used to specify a search that will retrieve a record if any one of the requirements joined by OR is true.

originate mode In computer communications over telephone lines, a condition in which a computer can initiate a connection. *See also* answer mode.

orphan Last line of a paragraph appears as the first line on a printed page.

output Sending information into the environment, e.g., when a human speaks or when a computer prints.

outside testing Verifying that the components of a system work effectively together.

oval A paint system input mode that allows the user to generate arbitrary oval or circular figures.

program product A software package that includes program modules, installation data, and documentation.

page breaks In word processing systems, an embedded command that terminates the printing of one page and begins subsequent text at the top of a new page.

pagination The process of numbering the pages of a document.

paintbrush A paint system input mode that lets the user draw arbitrary lines of varying width, color, and texture on the screen.

paint system One of the two major types of computer graphics systems, used to create arbitrary graphic images.

parallel communication Communication between two computing devices in which many bits of data are sent at the same time, each down its own communication line. *See also* serial communication.

parallel systems method A method of converting from one information system to another in which the old and the new systems are temporarily operated side by side to protect the client organization in case the new system fails during the shakedown period.

parameter A value given to a process that modifies how the process works. For example, the addition process produces one result when given the two parameters 2 and 2 and a different result when given the two parameters 5 and 7.

parameter passing The sending of data from one program to another.

parity A means of detecting errors during communication by adding an extra bit to each character sent and thus establishing an even number (for even parity) or odd number (for odd parity) of 1's in each character. If the receiving computer reads a number of 1's that differs from the parity, the transmission is suspect.

parity bit The extra bit added when using parity.

partial string match A data base search that retrieves all records in which part of the data in the specified field matches a designated string (e.g., a partial string match could find all records in which the field called "last name" begins with "Mc," like McDonald or McPhee).

Pascal A computer programming language with highly structured data types and control capabilities. It was originally developed for educational purposes but has increasingly been applied to scientific and engineering purposes as well.

password A confidential code word or number that enables a user to identify himself/herself to a computer and thus gain access to a computer system. Passwords are most frequently used by operating systems but may be required by any arbitrary software system.

paste process A process by which text, tables, or graphic images that have been cut at an earlier time are placed back into the document, table, or picture being created.

PDLC The Program Development Life Cycle is the set of steps taken in creating and operating a computer program: goal analyses, design, development, evaluation and maintenance.

PEARLS An acronym to remind systems managers to relate the system's *P*urpose to the users, *E*valuate the system's effectiveness, support user *A*ccess, provide *Repair* and maintenance, and find a convenient *Location* that is *Secure*.

pencil A paint system input mode that lets the user draw arbitrary lines on the screen, as if drawing with a pencil.

peripheral (external) hardware Hardware devices which are not directly a part of the motherboard/microprocessor combination. Include input and output devices and disk or tape storage. Peripherals are often interchangeable across com puters.

peripherals input, output, storage, and communications devices that are separate from, but attached to, the main circuit board of a microcomputer or to communication channels of main frames (e.g. printers, disk storage drives, video display monitors).

personal computer A computer designed primarily for use by an individual or a few individuals. The control and processing may be performed by more than one microprocessor chip. They typically cost less than $10,000.

phase-in/phase-out method A method of converting from one information system to another by allowing the old system to expire gradually while the new one is moved into full operation one stage at a time.

pie chart A type of graph in which data is represented by wedges of a circle. The total area within the circle represents the sum (100%) of the data, and the wedges represent percentages of the total.

pilot system method A method for converting from one information system to another by testing the new system on only a small part of the old system's information load.

pipes A special symbol in a command line that allows the user to direct that the output of one command be used as the input to another command.

pixel in graphics a picture element; the dots which make up a graphic image, that can be turned on, off, or set to a color.

planning horizon the time from the date of purchase of a new information system to the date of its replacement by another.

plotter A computer output device capable of presenting data in graphic form on paper by drawing lines much as a person would with pen and ink.

plug board A simple device for programming early computers. The pattern of electrical connections in the computer could be altered by a board with many plugs connected by wires. Changing the connections between the plugs changed the program.

portability The ease with which a program written for one particular hardware/software system can be transported to another hardware/software system.

precedence the prescribed order in which arithmetic and other operations are performed on the computer. Operators with precedence are executed first, e.g. * takes precedence over + smce 2 * 4 + 1 = 9 not 10.

primary key The set of fields on which the records of the data base are ordered for searching.

primitive storage types *see* data types.

primitive structures the elemental pieces of text or graphics out of which large documents and pictures are created e.g., characters and pixels, respectively.

priority commands On multiuser systems, these commands enable a user to select a balance between speed and cost, within an allowed range.

procedural programming languages Traditional programming languages like BASIC and Pascal. Control is mainly written into the program by means of control commands for sequence, selection, and iteration which are provided by the programmer.

processing The manipulation of information inside a computer or person.

processing register or accumulator A register in the CPU where processes are executed on data.

profiles A specific configuration of parameters commonly used by a particular user and saved for easy reference. For example, communications parameters can be saved into a file and called up as needed , thus sparing the user from having to re-enter the parameters one at a time each time a connection is made.

program A set of programming language instructions that direct the computer to perform ISPCO functions. needed by the user.

program break (or breakpoint) A specified point in a computer program where the program can be interrupted for checking and debugging.

program coding The process of translating design specifications into a computer program written in a specific computer programming language.

program design The translation of the goal analysis results into a design or plan for the development of a program.

program development The implementation of a computer program design, including the selection of a programming language and the actual programming.

program evaluation Testing a computer program to see if it performs as intended; its principal concerns are verification (does the program's performance match its design?) and validation (does the program solve the user's problem?).

program execution software The software that executes a translated program on data for the programmer and user.

program generators Programs that interact with a user through an interview process to complete goal analysis and program design and then independently compile the new program using a lower-level language.

program maintenance The process of modifying and adapting a computer program to fit with changes in hardware, other software and users needs.

programming *see* computer programming.

programming language An artificial language used to write instructions directing a computer to perform ISPCO functions. Traditional programming languages include commands for the explicit control of the order in which instructions are executed.

programming software Software that helps users create and manage computer programs. It usually includes a program preparation system (to help input, edit, save, and execute programs) and a translator (to translate from the user's programming language into a language the computer can process).

program module or **subprogram** A part of a computer program designed to perform a specific task for the program.

program preparation software Software that aids in the entry of newly designed computer programs into the computer; program preparation software has editing functions similar to those of a word processor.

program requirements document Documentation that specifies what a proposed program is supposed to do; a cohesive, integrated description of a problem and its context, drawn from the data generated by goal analysis.

program structure The arrangement of program elements that result from joining logical subprograms using sequence, selection, and iteration.

program structure chart A diagram of the hierarchy of programs and subprograms.

program trace A troubleshooting technique in which an output device makes a record of the execution of each step of a program to permit an analysis of the program.

program translation software The software that translates from the programming language used by the programmer into machine language that can be executed by the computer.

pseudo-code A technique used by program designers to describe a program in short, concise, English language phrases structured by keywords, such as *if-then-else*, *while-do*, and *end*.

pull-down menu A graphic form of a submenu that is displayed below a menu bar.

punched cards Small rectangular cards used as an input and storage medium; machine-readable programs and/or data is coded by a pattern of punched holes.

punched paper tape A continuous paper strip used as an input and storage medium; machine-readable programs and/or data is coded by a pattern of punched holes.

RAM (Random Access Memory) Electronic circuit memory built from integrated circuit chips. Its characteristics are random (equal speed) access, volatile retention (data retention requires electricity), read-write capable (contents can be changed), and fixed internal medium (can't be removed and replaced when filled).

random access a type of storage in which the time required to accessany data element is the same for all elements.

random files A file form where all data in a file can be accessed at about the same speed.

range search A data base search that retrieves all records in which the value of a particular field is between some upper and lower limits (e.g., all records in a personnel data base where the contents of the "age" field is between 40 and 70).

reboot the process of restarting the operating system. A reboot can be a "cold-start," in which the machine is turned off and then on again , or a "warm-start" in which reset keys are pressed. *See also* booting the system.

record A set of data organized into fields which is treated as the basic unit in the data base. Records are generated by entering data into the fields specified by the data record form or definition (e.g., Last Name = Brown and Telephone Number = 555-1234).

record definition mode The data base management mode in which the record form or definition is created. The first step in using data base software.

record entry and edit mode The data base management mode in which data records are entered or edited in the data base. This step requires a previously defined record form. Often the second step in using data bases.

record form (or record definition) A data record description giving the exact specifications for all fields to be used in the data records comprising the data base. Specifications include field names (e.g., Last Name or Telephone Number), the types of data to be entered in each field (e.g., letters or numbers) and other information.

record structure The format or arrangement of data elements in a record, e.g., the sequence of the data values entered into the various fields.

rectangle A paint system input mode that enables the user to form a rectangle on a graphic screen. The rectangle may be filled with a solid color or a colored pattern or left empty, as the user chooses.

reductionism *see* modularity.

redundancy principle The cost of operating and maintaining a system is related not so much to the number of identical systems purchased as to the number of different systems purchased, e.g. training costs can double if two different word processors are used in an organization.

relational operators Symbols used to perform comparing operations, e.g., $>$ (greater than) and $<=$ (less than or equal to).

relational search The use of relational operators ($=$, $>$, $<$, $<=$, $>=$, $<>$) in conjunction with specific data field values to search for and retrieve records in a data base.

relative path name In a file hierarchy or file tree, the name for a specific file determined by tracing the path from wherever the user is working to the file. Since the user can work in different places at different times, relative path names change. Different files can even have identical relative path names at different times.

relative reference When a formula is copied the coordinates are changed, i.e., copying $(A1+B1)$ from cell C1 to C10 places $(A10+B10)$ in cell C10.

relevance rule A principle of maximum system use that states that the value of a system depends on the overlap of its tasks and the tasks that the user must perform.

REM command BASIC programming statements that are included in a program but not executed; they document aspects of the program by allowing the programmer to explain its purpose in English.

remote mode In communications software, a mode of operation in which the input and output are associated with the remote computer to which the user has connected.

repeater circuits Circuits that amplify signals that are weakened by distance as they are transmitted between computer systems connected by their own private transmission lines (as opposed to telephone lines).

report A report generated by combining a report form or definition with a specific set of data records used in a particular order. To generate a report the user selects a previously defined report form, specifies the data records to be used (e.g., all records), and gives the order (e.g., in alphabetical order of the Last Name field).

report definition mode The data base management mode in which report forms or definitions are specified. These forms are used as the basis for report generation. Usually the third step in using data bases.

report form (or report definition) A report description giving the specifications for reports. Specifications include the names of fields to be used, where each field should appear, what types of summary statistics should be used with each field (e.g., sums or average), and other information.

report generation mode The data base management mode in which printed or screen reports are generated by combining report forms with particular sets of data records. Usually, the fourth step in using data bases.

requirements specifications language A formal computer-readable language with a restricted vocabulary and syntax, used for writing program requirements.

resident operating system functions Operating system functions performed by programs that are transferred into RAM and remain there during all subsequent computer processing until the machine is turned off, e.g., for copying single files.

resolution In computer graphic systems, resolution refers to the number of dots (pixels) in a given area on the screen. The more dots in a given area the higher the resolution or quality of the graphics.

resource manager The part of the operating system that insures hardware requests are of the proper form.

reverse video A switch in the coloring system on a two-color video screen; the lines and spaces using one color are switched to the other color, and vice versa.

ROM (Read Only Memory) Electronic circuit memory with the same characteristics as RAM, except that it is read-only (contents cannot be changed) and nonvolatile. Often used to provide built-in programs.

root directory The initial file directory in a file hierarchy; it points to all files in the tree, either directly or indirectly through other directories.

rotate process A paint graphics process that permits the user to change the position of a portion of a graphic by rotating it on an axis perpendicular to the screen.

rounded rectangle A paint system input mode identical to the rectangle mode, except the corners of the rectangles are rounded.

routine (or subroutine) a set of instructions used by a program to perform a desired task such as inputting or outputting specified data; also a subprogram, module, or procedure.

row/column selection In spreadsheets specifying a row or column for deleting, moving, or copying by inputing cell coordinates or moving the cursor.

ruler In word processing systems, a line across the top of the display screen that includes tic marks to count off characters and displays the position of tab characters, paragraph indentations, margins, and so forth.

saving A procedure for copying data from internal storage to an external storage device, e.g., saving data from RAM to magnetic disk.

scalar storage storage in a programming language in which only one piece of data can be held, in contrast to aggregate storage, which stores a set of related data together.

scatter plot In chart graphics systems, a variation of the line graph, in which the data points are plotted but are not connected by lines.

scientific notation A method used to represent fractional numbers. Numbers are represented as a number between 1 and 10, multiplied by a power of 10, e.g., $25 = 2.5 \times 10^1$ Computers use a similar notation.

screen editor A file editor that treats a file as a visual object displayed on the screen, where any changes are immediately reflected on the screen.

script (ISPCO script) A summary listing of the sequential steps required to complete a specific task using a computer.

scrolling The vertical movement of text on the display screen, up or down. Scrolling allows the user to see different parts of a document or text, since the screen is usually not large enough to hold all of the text at once.

SDLC The System Development Life Cycle (SDLC) is the process of applying the four steps (goal analysis, design, development, evaluation and maintenance) to an information system consisting of people, data, software, and hardware.

search language A formal language through which a set of records having certain characteristic field values can be retrieved from a data base.

search statements Statements setting the conditions for retrieving data records based upon the contents of fields (e.g., Age > 30 AND Salary < 3 0000).

search/replace Commands which find all instances of a string in text and optionally replaces it.

second generation computers Electronic computers that used the transistor as the technological base for electrical circuits.

secondary key Fields on which secondary index files will be created to speed the searching process for data in fields other than those in the primary key.

sequential control Performing computing tasks in the order given.

sequential files A file form where the data at the beginning of a file is much more rapidly accessed than data at the end.

serial communication A standard for communication in which only one bit of data at a time can be sent down a single communication line. *See also* parallel communication.

set brush process A paint graphics process that determines the size and shape of the brushes used in the paintbrush input mode.

set color process A paint graphics process that lets the user choose the background and paint colors used in a graphic.

set pattern process A paint graphics process that selects the pattern that will be painted by paintbrush.

shell The part of the operating system or applications software that reads user commands and then calls other programs to do what is requested.

show page process A paint graphics process that enables a user to reduce the size of a graphic so that the entire page containing the complete picture can be seen on the screen. Its purpose is to let the user see the layout of the entire page, but fine detail cannot be seen.

simplex communication Communication in which data is transmitted in only one direction.

simplification rule A principle of maximum system use that states that system effectiveness depends on the degree to which it reduces the information processing load of its users.

soft hyphen A word processing command that inserts a hyphen only when a word needs to be broken at the end of a line.

software Computer programs that contain sets of instructions for the computer to follow. When the computer follows the instructions, some desired task is performed. Software is often used to refer both to computer programs and to documentation for their use.

software compatibility The ability of devices to function correctly together at the software level, i.e., the ability of two devices to process data identically using the same software.

software environment the collection that serves as a resource upon which all programs can draw if they are mutually compatible.

solid-state machines computers that are fabricated from electronic components using transistors or silicon chips.

sort/merge programs An operating system utility that orders data in an alphabetic or numeric sequence or combines two ordered sets of data.

source language The programming language used to generate the instructions of a source program. The source program must be translated into an object program before it can be executed by a computer.

source program The initial form of a program written in a source language and entered through an input device for translation into machine language.

spreadsheet software An applications program that aids the user with the manipulation of tabular data like that found on an accountant's ledger sheet.

stacked bars In a chart graphics system bars that are placed on top of each other in a bar graph, generally used when the sum of the bars represents a constant.

start bit In a synchronous communication, a bit that precedes the code of a character to indicate to the receiving computer that a character is about to be received.

status commands On time-sharing systems, these commands enable users to determine current conditions pertaining to the computer system, such as the number of users currently logged on and number of tape drives available; then users can estimate the number of devices and amount of time available for completing their tasks.

status line In applications software systems, a line of text on the video screen that displays the current status of the system, e.g., for spreadsheets it displays the coordinates of the current cell (the position of the cursor), the contents of the cell, and the type of contents. Status lines for other software often display the amount of RAM available, the name of the file in RAM, and so on.

stop bit In asynchronous communication, a bit that follows the code for a character to indicate to the receiving computer that the character has been completed.

storage Retaining information.

string matching A data base search in which the computer is directed to find all records in which a text field holds a particular set of characters, e.g., Last Name = Jones.

string A sequence of characters drawn from the computer's ASCII code alphabet. Examples of strings include: "hello there," "h39x./12" and "123.23". Note that the string "123.23" is not the same as the number 123.23, just as a typewriter's "123" is different from a calculator's 123.

structure The arrangement or relationship of the component parts of a system.

structured programming A method of designing and constructing programs by breaking the program into logical modules and coherently combining the modules using a few well understood control structures, thus improving program clarity, reducing testing time and increasing productivity.

structured programming language a language that emphasizes separating a program into logical pieces or modules which are linked together by sequence, selection, and iteration control; structure makes programming, testing, and maintenance easier.

sub-menu part of a nested menu.

subroutine A subprogram referred to as a routine or subroutine in some languages (e.g., BASIC and FORTRAN) and as procedures in others (e.g. Pascal).

subsystem A component or element of an information system, e.g., the people, data, software, and hardware subsystems.

successive refinement A process in which a program is decomposed hierarchically; major features are described first, followed by successively more detailed layers of descriptions. Top down design.

supervisor The component of an operating system that controls controls turn taking, i.e., which program is using the hardware devices at any given time.

synchronous communication A standard for communication in which data transmission occurs at time intervals defined by a system clock.

syntax The structure of expressions in a language, or the rules governing the structure.

syntax checker A mechanism that applies syntax rules to determine whether statements in a computer program are in the proper form.

syntax-directed editor A program preparation software function that does not permit the entry of statements that are syntactically incorrect.

system operator The person who turns a multiuser computer on or off and activates the remote access lines going to the users.

systems analysis The process of breaking the design of a total system down into a set of simpler designs for the necessary component subsystems, e.g., as in top-down design.

systems analyst The person responsible for the goal analysis and design phase of the SDLC; may also supervise development and evaluation as well.

systems design The process of producing a set of valid, unambiguous design specifications for a proposed system. System design incorporates both the breaking of the system into modules (system, analysis) and the combination of the modules to form the system (system synthesis).

systems development The process of creating and operating an information system by executing the four steps in the System Development Life Cycle (SDLC), including goal analysis, design, development, evaluation and maintenance.

systems evaluation The process of determining how well an information system meets its intended purpose through procedures such as (1) deriving evaluative criteria from the systems requirements and design specifications, (2) translating these criteria into objective tests, (3) collecting and analyzing data, and (4) documentating the results.

systems requirement study an investigation to determine the requirements of a proposed system.

systems synthesis the process of creating the design of a total system by assembling the designs of the required component subsystems.

systems utility programs Programs often bundled with the operating system because of their frequent use, providing such commands as message, priority, status, calculator, calender, sort/merge, macro/abbreviations, and date/time. Utilities may also include programs to implement some storage commands such as disk copying and formatting.

tab A character analogous to the tab settings on a typewriter, used to align text in tables and other noncontinuous text formats.

tabular report format A particular style of data base report in which the data is used to create tables much like spreadsheet tables, with full use of formulas to operate on the data.

technical manual Documentation that describes the details of the implementation choices made during computer program development, for use by programmers and technicians for repairing and upgrading the program.

technology trap The tendency to build unneeded computer systems or subsystems simply because the technology is available, without regard to actual value to the user.

teleconferencing *see* computer conferencing

TELENET A widely used national network of computers with access to many data base and computer services.

teleprocessing The use of communication networks to permit users to interact with remotely located computers.

template or boilerplate file A word processing file containing a document framework into which specific text can be inserted.

terminal A single device that embodies both the input and output functions. It often includes a computer keyboard for input of data to the computer and a television screen or printer for output of data from the computer.

test data Data generated or acquired to determine whether a newly designed program works and how well it works.

test suite A set of data that tests all of the critical capabilities of a program.

text Any combination of characters such as A, B, . . . , Z, 0, 1, . . . , 9, *, ∧, and so forth.

text editor A computer routine that can modify text input prior to or during a computer run or on the output after a computer run.

text entry mode (or entry mode) An operational mode in word processing systems that permits written material to be typed into the document.

text file A file that contains an unspecified sequence of text data (arbitrary characters, e.g., ASCII codes) that cannot be interpreted as a directly executable program by the operating system. ASCII text files are widely used for computer communications, e.g., between applications programs such as two different word processors.

text justification A process in word processing for aligning text on a page. The text may be aligned so that it is flush on one or both margins of a page, or it may be centered.

thesaurus A book of classified synonyms and antonyms. A thesaurus may be stored on magnetic disk for use by word processors.

third generation computers Computers that used integrated circuits as the technological base for their electronic circuits.

timesharing The simultaneous use of one computer by more than one user, often accomplished by time-slicing, i.e., a very rapid turn-taking enforced by the operating system of the computer. In this turn-taking, each user gets a "slice" of time to run his or her program.

time-slicing *see* timesharing.

toggle A single command that permits one to switch from one mode to another and back again, e.g., in word processing, a command that switches from an insert-at-cursor to a replace-at-cursor mode of text entry.

top-down organization a method of designing an information system by first blocking out the major operations or tasks to be performed, then determining the tasks to accomplish each of the major operations, and continuing to work down to more and more detailed levels of the program.

top-down program design A hierarchial design process in which major operations are first determined, then simpler operations within each major operation, and so on, until the operations are simple enough to be written as program language commands.

transistor An electronic switch that determines whether the current is flowing or not, and can thus represent the required one (on) or zero (off) state in a computer; used in second generation computers.

turbo-PASCAL a version of the high-level programming language PASCAL published by Borland International, designed for greater ease of use by less sophisticated programmers.

turnkey system An applications program whose commands are executed automatically when the computer is turned on so that the user has little more to do than "turn the key" to start the system.

turn-taking On a time-sharing system, the determination of the sequence in which multiple users access the machine. Turn-taking is managed by the supervisory routine of an operating system.

unconditional branch A computer programming instruction that transfers control from the current statement to any other arbitrary statement in a program; also called a GOTO statement.

unconditional page break A command that causes a word processor to automatically terminate printing the current page and begin printing the next one.

undo process A process that allows the user to remove the effect of a process performed in error. In a paint graphics system, the undo process enables the user to correct mistaken inputs or processes made while developing a graphic.

UNIX A sophisticated multiuser operating system developed by Bell Laboratories. Advanced programming skills are necessary for its full use.

upstream problem Resistance to some aspect of a proposed information system by its intended users.

user A person responsible for applying a computer program to the processing of data and determining the usefulness of the program in solving his or her problems.

user friendly A computer program or system that has been designed for ease of use by ordinary, nontechnical people.

user/initiator Person or persons primarily responsible for stimulating the development of a computer programming project.

user's manual Documentation that describes how to use a program. Often includes installation instructions, a tutorial, and a list of all commands with instructions and examples of usage.

vacuum tube A basic electronic switching device used in first generation computers.

validation The process of determining the extent to which a program meets the needs of a user.

variable A portion of computer memory that has been given a name and is intended for the storage of a particular type of value, e.g., NUMBER _COATS (the name) = 10 (the value).

verification The process of ensuring that the computer program meets the objectives stated in the program design specifications.

very high-level languages (VHLLs) Nonprocedural programming languages that are problem specific, in which programmers deal primarily with goal analysis and program design, with the translation program performing the remaining tasks of development and evaluation.

very large scale integrated (VLSI) circuits Single silicon chips containing more than 1,000 gates (basic functional units). VLSI is the basis for current microprocessors (single-chip computers).

VHLL see very high level language.

video controller Electronic circuits that translate text or graphic images into a pattern of lighted dots on a video screen. Often provided by a controller board inserted in an expansion slot of the motherboard.

virtual memory system A system in which parts of programs not immediately needed are stored externally until needed, thus making it appear that primary storage has more memory capacity than it actually does.

walkthrough A manual simulation of a program design using real data.

widow The first line of a paragraph appears as the last line on a printed page.

window A part of the video screen used by some applications programs to display information, e.g., a word processor might display information from different files by splitting the screen into different windows.

word A set of adjacent bytes in computer storage; the fundamental unit of information manipulated by a microprocessor or mainframe central processor.

word processing software An applications program that enables a user to generate and edit arbitrary documents.

wordwrap An automatic feature of word processing systems that causes the computer to advance any word to the next line if it is too long to fit at the end of the current line.

working directory In a file hierarchy or tree, the directory in which the user is currently working. The only purpose of a working directory is to allow the user to use short relative path names rather than longer absolute path names.

workstation A computing resource for use by a professional that generally includes a personal computer linked to other computing devices in some type of network.

zooming in Viewing embedded commands on the display screen along with the rest of the text that is being word processed.

zooming out Hiding embedded commands so that they do not appear on the display screen with the text that is being word processed, but their effects on the text can be seen.

Index

A great deal of effort has been expended to provide an index that points to the important ideas in the text. Any page number that is followed by the letter "f" refers to a figure. Any page number that is followed by the letters "ci" refers to a computer insight. If you have any trouble finding a topic, consider looking under the following major headings of the index: Communications, Computer insights, Data base management, Graphic systems, Hardware, Operating systems, People, Programming, Spreadsheet software, Systems analysis and Word processing. Of course, within each area, consider looking for the concept you need under Input, Storage, Processing, Control or Output.